BUS 320 Corporate Finance
With Connect access

STONEHILL COLLEGE

Department of Business Administration

create.mheducation.com

ISBN-13: 9781307658743

ISBN-10: 1307658741

Contents

Part 1   Overview of Corporate Finance

Introduction to Corporate Finance

Chapter 1

THE CONTROL of a corporation typically rests with its shareholders, who receive one vote for each share of stock they own. However, Alphabet (the parent company of Google) and Facebook are two well-known companies with unusual voting rights. Both companies originally had two classes of stock: Class A, with 1 vote per share, and Class B, with 10 votes per share. The B shares were mostly held by the founding shareholders, so the voting structure meant that Mark Zuckerberg (Facebook) and Sergey Brin and Larry Page (Alphabet) retained control of the companies they started.

In 2016, Facebook announced that it would create Class C shares, similar to what Google had done in 2014. The Class C shares would have the same economic benefit as Class A and B shares, but no voting rights. So why would these two companies create shares of stock with different voting rights, and in the case of Class C stock, no voting rights? The answer leads us to the corporate form of organization, corporate goals, and corporate control, all of which we discuss in this chapter.

Learning Objectives

After studying this chapter, you should be able to:

LO1   Define the basic types of financial management decisions and the role of the financial manager.

LO2   Explain the goal of financial management.

LO3   Articulate the financial implications of the different forms of business organization.

LO4   Explain the conflicts of interest that can arise between managers and owners.

©by_adri/iStockPhoto/GettyImages

For updates on the latest happenings in finance, visit fundamentalsofcorporatefinance .blogspot.com.

To begin our study of modern corporate finance and financial management, we need to address two central issues. First, what is corporate finance and what is the role of the financial manager in the corporation? Second, what is the goal of financial management? To describe the financial management environment, we consider the corporate form of organization and discuss some conflicts that can arise within the corporation. We also take a brief look at financial markets in the United States.

1.1 Corporate Finance and the Financial Manager

In this section, we discuss where the financial manager fits in the corporation. We start by defining *corporate finance* and the financial manager's job.

WHAT IS CORPORATE FINANCE?

Imagine that you were to start your own business. No matter what type you started, you would have to answer the following three questions in some form or another:

1. What long-term investments should you take on? That is, what lines of business will you be in and what sorts of buildings, machinery, and equipment will you need?
2. Where will you get the long-term financing to pay for your investment? Will you bring in other owners or will you borrow the money?
3. How will you manage your everyday financial activities such as collecting from customers and paying suppliers?

These are not the only questions by any means, but they are among the most important. Corporate finance, broadly speaking, is the study of ways to answer these three questions. Accordingly, we'll be looking at each of them in the chapters ahead.

THE FINANCIAL MANAGER

A striking feature of large corporations is that the owners (the stockholders) are usually not directly involved in making business decisions, particularly on a day-to-day basis. Instead, the corporation employs managers to represent the owners' interests and make decisions on their behalf. In a large corporation, the financial manager would be in charge of answering the three questions we raised in the preceding section.

The financial management function is usually associated with a top officer of the firm, such as a vice president of finance or some other chief financial officer (CFO). Figure 1.1 is a simplified organizational chart that highlights the finance activity in a large firm. As shown, the vice president of finance coordinates the activities of the treasurer and the controller. The controller's office handles cost and financial accounting, tax payments, and management information systems. The treasurer's office is responsible for managing the firm's cash and credit, its financial planning, and its capital expenditures. These treasury activities are all related to the three general questions raised earlier, and the chapters ahead deal primarily with these issues. Our study thus bears mostly on activities usually associated with the treasurer's office.

For current issues facing CFOs, see **ww2.cfo.com**.

FINANCIAL MANAGEMENT DECISIONS

As the preceding discussion suggests, the financial manager must be concerned with three basic types of questions. We consider these in greater detail next.

capital budgeting
The process of planning and managing a firm's long-term investments.

Capital Budgeting   The first question concerns the firm's long-term investments. The process of planning and managing a firm's long-term investments is called **capital budgeting**. In capital budgeting, the financial manager tries to identify investment opportunities that are worth more to the firm than they cost to acquire. Loosely speaking, this means that the value of the cash flow generated by an asset exceeds the cost of that asset.

The types of investment opportunities that would typically be considered depend in part on the nature of the firm's business. For a large retailer such as Walmart, deciding whether to open another store would be an important capital budgeting decision. Similarly, for a

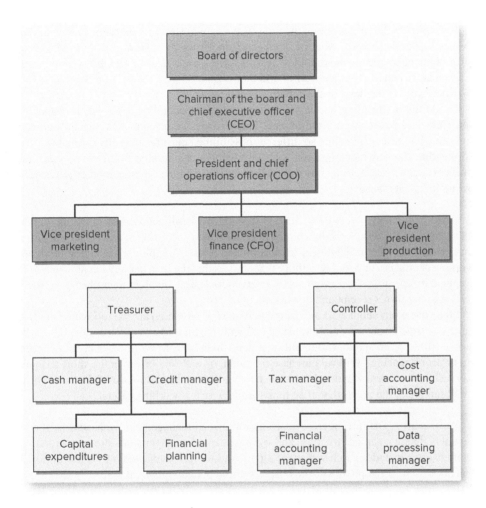

FIGURE 1.1

A Sample Simplified Organizational Chart

software company such as Oracle or Microsoft, the decision to develop and market a new spreadsheet program would be a major capital budgeting decision. Some decisions, such as what type of computer system to purchase, might not depend so much on a particular line of business.

Regardless of the specific nature of an opportunity under consideration, financial managers must be concerned not only with how much cash they expect to receive, but also with when they expect to receive it and how likely they are to receive it. Evaluating the *size, timing,* and *risk* of future cash flows is the essence of capital budgeting. In fact, as we will see in the chapters ahead, whenever we evaluate a business decision, the size, timing, and risk of the cash flows will be by far the most important things we will consider.

Capital Structure   The second question for the financial manager concerns ways in which the firm obtains and manages the long-term financing it needs to support its long-term investments. A firm's **capital structure** (or financial structure) is the specific mixture of long-term debt and equity the firm uses to finance its operations. The financial manager has two concerns in this area. First, how much should the firm borrow? That is, what mixture of debt and equity is best? The mixture chosen will affect both the risk and the value of the firm. Second, what are the least expensive sources of funds for the firm?

capital structure
The mixture of debt and equity maintained by a firm.

If we picture the firm as a pie, then the firm's capital structure determines how that pie is sliced—in other words, what percentage of the firm's cash flow goes to creditors and what percentage goes to shareholders. Firms have a great deal of flexibility in choosing a financial structure. The question of whether one structure is better than any other for a particular firm is the heart of the capital structure issue.

In addition to deciding on the financing mix, the financial manager has to decide exactly how and where to raise the money. The expenses associated with raising long-term financing can be considerable, so different possibilities must be carefully evaluated. Also, corporations borrow money from a variety of lenders in a number of different, and sometimes exotic, ways. Choosing among lenders and among loan types is another job handled by the financial manager.

working capital
A firm's short-term assets and liabilities.

Working Capital Management   The third question concerns **working capital** management. The term *working capital* refers to a firm's short-term assets, such as inventory, and its short-term liabilities, such as money owed to suppliers. Managing the firm's working capital is a day-to-day activity that ensures that the firm has sufficient resources to continue its operations and avoid costly interruptions. This involves a number of activities related to the firm's receipt and disbursement of cash.

Some questions about working capital that must be answered are the following: (1) How much cash and inventory should we keep on hand? (2) Should we sell on credit? If so, what terms will we offer, and to whom will we extend them? (3) How will we obtain any needed short-term financing? Will we purchase on credit, or will we borrow in the short term and pay cash? If we borrow in the short term, how and where should we do it? These are just a small sample of the issues that arise in managing a firm's working capital.

Conclusion   The three areas of corporate financial management we have described—capital budgeting, capital structure, and working capital management—are very broad categories. Each includes a rich variety of topics, and we have indicated only a few questions that arise in the different areas. The chapters ahead contain greater detail.

Concept Questions

1.1a   What is the capital budgeting decision?

1.1b   What do you call the specific mixture of long-term debt and equity that a firm chooses to use?

1.1c   Into what category of financial management does cash management fall?

1.2   Forms of Business Organization

Large firms in the United States, such as Ford and Microsoft, are almost all organized as corporations. We examine the three different legal forms of business organization—sole proprietorship, partnership, and corporation—to see why this is so. Each form has distinct advantages and disadvantages for the life of the business, the ability of the business to raise cash, and taxes. A key observation is that as a firm grows, the advantages of the corporate form may come to outweigh the disadvantages.

SOLE PROPRIETORSHIP

sole proprietorship
A business owned by a single individual.

A **sole proprietorship** is a business owned by one person. This is the simplest type of business to start and is the least regulated form of organization. Depending on where you live, you might be able to start a proprietorship by doing little more than getting a business license and opening your doors. For this reason, there are more proprietorships than any other type of business, and many businesses that later become large corporations start out as small proprietorships.

The owner of a sole proprietorship keeps all the profits. That's the good news. The bad news is that the owner has *unlimited liability* for business debts. This means that creditors can look beyond business assets to the proprietor's personal assets for payment. Similarly, there is no distinction between personal and business income, so all business income is taxed as personal income. However, with the passage of the Tax Cuts and Jobs Act of 2017, up to 20 percent of business income may be exempt from taxation (the specific rules are too complex to cover here).

The life of a sole proprietorship is limited to the owner's life span, and the amount of equity that can be raised is limited to the amount of the proprietor's personal wealth. This limitation often means that the business is unable to exploit new opportunities because of insufficient capital. Ownership of a sole proprietorship may be difficult to transfer because this transfer requires the sale of the entire business to a new owner.

PARTNERSHIP

A **partnership** is similar to a proprietorship except that there are two or more owners (partners). In a *general partnership*, all the partners share in gains or losses, and all have unlimited liability for *all* partnership debts, not just some particular share. The way partnership gains (and losses) are divided is described in the *partnership agreement*. This agreement can be an informal oral agreement, such as "let's start a lawn mowing business," or a lengthy, formal written document.

partnership
A business formed by two or more individuals or entities.

In a *limited partnership*, one or more *general partners* will run the business and have unlimited liability, but there will be one or more *limited partners* who will not actively participate in the business. A limited partner's liability for business debts is limited to the amount that partner contributes to the partnership. This form of organization is common in real estate ventures, for example.

The advantages and disadvantages of a partnership are basically the same as those of a proprietorship. Partnerships based on a relatively informal agreement are easy and inexpensive to form. General partners have unlimited liability for partnership debts, and the partnership terminates when a general partner wishes to sell out or dies. All income is taxed as personal income to the partners, and the amount of equity that can be raised is limited to the partners' combined wealth. As with sole proprietorships, beginning in 2018, up to 20 percent of a partner's income may be exempt depending on various rules spelled out in the Tax Cuts and Jobs Act of 2017. Ownership of a general partnership is not easily transferred because a transfer requires that a new partnership be formed. A limited partner's interest can be sold without dissolving the partnership, but finding a buyer may be difficult.

Because a partner in a general partnership can be held responsible for all partnership debts, having a written agreement is very important. Failure to spell out the rights and duties of the partners frequently leads to misunderstandings later on. Also, if you are a limited partner, you must not become deeply involved in business decisions unless you are willing to assume the obligations of a general partner. The reason is that if things go badly, you may be deemed to be a general partner even though you say you are a limited partner.

Based on our discussion, the primary disadvantages of sole proprietorships and partnerships as forms of business organization are (1) unlimited liability for business debts on the part of the owners, (2) limited life of the business, and (3) difficulty of transferring ownership. These three disadvantages add up to a single, central problem: The ability of such businesses to grow can be seriously limited by an inability to raise cash for investment.

CORPORATION

The **corporation** is the most important form (in terms of size) of business organization in the United States. A corporation is a legal "person," separate and distinct from its owners,

corporation
A business created as a distinct legal entity composed of one or more individuals or entities.

and it has many of the rights, duties, and privileges of an actual person. Corporations can borrow money and own property, sue and be sued, and enter into contracts. A corporation can even be a general partner or a limited partner in a partnership, and a corporation can own stock in another corporation.

Not surprisingly, starting a corporation is somewhat more complicated than starting the other forms of business organization. Forming a corporation involves preparing *articles of incorporation* (or a charter) and a set of *bylaws*. The articles of incorporation must contain a number of things, including the corporation's name, its intended life (which can be forever), its business purpose, and the number of shares that can be issued. This information must normally be supplied to the state in which the firm will be incorporated. For most legal purposes, the corporation is a "resident" of that state.

The bylaws are rules describing how the corporation regulates its existence. For example, the bylaws describe how directors are elected. These bylaws may be a simple statement of a few rules and procedures, or they may be quite extensive for a large corporation. The bylaws may be amended or extended from time to time by the stockholders.

In a large corporation, the stockholders and the managers are usually separate groups. The stockholders elect the board of directors, who then select the managers. Managers are charged with running the corporation's affairs in the stockholders' interests. In principle, stockholders control the corporation because they elect the directors.

As a result of the separation of ownership and management, the corporate form has several advantages. Ownership (represented by shares of stock) can be readily transferred, and the life of the corporation is therefore not limited. The corporation borrows money in its own name. As a result, the stockholders in a corporation have limited liability for corporate debts. The most they can lose is what they have invested.

The relative ease of transferring ownership, the limited liability for business debts, and the unlimited life of the business are why the corporate form is superior for raising cash. If a corporation needs new equity, for example, it can sell new shares of stock and attract new investors. Apple is an example. The company was a pioneer in the personal computer business. As demand for its products exploded, it had to convert to the corporate form of organization to raise the capital needed to fund growth and new product development. The number of owners can be huge; larger corporations have many thousands or even millions of stockholders. For example, in 2017, General Electric Company (better known as GE) had about 440,000 stockholders and about 8.7 billion shares outstanding. In such cases, ownership can change continuously without affecting the continuity of the business.

The corporate form has a significant disadvantage. Because a corporation is a legal person, it must pay taxes. Moreover, money paid out to stockholders in the form of dividends is taxed again as income to those stockholders. This is *double taxation*, meaning that corporate profits are taxed twice: First at the corporate level when they are earned and again at the personal level when they are paid out.[1]

Today, all 50 states have enacted laws allowing for the creation of a relatively new form of business organization, the limited liability company (LLC). The goal of this entity is to operate and be taxed like a partnership but retain limited liability for owners, so an LLC is essentially a hybrid of partnership and corporation. Although states have differing definitions for LLCs, the more important scorekeeper is the Internal Revenue Service (IRS). The IRS will consider an LLC a corporation, thereby subjecting it to double taxation, unless it meets certain specific criteria. In essence, an LLC cannot be too corporation-like, or it will be treated as one by the IRS. LLCs have become common. For example, Goldman, Sachs and Co., one of Wall Street's last remaining partnerships, decided to convert from a private

---

[1] An S corporation is a special type of small corporation that is essentially taxed like a partnership and thus avoids double taxation. In 2017, the maximum number of shareholders in an S corporation was 100.

TABLE 1.1   International Corporations

Company	Country of Origin	Type of Company	
		In Original Language	Translated
Bayerische Motoren Werke (BMW) AG	Germany	Aktiengesellschaft	Corporation
Dornier GmbH	Germany	Gesellschaft mit Beschränkter Haftung	Limited liability company
Rolls-Royce PLC	United Kingdom	Public limited company	Public limited company
Shell UK Ltd.	United Kingdom	Limited	Corporation
Unilever NV	Netherlands	Naamloze Vennootschap	Joint stock company
Fiat SpA	Italy	Società per Azioni	Joint stock company
Volvo AB	Sweden	Aktiebolag	Joint stock company
Peugeot SA	France	Société Anonyme	Joint stock company

partnership to an LLC (it later "went public," becoming a publicly held corporation). Large accounting firms and law firms by the score have converted to LLCs.

As the discussion in this section illustrates, because of their need for outside investors and creditors, the corporate form will generally be the best choice for large firms. We focus on corporations in the chapters ahead because of the importance of the corporate form in the United States and world economies. Also, a few important financial management issues, such as dividend policy, are unique to corporations. However, businesses of all types and sizes need financial management, so the majority of the subjects we discuss bear on any form of business.

A CORPORATION BY ANOTHER NAME . . .

The corporate form of organization has many variations around the world. The exact laws and regulations differ from country to country, of course, but the essential features of public ownership and limited liability remain. These firms are often called *joint stock companies*, *public limited companies*, or *limited liability companies*, depending on the specific nature of the firm and the country of origin.

Table 1.1 gives the names of a few well-known international corporations, their countries of origin, and a translation of the abbreviation that follows the company name.

Concept Questions

1.2a   What are the three forms of business organization?

1.2b   What are the primary advantages and disadvantages of sole proprietorships and partnerships?

1.2c   What is the difference between a general and a limited partnership?

1.2d   Why is the corporate form superior when it comes to raising cash?

The Goal of Financial Management   1.3

Assuming that we restrict ourselves to for-profit businesses, the goal of financial management is to make money or add value for the owners. This goal is a little vague, of course, so we examine some different ways of formulating it to come up with a more precise definition. Such a definition is important because it leads to an objective basis for making and evaluating financial decisions.

POSSIBLE GOALS

If we were to consider possible financial goals, we might come up with some ideas like the following:

Survive.

Avoid financial distress and bankruptcy.

Beat the competition.

Maximize sales or market share.

Minimize costs.

Maximize profits.

Maintain steady earnings growth.

These are only a few of the goals we could list. Furthermore, each of these possibilities presents problems as a goal for the financial manager.

For example, it's easy to increase market share or unit sales: All we have to do is lower our prices or relax our credit terms. Similarly, we can always cut costs simply by doing away with things such as research and development. We can avoid bankruptcy by never borrowing any money or never taking any risks, and so on. It's not clear that any of these actions are in the stockholders' best interests.

Profit maximization would probably be the most commonly cited goal, but even this is not a precise objective. Do we mean profits this year? If so, we should note that actions such as deferring maintenance, letting inventories run down, and taking other short-run cost-cutting measures will tend to increase profits now, but these activities aren't necessarily desirable.

The goal of maximizing profits may refer to some sort of "long-run" or "average" profits, but it's still unclear exactly what this means. First, do we mean something like accounting net income or earnings per share? As we will see in more detail in the next chapter, these accounting numbers may have little to do with what is good or bad for the firm. Second, what do we mean by the long run? As a famous economist once remarked, in the long run, we're all dead! More to the point, this goal doesn't tell us what the appropriate trade-off is between current and future profits.

The goals we've listed here are all different, but they tend to fall into two classes. The first of these relates to profitability. The goals involving sales, market share, and cost control all relate, at least potentially, to different ways of earning or increasing profits. The goals in the second group, involving bankruptcy avoidance, stability, and safety, relate in some way to controlling risk. Unfortunately, these two types of goals are somewhat contradictory. The pursuit of profit normally involves some element of risk, so it isn't really possible to maximize both safety and profit. What we need, therefore, is a goal that encompasses both factors.

THE GOAL OF FINANCIAL MANAGEMENT

The financial manager in a corporation makes decisions for the stockholders of the firm. Given this, instead of listing possible goals for the financial manager, we really need to answer a more fundamental question: From the stockholders' point of view, what is a good financial management decision?

If we assume that stockholders buy stock because they seek to gain financially, then the answer is obvious: Good decisions increase the value of the stock, and poor decisions decrease the value of the stock.

Given our observations, it follows that the financial manager acts in the shareholders' best interests by making decisions that increase the value of the stock. The appropriate goal for the financial manager can thus be stated quite easily:

> **The goal of financial management is to maximize the current value per share of the existing stock.**

The goal of maximizing the value of the stock avoids the problems associated with the different goals we listed earlier. There is no ambiguity in the criterion, and there is no short-run versus long-run issue. We explicitly mean that our goal is to maximize the *current* stock value.

If this goal seems a little strong or one-dimensional to you, keep in mind that the stockholders in a firm are residual owners. By this we mean that they are entitled to only what is left after employees, suppliers, and creditors (and anyone else with a legitimate claim) are paid their due. If any of these groups go unpaid, the stockholders get nothing. So, if the stockholders are winning in the sense that the leftover, residual portion is growing, it must be true that everyone else is winning also.

Because the goal of financial management is to maximize the value of the stock, we need to learn how to identify investments and financing arrangements that favorably impact the value of the stock. This is precisely what we will be studying. In fact, we could have defined *corporate finance* as the study of the relationship between business decisions and the value of the stock in the business.

A MORE GENERAL GOAL

Given our goal as stated in the preceding section (maximize the value of the stock), an obvious question comes up: What is the appropriate goal when the firm has no traded stock? Corporations are certainly not the only type of business; and the stock in many corporations rarely changes hands, so it's difficult to say what the value per share is at any given time.

As long as we are dealing with for-profit businesses, only a slight modification is needed. The total value of the stock in a corporation is simply equal to the value of the owners' equity. Therefore, a more general way of stating our goal is as follows: Maximize the market value of the existing owners' equity.

With this in mind, it doesn't matter whether the business is a proprietorship, a partnership, or a corporation. For each of these, good financial decisions increase the market value of the owners' equity and poor financial decisions decrease it. In fact, although we focus on corporations in the chapters ahead, the principles we develop apply to all forms of business. Many of them even apply to the not-for-profit sector.

Finally, our goal does not imply that the financial manager should take illegal or unethical actions in the hope of increasing the value of the equity in the firm. What we mean is that the financial manager best serves the owners of the business by identifying goods and services that add value to the firm because they are desired and valued in the free marketplace.

SARBANES-OXLEY

In response to corporate scandals at companies such as Enron, WorldCom, Tyco, and Adelphia, Congress enacted the Sarbanes-Oxley Act in 2002. The act, better known as "Sarbox," is intended to protect investors from corporate abuses. For example, one section of Sarbox prohibits personal loans from a company to its officers, such as the ones that were received by WorldCom CEO Bernie Ebbers.

One of the key sections of Sarbox took effect on November 15, 2004. Section 404 requires, among other things, that each company's annual report must have an assessment of the company's internal control structure and financial reporting. An independent auditor must then evaluate and attest to management's assessment of these issues.

Sarbox contains other key requirements. For example, the officers of the corporation must review and sign the annual reports. They must explicitly declare that the annual report does not contain any false statements or material omissions; that the financial statements fairly represent the financial results; and that they are responsible for all internal controls. Finally, the annual report must list any deficiencies in internal controls. In essence, Sarbox makes company management responsible for the accuracy of the company's financial statements.

Because of its extensive reporting requirements, compliance with Sarbox can be very costly, which has led to some unintended results. Since its implementation, hundreds of public firms have chosen to "go dark," meaning that their shares are no longer traded on the major stock exchanges, in which case Sarbox does not apply. Most of these companies stated that their reason was to avoid the cost of compliance. Ironically, in such cases, the law has had the effect of eliminating public disclosure instead of improving it.

For more about Sarbanes-Oxley, visit **www.soxlaw.com**.

Concept Questions

1.3a   What is the goal of financial management?
1.3b   What are some shortcomings of the goal of profit maximization?
1.3c   Can you give a definition of *corporate finance*?

1.4   The Agency Problem and Control of the Corporation

We've seen that the financial manager acts in the best interests of the stockholders by taking actions that increase the value of the stock. However, we've also seen that in large corporations ownership can be spread over a huge number of stockholders. This dispersion of ownership arguably means that management effectively controls the firm. In this case, will management necessarily act in the best interests of the stockholders? Put another way, might management choose to pursue its own goals at the stockholders' expense? In the following pages, we briefly consider some of the arguments relating to this question.

AGENCY RELATIONSHIPS

The relationship between stockholders and management is called an *agency relationship*. Such a relationship exists whenever someone (the principal) hires another (the agent) to represent his or her interests. For example, you might hire someone (an agent) to sell a car you own while you are away at school. In all such relationships, there is a possibility of conflict of interest between the principal and the agent. Such a conflict is called an **agency problem.**

agency problem
The possibility of conflict of interest between the stockholders and management of a firm.

Suppose you hire someone to sell your car and agree to pay that person a flat fee when he or she sells the car. The agent's incentive in this case is to make the sale, not necessarily to get you the best price. If you offer a commission of, say, 10 percent of the sales price instead of a flat fee, then this problem might not exist. This example illustrates that the way in which an agent is compensated is one factor that affects agency problems.

MANAGEMENT GOALS

To see how management and stockholder interests might differ, imagine that the firm is considering a new investment. The new investment is expected to favorably impact the share value, but it is also a relatively risky venture. The owners of the firm will wish to take the investment (because the stock value will rise), but management may not because there is the possibility that things will turn out badly and management jobs will be lost. If management does not take the investment, then the stockholders may lose a valuable opportunity. This is one example of an agency cost.

More generally, the term *agency costs* refers to the costs of the conflict of interest between stockholders and management. These costs can be indirect or direct. An indirect agency cost is a lost opportunity, such as the one we have just described.

Direct agency costs come in two forms. The first type is a corporate expenditure that benefits management but costs the stockholders. Perhaps the purchase of a luxurious and unneeded corporate jet would fall under this heading. The second type of direct agency cost is an expense that arises from the need to monitor management actions. Paying outside auditors to assess the accuracy of financial statement information could be one example.

It is sometimes argued that, left to themselves, managers would tend to maximize the amount of resources over which they have control or, more generally, corporate power or wealth. This goal could lead to an overemphasis on corporate size or growth. For example, cases in which management is accused of overpaying to buy another company just to increase the size of the business or to demonstrate corporate power are not uncommon. Obviously, if overpayment does take place, such a purchase does not benefit the stockholders of the purchasing company.

Our discussion indicates that management may tend to overemphasize organizational survival to protect job security. Also, management may dislike outside interference, so independence and corporate self-sufficiency may be important goals.

DO MANAGERS ACT IN THE STOCKHOLDERS' INTERESTS?

Whether managers will, in fact, act in the best interests of stockholders depends on two factors. First, how closely are management goals aligned with stockholder goals? This question relates, at least in part, to the way managers are compensated. Second, can managers be replaced if they do not pursue stockholder goals? This issue relates to control of the firm. As we will discuss, there are a number of reasons to think that even in the largest firms, management has a significant incentive to act in the interests of stockholders.

Managerial Compensation Management will frequently have a significant economic incentive to increase share value for two reasons. First, managerial compensation, particularly at the top, is usually tied to financial performance in general and often to share value in particular. For example, managers are frequently given the option to buy stock at a bargain price. The more the stock is worth, the more valuable is this option. In fact, options are often used to motivate employees of all types, not just top managers. For example, in late 2016, Alphabet's more than 72,000 employees owned enough options to buy 3.3 million shares in the company. Many other corporations, large and small, have adopted similar policies.

The second incentive managers have relates to job prospects. Better performers within the firm will tend to get promoted. More generally, managers who are successful in pursuing stockholder goals will be in greater demand in the labor market and thus command higher salaries.

In fact, managers who are successful in pursuing stockholder goals can reap enormous rewards. For example, according to Equilar, the best-paid executive in 2016 was Thomas Rutledge, the CEO of Charter Communications, who made about $98 million. By way of comparison, Rutledge made less than performer Katy Perry ($135 million) and way less than boxer Floyd Mayweather ($300 million). Information about executive compensation, along with lots of other information, can be easily found on the web for almost any public company. Our nearby *Work the Web* box shows you how to get started.

WORK THE WEB

The web is a great place to learn more about individual companies, and there are a slew of sites available to help you. Try pointing your web browser to finance.yahoo.com. Once you get there, you should see a link for a "Quote Lookup".

To look up a company, you can use its "ticker symbol" (or just ticker for short), which is a unique one-to five-letter identifier. You can even type the company name into the lookup box and Yahoo Finance will show you the ticker symbol. We typed in "PZZA", which is the ticker for pizza maker Papa John's. Here is a portion of what we found:

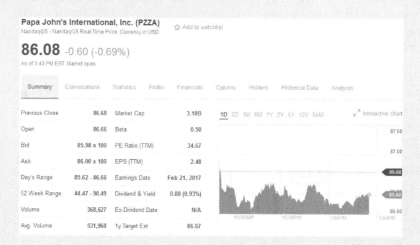

There's a lot of information here and many links for you to explore, so have at it. By the end of the term, we hope it all makes sense to you!

Questions
1. Go to finance.yahoo.com and find the current stock prices for Southwest Airlines (LUV), Harley-Davidson (HOG), and Anheuser-Busch InBev (BUD).
2. Get a quote for American Express (AXP) and follow the "Statistics" link. What information is available on this link? What do mrq, ttm, yoy, and lfy mean?

Business ethics are considered at **www.business-ethics.com**.

While the appropriate level of executive compensation can be debated, bonuses and other payments made to executives who receive payments due to illegal or unethical behavior are a problem. Recently, "clawbacks" and deferred compensation have been introduced to combat such questionable payments. With a clawback, a bonus can be reclaimed by the company for specific reasons, such as fraud. For example, in 2016, former Wells Fargo CEO John Stumpf was forced to forfeit $41 million and former retail banking head Carrie Tolstedt had to give up $19 million due to behavior while the two led the company. Then, in April 2017, Stumpf was forced to return another $28 million and Tolstedt was forced to return an additional $47.3 million. The use of deferred compensation has also increased. Deferred compensation is money paid to an executive several years after it is earned. With a deferred compensation agreement, if circumstances warrant, the payment can be canceled.

Control of the Firm   Control of the firm ultimately rests with stockholders. They elect the board of directors, who in turn hire and fire managers. The fact that stockholders control the corporation was made abundantly clear by Steve Jobs's experience at Apple. Even though he was a founder of the corporation and was largely responsible for its most successful products, there came a time when shareholders, through their elected directors, decided that Apple would be better off without him, so out he went. Of course, he was later rehired and helped turn Apple around with great new products such as the iPod, iPhone, and iPad. Going back to the chapter opener, why would Facebook, specifically Mark Zuckerberg, want to create new shares of stock with no voting rights? The answer is that Zuckerberg had pledged to give away 99 percent of his shares in Facebook during his lifetime. The new C shares he received with no voting rights were to be given to the Chan Zuckerberg Initiative, a philanthropic entity that he created. Therefore, even in giving away these shares, he still retained control of Facebook. In Alphabet's case, Brin and Page had seen their voting power drop to about 56 percent of votes because of the number of Class A shares issued to fund acquisitions and employee stock awards. The new Class C shares were to be used to fund these areas going forward.

An important mechanism by which unhappy stockholders can act to replace existing management is called a *proxy fight*. A proxy is the authority to vote someone else's stock. A proxy fight develops when a group solicits proxies in order to replace the existing board and thereby replace existing managers. For example, in 2016, activist investor Starboard Value LP launched a proxy battle with Yahoo!, arguing that Yahoo! should sell its core business. In response, Yahoo! agreed to a deal that granted four seats on its board of directors to Starboard's nominees—and thus a long proxy fight was defused. Several months later, Yahoo! announced that it would be purchased by Verizon for $4.8 billion, although the acquisition price was reduced by $350 million due to a 2013 e-mail hack experienced by Yahoo! that had not been made public.

Another way that managers can be replaced is by takeover. Firms that are poorly managed are more attractive as acquisitions because a greater profit potential exists. Thus, avoiding a takeover gives management another incentive to act in the stockholders' interests. For example, in 2016, Marriott completed its takeover of Starwood Hotels. Marriott expected to save $250 million per year in operating the combined companies, with much of the savings coming from job cuts in the executive ranks at Starwood. In short, Marriott bought Starwood and fired most of its top executives, eliminating those salaries and saving money.

Conclusion   The available theory and evidence are consistent with the view that stockholders control the firm and that stockholder wealth maximization is the relevant goal of the corporation. Even so, there will undoubtedly be times when management goals are pursued at the expense of the stockholders, at least temporarily.

STAKEHOLDERS

Our discussion thus far implies that management and stockholders are the only parties with an interest in the firm's decisions. This is an oversimplification, of course. Employees, customers, suppliers, and even the government all have a financial interest in the firm.

Taken together, these various groups are called **stakeholders** in the firm. In general, a stakeholder is someone other than a stockholder or creditor who potentially has a claim on the cash flows of the firm. Such groups will also attempt to exert control over the firm, perhaps to the detriment of the owners.

stakeholder
Someone other than a stockholder or creditor who potentially has a claim on the cash flows of the firm.

Concept Questions

1.4a What is an agency relationship?

1.4b What are agency problems and how do they come about? What are agency costs?

1.4c What incentives do managers in large corporations have to maximize share value?

1.5 Financial Markets and the Corporation

We've seen that the primary advantages of the corporate form of organization are that ownership can be transferred more quickly and easily than with other forms and that money can be raised more readily. Both of these advantages are significantly enhanced by the existence of financial markets, and financial markets play an extremely important role in corporate finance.

CASH FLOWS TO AND FROM THE FIRM

The interplay between the corporation and the financial markets is illustrated in Figure 1.2. The arrows in Figure 1.2 trace the passage of cash from the financial markets to the firm and from the firm back to the financial markets.

Suppose we start with the firm selling shares of stock and borrowing money to raise cash. Cash flows to the firm from the financial markets (A). The firm invests the cash in current and fixed assets (B). These assets generate cash (C), some of which goes to pay corporate taxes (D). After taxes are paid, some of this cash flow is reinvested in the firm (E). The rest goes back to the financial markets as cash paid to creditors and shareholders (F).

FIGURE 1.2

Cash Flows between the Firm and the Financial Markets

A. Firm issues securities to raise cash.
B. Firm invests in assets.
C. Firm's operations generate cash flow.
D. Cash is paid to government as taxes. Other stakeholders may receive cash.
E. Reinvested cash flows are plowed back into firm.
F. Cash is paid out to investors in the form of interest and dividends.

A financial market, like any market, is just a way of bringing buyers and sellers together. In financial markets, it is debt and equity securities that are bought and sold. Financial markets differ in detail, however. The most important differences concern the types of securities that are traded, how trading is conducted, and who the buyers and sellers are. Some of these differences are discussed next.

PRIMARY VERSUS SECONDARY MARKETS

Financial markets function as both primary and secondary markets for debt and equity securities. The term *primary market* refers to the original sale of securities by governments and corporations. The *secondary markets* are those in which these securities are bought and sold after the original sale. Equities are, of course, issued solely by corporations. Debt securities are issued by both governments and corporations. In the discussion that follows, we focus on corporate securities only.

Primary Markets   In a primary market transaction, the corporation is the seller, and the transaction raises money for the corporation. Corporations engage in two types of primary market transactions: public offerings and private placements. A public offering, as the name suggests, involves selling securities to the general public, whereas a private placement is a negotiated sale involving a specific buyer.

By law, public offerings of debt and equity must be registered with the Securities and Exchange Commission (SEC). Registration requires the firm to disclose a great deal of information before selling any securities. The accounting, legal, and selling costs of public offerings can be considerable.

To learn more about the SEC, visit **www.sec.gov**.

Partly to avoid the various regulatory requirements and the expense of public offerings, debt and equity are often sold privately to large financial institutions such as life insurance companies or mutual funds. Such private placements do not have to be registered with the SEC and do not require the involvement of underwriters (investment banks that specialize in selling securities to the public).

Secondary Markets   A secondary market transaction involves one owner or creditor selling to another. Therefore, the secondary markets provide the means for transferring ownership of corporate securities. Although a corporation is directly involved only in a primary market transaction (when it sells securities to raise cash), the secondary markets are still critical to large corporations. The reason is that investors are much more willing to purchase securities in a primary market transaction when they know that those securities can later be resold if desired.

Dealer versus Auction Markets   There are two kinds of secondary markets: *auction* markets and *dealer* markets. Generally speaking, dealers buy and sell for themselves, at their own risk. A car dealer, for example, buys and sells automobiles. In contrast, brokers and agents match buyers and sellers, but they do not actually own the commodity that is bought or sold. A real estate agent, for example, does not normally buy and sell houses.

Dealer markets in stocks and long-term debt are called *over-the-counter* (OTC) markets. Most trading in debt securities takes place over the counter. The expression *over the counter* refers to days of old when securities were literally bought and sold at counters in offices around the country. Today, a significant fraction of the market for stocks and almost all of the market for long-term debt have no central location; the many dealers are connected electronically.

Auction markets differ from dealer markets in two ways. First, an auction market or exchange has a physical location (like Wall Street). Second, in a dealer market, most of the buying and selling is done by the dealer. The primary purpose of an auction market, on the other hand, is to match those who wish to sell with those who wish to buy. Dealers play a limited role.

Trading in Corporate Securities   The equity shares of most of the large firms in the United States trade in organized auction markets. The largest such market is the New York Stock Exchange (NYSE). There is also a large OTC market for stocks. In 1971, the National Association of Securities Dealers (NASD) made available to dealers and brokers an electronic quotation system called NASDAQ (which originally stood for NASD Automated Quotation system and is pronounced "naz-dak"). NASDAQ-listed companies tend to be smaller and trade less actively. There are exceptions, of course. Both Microsoft and Intel trade OTC, for example. Nonetheless, the total value of NASDAQ stocks is much less than the total value of NYSE stocks.

There are many large and important financial markets outside the United States, of course, and U.S. corporations are increasingly looking to these markets to raise cash. The Tokyo Stock Exchange and the London Stock Exchange (TSE and LSE, respectively) are two well-known examples. The fact that OTC markets have no physical location means that national borders do not present a great barrier, and there is now a huge international OTC debt market. Because of globalization, financial markets have reached the point where trading in many investments never stops; it just travels around the world.

Listing   Stocks that trade on an organized exchange are said to be *listed* on that exchange. To be listed, firms must meet certain minimum criteria concerning, for example, asset size and number of shareholders. These criteria differ from one exchange to another.

The NYSE has the most stringent requirements of the exchanges in the United States. For example, to be listed on the NYSE, a company is expected to have a market value for its publicly held shares of at least $100 million. There are additional minimums on earnings, assets, and number of shares outstanding.

To learn more about the exchanges, visit **www.nyse.com** and **www.nasdaq.com**.

Concept Questions

1.5a   What is a dealer market? How do dealer and auction markets differ?

1.5b   What does *OTC* stand for? What is the large OTC market for stocks called?

1.5c   What is the largest auction market in the United States?

1.6 Summary and Conclusions

This chapter introduced you to some of the basic ideas in corporate finance:

1. Corporate finance has three main areas of concern:

    a. Capital budgeting: What long-term investments should the firm undertake?

    b. Capital structure: Where will the firm get the long-term financing to pay for its investments? In other words, what mixture of debt and equity should the firm use to fund operations?

    c. Working capital management: How should the firm manage its everyday financial activities?

2. The goal of financial management in a for-profit business is to make decisions that increase the value of the stock or, more generally, increase the market value of the equity.

3. The corporate form of organization is superior to other forms when it comes to raising money and transferring ownership interests, but it has the significant disadvantage of double taxation.

4. There is the possibility of conflicts between stockholders and management in a large corporation. We called these conflicts *agency problems* and discussed how they might be controlled and reduced.

5. The advantages of the corporate form are enhanced by the existence of financial markets. Financial markets function as both primary and secondary markets for corporate securities and can be organized as either dealer or auction markets.

Of the topics we've discussed thus far, the most important is the goal of financial management: Maximizing the value of the stock. Throughout the text, we will be analyzing many different financial decisions, but we will always ask the same question: How does the decision under consideration affect the value of the stock?

CONNECT TO FINANCE

 Connect Finance offers you plenty of opportunities to practice mastering these concepts. Log on to connect.mheducation.com to learn more. If you like what you see, ask your professor about using *Connect Finance*!

Can you answer the following *Connect* Quiz questions?

Section 1.1 Deciding which fixed assets should be purchased is an example of what type of decision?

Section 1.2 What form of ownership is easiest to transfer?

Section 1.3 What best describes the goal of financial management?

Section 1.4 In a corporation, the primary agency conflict arises between which two parties?

CONCEPTS REVIEW AND CRITICAL THINKING QUESTIONS

1. **The Financial Management Decision Process** [LO1] What are the three types of financial management decisions? For each type of decision, give an example of a business transaction that would be relevant.

2. **Sole Proprietorships and Partnerships** [LO3] What are the four primary disadvantages of the sole proprietorship and partnership forms of business organization? What benefits are there to these types of business organization as opposed to the corporate form?

3. **Corporations** [LO3] What is the primary disadvantage of the corporate form of organization? Name at least two advantages of corporate organization.

4. **Sarbanes-Oxley** [LO4] In response to the Sarbanes-Oxley Act, many small firms in the United States have opted to "go dark" and delist their stock. Why might a company choose this route? What are the costs of "going dark"?

5. **Corporate Finance Organization** [LO1] In a large corporation, what are the two distinct groups that report to the chief financial officer? Which group is the focus of corporate finance?

6. **Goal of Financial Management** [LO2] What goal should always motivate the actions of a firm's financial manager?

7. **Agency Problems** [LO4] Who owns a corporation? Describe the process whereby the owners control the firm's management. What is the main reason that an agency relationship exists in the corporate form of organization? In this context, what kinds of problems can arise?

8. **Primary versus Secondary Markets** [LO3] You've probably noticed coverage in the financial press of an initial public offering (IPO) of a company's securities. Is an IPO a primary market transaction or a secondary market transaction?

9. **Auction versus Dealer Markets** [LO3] What does it mean when we say the New York Stock Exchange is an auction market? How are auction markets different from dealer markets? What kind of market is NASDAQ?

10. **Not-for-Profit Firm Goals** [LO2] Suppose you were the financial manager of a not-for-profit business (a not-for-profit hospital, perhaps). What kinds of goals do you think would be appropriate?

11. **Goal of the Firm** [LO2] Evaluate the following statement: Managers should not focus on the current stock value because doing so will lead to an overemphasis on short-term profits at the expense of long-term profits.

12. **Ethics and Firm Goals** [LO2] Can our goal of maximizing the value of the stock conflict with other goals, such as avoiding unethical or illegal behavior? In particular, do you think subjects like customer and employee safety, the environment, and the general good of society fit in this framework, or are they essentially ignored? Think of some specific scenarios to illustrate your answer.

13. **International Firm Goal** [LO2] Would our goal of maximizing the value of the stock be different if we were thinking about financial management in a foreign country? Why or why not?

14. **Agency Problems** [LO4] Suppose you own stock in a company. The current price per share is $25. Another company has just announced that it wants to buy your company and will pay $35 per share to acquire all the outstanding stock. Your company's management immediately begins fighting off this hostile bid. Is management acting in the shareholders' best interests? Why or why not?

15. **Agency Problems and Corporate Ownership** [LO4] Corporate ownership varies around the world. Historically individuals have owned the majority of shares in public corporations in the United States. In Germany and Japan, however, banks, other large financial institutions, and other companies own most of the stock in public corporations. Do you think agency problems are likely to be more or less severe in Germany and Japan than in the United States? Why? Over the last few decades, large financial institutions such as mutual funds and pension funds have been becoming the dominant owners of stock in the United States, and these institutions are becoming more active in corporate affairs. What are the implications of this trend for agency problems and corporate control?

16. **Executive Compensation** [LO4] Critics have charged that compensation to top managers in the United States is simply too high and should be cut back. For example, focusing on large corporations, Mark Parker, CEO of Nike, earned about $47.6 million in 2016. Are such amounts excessive? In answering, it might be helpful to recognize that superstar athletes such as LeBron James, top entertainers such as Taylor Swift and Dwayne Johnson, and many others at the top of their respective fields earn at least as much, if not a great deal more.

MINICASE

The McGee Cake Company

In early 2013, Doc and Lyn McGee formed the McGee Cake Company. The company produced a full line of cakes, and its specialties included chess cake,* lemon pound cake, and double-iced, double-chocolate cake. The couple formed the company as an outside interest, and both continued to work at their current jobs. Doc did all the baking, and Lyn handled the marketing and distribution. With good product quality and a sound marketing plan, the company grew rapidly. In early 2016, the company was featured in a widely distributed entrepreneurial magazine. Later that year, the company was featured in *Gourmet Desserts*, a leading specialty food magazine. After the article appeared in *Gourmet Desserts*, sales exploded, and the company began receiving orders from all over the world.

Because of the increased sales, Doc left his other job, followed shortly by Lyn. The company hired additional workers to meet demand. Unfortunately, the fast growth experienced by the company led to cash flow and capacity problems. The company is currently producing as many cakes as possible with the assets it owns, but demand for its cakes is still growing. Further, the company has been approached by a national supermarket chain with a proposal to put four of its cakes in all of the chain's stores, and a national restaurant chain has contacted the company about selling McGee cakes in its restaurants. The restaurant would sell the cakes without a brand name.

Doc and Lyn have operated the company as a sole proprietorship. They have approached you to help manage and direct the company's growth. Specifically, they have asked you to answer the following questions.

QUESTIONS

1. What are the advantages and disadvantages of changing the company organization from a sole proprietorship to an LLC?

2. What are the advantages and disadvantages of changing the company organization from a sole proprietorship to a corporation?

3. Ultimately, what action would you recommend the company undertake? Why?

---

*Chess cake is quite delicious and distinct from cheesecake. The origin of the name is obscure.

Chapter

2 | Financial Statements, Taxes, and Cash Flow

IN DECEMBER 2017, the Tax Cuts and Jobs Act was enacted into law beginning in 2018. The new law was a sweeping change to corporate taxes in the U.S. For example, rather than depreciating an asset over time for tax purposes, companies are allowed to depreciate the entire purchase price in the first year. Another change was a limit to the tax deductibility of interest expense. However, possibly the biggest change was the switch from a graduated corporate income tax structure, which ranged from 15 percent to 39 percent, to a flat 21 percent corporate tax rate.

While the change in the corporate tax rate affects net income, there is a more important impact. Because taxes are a key consideration in making investment decisions, the change in the tax rate could lead to a significant change in corporate behavior. Understanding why ultimately leads us to the main subject of this chapter: That all-important substance known as *cash flow*.

Learning Objectives

After studying this chapter, you should be able to:

LO1 Describe the difference between accounting value (or *book value*) and market value.

LO2 Describe the difference between accounting income and cash flow.

LO3 Describe the difference between average and marginal tax rates.

LO4 Determine a firm's cash flow from its financial statements.

For updates on the latest happenings in finance, visit fundamentalsofcorporatefinance.blogspot.com.

In this chapter, we examine financial statements, taxes, and cash flow. Our emphasis is not on preparing financial statements. Instead, we recognize that financial statements are frequently a key source of information for financial decisions, so our goal is to briefly examine such statements and point out some of their more relevant features. We pay special attention to some of the practical details of cash flow.

As you read, pay particular attention to two important differences: (1) the difference between accounting value and market value and (2) the difference between accounting income and cash flow. These distinctions will be important throughout the book.

The Balance Sheet

The **balance sheet** is a snapshot of the firm. It is a convenient means of organizing and summarizing what a firm owns (its assets), what a firm owes (its liabilities), and the difference between the two (the firm's equity) at a given point in time. Figure 2.1 illustrates how the balance sheet is constructed. As shown, the left side lists the assets of the firm, and the right side lists the liabilities and equity.

ASSETS: THE LEFT SIDE

Assets are classified as either *current* or *fixed* assets. A fixed asset is one that has a relatively long life. Fixed assets can be either *tangible*, such as a truck or a computer, or *intangible*, such as a trademark or patent. A current asset has a life of less than one year. This means that the asset will convert to cash within 12 months. For example, inventory would normally be purchased and sold within a year and is classified as a current asset. Obviously, cash itself is a current asset. Accounts receivable (money owed to the firm by its customers) are also current assets.

LIABILITIES AND OWNERS' EQUITY: THE RIGHT SIDE

The firm's liabilities are the first thing listed on the right side of the balance sheet. These are classified as either *current* or *long-term*. Current liabilities, like current assets, have a life of less than one year (meaning they must be paid within the year) and are listed before long-term liabilities. Accounts payable (money the firm owes to its suppliers) are one example of a current liability.

A debt that is not due in the coming year is classified as a long-term liability. A loan that the firm will pay off in five years is one such long-term debt. Firms borrow in the long term from a variety of sources. We will tend to use the terms *bond* and *bondholders* generically to refer to long-term debt and long-term creditors, respectively.

Finally, by definition, the difference between the total value of the assets (current and fixed) and the total value of the liabilities (current and long-term) is the *shareholders' equity*, also called *common equity* or *owners' equity*. This feature of the balance sheet is intended to reflect the fact that, if the firm were to sell all its assets and use the money to pay off its debts, then whatever residual value remained would belong to the shareholders. So, the balance sheet "balances" because the value of the left side always equals the value

2.1

Excel Master It!
Excel Master coverage online

balance sheet
Financial statement showing a firm's accounting value on a particular date.

Three excellent sites for company financial information are **finance.yahoo.com**, **finance.google.com**, and **money.cnn.com**.

FIGURE 2.1

The Balance Sheet. Left Side: Total Value of Assets. Right Side: Total Value of Liabilities and Shareholders' Equity.

of the right side. That is, the value of the firm's assets is equal to the sum of its liabilities and shareholders' equity:[1]

Assets = Liabilities + Shareholders' equity

2.1

This is the *balance sheet identity*, or equation, and it always holds because shareholders' equity is defined as the difference between assets and liabilities.

NET WORKING CAPITAL

net working capital
Current assets less current liabilities.

As shown in Figure 2.1, the difference between a firm's current assets and its current liabilities is called **net working capital**. Net working capital is positive when current assets exceed current liabilities. Based on the definitions of current assets and current liabilities, this means the cash that will become available over the next 12 months exceeds the cash that must be paid over the same period. For this reason, net working capital is usually positive in a healthy firm.

EXAMPLE 2.1	Building the Balance Sheet

A firm has current assets of $100, net fixed assets of $500, short-term debt of $70, and long-term debt of $200. What does the balance sheet look like? What is shareholders' equity? What is net working capital?

In this case, total assets are $100 + 500 = $600 and total liabilities are $70 + 200 = $270, so shareholders' equity is the difference: $600 − 270 = $330. The balance sheet would look like this:

Assets		Liabilities and Shareholders' Equity	
Current assets	$100	Current liabilities	$ 70
Net fixed assets	500	Long-term debt	200
		Shareholders' equity	330
Total assets	$600	Total liabilities and shareholders' equity	$600

Net working capital is the difference between current assets and current liabilities, or $100 − 70 = $30.

Table 2.1 shows simplified balance sheets for the fictitious U.S. Corporation. The assets on the balance sheet are listed in order of the length of time it takes for them to convert to cash in the normal course of business. Similarly, the liabilities are listed in the order in which they would normally be paid.

The structure of the assets for a particular firm reflects the line of business the firm is in, as well as managerial decisions regarding how much cash and inventory to have on hand, the firm's credit policy, fixed-asset acquisitions, and so on.

The liabilities side of the balance sheet primarily reflects managerial decisions about capital structure and the use of short-term debt. For example, in 2018, total long-term debt for U.S. Corporation was $454 and total equity was $640 + 1,690 = $2,330, so total long-term financing was $454 + 2,330 = $2,784. (Note that, throughout, all figures are in millions of dollars.) Of this amount, $454/$2,784 = 16.31 percent was long-term debt. This percentage reflects capital structure decisions made in the past by the management of U.S.

Disney has a good investor relations site at **thewaltdisneycompany.com /investors**.

---

[1]The terms *owners' equity, shareholders' equity,* and *stockholders' equity* are used interchangeably to refer to the equity in a corporation. The term *net worth* is also used. Variations exist in addition to these.

TABLE 2.1

Balance Sheets

U.S. CORPORATION 2017 and 2018 Balance Sheets ($ in millions)					
Assets			**Liabilities and Owners' Equity**		
	2017	**2018**		**2017**	**2018**
Current assets			Current liabilities		
Cash	$ 104	$ 221	Accounts payable	$ 232	$ 266
Accounts receivable	455	688	Notes payable	196	123
Inventory	553	555	Total	$ 428	$ 389
Total	$1,112	$1,464			
Fixed assets					
Net plant and equipment	$1,644	$1,709	Long-term debt	$ 408	$ 454
			Owners' equity		
			Common stock and paid-in surplus	600	640
			Retained earnings	1,320	1,690
			Total	$1,920	$2,330
Total assets	$2,756	$3,173	Total liabilities and owners' equity	$2,756	$3,173

There are three particularly important things to keep in mind when examining a balance sheet: liquidity, debt versus equity, and market value versus book value.

LIQUIDITY

Liquidity refers to the speed and ease with which an asset can be converted to cash. Gold is a relatively liquid asset; a custom manufacturing facility is not. Liquidity actually has two dimensions: Ease of conversion versus loss of value. Any asset can be converted to cash quickly if we cut the price enough. A highly liquid asset is therefore one that can be quickly sold without significant loss of value. An illiquid asset is one that cannot be quickly converted to cash without a substantial price reduction.

Assets are normally listed on the balance sheet in order of decreasing liquidity, meaning that the most liquid assets are listed first. Current assets are relatively liquid and include cash and assets we expect to convert to cash over the next 12 months. Accounts receivable, for example, represent amounts not yet collected from customers on sales already made. Naturally, we hope these will convert to cash in the near future. Inventory is probably the least liquid of the current assets, at least for many businesses.

Fixed assets are, for the most part, relatively illiquid. These consist of tangible things such as buildings and equipment that don't convert to cash at all in normal business activity (they are, of course, used in the business to generate cash). Intangible assets, such as a trademark, have no physical existence but can be very valuable. Like tangible fixed assets, they won't ordinarily convert to cash and are generally considered illiquid.

Liquidity is valuable. The more liquid a business is, the less likely it is to experience financial distress (that is, difficulty in paying debts or buying needed assets). Unfortunately, liquid assets are generally less profitable to hold. Cash holdings are the most liquid of all investments, but they sometimes earn no return at all—they just sit there. There is therefore a trade-off between the advantages of liquidity and forgone potential profits.

Annual and quarterly financial statements (and lots more) for most public U.S. corporations can be found in the EDGAR database at **www.sec.gov**.

DEBT VERSUS EQUITY

To the extent that a firm borrows money, it usually gives first claim to the firm's cash flow to creditors. Equity holders are entitled to only the residual value, the portion left after creditors are paid. The value of this residual portion is the shareholders' equity in the firm, which is just the value of the firm's assets less the value of the firm's liabilities:

Shareholders' equity = Assets − Liabilities

This is true in an accounting sense because shareholders' equity is defined as this residual portion. More important, it is true in an economic sense: If the firm sells its assets and pays its debts, whatever cash is left belongs to the shareholders.

The use of debt in a firm's capital structure is called *financial leverage*. The more debt a firm has (as a percentage of assets), the greater is its degree of financial leverage. As we discuss in later chapters, debt acts like a lever in the sense that using it can greatly magnify both gains and losses. So, financial leverage increases the potential reward to shareholders, but it also increases the potential for financial distress and business failure.

MARKET VALUE VERSUS BOOK VALUE

Generally Accepted Accounting Principles (GAAP)
The common set of standards and procedures by which audited financial statements are prepared.

The home page for the Financial Accounting Standards Board (FASB) is **www.fasb.org**.

The values shown on the balance sheet for the firm's assets are *book values* and generally are not what the assets are actually worth. Under **Generally Accepted Accounting Principles (GAAP)**, audited financial statements in the United States mostly show assets at *historical cost*. In other words, assets are "carried on the books" at what the firm paid for them, no matter how long ago they were purchased or how much they are worth today.

For current assets, market value and book value might be somewhat similar because current assets are bought and converted into cash over a relatively short span of time. In other circumstances, the two values might differ quite a bit. Moreover, for fixed assets, it would be purely a coincidence if the actual market value of an asset (what the asset could be sold for) were equal to its book value. For example, a railroad might own enormous tracts of land purchased a century or more ago. What the railroad paid for that land could be hundreds or thousands of times less than what the land is worth today. The balance sheet would nonetheless show the historical cost.

The difference between market value and book value is important for understanding the impact of reported gains and losses. For example, from time to time, accounting rule changes take place that lead to reductions in the book value of certain types of assets. However, a change in accounting rules all by itself has no effect on what the assets in question are really worth. Instead, the market value of an asset depends on things like its riskiness and cash flows, neither of which have anything to do with accounting.

The balance sheet is potentially useful to many different parties. A supplier might look at the size of accounts payable to see how promptly the firm pays its bills. A potential creditor would examine the liquidity and degree of financial leverage. Managers within the firm can track things like the amount of cash and the amount of inventory the firm keeps on hand. Uses such as these are discussed in more detail in Chapter 3.

Managers and investors will frequently be interested in knowing the value of the firm. This information is not on the balance sheet. The fact that balance sheet assets are listed at cost means that there is no necessary connection between the total assets shown and the value of the firm. Indeed, many of the most valuable assets a firm might have—good management, a good reputation, talented employees—don't appear on the balance sheet at all.

Similarly, the shareholders' equity figure on the balance sheet and the true value of the stock need not be related. For example, in late 2017, the book value of IBM's equity was about $18 billion, while the market value was $142 billion. At the same time, Alphabet's book value was $139 billion, while the market value was $731 billion.

For financial managers, then, the accounting value of the stock is not an especially important concern; it is the market value that matters. Henceforth, whenever we speak of the value of an asset or the value of the firm, we will normally mean its *market value*. So, for example, when we say the goal of the financial manager is to increase the value of the stock, we mean the market value of the stock.

Market Value versus Book Value   EXAMPLE 2.2

The Klingon Corporation has net fixed assets with a book value of $700 and an appraised market value of about $1,000. Net working capital is $400 on the books, but approximately $600 would be realized if all the current accounts were liquidated. Klingon has $500 in long-term debt, both book value and market value. What is the book value of the equity? What is the market value?

We can construct two simplified balance sheets, one in accounting (book value) terms and one in economic (market value) terms:

KLINGON CORPORATION Balance Sheets Market Value versus Book Value					
Assets			**Liabilities and Shareholders' Equity**		
	Book	**Market**		**Book**	**Market**
Net working capital	$ 400	$ 600	Long-term debt	$ 500	$ 500
Net fixed assets	700	1,000	Shareholders' equity	600	1,100
	$1,100	$1,600		$1,100	$1,600

In this example, shareholders' equity is actually worth almost twice as much as what is shown on the books. The distinction between book and market values is important precisely because book values can be so different from true economic value.

Concept Questions

2.1a   What is the balance sheet identity?

2.1b   What is liquidity? Why is it important?

2.1c   What do we mean by financial leverage?

2.1d   Explain the difference between book value and market value. Which is more important to the financial manager? Why?

income statement
Financial statement summarizing a firm's performance over a period of time.

The Income Statement   2.2

The income statement measures performance over some period of time, usually a quarter or a year. The income statement equation is:

Revenues − Expenses = Income

If you think of the balance sheet as a snapshot, then you can think of the income statement as a video recording covering the period between before and after pictures. Table 2.2 gives a simplified income statement for U.S. Corporation.

Excel Master It!

Excel Master coverage online

TABLE 2.2

Income Statement

U.S. CORPORATION 2018 Income Statement ($ in millions)	
Net sales	$1,509
Cost of goods sold	750
Depreciation	65
Earnings before interest and taxes	$ 694
Interest paid	70
Taxable income	$ 624
Taxes (21%)	131
Net income	$ 493
Dividends	$123
Addition to retained earnings	370

The first thing reported on an income statement would usually be revenue and expenses from the firm's principal operations. Subsequent parts include, among other things, financing expenses such as interest paid. Taxes paid are reported separately. The last item is *net income* (the so-called bottom line). Net income is often expressed on a per-share basis and called *earnings per share* (EPS).

As indicated, U.S. Corporation paid cash dividends of $123. The difference between net income and cash dividends, $370, is the addition to retained earnings for the year. This amount is added to the cumulative retained earnings account on the balance sheet. If you look back at the two balance sheets for U.S. Corporation, you'll see that retained earnings did go up by this amount: $1,320 + 370 = $1,690.

EXAMPLE 2.3	**Calculating Earnings and Dividends per Share**

Suppose U.S. had 200 million shares outstanding at the end of 2018. Based on the income statement in Table 2.2, what was EPS? What were dividends per share?

From the income statement, we see that U.S. had a net income of $493 million for the year. Total dividends were $123 million. Because 200 million shares were outstanding, we can calculate earnings per share, or EPS, and dividends per share as follows:

Earnings per share = Net income/Total shares outstanding

= $493/200 = $2.46 per share

Dividends per share = Total dividends/Total shares outstanding

= $123/200 = $.615 per share

When looking at an income statement, the financial manager needs to keep three things in mind: GAAP, cash versus noncash items, and time and costs.

GAAP AND THE INCOME STATEMENT

An income statement prepared using GAAP will show revenue when it accrues. This is not necessarily when the cash comes in. The general rule (the *recognition* or *realization principle*) is to recognize revenue when the earnings process is virtually complete and the value of an exchange of goods or services is known or can be reliably determined. In practice, this principle usually means that revenue is recognized at the time of sale, which need not be the same as the time of collection.

Expenses shown on the income statement are based on the *matching principle*. The basic idea here is to first determine revenues as described previously and then match those revenues with the costs associated with producing them. So, if we manufacture a product and then sell it on credit, the revenue is realized at the time of sale. The production and other costs associated with the sale of that product will likewise be recognized at that time. Once again, the actual cash outflows may have occurred at some different time.

As a result of the way revenues and expenses are realized, the figures shown on the income statement may not be at all representative of the actual cash inflows and outflows that occurred during a particular period.

NONCASH ITEMS

A primary reason that accounting income differs from cash flow is that an income statement contains **noncash items**. The most important of these is *depreciation*. Suppose a firm purchases an asset for $5,000 and pays in cash. Obviously, the firm has a $5,000 cash outflow at the time of purchase. However, instead of deducting the $5,000 as an expense, an accountant might depreciate the asset over a five-year period.

If the depreciation is straight-line and the asset is written down to zero over that period, then $5,000/5 = $1,000 will be deducted each year as an expense.[2] The important thing to recognize is that this $1,000 deduction isn't cash—it's an accounting number. The actual cash outflow occurred when the asset was purchased.

The depreciation deduction is another application of the matching principle in accounting. The revenues associated with an asset generally occur over some length of time. So, the accountant seeks to match the expense of purchasing the asset with the benefits produced from owning it.

As we will see, for the financial manager, the actual timing of cash inflows and outflows is critical in coming up with a reasonable estimate of market value. For this reason, we need to learn how to separate the cash flows from the noncash accounting entries. In reality, the difference between cash flow and accounting income can be pretty dramatic. For example, consider the case of U.S. Steel, which reported a net loss of $340 million for the first quarter of 2016. Sounds bad, but U.S. Steel also reported a *positive* cash flow of $113 million, a difference of about $453 million!

noncash items
Expenses charged against revenues that do not directly affect cash flow, such as depreciation.

TIME AND COSTS

It is often useful to think of the future as having two distinct parts: The short run and the long run. These are not precise time periods. The distinction has to do with whether costs are fixed or variable. In the long run, all business costs are variable. Given sufficient time, assets can be sold, debts can be paid, and so on.

If our time horizon is relatively short, however, some costs are effectively fixed—they must be paid no matter what (property taxes, for example). Other costs, such as wages to laborers and payments to suppliers, are still variable. As a result, even in the short run, the firm can vary its output level by varying expenditures in these areas.

The distinction between fixed and variable costs is important, at times, to the financial manager, but the way costs are reported on the income statement is not a good guide to which costs are which. The reason is that, in practice, accountants tend to classify costs as either product costs or period costs.

---

[2]By *straight-line*, we mean that the depreciation deduction is the same every year. By *written down to zero*, we mean that the asset is assumed to have no value at the end of five years. Depreciation is discussed in more detail in Chapter 10.

WORK THE WEB

The U.S. Securities and Exchange Commission (SEC) requires that most public companies file regular reports, including annual and quarterly financial statements. The SEC has a public site named EDGAR that makes these free reports available at www.sec.gov. We went to "Search EDGAR" and looked up Alphabet:

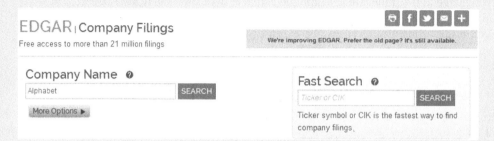

Here is a partial view of what we found:

The two reports we look at the most are the 10-K, which is the annual report filed with the SEC, and the 10-Q. The 10-K includes the list of officers and their salaries, financial statements for the previous fiscal year, and an explanation by the company of the financial results. The 10-Q is a smaller report that includes the financial statements for the quarter.

Questions

1. As you can imagine, electronic filing of documents with the SEC has not been around for very long. Go to www.sec.gov and find the filings for General Electric. What is the date of the oldest 10-K available on the website for General Electric? Look up the 10-K forms for IBM and Apple to see if the year of the first electronic filing is the same for these companies.

2. Go to www.sec.gov and find out when the following forms are used: Form DEF 14A, Form 8-K, and Form 6-K.

Product costs include such things as raw materials, direct labor expense, and manufacturing overhead. These are reported on the income statement as costs of goods sold, but they include both fixed and variable costs. Similarly, *period costs* are incurred during a particular time period and might be reported as selling, general, and administrative expenses. Once again, some of these period costs may be fixed and others may be variable. The company president's salary, for example, is a period cost and is probably fixed, at least in the short run.

The balance sheets and income statement we have been using thus far are hypothetical. Our nearby *Work the Web* box shows how to find actual balance sheets and income statements online for almost any company. Also, with the increasing globalization of business, there is a clear need for accounting standards to become more comparable across countries. Accordingly, in recent years, U.S. accounting standards have become more closely tied to International Financial Reporting Standards (IFRS). In particular, the Financial Accounting Standards Board (FASB), which is in charge of U.S. GAAP policies, and the International Accounting Standards Board, which is in charge of IFRS policies, have been working toward a convergence of policies since 2002. Although GAAP and IFRS have become similar in important ways, as of early 2018, it appears that a full convergence of accounting policies is off the table, at least for now.

For more information about IFRS, check out the website **www.ifrs.org**.

Concept Questions

2.2a What is the income statement equation?

2.2b What are the three things to keep in mind when looking at an income statement?

2.2c Why is accounting income not the same as cash flow? Give two reasons.

Taxes

2.3

Taxes can be one of the largest cash outflows a firm experiences. For example, for the fiscal year 2016, JPMorgan Chase's earnings before taxes were about $34.54 billion. Its tax bill, including all taxes paid worldwide, was a whopping $9.8 billion, or about 28 percent of its pretax earnings. Also for fiscal year 2016, Walmart had a taxable income of $20.50 billion, and the company paid $6.2 billion in taxes—an average tax rate of 30 percent.

The size of a company's tax bill is determined by the tax code, an often amended set of rules. In this section, we examine corporate tax rates and how taxes are calculated. If the various rules of taxation seem a little bizarre or convoluted to you, keep in mind that the tax code is the result of political, not economic, forces. As a result, there is no reason why it has to make economic sense.

Excel Master It!
Excel Master coverage online

CORPORATE TAX RATES

Corporate tax rates in effect for 2017 (but not 2018 and beyond) are shown in Table 2.3. As shown, corporate tax rates rise from 15 percent to 39 percent, but they drop back to 34 percent on income over $335,000. They then rise to 38 percent and subsequently fall to 35 percent.

The tax rate schedule in Table 2.3 was simplified considerably by the Tax Cuts and Jobs Act of 2017. Beginning in 2018, the corporate tax rate is 21 percent, and that rate applies regardless of the level of taxable income.

TABLE 2.3

Corporate Tax Rates for 2017

Taxable Income	Tax Rate
$ 0– 50,000	15%
50,001– 75,000	25
75,001– 100,000	34
100,001– 335,000	39
335,001–10,000,000	34
10,000,001–15,000,000	35
15,000,001–18,333,333	38
18,333,334+	35

AVERAGE VERSUS MARGINAL TAX RATES

average tax rate
Total taxes paid divided by total taxable income.

marginal tax rate
Amount of tax payable on the next dollar earned.

In making financial decisions, it is frequently important to distinguish between average and marginal tax rates. Your **average tax rate** is your tax bill divided by your taxable income—in other words, the percentage of your income that goes to pay taxes. Your **marginal tax rate** is the rate of the extra tax you would pay if you earned one more dollar. The percentage tax rates shown in Table 2.3 are all marginal rates. Put another way, the tax rates in Table 2.3 applied to the part of income in the indicated range only, not all income.

The difference between average and marginal tax rates can best be illustrated with an example. Suppose our corporation had a taxable income of $200,000 in 2017. What was the tax bill? Using Table 2.3, we can figure our tax bill:

$$
\begin{aligned}
.15(\$50{,}000) &= \$\ 7{,}500 \\
.25(\$75{,}000 - 50{,}000) &= \ 6{,}250 \\
.34(\$100{,}000 - 75{,}000) &= \ 8{,}500 \\
.39(\$200{,}000 - 100{,}000) &= \underline{\ 39{,}000} \\
&\ \ \ \$61{,}250
\end{aligned}
$$

The IRS has a great website! Check out **www.irs.gov**.

Our total tax was $61,250.

In our example, what is the average tax rate? We had a taxable income of $200,000 and a tax bill of $61,250, so the average tax rate is $61,250/$200,000 = 30.625 percent. What is the marginal tax rate? If we made one more dollar, the tax on that dollar would be 39 cents, so our marginal rate is 39 percent.

EXAMPLE 2.4   **Deep in the Heart of Taxes**

Algernon, Inc., has a taxable income of $85,000 for 2017. What is its tax bill? What is its average tax rate? Its marginal tax rate? What would these be in 2018 and beyond?

From Table 2.3, we see that the tax rate applied to the first $50,000 is 15 percent; the rate applied to the next $25,000 is 25 percent; and the rate applied after that up to $100,000 is 34 percent. So Algernon must pay .15 × $50,000 + .25 × $25,000 + .34 × ($85,000 − 75,000) = $17,150. The average tax rate is thus $17,150/$85,000 = 20.18 percent. The marginal rate is 34 percent because Algernon's taxes would rise by 34 cents if it had another dollar in taxable income.

In 2018 and beyond, the average rate and the marginal rate are the same, 21 percent. There is no need to do any calculations!

Table 2.4 summarizes some different taxable incomes, marginal tax rates, and average tax rates for corporations. Notice how the average and marginal tax rates come together at 35 percent.

(1) Taxable Income	(2) Marginal Tax Rate	(3) Total Tax	(3)/(1) Average Tax Rate
$ 45,000	15%	$ 6,750	15.00%
70,000	25	12,500	17.86
95,000	34	20,550	21.63
250,000	39	80,750	32.30
1,000,000	34	340,000	34.00
17,500,000	38	6,100,000	34.86
50,000,000	35	17,500,000	35.00
100,000,000	35	35,000,000	35.00

TABLE 2.4

Corporate Taxes and Tax Rates

With a *flat-rate* tax, there is only one tax rate, so the rate is the same for all income levels. The 21 percent corporate tax created by the Tax Cuts and Jobs Act of 2017 is such a tax. In this case, as Example 2.4 illustrates, the marginal tax rate is always the same as the average tax rate. As it stands now, corporate taxation in the United States shifted in 2018 from a modified flat-rate tax, which became a true flat rate for only the highest incomes, to a true flat rate.

Normally the marginal tax rate is relevant for financial decision making. The reason is that any new cash flows will be taxed at that marginal rate. Because financial decisions usually involve new cash flows or changes in existing ones, this rate will tell us the marginal effect of a decision on our tax bill.

We should note that we have simplified the U.S. tax code in our discussions. In reality, the tax code is much more complex and riddled with various tax deductions and loopholes allowed for certain industries. As a result, the average corporate tax rate may be far from 21 percent for many companies. Table 2.5 displays average tax rates for various industries. Note that these rates pre-date the 21 percent flat tax instituted for 2018, but we still expect to see a wide range of average tax rates in 2018 and beyond due to other features of the tax code.

Prior to 2018, with a tax rate of 35 percent for large, profitable companies, the U.S. corporate tax rate was the highest in the world among developed economies. As a result, several companies in recent years have undertaken a controversial reorganization called a *tax inversion*. In a tax inversion, a company transfers ownership of its U.S.-based operations to a corporation domiciled in a foreign country, typically by a merger. This maneuver allows the company to avoid paying taxes in the United States on earnings from outside the United

Industry	Number of Companies	Average Tax Rate
Electric utilities (Eastern U.S.)	24	33.8%
Trucking	33	32.7
Railroad	15	27.4
Securities brokerage	30	20.5
Banking	481	17.5
Medical supplies	264	11.2
Internet	239	5.9
Pharmaceutical	337	5.6
Biotechnology	121	4.5

TABLE 2.5

Average Tax Rates

States. The 2017 reduction in the corporate tax rate to 21 percent puts the United States more-or-less in the middle relative to other developed economies, and a primary reason for the reduction was to eliminate the incentive for tax inversions and other strategies to avoid the U.S. corporate tax.

Before moving on, we should note that the tax rates we have discussed in this section relate to federal taxes only. Overall tax rates can be higher if state, local, and any other taxes are considered.

Concept Questions

2.3a   What is the difference between a marginal and an average tax rate?

2.3b   What was the impact of the Tax Cuts and Jobs Act of 2017 on corporate tax rates?

2.4   Cash Flow

Excel Master It!

xlsx   Excel Master coverage online

At this point, we are ready to discuss perhaps one of the most important pieces of financial information that can be gleaned from financial statements: Cash flow. By *cash flow*, we mean the difference between the number of dollars that came in and the number of dollars that went out. For example, if you were the owner of a business, you might be very interested in how much cash you actually took out of your business in a given year. How to determine this amount is one of the things we discuss next.

No standard financial statement presents this information in the way that we wish. We will therefore discuss how to calculate cash flow for U.S. Corporation and point out how the result differs from that of standard financial statement calculations. There is a standard financial accounting statement called the *statement of cash flows*, but it is concerned with a somewhat different issue that should not be confused with what is discussed in this section. The accounting statement of cash flows is discussed in Chapter 3.

From the balance sheet identity, we know that the value of a firm's assets is equal to the value of its liabilities plus the value of its equity. Similarly, the cash flow from the firm's assets must equal the sum of the cash flow to creditors and the cash flow to stockholders (or owners):

Cash flow from assets = Cash flow to creditors + Cash flow to stockholders   **2.3**

This is the *cash flow identity*. It says that the cash flow from the firm's assets is equal to the cash flow paid to suppliers of capital to the firm. What it reflects is the fact that a firm generates cash through its various activities, and that cash is either used to pay creditors or paid out to the owners of the firm. We discuss the various things that make up these cash flows next.

cash flow from assets
The total of cash flow to creditors and cash flow to stockholders, consisting of the following: operating cash flow, capital spending, and change in net working capital.

operating cash flow
Cash generated from a firm's normal business activities.

CASH FLOW FROM ASSETS

Cash flow from assets involves three components: operating cash flow, capital spending, and change in net working capital. **Operating cash flow** refers to the cash flow that results from the firm's day-to-day activities of producing and selling. Expenses associated with the firm's financing of its assets are not included because they are not operating expenses.

As we discussed in Chapter 1, some portion of the firm's cash flow is reinvested in the firm. *Capital spending* refers to the net spending on fixed assets (purchases of fixed assets less sales of fixed assets). Finally, *change in net working capital* is measured as the net change in current assets relative to current liabilities for the period being examined and represents the amount spent on net working capital. The three components of cash flow are examined in more detail next.

Operating Cash Flow   To calculate operating cash flow (OCF), we want to calculate revenues minus costs, but we don't want to include depreciation because it's not a cash outflow, and we don't want to include interest because it's a financing expense. We do want to include taxes because taxes are (unfortunately) paid in cash.

If we look at U.S. Corporation's income statement (Table 2.2), we see that earnings before interest and taxes (EBIT) are $694. This is almost what we want because it doesn't include interest paid. However, we need to make two adjustments. First, recall that depreciation is a noncash expense. To get cash flow, we first add back the $65 in depreciation because it wasn't a cash deduction. The other adjustment is to subtract the $131 in taxes because these were paid in cash. The result is operating cash flow:

U.S. CORPORATION 2018 Operating Cash Flow	
Earnings before interest and taxes	$694
+ Depreciation	65
− Taxes	131
Operating cash flow	$628

U.S. Corporation had a 2018 operating cash flow of $628.

Operating cash flow is an important number because it tells us, on a very basic level, whether a firm's cash inflows from its business operations are sufficient to cover its everyday cash outflows. For this reason, a negative operating cash flow is often a sign of trouble.

There is an unpleasant possibility of confusion when we speak of operating cash flow. In accounting practice, operating cash flow is often defined as net income plus depreciation. For U.S. Corporation, this would amount to $493 + 65 = $558.

The accounting definition of operating cash flow differs from ours in one important way: Interest is deducted when net income is computed. Notice that the difference between the $628 operating cash flow we calculated and this $558 is $70, the amount of interest paid for the year. This definition of cash flow thus considers interest paid to be an operating expense. Our definition treats it properly as a financing expense. If there were no interest expense, the two definitions would be the same.

To finish our calculation of cash flow from assets for U.S. Corporation, we need to consider how much of the $628 operating cash flow was reinvested in the firm. We consider spending on fixed assets first.

Capital Spending   Net capital spending is money spent on fixed assets less money received from the sale of fixed assets. At the end of 2017, net fixed assets for U.S. Corporation (Table 2.1) were $1,644. During the year, U.S. wrote off (depreciated) $65 worth of fixed assets on the income statement. So, if the firm didn't purchase any new fixed assets, net fixed assets would have been $1,644 − 65 = $1,579 at year's end. The 2018 balance sheet shows $1,709 in net fixed assets, so U.S. must have spent a total of $1,709 − 1,579 = $130 on fixed assets during the year:

This $130 is the net capital spending for 2018.

Ending net fixed assets	$1,709
− Beginning net fixed assets	1,644
+ Depreciation	65
Net capital spending	$ 130

Could net capital spending be negative? The answer is yes. This would happen if the firm sold more assets than it purchased. The *net* here refers to purchases of fixed assets net of any sales of fixed assets. You will often see capital spending called CAPEX, which is an acronym for capital expenditures. It usually means the same thing.

Change in Net Working Capital   In addition to investing in fixed assets, a firm will also invest in current assets. For example, going back to the balance sheets in Table 2.1, we see that, at the end of 2018, U.S. had current assets of $1,464. At the end of 2017, current assets were $1,112; so, during the year, U.S. invested $1,464 − 1,112 = $352 in current assets.

As the firm changes its investment in current assets, its current liabilities will usually change as well. To determine the change in net working capital, the easiest approach is to take the difference between the beginning and ending net working capital (NWC) figures. Net working capital at the end of 2018 was $1,464 − 389 = $1,075. Similarly, at the end of 2017, net working capital was $1,112 − 428 = $684. Given these figures, we have the following:

Ending NWC	$1,075
− Beginning NWC	684
Change in NWC	$ 391

Net working capital thus increased by $391. Put another way, U.S. Corporation had a net investment of $391 in NWC for the year. This change in NWC is often referred to as the "addition to" NWC.

Conclusion   Given the figures we've come up with, we're ready to calculate cash flow from assets. The total cash flow from assets is given by operating cash flow less the amounts invested in fixed assets and net working capital. So, for U.S. Corporation, we have:

U.S. CORPORATION 2018 Cash Flow from Assets	
Operating cash flow	$628
− Net capital spending	130
− Change in NWC	391
Cash flow from assets	$107

From the cash flow identity given earlier, we know that this $107 cash flow from assets equals the sum of the firm's cash flow to creditors and its cash flow to stockholders. We consider these next.

It wouldn't be at all unusual for a growing corporation to have a negative cash flow. As we see next, a negative cash flow means that the firm raised more money by borrowing and selling stock than it paid out to creditors and stockholders during the year.

A Note about "Free" Cash Flow   Cash flow from assets sometimes goes by a different name, **free cash flow**. Of course, there is no such thing as "free" cash (we wish!). Instead the name refers to cash that the firm is free to distribute to creditors and stockholders because it is not needed for working capital or fixed asset investments. We will stick with "cash flow from assets" as our label for this important concept because, in practice, there is some variation in exactly how free cash flow is computed; different users calculate it in different ways. Nonetheless, whenever you hear the phrase "free cash flow," you should understand that what is being discussed is cash flow from assets or something quite similar.

free cash flow
Another name for cash flow from assets.

CASH FLOW TO CREDITORS AND STOCKHOLDERS

The cash flows to creditors and stockholders represent the net payments to creditors and owners during the year. Their calculation is similar to that of cash flow from assets. **Cash flow to creditors** is interest paid less net new borrowing; **cash flow to stockholders** is dividends paid less net new equity raised.

cash flow to creditors
A firm's interest payments to creditors less net new borrowing.

Cash Flow to Creditors   Looking at the income statement in Table 2.2, we see that U.S. Corporation paid $70 in interest to creditors. From the balance sheets in Table 2.1, we see that long-term debt rose by $454 − 408 = $46. So U.S. Corporation paid out $70 in interest, but it borrowed an additional $46. Thus, net cash flow to creditors is:

cash flow to stockholders
Dividends paid out by a firm less net new equity raised.

U.S. CORPORATION 2018 Cash Flow to Creditors	
Interest paid	$70
− Net new borrowing	46
Cash flow to creditors	$24

Cash flow to creditors is sometimes called *cash flow to bondholders*; we will use these terms interchangeably.

Cash Flow to Stockholders   From the income statement, we see that dividends paid to stockholders amounted to $123. To get net new equity raised, we need to look at the common stock and paid-in surplus account. This account tells us how much stock the company has sold. During the year, this account rose by $40, so $40 in net new equity was raised. Given this, we have the following:

U.S. CORPORATION 2018 Cash Flow to Stockholders	
Dividends paid	$123
− Net new equity raised	40
Cash flow to stockholders	$ 83

The cash flow to stockholders for 2018 was $83.

The last thing we need to do is to verify that the cash flow identity holds to be sure we didn't make any mistakes. From the previous section, we know that cash flow from assets is $107. Cash flow to creditors and stockholders is $24 + 83 = $107, so everything checks out. Table 2.6 contains a summary of the various cash flow calculations for future reference.

As our discussion indicates, it is essential that a firm keep an eye on its cash flow. The following serves as an excellent reminder of why doing so is a good idea, unless the firm's owners wish to end up in the "Po' " house:

QUOTH THE BANKER, "WATCH CASH FLOW"

Once upon a midnight dreary as I pondered weak and weary
Over many a quaint and curious volume of accounting lore,
Seeking gimmicks (without scruple) to squeeze through some new tax loophole,
Suddenly I heard a knock upon my door, Only this, and nothing more.

Then I felt a queasy tingling and I heard the cash a-jingling
As a fearsome banker entered whom I'd often seen before.
His face was money-green and in his eyes there could be seen
Dollar-signs that seemed to glitter as he reckoned up the score.
   "Cash flow," the banker said, and nothing more.

TABLE 2.6

Cash Flow Summary

I. The cash flow identity
Cash flow from assets = Cash flow to creditors (bondholders) + Cash flow to stockholders (owners)
II. Cash flow from assets
Cash flow from assets = Operating cash flow − Net capital spending − Change in net working capital (NWC) where: Operating cash flow = Earnings before interest and taxes (EBIT) + Depreciation − Taxes Net capital spending = Ending net fixed assets − Beginning net fixed assets + Depreciation Change in NWC = Ending NWC − Beginning NWC
III. Cash flow to creditors (bondholders)
Cash flow to creditors = Interest paid − Net new borrowing
IV. Cash flow to stockholders (owners)
Cash flow to stockholders = Dividends paid − Net new equity raised

I had always thought it fine to show a jet black bottom line.
But the banker sounded a resounding, "No.
Your receivables are high, mounting upward toward the sky;
Write-offs loom. What matters is cash flow."
 He repeated, "Watch cash flow."

Then I tried to tell the story of our lovely inventory
Which, though large, is full of most delightful stuff.
But the banker saw its growth, and with a mighty oath
He waved his arms and shouted, "Stop! Enough!
 Pay the interest, and don't give me any guff!"

Next I looked for noncash items which could add ad infinitum
To replace the ever-outward flow of cash,
But to keep my statement black I'd held depreciation back,
And my banker said that I'd done something rash.
 He quivered, and his teeth began to gnash.

When I asked him for a loan, he responded, with a groan,
That the interest rate would be just prime plus eight,
And to guarantee my purity he'd insist on some security—
All my assets plus the scalp upon my pate.
 Only this, a standard rate.

Though my bottom line is black, I am flat upon my back,
My cash flows out and customers pay slow.
The growth of my receivables is almost unbelievable:
The result is certain—unremitting woe!
And I hear the banker utter an ominous low mutter,
 "Watch cash flow."

Herbert S. Bailey Jr.

"Quoth the Banker, 'Watch Cash Flow,'" from *Publishers Weekly*, January 13, 1975. ©1975 by *Publishers Weekly*. All rights reserved. Used with permission.

To which we can only add, "Amen."

AN EXAMPLE: CASH FLOWS FOR DOLE COLA

This extended example covers the various cash flow calculations discussed in the chapter. It also illustrates a few variations that may arise.

Operating Cash Flow   During the year, Dole Cola, Inc., had sales and cost of goods sold of $600 and $300, respectively. Depreciation was $150 and interest paid was $30. Taxes were calculated at a straight 21 percent. Dividends were $36. (All figures are in millions of dollars.) What was operating cash flow for Dole? Why is this different from net income?

The easiest thing to do here is to create an income statement. We can then pick up the numbers we need. Dole Cola's income statement is given here:

DOLE COLA 2018 Income Statement	
Net sales	$600
Cost of goods sold	300
Depreciation	150
Earnings before interest and taxes	$150
Interest paid	30
Taxable income	$120
Taxes	25
Net income	$ 95
Dividends	$36
Addition to retained earnings	59

Net income for Dole was $95. We now have all the numbers we need. Referring back to the U.S. Corporation example and Table 2.6, we have this:

DOLE COLA 2018 Operating Cash Flow	
Earnings before interest and taxes	$150
+ Depreciation	150
− Taxes	25
Operating cash flow	$275

As this example illustrates, operating cash flow is not the same as net income because depreciation and interest are subtracted out when net income is calculated. If you recall our earlier discussion, we don't subtract these out in computing operating cash flow because depreciation is not a cash expense and interest paid is a financing expense, not an operating expense.

Net Capital Spending   Suppose beginning net fixed assets were $500 and ending net fixed assets were $750. What was the net capital spending for the year?

From the income statement for Dole, we know that depreciation for the year was $150. Net fixed assets rose by $250. Dole thus spent $250 along with an additional $150, for a total of $400.

Change in NWC and Cash Flow from Assets   Suppose Dole Cola started the year with $2,130 in current assets and $1,620 in current liabilities, and the corresponding ending figures were $2,276 and $1,710. What was the change in NWC during the year? What was cash flow from assets? How does this compare to net income?

Net working capital started out as $2,130 − 1,620 = $510 and ended up at $2,276 − 1,710 = $566. The addition to NWC was $566 − 510 = $56. Putting together all the information for Dole, we have the following:

DOLE COLA	
2018 Cash Flow from Assets	
Operating cash flow	$275
− Net capital spending	400
− Change in NWC	56
Cash flow from assets	−$181

Dole had a cash flow from assets of −$181. Net income was positive at $95. Is the fact that cash flow from assets was negative a cause for alarm? Not necessarily. The cash flow here is negative primarily because of a large investment in fixed assets. If these are good investments, the resulting negative cash flow is not a worry.

Cash Flow to Stockholders and Creditors   We saw that Dole Cola had cash flow from assets of −$181. The fact that this is negative means that Dole raised more money in the form of new debt and equity than it paid out for the year. For example, suppose we know that Dole didn't sell any new equity for the year. What was cash flow to stockholders? To creditors?

Because it didn't raise any new equity, Dole's cash flow to stockholders is equal to the cash dividend paid:

DOLE COLA	
2018 Cash Flow to Stockholders	
Dividends paid	$36
− Net new equity raised	0
Cash flow to stockholders	$36

Now, from the cash flow identity, we know that the total cash paid to creditors and stockholders was −$181. Cash flow to stockholders is $36, so cash flow to creditors must be equal to −$181 − 36 = −$217:

Cash flow to creditors + Cash flow to stockholders = −$181

Cash flow to creditors + $36   = −$181

Cash flow to creditors   = −$217

Because we know that cash flow to creditors is −$217 and interest paid is $30 (from the income statement), we can now determine net new borrowing. Dole must have borrowed $247 during the year to help finance the fixed asset expansion:

DOLE COLA	
2018 Cash Flow to Creditors	
Interest paid	$ 30
– Net new borrowing	– 247
Cash flow to creditors	–$217

Concept Questions

2.4a   What is the cash flow identity? Explain what it says.

2.4b   What are the components of operating cash flow?

2.4c   Why is interest paid not a component of operating cash flow?

Summary and Conclusions   2.5

This chapter has introduced some of the basics of financial statements, taxes, and cash flow:

1. The book values on an accounting balance sheet can be very different from market values. The goal of financial management is to maximize the market value of the stock, not its book value.

2. Net income as it is computed on the income statement is not cash flow. A primary reason is that depreciation, a noncash expense, is deducted when net income is computed.

3. Marginal and average tax rates can be different, and it is the marginal tax rate that is relevant for most financial decisions.

4. The tax rate paid by corporations is a flat tax of 21 percent, although state and local taxes can increase this rate.

5. There is a cash flow identity much like the balance sheet identity. It says that cash flow from assets equals cash flow to creditors and stockholders.

The calculation of cash flow from financial statements isn't difficult. Care must be taken in handling noncash expenses, such as depreciation, and operating costs must not be confused with financing costs. Most of all, it is important not to confuse book values with market values, or accounting income with cash flow.

CONNECT TO FINANCE

 Do you use *Connect Finance* to practice what you learned? If you don't, you should—we can help you master the topics presented in this material. Log on to connect.mheducation.com to learn more!

Can you answer the following *Connect* Quiz questions?

Section 2.1   What types of accounts are the most liquid?

Section 2.2   What is an example of a noncash expense?

Section 2.3   The marginal tax rate is the tax rate that _____.

Section 2.4   Interest expense is treated as what type of cash flow?

CHAPTER REVIEW AND SELF-TEST PROBLEM

2.1   Cash Flow for Mara Corporation   This problem will give you some practice working with financial statements and figuring cash flow. Based on the following information for Mara Corporation, prepare an income statement for 2018 and balance sheets for 2017 and 2018. Next, following our U.S. Corporation examples in the chapter, calculate cash flow from assets, cash flow to creditors, and cash flow to stockholders for Mara for 2018. Use a 21 percent tax rate throughout. You can check your answers against ours, found in the following section.

	2017	2018
Sales	$4,203	$4,507
Cost of goods sold	2,422	2,633
Depreciation	785	952
Interest	180	196
Dividends	275	352
Current assets	2,205	2,429
Net fixed assets	7,344	7,650
Current liabilities	1,003	1,255
Long-term debt	3,106	2,085

ANSWER TO CHAPTER REVIEW AND SELF-TEST PROBLEM

2.1   In preparing the balance sheets, remember that shareholders' equity is the residual. With this in mind, Mara's balance sheets are as follows:

MARA CORPORATION 2017 and 2018 Balance Sheets					
	2017	2018		2017	2018
Current assets	$2,205	$ 2,429	Current liabilities	$1,003	$ 1,255
Net fixed assets	7,344	7,650	Long-term debt	3,106	2,085
			Equity	5,440	6,739
Total assets	$9,549	$10,079	Total liabilities and shareholders' equity	$9,549	$10,079

The income statement is straightforward:

MARA CORPORATION 2018 Income Statement	
Sales	$4,507
Cost of goods sold	2,633
Depreciation	952
Earnings before interest and taxes	$ 922
Interest paid	196
Taxable income	$ 726
Taxes (21%)	152
Net income	$ 574
Dividends	$352
Addition to retained earnings	222

Notice that the addition to retained earnings is net income less cash dividends. We can now pick up the figures we need to get operating cash flow:

MARA CORPORATION 2018 Operating Cash Flow	
Earnings before interest and taxes	$ 922
+ Depreciation	952
− Taxes	152
Operating cash flow	$1,722

Next, we get the net capital spending for the year by looking at the change in fixed assets, remembering to account for depreciation:

Ending net fixed assets	$7,650
− Beginning net fixed assets	7,344
+ Depreciation	952
Net capital spending	$1,258

After calculating beginning and ending NWC, we take the difference to get the change in NWC:

Ending NWC	$1,174
− Beginning NWC	1,202
Change in NWC	−$ 28

We now combine operating cash flow, net capital spending, and the change in net working capital to get the total cash flow from assets:

MARA CORPORATION Cash Flow from Assets	
Operating cash flow	$1,722
− Net capital spending	1,258
− Change in NWC	−28
Cash flow from assets	$ 492

To get cash flow to creditors, notice that long-term borrowing decreased by $1,021 during the year and that interest paid was $196:

MARA CORPORATION 2018 Cash Flow to Creditors	
Interest paid	$ 196
− Net new borrowing	−1,021
Cash flow to creditors	$ 1,217

Finally, dividends paid were $352. To get net new equity raised, we have to do some extra calculating. Total equity was up by $6,739 − 5,440 = $1,299. Of this increase, $222 was from additions to retained earnings, so $1,077 in new equity was raised during the year. Cash flow to stockholders was thus:

MARA CORPORATION 2018 Cash Flow to Stockholders	
Dividends paid	$ 352
− Net new equity raised	1,077
Cash flow to stockholders	−$ 725

As a check, notice that cash flow from assets ($492) equals cash flow to creditors plus cash flow to stockholders ($1,217 − 725 = $492).

CONCEPTS REVIEW AND CRITICAL THINKING QUESTIONS

1. **Liquidity** [LO1] What does liquidity measure? Explain the trade-off a firm faces between high liquidity and low liquidity levels.

2. **Accounting and Cash Flows** [LO2] Why might the revenue and cost figures shown on a standard income statement not be representative of the actual cash inflows and outflows that occurred during a period?

3. **Book Values versus Market Values** [LO1] In preparing a balance sheet, why do you think standard accounting practice focuses on historical cost rather than market value?

4. **Operating Cash Flow** [LO2] In comparing accounting net income and operating cash flow, name two items you typically find in net income that are not in operating cash flow. Explain what each is and why it is excluded in operating cash flow.

5. **Book Values versus Market Values** [LO1] Under standard accounting rules, it is possible for a company's liabilities to exceed its assets. When this occurs, the owners' equity is negative. Can this happen with market values? Why or why not?

6. **Cash Flow from Assets** [LO4] Suppose a company's cash flow from assets is negative for a particular period. Is this necessarily a good sign or a bad sign?

7. **Operating Cash Flow** [LO4] Suppose a company's operating cash flow has been negative for several years running. Is this necessarily a good sign or a bad sign?

8. **Net Working Capital and Capital Spending** [LO4] Could a company's change in NWC be negative in a given year? (*Hint*: Yes.) Explain how this might come about. What about net capital spending?

9. **Cash Flow to Stockholders and Creditors** [LO4] Could a company's cash flow to stockholders be negative in a given year? (*Hint*: Yes.) Explain how this might come about. What about cash flow to creditors?

10. **Firm Values** [LO1] Referring back to the Boeing example used at the beginning of the chapter, note that we suggested that Boeing's stockholders probably didn't suffer as a result of the reported loss. What do you think was the basis for our conclusion?

11. **Enterprise Value** [LO1] A firm's *enterprise value* is equal to the market value of its debt and equity, less the firm's holdings of cash and cash equivalents. This figure is particularly relevant to potential purchasers of the firm. Why?

12. **Earnings Management** [LO2] Companies often try to keep accounting earnings growing at a relatively steady pace, thereby avoiding large swings in earnings from period to period. They also try to meet earnings targets. To do so, they use a variety of tactics. The simplest way is to control the timing of accounting revenues and costs, which all firms can do to at least some extent. For example, if earnings are looking too low this quarter, then some accounting costs can be deferred until next quarter. This practice is called *earnings management*. It is common, and it raises a lot of questions. Why do firms do it? Why are firms even allowed to do it under GAAP? Is it ethical? What are the implications for cash flow and shareholder wealth?

QUESTIONS AND PROBLEMS

1. **Building a Balance Sheet** [LO1] Wims, Inc., has current assets of $4,900, net fixed assets of $27,300, current liabilities of $4,100, and long-term debt of $10,200. What is the value of the shareholders' equity account for this firm? How much is net working capital?

BASIC
(Questions 1–10)

2. **Building an Income Statement** [LO1] Griffin's Goat Farm, Inc., has sales of $796,000, costs of $327,000, depreciation expense of $42,000, interest expense of $34,000, and a tax rate of 21 percent. What is the net income for this firm?

3. **Dividends and Retained Earnings** [LO1] Suppose the firm in Problem 2 paid out $95,000 in cash dividends. What is the addition to retained earnings?

4. **Per-Share Earnings and Dividends** [LO1] Suppose the firm in Problem 3 had 80,000 shares of common stock outstanding. What is the earnings per share, or EPS, figure? What is the dividends per share figure?

5. **Calculating OCF** [LO4] Pompeii, Inc., has sales of $46,200, costs of $23,100, depreciation expense of $2,200, and interest expense of $1,700. If the tax rate is 22 percent, what is the operating cash flow, or OCF?

6. **Calculating Net Capital Spending** [LO4] Logano Driving School's 2017 balance sheet showed net fixed assets of $2.4 million, and the 2018 balance sheet showed net fixed assets of $3.3 million. The company's 2018 income statement showed a depreciation expense of $319,000. What was net capital spending for 2018?

7. **Calculating Additions to NWC** [LO4] The 2017 balance sheet of Dream, Inc., showed current assets of $4,810 and current liabilities of $2,230. The 2018 balance sheet showed current assets of $5,360 and current liabilities of $2,970. What was the company's 2018 change in net working capital, or NWC?

8. **Cash Flow to Creditors** [LO4] The 2017 balance sheet of Kerber's Tennis Shop, Inc., showed long-term debt of $1.87 million, and the 2018 balance sheet showed long-term debt of $2.21 million. The 2018 income statement showed an interest expense of $255,000. What was the firm's cash flow to creditors during 2018?

9. **Cash Flow to Stockholders** [LO4] The 2017 balance sheet of Kerber's Tennis Shop, Inc., showed $650,000 in the common stock account and $3.98 million in the additional paid-in surplus account. The 2018 balance sheet showed $805,000 and $4.2 million in the same two accounts, respectively. If the company paid out $545,000 in cash dividends during 2018, what was the cash flow to stockholders for the year?

10. **Calculating Total Cash Flows** [LO4] Given the information for Kerber's Tennis Shop, Inc., in Problems 8 and 9, suppose you also know that the firm's net capital spending for 2018 was $1,250,000 and that the firm reduced its net working capital investment by $45,000. What was the firm's 2018 operating cash flow, or OCF?

INTERMEDIATE
(Questions 11–19)

11. **Market Values and Book Values** [LO1] Klingon Widgets, Inc., purchased new cloaking machinery three years ago for $6 million. The machinery can be sold to the Romulans today for $5.1 million. Klingon's current balance sheet shows net fixed assets of $3.4 million, current liabilities of $895,000, and net working capital of $235,000. If the current assets and current liabilities were liquidated today, the company would receive a total of $1.15 million cash. What is the book value of Klingon's total assets today? What is the sum of the market value of NWC and the market value of fixed assets?

12. **Calculating Total Cash Flows** [LO4] Square Hammer Corp. shows the following information on its 2018 income statement: Sales = $305,000; Costs = $176,000; Other expenses = $8,900; Depreciation expense = $18,700; Interest expense = $12,900; Taxes = $23,345; Dividends = $19,500. In addition, you're told that the firm issued $6,400 in new equity during 2018 and redeemed $4,900 in outstanding long-term debt.
   a. What is the 2018 operating cash flow?
   b. What is the 2018 cash flow to creditors?
   c. What is the 2018 cash flow to stockholders?
   d. If net fixed assets increased by $46,000 during the year, what was the addition to NWC?

13. **Using Income Statements** [LO1] Given the following information for Bowie Pizza Co., calculate the depreciation expense: Sales = $64,000; Costs = $30,700; Addition to retained earnings = $5,700; Dividends paid = $1,980; Interest expense = $4,400; Tax rate = 22 percent.

14. **Preparing a Balance Sheet** [LO1] Prepare a 2018 balance sheet for Rogers Corp. based on the following information: Cash = $127,000; Patents and copyrights = $660,000; Accounts payable = $210,000; Accounts receivable = $115,000; Tangible net fixed assets = $1,610,000; Inventory = $286,000; Notes payable = $155,000; Accumulated retained earnings = $1,368,000; Long-term debt = $830,000.

15. **Residual Claims** [LO1] Bishop, Inc., is obligated to pay its creditors $7,800 during the year.
   a. What is the market value of the shareholders' equity if assets have a market value of $9,400?
   b. What if assets equal $6,700?

16. **Net Income and OCF** [LO2] During 2018, Raines Umbrella Corp. had sales of $705,000. Cost of goods sold, administrative and selling expenses, and depreciation expenses were $445,000, $95,000, and $140,000, respectively. In addition, the company had an interest expense of $70,000 and a tax rate of 25 percent. (Ignore any tax loss carryforward provisions and assume interest expense is fully deductible.)
   a. What is the company's net income for 2018?
   b. What is its operating cash flow?
   c. Explain your results in (a) and (b).

17. **Accounting Values versus Cash Flows** [LO2] In Problem 16, suppose Raines Umbrella Corp. paid out $102,000 in cash dividends. Is this possible? If net capital spending and net working capital were both zero, and if no new stock was issued during the year, what do you know about the firm's long-term debt account?

18. **Calculating Cash Flows** [LO2] Cardinal Industries had the following operating results for 2018: Sales = $33,106; Cost of goods sold = $23,624; Depreciation expense = $5,877; Interest expense = $2,650; Dividends paid = $1,888. At the beginning of the year, net fixed assets were $19,820, current assets were $6,970, and current liabilities were $3,920. At the end of the year, net fixed assets were $24,394, current assets were $8,612, and current liabilities were $4,575. The tax rate for 2018 was 22 percent.

    a. What is net income for 2018?
    b. What is the operating cash flow for 2018?
    c. What is the cash flow from assets for 2018? Is this possible? Explain.
    d. If no new debt was issued during the year, what is the cash flow to creditors? What is the cash flow to stockholders? Explain and interpret the positive and negative signs of your answers in (a) through (d).

19. **Calculating Cash Flows** [LO4] Consider the following abbreviated financial statements for Parrothead Enterprises:

PARROTHEAD ENTERPRISES 2017 and 2018 Partial Balance Sheets					
Assets			**Liabilities and Owners' Equity**		
	2017	**2018**		**2017**	**2018**
Current assets	$1,206	$1,307	Current liabilities	$ 482	$ 541
Net fixed assets	4,973	5,988	Long-term debt	2,628	2,795

PARROTHEAD ENTERPRISES 2018 Income Statement	
Sales	$15,301
Costs	7,135
Depreciation	1,363
Interest paid	388

    a. What is owners' equity for 2017 and 2018?
    b. What is the change in net working capital for 2018?
    c. In 2018, Parrothead Enterprises purchased $2,496 in new fixed assets. How much in fixed assets did Parrothead Enterprises sell? What is the cash flow from assets for the year? The tax rate is 21 percent.
    d. During 2018, Parrothead Enterprises raised $504 in new long-term debt. How much long-term debt must Parrothead Enterprises have paid off during the year? What is the cash flow to creditors?

20. **Net Fixed Assets and Depreciation** [LO4] On the balance sheet, the net fixed assets (NFA) account is equal to the gross fixed assets (FA) account (which records the acquisition cost of fixed assets) minus the accumulated depreciation (AD) account (which records the total depreciation taken by the firm against its fixed assets). Using the fact that NFA = FA − AD, show that the expression given in the chapter for net capital spending, $NFA_{end} − NFA_{beg} + D$ (where D is the depreciation expense during the year), is equivalent to $FA_{end} − FA_{beg}$.

CHALLENGE
(Questions 20–22)

Use the following information for Taco Swell, Inc., for Problems 21 and 22 (assume the tax rate is 21 percent):

	2017	2018
Sales	$16,549	$18,498
Depreciation	2,376	2,484
Cost of goods sold	5,690	6,731
Other expenses	1,353	1,178
Interest	1,110	1,325
Cash	8,676	9,247
Accounts receivable	11,488	13,482
Short-term notes payable	1,674	1,641
Long-term debt	29,060	35,229
Net fixed assets	72,770	77,610
Accounts payable	6,269	6,640
Inventory	20,424	21,862
Dividends	1,979	2,314

21. **Financial Statements** [LO1] Draw up an income statement and balance sheet for this company for 2017 and 2018.

22. **Calculating Cash Flow** [LO4] For 2018, calculate the cash flow from assets, cash flow to creditors, and cash flow to stockholders.

EXCEL MASTER IT! PROBLEM

Using Excel to find the marginal tax rate can be accomplished using the VLOOKUP function. However, calculating the total tax bill is a little more difficult. Below we have shown a copy of the IRS tax table for an unmarried individual for 2018. Often, tax tables are presented in this format.

If taxable income is over ...	But not over ...	The tax is:
$ 0	$ 9,525	10% of the amount over $0
9,526	38,700	$952.50 plus 15% of the amount over $9,525
38,701	93,700	$5,328.75 plus 25% of the amount over $38,700
93,701	195,450	$19,078.75 plus 28% of the amount over $93,700
195,451	424,950	$47,568.75 plus 33% of the amount over $195,450
424,951	426,700	$123,303.75 plus 35% of the amount over $424,950
426,701		$123,916.25 plus 39.6% of the amount over $426,700

In reading this table, the marginal tax rate for taxable income less than $9,525 is 10 percent. If the taxable income is between $9,525 and $38,700, the tax bill is $952.50 plus the marginal taxes. The marginal taxes are calculated as the taxable income minus $9,525 times the marginal tax rate of 15 percent.

Below, we have the corporate tax table that was applicable 2017 and as shown in Table 2.3.

Taxable income is greater than or equal to...	But less than...	Tax rate
$ 0	$ 50,000	15%
50,001	75,000	25
75,001	100,000	34
100,001	335,000	39
335,001	10,000,000	34
10,000,001	15,000,000	35
15,000,001	18,333,333	38
18,333,334		35

a. Create a tax table in Excel for corporate taxes similar to the individual tax table shown above. Your spreadsheet should then calculate the marginal tax rate, the average tax rate, and the tax bill for any level of taxable income input by a user.

b. For a taxable income of $1,350,000, what is the marginal tax rate?

c. For a taxable income of $1,350,000, what is the total tax bill?

d. For a taxable income of $1,350,000, what is the average tax rate?

MINICASE

Cash Flows and Financial Statements at Sunset Boards, Inc.

Sunset Boards is a small company that manufactures and sells surfboards in Malibu. Tad Marks, the founder of the company, is in charge of the design and sale of the surfboards, but his background is in surfing, not business. As a result, the company's financial records are not well maintained.

The initial investment in Sunset Boards was provided by Tad and his friends and family. Because the initial investment was relatively small, and the company has made surfboards only for its own store, the investors haven't required detailed financial statements from Tad. But thanks to word of mouth among professional surfers, sales have picked up recently, and Tad is considering a major expansion. His plans include opening another surfboard store in Hawaii, as well as supplying his "sticks" (surfer lingo for boards) to other sellers.

Tad's expansion plans require a significant investment, which he plans to finance with a combination of additional funds from outsiders plus some money borrowed from banks. Naturally, the new investors and creditors require more organized and detailed financial statements than Tad has previously prepared. At the urging of his investors, Tad has hired financial analyst Christina Wolfe to evaluate the performance of the company over the past year.

After rooting through old bank statements, sales receipts, tax returns, and other records, Christina has assembled the following information:

	2017	2018
Cost of goods sold	$255,605	$322,742
Cash	36,884	55,725
Depreciation	72,158	81,559
Interest expense	15,687	17,980
Selling and administrative	50,268	65,610
Accounts payable	26,186	44,318
Net fixed assets	318,345	387,855
Sales	501,441	611,224
Accounts receivable	26,136	33,901
Notes payable	29,712	32,441
Long-term debt	160,689	175,340
Inventory	50,318	67,674
New equity	0	19,500

Sunset Boards currently pays out 40 percent of net income as dividends to Tad and the other original investors, and it has a 21 percent tax rate. You are Christina's assistant, and she has asked you to prepare the following:

1. An income statement for 2017 and 2018.
2. A balance sheet for 2017 and 2018.
3. Operating cash flow for each year.
4. Cash flow from assets for 2018.
5. Cash flow to creditors for 2018.
6. Cash flow to stockholders for 2018.

QUESTIONS

1. How would you describe Sunset Boards's cash flows for 2018? Write a brief discussion.
2. In light of your discussion in the previous question, what do you think about Tad's expansion plans?

Financial Statements and Long-Term Financial Planning

Part 2   Financial Statements and Long-Term Financial Planning

Working with Financial Statements

3 Chapter

THE PRICE OF A SHARE OF COMMON STOCK in corner pharmacy CVS Health closed at about $82 on January 6, 2017. At that price, CVS had a price-earnings (PE) ratio of 18. That is, investors were willing to pay $18 for every dollar in income earned by CVS. At the same time, investors were willing to pay $55, $34, and $6 for each dollar earned by Adobe Systems, Pfizer, and Ford, respectively. At the other extreme were Blackberry and Twitter. Both had negative earnings for the previous year, yet Blackberry was priced at about $8 per share and Twitter at about $17 per share. Because they had negative earnings, their PE ratios would have been negative, so they were not reported. At the time, the typical stock in the S&P 500 index of large company stocks was trading at a PE of about 16, or about 16 times earnings, as they say on Wall Street.

Price-to-earnings comparisons are examples of the use of financial ratios. As we will see in this chapter, there are a wide variety of financial ratios, all designed to summarize specific aspects of a firm's financial position. In addition to discussing how to analyze financial statements and compute financial ratios, we will have quite a bit to say about who uses this information and why.

Learning Objectives

After studying this chapter, you should be able to:

LO1   Standardize financial statements for comparison purposes.

LO2   Compute and, more importantly, interpret some common ratios.

LO3   Name the determinants of a firm's profitability.

LO4   Explain some of the problems and pitfalls in financial statement analysis.

©by_adri/iStockPhotoGettyImages

For updates on the latest happenings in finance, visit fundamentalsofcorporatefinance.blogspot.com.

In Chapter 2, we discussed some of the essential concepts of financial statements and cash flow. Part 2, this chapter and the next, continues where our earlier discussion left off. Our goal here is to expand your understanding of the uses (and abuses) of financial statement information.

Financial statement information will crop up in various places in the remainder of our book. Part 2 is not essential for understanding this material, but it will help give you an overall perspective on the role of financial statement information in corporate finance.

A good working knowledge of financial statements is desirable because such statements, and numbers derived from those statements, are the primary means of communicating financial information both within the firm and outside the firm. In short, much of the language of corporate finance is rooted in the ideas we discuss in this chapter.

Furthermore, as we will see, there are many different ways of using financial statement information and many different types of users. This diversity reflects the fact that financial statement information plays an important part in many types of decisions.

In the best of all worlds, the financial manager has full market value information about all of the firm's assets. This will rarely (if ever) happen. So, the reason we rely on accounting figures for much of our financial information is that we are almost always unable to obtain all (or even part) of the market information we want. The only meaningful yardstick for evaluating business decisions is whether they create economic value (see Chapter 1). However, in many important situations, it will not be possible to make this judgment directly because we can't see the market value effects of decisions.

We recognize that accounting numbers are often pale reflections of economic reality, but they are frequently the best available information. For privately held corporations, not-for-profit businesses, and smaller firms, for example, very little direct market value information exists at all. The accountant's reporting function is crucial in these circumstances.

Clearly, one important goal of the accountant is to report financial information to the user in a form useful for decision making. Ironically, the information frequently does not come to the user in such a form. In other words, financial statements don't come with a user's guide. This chapter and the next are first steps in filling this gap.

3.1 Cash Flow and Financial Statements: A Closer Look

Excel Master It!

xlsx Excel Master coverage online

At the most fundamental level, firms do two different things: They generate cash and they spend it. Cash is generated by selling a product, an asset, or a security. Selling a security involves either borrowing or selling an equity interest (shares of stock) in the firm. Cash is spent in paying for materials and labor to produce a product and in purchasing assets. Payments to creditors and owners also require the spending of cash.

In Chapter 2, we saw that the cash activities of a firm could be summarized by a simple identity:

Cash flow from assets = Cash flow to creditors + Cash flow to owners

This cash flow identity summarizes the total cash result of all transactions a firm engages in during the year. In this section, we return to the subject of cash flow by taking a closer look at the cash events during the year that led to these total figures.

SOURCES AND USES OF CASH

sources of cash
A firm's activities that generate cash.

uses of cash
A firm's activities in which cash is spent. Also called *applications of cash*.

Activities that bring in cash are called **sources of cash**. Activities that involve spending cash are called **uses** (or *applications*) **of cash**. What we need to do is to trace the changes in the firm's balance sheet to see how the firm obtained and spent its cash during some period.

To get started, consider the balance sheets for the Prufrock Corporation in Table 3.1. Notice that we have calculated the change in each of the items on the balance sheets.

Looking over the balance sheets for Prufrock, we see that quite a few things changed during the year. For example, Prufrock increased its net fixed assets by $149 and its inventory by $29. (Note that, throughout, all figures are in millions of dollars.) Where did the money come from? To answer this and related questions, we need to first identify those changes that used up cash (uses) and those that brought in cash (sources).

A little common sense is useful here. A firm uses cash by either buying assets or making payments. So, loosely speaking, an increase in an asset account means the firm, on a net basis, bought some assets—a use of cash. If an asset account went down, then on a net basis, the firm sold some assets. This would be a net source. Similarly, if a liability account goes down, then the firm has made a net payment—a use of cash.

TABLE 3.1

PRUFROCK CORPORATION 2017 and 2018 Balance Sheets ($ in millions)			
	2017	2018	Change
Assets			
Current assets			
Cash	$ 84	$ 146	+$ 62
Accounts receivable	165	188	+ 23
Inventory	393	422	+ 29
Total	$ 642	$ 756	+$114
Fixed assets			
Net plant and equipment	$2,731	$2,880	+$149
Total assets	$3,373	$3,636	+$263
Liabilities and Owners' Equity			
Current liabilities			
Accounts payable	$ 312	$ 344	+$ 32
Notes payable	231	196	− 35
Total	$ 543	$ 540	−$ 3
Long-term debt	$ 531	$ 457	−$ 74
Owners' equity			
Common stock and paid-in surplus	$ 500	$ 550	+$ 50
Retained earnings	1,799	2,089	+ 290
Total	$2,299	$2,639	+$340
Total liabilities and owners' equity	$3,373	$3,636	+$263

Given this reasoning, there is a simple, albeit mechanical, definition you may find useful. An increase in a left-side (asset) account or a decrease in a right-side (liability or equity) account is a use of cash. Likewise, a decrease in an asset account or an increase in a liability (or equity) account is a source of cash.

Looking again at Prufrock, we see that inventory rose by $29. This is a net use of cash because Prufrock effectively paid out $29 to increase inventories. Accounts payable rose by $32. This is a source of cash because Prufrock effectively has borrowed an additional $32 payable by the end of the year. Notes payable, on the other hand, went down by $35, so Prufrock effectively paid off $35 worth of short-term debt—a use of cash.

Based on our discussion, we can summarize the sources and uses of cash from the balance sheet as follows:

Company financial information can be found in many places on the web, including **finance.yahoo .com**, **finance.google.com**, and **money.msn.com**.

Sources of cash:	
Increase in accounts payable	$ 32
Increase in common stock	50
Increase in retained earnings	290
Total sources	$372
Uses of cash:	
Increase in accounts receivable	$ 23
Increase in inventory	29
Decrease in notes payable	35
Decrease in long-term debt	74
Net fixed asset acquisitions	149
Total uses	$310
Net addition to cash	$ 62

TABLE 3.2

PRUFROCK CORPORATION 2018 Income Statement ($ in millions)		
Sales		$2,311
Cost of goods sold		1,344
Depreciation		276
Earnings before interest and taxes		$ 691
Interest paid		141
Taxable income		$ 550
Taxes (21%)		116
Net income		$ 435
Dividends	$145	
Addition to retained earnings	290	

The net addition to cash is the difference between sources and uses, and our $62 result here agrees with the $62 change shown on the balance sheet.

This simple statement tells us much of what happened during the year, but it doesn't tell the whole story. For example, the increase in retained earnings is net income (a source of funds) less dividends (a use of funds). It would be more enlightening to have these reported separately so we could see the breakdown. Also, we have considered only net fixed asset acquisitions. Total or gross spending would be more interesting to know.

To further trace the flow of cash through the firm during the year, we need an income statement. For Prufrock, the results for the year are shown in Table 3.2.

Notice here that the $290 addition to retained earnings we calculated from the balance sheet is the difference between the net income of $435 and the dividends of $145.

THE STATEMENT OF CASH FLOWS

statement of cash flows
A firm's financial statement that summarizes its sources and uses of cash over a specified period.

There is some flexibility in summarizing the sources and uses of cash in the form of a financial statement. However it is presented, the result is called the **statement of cash flows**.

We present a particular format for this statement in Table 3.3. The basic idea is to group all the changes into three categories: operating activities, financing activities, and investment activities. The exact form differs in detail from one preparer to the next.

Don't be surprised if you come across different arrangements. The types of information presented will be similar; the exact order can differ. The key thing to remember in this case is that we started out with $84 in cash and ended up with $146, for a net increase of $62. We're trying to see what events led to this change.

Going back to Chapter 2, we note that there is a slight conceptual problem here. Interest paid should really go under financing activities, but unfortunately that's not the way the accounting is handled. The reason, you may recall, is that interest is deducted as an expense when net income is computed. Also, notice that the net purchase of fixed assets was $149. Because Prufrock wrote off $276 worth of assets (the depreciation), it must have actually spent a total of $149 + 276 = $425 on fixed assets.

Once we have this statement, it might seem appropriate to express the change in cash on a per-share basis, much as we did for net income. Ironically, despite the interest we might have in some measure of cash flow per share, standard accounting practice expressly prohibits reporting this information. The reason is that accountants feel that cash flow (or some component of cash flow) is not an alternative to accounting income, so only earnings per share are to be reported.

As shown in Table 3.4, it is sometimes useful to present the same information a bit differently. We will call this the "sources and uses of cash" statement. There is no such

TABLE 3.3

PRUFROCK CORPORATION 2018 Statement of Cash Flows ($ in millions)	
Cash, beginning of year	$ 84
Operating activity	
Net income	$ 435
Plus:	
Depreciation	276
Increase in accounts payable	32
Less:	
Increase in accounts receivable	− 23
Increase in inventory	− 29
Net cash from operating activity	$ 691
Investment activity	
Fixed asset acquisitions	−$ 425
Net cash from investment activity	−$ 425
Financing activity	
Decrease in notes payable	−$ 35
Decrease in long-term debt	− 74
Dividends paid	− 145
Increase in common stock	50
Net cash from financing activity	−$ 204
Net increase in cash	$ 62
Cash, end of year	$ 146

TABLE 3.4

PRUFROCK CORPORATION 2018 Sources and Uses of Cash ($ in millions)	
Cash, beginning of year	$ 84
Sources of cash	
Operations:	
Net income	$435
Depreciation	276
	$711
Working capital:	
Increase in accounts payable	$ 32
Long-term financing:	
Increase in common stock	50
Total sources of cash	$793
Uses of cash	
Working capital:	
Increase in accounts receivable	$ 23
Increase in inventory	29
Decrease in notes payable	35
Long-term financing:	
Decrease in long-term debt	74
Fixed asset acquisitions	425
Dividends paid	145
Total uses of cash	$731
Net addition to cash	$ 62
Cash, end of year	$146

statement in financial accounting, but this arrangement resembles one used many years ago. As we will discuss, this form can come in handy, but we emphasize again that it is not the way this information is normally presented.

Now that we have the various cash pieces in place, we can get a good idea of what happened during the year. Prufrock's major cash outlays were fixed asset acquisitions and cash dividends. It paid for these activities primarily with cash generated from operations.

Prufrock also retired some long-term debt and increased current assets. Finally, current liabilities were not greatly changed, and a relatively small amount of new equity was sold. Altogether, this short sketch captures Prufrock's major sources and uses of cash for the year.

Concept Questions

3.1a   What is a source of cash? Give three examples.

3.1b   What is a use, or application, of cash? Give three examples.

3.2   Standardized Financial Statements

Excel Master It!

xlsx Excel Master coverage online

The next thing we might want to do with Prufrock's financial statements is compare them to those of other similar companies. We would immediately have a problem, however. It's almost impossible to directly compare the financial statements for two companies because of differences in size.

For example, Ford and GM are serious rivals in the auto market, but GM is bigger (in terms of market share), so it is difficult to compare them directly. For that matter, it's difficult even to compare financial statements from different points in time for the same company if the company's size has changed. The size problem is compounded if we try to compare GM and, say, Toyota. If Toyota's financial statements are denominated in yen, then we have size *and* currency differences.

To start making comparisons, one obvious thing we might try to do is to somehow standardize the financial statements. One common and useful way of doing this is to work with percentages instead of total dollars. In this section, we describe two different ways of standardizing financial statements along these lines.

COMMON-SIZE STATEMENTS

common-size statement
A standardized financial statement presenting all items in percentage terms. Balance sheet items are shown as a percentage of assets and income statement items as a percentage of sales.

To get started, a useful way of standardizing financial statements is to express each item on the balance sheet as a percentage of assets and to express each item on the income statement as a percentage of sales. The resulting financial statements are called **common-size statements**. We consider these next.

Common-Size Balance Sheets   One way, though not the only way, to construct a common-size balance sheet is to express each item as a percentage of total assets. Prufrock's 2017 and 2018 common-size balance sheets are shown in Table 3.5.

Notice that some of the totals don't check exactly because of rounding. Also notice that the total change has to be zero because the beginning and ending numbers must add up to 100 percent.

In this form, financial statements are relatively easy to read and compare. For example, looking at the two balance sheets for Prufrock, we see that current assets

TABLE 3.5

PRUFROCK CORPORATION 2017 and 2018 Common-Size Balance Sheets			
	2017	**2018**	**Change**
Assets			
Current assets			
Cash	2.5%	4.0%	+1.5%
Accounts receivable	4.9	5.2	+ .3
Inventory	11.7	11.6	+ 0
Total	19.0	20.8	+1.8
Fixed assets			
Net plant and equipment	81.0	79.2	−1.8
Total assets	100.0%	100.0%	0
Liabilities and Owners' Equity			
Current liabilities			
Accounts payable	9.2%	9.5%	+ .2%
Notes payable	6.8	5.4	−1.5
Total	16.1	14.9	−1.2
Long-term debt	15.7	12.6	−3.2
Owners' equity			
Common stock and paid-in surplus	14.8	15.1	+ .3
Retained earnings	53.3	57.5	+4.1
Total	68.2	72.6	+4.4
Total liabilities and owners' equity	100.0%	100.0%	0

were 20.8 percent of total assets in 2018, up from 19.0 percent in 2017. Current liabilities declined from 16.1 percent to 14.9 percent of total liabilities and equity over that same time. Similarly, total equity rose from 68.2 percent of total liabilities and equity to 72.6 percent.

Overall, Prufrock's liquidity, as measured by current assets compared to current liabilities, increased over the year. Simultaneously, Prufrock's indebtedness diminished as a percentage of total assets. We might be tempted to conclude that the balance sheet has grown "stronger." We will say more about this later.

Common-Size Income Statements   A useful way of standardizing the income statement is to express each item as a percentage of total sales, as illustrated for Prufrock in Table 3.6.

This income statement tells us what happens to each dollar in sales. For Prufrock, interest expense eats up $.061 out of every sales dollar and taxes take another $.05. When all is said and done, $.188 of each dollar flows through to the bottom line (net income), and that amount is split into $.125 retained in the business and $.063 paid out in dividends.

These percentages are useful in comparisons. For example, a relevant figure is the cost percentage. For Prufrock, $.582 of each $1 in sales goes to pay for goods sold. It would be interesting to compute the same percentage for Prufrock's main competitors to see how Prufrock stacks up in terms of cost control.

TABLE 3.6

PRUFROCK CORPORATION 2018 Common-Size Income Statement	
Sales	100.0%
Cost of goods sold	58.2
Depreciation	11.9
Earnings before interest and taxes	29.9
Interest paid	6.1
Taxable income	23.8
Taxes (21%)	5.0
Net income	18.8%
Dividends 6.3%	
Addition to retained earnings 12.5	

Common-Size Statements of Cash Flows Although we have not presented it here, it is also possible and useful to prepare a common-size statement of cash flows. Unfortunately, with the current statement of cash flows, there is no obvious denominator such as total assets or total sales. However, if the information is arranged in a way similar to that in Table 3.4, then each item can be expressed as a percentage of total sources (or total uses). The results can then be interpreted as the percentage of total sources of cash supplied or as the percentage of total uses of cash for a particular item.

COMMON-BASE YEAR FINANCIAL STATEMENTS: TREND ANALYSIS

Imagine we were given balance sheets for the last 10 years for some company and we were trying to investigate trends in the firm's pattern of operations. Does the firm use more or less debt? Has the firm grown more or less liquid? A useful way of standardizing financial statements in this case is to choose a base year and then express each item relative to the base amount. We will call the resulting statements **common-base year statements**.

common-base year statement
A standardized financial statement presenting all items relative to a certain base year amount.

For example, from 2017 to 2018, looking at Table 3.1, Prufrock's inventory rose from $393 to $422. If we pick 2017 as our base year, then we would set inventory equal to 1.00 for that year. For the next year, we would calculate inventory relative to the base year as $422/$393 = 1.07. In this case, we could say inventory grew by about 7 percent during the year. If we had multiple years, we would divide the inventory figure for each one by $393. The resulting series is easy to plot, and it is then easy to compare companies. Table 3.7 summarizes these calculations for the asset side of the balance sheet.

COMBINED COMMON-SIZE AND BASE YEAR ANALYSIS

The trend analysis we have been discussing can be combined with the common-size analysis discussed earlier. The reason for doing this is that as total assets grow, most of the other accounts must grow as well. By first forming the common-size statements, we eliminate the effect of this overall growth.

For example, looking at Table 3.7, we see that Prufrock's accounts receivable were $165, or 4.9 percent of total assets, in 2017. In 2018, they had risen to $188, which was 5.2 percent of total assets. If we do our analysis in terms of dollars, then the 2018 figure would be $188/$165 = 1.14, representing a 14 percent increase in receivables. However, if we work with the common-size statements, then the 2018 figure would be 5.2%/4.9% = 1.06. This tells us accounts receivable, as a percentage of total assets, grew by 6 percent. Roughly speaking, what we see is that of the 14 percent total increase, about 8 percent (= 14% − 6%) is attributable to growth in total assets.

TABLE 3.7

PRUFROCK CORPORATION Summary of Standardized Balance Sheets (Asset Side Only)						
	Assets ($ in millions)		Common-Size Assets		Common-Base Year Assets	Combined Common-Size and Base Year Assets
	2017	2018	2017	2018	2018	2018
Current assets						
Cash	$ 84	$ 146	2.5%	4.0%	1.74	1.61
Accounts receivable	165	188	4.9	5.2	1.14	1.06
Inventory	393	422	11.7	11.6	1.07	1.00
Total current assets	$ 642	$ 756	19.0	20.8	1.18	1.09
Fixed assets						
Net plant and equipment	$2,731	$2,880	81.0	79.2	1.05	.98
Total assets	$3,373	$3,636	100.0%	100.0%	1.08	1.00

NOTE: The common-size numbers are calculated by dividing each item by total assets for that year. For example, the 2017 common-size cash amount is $84/$3,373 = .025, or 2.5%. The common-base year numbers are calculated by dividing each 2018 item by the base year (2017) dollar amount. The common-base year cash is thus $146/$84 = 1.74, representing a 74 percent increase. The combined common-size and base year figures are calculated by dividing each common-size amount by the base year (2017) common-size amount. The cash figure is therefore 4.0%/2.5% = 1.61, representing a 61 percent increase in cash holdings as a percentage of total assets. Columns may not total precisely due to rounding.

Concept Questions

3.2a   Why is it often necessary to standardize financial statements?

3.2b   Name two types of standardized statements and describe how each is formed.

Ratio Analysis

3.3

Another way of avoiding the problems involved in comparing companies of different sizes is to calculate and compare **financial ratios**. Such ratios are ways of comparing and investigating the relationships between different pieces of financial information. Using ratios eliminates the size problem because the size effectively divides out. We're then left with percentages, multiples, or time periods.

There is a problem in discussing financial ratios. Because a ratio is one number divided by another, and because there are so many accounting numbers out there, we could examine a huge number of possible ratios. Everybody has a favorite. We will restrict ourselves to a representative sampling.

In this section, we only want to introduce you to some commonly used financial ratios. These are not necessarily the ones we think are the best. In fact, some of them may strike you as illogical or not as useful as some alternatives. If they do, don't be concerned. As a financial analyst, you can always decide how to compute your own ratios.

What you do need to worry about is the fact that different people and different sources seldom compute these ratios in exactly the same way, and this leads to much confusion. The specific definitions we use here may or may not be the same as ones you have seen or will see elsewhere. If you are ever using ratios as a tool for analysis, you should be careful to document how you calculate each one. And if you are comparing your numbers to numbers from another source, be sure you know how those numbers have been computed.

Excel Master It!

xlsx Excel Master coverage online

financial ratios
Relationships determined from a firm's financial information and used for comparison purposes.

We will defer much of our discussion of how ratios are used and some problems that come up with using them until later in the chapter. For now, for each of the ratios we discuss, we consider several questions:

1. How is it computed?
2. What is it intended to measure, and why might we be interested?
3. What is the unit of measurement?
4. What might a high or low value tell us? How might such values be misleading?
5. How could this measure be improved?

Financial ratios are traditionally grouped into the following categories:

1. Short-term solvency, or liquidity, ratios.
2. Long-term solvency, or financial leverage, ratios.
3. Asset management, or turnover, ratios.
4. Profitability ratios.
5. Market value ratios.

We will consider each of these in turn. In calculating these numbers for Prufrock, we will use the ending balance sheet (2018) figures unless we say otherwise. Also notice that the various ratios are color keyed to indicate which numbers come from the income statement (blue) and which come from the balance sheet (green).

SHORT-TERM SOLVENCY, OR LIQUIDITY, MEASURES

As the name suggests, short-term solvency ratios as a group are intended to provide information about a firm's liquidity, and these ratios are sometimes called *liquidity measures*. The primary concern is the firm's ability to pay its bills over the short run without undue stress. Consequently, these ratios focus on current assets and current liabilities.

For obvious reasons, liquidity ratios are particularly interesting to short-term creditors. Because financial managers work constantly with banks and other short-term lenders, an understanding of these ratios is essential.

One advantage of looking at current assets and liabilities is that their book values and market values are likely to be similar. Often (though not always), these assets and liabilities don't live long enough for the two to get seriously out of step. On the other hand, like any type of near-cash, current assets and liabilities can and do change fairly rapidly, so today's amounts may not be a reliable guide to the future.

Go to **www.reuters.com** to examine comparative ratios for a huge number of companies.

Current Ratio   One of the best known and most widely used ratios is the *current ratio*. As you might guess, the current ratio is defined as follows:

$$\text{Current ratio} = \frac{\text{Current assets}}{\text{Current liabilities}}$$ **3.1**

Here is Prufrock's 2018 current ratio:

$$\text{Current ratio} = \frac{\$756}{\$540} = 1.40 \text{ times}$$

Because current assets and liabilities are, in principle, converted to cash over the following 12 months, the current ratio is a measure of short-term liquidity. The unit of measurement is either dollars or times. So, we could say Prufrock has $1.40 in current assets for every $1 in current liabilities, or we could say Prufrock has its current liabilities covered 1.40 times over.

To a creditor—particularly a short-term creditor such as a supplier—the higher the current ratio, the better. To the firm, a high current ratio indicates liquidity, but it also may indicate an inefficient use of cash and other short-term assets. Absent some extraordinary circumstances, we would expect to see a current ratio of at least 1 because a current ratio of less than 1 would mean that net working capital (current assets less current liabilities) is negative. This would be unusual in a healthy firm, at least for most types of businesses.

The current ratio, like any ratio, is affected by various types of transactions. For example, suppose the firm borrows over the long term to raise money. The short-run effect would be an increase in cash from the issue proceeds and an increase in long-term debt. Current liabilities would not be affected, so the current ratio would rise.

Finally, note that an apparently low current ratio may not be a bad sign for a company with a large reserve of untapped borrowing power.

Current Events	**EXAMPLE 3.1**

Suppose a firm pays off some of its suppliers and short-term creditors. What happens to the current ratio? Suppose a firm buys some inventory. What happens in this case? What happens if a firm sells some merchandise?

The first case is a trick question. What happens is that the current ratio moves away from 1. If it is greater than 1 (the usual case), it will get bigger. But if it is less than 1, it will get smaller. To see this, suppose the firm has $4 in current assets and $2 in current liabilities for a current ratio of 2. If we use $1 in cash to reduce current liabilities, then the new current ratio is ($4 − 1)/($2 − 1) = 3. If we reverse the original situation to $2 in current assets and $4 in current liabilities, then the change will cause the current ratio to fall to 1/3 from 1/2.

The second case is not quite as tricky. Nothing happens to the current ratio because cash goes down while inventory goes up—total current assets are unaffected.

In the third case, the current ratio will usually rise because inventory is normally shown at cost and the sale will normally be at something greater than cost (the difference is the markup). The increase in either cash or receivables is therefore greater than the decrease in inventory. This increases current assets, and the current ratio rises.

The Quick (or Acid-Test) Ratio   Inventory is often the least liquid current asset. It's also the one for which the book values are least reliable as measures of market value because the quality of the inventory isn't considered. Some of the inventory may later turn out to be damaged, obsolete, or lost.

More to the point, relatively large inventories are often a sign of short-term trouble. The firm may have overestimated sales and overbought or overproduced as a result. In this case, the firm may have a substantial portion of its liquidity tied up in slow-moving inventory.

To further evaluate liquidity, the *quick*, or *acid-test*, *ratio* is computed just like the current ratio, except inventory is omitted:

$$\text{Quick ratio} = \frac{\text{Current assets} - \text{Inventory}}{\text{Current liabilities}} \qquad \text{3.2}$$

Notice that using cash to buy inventory does not affect the current ratio, but it reduces the quick ratio. Again, the idea is that inventory is relatively illiquid compared to cash.

For Prufrock, this ratio for 2018 was:

$$\text{Quick ratio} = \frac{\$756 - 422}{\$540} = .62 \text{ times}$$

The quick ratio here tells a somewhat different story than the current ratio because inventory accounts for more than half of Prufrock's current assets. To exaggerate the point, if this inventory consisted of, say, unsold nuclear power plants, then this would be a cause for concern.

To give an example of current versus quick ratios, based on recent financial statements, Walmart and ManpowerGroup had current ratios of .85 and 1.39, respectively. However, Manpower carries no inventory to speak of, whereas Walmart's current assets are virtually all inventory. As a result, Walmart's quick ratio was only .22, whereas ManpowerGroup's was 1.39, the same as its current ratio.

Other Liquidity Ratios   We briefly mention three other measures of liquidity. A very short-term creditor might be interested in the *cash ratio*:

$$\text{Cash ratio} = \frac{\text{Cash}}{\text{Current liabilities}}$$ **3.3**

You can verify that for 2018 this works out to be .27 times for Prufrock.

Because net working capital, or NWC, is frequently viewed as the amount of short-term liquidity a firm has, we can consider the ratio of *NWC to total assets*:

$$\text{Net working capital to total assets} = \frac{\text{Net working capital}}{\text{Total assets}}$$ **3.4**

A relatively low value might indicate relatively low levels of liquidity. Here, this ratio works out to be ($756 − 540)/$3,636 = .06 times.

Finally, imagine that Prufrock was facing a strike and cash inflows began to dry up. How long could the business keep running? One answer is given by the *interval measure*:

$$\text{Interval measure} = \frac{\text{Current assets}}{\text{Average daily operating costs}}$$ **3.5**

Total costs for the year, excluding depreciation and interest, were $1,344. The average daily cost was $1,344/365 = $3.68 per day.[1] The interval measure is thus $756/$3.68 = 205 days. Based on this, Prufrock could hang on for six months or so.[2]

The interval measure (or something similar) is also useful for newly founded or start-up companies that often have little in the way of revenues. For such companies, the interval measure indicates how long the company can operate until it needs another round of financing. The average daily operating cost for start-up companies is often called the *burn rate*, meaning the rate at which cash is burned in the race to become profitable.

LONG-TERM SOLVENCY MEASURES

Long-term solvency ratios are intended to address the firm's long-term ability to meet its obligations, or, more generally, its financial leverage. These are sometimes called *financial leverage ratios* or *leverage ratios*. We consider three commonly used measures and some variations.

Total Debt Ratio   The *total debt ratio* takes into account all debts of all maturities to all creditors. It can be defined in several ways, the easiest of which is this:

$$\text{Total debt ratio} = \frac{\text{Total assets} - \text{Total equity}}{\text{Total assets}}$$ **3.6**
$$= \frac{\$3,636 - 2,639}{\$3,636} = .27 \text{ times}$$

---

[1]For many of these ratios that involve average daily amounts, a 360-day year is often used in practice. This so-called banker's year has exactly four quarters of 90 days each and was computationally convenient in the days before pocket calculators. We'll use 365 days.

[2]Sometimes depreciation and/or interest is included in calculating average daily costs. Depreciation isn't a cash expense, so its inclusion doesn't make a lot of sense. Interest is a financing cost, so we excluded it by definition (we looked at only operating costs). We could, of course, define a different ratio that included interest expense.

In this case, an analyst might say that Prufrock uses 27 percent debt.[3] Whether this is high or low or whether it even makes any difference depends on whether capital structure matters, a subject we discuss in Part 6.

Prufrock has $.27 in debt for every $1 in assets. Therefore, there is $.73 in equity (= $1 − .27) for every $.27 in debt. With this in mind, we can define two useful variations on the total debt ratio—the *debt-equity ratio* and the *equity multiplier*:

Debt-equity ratio = Total debt/Total equity

$$= \$.27/\$.73 = .38 \text{ times}$$

Equity multiplier = Total assets/Total equity

$$= \$1/\$.73 = 1.38 \text{ times}$$

The fact that the equity multiplier is 1 plus the debt-equity ratio is not a coincidence:

Equity multiplier = Total assets/Total equity = $1/$.73 = 1.38

$$= (\text{Total equity} + \text{Total debt})/\text{Total equity}$$

$$= 1 + \text{Debt-equity ratio} = 1.38 \text{ times}$$

The thing to notice here is that given any one of these three ratios, you can immediately calculate the other two; so, they all say exactly the same thing.

A Brief Digression: Total Capitalization versus Total Assets   Frequently, financial analysts are more concerned with a firm's long-term debt than its short-term debt because the short-term debt will be constantly changing. Also, a firm's accounts payable may reflect trade practice more than debt management policy. For these reasons, the *long-term debt ratio* is often calculated as follows:

Ratios used to analyze technology firms can be found at **www.chalfin.com** under the "Publications" link.

Long-term debt ratio $= \dfrac{\text{Long-term debt}}{\text{Long-term debt} + \text{Total equity}}$

$$= \frac{\$457}{\$457 + 2{,}639} = \frac{\$457}{\$3{,}096} = .15 \text{ times}$$

The $3,096 in total long-term debt and equity is sometimes called the firm's *total capitalization*, and the financial manager will frequently focus on this quantity rather than on total assets.

To complicate matters, different people (and different books) mean different things by the term *debt ratio*. Some mean a ratio of total debt, some mean a ratio of long-term debt only, and, unfortunately, a substantial number are vague about which one they mean.

This is a source of confusion, so we choose to give two separate names to the two measures. The same problem comes up in discussing the debt-equity ratio. Financial analysts frequently calculate this ratio using only long-term debt.

Times Interest Earned   Another common measure of long-term solvency is the *times interest earned* (TIE) *ratio*. Once again, there are several possible (and common) definitions, but we'll stick with the most traditional:

Times interest earned ratio $= \dfrac{\text{EBIT}}{\text{Interest}}$

$$= \frac{\$691}{\$141} = 4.9 \text{ times}$$

---

[3]Total equity here includes preferred stock (discussed in Chapter 8 and elsewhere), if there is any. An equivalent numerator in this ratio would be Current liabilities + Long-term debt.

As the name suggests, this ratio measures how well a company has its interest obligations covered, and it is often called the *interest coverage ratio*. For Prufrock, the interest bill is covered 4.9 times over.

Cash Coverage A problem with the TIE ratio is that it is based on EBIT, which is not really a measure of cash available to pay interest. The reason is that depreciation, a noncash expense, has been deducted out. Because interest is definitely a cash outflow (to creditors), one way to define the *cash coverage ratio* is this:

$$\text{Cash coverage ratio} = \frac{\text{EBIT} + \text{Depreciation}}{\text{Interest}}$$ **3.11**

$$= \frac{\$691 + 276}{\$141} = \frac{\$967}{\$141} = 6.86 \text{ times}$$

The numerator here, EBIT plus depreciation, is often abbreviated EBITD (earnings before interest, taxes, and depreciation—say "ebbit-dee"). It is a basic measure of the firm's ability to generate cash from operations, and it is frequently used as a measure of cash flow available to meet financial obligations.

A common variation on EBITD is earnings before interest, taxes, depreciation, and amortization (EBITDA—say "ebbit-dah"). Here *amortization* refers to a noncash deduction similar conceptually to depreciation, except it applies to an intangible asset (such as a patent) rather than a tangible asset (such as a machine). Note that the word *amortization* here does not refer to the repayment of debt, a subject we discuss in a later chapter.

ASSET MANAGEMENT, OR TURNOVER, MEASURES

We next turn our attention to the efficiency with which Prufrock uses its assets. The measures in this section are sometimes called *asset utilization ratios*. The specific ratios we discuss can all be interpreted as measures of turnover. What they are intended to describe is how efficiently or intensively a firm uses its assets to generate sales. We first look at two important current assets: inventory and receivables.

Inventory Turnover and Days' Sales in Inventory During the year, Prufrock had a cost of goods sold of $1,344. Inventory at the end of the year was $422. With these numbers, *inventory turnover* can be calculated as follows:

$$\text{Inventory turnover} = \frac{\text{Cost of goods sold}}{\text{Inventory}}$$ **3.12**

$$= \frac{\$1,344}{\$422} = 3.18 \text{ times}$$

In a sense, Prufrock sold off or turned over the entire inventory 3.18 times.[4] As long as we are not running out of stock and thereby forgoing sales, the higher this ratio is, the more efficiently we are managing inventory.

If we know we turned our inventory over 3.18 times during the year, we can immediately figure out how long it took us to turn it over on average. The result is the average *days' sales in inventory*:

$$\text{Days' sales in inventory} = \frac{365 \text{ days}}{\text{Inventory turnover}}$$ **3.13**

$$= \frac{365 \text{ days}}{3.18} = 115 \text{ days}$$

---

[4]Notice that we used cost of goods sold in the top of this ratio. For some purposes, it might be more useful to use sales instead of costs. For example, if we wanted to know the amount of sales generated per dollar of inventory, we could just replace the cost of goods sold with sales.

This tells us that, roughly speaking, inventory sits 115 days on average before it is sold. Alternatively, assuming we have used the most recent inventory and cost figures, it will take about 115 days to work off our current inventory.

To give an example, in September 2017, the U.S. automobile industry as a whole had a 74-day supply of cars, higher than the 60-day supply considered normal. This figure means that at the then-current rate of sales, it would have taken 62 days to deplete the available supply. Of course, there was significant variation among the auto manufacturers. For example, BMW had only a 40-day supply of inventory, while Mitsubishi's days' sales in inventory was 125 days.

It might make more sense to use the average inventory in calculating turnover. Inventory turnover would then be $1,344/[($393 + 422)/2] = 3.3$ times.[5] It depends on the purpose of the calculation. If we are interested in how long it will take us to sell our current inventory, then using the ending figure (as we did initially) is probably better.

In many of the ratios we discuss in this chapter, average figures could just as well be used. Again, it depends on whether we are worried about the past, in which case averages are appropriate, or the future, in which case ending figures might be better. Also, using ending figures is common in reporting industry averages; so, for comparison purposes, ending figures should be used in such cases. In any event, using ending figures is definitely less work, so we'll continue to use them.

Receivables Turnover and Days' Sales in Receivables   Our inventory measures give some indication of how fast we can sell product. We now look at how fast we collect on those sales. The *receivables turnover* is defined much like inventory turnover:

$$\text{Receivables turnover} = \frac{\text{Sales}}{\text{Accounts receivable}} \quad \text{[3.14]}$$

$$= \frac{\$2,311}{\$188} = 12.29 \text{ times}$$

Loosely speaking, Prufrock collected its outstanding credit accounts and reloaned the money 12.29 times during the year.[6]

This ratio makes more sense if we convert it to days, so here is the *days' sales in receivables*:

$$\text{Days' sales in receivables} = \frac{365 \text{ days}}{\text{Receivables turnover}} \quad \text{[3.15]}$$

$$= \frac{365}{12.29} = 30 \text{ days}$$

Therefore, on average, Prufrock collects on its credit sales in 30 days. For obvious reasons, this ratio is frequently called the *average collection period* (ACP).

Note that if we are using the most recent figures, we could also say that we have 30 days' worth of sales currently uncollected. We will learn more about this subject when we study credit policy in a later chapter.

---

[5]Notice that we calculated the average as (Beginning value + Ending value)/2.

[6]Here we have implicitly assumed that all sales are credit sales. If they were not, we would simply use total credit sales in these calculations, not total sales.

Payables Turnover   **EXAMPLE 3.2**

Here is a variation on the receivables collection period. How long, on average, does it take for Prufrock Corporation to pay its bills? To answer, we need to calculate the accounts payable turnover rate using cost of goods sold. We will assume that Prufrock purchases everything on credit.

> The cost of goods sold is $1,344, and accounts payable are $344. The turnover is therefore $1,344/$344 = 3.91 times. So, payables turned over about every 365/3.91 = 94 days. On average, then, Prufrock takes 94 days to pay. As a potential creditor, we might take note of this fact.

Asset Turnover Ratios   Moving away from specific accounts like inventory or receivables, we can consider several "big picture" ratios. For example, *NWC turnover* is:

$$\text{NWC turnover} = \frac{\text{Sales}}{\text{NWC}}$$

$$= \frac{\$2,311}{\$756 - 540} = 10.7 \text{ times}$$

[3.16]

This ratio measures how much "work" we get out of our working capital. Once again, assuming we aren't missing out on sales, a high value is preferred. (Why?)

Similarly, *fixed asset turnover* is:

$$\text{Fixed asset turnover} = \frac{\text{Sales}}{\text{Net fixed assets}}$$

$$= \frac{\$2,311}{\$2,880} = .80 \text{ times}$$

[3.17]

With this ratio, it probably makes more sense to say that for every dollar in fixed assets, Prufrock generated $.80 in sales.

Our final asset management ratio, *total asset turnover*, comes up quite a bit. We will see it later in this chapter and in the next chapter. As the name suggests, the total asset turnover is:

$$\text{Total asset turnover} = \frac{\text{Sales}}{\text{Total assets}}$$

$$= \frac{\$2,311}{\$3,588} = .64 \text{ times}$$

[3.18]

In other words, for every dollar in assets, Prufrock generated $.64 in sales.

To give an example of fixed and total asset turnover, based on recent financial statements, Southwest Airlines had a total asset turnover of .85, compared to .74 for IBM. However, the much higher investment in fixed assets in an airline is reflected in Southwest's fixed asset turnover of 1.03, compared to IBM's 1.20.

EXAMPLE 3.3   **More Turnover**

Suppose you find that a particular company generates $.40 in sales for every dollar in total assets. How often does this company turn over its total assets?

The total asset turnover here is .40 times per year. It takes 1/.40 = 2.5 years to turn total assets over completely.

PROFITABILITY MEASURES

The three measures we discuss in this section are probably the best known and most widely used of all financial ratios. In one form or another, they are intended to measure how efficiently a firm uses its assets and manages its operations. The focus in this group is on the bottom line, net income.

Profit Margin   Companies pay a great deal of attention to their *profit margins*:

3.19

$$\text{Profit margin} = \frac{\text{Net income}}{\text{Sales}}$$

$$= \frac{\$435}{\$2,311} = .1880, \text{ or } 18.80\%$$

This tells us that Prufrock, in an accounting sense, generates a little less than 19 cents in profit for every dollar in sales.

All other things being equal, a relatively high profit margin is obviously desirable. This situation corresponds to low expense ratios relative to sales. However, we hasten to add that other things are often not equal.

For example, lowering our sales price will usually increase unit volume but will normally cause profit margins to shrink. Total profit (or, more important, operating cash flow) may go up or down; so the fact that margins are smaller isn't necessarily bad. After all, isn't it possible that, as the saying goes, "Our prices are so low that we lose money on everything we sell, but we make it up in volume"?[7]

Return on Assets   *Return on assets* (ROA) is a measure of profit per dollar of assets. It can be defined several ways, but the most common is this:

3.20

$$\text{Return on assets} = \frac{\text{Net income}}{\text{Total assets}}$$

$$= \frac{\$435}{\$3,636} = .1195, \text{ or } 11.95\%$$

Return on Equity   *Return on equity* (ROE) is a measure of how the stockholders fared during the year. Because benefiting shareholders is our goal, ROE is, in an accounting sense, the true bottom-line measure of performance. ROE is usually measured as follows:

3.21

$$\text{Return on equity} = \frac{\text{Net income}}{\text{Total equity}}$$

$$= \frac{\$435}{\$2,639} = .1646, \text{ or } 16.46\%$$

For every dollar in equity, therefore, Prufrock generated 16.46 cents in profit; but this is correct only in accounting terms.

Because ROA and ROE are such commonly cited numbers, we stress that it is important to remember they are accounting rates of return. For this reason, these measures should properly be called *return on book assets* and *return on book equity*. In fact, ROE is sometimes called *return on net worth*. Whatever it's called, it would be inappropriate to compare the result to, for example, an interest rate observed in the financial markets. We will have more to say about accounting rates of return in later chapters.

The fact that ROE exceeds ROA reflects Prufrock's use of financial leverage. We will examine the relationship between these two measures in more detail shortly.

---

[7]No, it's not.

ROE and ROA	**EXAMPLE 3.4**

Because ROE and ROA are usually intended to measure performance over a prior period, it makes a certain amount of sense to base them on average equity and average assets, respectively. For Prufrock, how would you calculate these?

We first need to calculate average assets and average equity:

Average assets = ($3,373 + 3,636)/2 = $3,505
Average equity = ($2,299 + 2,639)/2 = $2,469

With these averages, we can recalculate ROA and ROE as follows:

$$\text{ROA} = \frac{\$435}{\$3,505} = .1240, \text{ or } 12.40\%$$

$$\text{ROE} = \frac{\$435}{\$2,469} = .1760, \text{ or } 17.60\%$$

These are slightly higher than our previous calculations because assets and equity grew during the year, so the average values are below the ending values.

MARKET VALUE MEASURES

Our final group of measures is based, in part, on information not necessarily contained in financial statements—the market price per share of stock. Obviously, these measures can be calculated directly only for publicly traded companies.

We assume that Prufrock has 33 million shares outstanding and the stock sold for $88 per share at the end of the year. If we recall that Prufrock's net income was $435 million, we can calculate its earnings per share:

$$\text{EPS} = \frac{\text{Net income}}{\text{Shares outstanding}} = \frac{\$435}{33} = \$13.17$$

Price-Earnings Ratio The first of our market value measures, the *price-earnings* (PE) *ratio* (or multiple), is defined here:

$$\textbf{PE ratio} = \frac{\textbf{Price per share}}{\textbf{Earnings per share}}$$

$$= \frac{\$88}{\$13.17} = 6.68 \text{ times}$$

3.22

In the vernacular, we would say that Prufrock shares sell for almost seven times earnings, or we might say that Prufrock shares have or "carry" a PE multiple of 6.68.

PE ratios vary substantially across companies, but, in 2017, a typical large company in the United States had a PE in the 15–20 range. This is on the high side by historical standards, but not dramatically so. A low point for PEs was about 5 in 1974. PEs also vary across countries. For example, Japanese PEs have historically been much higher than those of their U.S. counterparts.

Because the PE ratio measures how much investors are willing to pay per dollar of current earnings, higher PEs are often taken to mean the firm has significant prospects for future growth. Of course, if a firm had no or almost no earnings, its PE would probably be quite large; so, as always, care is needed in interpreting this ratio.

Sometimes analysts divide PE ratios by expected future earnings growth rates (after multiplying the growth rate by 100). The result is the PEG ratio. Suppose Prufrock's anticipated growth rate in EPS was 6 percent. Its PEG ratio would then be 6.68/6 = 1.11. The idea behind the PEG ratio is that whether a PE ratio is high or low depends on expected future growth. High PEG ratios suggest that the PE is too high relative to growth, and vice versa.

Price-Sales Ratio In some cases, companies will have negative earnings for extended periods, so their PE ratios are not very meaningful. A good example is a recent start-up. Such companies usually do have some revenues, so analysts will often look at the *price-sales ratio*:

Price-sales ratio = Price per share/Sales per share

In Prufrock's case, sales were \$2,311, so here is the price-sales ratio:

Price-sales ratio = \$88/(\$2,311/33) = \$88/\$70 = 1.26 times

As with PE ratios, whether a particular price-sales ratio is high or low depends on the industry involved.

Market-to-Book Ratio   A third commonly quoted market value measure is the *market-to-book ratio*:

$$\text{Market-to-book ratio} = \frac{\text{Market value per share}}{\text{Book value per share}}$$

$$= \frac{\$88}{(\$2,639/33)} = \frac{\$88}{\$80.0} = 1.10 \text{ times}$$ **3.23**

Notice that book value per share is total equity (not just common stock) divided by the number of shares outstanding.

Because book value per share is an accounting number, it reflects historical costs. In a loose sense, the market-to-book ratio compares the market value of the firm's investments to their cost. A value less than 1 could mean that the firm has not been successful overall in creating value for its stockholders.

Market-to-book ratios in recent years appear high relative to past values. For example, for the 30 blue-chip companies that make up the widely followed Dow Jones Industrial Average, the historical norm is about 1.7; however, the market-to-book ratio for this group has recently been twice this size.

Another ratio, called *Tobin's Q ratio*, is much like the market-to-book ratio. Tobin's Q is the market value of a firm's assets divided by their replacement cost:

Tobin's Q = Market value of firm's assets/Replacement cost of firm's assets

= Market value of firm's debt and equity/Replacement cost of firm's assets

Notice that we used two equivalent numerators here: the market value of the firm's assets and the market value of its debt and equity.

Conceptually, the Q ratio is superior to the market-to-book ratio because it focuses on what the firm is worth today relative to what it would cost to replace it today. Firms with high Q ratios tend to be those with attractive investment opportunities or significant competitive advantages (or both). In contrast, the market-to-book ratio focuses on historical costs, which are less relevant.

As a practical matter, however, Q ratios are difficult to calculate with accuracy because estimating the replacement cost of a firm's assets is not an easy task. Also, market values for a firm's debt are often unobservable. Book values can be used instead in such cases, but accuracy may suffer.

Enterprise Value-EBITDA Ratio   A company's enterprise value is an estimate of the market value of the company's operating assets. By operating assets, we mean all the assets of the firm except cash. Of course, it's not practical to work with the individual assets of a firm because market values would usually not be available. Instead, we can use the right-hand side of the balance sheet and calculate the enterprise value as:

Enterprise value = Total market value of the stock   **3.24**

+ Book value of all liabilities − Cash

We use the book value for liabilities because we typically can't get the market values, at least not for all of them. However, book value is usually a reasonable approximation for market value when it comes to liabilities, particularly short-term debts. Notice that the sum of the value of the market values of the stock and all liabilities equals the value of the firm's assets from the balance sheet identity. Once we have this number, we subtract the cash to get the enterprise value.

TABLE 3.8   **Common Financial Ratios**

I. Short-term solvency, or liquidity, ratios	II. Long-term solvency, or financial leverage, ratios
$\text{Current ratio} = \dfrac{\text{Current assets}}{\text{Current liabilities}}$	$\text{Total debt ratio} = \dfrac{\text{Total assets} - \text{Total equity}}{\text{Total assets}}$
$\text{Quick ratio} = \dfrac{\text{Current assets} - \text{Inventory}}{\text{Current liabilities}}$	$\text{Debt-equity ratio} = \text{Total debt/Total equity}$
$\text{Cash ratio} = \dfrac{\text{Cash}}{\text{Current liabilities}}$	$\text{Equity multiplier} = \text{Total assets/Total equity}$
$\text{Net working capital to total assets} = \dfrac{\text{Net working capital}}{\text{Total assets}}$	$\text{Long-term debt ratio} = \dfrac{\text{Long-term debt}}{\text{Long-term debt} + \text{Total equity}}$
$\text{Interval measure} = \dfrac{\text{Current assets}}{\text{Average daily operating costs}}$	$\text{Times interest earned ratio} = \dfrac{\text{EBIT}}{\text{Interest}}$
	$\text{Cash coverage ratio} = \dfrac{\text{EBIT} + \text{Depreciation}}{\text{Interest}}$

III. Asset management, or turnover, ratios	IV. Profitability ratios
$\text{Inventory turnover} = \dfrac{\text{Cost of goods sold}}{\text{Inventory}}$	$\text{Profit margin} = \dfrac{\text{Net income}}{\text{Sales}}$
$\text{Days' sales in inventory} = \dfrac{365 \text{ days}}{\text{Inventory turnover}}$	$\text{Return on assets (ROA)} = \dfrac{\text{Net income}}{\text{Total assets}}$
$\text{Receivables turnover} = \dfrac{\text{Sales}}{\text{Accounts receivable}}$	$\text{Return on equity (ROE)} = \dfrac{\text{Net income}}{\text{Total equity}}$
$\text{Days' sales in receivables} = \dfrac{365 \text{ days}}{\text{Receivables turnover}}$	$\text{ROE} = \dfrac{\text{Net income}}{\text{Sales}} \times \dfrac{\text{Sales}}{\text{Assets}} \times \dfrac{\text{Assets}^*}{\text{Equity}}$
$\text{NWC turnover} = \dfrac{\text{Sales}}{\text{NWC}}$	**V. Market value ratios**
$\text{Fixed asset turnover} = \dfrac{\text{Sales}}{\text{Net fixed assets}}$	$\text{Price-earnings ratio} = \dfrac{\text{Price per share}}{\text{Earnings per share}}$
$\text{Total asset turnover} = \dfrac{\text{Sales}}{\text{Total assets}}$	$\text{PEG ratio} = \dfrac{\text{Price-earnings ratio}}{\text{Earnings growth rate (\%)}}$
	$\text{Price-sales ratio} = \dfrac{\text{Price per share}}{\text{Sales per share}}$
	$\text{Market-to-book-ratio} = \dfrac{\text{Market value per share}}{\text{Book value per share}}$
	$\text{Tobin's Q ratio} = \dfrac{\text{Market value of assets}}{\text{Replacement cost of assets}}$
	$\text{Enterprise value-EBITDA ratio} = \dfrac{\text{Enterprise value}}{\text{EBITDA}}$

*This ROE decomposition is covered in Section 3.4.

Enterprise value is frequently used to calculate the EBITDA ratio (or enterprise multiple):

EBITDA ratio = Enterprise value/EBITDA   **3.25**

This ratio is similar in spirit to the PE ratio, but it relates the value of all the operating assets (the enterprise value) to a measure of the operating cash flow generated by those assets (EBITDA).

CONCLUSION

This completes our definitions of some common ratios. We could tell you about more of them, but these are enough for now. We'll go on to discuss some ways of using these ratios instead of just how to calculate them. Table 3.8 summarizes the ratios we've discussed.

The DuPont Identity   **3.4**

As we mentioned in discussing ROA and ROE, the difference between these two profitability measures is a reflection of the use of debt financing, or financial leverage. We illustrate the relationship between these measures in this section by investigating a famous way of decomposing ROE into its component parts.

Excel Master It!
Excel Master coverage online

A CLOSER LOOK AT ROE

To begin, let's recall the definition of ROE:

$$\text{Return on equity} = \frac{\text{Net income}}{\text{Total equity}}$$

If we were so inclined, we could multiply this ratio by Assets/Assets without changing anything:

$$\text{Return on equity} = \frac{\text{Net income}}{\text{Total equity}} = \frac{\text{Net income}}{\text{Total equity}} \times \frac{\text{Assets}}{\text{Assets}}$$

$$= \frac{\text{Net income}}{\text{Assets}} \times \frac{\text{Assets}}{\text{Total equity}}$$

Notice that we have expressed the ROE as the product of two other ratios—ROA and the equity multiplier:

$$\text{ROE} = \text{ROA} \times \text{Equity multiplier} = \text{ROA} \times (1 + \text{Debt-equity ratio})$$

Looking back at Prufrock, for example, we see that the debt-equity ratio was .38 and ROA was 11.95 percent. Our work here implies that Prufrock's ROE, as we previously calculated, is this:

$$\text{ROE} = .1195 \times 1.38 = .1646, \text{ or } 16.46\%$$

The difference between ROE and ROA can be substantial, particularly for certain businesses. For example, in 2016, American Express had an ROA of 3.40 percent, which is fairly typical for financial institutions. However, financial institutions tend to borrow a lot of money and, as a result, have relatively large equity multipliers. For American Express, ROE was about 26.38 percent, implying an equity multiplier of 7.75 times.

We can further decompose ROE by multiplying the top and bottom by total sales:

$$\text{ROE} = \frac{\text{Sales}}{\text{Sales}} \times \frac{\text{Net income}}{\text{Assets}} \times \frac{\text{Assets}}{\text{Total equity}}$$

If we rearrange things a bit, ROE looks like this:

$$\text{ROE} = \underbrace{\frac{\text{Net income}}{\text{Sales}} \times \frac{\text{Sales}}{\text{Assets}}}_{\text{Return on assets}} \times \frac{\text{Assets}}{\text{Total equity}}$$ **3.26**

$$= \text{Profit margin} \times \text{Total asset turnover} \times \text{Equity multiplier}$$

DuPont identity
Popular expression breaking ROE into three parts: operating efficiency, asset use efficiency, and financial leverage.

What we have now done is to partition ROA into its two component parts, profit margin and total asset turnover. The last expression of the preceding equation is called the **DuPont identity**, after the DuPont Corporation, which popularized its use.

We can check this relationship for Prufrock by noting that the profit margin was 15.71 percent and the total asset turnover was .64:

$$\text{ROE} = \text{Profit margin} \times \text{Total asset turnover} \times \text{Equity multiplier}$$
$$= \quad .1880 \quad \times \quad .64 \quad \times \quad 1.38$$
$$= .1646, \text{ or } 16.46\%$$

This 16.46 percent ROE is exactly what we had before.

The DuPont identity tells us that ROE is affected by three things:

1. Operating efficiency (as measured by profit margin).
2. Asset use efficiency (as measured by total asset turnover).
3. Financial leverage (as measured by the equity multiplier).

Weakness in either operating or asset use efficiency (or both) will show up in a diminished return on assets, which will translate into a lower ROE.

Considering the DuPont identity, it appears that the ROE could be leveraged up by increasing the amount of debt in the firm. However, notice that increasing debt also increases interest expense, which reduces profit margins, which acts to reduce ROE. So, ROE could go up or down, depending on other variables. More important, the use of debt financing has a number of other effects, and, as we discuss at some length in Part 6, the amount of leverage a firm uses is governed by its capital structure policy.

The decomposition of ROE we've discussed in this section is a convenient way of systematically approaching financial statement analysis. If ROE is unsatisfactory by some measure, then the DuPont identity tells you where to start looking for the reasons.

General Motors provides a good example of how DuPont analysis can be very useful and also illustrates why care must be taken in interpreting ROE values. In 1989, GM had an ROE of 12.1 percent. By 1993, its ROE had improved to 44.1 percent, a dramatic improvement. On closer inspection, however, we find that over the same period GM's profit margin had declined from 3.4 to 1.8 percent, and ROA had declined from 2.4 to 1.3 percent. The decline in ROA was moderated only slightly by an increase in total asset turnover from .71 to .73 over the period.

Given this information, how is it possible for GM's ROE to have climbed so sharply? From our understanding of the DuPont identity, it must be the case that GM's equity multiplier increased substantially. In fact, what happened was that GM's book equity value was almost wiped out overnight in 1992 by changes in the accounting treatment of pension liabilities. If a company's equity value declines sharply, its equity multiplier rises. In GM's case, the multiplier went from 4.95 in 1989 to 33.62 in 1993. In sum, the dramatic "improvement" in GM's ROE was almost entirely due to an accounting change that affected the equity multiplier and didn't really represent an improvement in financial performance at all.

DuPont analysis (and ratio analysis in general) can be used to compare two companies as well. Yahoo! and Alphabet are among the most important Internet companies in the world. We will use them to illustrate how DuPont analysis can be useful in helping to ask the right questions about a firm's financial performance. The DuPont breakdowns for Yahoo! and Alphabet are summarized in Table 3.9.

As shown, in 2015, Yahoo! had an ROE of −15.0 percent, well down from its ROE in 2013 of 10.4 percent. In contrast, in 2015, Alphabet had an ROE of 13.6 percent, about the same as its ROE in 2013 of 14.8 percent. Given this information, how is it possible that

	ROE		Profit margin		Total asset turnover		Equity multiplier
Yahoo!							
2015	−15.0%	=	−87.5%	×	.110	×	1.56
2014	.4	=	3.1	×	.075	×	1.59
2013	10.4	=	29.2	×	.279	×	1.29
Alphabet							
2015	13.6%	=	21.8%	×	.509	×	1.23
2014	13.6	=	21.4	×	.511	×	1.24
2013	14.8	=	21.6	×	.539	×	1.27

TABLE 3.9

Alphabet's ROE could be so much higher during this period of time, and what accounts for the decrease in Yahoo!'s ROE?

On closer inspection of the DuPont breakdown, we see that Yahoo!'s profit margin in 2015 was −87.5 percent, really poor performance. Meanwhile, Alphabet's profit margin was 21.8 percent. While much of the difference in ROE can be explained by the difference in the profit margin, Yahoo! and Alphabet have similar financial leverage. However, it is also important to note that Alphabet has another advantage over Yahoo! in ROE—namely, the much higher asset utilization.

AN EXPANDED DUPONT ANALYSIS

So far, we've seen how the DuPont equation lets us break down ROE into its basic three components: profit margin, total asset turnover, and financial leverage. We now extend this analysis to take a closer look at how key parts of a firm's operations feed into ROE. To get going, we went to finance.yahoo.com and found financial statements for science and technology giant DuPont. What we found is summarized in Table 3.10.

Using the information in Table 3.10, Figure 3.1 shows how we can construct an expanded DuPont analysis for DuPont and present that analysis in chart form. The advantage of the extended DuPont chart is that it lets us examine several ratios at once, thereby getting a better overall picture of a company's performance and also allowing us to determine possible items to improve.

TABLE 3.10

FINANCIAL STATEMENTS FOR DUPONT 12 months ending December 31, 2016 (All numbers are in millions)					
Income Statement		**Balance Sheet**			
Sales	$24,750	Current assets		Current liabilities	
CoGS	14,469	Cash	$ 5,967	Accounts payable	$ 8,468
Gross profit	$10,281	Accounts receivable	4,971	Other	429
SG&A expenses	5,005	Inventory	6,179	Total	$ 8,897
R&D expenses	1,641	Total	$17,117		
EBIT	$ 3,635				
Interest	370	Fixed assets	$22,847	Total long-term debt	$21,069
EBT	$ 3,265				
Taxes	744			Total equity	$ 9,998
Net income	$ 2,521	Total assets	$39,964	Total liabilities and equity	$39,964

FIGURE 3.1   Extended DuPont Chart for DuPont

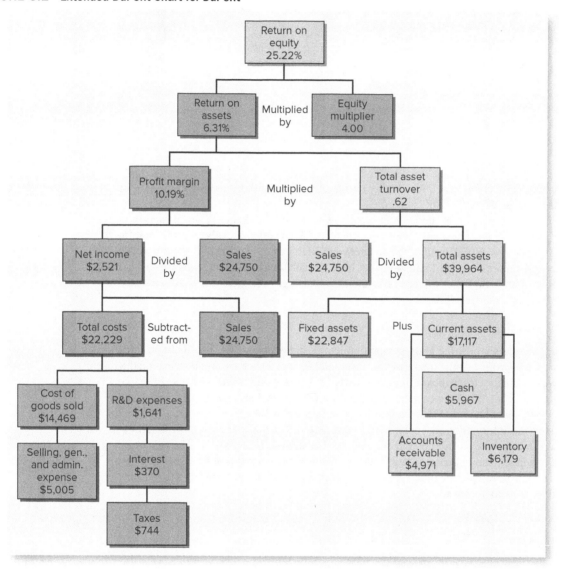

Looking at the left side of our DuPont chart in Figure 3.1, we see items related to profitability. As always, profit margin is calculated as net income divided by sales. But as our chart emphasizes, net income depends on sales and a variety of costs, such as cost of goods sold (CoGS) and selling, general, and administrative expenses (SG&A expense). DuPont can increase its ROE by increasing sales and also by reducing one or more of these costs. In other words, if we want to improve profitability, our chart clearly shows us the areas on which we should focus.

Turning to the right side of Figure 3.1, we have an analysis of the key factors underlying total asset turnover. Thus, for example, we see that reducing inventory holdings through more efficient management reduces current assets, which reduces total assets, which then improves total asset turnover.

Concept Questions

3.4a   Return on assets, or ROA, can be expressed as the product of two ratios. Which two?

3.4b   Return on equity, or ROE, can be expressed as the product of three ratios. Which three?

Using Financial Statement Information   3.5

Our last task in this chapter is to discuss in more detail some practical aspects of financial statement analysis. In particular, we will look at reasons for analyzing financial statements, how to get benchmark information, and some problems that come up in the process.

Excel Master It!

xlsx   Excel Master coverage online

WHY EVALUATE FINANCIAL STATEMENTS?

As we have discussed, the primary reason for looking at accounting information is that we don't have, and can't reasonably expect to get, market value information. We stress that whenever we have market information, we will use it instead of accounting data. Also, if there is a conflict between accounting and market data, market data should be given precedence.

Financial statement analysis is essentially an application of "management by exception." In many cases, such analysis will boil down to comparing ratios for one business with average or representative ratios. Those ratios that seem to differ the most from the averages are tagged for further study.

Internal Uses   Financial statement information has a variety of uses within a firm. Among the most important of these is performance evaluation. For example, managers are frequently evaluated and compensated on the basis of accounting measures of performance such as profit margin and return on equity. Also, firms with multiple divisions frequently compare the performance of those divisions using financial statement information.

Another important internal use we will explore in the next chapter is planning for the future. As we will see, historical financial statement information is useful for generating projections about the future and for checking the realism of assumptions made in those projections.

External Uses   Financial statements are useful to parties outside the firm, including short-term and long-term creditors and potential investors. For example, we would find such information quite useful in deciding whether to grant credit to a new customer.

We would also use this information to evaluate suppliers, and suppliers would review our statements before deciding to extend credit to us. Large customers use this information to decide if we are likely to be around in the future. Credit-rating agencies rely on financial statements in assessing a firm's overall creditworthiness. The common theme here is that financial statements are a prime source of information about a firm's financial health.

We would also find such information useful in evaluating our main competitors. We might be thinking of launching a new product. A prime concern would be whether the competition would jump in shortly thereafter. In this case, we would be interested in learning about our competitors' financial strength to see if they could afford the necessary development.

Finally, we might be thinking of acquiring another firm. Financial statement information would be essential in identifying potential targets and deciding what to offer.

CHOOSING A BENCHMARK

Given that we want to evaluate a division or a firm based on its financial statements, a basic problem immediately comes up. How do we choose a benchmark, or a standard of comparison? We describe some ways of getting started in this section.

Time Trend Analysis One standard we could use is history. Suppose we found that the current ratio for a particular firm is 2.4 based on the most recent financial statement information. Looking back over the last 10 years, we might find that this ratio had declined fairly steadily over that period.

Based on this, we might wonder if the liquidity position of the firm has deteriorated. It could be, of course, that the firm has made changes that allow it to more efficiently use its current assets, the nature of the firm's business has changed, or business practices have changed. If we investigate, we might find any of these possible explanations behind the decline. This is an example of what we mean by management by exception—a deteriorating time trend may not be bad, but it does merit investigation.

Peer Group Analysis The second means of establishing a benchmark is to identify firms similar in the sense that they compete in the same markets, have similar assets, and operate in similar ways. In other words, we need to identify a *peer group*. There are obvious problems with doing this because no two companies are identical. Ultimately, the choice of which companies to use as a basis for comparison is subjective.

One common way of identifying potential peers is based on **Standard Industrial Classification (SIC) codes**. These are four-digit codes established by the U.S. government for statistical reporting. Firms with the same SIC code are frequently assumed to be similar.

The first digit in an SIC code establishes the general type of business. For example, firms engaged in finance, insurance, and real estate have SIC codes beginning with 6. Each additional digit narrows down the industry. So, companies with SIC codes beginning with 60 are mostly banks and banklike businesses; those with codes beginning with 602 are mostly commercial banks; and SIC code 6025 is assigned to national banks that are members of the Federal Reserve system. Table 3.11 lists selected two-digit codes (the first two digits of the four-digit SIC codes) and the industries they represent.

Standard Industrial Classification (SIC) code
A U.S. government code used to classify a firm by its type of business operations.

TABLE 3.11

Selected Two-Digit SIC Codes

Agriculture, Forestry, and Fishing	Transportation, Communication, Electric, Gas, and Sanitary Service
01 Agriculture production—crops	40 Railroad transportation
08 Forestry	45 Transportation by air
09 Fishing, hunting, and trapping	49 Electric, gas, and sanitary services
Mining	**Retail Trade**
10 Metal mining	54 Food stores
12 Bituminous coal and lignite mining	55 Automobile dealers and gas stations
13 Oil and gas extraction	58 Eating and drinking places
Construction	**Finance, Insurance, and Real Estate**
15 Building construction	60 Banking
16 Construction other than building	63 Insurance
17 Construction—special trade contractors	65 Real estate
Manufacturing	**Services**
28 Chemicals and allied products	78 Motion pictures
29 Petroleum refining and related industries	80 Health services
37 Transportation equipment	82 Educational services

SIC codes are far from perfect. For example, suppose you were examining financial statements for Walmart, the largest retailer in the United States. The relevant two-digit SIC code is 53, General Merchandise Stores. In a quick scan of the nearest financial database, you would find about 20 large, publicly owned corporations with a similar SIC code, but you might not be comfortable with some of them. Target would seem to be a reasonable peer, but Neiman Marcus also carries the same industry code. Are Walmart and Neiman Marcus really comparable?

As this example illustrates, it is probably not appropriate to blindly use SIC code-based averages. Instead, analysts often identify a set of primary competitors and then compute a set of averages based on just this group. Also, we may be more concerned with a group of the top firms in an industry, not the average firm. Such a group is called an *aspirant group* because we aspire to be like its members. In this case, a financial statement analysis reveals how far we have to go.

Beginning in 1997, a new industry classification system was initiated. Specifically, the North American Industry Classification System (NAICS, pronounced "nakes") is intended to replace the older SIC codes, and it will eventually. Currently, however, SIC codes are still widely used.

With these caveats about industry codes in mind, we can now take a look at a specific industry. Suppose we are in the wine making business. Table 3.12 contains some condensed common-size financial statements for this industry from the Risk Management Association (RMA, formerly known as Robert Morris Associates), one of many sources of such information. Table 3.13 contains selected ratios from the same source.

Learn more about NAICS at **www.naics.com**.

There is a large amount of information here, most of which is self-explanatory. On the right in Table 3.12, we have current information reported for different groups based on sales. Within each sales group, common-size information is reported. For example, firms with sales in the $10 million to $25 million range have cash and equivalents equal to 2.0 percent of total assets. There are 48 companies in this group, out of 258 in all.

On the left, we have three years' worth of summary historical information for the entire group. For example, operating profit decreased slightly from 11.7 percent of sales to 11.4 percent over that time.

Table 3.13 contains some selected ratios, again reported by sales groups on the right and time period on the left. To see how we might use this information, suppose our firm has a current ratio of 2. Based on these ratios, is this value unusual?

Looking at the current ratio for the overall group for the most recent year (third column from the left in Table 3.13), we see that three numbers are reported. The one in the middle, 2.1, is the median, meaning that half of the 258 firms had current ratios that were lower and half had higher current ratios. The other two numbers are the upper and lower quartiles. So, 25 percent of the firms had a current ratio larger than 4.0 and 25 percent had a current ratio smaller than 1.4. Our value of 2 falls comfortably within these bounds, so it doesn't appear too unusual. This comparison illustrates how knowledge of the range of ratios is important in addition to knowledge of the average. Notice how stable the current ratio has been for the last three years.

| **More Ratios** | **EXAMPLE 3.5** |

Take a look at the most recent numbers reported for Cost of Sales/Inventory and EBIT/ Interest in Table 3.13. What are the overall median values? What are these ratios?

If you look back at our discussion, you will see that these are the inventory turnover and the times interest earned, or TIE, ratios. The median value for inventory turnover for the entire group is .7 times. So, the days' sales in inventory would be 365/.7 = 521 days, which is the boldfaced number reported. While this is long compared to other industries, this doesn't seem like very long for fine wines. The median for the TIE is 3.7 times. The number in parentheses indicates that the calculation is meaningful for, and therefore based on, only 235 of the 258 companies. In this case, the reason is that only 235 companies paid any significant amount of interest.

TABLE 3.12 Selected Financial Statement Information

Manufacturing—Wineries (NAICS 312130)									
COMPARATIVE HISTORICAL DATA				CURRENT DATA SORTED BY SALES					
			Type of Statement						
38	33	29	Unqualified	1			2	4	22
40	53	41	Reviewed		2		15	15	9
17	15	12	Compiled	1	2	3	3	2	1
24	25	26	Tax Returns	11	6	4	4	1˙	
100	150	150	Other	24	35	20	18	26	27
4/1/13–3/31/14	4/1/14–3/31/15	4/1/15–3/31/16		31 (4/1–9/30/15)		227 (10/1/15–3/31/16)			
ALL 219	ALL 276	ALL 258	**NUMBER OF STATEMENTS**	0–1MM 37	1–3MM 45	3–5MM 27	5–10MM 42	10–25MM 48	25MM & OVER 59
%	%	%	**Assets**	%	%	%	%	%	%
5.2	5.3	5.0	Cash & Equivalents	6.8	5.0	8.7	5.2	2.0	4.4
8.4	8.1	9.2	Trade Receivables (net)	5.6	7.3	7.5	9.0	11.0	12.3
44.4	47.4	47.3	Inventory	52.0	50.1	49.4	42.6	47.0	44.9
2.4	1.9	1.7	All Other Current	.6	1.6	.7	1.8	1.6	2.8
60.5	62.7	63.1	Total Current	65.0	64.0	66.3	58.6	61.6	64.3
32.0	29.2	29.8	Fixed Assets (net)	28.4	32.6	22.9	36.3	29.4	27.6
3.5	4.0	3.7	Intangibles (net)	4.5	1.5	3.7	3.1	5.0	4.1
4.0	4.1	3.4	All Other Non-current	2.0	2.0	7.1	2.0	3.9	4.0
100.0	100.0	100.0	Total	100.0	100.0	100.0	100.0	100.0	100.0
			Liabilities						
14.1	16.8	15.7	Notes Payable-Short term	17.7	14.3	10.0	12.3	18.8	18.1
2.1	1.8	1.3	Cur. Mat.-L.T.D	.9	1.0	.9	2.0	1.4	1.6
8.8	8.9	8.8	Trade Payables	5.9	9.0	7.2	7.8	12.2	9.3
.2	.2	.2	Income Taxes Payable	.4	.3	.0	.3	.0	.1
6.0	6.0	6.5	All Other Current	7.6	4.8	6.0	4.1	8.7	7.4
31.2	33.8	32.6	Total Current	32.5	29.3	24.1	26.5	41.2	36.5
19.8	17.4	18.5	Long-Term Debt	20.5	17.5	17.8	22.5	17.4	16.6
.4	.3	.4	Deferred Taxes	.0	.0	.2	.7	.7	.4
6.3	6.7	6.6	All Other Non-current	13.5	5.6	7.8	7.5	4.4	3.6
42.2	41.8	41.9	Net Worth	33.5	47.6	50.1	42.8	36.3	42.9
100.0	100.0	100.0	Total Liabilities & Net Worth	100.0	100.0	100.0	100.0	100.0	100.0
			Income Data						
100.0	100.0	100.0	Net Sales	100.0	100.0	100.0	100.0	100.0	100.0
48.9	50.0	49.3	Gross Profit	57.1	54.1	55.8	49.5	45.0	41.0
37.2	37.9	37.9	Operating Expenses	51.4	44.5	39.4	38.2	32.5	27.8
11.7	12.0	11.4	Operating Profit	5.7	9.7	16.4	11.3	12.5	13.3
2.7	2.6	2.6	All Other Expenses (net)	3.4	1.9	1.1	4.3	2.9	2.1
9.0	9.5	8.8	Profit Before Taxes	2.3	7.8	15.3	7.1	9.6	11.2

M = $ thousand; MM = $ million.

Interpretation of Statement Studies Figures: RMA cautions that the studies be regarded only as a general guideline and not as an absolute industry norm. This is due to limited samples within categories, the categorization of companies by their primary Standard Industrial Classification (SIC) number only, and different methods of operations by companies within the same industry. For these reasons, RMA recommends that the figures be used only as general guidelines in addition to other methods of financial analysis.

TABLE 3.13 Selected Ratios

Manufacturing—Wineries (NAICS 312130)										
COMPARATIVE HISTORICAL DATA					CURRENT DATA SORTED BY SALES					
			Type of Statement							
38	33	29	Unqualified		1			2	4	22
40	53	41	Reviewed			2		15	15	9
17	15	12	Compiled		1	2	3	3	2	1
24	25	26	Tax Returns		11	6	4	4	1	
100	150	150	Other		24	35	20	18	26	27

4/1/13–3/31/14 ALL 219	4/1/14–3/31/15 ALL 276	4/1/15–3/31/16 ALL 258	NUMBER OF STATEMENTS	31 (4/1–9/30/15)			227 (10/1/15–3/31/16)			25MM & OVER 59
				0–1MM 37	1–3MM 45	3–5MM 27	5–10MM 42	10–25MM 48		
			Ratios							
4.0	4.5	4.0	Current	4.1	5.8	5.9	3.8	2.4		3.4
2.1	2.0	2.1		2.7	2.3	3.3	2.3	1.5		1.9
1.4	1.4	1.4		1.4	1.5	1.8	1.8	1.2		1.3
.9	.9	.9	Quick	1.2	1.1	1.9	1.2	.6		.7
.3	.3	.3		.3	.3	.5	.4	.3		.4
.2	.2	.2		.1	.2	.2	.2	.1		.2
16 23.0	15 24.8	15 23.7	Sales/	0 UND	7 49.3	11 32.8	16 22.4	21 17.2		28 13.1
30 12.2	34 10.6	31 11.8	Receivables	10 35.6	28 12.9	20 18.3	29 12.6	37 9.8		41 8.9
51 7.1	52 7.0	52 7.0		46 7.9	50 7.3	39 9.4	57 6.4	56 6.5		59 6.2
261 1.4	332 1.1	304 1.2	Cost of Sales/	192 1.9	304 1.2	261 1.4	304 1.2	365 1.0		261 1.4
456 .8	521 .7	521 .7	Inventory	608 .6	608 .6	608 .6	608 .6	521 .7		365 1.0
730 .5	912 .4	730 .5		912 .4	912 .4	730 .5	730 .5	730 .5		608 .6
25 14.4	26 14.0	21 17.3	Cost of Sales/	0 UND	10 36.2	21 17.2	23 16.0	36 10.1		23 16.1
55 6.6	59 6.2	51 7.2	Payables	48 7.6	53 6.9	35 10.3	47 7.8	69 5.3		51 7.2
101 3.6	122 3.0	107 3.4		166 2.2	146 2.5	70 5.2	122 3.0	122 3.0		76 4.8
1.4	1.3	1.3	Sales/Working	1.2	1.2	1.1	1.3	2.0		1.9
2.7	2.4	2.6	Capital	2.0	2.8	2.3	2.1	3.7		2.9
6.6	5.1	5.2		7.8	5.8	4.0	2.8	6.7		6.0
9.7	11.4	14.3	EBIT/Interest	4.5	7.9	31.5	12.3	13.0		19.9
(200) 3.9	(252) 4.7	(235) 3.7		(31) 1.0	(36) 3.6	(25) 9.0	(40) 2.3	(46) 4.1		(57) 5.7
1.4	1.7	1.3		−2.1	1.2	2.1	1.1	1.2		2.8
8.0	9.1	9.5	Net Profit +					6.9		17.3
(42) 4.8	(55) 5.0	(45) 5.9	Depr., Dep,.				(10) 3.5	(24) 7.7		
1.9	2.6	2.6	Amort./Cur. Mat. L/T/D				1.8	4.3		
.3	.2	.2	Fixed/Worth	.2	.2	.1	.4	.2		.3
.8	.7	.7		.6	.7	.4	1.0	.8		.8
1.6	1.4	1.5		4.5	1.5	1.1	1.5	1.9		1.3
.6	.6	.6	Debt/Worth	.5	.5	.4	.6	1.2		.8
1.5	1.4	1.4		2.6	1.0	1.2	1.4	2.1		1.1
4.1	3.0	3.9		24.2	2.7	4.3	2.8	4.3		3.2
32.8	33.9	32.7	% Profit Before	34.2	25.0	47.0	20.0	42.2		27.9
(194) 14.8	(253) 15.6	(230) 13.6	Taxes/Tangible	(29) 5.5	(41) 11.8	(25) 20.5	(38) 7.4	(43) 19.6		(54) 18.3
2.7	3.3	2.7	Net Worth	−8.9	4.6	3.3	.4	3.7		10.2

(continued)

TABLE 3.13 *(continued)*

4/1/13–3/31/14 ALL 219	4/1/14–3/31/15 ALL 276	4/1/15–3/31/16 ALL 258	NUMBER OF STATEMENTS	31 (4/1–9/30/15)			227 (10/1/15–3/31/16)		
				0–1MM 37	1–3MM 45	3–5MM 27	5–10MM 42	10–25MM 48	25MM & OVER 59
12.0	12.8	12.1	% Profit Before Taxes/Total Assets	13.6	9.1	23.9	8.7	13.4	13.1
5.1	5.6	4.8		1.4	5.2	7.2	2.7	4.4	7.0
.7	.9	.6		−5.0	.8	1.5	.2	.8	3.0
7.4	9.5	8.6	Sales/Net Fixed Assets	7.3	6.8	13.9	3.9	33.5	9.0
2.5	3.0	2.9		5.0	2.3	5.1	1.4	2.1	3.3
1.1	1.1	1.2		2.4	1.5	1.7	.9	1.0	1.4
1.1	1.0	1.1	Sales/Total Assets	1.1	1.1	1.2	1.0	1.1	1.1
.7	.7	.7		.7	.7	.8	.6	.7	.7
.5	.5	.5		.5	.5	.5	.4	.4	.5
2.4	2.4	2.1	% Depr., Dep., Amort./Sales	3.4	1.6	1.1	2.7	2.3	1.4
(171) 5.2	(214) 5.1	(199) 5.3		(22) 5.9	(31) 5.8	(18) 3.9	(35) 7.1	(37) 6.1	(56) 4.0
8.3	8.1	8.4		14.3	8.7	9.6	9.1	9.3	7.1
3.1	2.7	2.6	% Officers', Directors', Owners' Comp/Sales						
(27) 4.3	(35) 4.1	(33) 4.1							
7.7	9.5	7.3							
4892971M	8360552M	5519014M	Net Sales ($)	19825M	82307M	103312M	287163M	774866M	4251541M
6963108M	8811913M	8435750M	Total Assets ($)	49293M	161278M	147637M	602723M	1722233M	5752586M

M = $ thousand; MM = $ million.

There are many sources of ratio information in addition to the one we examine here. Our nearby *Work the Web* box shows how to get this information for just about any company, along with some useful benchmarking information. Be sure to look it over and then benchmark your favorite company.

PROBLEMS WITH FINANCIAL STATEMENT ANALYSIS

We close our chapter on financial statements by discussing some additional problems that can arise in using financial statements. In one way or another, the basic problem with financial statement analysis is that there is no underlying theory to help us identify which quantities to look at and to use in establishing benchmarks.

As we discuss in other chapters, there are many cases in which financial theory and economic logic provide guidance in making judgments about value and risk. Little such help exists with financial statements. This is why we can't say which ratios matter the most and what may be considered a high or low value.

Other websites provide different information about a company's ratios. For example, check out **www.marketwatch.com** and **www.morningstar.com**.

One particularly severe problem is that many firms are conglomerates, owning more or less unrelated lines of business. The consolidated financial statements for such firms don't fit any neat industry category. Well-known companies like General Electric (GE) and 3M fall into this category. More generally, the kind of peer group analysis we have been describing works best when the firms are strictly in the same line of business, the industry is competitive, and there is only one way of operating.

Another problem that is becoming increasingly common is that major competitors and natural peer group members in an industry may be scattered around the globe. The automobile industry is an obvious example. The problem here is that financial statements from outside the United States do not necessarily conform at all to generally accepted accounting

WORK THE WEB

As we discussed in this chapter, ratios are an important tool for examining a company's performance. Gathering the necessary financial statements to calculate ratios can be tedious and time-consuming. Fortunately, many sites on the web provide this information for free. One of the best is www.reuters.com. We went there, entered the ticker symbol "HD" (for Home Depot), and then went to the "Financials" page. Here is an abbreviated look at the results:

	Company	industry	sector
Quick Ratio (MRQ)	0.42	1.03	1.26
Current Ratio (MRQ)	1.34	1.91	1.58
LT Debt to Equity (MRQ)	397.33	84.80	34.40
Total Debt to Equity (MRQ)	406.99	98.04	64.39
Interest Coverage (TTM)	18.56	14.73	3.63

The website reports the company, industry, and sector ratios. As you can see, Home Depot has lower quick and current ratios than the industry.

Questions

1. Go to www.reuters.com and find the major ratio categories listed on this website. How do the categories differ from the categories listed in this textbook?

2. Go to www.reuters.com and find all the ratios for Home Depot. How does the company compare to the industry for the ratios presented on this website?

---

principles (GAAP). The existence of different standards and procedures makes it difficult to compare financial statements across national borders.

Even companies that are clearly in the same line of business may not be comparable. For example, electric utilities engaged primarily in power generation are all classified in the same group (SIC 4911). This group is often thought to be relatively homogeneous. However, most utilities operate as regulated monopolies, so they don't compete much with each other, at least not historically. Many have stockholders, and many are organized as cooperatives with no stockholders. There are several different ways of generating power, ranging from hydroelectric to nuclear, so the operating activities of these utilities can differ quite a bit. Finally, profitability is strongly affected by the regulatory environment, so utilities in different locations can be similar but show different profits.

Several other general problems frequently crop up. First, different firms use different accounting procedures—for inventory, for example. This makes it difficult to compare statements. Second, different firms end their fiscal years at different times. For firms in seasonal businesses (such as a retailer with a large Christmas season), this can lead to difficulties in comparing balance sheets because of fluctuations in accounts during the year. Finally, for any particular firm, unusual or transient events, such as a one-time profit from an asset sale, may affect financial performance. In comparing firms, such events can give misleading signals.

80   **PART 2**   Financial Statements and Long-Term Financial Planning

3.6   Summary and Conclusions

This chapter has discussed aspects of financial statement analysis:

1. *Sources and uses of cash*: We discussed how to identify the ways in which businesses obtain and use cash, and we described how to trace the flow of cash through a business over the course of the year. We briefly looked at the statement of cash flows.

2. *Standardized financial statements*: We explained that differences in size make it difficult to compare financial statements, and we discussed how to form common-size and common-base period statements to make comparisons easier.

3. *Ratio analysis*: Evaluating ratios of accounting numbers is another way of comparing financial statement information. We defined and discussed a number of the most commonly reported and used financial ratios. We also discussed the famous DuPont identity as a way of analyzing financial performance.

4. *Using financial statements*: We described how to establish benchmarks for comparison and discussed some types of information that are available. We then examined potential problems that can arise.

After you have studied this chapter, we hope that you have some perspective on the uses and abuses of financial statements. You should also find that your vocabulary of business and financial terms has grown substantially.

CONNECT TO FINANCE

 For more practice, you should be in Connect Finance. Log on to connect.mheducation.com to get started!

Can you answer the following *Connect* Quiz questions?

Section 3.1   What is an example of a source of cash?

Section 3.2   Pioneer Aviation has total liabilities of $23,800 and total equity of $46,200. Current assets are $8,600. What is the common-size percentage for the current assets?

Section 3.3   What ratio measures the number of days that a firm can operate based on its current assets?

Section 3.4   What is the correct formula for computing the return on equity?

Section 3.5   If you want to identify other firms that have assets and operations that are similar to those of your firm, what should you refer to?

CHAPTER REVIEW AND SELF-TEST PROBLEMS

3.1   Sources and Uses of Cash Consider the following balance sheets for the Philippe Corporation. Calculate the changes in the various accounts and, where applicable, identify the change as a source or use of cash. What were the major sources and uses of cash? Did the company become more or less liquid during the year? What happened to cash during the year?

PHILIPPE CORPORATION 2017 and 2018 Balance Sheets ($ in millions)		
	2017	**2018**
Assets		
Current assets		
Cash	$ 210	$ 215
Accounts receivable	355	310
Inventory	507	328
Total	$1,072	$ 853
Fixed assets		
Net plant and equipment	$6,085	$6,527
Total assets	$7,157	$7,380
Liabilities and Owners' Equity		
Current liabilities		
Accounts payable	$ 207	$ 298
Notes payable	1,715	1,427
Total	$1,922	$1,725
Long-term debt	$1,987	$2,308
Owners' equity		
Common stock and paid-in surplus	$1,000	$1,000
Retained earnings	2,248	2,347
Total	$3,248	$3,347
Total liabilities and owners' equity	$7,157	$7,380

3.2   Common-Size Statements Here is the most recent income statement for Philippe. Prepare a common-size income statement based on this information. How do you interpret the standardized net income? What percentage of sales goes to cost of goods sold?

PHILIPPE CORPORATION 2018 Income Statement ($ in millions)	
Sales	$4,053
Cost of goods sold	2,816
Depreciation	550
Earnings before interest and taxes	$ 687
Interest paid	502
Taxable income	$ 185
Taxes (21%)	39
Net income	$ 146
Dividends	$47
Addition to retained earnings	99

3.3 **Financial Ratios** Based on the balance sheets and income statement in the previous two problems, calculate the following ratios for 2018:

Current ratio _____

Quick ratio _____

Cash ratio _____

Inventory turnover _____

Receivables turnover _____

Days' sales in inventory _____

Days' sales in receivables _____

Total debt ratio _____

Long-term debt ratio _____

Times interest earned ratio _____

Cash coverage ratio _____

3.4 **ROE and the DuPont Identity** Calculate the 2018 ROE for the Philippe Corporation and then break down your answer into its component parts using the DuPont identity.

ANSWERS TO CHAPTER REVIEW AND SELF-TEST PROBLEMS

3.1 We've filled in the answers in the following table. Remember, increases in assets and decreases in liabilities indicate that we spent some cash. Decreases in assets and increases in liabilities are ways of getting cash.

Philippe used its cash primarily to purchase fixed assets and to pay off short-term debt. The major sources of cash to do this were additional long-term borrowing, reductions in current assets, and additions to retained earnings.

PHILIPPE CORPORATION 2017 and 2018 Balance Sheets ($ in millions)				
	2017	2018	Change	Source or Use of Cash
Assets				
Current assets				
Cash	$ 210	$ 215	+$ 5	
Accounts receivable	355	310	− 45	Source
Inventory	507	328	− 179	Source
Total	$1,072	$ 853	−$219	
Fixed assets				
Net plant and equipment	$6,085	$6,527	+$442	Use
Total assets	$7,157	$7,380	+$223	
Liabilities and Owners' Equity				
Current liabilities				
Accounts payable	$ 207	$ 298	+$ 91	Source
Notes payable	1,715	1,427	− 288	Use
Total	$1,922	$1,725	−$197	
Long-term debt	$1,987	$2,308	+$321	Source
Owners' equity				
Common stock and paid-in surplus	$1,000	$1,000	+$ 0	—
Retained earnings	2,248	2,347	+ 99	Source
Total	$3,248	$3,347	+$ 99	
Total liabilities and owners' equity	$7,157	$7,380	+$223	

The current ratio went from $1,072/$1,922 = .56 to $853/$1,725 = .49, so the firm's liquidity appears to have declined somewhat. Overall, however, the amount of cash on hand increased by $5.

3.2 We've calculated the common-size income statement here. Remember that we simply divide each item by total sales.

PHILIPPE CORPORATION	
2018 Common-Size Income Statement	
Sales	100.0%
Cost of goods sold	69.5
Depreciation	13.6
Earnings before interest and taxes	17.0
Interest paid	12.4
Taxable income	4.6
Taxes (21%)	1.0
Net income	3.6
Dividends	1.2%
Addition to retained earnings	2.4

Net income is 3.6 percent of sales. Because this is the percentage of each sales dollar that makes its way to the bottom line, the standardized net income is the firm's profit margin. Cost of goods sold is 69.5 percent of sales.

3.3 We've calculated the following ratios based on the ending figures. If you don't remember a definition, refer back to Table 3.8.

Current ratio	$853/$1,725	= .49 times
Quick ratio	$525/$1,725	= .30 times
Cash ratio	$215/$1,725	= .12 times
Inventory turnover	$2,816/$328	= 8.59 times
Receivables turnover	$4,053/$310	= 13.07 times
Days' sales in inventory	365/8.59	= 42.51 days
Days' sales in receivables	365/13.07	= 27.92 days
Total debt ratio	$4,033/$7,380	= .546, or 54.6%
Long-term debt ratio	$2,308/$5,655	= .408, or 40.8%
Times interest earned ratio	$687/$502	= 1.37 times
Cash coverage ratio	$1,237/$502	= 2.46 times

3.4 The return on equity is the ratio of net income to total equity. For Philippe, this is $146/$3,347 = 4.4 percent, which is not outstanding.

Given the DuPont identity, ROE can be written as follows:

ROE = Profit margin × Total asset turnover × Equity multiplier

= $146/$4,053   × $4,053/$7,380   × $7,380/$3,347

=   .036%   ×   .549   ×   2.20

=   .044, or 4.4%

Notice that return on assets, ROA, is .036% × .549 = 1.98 percent.

CONCEPTS REVIEW AND CRITICAL THINKING QUESTIONS

1. **Current Ratio** [LO2] What effect would the following actions have on a firm's current ratio? Assume that net working capital is positive.
    a. Inventory is purchased.
    b. A supplier is paid.
    c. A short-term bank loan is repaid.
    d. A long-term debt is paid off early.
    e. A customer pays off a credit account.
    f. Inventory is sold at cost.
    g. Inventory is sold for a profit.

2. **Current Ratio and Quick Ratio** [LO2] In recent years, Dixie Co. has greatly increased its current ratio. At the same time, the quick ratio has fallen. What has happened? Has the liquidity of the company improved?

3. **Current Ratio** [LO2] Explain what it means for a firm to have a current ratio equal to .50. Would the firm be better off if the current ratio were 1.50? What if it were 15.0? Explain your answers.

4. **Financial Ratios** [LO2] Fully explain the kind of information the following financial ratios provide about a firm:
    a. Quick ratio.
    b. Cash ratio.
    c. Total asset turnover.
    d. Equity multiplier.
    e. Long-term debt ratio.
    f. Times interest earned ratio.
    g. Profit margin.
    h. Return on assets.
    i. Return on equity.
    j. Price–earnings ratio.

5. **Standardized Financial Statements** [LO1] What types of information do common-size financial statements reveal about the firm? What is the best use for these common-size statements? What purpose do common-base year statements have? When would you use them?

6. **Peer Group Analysis** [LO2] Explain what peer group analysis is. As a financial manager, how could you use the results of peer group analysis to evaluate the performance of your firm? How is a peer group different from an aspirant group?

7. **DuPont Identity** [LO3] Why is the DuPont identity a valuable tool for analyzing the performance of a firm? Discuss the types of information it reveals compared to ROE considered by itself.

8. **Industry-Specific Ratios** [LO2] Specialized ratios are sometimes used in specific industries. For example, the so-called book-to-bill ratio is closely watched for semiconductor manufacturers. A ratio of .93 indicates that for every $100 worth of chips shipped over some period, only $93 worth of new orders were received. In November 2016, the semiconductor equipment industry's book-to-bill ratio was .96, compared to .91 during the month of October 2016. The book-to-bill ratio reached a recent low of .47 during January 2009 and a recent high of 1.23 during July 2010. What is this ratio intended to measure? Why do you think it is so closely followed?

9. **Industry-Specific Ratios** [LO2] So-called same-store sales are a very important measure for companies as diverse as McDonald's and Sears. As the name suggests, examining same-store sales means comparing revenues from the same stores or restaurants at two different points in time. Why might companies focus on same-store sales rather than total sales?

10. **Industry-Specific Ratios** [LO2] There are many ways of using standardized financial information beyond those discussed in this chapter. The usual goal is to put firms

on an equal footing for comparison purposes. For example, for auto manufacturers, it is common to express sales, costs, and profits on a per-car basis. For each of the following industries, give an example of an actual company and discuss one or more potentially useful means of standardizing financial information:

a. Public utilities.

b. Large retailers.

c. Airlines.

d. Online services.

e. Hospitals.

f. College textbook publishers.

11. **Statement of Cash Flows** [LO4] In recent years, several manufacturing companies have reported the cash flow from the sale of Treasury securities in the cash from operations section of the statement of cash flows. What is the problem with this practice? Is there any situation in which this practice would be acceptable?

12. **Statement of Cash Flows** [LO4] Suppose a company lengthens the time it takes to pay suppliers. How would this affect the statement of cash flows? How sustainable is the change in cash flows from this practice?

QUESTIONS AND PROBLEMS

1. **Calculating Liquidity Ratios** [LO2] SDJ, Inc., has net working capital of $2,170, current liabilities of $4,590, and inventory of $3,860. What is the current ratio? What is the quick ratio?

2. **Calculating Profitability Ratios** [LO2] DTO, Inc., has sales of $16.7 million, total assets of $12.9 million, and total debt of $5.7 million. If the profit margin is 5 percent, what is net income? What is ROA? What is ROE?

BASIC
(Questions 1–17)

3. **Calculating the Average Collection Period** [LO2] Twist Corp. has a current accounts receivable balance of $537,810. Credit sales for the year just ended were $5,473,640. What is the receivables turnover? The days' sales in receivables? How long did it take on average for credit customers to pay off their accounts during the past year?

4. **Calculating Inventory Turnover** [LO2] The King Corporation has ending inventory of $386,735, and cost of goods sold for the year just ended was $4,981,315. What is the inventory turnover? The days' sales in inventory? How long on average did a unit of inventory sit on the shelf before it was sold?

5. **Calculating Leverage Ratios** [LO2] Queen, Inc., has a total debt ratio of .46. What is its debt-equity ratio? What is its equity multiplier?

6. **Calculating Market Value Ratios** [LO2] Makers Corp. had additions to retained earnings for the year just ended of $415,000. The firm paid out $220,000 in cash dividends, and it has ending total equity of $5.6 million. If the company currently has 170,000 shares of common stock outstanding, what are earnings per share? Dividends per share? Book value per share? If the stock currently sells for $65 per share, what is the market-to-book ratio? The price-earnings ratio? If the company had sales of $7.45 million, what is the price-sales ratio?

7. **DuPont Identity** [LO3] If Roten Rooters, Inc., has an equity multiplier of 1.27, total asset turnover of 2.10, and a profit margin of 6.1 percent, what is its ROE?

8. **DuPont Identity** [LO3] Jack Corp. has a profit margin of 6.4 percent, total asset turnover of 1.77, and ROE of 15.84 percent. What is this firm's debt-equity ratio?

9. **Sources and Uses of Cash** [LO1] Based only on the following information for Thrice Corp., did cash go up or down? By how much? Classify each event as a source or use of cash.

Decrease in inventory	$375
Decrease in accounts payable	220
Increase in notes payable	290
Increase in accounts receivable	270

10. **Calculating Average Payables Period** [LO2] Heritage, Inc., had a cost of goods sold of $68,314. At the end of the year, the accounts payable balance was $15,486. How long on average did it take the company to pay off its suppliers during the year? What might a large value for this ratio imply?

11. **Enterprise Value-EBITDA Multiple** [LO2] The market value of the equity of Hudgins, Inc., is $645,000. The balance sheet shows $53,000 in cash and $215,000 in debt, while the income statement has EBIT of $91,000 and a total of $157,000 in depreciation and amortization. What is the enterprise value-EBITDA multiple for this company?

12. **Equity Multiplier and Return on Equity** [LO3] SME Company has a debt-equity ratio of .57. Return on assets is 7.9 percent, and total equity is $620,000. What is the equity multiplier? Return on equity? Net income?

Just Dew It Corporation reports the following balance sheet information for 2017 and 2018. Use this information to work Problems 13 through 17.

JUST DEW IT CORPORATION 2017 and 2018 Balance Sheets					
Assets			**Liabilities and Owners' Equity**		
	2017	**2018**		**2017**	**2018**
Current assets			Current liabilities		
Cash	$ 12,157	$ 14,105	Accounts payable	$ 46,382	$ 49,276
Accounts receivable	29,382	32,815	Notes payable	18,246	19,784
Inventory	54,632	57,204	Total	$ 64,628	$ 69,060
Total	$ 96,171	$104,124			
			Long-term debt	$ 49,000	$ 45,000
			Owners' equity		
			Common stock and		
			paid-in surplus	$ 50,000	$ 50,000
			Retained earnings	299,784	315,894
Net plant and equipment	$367,241	$375,830	Total	$349,784	$365,894
			Total liabilities and		
Total assets	$463,412	$479,954	owners' equity	$463,412	$479,954

13. **Preparing Standardized Financial Statements** [LO1] Prepare the 2017 and 2018 common-size balance sheets for Just Dew It.

14. **Preparing Standardized Financial Statements** [LO1] Prepare the 2018 common-base year balance sheet for Just Dew It.

15. **Preparing Standardized Financial Statements** [LO1] Prepare the 2018 combined common-size, common-base year balance sheet for Just Dew It.

16. **Sources and Uses of Cash** [LO1] For each account on this company's balance sheet, show the change in the account during 2018 and note whether this change was a

source or use of cash. Do your numbers add up and make sense? Explain your answer for total assets as compared to your answer for total liabilities and owners' equity.

17. **Calculating Financial Ratios** [LO2] Based on the balance sheets given for Just Dew It, calculate the following financial ratios for each year:

    a Current ratio.

    b Quick ratio.

    c Cash ratio.

    d NWC to total assets ratio

    e Debt-equity ratio and equity multiplier.

    f Total debt ratio and long-term debt ratio.

18. **Using the DuPont Identity** [LO3] Y3K, Inc., has sales of $6,183, total assets of $2,974, and a debt-equity ratio of .57. If its return on equity is 11 percent, what is its net income?

19. **Days' Sales in Receivables** [LO2] A company has net income of $196,500, a profit margin of 6.8 percent, and an accounts receivable balance of $119,630. Assuming 65 percent of sales are on credit, what is the company's days' sales in receivables?

20. **Ratios and Fixed Assets** [LO2] The Maurer Company has a long-term debt ratio of .35 and a current ratio of 1.30. Current liabilities are $955, sales are $7,210, profit margin is 8.3 percent, and ROE is 17.5 percent. What is the amount of the firm's net fixed assets?

21. **Profit Margin** [LO4] In response to complaints about high prices, a grocery chain runs the following advertising campaign: "If you pay your child $1.50 to go buy $50 worth of groceries, then your child makes twice as much on the trip as we do." You've collected the following information from the grocery chain's financial statements:

($ in millions)	
Sales	$680
Net income	10.2
Total assets	380
Total debt	270

Evaluate the grocery chain's claim. What is the basis for the statement? Is this claim misleading? Why or why not?

22. **Return on Equity** [LO2] Firm A and Firm B have debt-total asset ratios of 65 percent and 45 percent, respectively, and returns on total assets of 5 percent and 9 percent, respectively. Which firm has a greater return on equity?

23. **Calculating the Cash Coverage Ratio** [LO2] Pop Evil Inc.'s net income for the most recent year was $16,481. The tax rate was 21 percent. The firm paid $3,681 in total interest expense and deducted $4,385 in depreciation expense. What was the cash coverage ratio for the year?

24. **Cost of Goods Sold** [LO2] Highly Suspect Corp. has current liabilities of $415,000, a quick ratio of .79, inventory turnover of 9.5, and a current ratio of 1.25. What is the cost of goods sold for the company?

25. **Ratios and Foreign Companies** [LO2] Prince Albert Canning PLC had a net loss of £29,157 on sales of £315,650. What was the company's profit margin? Does the fact that these figures are quoted in a foreign currency make any difference? Why? In dollars, sales were $395,183. What was the net loss in dollars?

    Some recent financial statements for Smolira Golf Corp. follow. Use this information to work Problems 26 through 30.

INTERMEDIATE
(Questions 18–30)

SMOLIRA GOLF CORP. 2017 and 2018 Balance Sheets					
Assets			**Liabilities and Owners' Equity**		
	2017	2018		2017	2018
Current assets			Current liabilities		
Cash	$ 34,385	$ 37,837	Accounts payable	$ 36,722	$ 42,582
Accounts receivable	17,801	27,766	Notes payable	19,008	16,200
Inventory	36,310	42,632	Other	19,864	24,634
Total	$ 88,496	$108,235	Total	$ 75,594	$ 83,416
			Long-term debt	$115,000	$145,000
			Owners' equity		
			Common stock and paid-in surplus	$ 55,000	$ 55,000
Fixed assets			Accumulated retained earnings	307,217	344,452
Net plant and equipment	464,315	519,633	Total	$362,217	$399,452
Total assets	$552,811	$627,868	Total liabilities and owners' equity	$552,811	$627,868

SMOLIRA GOLF CORP. 2018 Income Statement	
Sales	$506,454
Cost of goods sold	359,328
Depreciation	44,463
Earnings before interest and taxes	$102,663
Interest paid	19,683
Taxable income	$ 82,980
Taxes (25%)	20,745
Net income	$ 62,235
Dividends	$25,000
Retained earnings	37,235

26. **Calculating Financial Ratios** [LO2] Find the following financial ratios for Smolira Golf Corp. (use year-end figures rather than average values where appropriate):

Short-term solvency ratios:
a. Current ratio. _____
b. Quick ratio. _____
c. Cash ratio. _____

Asset utilization ratios:
d. Total asset turnover. _____
e. Inventory turnover. _____
f. Receivables turnover. _____

Long-term solvency ratios:
g. Total debt ratio. _____
h. Debt-equity ratio. _____

i. Equity multiplier.   _____

j. Times interest earned ratio.   _____

k. Cash coverage ratio.   _____

Profitability ratios:

l. Profit margin.   _____

m. Return on assets.   _____

n. Return on equity.   _____

27. **DuPont Identity** [LO3] Construct the DuPont identity for Smolira Golf Corp.

28. **Statement of Cash Flows** [LO1] Prepare the 2018 statement of cash flows for Smolira Golf Corp.

29. **Market Value Ratios** [LO2] Smolira Golf Corp. has 20,000 shares of common stock outstanding, and the market price for a share of stock at the end of 2018 was $58. What is the price-earnings ratio? What are the dividends per share? What is the market-to-book ratio at the end of 2018? If the company's growth rate is 9 percent, what is the PEG ratio?

30. **Tobin's Q** [LO2] What is Tobin's Q for Smolira Golf? What assumptions are you making about the book value of debt and the market value of debt? What about the book value of assets and the market value of assets? Are these assumptions realistic? Why or why not?

EXCEL MASTER IT! PROBLEM

The eXtensible Business Reporting Language (XBRL) is the future of financial reporting. XBRL is a computer language that "tags" each item and specifies what that item is. XBRL reporting has also been adopted for use in Australia, Japan, and the United Kingdom. The Securities and Exchange Commission (SEC) requires that U.S. companies submit financial reports to the SEC in XBRL format. XBRL reporting allows investors to quickly download financial statements for analysis.

For this assignment, go to the SEC website at www.sec.gov. Once there, look up the financials for a company. Next to the 10-Q (quarterly) and 10-K (annual) reports, you should notice a link that says "InteractiveData." Click on this link, follow the "Financial Statements" link, and select "View Excel Document." This link will allow you to download all of the financial statements in one Excel document. Download the Excel document and copy into the next worksheet. Use these statements to calculate the ratios on that worksheet. Do you notice any changes in these ratios that might indicate further investigation?

MINICASE

Ratio Analysis at S&S Air, Inc.

Chris Guthrie was recently hired by S&S Air, Inc., to assist the company with its financial planning and to evaluate the company's performance. Chris graduated from college five years ago with a finance degree. He has been employed in the finance department of a *Fortune* 500 company since then.

S&S Air was founded 10 years ago by friends Mark Sexton and Todd Story. The company has manufactured and sold light airplanes over this period, and the company's products have received high reviews for safety and reliability. The company has a niche market in that it sells primarily to individuals who own and fly their own airplanes. The company has two models: the Birdie, which sells for $103,000, and the Eagle, which sells for $178,000.

Although the company manufactures aircraft, its operations are different from commercial aircraft companies. S&S Air builds aircraft to order. By using prefabricated parts, the company can complete the manufacture of an airplane in only five weeks. The company also receives a deposit on each order, as well as another partial payment before the order is complete. In contrast, a commercial airplane may take one and one-half to two years to manufacture once the order is placed.

Mark and Todd have provided the following financial statements. Chris has gathered the industry ratios for the light airplane manufacturing industry.

S&S AIR, INC. 2018 Income Statement		
Sales		$46,298,115
Cost of goods sold		34,536,913
Other expenses		5,870,865
Depreciation		2,074,853
EBIT		$ 3,815,484
Interest		725,098
Taxable income		$ 3,090,386
Taxes (25%)		772,597
Net income		$ 2,317,789
Dividends	$ 705,000	
Add to retained earnings	1,612,789	

S&S AIR, INC. 2018 Balance Sheet			
Assets		**Liabilities and Equity**	
Current assets		Current liabilities	
Cash	$ 524,963	Accounts payable	$ 1,068,356
Accounts receivable	843,094	Notes payable	2,439,553
Inventory	1,235,161	Total current liabilities	$ 3,507,909
Total current assets	$ 2,603,218		
		Long-term debt	$ 6,300,000
Fixed assets			
Net plant and equipment	$20,381,945	Shareholder equity	
		Common stock	$ 460,000
		Retained earnings	12,717,254
		Total equity	$13,177,254
Total assets	$22,985,163	Total liabilities and equity	$22,985,163

Light Airplane Industry Ratios			
	Lower Quartile	Median	Upper Quartile
Current ratio	.50	1.43	1.89
Quick ratio	.21	.35	.62
Cash ratio	.08	.21	.39
Total asset turnover	.68	.85	1.38
Inventory turnover	4.89	6.15	10.89
Receivables turnover	6.27	9.82	14.11
Total debt ratio	.41	.52	.61
Debt-equity ratio	.68	1.08	1.56
Equity multiplier	1.68	2.08	2.56
Times interest earned	5.18	8.06	9.83
Cash coverage ratio	5.84	9.41	10.27
Profit margin	4.05%	5.10%	7.15%
Return on assets	6.05%	9.53%	13.21%
Return on equity	9.93%	15.14%	19.15%

QUESTIONS

1. Using the financial statements provided for S&S Air, calculate each of the ratios listed in the table for the light aircraft industry.

2. Mark and Todd agree that a ratio analysis can provide a measure of the company's performance. They have chosen Boeing as an aspirant company. Would you choose Boeing as an aspirant company? Why or why not? There are other aircraft manufacturers S&S Air could use as aspirant companies. Discuss whether it is appropriate to use any of the following companies: Bombardier, Embraer, Cirrus Aircraft Corporation, and Cessna Aircraft Company.

3. Compare the performance of S&S Air to the industry. For each ratio, comment on why it might be viewed as positive or negative relative to the industry. Suppose you create an inventory ratio calculated as inventory divided by current liabilities. How do you think S&S Air's ratio would compare to the industry average?

Long-Term Financial Planning and Growth

4 Chapter

GROWTH RATES ARE IMPORTANT TOOLS for evaluating a company and, as we will see later, for valuing a company's stock. When thinking about (and calculating) growth rates, a little common sense goes a long way. For example, in 2017, retailing giant Walmart had about 1.156 billion square feet of stores, distribution centers, and so forth. The company expected to increase its square footage by about 4 percent over the next year. This doesn't sound too outrageous, but can Walmart grow its square footage at 4 percent indefinitely?

We'll get into the calculation in our next chapter, but if you assume that Walmart grows at 4 percent per year over the next 291 years, the company will have about 105 trillion square feet of property, which is about the total land mass of the entire United States! In other words, if Walmart keeps growing at 4 percent, the entire country will eventually be one big Walmart. Scary.

Sirius XM Satellite Radio is another example in which common sense comes in handy. The company had total revenues of about $805,000 in 2002 and $4.9 billion in 2016. This represents an annual increase of about 86 percent! How likely do you think it is that the company can continue this growth rate? If this growth continued, the company would have revenues of about $16.01 trillion in just 13 years, which is about the same as the gross domestic product (GDP) of the United States. Obviously, Sirius XM Radio's growth rate will slow substantially in the next several years. So, long-term growth rate estimates must be chosen very carefully. As a rule of thumb, for really long-term growth estimates, you should probably assume that a company will not grow much faster than the economy as a whole, which is about 1 to 3 percent (inflation-adjusted).

Proper management of growth is vital. Thus, this chapter emphasizes the importance of planning for the future and discusses some tools firms use to think about, and manage, growth.

Learning Objectives

After studying this chapter, you should be able to:

LO1 Apply the percentage of sales method.

LO2 Compute the external financing needed to fund a firm's growth.

LO3 Name the determinants of a firm's growth.

LO4 Anticipate some of the problems in planning for growth.

©by_adri/iStockPhoto/GettyImages

For updates on the latest happenings in finance, visit fundamentalsofcorporatefinance.blogspot.com.

A lack of effective long-range planning is a commonly cited reason for financial distress and failure. As we discuss in this chapter, long-range planning is a means of systematically thinking about the future and anticipating possible problems before they arrive. There are no magic mirrors, of course, so the best we can hope for is a logical and organized procedure for exploring the unknown. As one member of GM's board was heard to say, "Planning is a process that at best helps the firm avoid stumbling into the future backward."

Financial planning establishes guidelines for change and growth in a firm. It normally focuses on the big picture. This means it is concerned with the major elements of a firm's financial and investment policies without examining the individual components of those policies in detail.

Our primary goals in this chapter are to discuss financial planning and to illustrate the interrelatedness of the various investment and financing decisions a firm makes. In the chapters ahead, we will examine in much more detail how these decisions are made.

We first describe what is usually meant by *financial planning*. For the most part, we talk about long-term planning. Short-term financial planning is discussed in a later chapter. We examine what the firm can accomplish by developing a long-term financial plan. To do this, we develop a simple but useful long-range planning technique: The percentage of sales approach. We describe how to apply this approach in some simple cases, and we discuss some extensions.

To develop an explicit financial plan, managers must establish certain basic elements of the firm's financial policy:

1. *The firm's needed investment in new assets*: This will arise from the investment opportunities the firm chooses to undertake, and it is the result of the firm's capital budgeting decisions.

2. *The degree of financial leverage the firm chooses to employ*: This will determine the amount of borrowing the firm will use to finance its investments in real assets. This is the firm's capital structure policy.

3. *The amount of cash the firm thinks is necessary and appropriate to pay shareholders*: This is the firm's dividend policy.

4. *The amount of liquidity and working capital the firm needs on an ongoing basis*: This is the firm's net working capital decision.

As we will see, the decisions a firm makes in these four areas will directly affect its future profitability, its need for external financing, and its opportunities for growth.

A key lesson to be learned from this chapter is that a firm's investment and financing policies interact and thus cannot truly be considered in isolation from one another. The types and amounts of assets a firm plans on purchasing must be considered along with the firm's ability to raise the capital necessary to fund those investments. Many business students are aware of the classic three *P*s (or even four *P*s) of marketing. Not to be outdone, financial planners have no fewer than six *P*s: *P*roper *P*rior *P*lanning *P*revents *P*oor *P*erformance.

Financial planning forces the corporation to think about goals. A goal frequently espoused by corporations is growth, and almost all firms use an explicit, companywide growth rate as a major component of their long-term financial planning. For example, in September 2007, Toyota Motor announced that it planned to sell about 9.8 million vehicles in 2008 and 10.4 million vehicles in 2009, becoming the first auto manufacturer to sell more than 10 million vehicles in a year. Of course, Toyota's plans didn't come to fruition. In 2009, the company sold only 7.2 million cars, and it sold 8.6 million in 2010. In 2013, the company sold 9.98 million cars, almost reaching the goal set four years prior, before selling 10.14 million vehicles in 2014 and 10.15 million vehicles in 2015.

There are direct connections between the growth a company can achieve and its financial policy. In the following sections, we show how financial planning models can be used to better understand how growth is achieved. We also show how such models can be used to establish the limits on possible growth.

What Is Financial Planning?

4.1

Financial planning formulates the way in which financial goals are to be achieved. A financial plan is thus a statement of what is to be done in the future. Many decisions have long lead times, which means they take a long time to implement. In an uncertain world, this requires that decisions be made far in advance of their implementation. If a firm wants to build a factory in 2020, for example, it might have to begin lining up contractors and financing in 2018 or even earlier.

GROWTH AS A FINANCIAL MANAGEMENT GOAL

Because the subject of growth will be discussed in various places in this chapter, we need to start out with an important warning: Growth, by itself, is not an appropriate goal for the financial manager. Clothing retailer J. Peterman Co., whose quirky catalogs were made famous on the TV show *Seinfeld*, learned this lesson the hard way. Despite its strong brand name and years of explosive revenue growth, the company was ultimately forced to file for bankruptcy—the victim of an overly ambitious, growth-oriented expansion plan.

Amazon.com, the big online retailer, is another example. At one time, Amazon's motto seemed to be "growth at any cost." Unfortunately, what really grew rapidly for the company were losses. As a result, Amazon refocused its business, explicitly sacrificing growth in the hope of achieving profitability. The plan seems to be working, as Amazon has become a profitable retailing giant.

As we discussed in Chapter 1, the appropriate goal for a firm is increasing the market value of the owners' equity. Of course, if a firm is successful in doing this, then growth will usually result. Growth may thus be a desirable consequence of good decision making, but it is not an end unto itself. We discuss growth because growth rates are so commonly used in the planning process. As we will see, growth is a convenient means of summarizing various aspects of a firm's financial and investment policies. Also, if we think of growth as growth in the market value of the equity in the firm, then goals of growth and increasing the market value of the equity in the firm are not all that different.

You can find growth rates at **www.reuters.com** and **finance.yahoo.com**.

DIMENSIONS OF FINANCIAL PLANNING

It is often useful for planning purposes to think of the future as having a short run and a long run. The short run, in practice, is usually the coming 12 months. We focus our attention on financial planning over the long run, which is usually taken to be the coming two to five years. This time period is called the **planning horizon**, and it is the first dimension of the planning process that must be established.

In drawing up a financial plan, all of the individual projects and investments the firm will undertake are combined to determine the total needed investment. In effect, the smaller investment proposals of each operational unit are added up, and the sum is treated as one big project. This process is called **aggregation**. The level of aggregation is the second dimension of the planning process that needs to be determined.

Once the planning horizon and level of aggregation are established, a financial plan requires inputs in the form of alternative sets of assumptions about important variables. For example, suppose a company has two separate divisions: One for consumer products and

planning horizon
The long-range time period on which the financial planning process focuses (usually the next two to five years).

aggregation
The process by which smaller investment proposals of each of a firm's operational units are added up and treated as one big project.

one for gas turbine engines. The financial planning process might require each division to prepare three alternative business plans for the next three years:

1. *A worst case*: This plan would require making relatively pessimistic assumptions about the company's products and the state of the economy. This kind of disaster planning would emphasize a division's ability to withstand significant economic adversity, and it would require details concerning cost cutting and even divestiture and liquidation. For example, in 2016, Lenovo announced that it had written off $173 million in smartphone inventory. The company had evidently overestimated the demand for its products.

2. *A normal case*: This plan would require making the most likely assumptions about the company and the economy.

3. *A best case*: Each division would be required to work out a case based on optimistic assumptions. It could involve new products and expansion and then detail the financing needed to fund the expansion. For example, in 2016, Amazon ran out of its Echo hands-free speaker on December 9. The company didn't expect to get any back in stock until at least December 30th, missing much of the Christmas shopping season. The smaller Echo Dot was also sold out and not expected to be back in stock until December 27th. In fact, because of the shortage, Echos were selling on eBay for $399, almost triple the Amazon retail price of $139. Evidently, Amazon underestimated the best case.

In this discussion, business activities are aggregated along divisional lines, and the planning horizon is three years. This type of planning, which considers all possible events, is particularly important for cyclical businesses (businesses with sales that are strongly affected by the overall state of the economy or business cycles).

WHAT CAN PLANNING ACCOMPLISH?

Because a company is likely to spend a lot of time examining the different scenarios that will become the basis for its financial plan, it seems reasonable to ask what the planning process will accomplish.

Examining Interactions   As we discuss in greater detail in the following pages, the financial plan must make explicit the linkages between investment proposals for the different operating activities of the firm and its available financing choices. In other words, if the firm is planning on expanding and undertaking new investments and projects, where will the financing be obtained to pay for this activity?

Exploring Options   The financial plan allows the firm to develop, analyze, and compare many different scenarios in a consistent way. Various investment and financing options can be explored, and their impact on the firm's shareholders can be evaluated. Questions concerning the firm's future lines of business and optimal financing arrangements are addressed. Options such as marketing new products or closing plants might be evaluated.

Avoiding Surprises   Financial planning should identify what may happen to the firm if different events take place. In particular, it should address what actions the firm will take if things go seriously wrong or, more generally, if assumptions made today about the future are seriously in error. As physicist Niels Bohr once observed, "Prediction is very difficult, particularly when it concerns the future."* Thus, one purpose of financial planning is to avoid surprises and develop contingency plans.

---

*Source: Niels Bohr (1885–1962)

For example, when Tesla Motors announced its new Model X in February 2012, the company promised that production would begin in 2013. In 2013, when production had yet to start, Tesla pushed back production until late 2014. A company spokesperson stated that production was being delayed "to allow ourselves to focus on production and enhancements in Model S." Of course, even though production of the Model S had begun on time several years earlier, production of that model was below expectations for at least a year. And Tesla didn't meet its revised goal; the first Model X didn't hit the market until September 2015. Thus, a lack of proper planning can be a problem for even the most high-tech companies.

Ensuring Feasibility and Internal Consistency   Beyond a general goal of creating value, a firm will normally have many specific goals. Such goals might be couched in terms of market share, return on equity, financial leverage, and so on. At times, the linkages between different goals and different aspects of a firm's business are difficult to see. A financial plan makes these linkages explicit, while also imposing a unified structure for reconciling goals and objectives. In other words, financial planning is a way of verifying that the goals and plans made for specific areas of a firm's operations are feasible and internally consistent. Conflicting goals will often exist. To generate a coherent plan, goals and objectives will have to be modified, and priorities will have to be established.

For example, one goal a firm might have is 12 percent growth in unit sales per year. Another goal might be to reduce the firm's total debt ratio from 40 to 20 percent. Are these two goals compatible? Can they be accomplished simultaneously? Maybe yes, maybe no. As we will discuss, financial planning is a way of finding out what is possible—and, by implication, what is not.

Conclusion   Probably the most important result of the planning process is that it forces managers to think about goals and establish priorities. In fact, conventional business wisdom holds that financial plans don't work, but financial planning does. The future is inherently unknown. What we can do is establish the direction in which we want to travel and make some educated guesses about what we will find along the way. If we do a good job, we won't be caught off guard when the future rolls around.

Concept Questions

4.1a   What are the two dimensions of the financial planning process?

4.1b   Why should firms draw up financial plans?

Financial Planning Models: A First Look   4.2

Just as companies differ in size and products, the financial planning process will differ from firm to firm. In this section, we discuss some common elements in financial plans and develop a basic model to illustrate these elements. What follows is a quick overview; later sections will take up the various topics in more detail.

Excel Master It!
Excel Master
coverage online

A FINANCIAL PLANNING MODEL: THE INGREDIENTS

Most financial planning models require the user to specify some assumptions about the future. Based on those assumptions, the model generates predicted values for many other variables. Models can vary quite a bit in complexity, but almost all have the elements we discuss next.

Sales Forecast Almost all financial plans require an externally supplied sales forecast. In our models that follow, for example, the sales forecast will be the "driver," meaning that the user of the planning model will supply this value, and most other values will be calculated based on it. This arrangement is common for many types of business; planning will focus on projected future sales and the assets and financing needed to support those sales.

Frequently, the sales forecast will be given as the growth rate in sales rather than as an explicit sales figure. These two approaches are essentially the same because we can calculate projected sales once we know the growth rate. Perfect sales forecasts are not possible, of course, because sales depend on the uncertain future state of the economy. To help a firm come up with its projections, some businesses specialize in macroeconomic and industry projections.

As we discussed previously, we frequently will be interested in evaluating alternative scenarios, so it isn't necessarily crucial that the sales forecast be accurate. In such cases, our goal is to examine the interplay between investment and financing needs at different possible sales levels, not to pinpoint what we expect to happen.

Pro Forma Statements A financial plan will have a forecast balance sheet, income statement, and statement of cash flows. These are called *pro forma statements*, or *pro formas* for short. The phrase *pro forma* literally means "as a matter of form." In our case, this means the financial statements are the form we use to summarize the different events projected for the future. At a minimum, a financial planning model will generate these statements based on projections of key items such as sales.

In the planning models we will describe, the pro formas are the output from the financial planning model. The user will supply a sales figure, and the model will generate the resulting income statement and balance sheet.

Asset Requirements The plan will describe projected capital spending. At a minimum, the projected balance sheet will contain changes in total fixed assets and net working capital. These changes are effectively the firm's total capital budget. Proposed capital spending in different areas must be reconciled with the overall increases contained in the long-range plan.

Financial Requirements The plan will include a section about the necessary financing arrangements. This part of the plan should discuss dividend policy and debt policy. Sometimes firms will expect to raise cash by selling new shares of stock or by borrowing. In this case, the plan will have to consider what kinds of securities have to be sold and what methods of issuance are most appropriate. These are subjects we consider in Part 6 of our book, where we discuss long-term financing, capital structure, and dividend policy.

The Plug After the firm has a sales forecast and an estimate of the required spending on assets, some amount of new financing will often be necessary because projected total assets will exceed projected total liabilities and equity. In other words, the balance sheet will no longer balance.

Because new financing may be necessary to cover all of the projected capital spending, a financial "plug" variable must be selected. The plug is the designated source or sources of external financing needed to deal with any shortfall (or surplus) in financing and thereby bring the balance sheet into balance.

For example, a firm with a great number of investment opportunities and limited cash flow may have to raise new equity. Other firms with few growth opportunities and ample cash flow will have a surplus and thus might pay an extra dividend. In the first case, external equity is the plug variable. In the second, the dividend is used.

Economic Assumptions   The plan will have to state explicitly the economic environment in which the firm expects to reside over the life of the plan. Among the more important economic assumptions that will have to be made are the level of interest rates and the firm's tax rate.

A SIMPLE FINANCIAL PLANNING MODEL

We can begin our discussion of long-term planning models with a relatively simple example. The Computerfield Corporation's financial statements from the most recent year are as follows:

COMPUTERFIELD CORPORATION Financial Statements					
Income Statement			**Balance Sheet**		
Sales	$1,000	Assets	$500	Debt	$250
Costs	800			Equity	250
Net income	$ 200	Total	$500	Total	$500

Unless otherwise stated, the financial planners at Computerfield assume that all variables are tied directly to sales and current relationships are optimal. This means that all items will grow at exactly the same rate as sales. This is obviously oversimplified; we use this assumption only to make a point.

Suppose sales increase by 20 percent, rising from $1,000 to $1,200. Planners would then also forecast a 20 percent increase in costs, from $800 to $800 × 1.2 = $960. The pro forma income statement would be:

Pro Forma Income Statement	
Sales	$1,200
Costs	960
Net income	$ 240

The assumption that all variables will grow by 20 percent lets us easily construct the pro forma balance sheet as well:

Pro Forma Balance Sheet			
Assets	$600 (+100)	Debt	$300 (+ 50)
		Equity	300 (+ 50)
Total	$600 (+100)	Total	$600 (+100)

Notice that we have increased every item by 20 percent. The numbers in parentheses are the dollar changes for the different items.

Now we have to reconcile these two pro formas. How, for example, can net income be equal to $240 and equity increase by only $50? The answer is that Computerfield must have paid out the difference of $240 − 50 = $190, possibly as a cash dividend. In this case, dividends are the plug variable.

Suppose Computerfield does not pay out the $190. In this case, the addition to retained earnings is the full $240. Computerfield's equity will grow to $250 (the starting amount) plus $240 (net income), or $490, and debt must be retired to keep total assets equal to $600.

Planware provides insight into cash flow forecasting (**www.planware.org**).

With $600 in total assets and $490 in equity, debt will have to be $600 − 490 = $110. Because we started with $250 in debt, Computerfield will have to retire $250 − 110 = $140 in debt. The resulting pro forma balance sheet would look like this:

Pro Forma Balance Sheet			
Assets	$600 (+100)	Debt	$110 (−140)
		Equity	490 (+240)
Total	$600 (+100)	Total	$600 (+100)

In this case, debt is the plug variable used to balance projected total assets and liabilities.

This example shows the interaction between sales growth and financial policy. As sales increase, so do total assets. This occurs because the firm must invest in net working capital and fixed assets to support higher sales levels. Because assets are growing, total liabilities and equity (the right side of the balance sheet) will grow as well.

The thing to notice from our simple example is that the way the liabilities and owners' equity change depends on the firm's financing policy and its dividend policy. The growth in assets requires that the firm decide on how to finance that growth. This is strictly a managerial decision. Note that in our example, the firm needed no outside funds. This won't usually be the case, so we explore a more detailed situation in the next section.

Concept Questions

4.2a What are the basic components of a financial plan?
4.2b Why is it necessary to designate a plug in a financial planning model?

4.3 The Percentage of Sales Approach

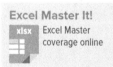
In the previous section, we described a simple planning model in which every item increased at the same rate as sales. This may be a reasonable assumption for some elements. For others, such as long-term borrowing, it probably is not: The amount of long-term borrowing is something set by management, and it does not necessarily relate directly to the level of sales.

In this section, we describe an extended version of our simple model. The basic idea is to separate the income statement and balance sheet accounts into two groups—those that vary directly with sales and those that do not. Given a sales forecast, we will then be able to calculate how much financing the firm will need to support the predicted sales level.

percentage of sales approach
A financial planning method in which accounts are varied depending on a firm's predicted sales level.

The financial planning model we describe next is based on the **percentage of sales approach**. Our goal here is to develop a quick and practical way of generating pro forma statements. We defer discussion of some "bells and whistles" to a later section.

THE INCOME STATEMENT

We start out with the most recent income statement for the Rosengarten Corporation, as shown in Table 4.1. Notice we have still simplified things by including costs, depreciation, and interest in a single cost figure.

Rosengarten has projected a 25 percent increase in sales for the coming year, so we are anticipating sales of $1,000 × 1.25 = $1,250. To generate a pro forma income statement, we assume that total costs will continue to run at $833/$1,000 = .833, or 83.3% of sales. With this assumption, Rosengarten's pro forma income statement is shown in Table 4.2. The effect

ROSENGARTEN CORPORATION Income Statement	
Sales	$1,000
Costs	833
Taxable income	$ 167
Taxes (21%)	35
Net income	$ 132
Dividends	$44
Addition to retained earnings	88

TABLE 4.1

Rosengarten Corporation Income Statement

ROSENGARTEN CORPORATION Pro Forma Income Statement	
Sales (projected)	$1,250
Costs (83.3% of sales)	1,041
Taxable income	$ 209
Taxes (21%)	44
Net income	$ 165

TABLE 4.2

Rosengarten Corporation Pro Forma Income Statement

here of assuming that costs are a constant percentage of sales is to assume that the profit margin is constant. To check this, notice that the profit margin was $132/$1,000 = .132, or 13.2%. In our pro forma, the profit margin is $165/$1,250 = .132, or 13.2%, so it is unchanged.

Next, we need to project the dividend payment. This amount is up to Rosengarten's management. We will assume Rosengarten has a policy of paying out a constant fraction of net income in the form of a cash dividend. For the most recent year, the **dividend payout ratio** was this:

dividend payout ratio
The amount of cash paid out to shareholders divided by net income.

Dividend payout ratio = Cash dividends/Net income
$$= \$44/\$132 = 1/3$$

  4.1

We can also calculate the ratio of the addition to retained earnings to net income:

Addition to retained earnings/Net income = $88/$132 = 2/3

This ratio is called the **retention ratio** or **plowback ratio**, and it is equal to 1 minus the dividend payout ratio because everything not paid out is retained. Assuming that the payout ratio is constant, here are the projected dividends and addition to retained earnings:

retention ratio
The addition to retained earnings divided by net income. Also called the *plowback ratio*.

Projected dividends paid to shareholders = $165 × 1/3 = $ 55
Projected addition to retained earnings = $165 × 2/3 = 110
$165

THE BALANCE SHEET

To generate a pro forma balance sheet, we start with the most recent statement, as shown in Table 4.3.

On our balance sheet, we assume that some items vary directly with sales and others do not. For items that vary with sales, we express each as a percentage of sales for the year just completed. When an item does not vary directly with sales, we write "n/a" for "not applicable."

TABLE 4.3   Rosengarten Corporation Balance Sheet

ROSENGARTEN CORPORATION Balance Sheet					
Assets			**Liabilities and Owners' Equity**		
	$	Percentage of Sales		$	Percentage of Sales
Current assets			Current liabilities		
Cash	$ 160	16%	Accounts payable	$ 300	30%
Accounts receivable	440	44	Notes payable	100	n/a
Inventory	600	60	Total	$ 400	n/a
Total	$1,200	120	Long-term debt	$ 800	n/a
Fixed assets			Owners' equity		
Net plant and equipment	$1,800	180	Common stock and paid-in surplus	$ 800	n/a
			Retained earnings	1,000	n/a
			Total	$1,800	n/a
Total assets	$3,000	300%	Total liabilities and owners' equity	$3,000	n/a

For example, on the asset side, inventory is equal to 60 percent of sales (= $600/$1,000) for the year just ended. We assume this percentage applies to the coming year, so for each $1 increase in sales, inventory will rise by $.60. More generally, the ratio of total assets to sales for the year just ended is $3,000/$1,000 = 3, or 300%.

capital intensity ratio
A firm's total assets divided by its sales, or the amount of assets needed to generate $1 in sales.

This ratio of total assets to sales is sometimes called the **capital intensity ratio**. It tells us the amount of assets needed to generate $1 in sales; so the higher the ratio is, the more capital-intensive is the firm. Notice also that this ratio is the reciprocal of the total asset turnover ratio we defined in the last chapter.

For Rosengarten, assuming that this ratio is constant, it takes $3 in total assets to generate $1 in sales (apparently Rosengarten is in a relatively capital-intensive business). Therefore, if sales are to increase by $100, Rosengarten will have to increase total assets by three times this amount, or $300.

On the liability side of the balance sheet, we show accounts payable varying with sales. The reason is that we expect to place more orders with our suppliers as sales volume increases, so payables will change "spontaneously" with sales. Notes payable, on the other hand, represent short-term debt such as bank borrowing. This item will not vary unless we take specific actions to change the amount, so we mark it as "n/a."

Similarly, we use "n/a" for long-term debt because it won't automatically change with sales. The same is true for common stock and paid-in surplus. The last item on the right side, retained earnings, will vary with sales, but it won't be a simple percentage of sales. Instead, we will explicitly calculate the change in retained earnings based on our projected net income and dividends.

We can now construct a partial pro forma balance sheet for Rosengarten. We do this by using the percentages we have just calculated wherever possible to calculate the projected amounts. For example, net fixed assets are 180 percent of sales; so, with a new sales level of $1,250, the net fixed asset amount will be 1.80 × $1,250 = $2,250, representing an increase of $2,250 − 1,800 = $450 in plant and equipment. It is important to note that for items that don't vary directly with sales, we initially assume no change and write in the

TABLE 4.4

			ROSENGARTEN CORPORATION Partial Pro Forma Balance Sheet			
Assets				**Liabilities and Owners' Equity**		
	Projected	**Change from Previous Year**			**Projected**	**Change from Previous Year**
Current assets			Current liabilities			
Cash	$ 200	$ 40	Accounts payable		$ 375	$ 75
Accounts receivable	550	110	Notes payable		100	0
Inventory	750	150	Total		$ 475	$ 75
Total	$1,500	$300	Long-term debt		$ 800	$ 0
Fixed assets						
Net plant and equipment	$2,250	$450	Owners' equity			
			Common stock and paid-in surplus		$ 800	$ 0
			Retained earnings		1,110	110
			Total		$1,910	$110
Total assets	$3,750	$750	Total liabilities and owners' equity		$3,185	$185
			External financing needed		$ 565	$565

original amounts. The result is shown in Table 4.4. Notice that the change in retained earnings is equal to the $110 addition to retained earnings we calculated earlier.

Inspecting our pro forma balance sheet, we notice that assets are projected to increase by $750. However, without additional financing, liabilities and equity will increase by only $185, leaving a shortfall of $750 − 185 = $565. We label this amount *external financing needed* (EFN).

A PARTICULAR SCENARIO

Our financial planning model now reminds us of one of those good news–bad news jokes. The good news is we're projecting a 25 percent increase in sales. The bad news is that this isn't going to happen unless Rosengarten can somehow raise $565 in new financing.

This is a good example of how the planning process can point out problems and potential conflicts. If, for example, Rosengarten has a goal of not borrowing any additional funds and not selling any new equity, then a 25 percent increase in sales is probably not feasible.

If we take the need for $565 in new financing as given, we know that Rosengarten has three possible sources: short-term borrowing, long-term borrowing, and new equity. The choice of some combination among these three is up to management; we will illustrate only one of the many possibilities.

Suppose Rosengarten decides to borrow the needed funds. In this case, the firm might choose to borrow some over the short term and some over the long term. For example, current assets increased by $300, whereas current liabilities rose by only $75. Rosengarten could borrow $300 − 75 = $225 in short-term notes payable and leave total net working capital unchanged. With $565 needed, the remaining $565 − 225 = $340 would have to come from long-term debt. Table 4.5 shows the completed pro forma balance sheet for Rosengarten.

TABLE 4.5

ROSENGARTEN CORPORATION Pro Forma Balance Sheet					
Assets			**Liabilities and Owners' Equity**		
	Projected	Change from Previous Year		Projected	Change from Previous Year
Current assets			Current liabilities		
Cash	$ 200	$ 40	Accounts payable	$ 375	$ 75
Accounts receivable	550	110	Notes payable	325	225
Inventory	750	150	Total	$ 700	$300
Total	$1,500	$300	Long-term debt	$1,140	$340
Fixed assets					
Net plant and equipment	$2,250	$450	Owners' equity		
			Common stock and paid-in surplus	$ 800	$ 0
			Retained earnings	1,110	110
			Total	$1,910	$110
Total assets	$3,750	$750	Total liabilities and owners' equity	$3,750	$750

We have used a combination of short- and long-term debt as the plug here, but we emphasize that this is just one possible strategy; it is not necessarily the best one by any means. There are many other scenarios we could (and should) investigate. The various ratios we discussed in Chapter 3 come in handy here. For example, with the scenario we have just examined, we would surely want to examine the current ratio and the total debt ratio to see if we were comfortable with the new projected debt levels.

Now that we have finished our balance sheet, we have all of the projected sources and uses of cash. We could finish off our pro formas by drawing up the projected statement of cash flows along the lines discussed in Chapter 3. We will leave this as an exercise and instead investigate an important alternative scenario.

AN ALTERNATIVE SCENARIO

The assumption that assets are a fixed percentage of sales is convenient, but it may not be suitable in many cases. In particular, note that we effectively assumed that Rosengarten was using its fixed assets at 100 percent of capacity because any increase in sales led to an increase in fixed assets. For most businesses, there would be some slack or excess capacity, and production could be increased by perhaps running an extra shift.

For example, in July 2016, Fiat Chrysler announced that it would spend $1.05 billion in assembly plants in Ohio and Illinois to expand production of its Jeep product line. Later that year, Ford announced plans to close two Mexican plants. Ford also announced that it would idle four of its plants for a week, or longer. Evidently Ford had excess capacity, whereas Fiat Chrysler did not.

In another example, in November 2016, automotive replacement parts manufacturer Standard Motor Products announced that it was closing a plant in Texas. The company stated that it would increase production at other plants to compensate for the closings. Apparently, Standard Motor had significant excess capacity at its production facilities. Overall, according to the Federal Reserve, capacity utilization for U.S. manufacturing companies in September 2017 was 76.2 percent, up slightly from the 76.1 percent in the previous month.

If we assume that Rosengarten is operating at only 70 percent of capacity, then the need for external funds will be quite different. When we say "70 percent of capacity," we mean that the current sales level is 70 percent of the full-capacity sales level:

Current sales = $1,000 = .70 × Full-capacity sales

Full-capacity sales = $1,000/.70 = $1,429

This tells us that sales could increase by almost 43 percent—from $1,000 to $1,429— before any new fixed assets would be needed.

In our previous scenario, we assumed it would be necessary to add $450 in net fixed assets. In the current scenario, no spending on net fixed assets is needed because sales are projected to rise only to $1,250, which is substantially less than the $1,429 full-capacity level.

As a result, our original estimate of $565 in external funds needed is too high. We estimated that $450 in new net fixed assets would be needed. Instead, no spending on new net fixed assets is necessary. Thus, if we are currently operating at 70 percent capacity, we need only $565 − 450 = $115 in external funds. The excess capacity thus makes a considerable difference in our projections.

EFN and Capacity Usage	**EXAMPLE 4.1**

Suppose Rosengarten is operating at 90 percent capacity. What would sales be at full capacity? What is the capital intensity ratio at full capacity? What is EFN in this case?

Full-capacity sales would be $1,000/.90 = $1,111. From Table 4.3, we know that fixed assets are $1,800. At full capacity, the ratio of fixed assets to sales is this:

Fixed assets/Full-capacity sales = $1,800/$1,111 = 1.62

So, Rosengarten needs $1.62 in fixed assets for every $1 in sales once it reaches full capacity. At the projected sales level of $1,250, then, it needs $1,250 × 1.62 = $2,025 in fixed assets. Compared to the $2,250 we originally projected, this is $225 less, so EFN is $565 − 225 = $340.

Current assets would still be $1,500, so total assets would be $1,500 + 2,025 = $3,525. The capital intensity ratio would thus be $3,525/$1,250 = 2.82, which is less than our original value of 3 because of the excess capacity.

These alternative scenarios illustrate that it is inappropriate to blindly manipulate financial statement information in the planning process. The results depend critically on the assumptions made about the relationships between sales and asset needs. We return to this point a little later.

One thing should be clear by now. Projected growth rates play an important role in the planning process. They are also important to outside analysts and potential investors. Our nearby *Work the Web* box shows you how to obtain growth rate estimates for real companies.

Concept Questions

4.3a   What is the basic idea behind the percentage of sales approach?

4.3b   Unless it is modified, what does the percentage of sales approach assume about fixed asset capacity usage?

WORK THE WEB

Calculating company growth rates can involve detailed research, and a major part of a stock analyst's job is to estimate them. One place to find earnings and sales growth rates on the web is Yahoo! Finance at finance.yahoo.com. We pulled up a quote for 3M Company and followed the "Analysts" link. Here is an abbreviated look at the results:

Revenue Estimate	Current Qtr. (Mar 2017)	Next Qtr. (Jun 2017)	Current Year	Next Year
No. of Analysts	12	12	16	15
Avg. Estimate	7.47B	7.71B	30.44B	31.44B
Low Estimate	7.33B	7.58B	30.14B	31.1B
High Estimate	7.57B	7.85B	30.91B	31.89B
Year Ago Sales	7.41B	7.66B	30.11B	30.44B
Sales Growth (year/est)	0.90%	0.70%	1.10%	3.30%

As shown, analysts expect, on average, revenue (sales) of $30.44 billion in 2017, growing to $31.44 billion in 2018, an increase of 3.3 percent. We also have the following table showing estimates for estimated growth in 3M's EPS:

Earnings Estimate	Current Qtr. (Mar 2017)	Next Qtr. (Jun 2017)	Current Year	Next Year
No. of Analysts	16	15	18	17
Avg. Estimate	2.06	2.23	8.62	9.38
Low Estimate	2.02	2.14	8.4	9
High Estimate	2.14	2.29	8.8	10.2
Year Ago EPS	2.05	2.08	8.16	8.62

As you can see, the average EPS estimate for 3M in 2017 is $8.62, while the average EPS estimate for 2018 is $9.38, an increase of 8.8 percent. What does this mean for 3M stock? We'll get to that in a later chapter.

Questions

1. One of the things shown here is the projected sales growth for 3M during 2017 at the time this was captured from finance.yahoo.com. How does the current sales projection or the actual sales number differ from this projection? Can you think of any reasons for the difference?

2. On the same web page, you can find the earnings history for 3M. How close have analysts been to estimating 3M's earnings? In other words, what has the "surprise" been in 3M's earnings?

External Financing and Growth

4.4

External financing needed and growth are obviously related. All other things staying the same, the higher the rate of growth in sales or assets, the greater will be the need for external financing. In the previous section, we took a growth rate as given, and then we determined the amount of external financing needed to support that growth. In this section, we turn things around a bit. We will take the firm's financial policy as given and then examine the relationship between that financial policy and the firm's ability to finance new investments and thereby grow.

Once again, we emphasize that we are focusing on growth but not because growth is an appropriate goal; instead, for our purposes, growth is a convenient means of examining the interactions between investment and financing decisions. In effect, we assume that the use of growth as a basis for planning is a reflection of the very high level of aggregation used in the planning process.

EFN AND GROWTH

The first thing we need to do is establish the relationship between EFN and growth. To do this, we introduce the simplified income statement and balance sheet for the Hoffman Company in Table 4.6. Notice that we have simplified the balance sheet by combining short-term and long-term debt into a single total debt figure. Effectively, we are assuming that none of the current liabilities varies spontaneously with sales. This assumption isn't as restrictive as it sounds. If any current liabilities (such as accounts payable) vary with sales, we can assume that any such accounts have been netted out in current assets. Also, we continue to combine depreciation, interest, and costs on the income statement.

Suppose the Hoffman Company is forecasting next year's sales level at $600, a $100 increase. Notice that the percentage increase in sales is $100/$500 = .20, or 20%. Using the percentage of sales approach and the figures in Table 4.6, we can prepare a pro forma income statement and balance sheet as in Table 4.7. As Table 4.7 illustrates, at a 20 percent growth

TABLE 4.6

HOFFMAN COMPANY Income Statement and Balance Sheet					
Income Statement					
Sales			$500.0		
Costs			416.5		
Taxable income			$ 83.5		
Taxes (21%)			17.5		
Net income			$ 66.0		
Dividends		$22			
Addition to retained earnings		44			
Balance Sheet					
Assets			**Liabilities and Owners' Equity**		
	$	**Percentage of Sales**		**$**	**Percentage of Sales**
Current assets	$200	40%	Total debt	$250	n/a
Net fixed assets	300	60	Owners' equity	250	n/a
Total assets	$500	100%	Total liabilities and owners' equity	$500	n/a

TABLE 4.7

HOFFMAN COMPANY Pro Forma Income Statement and Balance Sheet					
Income Statement					
Sales (projected)			$600.0		
Costs (83.3% of sales)			499.8		
Taxable income			$100.2		
Taxes (21%)			21.0		
Net income			$ 79.2		
Dividends		$26.4			
Addition to retained earnings		52.8			
Balance Sheet					
Assets			**Liabilities and Owners' Equity**		
	$	Percentage of Sales		$	Percentage of Sales
Current assets	$240.0	40%	Total debt	$250.0	n/a
Net fixed assets	360.0	60	Owners' equity	302.8	n/a
Total assets	$600.0	100%	Total liabilities and owners' equity	$552.8	n/a
			External financing needed	$ 47.2	n/a

rate, Hoffman needs $100 in new assets (assuming full capacity). The projected addition to retained earnings is $52.8, so the external financing needed (EFN) is $100 − 52.8 = $47.2.

Notice that the debt-equity ratio for Hoffman was originally (from Table 4.6) equal to $250/$250 = 1.0. We will assume that the Hoffman Company does not wish to sell new equity. In this case, the $47.2 in EFN will have to be borrowed. What will the new debt-equity ratio be? From Table 4.7, we know that total owners' equity is projected at $302.8. The new total debt will be the original $250 plus $47.2 in new borrowing, or $297.2 total. The debt-equity ratio thus falls from 1.0 to $297.2/$302.8 = .98.

Table 4.8 shows EFN for several different growth rates. The projected addition to retained earnings and the projected debt-equity ratio for each scenario are also given (you should probably calculate a few of these for practice). In determining the debt-equity ratios, we assumed that any needed funds were borrowed, and we also assumed any surplus funds were used to pay off debt. Thus, for the zero growth case, debt falls by $44, from $250 to $206. In Table 4.8, notice that the increase in assets required is equal to the original assets

TABLE 4.8

Growth and Projected EFN for the Hoffman Company

Projected Sales Growth	Increase in Assets Required	Addition to Retained Earnings	External Financing Needed, EFN	Projected Debt-Equity Ratio
0%	$ 0	$44.0	−$44.0	.70
5	25	46.2	−21.2	.77
10	50	48.4	1.6	.84
15	75	50.6	24.4	.91
20	100	52.8	47.2	.98
25	125	55.0	70.0	1.05

FIGURE 4.1

**Growth and Related
Financing Needed for
the Hoffman Company**

of $500 multiplied by the growth rate. Similarly, the addition to retained earnings is equal to the original $44 plus $44 times the growth rate.

Table 4.8 shows that for relatively low growth rates, Hoffman will run a surplus, and its debt-equity ratio will decline. Once the growth rate increases to about 10 percent, however, the surplus becomes a deficit. Furthermore, as the growth rate exceeds approximately 20 percent, the debt-equity ratio surpasses its original value of 1.0.

Figure 4.1 illustrates the connection between growth in sales and external financing needed in more detail by plotting asset needs and additions to retained earnings from Table 4.8 against the growth rates. As shown, the need for new assets grows at a much faster rate than the addition to retained earnings, so the internal financing provided by the addition to retained earnings rapidly disappears.

As this discussion shows, whether a firm runs a cash surplus or deficit depends on growth. Microsoft is a good example. Its revenue growth in the 1990s was amazing, averaging well over 30 percent per year for the decade. Growth slowed down noticeably over the 2000–2010 period; nonetheless, Microsoft's combination of growth and substantial profit margins led to enormous cash surpluses. In part because Microsoft pays a relatively small dividend, the cash really piled up; in 2017, Microsoft's cash horde exceeded $137 billion.

FINANCIAL POLICY AND GROWTH

Based on our preceding discussion, we see that there is a direct link between growth and external financing. In this section, we discuss two growth rates that are particularly useful in long-range planning.

The Internal Growth Rate   The first growth rate of interest is the maximum growth rate that can be achieved with no external financing of any kind. We will call this the **internal growth rate** because this is the rate the firm can maintain with internal financing only. In Figure 4.1, this internal growth rate is represented by the point where the two lines cross. At this point, the required increase in assets is exactly equal to the addition

internal growth rate
The maximum growth rate a firm can achieve without external financing of any kind.

to retained earnings, and EFN is therefore zero. We have seen that this happens when the growth rate is slightly less than 10 percent. With a little algebra (see Problem 31 at the end of the chapter), we can define this growth rate more precisely:

$$\text{Internal growth rate} = \frac{\text{ROA} \times b}{1 - \text{ROA} \times b} \qquad \text{4.2}$$

Here, ROA is the return on assets we discussed in Chapter 3, and b is the plowback, or retention, ratio defined earlier in this chapter.

For the Hoffman Company, net income was $66 and total assets were $500. ROA is thus $66/$500 = .132, or 13.2%. Of the $66 net income, $44 was retained, so the plowback ratio, b, is $44/$66 = 2/3. With these numbers, we can calculate the internal growth rate:

$$
\begin{aligned}
\text{Internal growth rate} &= \frac{\text{ROA} \times b}{1 - \text{ROA} \times b} \\
&= \frac{.132 \times (2/3)}{1 - .132 \times (2/3)} \\
&= .0964, \text{ or } 9.64\%
\end{aligned}
$$

Thus, the Hoffman Company can expand at a maximum rate of 9.64 percent per year without external financing.

The Sustainable Growth Rate   We have seen that if the Hoffman Company wishes to grow more rapidly than at a rate of 9.64 percent per year, external financing must be arranged. The second growth rate of interest is the maximum growth rate a firm can achieve with no external *equity* financing while it maintains a constant debt-equity ratio. This rate is commonly called the **sustainable growth rate** because it is the maximum rate of growth a firm can maintain without increasing its financial leverage.

There are various reasons why a firm might wish to avoid equity sales. For example, as we discuss in Chapter 15, new equity sales can be expensive. Alternatively, the current owners may not wish to bring in new owners or contribute additional equity. Why a firm might view a particular debt-equity ratio as optimal is discussed in Chapters 14 and 16; for now, we will take it as given.

Based on Table 4.8, the sustainable growth rate for Hoffman is approximately 20 percent because the debt-equity ratio is near 1.0 at that growth rate. The precise value can be calculated (see Problem 31 at the end of the chapter):

$$\text{Sustainable growth rate} = \frac{\text{ROE} \times b}{1 - \text{ROE} \times b} \qquad \text{4.3}$$

This is identical to the internal growth rate except that ROE, return on equity, is used instead of ROA.

For the Hoffman Company, net income was $66 and total equity was $250; ROE is thus $66/$250 = .264, or 26.4%. The plowback ratio, b, is still 2/3, so we can calculate the sustainable growth rate as follows:

$$
\begin{aligned}
\text{Sustainable growth rate} &= \frac{\text{ROE} \times b}{1 - \text{ROE} \times b} \\
&= \frac{.264 \times (2/3)}{1 - .264 \times (2/3)} \\
&= .2135, \text{ or } 21.35\%
\end{aligned}
$$

Thus, the Hoffman Company can expand at a maximum rate of 21.35 percent per year without external equity financing.

sustainable growth rate
The maximum growth rate a firm can achieve without external equity financing while maintaining a constant debt-equity ratio.

| | Sustainable Growth | **EXAMPLE 4.2** |

Suppose Hoffman grows at exactly the sustainable growth rate of 21.35 percent. What will the pro forma statements look like?

At a 21.35 percent growth rate, sales will rise from $500 to $606.7. The pro forma income statement will look like this:

HOFFMAN COMPANY Pro Forma Income Statement	
Sales (projected)	$606.7
Costs (83.3% of sales)	505.4
Taxable income	$101.3
Taxes (21%)	21.3
Net income	$ 80.0
Dividends	$26.7
Addition to retained earnings	53.4

We construct the balance sheet as we did before. Notice, in this case, that owners' equity will rise from $250 to $303.4 because the addition to retained earnings is $53.4.

HOFFMAN COMPANY Pro Forma Balance Sheet					
Assets			**Liabilities and Owners' Equity**		
	$	Percentage of Sales		$	Percentage of Sales
Current assets	$242.7	40%	Total debt	$250.0	n/a
Net fixed assets	364.0	60	Owners' equity	303.4	n/a
Total assets	$606.7	100%	Total liabilities and owners' equity	$553.4	n/a
			External financing needed	$ 53.4	n/a

As illustrated, EFN is $53.4. If Hoffman borrows this amount, then total debt will rise to $303.4, and the debt-equity ratio will be exactly 1.0, which verifies our earlier calculation. At any other growth rate, something would have to change.

Determinants of Growth In the last chapter, we saw that the return on equity, ROE, could be decomposed into its various components using the DuPont identity. Because ROE appears so prominently in the determination of the sustainable growth rate, it is obvious that the factors important in determining ROE are also important determinants of growth.

From Chapter 3, we know that ROE can be written as the product of three factors:

ROE = Profit margin × Total asset turnover × Equity multiplier

If we examine our expression for the sustainable growth rate, we see that anything that increases ROE will increase the sustainable growth rate by making the top bigger and the bottom smaller. Increasing the plowback ratio will have the same effect.

Putting it all together, what we have is that a firm's ability to sustain growth depends explicitly on the following four factors:

1. *Profit margin*: An increase in profit margin will increase the firm's ability to generate funds internally and thereby increase its sustainable growth.

2. *Dividend policy*: A decrease in the percentage of net income paid out as dividends will increase the retention ratio. This increases internally generated equity and thus increases sustainable growth.

3. *Financial policy*: An increase in the debt-equity ratio increases the firm's financial leverage. Because this makes additional debt financing available, it increases the sustainable growth rate.

4. *Total asset turnover*: An increase in the firm's total asset turnover increases the sales generated for each dollar in assets. This decreases the firm's need for new assets as sales grow and thereby increases the sustainable growth rate. Notice that increasing total asset turnover is the same thing as decreasing capital intensity.

The sustainable growth rate is a very useful planning number. What it illustrates is the explicit relationship between the firm's four major areas of concern: Its operating efficiency as measured by profit margin, its asset use efficiency as measured by total asset turnover, its dividend policy as measured by the retention ratio, and its financial policy as measured by the debt-equity ratio.

Given values for all four of these, there is only one growth rate that can be achieved. This is an important point, so it bears restating:

> **If a firm does not wish to sell new equity and its profit margin, dividend policy, financial policy, and total asset turnover (or capital intensity) are all fixed, then there is only one possible growth rate.**

As we described early in this chapter, one of the primary benefits of financial planning is that it ensures internal consistency among the firm's various goals. The concept of the sustainable growth rate captures this element nicely. Also, we now see how a financial planning model can be used to test the feasibility of a planned growth rate. If sales are to grow at a rate higher than the sustainable growth rate, the firm must increase profit margins, increase total asset turnover, increase financial leverage, increase earnings retention, or sell new shares.

The two growth rates, internal and sustainable, are summarized in Table 4.9.

TABLE 4.9

Summary of Internal and Sustainable Growth Rates

I.   **Internal Growth Rate**

Internal growth rate $= \dfrac{\text{ROA} \times b}{1 - \text{ROA} \times b}$
 where
    ROA = Return on assets = Net income/Total assets
     b = Plowback (retention) ratio
      = Addition to retained earnings/Net income
 The internal growth rate is the maximum growth rate that can be achieved with no external financing of any kind.

II.   **Sustainable Growth Rate**

Sustainable growth rate $= \dfrac{\text{ROE} \times b}{1 - \text{ROE} \times b}$
 where
    ROE = Return on equity = Net income/Total equity
     b = Plowback (retention) ratio
      = Addition to retained earnings/Net income
 The sustainable growth rate is the maximum growth rate that can be achieved with no external equity financing while maintaining a constant debt-equity ratio.

IN THEIR OWN WORDS ...

Robert C. Higgins on Sustainable Growth

Most financial officers know intuitively that it takes money to make money. Rapid sales growth requires increased assets in the form of accounts receivable, inventory, and fixed plant, which, in turn, require money to pay for assets. They also know that if their company does not have the money when needed, it can literally "grow broke." The sustainable growth equation states these intuitive truths explicitly.

Sustainable growth is often used by bankers and other external analysts to assess a company's creditworthiness. They are aided in this exercise by several sophisticated computer software packages that provide detailed analyses of the company's past financial performance, including its annual sustainable growth rate.

Bankers use this information in several ways. Quick comparison of a company's actual growth rate to its sustainable rate tells the banker what issues will be at the top of management's financial agenda. If actual growth consistently exceeds sustainable growth, management's problem will be where to get the cash to finance growth. The banker thus can anticipate interest in loan products. Conversely, if sustainable growth consistently exceeds actual, the banker had best be prepared to talk about investment products, because management's problem will be what to do with all the cash that keeps piling up in the till.

Bankers also find the sustainable growth equation useful for explaining to financially inexperienced small business owners and overly optimistic entrepreneurs that, for the long-run viability of their business, it is necessary to keep growth and profitability in proper balance.

Finally, comparison of actual to sustainable growth rates helps a banker understand why a loan applicant needs money and for how long the need might continue. In one instance, a loan applicant requested $100,000 to pay off several insistent suppliers and promised to repay in a few months when he collected some accounts receivable that were coming due. A sustainable growth analysis revealed that the firm had been growing at four to six times its sustainable growth rate and that this pattern was likely to continue in the foreseeable future. This alerted the banker to the fact that impatient suppliers were only a symptom of the much more fundamental disease of overly rapid growth, and that a $100,000 loan would likely prove to be only the down payment on a much larger, multiyear commitment.

Robert C. Higgins is the Marguerite Reimers Professor of Finance, Emeritus, at the Foster School of Business at the University of Washington. He pioneered the use of sustainable growth as a tool for financial analysis.

A NOTE ABOUT SUSTAINABLE GROWTH RATE CALCULATIONS

Very commonly, the sustainable growth rate is calculated using just the numerator in our expression, ROE $\times b$. This causes some confusion, which we can clear up here. The issue has to do with how ROE is computed. Recall that ROE is calculated as net income divided by total equity. If total equity is taken from an ending balance sheet (as we have done consistently, and is commonly done in practice), then our formula is the right one. However, if total equity is from the beginning of the period, then the simpler formula is the correct one.

In principle, you'll get exactly the same sustainable growth rate regardless of which way you calculate it (as long as you match up the ROE calculation with the right formula). In reality, you may see some differences because of accounting-related complications. By the way, if you use the average of beginning and ending equity (as some advocate), yet another formula is needed. Also, all of our comments here apply to the internal growth rate as well.

A simple example is useful to illustrate these points. Suppose a firm has a net income of $20 and a retention ratio of .60. Beginning assets are $100. The debt-equity ratio is .25, so beginning equity is $80.

If we use beginning numbers, we get the following:

ROE = $20/$80 = .25, or 25%

Sustainable growth = .60 $\times$ .25 = .15, or 15%

For the same firm, ending equity is $80 + .60 $\times$ $20 = $92. So, we can calculate this:

ROE = $20/$92 = .2174, or 21.74%

Sustainable growth = .60 $\times$ .2174/(1 − .60 $\times$ .2174) = .15, or 15%

These growth rates are exactly the same (after accounting for a small rounding error in the second calculation). See if you don't agree that the internal growth rate is 12 percent.

EXAMPLE 4.3	**Profit Margins and Sustainable Growth**

The Sandar Co. has a debt-equity ratio of .5, a profit margin of 3 percent, a dividend payout ratio of 40 percent, and a capital intensity ratio of 1. What is its sustainable growth rate? If Sandar desired a 10 percent sustainable growth rate and planned to achieve this goal by improving profit margins, what would you think?

ROE is $.03 \times 1 \times 1.5 = .045$, or 4.5%. The retention ratio is $1 - .40 = .60$. Sustainable growth is thus $.045(.60)/[1 - .045(.60)] = .0277$, or 2.77%.

For the company to achieve a 10 percent growth rate, the profit margin will have to rise. To see this, assume that sustainable growth is equal to 10 percent and then solve for profit margin, PM:

$.10 = PM(1.5)(.6)/[1 - PM(1.5)(.6)]$
$PM = .1/.99 = .101$, or 10.1%

For the plan to succeed, the necessary increase in profit margin is substantial, from 3 percent to about 10 percent. This may not be feasible.

Concept Questions

4.4a How is a firm's sustainable growth related to its accounting return on equity (ROE)?

4.4b What are the determinants of growth?

4.5 Some Caveats Regarding Financial Planning Models

Financial planning models do not always ask the right questions. A primary reason is that they tend to rely on accounting relationships and not financial relationships. In particular, the three basic elements of firm value tend to get left out—namely, cash flow size, risk, and timing.

Because of this, financial planning models sometimes do not produce meaningful clues about what strategies will lead to increases in value. Instead, they divert the user's attention to questions concerning the association of, say, the debt-equity ratio and firm growth.

The financial model we used for the Hoffman Company was simple—in fact, too simple. Our model, like many in use today, is really an accounting statement generator at heart. Such models are useful for pointing out inconsistencies and reminding us of financial needs, but they offer little guidance concerning what to do about these problems.

In closing our discussion, we should add that financial planning is an iterative process. Plans are created, examined, and modified over and over. The final plan will be a result negotiated between all the different parties to the process. In fact, long-term financial planning in most corporations relies on what might be called the Procrustes approach.[1] Upper-level managers have a goal in mind, and it is up to the planning staff to rework and ultimately deliver a feasible plan that meets that goal.

---

[1] In Greek mythology, Procrustes is a giant who seizes travelers and ties them to an iron bed. He stretches them or cuts off their legs as needed to make them fit the bed.

The final plan will therefore implicitly contain different goals in different areas and also satisfy many constraints. For this reason, such a plan need not be a dispassionate assessment of what we think the future will bring; it may instead be a means of reconciling the planned activities of different groups and a way of setting common goals for the future.

Concept Questions

4.5a What are some important elements that are often missing in financial planning models?

4.5b Why do we say planning is an iterative process?

Summary and Conclusions   4.6

Financial planning forces the firm to think about the future. We have examined a number of features of the planning process. We described what financial planning can accomplish and the components of a financial model. We went on to develop the relationship between growth and financing needs, and we discussed how a financial planning model is useful in exploring that relationship.

Corporate financial planning should not become a purely mechanical activity. If it does, it will probably focus on the wrong things. In particular, plans all too often are formulated in terms of a growth target with no explicit linkage to value creation, and they frequently are overly concerned with accounting statements. Nevertheless, the alternative to financial planning is stumbling into the future. Perhaps the immortal Yogi Berra (the baseball catcher, not the cartoon character) put it best when he said, "Ya gotta watch out if you don't know where you're goin'. You just might not get there."[2]

CONNECT TO FINANCE

 If you are using *Connect* Finance in your course, get online to take a Practice Test, check out study tools, and find out where you need additional practice.

Can you answer the following *Connect* Quiz questions?

Section 4.1 Murphy's, Inc., is in the process of preparing a financial plan for the firm for the next five years. This five-year period is referred to as the
_____.

Section 4.2 What is generally the first step in the financial planning process?

Section 4.3 A firm has current sales of $272,600 with total assets of $311,000. What is the full-capacity capital intensity ratio if the firm is currently operating at 68 percent capacity?

Section 4.4 What growth rate assumes that the debt-equity ratio is held constant?

Section 4.5 What is generally considered when compiling a financial plan?

---

[2] We're not *exactly* sure what this means either, but we like the sound of it.

CHAPTER REVIEW AND SELF-TEST PROBLEMS

4.1   Calculating EFN Based on the following information for the Skandia Mining Company, what is EFN if sales are predicted to grow by 10 percent? Use the percentage of sales approach and assume the company is operating at full capacity. The payout ratio is constant.

SKANDIA MINING COMPANY Financial Statements					
Income Statement		**Balance Sheet**			
		Assets		**Liabilities and Owners' Equity**	
Sales	$4,250.0	Current assets	$ 900.0	Current liabilities	$ 500.0
Costs	3,936.7	Net fixed assets	2,200.0	Long-term debt	1,800.0
Taxable income	$ 313.3			Owners' equity	800.0
Taxes (21%)	65.8			Total liabilities and owners'	
Net income	$ 247.5	Total assets	$3,100.0	equity	$3,100.0
Dividends	$ 82.6				
Addition to retained earnings	164.9				

4.2   EFN and Capacity Use Based on the information in Problem 4.1, what is EFN, assuming 60 percent capacity usage for net fixed assets? Assuming 95 percent capacity?

4.3   Sustainable Growth Based on the information in Problem 4.1, what growth rate can Skandia maintain if no external financing is used? What is the sustainable growth rate?

ANSWERS TO CHAPTER REVIEW AND SELF-TEST PROBLEMS

4.1   We can calculate EFN by preparing the pro forma statements using the percentage of sales approach. Note that sales are forecast to be $4,250 × 1.10 = $4,675.

SKANDIA MINING COMPANY Pro Forma Financial Statements					
Income Statement					
Sales	$4,675.0	Forecast			
Costs	4,330.4	92.63% of sales			
Taxable income	$ 344.6				
Taxes (21%)	72.4				
Net income	$ 272.3				
Dividends	$ 90.9	33.37% of net income			
Addition to retained earnings	181.4				
Balance Sheet					
Assets			**Liabilities and Owners' Equity**		
Current assets	$ 990.0	21.18%	Current liabilities	$ 550.0	11.76%
Net fixed assets	2,420.0	51.76%	Long-term debt	1,800.0	n/a
			Owners' equity	981.4	n/a
Total assets	$3,410.0	72.94%	Total liabilities and owners' equity	$3,331.4	n/a
			EFN	$ 78.6	n/a

4.2 Full-capacity sales are equal to current sales divided by the capacity utilization. At 60 percent of capacity:

$4,250 = .60 × Full-capacity sales

$7,083 = Full-capacity sales

With a sales level of $4,675, no net new fixed assets will be needed, so our earlier estimate is too high. We estimated an increase in fixed assets of $2,420 − 2,200 = $220. The new EFN will thus be $78.6 − 220 = −$141.4, a surplus. No external financing is needed in this case.

At 95 percent capacity, full-capacity sales are $4,474. The ratio of fixed assets to full-capacity sales is thus $2,200/$4,474 = .4918, or 49.18%. At a sales level of $4,675, we will thus need $4,675 × .4918 = $2,299.0 in net fixed assets, an increase of $99.0. This is $220 − 99 = $121 less than we originally predicted, so the EFN is now $78.6 − 121 = −$42.4, a surplus. No additional financing is needed.

4.3 Skandia retains $b = 1 − .3337 = .6663$, or 66.63% of net income. Return on assets is $247.5/$3,100 = .0798, or 7.98%. The internal growth rate is thus:

$$\frac{\text{ROA} \times b}{1 - \text{ROA} \times b} = \frac{.0798 \times .6663}{1 - .0798 \times .6663}$$

$$= .0562, \text{ or } 5.62\%$$

Return on equity for Skandia is $247.5/$800 = .3094, or 30.94%, so we can calculate the sustainable growth rate as follows:

$$\frac{\text{ROE} \times b}{1 - \text{ROE} \times b} = \frac{.3094 \times .6663}{1 - .3094 \times .6663}$$

$$= .2597, \text{ or } 25.97\%$$

CONCEPTS REVIEW AND CRITICAL THINKING QUESTIONS

1. **Sales Forecast** [LO1] Why do you think most long-term financial planning begins with sales forecasts? Put differently, why are future sales the key input?

2. **Sustainable Growth** [LO3] In the chapter, we used Rosengarten Corporation to demonstrate how to calculate EFN. The ROE for Rosengarten is about 7.3 percent, and the plowback ratio is about 67 percent. If you calculate the sustainable growth rate for Rosengarten, you will find it is only 5.14 percent. In our calculation for EFN, we used a growth rate of 25 percent. Is this possible? (*Hint*: Yes. How?)

3. **External Financing Needed** [LO2] Testaburger, Inc., uses no external financing and maintains a positive retention ratio. When sales grow by 15 percent, the firm has a negative projected EFN. What does this tell you about the firm's internal growth rate? How about the sustainable growth rate? At this same level of sales growth, what will happen to the projected EFN if the retention ratio is increased? What if the retention ratio is decreased? What happens to the projected EFN if the firm pays out all of its earnings in the form of dividends?

4. **EFN and Growth Rates** [LO2, 3] Broslofski Co. maintains a positive retention ratio and keeps its debt-equity ratio constant every year. When sales grow by 20 percent, the firm has a negative projected EFN. What does this tell you about the firm's sustainable growth rate? Do you know, with certainty, if the internal growth rate is greater than or less than 20 percent? Why? What happens to the projected EFN if the retention ratio is increased? What if the retention ratio is decreased? What if the retention ratio is zero?

Use the following information to answer Questions 5–10: A small business called The Grandmother Calendar Company began selling personalized photo calendar kits. The kits were a hit, and sales soon sharply exceeded forecasts. The rush of orders created a huge backlog, so the company leased more space and expanded capacity; but it still could not keep up with demand. Equipment failed from overuse and quality suffered. Working capital was drained to expand production, and, at the same time, payments from customers were often delayed until the product was shipped. Unable to deliver on orders, the company became so strapped for cash that employee paychecks began to bounce. Finally, out of cash, the company ceased operations entirely three years later.

5. **Product Sales** [LO4] Do you think the company would have suffered the same fate if its product had been less popular? Why or why not?

6. **Cash Flow** [LO4] The Grandmother Calendar Company clearly had a cash flow problem. In the context of the cash flow analysis we developed in Chapter 2, what was the impact of customers not paying until orders were shipped?

7. **Product Pricing** [LO4] The firm actually priced its product to be about 20 percent less than that of competitors, even though the Grandmother calendar was more detailed. In retrospect, was this a wise choice?

8. **Corporate Borrowing** [LO4] If the firm was so successful at selling, why wouldn't a bank or some other lender step in and provide it with the cash it needed to continue?

9. **Cash Flow** [LO4] Which was the biggest culprit here: Too many orders, too little cash, or too little production capacity?

10. **Cash Flow** [LO4] What are some of the actions that a small company like The Grandmother Calendar Company can take if it finds itself in a situation in which growth in sales outstrips production capacity and available financial resources? What other options (besides expansion of capacity) are available to a company when orders exceed capacity?

QUESTIONS AND PROBLEMS

1. **Forma Statements** [LO1] Consider the following simplified financial statements for the Wims Corporation (assuming no income taxes):

BASIC
(Questions 1–15)

Income Statement		Balance Sheet			
Sales	$38,000	Assets	$27,300	Debt	$ 6,700
Costs	32,600			Equity	20,600
Net income	$ 5,400	Total	$27,300	Total	$27,300

The company has predicted a sales increase of 15 percent. It has predicted that every item on the balance sheet will increase by 15 percent as well. Create the pro forma statements and reconcile them. What is the plug variable here?

2. **Pro Forma Statements and EFN** [LO1, 2] In Question 1, assume the company pays out half of net income in the form of a cash dividend. Costs and assets vary with sales, but debt and equity do not. Prepare the pro forma statements and determine the external financing needed.

3. **Calculating EFN** [LO2] The most recent financial statements for Kerch, Inc., are shown here (assuming no income taxes):

Income Statement			Balance Sheet			
Sales	$7,200	Assets	$21,700	Debt	$ 9,100
Costs	4,730			Equity	12,600
Net income	$2,470	Total	$21,700	Total	$21,700

Assets and costs are proportional to sales. Debt and equity are not. No dividends are paid. Next year's sales are projected to be $8,424. What is the external financing needed?

4. **EFN** [LO2] The most recent financial statements for Cardinal, Inc., are shown here:

Income Statement			Balance Sheet		
Sales	$25,400	Assets	$61,000	Debt	$26,900
Costs	17,300			Equity	34,100
Taxable income	$ 8,100	Total	$61,000	Total	$61,000
Taxes (21%)	1,701				
Net income	$ 6,399				

Assets and costs are proportional to sales. Debt and equity are not. A dividend of $2,100 was paid, and the company wishes to maintain a constant payout ratio. Next year's sales are projected to be $29,210. What is the external financing needed?

5. **EFN** [LO2] The most recent financial statements for Assoud, Inc., are shown here: X

Income Statement			Balance Sheet		
Sales	$7,900	Current assets	$ 3,900	Current liabilities	$ 2,100
Costs	5,500	Fixed assets	8,600	Long-term debt	3,700
Taxable income	$2,400			Equity	6,700
Taxes (25%)	600	Total	$12,500	Total	$12,500
Net income	$1,800				

Assets, costs, and current liabilities are proportional to sales. Long-term debt and equity are not. The company maintains a constant 40 percent dividend payout ratio. As with every other firm in its industry, next year's sales are projected to increase by exactly 15 percent. What is the external financing needed?

6. **Calculating Internal Growth** [LO3] The most recent financial statements for X Bello Co. are shown here:

Income Statement			Balance Sheet		
Sales	$18,900	Current assets	$11,700	Debt	$15,700
Costs	12,800	Fixed assets	26,500	Equity	22,500
Taxable income	$ 6,100	Total	$38,200	Total	$38,200
Taxes (21%)	1,281				
Net income	$ 4,819				

Assets and costs are proportional to sales. Debt and equity are not. The company maintains a constant 30 percent dividend payout ratio. What is the internal growth rate?

7. **Calculating Sustainable Growth** [LO3] For the company in Problem 6, what is the sustainable growth rate?

8. **Sales and Growth** [LO2] The most recent financial statements for Alexander Co. are shown here:

Income Statement		Balance Sheet			
Sales	$42,800	Current assets	$17,500	Long-term debt	$37,000
Costs	35,500	Fixed assets	68,300	Equity	48,800
Taxable income	$ 7,300	Total	$85,800	Total	$85,800
Taxes (23%)	1,679				
Net income	$ 5,621				

Assets and costs are proportional to sales. The company maintains a constant 40 percent dividend payout ratio and a constant debt-equity ratio. What is the maximum increase in sales that can be sustained assuming no new equity is issued?

9. **Calculating Retained Earnings from Pro Forma Income** [LO1] Consider the following income statement for the Heir Jordan Corporation:

HEIR JORDAN CORPORATION Income Statement	
Sales	$49,000
Costs	40,300
Taxable income	$ 8,700
Taxes (22%)	1,914
Net income	$ 6,786
Dividends	$2,400
Addition to retained earnings	4,386

A 20 percent growth rate in sales is projected. Prepare a pro forma income statement assuming costs vary with sales and the dividend payout ratio is constant. What is the projected addition to retained earnings?

10. **Applying Percentage of Sales** [LO1] The balance sheet for the Heir Jordan Corporation follows. Based on this information and the income statement in the previous problem, supply the missing information using the percentage of sales approach. Assume that accounts payable vary with sales, whereas notes payable do not. Put "n/a" where needed.

HEIR JORDAN CORPORATION Balance Sheet					
Assets			**Liabilities and Owners' Equity**		
	$	Percentage of Sales		$	Percentage of Sales
Current assets			Current liabilities		
Cash	$ 2,950	—	Accounts payable	$ 2,400	—
Accounts receivable	4,100	—	Notes payable	5,400	—
Inventory	6,400	—	Total	$ 7,800	—
Total	$13,450	—	Long-term debt	$28,000	—
Fixed assets					
Net plant and equipment	$41,300	—	Owners' equity		
			Common stock and paid-in surplus	$15,000	—
			Retained earnings	3,950	—
			Total	$18,950	—
Total assets	$54,750	—	Total liabilities and owners' equity	$54,750	—

11. **EFN and Sales** [LO2] From the previous two questions, prepare a pro forma balance sheet showing EFN, assuming an increase in sales of 15 percent, no new external debt or equity financing, and a constant payout ratio.

12. **Internal Growth** [LO3] If A7X Co. has an ROA of 7.6 percent and a payout ratio of 25 percent, what is its internal growth rate?

13. **Sustainable Growth** [LO3] If Synyster Corp. has an ROE of 14.7 percent and a payout ratio of 30 percent, what is its sustainable growth rate?

14. **Sustainable Growth** [LO3] Based on the following information, calculate the sustainable growth rate for Kaleb's Heavy Equipment:

Profit margin	= 7.3%
Capital intensity ratio	= .80
Debt–equity ratio	= .95
Net income	= $73,000
Dividends	= $24,000

15. **Sustainable Growth** [LO3] Assuming the following ratios are constant, what is the sustainable growth rate?

Total asset turnover	= 2.90
Profit margin	= 5.2%
Equity multiplier	= 1.10
Payout ratio	= 35%

16. **Full-Capacity Sales** [LO1] Hodgkiss Mfg., Inc., is currently operating at only 91 percent of fixed asset capacity. Current sales are $715,000. How fast can sales grow before any new fixed assets are needed?

INTERMEDIATE (Questions 16–26)

17. **Fixed Assets and Capacity Usage** [LO1] For the company in Problem 16, suppose fixed assets are $520,000 and sales are projected to grow to $790,000. How much in new fixed assets are required to support this growth in sales? Assume the company wants to operate at full capacity.

18. **Growth and Profit Margin** [LO3] Ramble On Co. wishes to maintain a growth rate of 12 percent per year, a debt-equity ratio of .90, and a dividend payout ratio of 25 percent. The ratio of total assets to sales is constant at .85. What profit margin must the firm achieve?

19. **Growth and Assets** [LO3] A firm wishes to maintain an internal growth rate of 7.1 percent and a dividend payout ratio of 25 percent. The current profit margin is 6.5 percent, and the firm uses no external financing sources. What must total asset turnover be?

20. **Sustainable Growth** [LO3] Based on the following information, calculate the sustainable growth rate for Hendrix Guitars, Inc.:

Profit margin	= 6.3%
Total asset turnover	= 1.75
Total debt ratio	= .35
Payout ratio	= 30%

21. **Sustainable Growth and Outside Financing** [LO3] You've collected the following information about Molino, Inc.:

Sales	= $215,000
Net income	= $17,300
Dividends	= $9,400
Total debt	= $77,000
Total equity	= $59,000

What is the sustainable growth rate for the company? If it does grow at this rate, how much new borrowing will take place in the coming year, assuming a constant debt-equity ratio? What growth rate could be supported with no outside financing at all?

22. **Sustainable Growth Rate** [LO3] Gilmore, Inc., had equity of $145,000 at the beginning of the year. At the end of the year, the company had total assets of $210,000. During the year, the company sold no new equity. Net income for the year was $27,000 and dividends were $5,800. What is the sustainable growth rate for the company? What is the sustainable growth rate if you use the formula ROE × b and beginning of period equity? What is the sustainable growth rate if you use end of period equity in this formula? Is this number too high or too low? Why?

23. **Internal Growth Rates** [LO3] Calculate the internal growth rate for the company in Problem 22. Now calculate the internal growth rate using ROA × b for both beginning of period and end of period total assets. What do you observe?

24. **Calculating EFN** [LO2] The most recent financial statements for Crosby, Inc., follow. Sales for 2018 are projected to grow by 20 percent. Interest expense will remain constant; the tax rate and the dividend payout rate will also remain constant. Costs, other expenses, current assets, fixed assets, and accounts payable increase spontaneously with sales. If the firm is operating at full capacity and no new debt or equity is issued, what external financing is needed to support the 20 percent growth rate in sales?

CROSBY, INC.
2017 Income Statement

Sales	$980,760
Costs	792,960
Other expenses	20,060
Earnings before interest and taxes	$167,740
Interest paid	14,740
Taxable income	$153,000
Taxes (21%)	32,130
Net income	$120,870
Dividends	$39,250
Addition to retained earnings	81,620

CROSBY, INC.
Balance Sheet as of December 31, 2017

Assets		Liabilities and Owners' Equity	
Current assets		Current liabilities	
Cash	$ 27,920	Accounts payable	$ 71,720
Accounts receivable	42,630	Notes payable	17,620
Inventory	95,910	Total	$ 89,340
Total	$166,460	Long-term debt	$170,000
Fixed assets		Owners' equity	
Net plant and equipment	$455,980	Common stock and paid-in surplus	$140,000
		Retained earnings	223,100
		Total	$363,100
Total assets	$622,440	Total liabilities and owners' equity	$622,440

25. **Capacity Usage and Growth** [LO2] In the previous problem, suppose the firm was operating at only 80 percent capacity in 2017. What is EFN now?

26. **Calculating EFN** [LO2] In Problem 24, suppose the firm wishes to keep its debt-equity ratio constant. What is EFN now?

27. **EFN and Internal Growth** [LO2, 3] Redo Problem 24 using sales growth rates of 15 and 25 percent in addition to 20 percent. Illustrate graphically the relationship between EFN and the growth rate, and use this graph to determine the relationship between them. At what growth rate is the EFN equal to zero? Why is this internal growth rate different from that found by using the equation in the text?

CHALLENGE
(Questions 27–32)

28. **EFN and Sustainable Growth** [LO2, 3] Redo Problem 26 using sales growth rates of 30 and 35 percent in addition to 20 percent. Assume the firm wishes to maintain its debt-equity ratio. Illustrate graphically the relationship between EFN and the growth rate, and use this graph to determine the relationship between them. At what growth rate is the EFN equal to zero? Why is this sustainable growth rate different from that found by using the equation in the text?

29. **Constraints on Growth** [LO3] Sig, Inc., wishes to maintain a growth rate of 12 percent per year and a debt-equity ratio of .43. The profit margin is 5.9 percent, and the ratio of total assets to sales is constant at 1.80. Is this growth rate possible? To answer, determine what the dividend payout ratio must be. How do you interpret the result?

30. **EFN** [LO2] Define the following:

   S = Previous year's sales

   A = Total assets

   E = Total equity

   g = Projected growth in sales

   PM = Profit margin

   b = Retention (plowback) ratio

   Assuming all debt is constant, show that EFN can be written as follows:

   $$\text{EFN} = -\text{PM}(S)b + (A - \text{PM}(S)b) \times g$$

   Hint: Asset needs will equal $A \times g$. The addition to retained earnings will equal $\text{PM}(S)b \times (1 + g)$.

31. **Growth Rates** [LO3] Based on the result in Problem 30, show that the internal and sustainable growth rates are as given in the chapter. *Hint*: For the internal growth rate, set EFN equal to zero and solve for g.

32. **Sustainable Growth Rate** [LO3] In the chapter, we discussed the two versions of the sustainable growth rate formula. Derive the formula ROE × b from the formula given in the chapter, where ROE is based on beginning of period equity. Also, derive the formula ROA × b from the internal growth rate formula.

EXCEL MASTER IT! PROBLEM

Financial planning can be more complex than the percentage of sales approach indicates. Often, the assumptions behind the percentage of sales approach may be too simple. A more sophisticated model allows important items to vary without being a strict percentage of sales.

Consider a new model in which depreciation is calculated as a percentage of beginning fixed assets and interest expense depends directly on the amount of debt. Debt is still the plug variable. Note that since depreciation and interest now do not necessarily vary directly with sales, the profit margin is no longer constant. Also, for the same reason, taxes and dividends will no longer be a fixed percentage of sales. The parameter estimates used in the new model are:

Cost percentage   = Costs / Sales
Depreciation rate   = Depreciation / Beginning fixed assets
Interest rate   = Interest paid / Total debt
Tax rate   = Taxes / Net income
Payout ratio   = Dividends / Net income
Capital intensity ratio = Fixed assets / Sales
Fixed assets ratio   = Fixed assets / Total assets

The model parameters can be determined by whatever methods the company deems appropriate. For example, they might be based on average values for the last several years, industry standards, subjective estimates, or even company targets. Alternatively, sophisticated statistical techniques can be used to estimate them.

The Moore Company is preparing its pro forma financial statements for the next year using this model. The abbreviated financial statements are presented below.

Sales growth	20%
Tax rate	21%
Income Statement	
Sales	$780,000
Costs	415,000
Depreciation	135,000
Interest	68,000
Taxable income	$162,000
Taxes	34,020
Net income	$127,980
Dividends	$ 30,000
Additions to retained earnings	$ 97,980

Balance Sheet			
Assets		**Liabilities and Equity**	
Current assets	$ 240,000	Total debt	$ 880,000
Net fixed assets	1,350,000	Owners' equity	710,000
Total assets	$1,590,000	Total debt and equity	$1,590,000

a. Calculate each of the parameters necessary to construct the pro forma balance sheet.

b. Construct the pro forma balance sheet. What is the total debt necessary to balance the pro forma balance sheet?

c. In this financial planning model, show that it is possible to solve algebraically for the amount of new borrowing.

MINICASE

Planning for Growth at S&S Air

After Chris completed the ratio analysis for S&S Air (see Chapter 3), Mark and Todd approached him about planning for next year's sales. The company had historically used little planning for investment needs. As a result, the company experienced some challenging times because of cash flow problems. The lack of planning resulted in missed sales, as well as

periods when Mark and Todd were unable to draw salaries. To this end, they would like Chris to prepare a financial plan for the next year so the company can begin to address any outside investment requirements. The income statement and balance sheet are shown here:

S&S AIR, INC. 2018 Income Statement	
Sales	$46,298,115
Cost of goods sold	34,536,913
Other expenses	5,870,865
Depreciation	2,074,853
EBIT	$ 3,815,484
Interest	725,098
Taxable income	$ 3,090,386
Taxes (21%)	772,597
Net income	$ 2,317,789
Dividends	$ 705,000
Add to retained earnings	1,612,789

S&S AIR, INC. 2018 Balance Sheet			
Assets		**Liabilities and Equity**	
Current assets		Current liabilities	
Cash	$ 524,963	Accounts payable	$ 1,068,356
Accounts receivable	843,094	Notes payable	2,439,553
Inventory	1,235,161	Total current liabilities	$ 3,507,909
Total current assets	$ 2,603,218	Long-term debt	$ 6,300,000
Fixed assets			
Net plant and equipment	$20,381,945	Shareholder equity	
		Common stock	$ 460,000
		Retained earnings	12,717,254
		Total equity	$13,177,254
Total assets	$22,985,163	Total liabilities and equity	$22,985,163

QUESTIONS

1. Calculate the internal growth rate and sustainable growth rate for S&S Air. What do these numbers mean?

2. S&S Air is planning for a growth rate of 12 percent next year. Calculate the EFN for the company assuming the company is operating at full capacity. Can the company's sales increase at this growth rate?

3. Most assets can be increased as a percentage of sales. For instance, cash can be increased by any amount. However,

fixed assets must be increased in specific amounts because it is impossible, as a practical matter, to buy part of a new plant or machine. In this case, a company has a "staircase" or "lumpy" fixed cost structure. Assume S&S Air is currently producing at 100 percent capacity. As a result, to increase production, the company must set up an entirely new line at a cost of $5,000,000. Calculate the new EFN with this assumption. What does this imply about capacity utilization for the company next year?

Valuation of Future Cash Flows

Part 3   Valuation of Future Cash Flows

Chapter

5 | Introduction to Valuation: The Time Value of Money

AS YOU ARE PROBABLY AWARE, the United States government has a significant amount of debt. That debt, which is widely owned by investors, comes in different varieties, including Series EE U.S. Treasury savings bonds. With a Series EE bond, you pay a particular amount today of, say, $25, and the bond accrues interest over the time you hold it. In early 2017, the U.S. Treasury promised to pay .10 percent per year on EE savings bonds. In an interesting (and important) wrinkle, if you hold the bond for 20 years, the Treasury promises to "step up" the value to double your cost. That is, if the $25 bond you purchased and all the accumulated interest earned are worth less than $50, the Treasury will automatically increase the value of the bond to $50.

Is giving up $25 in exchange for $50 in 20 years a good deal? On the plus side, you get back $2 for every $1 you put up. That probably sounds good, but, on the downside, you have to wait 20 years to get it. What you need to know is how to analyze this trade-off. This chapter gives you the tools you need.

Learning Objectives

After studying this chapter, you should be able to:

LO1   Determine the future value of an investment made today.

LO2   Determine the present value of cash to be received at a future date.

LO3   Find the return on an investment.

LO4   Calculate how long it takes for an investment to reach a desired value.

For updates on the latest happenings in finance, visit fundamentalsofcorporatefinance.blogspot.com.

One of the basic problems faced by the financial manager is how to determine the value today of cash flows expected in the future. For example, the jackpot in a Powerball™ lottery drawing was $110 million. Does this mean the winning ticket was worth $110 million? The answer is no because the jackpot was actually going to pay out over a 20-year period at a rate of $5.5 million per year. How much was the ticket worth then? The answer depends on the time value of money, the subject of this chapter.

In the most general sense, the phrase *time value of money* refers to the fact that a dollar in hand today is worth more than a dollar promised at some time in the future. On a practical level, one reason for this is that you could earn interest while you waited; so, a dollar today would grow to more than a dollar later. The trade-off between money now and money

Chapter 5   Introduction to Valuation: The Time Value of Money   **125**

later thus depends on, among other things, the rate you can earn by investing. Our goal in this chapter is to explicitly evaluate this trade-off between dollars today and dollars at some future time.

A thorough understanding of the material in this chapter is critical to understanding material in subsequent chapters, so you should study it with particular care. We will present a number of examples in this chapter. In many problems, your answer may differ from ours slightly. This can happen because of rounding and is not a cause for concern.

Future Value and Compounding

5.1

The first thing we will study is future value. **Future value (FV)** refers to the amount of money an investment will grow to over some period of time at some given interest rate. Put another way, future value is the cash value of an investment at some time in the future. We start out by considering the simplest case: A single-period investment.

Excel Master It!

xlsx Excel Master
coverage online

INVESTING FOR A SINGLE PERIOD

Suppose you invest $100 in a savings account that pays 10 percent interest per year. How much will you have in one year? You will have $110. This $110 is equal to your original *principal* of $100 plus $10 in interest that you earn. We say that $110 is the future value of $100 invested for one year at 10 percent, and we mean that $100 today is worth $110 in one year, given that 10 percent is the interest rate.

In general, if you invest for one period at an interest rate of r, your investment will grow to $(1 + r)$ per dollar invested. In our example, r is 10 percent, so your investment grows to $1 + .10 = 1.1$ dollars per dollar invested. You invested $100 in this case, so you ended up with $100 \times 1.10 = $110.

future value (FV)
The amount an investment is worth after one or more periods.

INVESTING FOR MORE THAN ONE PERIOD

Going back to our $100 investment, what will you have after two years, assuming the interest rate doesn't change? If you leave the entire $110 in the bank, you will earn $110 \times .10 = $11 in interest during the second year, so you will have a total of $110 + 11 = $121. This $121 is the future value of $100 in two years at 10 percent. Another way of looking at it is that one year from now you are effectively investing $110 at 10 percent for a year. This is a single-period problem, so you'll end up with $1.10 for every dollar invested, or $110 \times 1.1 = $121 total.

This $121 has four parts. The first part is the $100 original principal. The second part is the $10 in interest you earned in the first year, and the third part is another $10 you earned in the second year, for a total of $120. The last $1 you end up with (the fourth part) is interest you earned in the second year on the interest paid in the first year: $10 \times .10 = $1.

This process of leaving your money and any accumulated interest in an investment for more than one period, thereby *reinvesting* the interest, is called **compounding**. Compounding the interest means earning **interest on interest**, so we call the result **compound interest**. With **simple interest**, the interest is not reinvested, so interest is earned each period only on the original principal.

compounding
The process of accumulating interest on an investment over time to earn more interest.

interest on interest
Interest earned on the reinvestment of previous interest payments.

compound interest
Interest earned on both the initial principal and the interest reinvested from prior periods.

simple interest
Interest earned only on the original principal amount invested.

Interest on Interest	**EXAMPLE 5.1**

Suppose you locate a two-year investment that pays 14 percent per year. If you invest $325, how much will you have at the end of the two years? How much of this is simple interest? How much is compound interest?

At the end of the first year, you will have $325 × (1 + .14) = $370.50. If you reinvest this entire amount and thereby compound the interest, you will have $370.50 × 1.14 = $422.37 at the end of the second year. The total interest you earn is thus $422.37 − 325 = $97.37. Your $325 original principal earns $325 × .14 = $45.50 in interest each year, for a two-year total of $91 in simple interest. The remaining $97.37 − 91 = $6.37 results from compounding. You can check this by noting that the interest earned in the first year is $45.50. The interest on interest earned in the second year thus amounts to $45.50 × .14 = $6.37, as we calculated.

We now take a closer look at how we calculated the $121 future value. We multiplied $110 by 1.1 to get $121. The $110, however, was $100 also multiplied by 1.1. In other words:

$$\$121 = \$110 \times 1.1$$
$$= (\$100 \times 1.1) \times 1.1$$
$$= \$100 \times (1.1 \times 1.1)$$
$$= \$100 \times 1.1^2$$
$$= \$100 \times 1.21$$

At the risk of belaboring the obvious, let's ask: How much would our $100 grow to after three years? Once again, in two years, we'll be investing $121 for one period at 10 percent. We'll end up with $1.10 for every dollar we invest, or $121 × 1.1 = $133.10 total. This $133.10 is thus:

$$\$133.10 = \$121 \times 1.1$$
$$= (\$110 \times 1.1) \times 1.1$$
$$= (\$100 \times 1.1) \times 1.1 \times 1.1$$
$$= \$100 \times (1.1 \times 1.1 \times 1.1)$$
$$= \$100 \times 1.1^3$$
$$= \$100 \times 1.331$$

You're probably noticing a pattern to these calculations, so we can now go ahead and state the general result. As our examples suggest, the future value of $1 invested for t periods at a rate of r per period is this:

Future value = $1 × $(1 + r)^t$ [5.1]

The expression $(1 + r)^t$ is sometimes called the *future value interest factor* (or just *future value factor*) for $1 invested at r percent for t periods and can be abbreviated as FVIF(r, t).

In our example, what would your $100 be worth after five years? We can first compute the relevant future value factor as follows:

$$(1 + r)^t = (1 + .10)^5 = 1.1^5 = 1.6105$$

Your $100 will thus grow to:

$$\$100 \times 1.6105 = \$161.05$$

The growth of your $100 each year is illustrated in Table 5.1. As shown, the interest earned in each year is equal to the beginning amount multiplied by the interest rate of 10 percent.

In Table 5.1, notice the total interest you earn is $61.05. Over the five-year span of this investment, the simple interest is $100 × .10 = $10 per year, so you accumulate $50 this way. The other $11.05 is from compounding.

Year	Beginning Amount	Simple Interest	Compound Interest	Total Interest Earned	Ending Amount
1	$100.00	$10	$ .00	$10.00	$110.00
2	110.00	10	1.00	11.00	121.00
3	121.00	10	2.10	12.10	133.10
4	133.10	10	3.31	13.31	146.41
5	146.41	10	4.64	14.64	161.05
Total		$50	$11.05	$61.05	

TABLE 5.1

Future Value of $100 at 10 percent

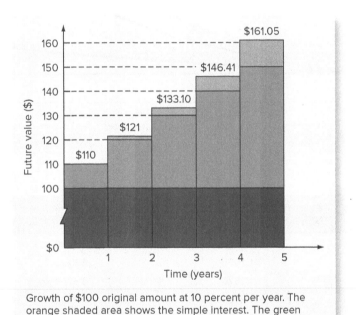

FIGURE 5.1

Future Value, Simple Interest, and Compound Interest

Growth of $100 original amount at 10 percent per year. The orange shaded area shows the simple interest. The green shaded area represents the portion of the total that results from compounding of interest.

Figure 5.1 illustrates the growth of the compound interest in Table 5.1. Notice how the simple interest is constant each year, but the amount of compound interest you earn gets bigger every year. The amount of the compound interest keeps increasing because more and more interest builds up and there is thus more to compound.

Future values depend critically on the assumed interest rate, particularly for long-lived investments. Figure 5.2 illustrates this relationship by plotting the growth of $1 for different rates and lengths of time. Notice the future value of $1 after 10 years is about $6.20 at a 20 percent rate, but it is only about $2.60 at 10 percent. In this case, doubling the interest rate more than doubles the future value.

To solve future value problems, we need to come up with the relevant future value factors. There are several different ways of doing this. In our example, we could have multiplied 1.1 by itself five times. This would work just fine, but it would get to be very tedious for, say, a 30-year investment.

A brief introduction to key financial concepts is available at **www.teachmefinance.com**.

FIGURE 5.2

Future Value of $1 for Different Periods and Rates

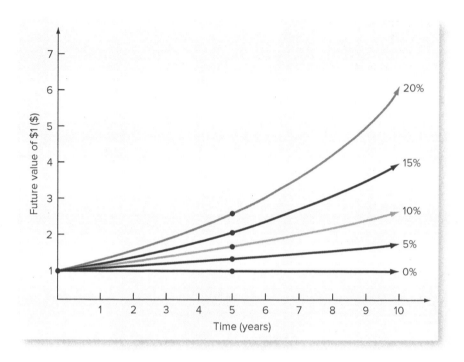

TABLE 5.2

Future Value Interest Factors

Number of Periods	Interest Rate			
	5%	10%	15%	20%
1	1.0500	1.1000	1.1500	1.2000
2	1.1025	1.2100	1.3225	1.4400
3	1.1576	1.3310	1.5209	1.7280
4	1.2155	1.4641	1.7490	2.0736
5	1.2763	1.6105	2.0114	2.4883

Fortunately, there are several easier ways to get future value factors. Most calculators have a key labeled "y^x". You can usually just enter 1.1, press this key, enter 5, and press the "=" key to get the answer. This is an easy way to calculate future value factors because it's quick and accurate.

Alternatively, you can use a table that contains future value factors for some common interest rates and time periods. Table 5.2 contains some of these factors. Table A.1 in the appendix at the end of book contains a much larger set. To use the table, find the column that corresponds to 10 percent. Then look down the rows until you come to five periods. You should find the factor that we calculated, 1.6105.

Future value interest factor tables such as Table 5.2 are not as common as they once were because they predate inexpensive calculators and are available only for a relatively small number of rates. Interest rates are often quoted to three or four decimal places, so the tables needed to deal with these accurately would be quite large. As a result, the real world has moved away from using them. We will emphasize the use of a calculator in this chapter.

These tables still serve a useful purpose, however. To make sure you are doing the calculations correctly, pick a factor from the table and then calculate it yourself to see that you get the same answer. There are plenty of numbers to choose from.

Compound Interest	**EXAMPLE 5.2**

You've located an investment that pays 12 percent per year. That rate sounds good to you, so you invest $400. How much will you have in three years? How much will you have in seven years? At the end of seven years, how much interest will you have earned? How much of that interest results from compounding?

Based on our discussion, we can calculate the future value factor for 12 percent and three years as follows:

$$(1 + r)^t = 1.12^3 = 1.4049$$

Your $400 thus grows to:

$$\$400 \times 1.4049 = \$561.97$$

After seven years, you will have:

$$\$400 \times 1.12^7 = \$400 \times 2.2107 = \$884.27$$

Thus, you will more than double your money over seven years.

Because you invested $400, the interest in the $884.27 future value is $884.27 − 400 = $484.27. At 12 percent, your $400 investment earns $400 × .12 = $48 in simple interest every year. Over seven years, the simple interest thus totals 7 × $48 = $336. The other $484.27 − 336 = $148.27 is from compounding.

The effect of compounding is not great over short time periods, but it really starts to add up as the horizon grows. To take an extreme case, suppose one of your more frugal ancestors had invested $5 for you at a 6 percent interest rate 200 years ago. How much would you have today? The future value factor is a substantial $1.06^{200} = 115,125.90$ (you won't find this one in a table), so you would have $5 × 115,125.90 = $575,629.52 today. Notice that the simple interest is just $5 × .06 = $.30 per year. After 200 years, this amounts to $60. The rest is from reinvesting. Such is the power of compound interest!

How Much for That Island?	**EXAMPLE 5.3**

To further illustrate the effect of compounding for long horizons, consider the case of Peter Minuit and the American Indians. In 1626, Minuit bought all of Manhattan Island for about $24 in goods and trinkets. This sounds cheap, but the Indians may have gotten the better end of the deal. To see why, suppose the Indians had sold the goods and invested the $24 at 10 percent. How much would it be worth today?

About 391 years have passed since the transaction. At 10 percent, $24 will grow by quite a bit over that time. How much? The future value factor is roughly:

$$(1 + r)^t = 1.1^{391} \approx 15,295,000,000,000,000$$

That is, 15.295 followed by 12 zeroes. The future value is thus on the order of $24 × 15.295 = $367 *quadrillion* (give or take a few hundreds of trillions).

Well, $367 quadrillion is a lot of money. How much? If you had it, you could buy the United States. All of it. Cash. With money left over to buy Canada, Mexico, and the rest of the world, for that matter.

This example is something of an exaggeration, of course. In 1626, it would not have been easy to locate an investment that would pay 10 percent every year without fail for the next 391 years.

CALCULATOR HINTS

Using a Financial Calculator

Although there are the various ways of calculating future values we have described so far, many of you will decide that a financial calculator is the way to go. If you are planning on using one, you should read this extended hint; otherwise, skip it.

A financial calculator is an ordinary calculator with a few extra features. In particular, it knows some of the most commonly used financial formulas, so it can directly compute things like future values.

Financial calculators have the advantage that they handle a lot of the computation, but that is really all. In other words, you still have to understand the problem; the calculator just does some of the arithmetic. In fact, there is an old joke (somewhat modified) that goes like this: Anyone can make a mistake on a time value of money problem, but to really screw one up takes a financial calculator! We therefore have two goals for this section. First, we'll discuss how to compute future values. After that, we'll show you how to avoid the most common mistakes people make when they start using financial calculators.

How to Calculate Future Values with a Financial Calculator

Examining a typical financial calculator, you will find five keys of particular interest. They usually look like this:

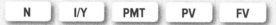

For now, we need to focus on four of these. The keys labeled **PV** and **FV** are just what you would guess: present value and future value. The key labeled **N** refers to the number of periods, which is what we have been calling t. Finally, **I/Y** stands for the interest rate, which we have called r[1].

If we have the financial calculator set up right (see our next section), then calculating a future value is very simple. Take a look back at our question involving the future value of $100 at 10 percent for five years. We have seen that the answer is $161.05. The exact keystrokes will differ depending on what type of calculator you use, but here is basically all you do:

1. Enter −100. Press the **PV** key. (The negative sign is explained in the next section.)
2. Enter 10. Press the **I/Y** key. (Notice that we entered 10, not .10; see the next section.)
3. Enter 5. Press the **N** key.

Now we have entered all of the relevant information. To solve for the future value, we need to ask the calculator what the FV is. Depending on your calculator, either you press the button labeled "CPT" (for compute) and then press **FV**, or you just press **FV**. Either way, you should get 161.05. If you don't (and you probably won't if this is the first time you have used a financial calculator!), we will offer some help in our next section.

Before we explain the kinds of problems you are likely to run into, we want to establish a standard format for showing you how to use a financial calculator. Using the example we just looked at, in the future, we will illustrate such problems like this:

Here is an important tip: Appendix D contains more detailed instructions for the most common types of financial calculators. See if yours is included; if it is, follow the instructions there if you need help. Of course, if all else fails, you can read the manual that came with the calculator.

How to Get the Wrong Answer Using a Financial Calculator

There are a couple of common (and frustrating) problems that cause a lot of trouble with financial calculators. In this section, we provide some important *dos* and *don'ts*. If you just can't seem to get a problem to work out, you should refer back to this section.

---

[1]The reason financial calculators use N and I/Y is that the most common use for these calculators is determining loan payments. In this context, N is the number of payments and I/Y is the interest rate on the loan. But as we will see, there are many other uses of financial calculators that don't involve loan payments and interest rates.

There are two categories we examine: Three things you need to do only once and three things you need to do every time you work a problem. The things you need to do just once deal with the following calculator settings:

1. *Make sure your calculator is set to display a large number of decimal places.* Most financial calculators display only two decimal places; this causes problems because we frequently work with numbers—like interest rates—that are very small.

2. *Make sure your calculator is set to assume only one payment per period or per year.* Most financial calculators assume monthly payments (12 per year) unless you specify otherwise.

3. *Make sure your calculator is in "end" mode.* This is usually the default, but you can accidentally change to "begin" mode.

If you don't know how to set these three things, see Appendix D or your calculator's operating manual. There are also three things you need to do *every time you work a problem*:

1. *Before you start, completely clear out the calculator.* This is very important. Failure to do this is the number one reason for wrong answers; you must get in the habit of clearing the calculator every time you start a problem. How you do this depends on the calculator (see Appendix D), but you must do more than just clear the display. For example, on a Texas Instruments BA II Plus you must press **2nd** then **CLR TVM** for *clear time value of money.* There is a similar command on your calculator. Learn it!

   Note that turning the calculator off and back on won't do it. Most financial calculators remember everything you enter, even after you turn them off. In other words, they remember all your mistakes unless you explicitly clear them out. Also, if you are in the middle of a problem and make a mistake, *clear it out and start over.* Better to be safe than sorry.

2. *Put a negative sign on cash outflows.* Most financial calculators require you to put a negative sign on cash outflows and a positive sign on cash inflows. As a practical matter, this usually just means that you should enter the present value amount with a negative sign (because normally the present value represents the amount you give up today in exchange for cash inflows later). By the same token, when you solve for a present value, you shouldn't be surprised to see a negative sign.

3. *Enter the rate correctly.* Financial calculators assume that rates are quoted in percent, so if the rate is .08 (or 8 percent), you should enter 8, not .08.

If you follow these guidelines (especially the one about clearing out the calculator), you should have no problem using a financial calculator to work almost all of the problems in this and the next few chapters. We'll provide some additional examples and guidance where appropriate.

A NOTE ABOUT COMPOUND GROWTH

If you are considering depositing money in an interest-bearing account, then the interest rate on that account is just the rate at which your money grows, assuming you don't remove any of it. If that rate is 10 percent, then each year you have 10 percent more money than you had the year before. In this case, the interest rate is just an example of a compound growth rate.

The way we calculated future values is actually quite general and lets you answer some other types of questions related to growth. For example, say your company currently has 10,000 employees. You've estimated that the number of employees grows by 3 percent per year. How many employees will there be in five years? Here, we start with 10,000 people instead of dollars, and we don't think of the growth rate as an interest rate, but the calculation is exactly the same:

$$10,000 \times 1.03^5 = 10,000 \times 1.1593 = 11,593 \text{ employees}$$

There will be about 1,593 net new hires over the coming five years.

To give another example, according to the company, Walmart's 2016 sales were about $481 billion. Suppose sales are projected to increase at a rate of 15 percent per year. What will Walmart's sales be in the year 2021 if this is correct? Verify for yourself that the answer is about $968 billion—just over twice as large.

EXAMPLE 5.4   **Dividend Growth**

The TICO Corporation currently pays a cash dividend of $5 per share. You believe the dividend will be increased by 4 percent each year indefinitely. How big will the dividend be in eight years?

Here we have a cash dividend growing because it is being increased by management; but once again the calculation is the same:

Future value = $5 × 1.04^8 = $5 × 1.3686 = $6.84

The dividend will grow by $1.84 over that period. Dividend growth is a subject we will return to in a later chapter.

Concept Questions

5.1a   What do we mean by the future value of an investment?

5.1b   What does it mean to compound interest? How does compound interest differ from simple interest?

5.1c   In general, what is the future value of $1 invested at r per period for t periods?

5.2 Present Value and Discounting

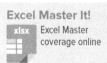

Excel Master It!

Excel Master coverage online

When we discuss future value, we are thinking of questions like: What will my $2,000 investment grow to if it earns a 6.5 percent return every year for the next six years? The answer to this question is what we call the future value of $2,000 invested at 6.5 percent for six years (verify that the answer is about $2,918).

Another type of question that comes up even more often in financial management is obviously related to future value. Suppose you need to have $10,000 in 10 years, and you can earn 6.5 percent on your money. How much do you have to invest today to reach your goal? You can verify that the answer is $5,327.26. How do we know this? Read on.

THE SINGLE-PERIOD CASE

We've seen that the future value of $1 invested for one year at 10 percent is $1.10. We now ask a slightly different question: How much do we have to invest today at 10 percent to get $1 in one year? In other words, we know the future value here is $1, but what is the **present value (PV)**? The answer isn't too hard to figure out. Whatever we invest today will be 1.1 times bigger at the end of the year. Because we need $1 at the end of the year:

present value (PV)
The current value of future cash flows discounted at the appropriate discount rate.

Present value × 1.1 = $1

Or solving for the present value:

Present value = $1/1.1 = $.909

In this case, the present value is the answer to the following question: What amount, invested today, will grow to $1 in one year if the interest rate is 10 percent? Present value is thus the reverse of future value. Instead of compounding the money forward into the future, we **discount** it back to the present.

discount
Calculate the present value of some future amount.

Single-Period PV	EXAMPLE 5.5

Suppose you need $400 to buy textbooks next year. You can earn 7 percent on your money. How much do you have to put up today?

We need to know the PV of $400 in one year at 7 percent. Proceeding as in the previous example:

Present value × 1.07 = $400

We can now solve for the present value:

Present value = $400 × (1/1.07) = $373.83

Thus, $373.83 is the present value. Again, this means that investing this amount for one year at 7 percent will give you a future value of $400.

From our examples, the present value of $1 to be received in one period is generally given as follows:

$$PV = \$1 \times [1/(1 + r)] = \$1/(1 + r)$$

We next examine how to get the present value of an amount to be paid in two or more periods into the future.

PRESENT VALUES FOR MULTIPLE PERIODS

Suppose you need to have $1,000 in two years. If you can earn 7 percent, how much do you have to invest to make sure you have the $1,000 when you need it? In other words, what is the present value of $1,000 in two years if the relevant rate is 7 percent?

Based on your knowledge of future values, you know the amount invested must grow to $1,000 over the two years. In other words, it must be the case that:

$$\begin{aligned}\$1,000 &= PV \times 1.07 \times 1.07 \\ &= PV \times 1.07^2 \\ &= PV \times 1.1449\end{aligned}$$

Given this, we can solve for the present value:

Present value = $1,000/1.1449 = $873.44

Therefore, $873.44 is the amount you must invest to achieve your goal.

Saving Up	EXAMPLE 5.6

You would like to buy a new automobile. You have $50,000 or so, but the car costs $68,500. If you can earn 9 percent, how much do you have to invest today to buy the car in two years? Do you have enough? Assume the price will stay the same.

What we need to know is the present value of $68,500 to be paid in two years, assuming a 9 percent rate. Based on our discussion, this is:

PV = $68,500/1.09² = $68,500/1.1881 = $57,655.08

You're still about $7,655 short, even if you're willing to wait two years.

TABLE 5.3

Present Value Interest Factors

Number of Periods	Interest Rate			
	5%	10%	15%	20%
1	.9524	.9091	.8696	.8333
2	.9070	.8264	.7561	.6944
3	.8638	.7513	.6575	.5787
4	.8227	.6830	.5718	.4823
5	.7835	.6209	.4972	.4019

As you have probably recognized by now, calculating present values is quite similar to calculating future values, and the general result looks much the same. The present value of $1 to be received t periods into the future at a discount rate of r is:

$$PV = \$1 \times [1/(1 + r)^t] = \$1/(1 + r)^t \qquad 5.2$$

The quantity in brackets, $1/(1 + r)^t$, goes by several different names. Because it's used to discount a future cash flow, it is often called a *discount factor*. With this name, it is not surprising that the rate used in the calculation is often called the **discount rate**. We will tend to call it this in talking about present values. The quantity in brackets is also called the *present value interest factor* (or just *present value factor*) for $1 at r percent for t periods and is sometimes abbreviated as PVIF(r, t). Finally, calculating the present value of a future cash flow to determine its worth today is commonly called **discounted cash flow (DCF) valuation**.

discount rate
The rate used to calculate the present value of future cash flows.

discounted cash flow (DCF) valuation
Calculating the present value of a future cash flow to determine its value today.

To illustrate, suppose you need $1,000 in three years. You can earn 15 percent on your money. How much do you have to invest today? To find out, we have to determine the present value of $1,000 in three years at 15 percent. We do this by discounting $1,000 back three periods at 15 percent. With these numbers, the discount factor is:

$$1/(1 + .15)^3 = 1/1.5209 = .6575$$

The amount you must invest is thus:

$$\$1,000 \times .6575 = \$657.50$$

We say that $657.50 is the present or discounted value of $1,000 to be received in three years at 15 percent.

There are tables for present value factors just as there are tables for future value factors, and you use them in the same way (if you use them at all). Table 5.3 contains a small set. A much larger set can be found in Table A.2 in the book's appendix.

In Table 5.3, the discount factor we just calculated (.6575) can be found by looking down the column labeled "15%" until you come to the third row.

CALCULATOR HINTS

You solve present value problems on a financial calculator just as you do future value problems. For the example we just examined (the present value of $1,000 to be received in three years at 15 percent), you would do the following:

Enter	3	15			1,000
	N	I/Y	PMT	PV	FV
Solve for				−657.52	

Notice that the answer has a negative sign; as we discussed earlier, that's because it represents an outflow today in exchange for the $1,000 inflow later.

| **Deceptive Advertising?** | **EXAMPLE 5.7** |

Businesses sometimes advertise that you should "Come try our product. If you do, we'll give you $100 just for coming by!" If you read the fine print, what you find out is that they will give you a savings certificate that will pay you $100 in 25 years or so. If the going interest rate on such certificates is 10 percent per year, how much are they really giving you today?

What you're actually getting is the present value of $100 to be paid in 25 years. If the discount rate is 10 percent per year, then the discount factor is:

$$1/1.1^{25} = 1/10.8347 = .0923$$

This tells you that a dollar in 25 years is worth a little more than nine cents today, assuming a 10 percent discount rate. Given this, the promotion is actually paying you about .0923 × $100 = $9.23. Maybe this is enough to draw customers, but it's not $100.

As the length of time until payment grows, present values decline. As Example 5.7 illustrates, present values tend to become small as the time horizon grows. If you look out far enough, they will always approach zero. Also, for a given length of time, the higher the discount rate is, the lower the present value will be. Put another way, present values and discount rates are inversely related. Increasing the discount rate decreases the PV and vice versa.

The relationship between time, discount rates, and present values is illustrated in Figure 5.3. Notice that by the time we get to 10 years, the present values are all substantially smaller than the future amounts.

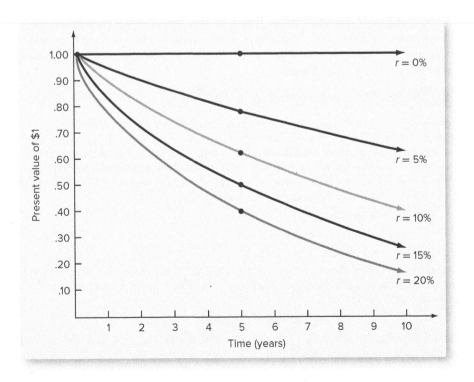

FIGURE 5.3

Present Value of $1 for Different Periods and Rates

Concept Questions

5.2a What do we mean by the *present value* of an investment?

5.2b The process of discounting a future amount back to the present is the opposite of doing what?

5.2c What do we mean by *discounted cash flow*, or *DCF, valuation*?

5.2d In general, what is the present value of $1 to be received in t periods, assuming a discount rate of r per period?

5.3 More about Present and Future Values

Excel Master It!

xlsx Excel Master coverage online

If you look back at the expressions we came up with for present and future values, you will see a simple relationship between the two. We explore this relationship and some related issues in this section.

PRESENT VERSUS FUTURE VALUE

What we called the present value factor is the reciprocal of (that is, 1 divided by) the future value factor:

$$\text{Future value factor} = (1 + r)^t$$

$$\text{Present value factor} = 1/(1 + r)^t$$

In fact, the easy way to calculate a present value factor on many calculators is to first calculate the future value factor and then press the "$1/x$" key to flip it over.

If we let FV_t stand for the future value after t periods, then the relationship between future value and present value can be written as one of the following:

$$PV \times (1 + r)^t = FV_t$$

$$PV = FV_t/(1 + r)^t = FV_t \times [1/(1 + r)^t]$$

This last result we will call the *basic present value equation*. We will use it throughout the text. A number of variations come up, but this simple equation underlies many of the most important ideas in corporate finance.

5.3

EXAMPLE 5.8 | **Evaluating Investments**

To give you an idea of how we will be using present and future values, consider the following simple investment. Your company proposes to buy an asset for $335. This investment is very safe. You would sell off the asset in three years for $400. You know you could invest the $335 elsewhere at 10 percent with very little risk. What do you think of the proposed investment?

This is not a good investment. Why not? Because you can invest the $335 elsewhere at 10 percent. If you do, after three years it will grow to:

$$
\begin{aligned}
\$335 \times (1 + r)^t &= \$335 \times 1.1^3 \\
&= \$335 \times 1.331 \\
&= \$445.89
\end{aligned}
$$

Because the proposed investment pays out only $400, it is not as good as other alternatives we have. Another way of seeing the same thing is to notice that the present value of $400 in three years at 10 percent is:

$$\$400 \times [1/(1 + r)^t] = \$400/1.1^3 = \$400/1.331 = \$300.53$$

This tells us that we have to invest only about $300 to get $400 in three years, not $335. We will return to this type of analysis later on.

DETERMINING THE DISCOUNT RATE

We frequently need to determine what discount rate is implicit in an investment. We can do this by looking at the basic present value equation:

$$PV = FV_t/(1 + r)^t$$

There are only four parts to this equation: The present value (PV), the future value (FV_t), the discount rate (r), and the life of the investment (t). Given any three of these, we can always find the fourth.

For a downloadable, Windows-based financial calculator, go to **www.calculator.org**.

Finding *r* for a Single-Period Investment	**EXAMPLE 5.9**

You are considering a one-year investment. If you put up $1,250, you will get back $1,350. What rate is this investment paying?

First, in this single-period case, the answer is fairly obvious. You are getting a total of $100 in addition to your $1,250. The implicit rate on this investment is thus $100/$1,250 = 8 percent.

More formally, from the basic present value equation, the present value (the amount you must put up today) is $1,250. The future value (what the present value grows to) is $1,350. The time involved is one period, so we have:

$$\$1,250 = \$1,350/(1 + r)^1$$
$$1 + r = \$1,350/\$1,250 = 1.08$$
$$r = .08, \text{ or } 8\%$$

In this simple case, of course, there was no need to go through this calculation. But as we describe next, it gets a little harder with more than one period.

To illustrate what happens with multiple periods, let's say we are offered an investment that costs us $100 and will double our money in eight years. To compare this to other investments, we would like to know what discount rate is implicit in these numbers. This discount rate is called the *rate of return*, or sometimes just the *return*, on the investment. In this case, we have a present value of $100, a future value of $200 (double our money), and an eight-year life. To calculate the return, we can write the basic present value equation as:

$$PV = FV_t /(1 + r)^t$$
$$\$100 = \$200/(1 + r)^8$$

It could also be written as:

$$(1 + r)^8 = \$200/\$100 = 2$$

We now need to solve for r. There are three ways to do this:

1. Use a financial calculator.
2. Solve the equation for $1 + r$ by taking the eighth root of both sides. Because this is the same thing as raising both sides to the power of ⅛ or .125, this is actually easy to do with the "y^x" key on a calculator. Just enter 2, then press "y^x," enter .125, and press the "=" key. The eighth root should be about 1.09, which implies that r is 9 percent.
3. Use a future value table. The future value factor after eight years is equal to 2. If you look across the row corresponding to eight periods in Table A.1, you will see that a future value factor of 2 corresponds to the 9 percent column, again implying that the return here is 9 percent.

Actually, in this particular example, there is a useful "back of the envelope" means of solving for r—the Rule of 72. For reasonable rates of return, the time it takes to double your money is given approximately by $72/r\%$. In our example, this means that $72/r\% = 8$ years, implying that r is 9 percent, as we calculated. This rule is fairly accurate for discount rates in the 5 percent to 20 percent range.

EXAMPLE 5.10   **Sneakers as Investments**

In December 2016, a pair of game-worn shoes with graffiti-style writing that said "Oakland Strong" used by Stephen Curry were auctioned off to benefit the Oakland Fire Relief Fund. The shoes sold for $30,101. The record for game-worn shoes by an active NBA player is $37,740 for a pair of Kobe Bryant shoes used in the 2008 Olympics. "Experts" often argue that collectibles such as this will double in value over a 10-year period.

So were the sneakers a good investment? By the Rule of 72, you already know the experts were predicting that the sneakers would double in value in 10 years; so the return predicted would be about $72/10 = 7.2$ percent per year, which is only so-so.

Why does the Rule
of 72 work? See
www.moneychimp.com.

At one time at least, a rule of thumb in the rarefied world of fine art collecting was "your money back in 5 years, double your money in 10 years." Given this, let's see how an investment stacked up. In 2013, the Pablo Picasso painting *Le Rêve* was sold for $155 million. The painting had reached a level of notoriety in part because its owner, casino magnate Steve Wynn, had put his elbow through the middle of the painting. Wynn had purchased the painting 12 years earlier in 2001 for an estimated $60 million. So was Wynn's gamble a winner?

The rule of thumb has us doubling our money in 10 years; so, from the Rule of 72, we have that 7.2 percent per year was the norm. The painting was resold in about 12 years. The present value is $60 million, and the future value is $155 million. We need to solve for the unknown rate, r, as follows:

$$\$60,000,000 = \$155,000,000/(1 + r)^{12}$$
$$(1 + r)^{12} = 2.5833$$

Solving for r, we find that Wynn earned about 8.23 percent per year—a little better than the 7.2 percent rule of thumb.

What about other collectibles? To a philatelist (a stamp collector to you and us), one of the most prized stamps is the 1918 24-cent inverted Jenny C3a. The stamp is a collectible because it has a picture of an upside-down biplane. One of these stamps sold at auction for $1,175,000 in 2016. At what rate did its value grow? Verify for yourself that the answer is about 17.02 percent, assuming a 98-year period.

Collectible autos can also have good returns. For example, a 1939 Alfa Romeo 8C 2900B Lungo Spider was reported to have sold for £1,150 when it was brand new. When it was auctioned in 2016, it became the most expensive prewar car to date when it sold for £19.8 million. Assuming that 77 years had passed, see if you don't agree that the increase in the value of the car was 13.50 percent per year.

Not all collectibles do as well. In 2016, a 1792 Silver Center Cent, believed to be the first coin produced outside the U.S. Mint, was auctioned for $352,500. While this seems like a huge return to the untrained eye, check that, over the 224-year period, the gain was only about 8.07 percent.

One of the rarest coins is the 1894-S dime, struck at the San Francisco mint. Only 24 were ever produced, with nine believed to be still in existence. In 2016, one of these dimes sold at auction for $2 million. See if you agree that this collectible gained about 14.77 percent per year.

A slightly more extreme example involves money bequeathed by Benjamin Franklin, who died on April 17, 1790. In his will, he gave 1,000 pounds sterling to Massachusetts and the city of Boston. He gave a like amount to Pennsylvania and the city of Philadelphia. The money had been paid to Franklin when he held political office, but he believed that politicians should not be paid for their service (it appears that this view is not widely shared by modern politicians).

Franklin originally specified that the money should be paid out 100 years after his death and used to train young people. Later, however, after some legal wrangling, it was agreed that the money would be paid out in 1990, 200 years after Franklin's death. By that time, the Pennsylvania bequest had grown to about $2 million; the Massachusetts bequest had grown to $4.5 million. The money was used to fund the Franklin Institutes in Boston and Philadelphia. Assuming that 1,000 pounds sterling was equivalent to $1,000, what rate of return did the two states earn? (The dollar did not become the official U.S. currency until 1792.)

For Pennsylvania, the future value is $2 million and the present value is $1,000. There are 200 years involved, so we need to solve for r in the following:

$$\$1,000 = \$2 \text{ million}/(1 + r)^{200}$$

$$(1 + r)^{200} = 2,000$$

Solving for r, we see that the Pennsylvania money grew at about 3.87 percent per year. The Massachusetts money did better; verify that the rate of return in this case was 4.3 percent. Small differences in returns can add up!

CALCULATOR HINTS

We can illustrate how to calculate unknown rates using a financial calculator with these numbers. For Pennsylvania, you would do the following:

Enter	200			−1,000	2,000,000
	N	I/Y	PMT	PV	FV
Solve for		3.87			

As in our previous examples, notice the minus sign on the present value, representing Franklin's outlay made many years ago. What do you change to work the problem for Massachusetts?

Saving for College   EXAMPLE 5.11

You estimate that you will need about $80,000 to send your child to college in eight years. You have about $35,000 now. If you can earn 20 percent per year, will you make it? At what rate will you just reach your goal?

If you can earn 20 percent, the future value of your $35,000 in eight years will be:

$$FV = \$35,000 \times 1.20^8 = \$35,000 \times 4.2998 = \$150,493.59$$

So, you will make it easily. The minimum rate is the unknown r in the following:

$$FV = \$35{,}000 \times (1 + r)^8 = \$80{,}000$$

$$(1 + r)^8 = \$80{,}000 / \$35{,}000 = 2.2857$$

Therefore, the future value factor is 2.2857. Looking at the row in Table A.1 that corresponds to eight periods, we see that our future value factor is roughly halfway between the ones shown for 10 percent (2.1436) and 12 percent (2.4760), so you will just reach your goal if you earn approximately 11 percent. To get the exact answer, we could use a financial calculator or we could solve for r:

$$(1 + r)^8 = \$80{,}000 / \$35{,}000 = 2.2857$$

$$1 + r = 2.2857^{1/8} = 2.2857^{.125} = 1.1089$$

$$r = .1089, \text{ or } 10.89\%$$

EXAMPLE 5.12   **Only 18,262.5 Days to Retirement**

You would like to retire in 50 years as a millionaire. If you have $10,000 today, what rate of return do you need to earn to achieve your goal?

The future value is $1,000,000. The present value is $10,000, and there are 50 years until payment. We need to calculate the unknown discount rate in the following:

$$\$10{,}000 = \$1{,}000{,}000 / (1 + r)^{50}$$

$$(1 + r)^{50} = 100$$

The future value factor is thus 100. You can verify that the implicit rate is about 9.65 percent.

Not taking the time value of money into account when computing growth rates or rates of return often leads to some misleading numbers in the real world. For example, the most loved (and hated) team in baseball, the New York Yankees, had the highest payroll during the 1988 season, about $19 million. In 2016, the Los Angeles Dodgers had the highest payroll, a staggering $223 million—an increase of 1,074 percent! If history is any guide, we can get a rough idea of the future growth in baseball payrolls. See if you don't agree that this represents an annual increase of 9.19 percent, a substantial growth rate, but much less than the gaudy 1,074 percent.

How about classic maps? A few years ago, the first map of America, printed in Rome in 1507, was valued at about $135,000, 69 percent more than the $80,000 it was worth 10 years earlier. Your return on investment if you were the proud owner of the map over those 10 years? Verify that it's about 5.4 percent per year—far worse than the 69 percent reported increase in price.

Whether with maps or baseball payrolls, it's easy to be misled when returns are quoted without considering the time value of money. However, it's not just the uninitiated who are guilty of this slight form of deception. The title of a feature article in a leading business magazine predicted the Dow Jones Industrial Average would soar to a 70 percent gain over the coming five years. Do you think it meant a 70 percent return per year on your money? Think again!

FINDING THE NUMBER OF PERIODS

Suppose we are interested in purchasing an asset that costs $50,000. We currently have $25,000. If we can earn 12 percent on this $25,000, how long until we have the $50,000?

Finding the answer involves solving for the last variable in the basic present value equation, the number of periods. You already know how to get an approximate answer to this particular problem. Notice that we need to double our money. From the Rule of 72, this will take about $72/12 = 6$ years at 12 percent.

To come up with the exact answer, we can again manipulate the basic present value equation. The present value is $25,000, and the future value is $50,000. With a 12 percent discount rate, the basic equation takes one of the following forms:

$$\$25,000 = \$50,000/1.12^t$$

$$\$50,000/\$25,000 = 1.12^t = 2$$

We thus have a future value factor of 2 for a 12 percent rate. We now need to solve for t. If you look down the column in Table A.1 that corresponds to 12 percent, you will see that a future value factor of 1.9738 occurs at six periods. It will thus take about six years, as we calculated. To get the exact answer, we have to explicitly solve for t (or use a financial calculator). If you do this, you will see that the answer is 6.1163 years, so our approximation was quite close in this case.

CALCULATOR HINTS

If you use a financial calculator, here are the relevant entries:

Enter		12		−25,000	50,000
	N	I/Y	PMT	PV	FV
Solve for	6.1163				

Waiting for Godot   EXAMPLE 5.13

You've been saving up to buy the Godot Company. The total cost will be $10 million. You currently have about $2.3 million. If you can earn 5 percent on your money, how long will you have to wait? At 16 percent, how long must you wait?

At 5 percent, you'll have to wait a long time. From the basic present value equation:

$$\$2.3 \text{ million} = \$10 \text{ million}/1.05^t$$

$$1.05^t = 4.35$$

$$t = 30 \text{ years}$$

At 16 percent, things are a little better. Verify for yourself that it will take about 10 years.

Consider the U.S. EE Savings Bonds that we discussed at the beginning of the chapter. You purchase them for half of their $50 face value. In other words, you pay $25 today and get $50 at some point in the future when the bond "matures." You receive no interest in between, and the interest rate is adjusted every six months, so the length of time until your $25 grows to $50 depends on future interest rates. However, at worst, the bonds are guaranteed to be worth $50 at the end of 20 years, so this is the longest you would ever have to wait. If you do have to wait the full 20 years, what rate do you earn?

Learn more about using Excel for time value and other calculations at **www.studyfinance.com**.

142   **PART 3**   Valuation of Future Cash Flows

TABLE 5.4

Summary of Time Value Calculations

I. Symbols:	
PV = Present value, what future cash flows are worth today	
FV_t = Future value, what cash flows are worth in the future	
r = Interest rate, rate of return, or discount rate per period—typically, but not always, one year	
t = Number of periods—typically, but not always, the number of years	
C = Cash amount	
II. Future Value of C Invested at r Percent for t Periods:	
$FV_t = C \times (1 + r)^t$	
The term $(1 + r)^t$ is called the *future value factor*.	
III. Present Value of C to Be Received in t Periods at r Percent per Period:	
$PV = C/(1 + r)^t$	
The term $1/(1 + r)^t$ is called the *present value factor*.	
IV. The Basic Present Value Equation Giving the Relationship between Present and Future Value:	
$PV = FV_t/(1 + r)^t$	

Because this investment is doubling in value in 20 years, the Rule of 72 tells you the answer right away: $72/20 = .036$, or 3.6%. Remember, this is the *minimum* guaranteed return, so you might do better. This example finishes our introduction to basic time value concepts. Table 5.4 summarizes present and future value calculations for future reference. As our nearby *Work the Web* box shows, online calculators are widely available to handle these calculations; however, it is still important to know what is really going on.

SPREADSHEET STRATEGIES

Using a Spreadsheet for Time Value of Money Calculations

More and more, businesspeople from many different areas (not just finance and accounting) rely on spreadsheets to do all the different types of calculations that come up in the real world. As a result, in this section, we will show you how to use a spreadsheet to handle the various time value of money problems we presented in this chapter. We will use Microsoft Excel™, but the commands are similar for other types of software. We assume you are already familiar with basic spreadsheet operations.

As we have seen, you can solve for any one of the following four potential unknowns: Future value, present value, the discount rate, or the number of periods. With a spreadsheet, there is a separate formula for each. In Excel, these are shown in a nearby box.

In these formulas, *pv* and *fv* are present and future value, respectively; *nper* is the number of periods; and *rate* is the discount, or interest, rate. We will talk about *pmt* in the next chapter.

Two things are a little tricky here. First, unlike a financial calculator, the spreadsheet requires that the rate be entered as a decimal. Second, as with most financial

To Find	Enter This Formula
Future value	= FV (rate,nper,pmt,pv)
Present value	= PV (rate,nper,pmt,fv)
Discount rate	= RATE (nper,pmt,pv,fv)
Number of periods	= NPER (rate,pmt,pv,fv)

calculators, you have to put a negative sign on either the present value or the future value to solve for the rate or the number of periods. For the same reason, if you solve for a present value, the answer will have a negative sign unless you input a negative future value. The same is true when you compute a future value.

To illustrate how you might use these formulas, we will go back to an example in the chapter. If you invest $25,000 at 12 percent per year, how long until you have $50,000? You might set up a spreadsheet like this:

	A	B	C	D	E	F	G	H
1								
2	**Using a spreadsheet for time value of money calculations**							
3								
4	If we invest $25,000 at 12 percent, how long until we have $50,000? We need to solve							
5	for the unknown number of periods, so we use the formula NPER(rate,pmt,pv,fv).							
6								
7	Present value (pv):	$25,000						
8	Future value (fv):	$50,000						
9	Rate (rate):	.12						
10								
11	Periods:	**6.1162554**						
12								
13	The formula entered in cell B11 is =NPER(B9,0,-B7,B8); notice that pmt is zero and that pv							
14	has a negative sign on it. Also notice that rate is entered as a decimal, not a percentage.							

SOURCE: Microsoft Excel

Concept Questions

5.3a   What is the basic present value equation?

5.3b   What is the Rule of 72?

WORK THE WEB

How important is the time value of money? A recent search on one web search engine returned over 689 million hits! Although you must understand the calculations behind the time value of money, the advent of financial calculators and spreadsheets has eliminated the need for tedious calculations. In fact, many websites offer time value of money calculators. The following is one example from www .investopedia.com.

You have $20,000 today and will invest it at 9.75 percent for 40 years. How much will it be worth at that time? With the Investopedia calculator, you enter the values and hit "Calculate". The results look like this:

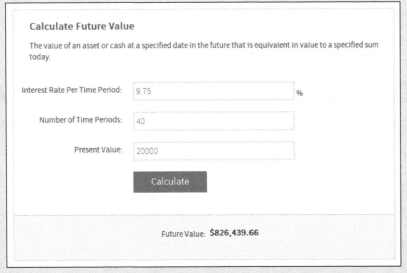

Calculate Future Value

The value of an asset or cash at a specified date in the future that is equivalent in value to a specified sum today.

Interest Rate Per Time Period: 9.75   %

Number of Time Periods: 40

Present Value: 20000

Calculate

Future Value: **$826,439.66**

Who said time value of money calculations are hard?

Questions

1. *Use the present value calculator on this website to answer the following: Suppose you want to have $140,000 in 25 years. If you can earn a 10 percent return, how much do you have to invest today?*

2. *Use the future value calculator on this website to answer the following question: Suppose you have $8,000 today that you plan to save for your retirement in 40 years. If you earn a return of 10.8 percent per year, how much will this account be worth when you are ready to retire?*

5.4 Summary and Conclusions

This chapter has introduced you to the basic principles of present value and discounted cash flow valuation. In it, we explained a number of things about the time value of money, including these:

1. For a given rate of return, we can determine the value at some point in the future of an investment made today by calculating the future value of that investment.

2. We can determine the current worth of a future cash flow or series of cash flows for a given rate of return by calculating the present value of the cash flow(s) involved.

3. The relationship between present value (PV) and future value (FV) for a given rate r and time t is given by the basic present value equation:

$$PV = FV_t/(1 + r)^t$$

As we have shown, it is possible to find any one of the four components (PV, FV_t, r, or t) given the other three.

The principles developed in this chapter will figure prominently in the chapters to come. The reason for this is that most investments, whether they involve real assets or financial assets, can be analyzed using the discounted cash flow (DCF) approach. As a result, the DCF approach is broadly applicable and widely used in practice. Before going on you might want to do some of the problems that follow.

CONNECT TO FINANCE

 Connect Finance offers you plenty of opportunities to practice mastering time value of money concepts. Log on to connect.mheducation.com to learn more. If you like what you see, ask your professor about using *Connect Finance!*

Can you answer the following *Connect* Quiz questions?

Section 5.1   You deposited $2,000 in a bank account that pays 5 percent simple interest. How much will you have in this account after three years?

Section 5.2   What is the present value of $11,500 discounted at 9 percent for 11 years?

Section 5.3   Charlie invested $6,200 in a stock last year. Currently, this investment is worth $6,788.38. What is the rate of return on this investment?

CHAPTER REVIEW AND SELF-TEST PROBLEMS

5.1 **Calculating Future Values** Assume you deposit $10,000 today in an account that pays 6 percent interest. How much will you have in five years?

5.2 **Calculating Present Values** Suppose you have just celebrated your 19th birthday. A rich uncle has set up a trust fund for you that will pay you $150,000 when you turn 30. If the relevant discount rate is 9 percent, how much is this fund worth today?

5.3 **Calculating Rates of Return** You've been offered an investment that will double your money in 10 years. What rate of return are you being offered? Check your answer using the Rule of 72.

5.4 **Calculating the Number of Periods** You've been offered an investment that will pay you 9 percent per year. If you invest $15,000, how long until you have $30,000? How long until you have $45,000?

ANSWERS TO CHAPTER REVIEW AND SELF-TEST PROBLEMS

5.1 We need to calculate the future value of $10,000 at 6 percent for five years. The future value factor is:

$$1.06^5 = 1.3382$$

The future value is thus $10,000 × 1.3382 = $13,382.26.

5.2 We need the present value of $150,000 to be paid in 11 years at 9 percent. The discount factor is:

$$1/1.09^{11} = 1/2.5804 = .3875$$

The present value is thus about $58,130.

5.3 Suppose you invest $1,000. You will have $2,000 in 10 years with this investment. So, $1,000 is the amount you have today, or the present value, and $2,000 is the amount you will have in 10 years, or the future value. From the basic present value equation, we have:

$$\$2,000 = \$1,000 \times (1 + r)^{10}$$
$$2 = (1 + r)^{10}$$

From here, we need to solve for r, the unknown rate. As shown in the chapter, there are several different ways to do this. We will take the 10th root of 2 (by raising 2 to the power of 1/10):

$$2^{1/10} = 1 + r$$
$$1.0718 = 1 + r$$
$$r = .0718, \text{ or } 7.18\%$$

Using the Rule of 72, we have $72/t = r\%$, or $72/10 = .072$, or 7.2%; so, our answer looks good (remember that the Rule of 72 is only an approximation).

5.4 The basic equation is this:

$$\$30,000 = \$15,000 \times (1 + .09)^t$$
$$2 = (1 + .09)^t$$

If we solve for t, we find that $t = 8.04$ years. Using the Rule of 72, we get $72/9 = 8$ years, so once again our answer looks good. To get $45,000, verify for yourself that you will have to wait 12.75 years.

CONCEPTS REVIEW AND CRITICAL THINKING QUESTIONS

1. **Present Value** [LO2] The basic present value equation has four parts. What are they?

2. **Compounding** [LO1, 2] What is compounding? What is discounting?

3. **Compounding and Periods** [LO1, 2] As you increase the length of time involved, what happens to future values? What happens to present values?

4. **Compounding and Interest Rates** [LO1, 2] What happens to a future value if you increase the rate r? What happens to a present value?

5. **Ethical Considerations** [LO2] Take a look back at Example 5.7. Is it deceptive advertising? Is it unethical to advertise a future value like this without a disclaimer?

Use the following information for Questions 6–10:

On March 28, 2008, Toyota Motor Credit Corporation (TMCC), a subsidiary of Toyota Motor, offered some securities for sale to the public. Under the terms of the deal, TMCC promised to repay the owner of one of these securities $100,000 on March 28, 2038, but investors would receive nothing until then. Investors paid TMCC $24,099 for each of these securities; so they gave up $24,099 on March 28, 2008, for the promise of a $100,000 payment 30 years later.

6. **Time Value of Money** [LO2] Why would TMCC be willing to accept such a small amount today ($24,099) in exchange for a promise to repay about four times that amount ($100,000) in the future?

7. **Call Provisions** [LO2] TMCC has the right to buy back the securities on the anniversary date at a price established when the securities were issued (this feature is a term of this particular deal). What impact does this feature have on the desirability of this security as an investment?

8. **Time Value of Money** [LO2] Would you be willing to pay $24,099 today in exchange for $100,000 in 30 years? What would be the key considerations in answering yes or no? Would your answer depend on who is making the promise to repay?

9. **Investment Comparison** [LO2] Suppose that when TMCC offered the security for $24,099, the U.S. Treasury had offered an essentially identical security. Do you think it would have had a higher or lower price? Why?

10. **Length of Investment** [LO2] The TMCC security is bought and sold on the New York Stock Exchange. If you looked at the price today, do you think the price would exceed the $24,099 original price? Why? If you looked in the year 2019, do you think the price would be higher or lower than today's price? Why?

QUESTIONS AND PROBLEMS

BASIC
(Questions 1–14)

1. **Simple Interest versus Compound Interest** [LO1] First City Bank pays 9 percent simple interest on its savings account balances, whereas Second City Bank pays 9 percent interest compounded annually. If you made a deposit of $7,500 in each bank, how much more money would you earn from your Second City Bank account at the end of eight years?

2. **Calculating Future Values** [LO1] For each of the following, compute the future value:

Present Value	Years	Interest Rate	Future Value
$ 2,328	11	13%	
7,513	7	9	
74,381	14	12	
192,050	16	6	

3. Calculating Present Values [LO2] For each of the following, compute the present ✗ value:

Present Value	Years	Interest Rate	Future Value
	13	9%	$ 16,832
	4	7	48,318
	29	13	886,073
	40	21	550,164

4. Calculating Interest Rates [LO3] Solve for the unknown interest rate in each of ✗ the following:

Present Value	Years	Interest Rate	Future Value
$ 181	5		$ 317
335	17		1,080
48,000	13		185,382
40,353	30		531,618

5. Calculating the Number of Periods [LO4] Solve for the unknown number of years ✗ in each of the following:

Present Value	Years	Interest Rate	Future Value
$ 560		7%	$ 1,389
810		8	1,821
18,400		9	289,715
21,500		11	430,258

6. Calculating Interest Rates [LO3] Assume the total cost of a college education will be $345,000 when your child enters college in 18 years. You presently have $73,000 to invest. What annual rate of interest must you earn on your investment to cover the cost of your child's college education?

7. Calculating the Number of Periods [LO4] At 6.1 percent interest, how long does it take to double your money? To quadruple it?

8. Calculating Interest Rates [LO3] According to the Census Bureau, in October 2016, the average house price in the United States was $354,900. In October 2000, the average price was $215,100. What was the annual increase in the price of the average house sold?

9. Calculating the Number of Periods [LO4] You're trying to save to buy a new $245,000 Ferrari. You have $50,000 today that can be invested at your bank. The bank pays 4.3 percent annual interest on its accounts. How long will it be before you have enough to buy the car?

10. Calculating Present Values [LO2] Imprudential, Inc., has an unfunded pension liability of $415 million that must be paid in 20 years. To assess the value of the firm's stock, financial analysts want to discount this liability back to the present. If the relevant discount rate is 5.2 percent, what is the present value of this liability?

11. Calculating Present Values [LO2] You have just received notification that you have won the $2 million first prize in the Centennial Lottery. However, the prize will be awarded on your 100th birthday (assuming you're around to collect), 80 years from now. What is the present value of your windfall if the appropriate discount rate is 8.4 percent?

12. Calculating Future Values [LO1] Your coin collection contains fifty 1952 silver dollars. If your grandparents purchased them for their face value when they were new, how much will your collection be worth when you retire in 2067, assuming they appreciate at an annual rate of 4.3 percent?

13. Calculating Interest Rates and Future Values [LO1, 3] In 1895, the first U.S. Open Golf Championship was held. The winner's prize money was $150. In 2016, the winner's check was $1,800,000. What was the percentage increase per year in the winner's check over this period? If the winner's prize increases at the same rate, what will it be in 2040?

14. Calculating Rates of Return [LO3] Although appealing to more refined tastes, art as a collectible has not always performed so profitably. During 2003, Sotheby's sold the Edgar Degas bronze sculpture *Petite Danseuse de Quatorze Ans* at auction for a price of $10,311,500. Unfortunately for the previous owner, he had purchased it in 1999 at a price of $12,377,500. What was his annual rate of return on this sculpture?

15. Calculating Rates of Return [LO3] The "Brasher doubloon," which was featured in the plot of the Raymond Chandler novel, *The High Window*, was sold at auction in 2014 for $4,582,500. The coin had a face value of $15 when it was first issued in 1787 and had been previously sold for $430,000 in 1979. At what annual rate did the coin appreciate from its minting to the 1979 sale? What annual rate did the 1979 buyer earn on his purchase? At what annual rate did the coin appreciate from its minting to the 2014 sale?

16. Calculating Rates of Return [LO3] Refer back to the Series EE savings bonds we discussed at the very beginning of the chapter.

a. Assuming you purchased a $50 face value bond, what is the exact rate of return you would earn if you held the bond for 20 years until it doubled in value?

b. If you purchased a $50 face value bond in early 2017 at the then current interest rate of .10 percent per year, how much would the bond be worth in 2027?

c. In 2027, instead of cashing the bond in for its then current value, you decide to hold the bond until it doubles in face value in 2037. What rate of return will you earn over the last 10 years?

17. Calculating Present Values [LO2] Suppose you are still committed to owning a $245,000 Ferrari (see Problem 9). If you believe your mutual fund can achieve an annual rate of return of 11.2 percent and you want to buy the car in 9 years (on the day you turn 30), how much must you invest today?

18. Calculating Future Values [LO1] You have just made your first $5,500 contribution to your retirement account. Assuming you earn a return of 10 percent per year and make no additional contributions, what will your account be worth when you retire in 45 years? What if you wait 10 years before contributing? (Does this suggest an investment strategy?)

19. Calculating Future Values [LO1] You are scheduled to receive $20,000 in two years. When you receive it, you will invest it for six more years at 6.8 percent per year. How much will you have in eight years?

20. Calculating the Number of Periods [LO4] You expect to receive $10,000 at graduation in two years. You plan on investing it at 9 percent until you have $60,000. How long will you wait from now?

Discounted Cash Flow Valuation

6 Chapter

THE SIGNING OF BIG-NAME ATHLETES is frequently accompanied by great fanfare, but the numbers are often misleading. For example, in late 2016, catcher Jason Castro reached a deal with the Minnesota Twins, signing a contract with a reported value of $24.5 million. Not bad, especially for someone who makes a living using the "tools of ignorance" (jock jargon for a catcher's equipment). Another example is the contract signed by DeMar DeRozan with the Toronto Raptors, which had a stated value of $139 million.

It looks like Jason and DeMar did pretty well, but now consider Andrew Luck, who signed to play in front of the Indianapolis Colts' fans. Andrew's contract also had a stated value of about $139 million, but this amount was actually payable over several years. The contract consisted of a $6.4 million signing bonus, along with $12 million in salary in the first year plus $120.725 million in future salary to be paid in the years 2017 through 2021. The payments to Jason and DeMar were similarly spread over time.

Because all three contracts call for payments to be made at future dates, we must consider the time value of money, which means none of these players received the quoted amounts. How much did they really get? This chapter gives you the "tools of knowledge" to answer this question.

Learning Objectives

After studying this chapter, you should be able to:

LO1 Determine the future and present value of investments with multiple cash flows.

LO2 Explain how loan payments are calculated and how to find the interest rate on a loan.

LO3 Describe how loans are amortized or paid off.

LO4 Show how interest rates are quoted (and misquoted).

©by_adri/iStockPhoto/GettyImages

For updates on the latest happenings in finance, visit fundamentalsofcorporatefinance.blogspot.com.

In our previous chapter, we covered the basics of discounted cash flow valuation. However, so far, we have dealt with only single cash flows. In reality, most investments have multiple cash flows. For example, if Target is thinking of opening a new department store, there will be a large cash outlay in the beginning and then cash inflows for many years. In this chapter, we begin to explore how to value such investments.

When you finish this chapter, you should have some very practical skills. For example, you will know how to calculate your own car payments or student loan payments. You will also be able to determine how long it will take to pay off a credit card if you make the minimum payment each month (a practice we do not recommend). We will show you how to compare interest rates to determine which are the highest and which are the lowest, and we will also show you how interest rates can be quoted in different—and at times deceptive—ways.

FIGURE 6.1

Drawing and Using a Time Line

6.1 Future and Present Values of Multiple Cash Flows

Excel Master It!

Excel Master coverage online

Thus far, we have restricted our attention to either the future value of a lump sum present amount or the present value of some single future cash flow. In this section, we begin to study ways to value multiple cash flows. We start with future value.

FUTURE VALUE WITH MULTIPLE CASH FLOWS

Suppose you deposit $100 today in an account paying 8 percent interest. In one year, you will deposit another $100. How much will you have in two years? This particular problem is relatively easy. At the end of the first year, you will have $108 plus the second $100 you deposit, for a total of $208. You leave this $208 on deposit at 8 percent for another year. At the end of this second year, it is worth:

$208 × 1.08 = $224.64

Figure 6.1 is a *time line* that illustrates the process of calculating the future value of these two $100 deposits. Figures such as this are useful for solving complicated problems. Almost anytime you are having trouble with a present or future value problem, drawing a time line will help you see what is happening.

In the first part of Figure 6.1, we show the cash flows on the time line. The most important thing is that we write them down where they actually occur. Here, the first cash flow occurs today, which we label as Time 0. We therefore put $100 at Time 0 on the time line. The second $100 cash flow occurs one year from today, so we write it down at the point labeled as Time 1. In the second part of Figure 6.1, we calculate the future values one period at a time to come up with the final $224.64.

EXAMPLE 6.1	**Saving Up Revisited**

You think you will be able to deposit $4,000 at the end of each of the next three years in a bank account paying 8 percent interest. You currently have $7,000 in the account. How much will you have in three years? In four years?

At the end of the first year, you will have:

$7,000 × 1.08 + 4,000 = $11,560

At the end of the second year, you will have:

$11,560 \times 1.08 + 4,000 = \$16,484.80$

Repeating this for the third year gives:

$16,484.80 \times 1.08 + 4,000 = \$21,803.58$

Therefore, you will have $21,803.58 in three years. If you leave this on deposit for one more year (and don't add to it), at the end of the fourth year, you'll have:

$21,803.58 \times 1.08 = \$23,547.87$

When we calculated the future value of the two $100 deposits, we calculated the balance as of the beginning of each year and then rolled that amount forward to the next year. We could have done it another, quicker way. The first $100 is on deposit for two years at 8 percent, so its future value is:

$100 \times 1.08^2 = \$100 \times 1.1664 = \$116.64$

The second $100 is on deposit for one year at 8 percent, and its future value is thus:

$100 \times 1.08 = \$108$

The total future value, as we previously calculated, is equal to the sum of these two future values:

$116.64 + 108 = \$224.64$

Based on this example, there are two ways to calculate future values for multiple cash flows: (1) Compound the accumulated balance forward one year at a time or (2) calculate the future value of each cash flow first and then add them up. Both give the same answer, so you can do it either way.

To illustrate the two different ways of calculating future values, consider the future value of $2,000 invested at the end of each of the next five years. The current balance is zero, and the rate is 10 percent. We first draw a time line, as shown in Figure 6.2.

On the time line, notice that nothing happens until the end of the first year, when we make the first $2,000 investment. This first $2,000 earns interest for the next four (not five) years. Also notice that the last $2,000 is invested at the end of the fifth year, so it earns no interest at all.

Figure 6.3 illustrates the calculations involved if we compound the investment one period at a time. As illustrated, the future value is $12,210.20.

FIGURE 6.2

Time Line for $2,000 per Year for Five Years

FIGURE 6.3   **Future Value Calculated by Compounding Forward One Period at a Time**

FIGURE 6.4 **Future Value Calculated by Compounding Each Cash Flow Separately**

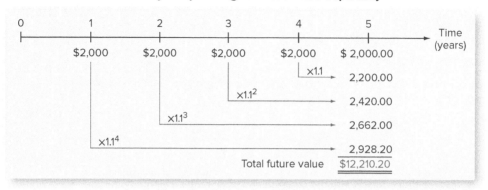

Figure 6.4 goes through the same calculations, but the second technique is used. Naturally, the answer is the same.

EXAMPLE 6.2	Saving Up Once Again

If you deposit $100 in one year, $200 in two years, and $300 in three years, how much will you have in three years? How much of this is interest? How much will you have in five years if you don't add additional amounts? Assume a 7 percent interest rate throughout.

We will calculate the future value of each amount in three years. Notice that the $100 earns interest for two years, and the $200 earns interest for one year. The final $300 earns no interest. The future values are thus:

$$
\begin{array}{ll}
\$100 \times 1.07^2 & = \$114.49 \\
\$200 \times 1.07 & = \ \ 214.00 \\
+\$300 & = \ \underline{\ \ 300.00} \\
\text{Total future value} & = \underline{\$628.49}
\end{array}
$$

The total future value is thus $628.49. The total interest is:

$628.49 − (100 + 200 + 300) = $28.49

How much will you have in five years? We know that you will have $628.49 in three years. If you leave that in for two more years, it will grow to:

$628.49 × 1.07² = $628.49 × 1.1449 = $719.56

Notice that we could have calculated the future value of each amount separately. Once again, be careful about the lengths of time. As we previously calculated, the first $100 earns interest for only four years, the second ($200) deposit earns three years' interest, and the last ($300) deposit earns two years' interest:

$$
\begin{array}{lll}
\$100 \times 1.07^4 = \$100 \times 1.3108 & = \$131.08 \\
\$200 \times 1.07^3 = \$200 \times 1.2250 & = \ \ 245.01 \\
+\$300 \times 1.07^2 = \$300 \times 1.1449 & = \ \underline{\ \ 343.47} \\
\hspace{2cm} \text{Total future value} & = \underline{\$719.56}
\end{array}
$$

PRESENT VALUE WITH MULTIPLE CASH FLOWS

We often need to determine the present value of a series of future cash flows. As with future values, there are two ways we can do it. We can either discount back one period at a time, or we can calculate the present values individually and add them up.

Suppose you need $1,000 in one year and $2,000 more in two years. If you can earn 9 percent on your money, how much do you have to put up today to exactly cover these amounts in the future? In other words, what is the present value of the two cash flows at 9 percent?

The present value of $2,000 in two years at 9 percent is:

$2,000/1.09^2 = $1,683.36

The present value of $1,000 in one year at 9 percent is:

$1,000/1.09 = $917.43

Therefore, the total present value is:

$1,683.36 + 917.43 = $2,600.79

To see why $2,600.79 is the right answer, we can check to see that after the $2,000 is paid out in two years, there is no money left. If we invest $2,600.79 for one year at 9 percent, we will have:

$2,600.79 × 1.09 = $2,834.86

We take out $1,000, leaving $1,834.86. This amount earns 9 percent for another year, leaving us with:

$1,834.86 × 1.09 = $2,000

This is just as we planned. As this example illustrates, the present value of a series of future cash flows is the amount you would need today to exactly duplicate those future cash flows (for a given discount rate).

An alternative way of calculating present values for multiple future cash flows is to discount back to the present, one period at a time. To illustrate, suppose we had an investment that was going to pay $1,000 at the end of every year for the next five years. To find the present value, we could discount each $1,000 back to the present separately and then add them up. Figure 6.5 illustrates this approach for a 6 percent discount rate; as shown, the answer is $4,212.37 (ignoring a small rounding error).

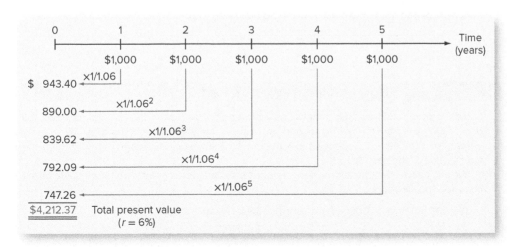

FIGURE 6.5

Present Value Calculated by Discounting Each Cash Flow Separately

FIGURE 6.6 **Present Value Calculated by Discounting Back One Period at a Time**

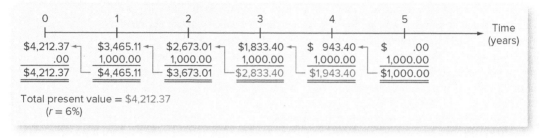

Alternatively, we could discount the last cash flow back one period and add it to the next-to-the-last cash flow:

$$(\$1,000/1.06) + 1,000 = \$943.40 + 1,000 = \$1,943.40$$

We could then discount this amount back one period and add it to the Year 3 cash flow:

$$(\$1,943.40/1.06) + 1,000 = \$1,833.40 + 1,000 = \$2,833.40$$

This process could be repeated as necessary. Figure 6.6 illustrates this approach and the remaining calculations.

EXAMPLE 6.3	How Much Is It Worth?

You are offered an investment that will pay you $200 in one year, $400 the next year, $600 the next year, and $800 at the end of the fourth year. You can earn 12 percent on very similar investments. What is the most you should pay for this one?

We need to calculate the present value of these cash flows at 12 percent. Taking them one at a time gives:

$$
\begin{aligned}
\$200 \times 1/1.12^1 &= \$200/1.1200 = \$\ \ 178.57 \\
\$400 \times 1/1.12^2 &= \$400/1.2544 = \ \ \ 318.88 \\
\$600 \times 1/1.12^3 &= \$600/1.4049 = \ \ \ 427.07 \\
+\$800 \times 1/1.12^4 &= \$800/1.5735 = \ \ \underline{508.41} \\
&\text{Total present value} = \underline{\underline{\$1,432.93}}
\end{aligned}
$$

If you can earn 12 percent on your money, then you can duplicate this investment's cash flows for $1,432.93, so this is the most you should be willing to pay.

EXAMPLE 6.4	How Much Is It Worth? Part 2

You are offered an investment that will make three $5,000 payments. The first payment will occur four years from today. The second will occur in five years, and the third will follow in six years. If you can earn 11 percent, what is the most this investment is worth today? What is the future value of the cash flows?

We will answer the questions in reverse order to illustrate a point. The future value of the cash flows in six years is:

$$(\$5,000 \times 1.11^2) + (5,000 \times 1.11) + 5,000 = \$6,160.50 + 5,550 + 5,000$$
$$= \$16,710.50$$

The present value must be:

$16,710.50/1.11^6 = \$8,934.12$

Let's check this. Taking them one at a time, the PVs of the cash flows are:

$$\$5,000 \times 1/1.11^6 = \$5,000/1.8704 = \$2,673.20$$
$$\$5,000 \times 1/1.11^5 = \$5,000/1.6851 = \ \ 2,967.26$$
$$+\$5,000 \times 1/1.11^4 = \$5,000/1.5181 = \ \underline{\ 3,293.65}$$
$$\text{Total present value} = \underline{\$8,934.12}$$

This is as we previously calculated. The point we want to make is that we can calculate present and future values in any order and convert between them using whatever way seems most convenient. The answers will always be the same as long as we stick with the same discount rate and are careful to keep track of the right number of periods.

CALCULATOR HINTS

How to Calculate Present Values with Multiple Future Cash Flows Using a Financial Calculator

To calculate the present value of multiple cash flows with a financial calculator, we will discount the individual cash flows one at a time using the same technique we used in our previous chapter, so this is not really new. However, we can show you a shortcut. We will use the numbers in Example 6.3 to illustrate.

To begin, of course, we first remember to clear out the calculator! Next, from Example 6.3, the first cash flow is $200 to be received in one year and the discount rate is 12 percent, so we do the following:

Enter | 1 | 12 | | | 200
| N | I/Y | PMT | PV | FV

Solve for − 178.57

Now, you can write down this answer to save it, but that's inefficient. All calculators have a memory where you can store numbers. Why not just save it there? Doing so cuts down on mistakes because you don't have to write down and/or rekey numbers, and it's much faster.

Next, we value the second cash flow. We need to change N to 2 and FV to 400. As long as we haven't changed anything else, we don't have to reenter I/Y or clear out the calculator, so we have:

Enter | 2 | | | | 400
| N | I/Y | PMT | PV | FV

Solve for − 318.88

You save this number by adding it to the one you saved in your first calculation, and so on for the remaining two calculations.

As we will see in a later chapter, some financial calculators will let you enter all of the future cash flows at once, but we'll discuss that subject when we get to it.

SPREADSHEET STRATEGIES

How to Calculate Present Values with Multiple Future Cash Flows Using a Spreadsheet

Just as we did in our previous chapter, we can set up a basic spreadsheet to calculate the present values of the individual cash flows as follows. Notice that we have calculated the present values one at a time and added them up:

	A	B	C	D	E
1					
2			Using a spreadsheet to value multiple future cash flows		
3					
4	What is the present value of $200 in one year, $400 the next year, $600 the next year, and				
5	$800 the last year if the discount rate is 12 percent?				
6					
7	Rate:	.12			
8					
9	Year	Cash flows	Present values	Formula used	
10	1	$200	$178.57	=PV($B$7,A10,0,−B10)	
11	2	$400	$318.88	=PV($B$7,A11,0,−B11)	
12	3	$600	$427.07	=PV($B$7,A12,0,−B12)	
13	4	$800	$508.41	=PV($B$7,A13,0,−B13)	
14					
15		Total PV:	$1,432.93	=SUM(C10:C13)	
16					
17	Notice the negative signs inserted in the PV formulas. These just make the present values have				
18	positive signs. Also, the discount rate in cell B7 is entered as $B$7 (an "absolute" reference)				
19	because it is used over and over. We could have just entered ".12" instead, but our approach is				
20	more flexible.				
21					
22					

SOURCE: Microsoft Excel

A NOTE ABOUT CASH FLOW TIMING

In working present and future value problems, cash flow timing is critically important. In almost all such calculations, it is implicitly assumed that the cash flows occur at the *end* of each period. In fact, all the formulas we have discussed, all the numbers in a standard present value or future value table, and (very important) all the preset (or default) settings on a financial calculator assume that cash flows occur at the end of each period. Unless you are explicitly told otherwise, you should always assume that this is what is meant.

As a quick illustration of this point, suppose you are told that a three-year investment has a first-year cash flow of $100, a second-year cash flow of $200, and a third-year cash flow of $300. You are asked to draw a time line. Without further information, you should always assume that the time line looks like this:

On our time line, notice how the first cash flow occurs at the end of the first period, the second at the end of the second period, and the third at the end of the third period.

We will close this section by answering the question we posed at the beginning of the chapter concerning quarterback Andrew Luck's contract. Recall that the contract called for a $6.4 million signing bonus and $12 million in salary in 2016. The remaining $120.725 million was to be paid as $19.4 million in 2017, $24.4 million in 2018, $27.525 million

This approach works just fine. However, we will often encounter situations in which the number of cash flows is quite large. For example, a typical home mortgage calls for monthly payments over 30 years, for a total of 360 payments. If we were trying to determine the present value of those payments, it would be useful to have a shortcut.

Because the cash flows of an annuity are all the same, we can come up with a handy variation on the basic present value equation. The present value of an annuity of C dollars per period for t periods when the rate of return or interest rate is r is given by:

$$\textbf{Annuity present value} = C \times \left(\frac{\textbf{1 - Present value factor}}{r}\right)$$

$$= C \times \left\{\frac{\textbf{1} - [\textbf{1}/(\textbf{1} + r)^t]}{r}\right\}$$

6.1

The term in parentheses on the first line is sometimes called the *present value interest factor for annuities* and abbreviated PVIFA(r, t).

The expression for the annuity present value may look a little complicated, but it isn't difficult to use. Notice that the term in square brackets on the second line, $1/(1 + r)^t$, is the same present value factor we've been calculating. In our example from the beginning of this section, the interest rate is 10 percent and there are three years involved. The usual present value factor is:

Present value factor $= 1/1.1^3 = 1/1.331 = .751315$

To calculate the annuity present value factor, we just plug this in:

Annuity present value factor $= (1 - \text{Present value factor})/r$

$$= (1 - .751315)/.10$$

$$= .248685/.10 = 2.48685$$

As we calculated before, the present value of our $500 annuity is therefore:

Annuity present value $= \$500 \times 2.48685 = \$1,243.43$

EXAMPLE 6.5	**How Much Can You Afford?**

After carefully going over your budget, you have determined you can afford to pay $632 per month toward a new sports car. You call your local bank and find out that the going rate is 1 percent per month for 48 months. How much can you borrow?

To determine how much you can borrow, we need to calculate the present value of $632 per month for 48 months at 1 percent per month. The loan payments are in ordinary annuity form, so the annuity present value factor is:

Annuity PV factor $= (1 - \text{Present value factor})/r$

$$= [1 - (1/1.01^{48})]/.01$$

$$= (1 - .6203)/.01 = 37.9740$$

With this factor, we can calculate the present value of the 48 payments of $632 each as:

Present value $= \$632 \times 37.9740 = \$24,000$

Therefore, $24,000 is what you can afford to borrow and repay.

Annuity Tables   Just as there are tables for ordinary present value factors, there are tables for annuity factors as well. Table 6.1 contains a few such factors; Table A.3 in the appendix to the book contains a larger set. To find the annuity present value factor we calculated just before Example 6.5, look for the row corresponding to three periods and then find the column for 10 percent. The number you see at that intersection should be 2.4869 (rounded to four decimal places), as we calculated. Once again, try calculating a few of

	Interest Rate			
Number of Periods	**5%**	**10%**	**15%**	**20%**
1	.9524	.9091	.8696	.8333
2	1.8594	1.7355	1.6257	1.5278
3	2.7232	2.4869	2.2832	2.1065
4	3.5460	3.1699	2.8550	2.5887
5	4.3295	3.7908	3.3522	2.9906

TABLE 6.1

Annuity Present Value Interest Factors

these factors yourself and compare your answers to the ones in the table to make sure you know how to do it. If you are using a financial calculator, just enter $1 as the payment and calculate the present value; the result should be the annuity present value factor.

CALCULATOR HINTS

Annuity Present Values

To find annuity present values with a financial calculator, we need to use the **PMT** key (you were probably wondering what it was for). Compared to finding the present value of a single amount, there are two important differences. First, we enter the annuity cash flow using the **PMT** key. Second, we don't enter anything for the future value, **FV**. So, for example, the problem we have been examining is a three-year, $500 annuity. If the discount rate is 10 percent, we need to do the following (after clearing out the calculator!):

Enter	3	10	500		
	N	**I/Y**	**PMT**	**PV**	**FV**
Solve for				−1,243.43	

As usual, we get a negative sign on the PV.

SPREADSHEET STRATEGIES

Annuity Present Values

Using a spreadsheet to find annuity present values goes like this:

	A	B	C	D	E	F	G
1							
2	**Using a spreadsheet to find annuity present values**						
3							
4	What is the present value of $500 per year for three years if the discount rate is 10 percent?						
5	We need to solve for the unknown present value, so we use the formula PV(rate,nper,pmt,fv).						
6							
7	Payment amount per period:	$500					
8	Number of payments:	3					
9	Discount rate:	.1					
10							
11	Annuity present value:	$1,243.43					
12							
13	The formula entered in cell B11 is =PV(B9,B8,-B7,0); notice that fv is zero and that						
14	pmt has a negative sign on it. Also notice that rate is entered as a decimal, not a percentage.						
15							
16							
17							

SOURCE: Microsoft Excel

Finding the Payment Suppose you wish to start up a new business that specializes in the latest of health food trends, frozen yak milk. To produce and market your product, the Yakkee Doodle Dandy, you need to borrow $100,000. Because it strikes you as unlikely that this particular fad will be long-lived, you propose to pay off the loan quickly by making five equal annual payments. If the interest rate is 18 percent, what will the payment be?

In this case, we know the present value is $100,000. The interest rate is 18 percent, and there are five years. The payments are all equal, so we need to find the relevant annuity factor and solve for the unknown cash flow:

$$\text{Annuity present value} = \$100,000 = C \times [(1 - \text{Present value factor})/r]$$
$$= C \times \{[1 - (1/1.18^5)]/.18\}$$
$$= C \times [(1 - .4371)/.18]$$
$$= C \times 3.1272$$
$$C = \$100,000/3.1272 = \$31,977.78$$

Therefore, you'll make five payments of just under $32,000 each.

CALCULATOR HINTS

Annuity Payments

Finding annuity payments is easy with a financial calculator. In our yak milk example, the PV is $100,000, the interest rate is 18 percent, and there are five years. We find the payment as follows:

Enter	5	18		100,000	
	N	**I/Y**	**PMT**	**PV**	**FV**
Solve for			−31,977.78		

Here, we get a negative sign on the payment because the payment is an outflow for us.

SPREADSHEET STRATEGIES

Annuity Payments

Using a spreadsheet to work the same problem goes like this:

	A	B	C	D	E	F	G
1							
2		Using a spreadsheet to find annuity payments					
3							
4	What is the annuity payment if the present value is $100,000, the interest rate is 18 percent, and						
5	there are five periods? We need to solve for the unknown payment in an annuity, so we use the						
6	formula PMT(rate,nper,pv,fv).						
7							
8	Annuity present value:	$100,000					
9	Number of payments:	5					
10	Discount rate:	.18					
11							
12	Annuity payment:	-$31,977.78					
13							
14	The formula entered in cell B12 is =PMT(B10,B9,B8,0); notice that fv is zero and that the payment						
15	has a negative sign because it is an outflow for us.						
16							

SOURCE: Microsoft Excel

Finding the Number of Payments	**EXAMPLE 6.6**

You ran a little short on your spring break vacation, so you put $1,000 on your credit card. You can afford only the minimum payment of $20 per month. The interest rate on the credit card is 1.5 percent per month. How long will you need to pay off the $1,000?

What we have here is an annuity of $20 per month at 1.5 percent per month for some unknown length of time. The present value is $1,000 (the amount you owe today). We need to do a little algebra (or use a financial calculator):

$$\$1,000 = \$20 \times [(1 - \text{Present value factor})/.015]$$
$$(\$1,000/20) \times .015 = 1 - \text{Present value factor}$$
$$\text{Present value factor} = .25 = 1/(1 + r)^t$$
$$1.015^t = 1/.25 = 4$$

At this point, the problem boils down to asking: How long does it take for your money to quadruple at 1.5 percent per month? Based on our previous chapter, the answer is about 93 months:

$$1.015^{93} = 3.99 \approx 4$$

It will take you about 93/12 = 7.75 years to pay off the $1,000 at this rate. If you use a financial calculator for problems like this, you should be aware that some automatically round up to the next whole period.

CALCULATOR HINTS

Finding the Number of Payments

To solve Example 6.6 on a financial calculator, do the following:

Enter		1.5	−20	1,000	
	N	**I/Y**	**PMT**	**PV**	**FV**
Solve for	93.11				

Notice that we put a negative sign on the payment you must make, and we have solved for the number of months. You still have to divide by 12 to get our answer. Also, some financial calculators won't report a fractional value for N; they automatically (without telling you) round up to the next whole period (not to the nearest value). With a spreadsheet, use the function =NPER(rate,pmt,pv,fv); be sure to put in a zero for fv and to enter −20 as the payment.

Finding the Rate   The last question we might want to ask concerns the interest rate implicit in an annuity. For example, an insurance company offers to pay you $1,000 per year for 10 years if you will pay $6,710 up front. What rate is implicit in this 10-year annuity?

In this case, we know the present value ($6,710), we know the cash flows ($1,000 per year), and we know the life of the investment (10 years). What we don't know is the discount rate:

$$\$6,710 = \$1,000 \times [(1 - \text{Present value factor})/r]$$
$$\$6,710/\$1,000 = 6.71 = \{1 - [1/(1 + r)^{10}]\}/r$$

So, the annuity factor for 10 periods is equal to 6.71, and we need to solve this equation for the unknown value of r. Unfortunately, this is mathematically impossible to do directly. The only way to do it is to use a table or trial and error to find a value for r.

If you look across the row corresponding to 10 periods in Table A.3, you will see a factor of 6.7101 for 8 percent, so we see right away that the insurance company is offering just about 8 percent. Alternatively, we could start trying different values until we got very close to the answer. Using this trial-and-error approach can be a little tedious, but fortunately machines are good at that sort of thing.[1]

To illustrate how to find the answer by trial and error, suppose a relative of yours wants to borrow $3,000. She offers to repay you $1,000 every year for four years. What interest rate are you being offered?

The cash flows here have the form of a four-year, $1,000 annuity. The present value is $3,000. We need to find the discount rate, r. Our goal in doing so is primarily to give you a feel for the relationship between annuity values and discount rates.

We need to start somewhere, and 10 percent is probably as good a place as any to begin. At 10 percent, the annuity factor is:

Annuity present value factor $= [1 - (1/1.10^4)]/.10 = 3.1699$

The present value of the cash flows at 10 percent is thus:

Present value $= \$1,000 \times 3.1699 = \$3,169.90$

You can see that we're already in the right ballpark.

Is 10 percent too high or too low? Recall that present values and discount rates move in opposite directions: Increasing the discount rate lowers the PV and vice versa. Our present value here is too high, so the discount rate is too low. If we try 12 percent, we're almost there:

Present value $= \$1,000 \times \{[1 - (1/1.12^4)]/.12\} = \$3,037.35$

We are still a little low on the discount rate (because the PV is a little high), so we'll try 13 percent:

Present value $= \$1,000 \times \{[1 - (1/1.13^4)]/.13\} = \$2,974.47$

This is less than $3,000, so we now know that the answer is between 12 percent and 13 percent, and it looks to be about 12.5 percent. For practice, work at it for a while longer and see if you find that the answer is about 12.59 percent.

CALCULATOR HINTS

Finding the Rate

Alternatively, you could use a financial calculator to do the following:

Enter	4		1,000	−3,000	
	N	**I/Y**	**PMT**	**PV**	**FV**
Solve for		12.59			

Notice that we put a negative sign on the present value (why?). With a spreadsheet, use the function =RATE(nper,pmt,pv,fv); be sure to put in a zero for fv and to enter 1,000 as the payment and −3,000 as the pv.

To illustrate a situation in which finding the unknown rate can be useful, let us consider that the Tri-State Megabucks lottery in Maine, Vermont, and New Hampshire offers you a choice of how to take your winnings (most lotteries do this). In a recent drawing, participants were offered the option of receiving a lump sum payment of $250,000 or an annuity

---

[1] Financial calculators rely on trial and error to find the answer. That's why they sometimes appear to be "thinking" before coming up with the answer. Actually, it is possible to directly solve for r if there are fewer than five periods, but it's usually not worth the trouble.

of $500,000 to be received in equal installments over a 25-year period. (At the time, the lump sum payment was always half the annuity option.) Which option was better?

To answer, suppose you were to compare $250,000 today to an annuity of $500,000/25 = $20,000 per year for 25 years. At what rate do these have the same value? This is the same type of problem we've been looking at; we need to find the unknown rate, r, for a present value of $250,000, a $20,000 payment, and a 25-year period. If you grind through the calculations (or get a little machine assistance), you should find that the unknown rate is about 6.24 percent. You should take the annuity option if that rate is attractive relative to other investments available to you. Notice that we have ignored taxes in this example, and taxes can significantly affect our conclusion. Be sure to consult your tax adviser anytime you win the lottery.

In another example, in early 2014, Warren Buffett and Dan Gilbert, founder of Quicken Loans, teamed up to offer $1 billion to anyone who could correctly predict a perfect NCAA March Madness bracket. The odds of winning: 1 in 9.2 quintillion! Of course, you wouldn't receive the $1 billion today, but rather $25 million per year for 40 years, or a lump sum of $500 million. See if you don't agree that the rate of return on this arrangement is 3.93 percent. Unfortunately, this was a one-time event, as legal and financial disagreements squashed the challenge.

FUTURE VALUE FOR ANNUITIES

On occasion, it's also handy to know a shortcut for calculating the future value of an annuity. As you might guess, there are future value factors for annuities as well as present value factors. In general, here is the future value factor for an annuity:

Annuity FV factor = (Future value factor − 1)/r   **6.2**
$$= [(1 + r)^t − 1]/r$$

To see how we use annuity future value factors, suppose you plan to contribute $2,000 every year to a retirement account paying 8 percent. If you retire in 30 years, how much will you have?

The number of years here, t, is 30, and the interest rate, r, is 8 percent; so we can calculate the annuity future value factor as:

Annuity FV factor = (Future value factor − 1)/r

$$= (1.08^{30} − 1)/.08$$
$$= (10.0627 − 1)/.08$$
$$= 113.2832$$

The future value of this 30-year, $2,000 annuity is thus:

Annuity future value = $2,000 × 113.28
$$= \$226,566.42$$

CALCULATOR HINTS

Future Values of Annuities

Of course, you could solve this problem using a financial calculator by doing the following:

Enter	30	8	−2,000		
	N	**I/Y**	**PMT**	**PV**	**FV**
Solve for					226,566.42

Notice that we put a negative sign on the payment (why?). With a spreadsheet, use the function =FV(rate,nper, pmt,pv); be sure to put in a zero for pv and to enter −2,000 as the payment.

Sometimes we need to find the unknown rate, r, in the context of an annuity future value. For example, if you had invested $100 per month in stocks over the 25-year period ended December 1978, your investment would have grown to $76,374. This period had the *worst* stretch of stock returns of any 25-year period between 1925 and 2016. How bad was it?

Here we have the cash flows ($100 per month), the *future* value ($76,374), and the time period (25 years, or 300 months). We need to find the implicit rate, r:

$76,374 = $100 \times [(\text{Future value factor} - 1)/r]$
$763.74 = [(1 + r)^{300} - 1]/r$

Because this is the worst period, let's try 1 percent:

Annuity future value factor $= (1.01^{300} - 1)/.01 = 1,878.85$

We see that 1 percent is too high. From here, it's trial and error. See if you agree that r is about .55 percent per month. As you will see later in the chapter, this works out to be about 6.8 percent per year.

A NOTE ABOUT ANNUITIES DUE

So far we have only discussed ordinary annuities. These are the most important, but there is a fairly common variation. Remember that with an ordinary annuity, the cash flows occur at the end of each period. When you take out a loan with monthly payments, for example, the first loan payment normally occurs one month after you get the loan. However, when you lease an apartment, the first lease payment is usually due immediately. The second payment is due at the beginning of the second month, and so on. A lease is an example of an **annuity due**. An annuity due is an annuity for which the cash flows occur at the beginning of each period. Almost any type of arrangement in which we have to prepay the same amount each period is an annuity due.

There are several different ways to calculate the value of an annuity due. With a financial calculator, you switch it into "due" or "beginning" mode. (Remember to switch it back when you are done!) Another way to calculate the present value of an annuity due can be illustrated with a time line. Suppose an annuity due has five payments of $400 each, and the relevant discount rate is 10 percent. The time line looks like this:

0	1	2	3	4	5
$400	$400	$400	$400	$400	

Notice how the cash flows here are the same as those for a *four*-year ordinary annuity, except that there is an extra $400 at Time 0. For practice, check to see that the value of a four-year ordinary annuity at 10 percent is $1,267.95. If we add on the extra $400, we get $1,667.95, which is the present value of this annuity due.

There is an even easier way to calculate the present or future value of an annuity due. If we assume cash flows occur at the end of each period when they really occur at the beginning, then we discount each one by one period too many. We could fix this by multiplying our answer by $(1 + r)$, where r is the discount rate. In fact, the relationship between the value of an annuity due and an ordinary annuity is:

Annuity due value = Ordinary annuity value $\times$ (1 + r)   [6.3]

This works for both present and future values, so calculating the value of an annuity due involves two steps: (1) Calculate the present or future value as though it were an ordinary annuity and (2) multiply your answer by $(1 + r)$.

annuity due
An annuity for which the cash flows occur at the beginning of the period.

Time value applications abound on the web. See, for example, **www .collegeboard.org** and **personal.fidelity.com**.

I.	**Symbols:**	

PV = Present value, what future cash flows are worth today

FV$_t$ = Future value, what cash flows are worth in the future

r = Interest rate, rate of return, or discount rate per period—typically, but not always, one year

t = Number of periods—typically, but not always, the number of years

C = Cash amount

II.	**Future Value of C per Period for t Periods at r Percent per Period:**

FV$_t$ = C × [[(1 + r)^t − 1]/r]

A series of identical cash flows is called an *annuity*, and the term [(1 + r)^t − 1]/r is called the *annuity future value factor.*

III.	**Present Value of C per Period for t Periods at r Percent per Period:**

PV = C × {1 − [1/(1 + r)^t]}/r

The term {1 − [1/(1 + r)^t]}/r is called the *annuity present value factor.*

IV.	**Present Value of a Perpetuity of C per Period:**

PV = C/r

A *perpetuity* has the same cash flow every year forever.

TABLE 6.2

Summary of Annuity and Perpetuity Calculations

PERPETUITIES

We've seen that a series of level cash flows can be valued by treating those cash flows as an annuity. An important special case of an annuity arises when the level stream of cash flows continues forever. Such an asset is called a **perpetuity** because the cash flows are perpetual. Perpetuities are also called **consols**, particularly in Canada and the United Kingdom. See Example 6.7 for an important example of a perpetuity.

Because a perpetuity has an infinite number of cash flows, we obviously can't compute its value by discounting each one. Fortunately, valuing a perpetuity turns out to be the easiest possible case. The present value of a perpetuity is:

perpetuity
An annuity in which the cash flows continue forever.

consol
A type of perpetuity.

PV for a perpetuity = C/r

For example, an investment offers a perpetual cash flow of $500 every year. The return you require on such an investment is 8 percent. What is the value of this investment? The value of this perpetuity is:

Perpetuity PV = C/r = $500/.08 = $6,250

For future reference, Table 6.2 contains a summary of the annuity and perpetuity basic calculations we have described in this section. By now, you probably think that you'll just use online calculators to handle annuity problems. Before you do, see our nearby *Work the Web* box!

Preferred Stock	**EXAMPLE 6.7**

Preferred stock (or preference stock) is an important example of a perpetuity. When a corporation sells preferred stock, the buyer is promised a fixed cash dividend every period (usually every quarter) forever. This dividend must be paid before any dividend can be paid to regular stockholders—hence the term *preferred*.

Suppose the Fellini Co. wants to sell preferred stock at $100 per share. A similar issue of preferred stock already outstanding has a price of $40 per share and offers a dividend of $1 every quarter. What dividend will Fellini have to offer if the preferred stock is going to sell?

166　　　　**PART 3**　Valuation of Future Cash Flows

The issue that is already out has a present value of $40 and a cash flow of $1 every quarter forever. Because this is a perpetuity:

Present value = $40 = $1 × (1/$r$)

$$r = .025, \text{ or } 2.5\%$$

To be competitive, the new Fellini issue will also have to offer 2.5 percent *per quarter*; so if the present value is to be $100, the dividend must be such that:

Present value = $100 = C × (1/.025)

$$C = \$2.50 \text{ (per quarter)}$$

WORK THE WEB

As we discussed in our previous chapter, many websites have financial calculators. One of these sites is Calculatoredge, which is located at www.calculatoredge.com. Suppose you retire with $1,750,000 and want to withdraw an equal amount each year for the next 30 years. If you can earn a 7 percent return, how much can you withdraw each year? Here is what Calculatoredge says:

Enter your values:

Currency:	US Dollars ▾
Starting Principal	1750000　**US Dollars**
Annual Interest Rate:	7　**%**
Repayment Period:	30　**Years**

[Calculate]　　[Clear]

Results:

Annuity Payment: 131800.19　**US Dollars / Year**

According to the Calculatoredge calculator, the answer is $131,800.19. How important is it to understand what you are doing? Calculate this one for yourself, and you should get $141,026.21. Who is right? You are, of course! What's going on is that Calculatoredge assumes (but does not tell you) that the annuity is in the form of an annuity due, not an ordinary annuity. Recall that with an annuity due, the payments occur at the beginning of the period rather than the end of the period. The moral of the story is clear: *Caveat calculator.*

Questions

1. Go to the calculator at www.calculatoredge.com and find out how much the website says you could withdraw each year if you have $2,500,000, earn an 8 percent interest rate, and make annual withdrawals for 35 years. How much more are the withdrawals if they are in the form of an ordinary annuity?

2. Suppose you have $500,000 and want to make withdrawals each month for the next 10 years. The first withdrawal is today and the appropriate interest rate is 9 percent compounded monthly. Using the calculator at this website, how much are your withdrawals?

GROWING ANNUITIES AND PERPETUITIES

Annuities commonly have payments that grow over time. Suppose, for example, that we are looking at a lottery payout over a 20-year period. The first payment, made one year from now, will be $200,000. Every year thereafter, the payment will grow by 5 percent, so the payment in the second year will be $200,000 × 1.05 = $210,000. The payment in the third year will be $210,000 × 1.05 = $220,500, and so on. What's the present value if the appropriate discount rate is 11 percent?

If we use the symbol g to represent the growth rate, we can calculate the value of a growing annuity using a modified version of our regular annuity formula:

$$\text{Growing annuity present value} = C \times \left[\frac{1 - \left(\frac{1+g}{1+r} \right)^t}{r - g} \right]$$

 6.5

Plugging in the numbers from our lottery example (and letting $g = .05$), we get:

$$\text{PV} = \$200,000 \times \left[\frac{1 - \left(\frac{1 + .05}{1 + .11} \right)^{20}}{.11 - .05} \right] = \$200,000 \times 11.18169 = \$2,236,337.06$$

There is also a formula for the present value of a growing perpetuity:

$$\text{Growing perpetuity present value} = C \times \left[\frac{1}{r - g} \right] = \frac{C}{r - g}$$

 6.6

Returning to our lottery example, now suppose the payments continue forever. In this case, the present value is:

$$\text{PV} = \$200,000 \times \frac{1}{.11 - .05} = \$200,000 \times 16.6667 = \$3,333,333.33$$

The notion of a growing perpetuity may seem a little odd because the payments get bigger every period forever; but, as we will see in a later chapter, growing perpetuities play a key role in our analysis of stock prices.

Before we go on, there is one important item to note in regard to our formulas for growing annuities and perpetuities. In both cases, the cash flow in the formula, C, is the cash flow that is going to occur exactly one period from today.

Concept Questions

6.2a   In general, what is the present value of an annuity of C dollars per period at a discount rate of r per period? The future value?

6.2b   In general, what is the present value of a perpetuity?

Comparing Rates: The Effect of Compounding   6.3

The next issue we need to discuss has to do with the way interest rates are quoted. This subject causes a fair amount of confusion because rates are quoted in many different ways. Sometimes the way a rate is quoted is the result of tradition, and sometimes it's the result of legislation. Unfortunately, at times, rates are quoted in deliberately deceptive ways to mislead borrowers and investors. We will discuss these topics in this section.

Excel Master It!
 Excel Master
coverage online

EFFECTIVE ANNUAL RATES AND COMPOUNDING

If a rate is quoted as 10 percent compounded semiannually, this means the investment actually pays 5 percent every six months. A natural question then arises: Is 5 percent every six months the same thing as 10 percent per year? It's easy to see that it is not. If you invest $1 at 10 percent per year, you will have $1.10 at the end of the year. If you invest at 5 percent every six months, then you'll have the future value of $1 at 5 percent for two periods:

$$\$1 \times 1.05^2 = \$1.1025$$

This is $.0025 more. The reason is simple: Your account was credited with $1 × .05 = 5 cents in interest after six months. In the following six months, you earned 5 percent on that nickel, for an extra 5 × .05 = .25 cents.

As our example illustrates, 10 percent compounded semiannually is actually equivalent to 10.25 percent per year. Put another way, we would be indifferent between 10 percent compounded semiannually and 10.25 percent compounded annually. Anytime we have compounding during the year, we need to be concerned about what the rate really is.

In our example, the 10 percent is called a **stated**, or **quoted**, **interest rate**. Other names are used as well. The 10.25 percent, which is actually the rate you will earn, is called the **effective annual rate (EAR)**. To compare different investments or interest rates, we will always need to convert to effective rates. Some general procedures for doing this are discussed next.

CALCULATING AND COMPARING EFFECTIVE ANNUAL RATES

To see why it is important to work only with effective rates, suppose you've shopped around and come up with the following three rates:

    Bank A: 15 percent compounded daily
    Bank B: 15.5 percent compounded quarterly
    Bank C: 16 percent compounded annually

Which of these is the best if you are thinking of opening a savings account? Which of these is best if they represent loan rates?

To begin, Bank C is offering 16 percent per year. Because there is no compounding during the year, this is the effective rate. Bank B is actually paying .155/4 = .03875 or 3.875 percent per quarter. At this rate, an investment of $1 for four quarters would grow to:

$$\$1 \times 1.03875^4 = \$1.1642$$

The EAR, therefore, is 16.42 percent. For a saver, this is much better than the 16 percent rate Bank C is offering; for a borrower, it's worse.

Bank A is compounding every day. This may seem a little extreme, but it is common to calculate interest daily. In this case, the daily interest rate is actually:

$$.15/365 = .000411$$

This is .0411 percent per day. At this rate, an investment of $1 for 365 periods would grow to:

$$\$1 \times 1.000411^{365} = \$1.1618$$

The EAR is 16.18 percent. This is not as good as Bank B's 16.42 percent for a saver, and not as good as Bank C's 16 percent for a borrower.

This example illustrates two things. First, the highest quoted rate is not necessarily the best. Second, compounding during the year can lead to a significant difference between the quoted rate and the effective rate. Remember that the effective rate is what you actually get or what you pay.

stated interest rate
The interest rate expressed in terms of the interest payment made each period. Also known as the *quoted interest rate*.

effective annual rate (EAR)
The interest rate expressed as if it were compounded once per year.

If you look at our examples, you see that we computed the EARs in three steps. We first divided the quoted rate by the number of times that the interest is compounded. We then added 1 to the result and raised it to the power of the number of times the interest is compounded. Finally, we subtracted the 1. If we let m be the number of times the interest is compounded during the year, these steps can be summarized as:

EAR = [1 + (Quoted rate/m)]^m − 1   6.7

For example, suppose you are offered 12 percent compounded monthly. In this case, the interest is compounded 12 times a year; so m is 12. You can calculate the effective rate as:

$$
\begin{aligned}
\text{EAR} &= [1 + (\text{Quoted rate}/m)]^m - 1 \\
&= [1 + (.12/12)]^{12} - 1 \\
&= 1.01^{12} - 1 \\
&= 1.126825 - 1 \\
&= .126825, \text{ or } 12.6825\%
\end{aligned}
$$

What's the EAR?	**EXAMPLE 6.8**

A bank is offering 12 percent compounded quarterly. If you put $100 in an account, how much will you have at the end of one year? What's the EAR? How much will you have at the end of two years?

The bank is effectively offering 12%/4 = 3% every quarter. If you invest $100 for four periods at 3 percent per period, the future value is:

$$
\begin{aligned}
\text{Future value} &= \$100 \times 1.03^4 \\
&= \$100 \times 1.1255 \\
&= \$112.55
\end{aligned}
$$

The EAR is 12.55 percent: $100 × (1 + .1255) = $112.55.

We can determine what you would have at the end of two years in two different ways. One way is to recognize that two years is the same as eight quarters. At 3 percent per quarter, after eight quarters, you would have:

$100 × 1.03^8 = $100 × 1.2668 = $126.68

Alternatively, we could determine the value after two years by using an EAR of 12.55 percent; so after two years you would have:

$100 × 1.1255^2 = $100 × 1.2668 = $126.68

Thus, the two calculations produce the same answer. This illustrates an important point. Anytime we do a present or future value calculation, the rate we use must be an actual or effective rate. In this case, the actual rate is 3 percent per quarter. The effective annual rate is 12.55 percent. It doesn't matter which one we use once we know the EAR.

Quoting a Rate	**EXAMPLE 6.9**

Now that you know how to convert a quoted rate to an EAR, consider going the other way. As a lender, you know you want to actually earn 18 percent on a particular loan. You want to quote a rate that features monthly compounding. What rate do you quote?

In this case, we know the EAR is 18 percent, and we know this is the result of monthly compounding. Let q stand for the quoted rate. We have:

$$EAR = [1 + (Quoted\ rate/m)]^m - 1$$
$$.18 = [1 + (q/12)]^{12} - 1$$
$$1.18 = [1 + (q/12)]^{12}$$

We need to solve this equation for the quoted rate. This calculation is the same as the ones we did to find an unknown interest rate in Chapter 5:

$$1.18^{(1/12)} = 1 + (q/12)$$
$$1.18^{.08333} = 1 + (q/12)$$
$$1.0139 = 1 + (q/12)$$
$$q = .0139 \times 12$$
$$= .1667, or\ 16.67\%$$

Therefore, the rate you would quote is 16.67 percent, compounded monthly.

EARs AND APRs

annual percentage rate (APR)

The interest rate charged per period multiplied by the number of periods per year.

Sometimes it's not altogether clear whether a rate is an effective annual rate. A case in point concerns what is called the **annual percentage rate (APR)** on a loan. Truth-in-lending laws in the United States require that lenders disclose an APR on virtually all consumer loans. This rate must be displayed on a loan document in a prominent and unambiguous way.[2]

Given that an APR must be calculated and displayed, an obvious question arises: Is an APR an effective annual rate? Put another way, if a bank quotes a car loan at 12 percent APR, is the consumer actually paying 12 percent interest? Surprisingly, the answer is no. There is some confusion over this point, which we discuss next.

The confusion over APRs arises because lenders are required by law to compute the APR in a particular way. By law, the APR is equal to the interest rate per period multiplied by the number of periods in a year. For example, if a bank is charging 1.2 percent per month on car loans, then the APR that must be reported is $1.2\% \times 12 = 14.4\%$. So, an APR is in fact a quoted, or stated, rate in the sense we've been discussing. For example, an APR of 12 percent on a loan calling for monthly payments is really 1 percent per month. The EAR on such a loan is thus:

$$EAR = [1 + (APR/12)]^{12} - 1$$
$$= 1.01^{12} - 1 = .126825, or\ 12.6825\%$$

---

[2] By law, lenders are required to report the APR on all consumer loans. In this text, we compute the APR as the interest rate per period multiplied by the number of periods in a year. According to federal law, the APR is a measure of the cost of consumer credit expressed as a yearly rate, and it includes interest and certain noninterest charges and fees. In practice, the APR can be much higher than the interest rate on the loan if the lender charges substantial fees that must be included in the federally mandated APR calculation.

EXAMPLE 6.10	**What Rate Are You Paying?**

Depending on the issuer, a typical credit card agreement quotes an interest rate of 18 percent APR. Monthly payments are required. What is the actual interest rate you pay on such a credit card?

Based on our discussion, an APR of 18 percent with monthly payments is really .18/12 = .015 or 1.5 percent per month. The EAR is thus:

$$EAR = [1 + (.18/12)]^{12} - 1$$
$$= 1.015^{12} - 1$$
$$= 1.1956 - 1$$
$$= .1956, \text{ or } 19.56\%$$

This is the rate you actually pay.

It is somewhat ironic that truth-in-lending laws sometimes require lenders to be *un*truthful about the actual rate on a loan. There are also truth-in-savings laws that require banks and other borrowers to quote an "annual percentage yield," or APY, on things like savings accounts. To make things a little confusing, an APY is an EAR. As a result, by law, the rates quoted to borrowers (APRs) and those quoted to savers (APYs) are not computed the same way.

There can be a huge difference between the APR and EAR when interest rates are large. For example, consider "payday loans." Payday loans are short-term loans made to consumers, often for less than two weeks, and are offered by companies such as AmeriCash Advance and National Payday. The loans work like this: You write a check today that is postdated (the date on the check is in the future) and give it to the company. They give you some cash. When the check date arrives, you either go to the store and pay the cash amount of the check, or the company cashes it (or else automatically renews the loan).

For example, in one particular state, Check Into Cash allows you to write a check for $115 dated 14 days in the future, for which you get $100 today. So what are the APR and EAR on this arrangement? First, we need to find the interest rate, which we can find by the FV equation as follows:

$$FV = PV \times (1 + r)^1$$
$$\$115 = \$100 \times (1 + r)^1$$
$$1.15 = (1 + r)$$
$$r = .15, \text{ or } 15\%$$

That doesn't seem too bad until you remember this is the interest rate for *14 days*! The APR of the loan is:

$$APR = .15 \times 365/14$$
$$APR = 3.9107, \text{ or } 391.07\%$$

And the EAR for this loan is:

$$EAR = (1 + \text{Quoted rate}/m)^m - 1$$
$$EAR = (1 + .15)^{365/14} - 1$$
$$EAR = 37.2366, \text{ or } 3{,}723.66\%$$

Now that's an interest rate! Just to see what a difference a small difference in fees can make, Advance America Cash Advance will let you write a check for $117.50 in exchange for the same $100 amount. Check for yourself that the APR of this arrangement is 456.25 percent and the EAR is 6,598.65 percent—not a loan we would like to take out!

TABLE 6.3

Compounding Frequency and Effective Annual Rates

Compounding Period	Number of Times Compounded	Effective Annual Rate
Year	1	10.00000%
Quarter	4	10.38129
Month	12	10.47131
Week	52	10.50648
Day	365	10.51558
Hour	8,760	10.51703
Minute	525,600	10.51709

TAKING IT TO THE LIMIT: A NOTE ABOUT CONTINUOUS COMPOUNDING

If you made a deposit in a savings account, how often could your money be compounded during the year? If you think about it, there isn't really any upper limit. We've seen that daily compounding, for example, isn't a problem. There is no reason to stop here, however. We could compound every hour or minute or second. How high would the EAR get in this case? Table 6.3 illustrates the EARs that result as 10 percent is compounded at shorter and shorter intervals. Notice that the EARs do keep getting larger, but the differences get very small.

As the numbers in Table 6.3 seem to suggest, there is an upper limit to the EAR. If we let q stand for the quoted rate, then, as the number of times the interest is compounded gets extremely large, the EAR approaches:

$$EAR = e^q - 1 \qquad \text{6.8}$$

where e is the number 2.71828 (look for a key labeled "e^x" on your calculator). For example, with our 10 percent rate, the highest possible EAR is:

$$
\begin{aligned}
EAR &= e^q - 1 \\
&= 2.71828^{.10} - 1 \\
&= 1.1051709 - 1 \\
&= .1051709, \text{ or } 10.51709\%
\end{aligned}
$$

In this case, we say that the money is continuously, or instantaneously, compounded. Interest is being credited the instant it is earned, so the amount of interest grows continuously.

EXAMPLE 6.11	**What's the Law?**

At one time, commercial banks and savings and loan associations (S&Ls) were restricted in the interest rates they could offer on savings accounts. Under what was known as Regulation Q, S&Ls were allowed to pay at most 5.5 percent, and banks were not allowed to pay more than 5.25 percent (the idea was to give the S&Ls a competitive advantage; it didn't work). The law did not say how often these rates could be compounded, however. Under Regulation Q, then, what were the maximum allowed interest rates?

The maximum allowed rates occurred with continuous, or instantaneous, compounding. For the commercial banks, 5.25 percent compounded continuously would be:

$$
\begin{aligned}
EAR &= e^{.0525} - 1 \\
&= 2.71828^{.0525} - 1 \\
&= 1.0539026 - 1 \\
&= .0539026, \text{ or } 5.39026\%
\end{aligned}
$$

This is what banks could actually pay. Check for yourself to see that S&Ls could effectively pay 5.65406 percent.

> **Concept Questions**
>
> **6.3a** If an interest rate is given as 12 percent compounded daily, what do we call this rate?
>
> **6.3b** What is an APR? What is an EAR? Are they the same thing?
>
> **6.3c** In general, what is the relationship between a stated interest rate and an effective interest rate? Which is more relevant for financial decisions?
>
> **6.3d** What does continuous compounding mean?

Loan Types and Loan Amortization   6.4

Whenever a lender extends a loan, some provision will be made for repayment of the principal (the original loan amount). A loan might be repaid in equal installments, for example, or it might be repaid in a single lump sum. Because the way that the principal and interest are paid is up to the parties involved, there are actually an unlimited number of possibilities.

Excel Master It!

Excel Master coverage online

In this section, we describe a few forms of repayment that come up quite often, and more complicated forms can usually be built up from these. The three basic types of loans are pure discount loans, interest-only loans, and amortized loans. Working with these loans is a very straightforward application of the present value principles that we have already developed.

PURE DISCOUNT LOANS

The *pure discount loan* is the simplest form of loan. With such a loan, the borrower receives money today and repays a single lump sum at some time in the future. A one-year, 10 percent pure discount loan, for example, would require the borrower to repay $1.10 in one year for every dollar borrowed today.

Because a pure discount loan is so simple, we already know how to value one. Suppose a borrower was able to repay $25,000 in five years. If we, acting as the lender, wanted a 12 percent interest rate on the loan, how much would we be willing to lend? Put another way, what value would we assign today to that $25,000 to be repaid in five years? Based on our work in Chapter 5, we know the answer is the present value of $25,000 at 12 percent for five years:

$$\text{Present value} = \$25,000/1.12^5$$
$$= \$25,000/1.7623$$
$$= \$14,186$$

Pure discount loans are common when the loan term is short—say a year or less. In recent years, they have become increasingly common for much longer periods.

Treasury Bills	**EXAMPLE 6.12**

When the U.S. government borrows money on a short-term basis (a year or less), it does so by selling what are called *Treasury bills*, or *T-bills* for short. A T-bill is a promise by the government to repay a fixed amount at some time in the future—for example, in 3 months or 12 months.

Treasury bills are pure discount loans. If a T-bill promises to repay $10,000 in 12 months, and the market interest rate is 7 percent, how much will the bill sell for in the market?

Because the going rate is 7 percent, the T-bill will sell for the present value of $10,000 to be repaid in one year at 7 percent:

Present value = $10,000/1.07 = $9,345.79

INTEREST-ONLY LOANS

A second type of loan repayment plan calls for the borrower to pay interest each period and to repay the entire principal (the original loan amount) at some point in the future. Loans with such a repayment plan are called *interest-only loans*. Notice that if there is just one period, a pure discount loan and an interest-only loan are the same thing.

For example, with a three-year, 10 percent, interest-only loan of $1,000, the borrower would pay $1,000 × .10 = $100 in interest at the end of the first and second years. At the end of the third year, the borrower would return the $1,000 along with another $100 in interest for that year. Similarly, a 50-year interest-only loan would call for the borrower to pay interest every year for the next 50 years and then repay the principal. In the extreme, the borrower pays the interest every period forever and never repays any principal. As we discussed earlier in the chapter, the result is a perpetuity.

Most corporate bonds have the general form of an interest-only loan. Because we will be considering bonds in some detail in the next chapter, we will defer further discussion of them for now.

AMORTIZED LOANS

With a pure discount or interest-only loan, the principal is repaid all at once. An alternative is an *amortized loan*, with which the lender may require the borrower to repay parts of the loan amount over time. The process of providing for a loan to be paid off by making regular principal reductions is called *amortizing* the loan.

A simple way of amortizing a loan is to have the borrower pay the interest each period plus some fixed amount. This approach is common with medium-term business loans. For example, suppose a business takes out a $5,000, five-year loan at 9 percent. The loan agreement calls for the borrower to pay the interest on the loan balance each year and to reduce the loan balance each year by $1,000. Because the loan amount declines by $1,000 each year, it is fully paid in five years.

In the case we are considering, notice that the total payment will decline each year. The reason is that the loan balance goes down, resulting in a lower interest charge each year, whereas the $1,000 principal reduction is constant. For example, the interest in the first year will be $5,000 × .09 = $450. The total payment will be $1,000 + 450 = $1,450. In the second year, the loan balance is $4,000, so the interest is $4,000 × .09 = $360, and the total payment is $1,360. We can calculate the total payment in each of the remaining years by preparing a simple *amortization schedule* as follows:

Year	Beginning Balance	Total Payment	Interest Paid	Principal Paid	Ending Balance
1	$5,000	$1,450	$ 450	$1,000	$4,000
2	4,000	1,360	360	1,000	3,000
3	3,000	1,270	270	1,000	2,000
4	2,000	1,180	180	1,000	1,000
5	1,000	1,090	90	1,000	0
Totals		$6,350	$1,350	$5,000	

Notice that in each year, the interest paid is given by the beginning balance multiplied by the interest rate. Also notice that the beginning balance is given by the ending balance from the previous year.

Probably the most common way of amortizing a loan is to have the borrower make a single, fixed payment every period. Almost all consumer loans (such as car loans) and mortgages work this way. For example, suppose our five-year, 9 percent, $5,000 loan was amortized this way. How would the amortization schedule look?

We first need to determine the payment. From our discussion earlier in the chapter, we know that this loan's cash flows are in the form of an ordinary annuity. In this case, we can solve for the payment as follows:

$$\$5,000 = C \times \{[1 - (1/1.09^5)]/.09\}$$
$$= C \times [(1 - .6499)/.09]$$

This gives us:

$$C = \$5,000/3.8897$$
$$= \$1,285.46$$

The borrower will therefore make five equal payments of $1,285.46. Will this pay off the loan? We will check by filling in an amortization schedule.

In our previous example, we knew the principal reduction each year. We then calculated the interest owed to get the total payment. In this example, we know the total payment. We will calculate the interest and then subtract it from the total payment to calculate the principal portion in each payment.

In the first year, the interest is $450, as we calculated before. Because the total payment is $1,285.46, the principal paid in the first year must be:

Principal paid = $1,285.46 − 450 = $835.46

The ending loan balance is:

Ending balance = $5,000 − 835.46 = $4,164.54

The interest in the second year is $4,164.54 × .09 = $374.81, and the loan balance declines by $1,285.46 − 374.81 = $910.65. We can summarize all of the relevant calculations in the following schedule:

Year	Beginning Balance	Total Payment	Interest Paid	Principal Paid	Ending Balance
1	$5,000.00	$1,285.46	$ 450.00	$ 835.46	$4,164.54
2	4,164.54	1,285.46	374.81	910.65	3,253.88
3	3,253.88	1,285.46	292.85	992.61	2,261.27
4	2,261.27	1,285.46	203.51	1,081.95	1,179.32
5	1,179.32	1,285.46	106.14	1,179.32	0.00
Totals		$6,427.31	$1,427.31	$5,000.00	

Because the loan balance declines to zero, the five equal payments do pay off the loan. Notice that the interest paid declines each period. This isn't surprising because the loan balance is going down. Given that the total payment is fixed, the principal paid must be rising each period.

If you compare the two loan amortizations in this section, you will see that the total interest is greater for the equal total payment case: $1,427.31 versus $1,350. The reason for this is that the loan is repaid more slowly early on, so the interest is somewhat higher. This doesn't mean that one loan is better than the other; it means that one is effectively paid off faster than the other. For example, the principal reduction in the first year is $835.46 in the equal total payment case as compared to $1,000 in the first case. Many websites offer loan amortization schedules. See our nearby *Work the Web* box for an example.

WORK THE WEB

Preparing an amortization table is one of the more tedious time value of money applications. Using a spreadsheet makes it relatively easy, but there are also websites available that will prepare an amortization schedule very quickly. One such site is www.bankrate.com. This site has a mortgage calculator for home loans, but the same calculations apply to most other types of loans such as car loans and student loans. Suppose you graduate with a student loan of $25,000 and will repay the loan over the next 10 years at 5.3 percent. What are your monthly payments? Using the calculator we get:

Home price ⑦

$ 25,000

Down payment ⑦

$ 0   0.00 %

Mortgage term ⑦

10.000 years   120 months

Annual interest rate ⑦

5.30 %   TODAY'S RATES

CALCULATE

Your estimated monthly payment ⑦

$268.84

Try this example yourself and click the "Show Amortization Schedule" button. You will find that your first payment will consist of $158.43 in principal and $110.42 in interest. Over the life of the loan you will pay a total of $7,261 in interest.

Questions

1. Suppose you take out a 30-year mortgage for $250,000 at an interest rate of 6.8 percent. Use this website to construct an amortization table for the loan. What are the interest payment and principal amounts in the 110th payment? How much in total interest will you pay over the life of the loan?

2. You take out a 30-year mortgage for $275,000 at an interest rate of 7.3 percent. How much will you pay in interest over the life of this loan? Now assume you pay an extra $100 per month on this loan. How much is your total interest now? How much sooner will the mortgage be paid off?

We will close this chapter with an example that may be of particular relevance. Federal Stafford loans are an important source of financing for many college students, helping to cover the cost of tuition, books, new cars, condominiums, and many other things. Sometimes students do not seem to fully realize that Stafford loans have a serious drawback: They must be repaid in monthly installments, usually beginning six months after the student leaves school.

Some Stafford loans are subsidized, meaning that the interest does not begin to accrue until repayment begins (this is a good thing). If you are a dependent undergraduate student under this particular option, the total debt you can run up is, at most, $23,000. The interest rate in 2017–2018 is 4.45 percent, or $4.45/12 = .3708$ percent per month. Under the "standard repayment plan," the loans are amortized over 10 years (subject to a minimum payment of $50).

Suppose you max out borrowing under this program. Beginning six months after you graduate (or otherwise depart the ivory tower), what will your monthly payment be? How much will you owe after making payments for four years?

Given our earlier discussions, see if you don't agree that your monthly payment (assuming a $23,000 total loan) is $237.81 per month. Also, as explained in Example 6.13, after making payments for four years, you still owe the present value of the remaining payments. There are 120 payments in all. After you make 48 of them (the first four years), you have 72 to go. By now, it should be easy for you to verify that the present value of $237.81 per month for 72 months at .3708 percent per month is about $15,003.07, so you still have a long way to go.

Partial Amortization, or "Bite the Bullet"   EXAMPLE 6.13

A common arrangement in real estate lending might call for a 5-year loan with, say, a 15-year amortization. What this means is that the borrower makes a payment every month of a fixed amount based on a 15-year amortization. However, after 60 months, the borrower makes a single, much larger payment called a "balloon" or "bullet" to pay off the loan. Because the monthly payments don't fully pay off the loan, the loan is said to be partially amortized.

Suppose we have a $100,000 commercial mortgage with a 12 percent APR and a 20-year (240-month) amortization. Further suppose the mortgage has a five-year balloon. What will the monthly payment be? How big will the balloon payment be?

The monthly payment can be calculated based on an ordinary annuity with a present value of $100,000. There are 240 payments, and the interest rate is 1 percent per month. The payment is:

$$\$100,000 = C \times [(1 - 1/1.01^{240})/.01]$$
$$= C \times 90.8194$$
$$C = \$1,101.09$$

Now, there is an easy way and a hard way to determine the balloon payment. The hard way is to actually amortize the loan for 60 months to see what the balance is at that time. The easy way is to recognize that after 60 months, we have a $240 - 60 = 180$-month loan. The payment is still $1,101.09 per month, and the interest rate is still 1 percent per month. The loan balance is thus the present value of the remaining payments:

$$\text{Loan balance} = \$1,101.09 \times [(1 - 1/1.01^{180})/.01]$$
$$= \$1,101.09 \times 83.3217$$
$$= \$91,744.33$$

The balloon payment is a substantial $91,744.33. Why is it so large? To get an idea, consider the first payment on the mortgage. The interest in the first month is $100,000 \times .01 = \$1,000$. Your payment is $1,101.09, so the loan balance declines by only $101.09. Because the loan balance declines so slowly, the cumulative "pay down" over five years is not great.

SPREADSHEET STRATEGIES

Loan Amortization Using a Spreadsheet

Loan amortization is a common spreadsheet application. To illustrate, we will set up the problem that we examined earlier in this section: a five-year, $5,000, 9 percent loan with constant payments. Our spreadsheet looks like this:

	A	B	C	D	E	F	G	H
1								
2			**Using a spreadsheet to amortize a loan**					
3								
4			Loan amount:	$5,000				
5			Interest rate:	.09				
6			Loan term:	5				
7			Loan payment:	**$1,285.46**				
8				*Note:* Payment is calculated using PMT(rate,nper,-pv,fv).				
9		*Amortization table:*						
10								
11		Year	Beginning	Total	Interest	Principal	Ending	
12			Balance	Payment	Paid	Paid	Balance	
13		1	$5,000.00	$1,285.46	$450.00	$835.46	$4,164.54	
14		2	4,164.54	1,285.46	374.81	910.65	3,253.88	
15		3	3,253.88	1,285.46	292.85	992.61	2,261.27	
16		4	2,261.27	1,285.46	203.51	1,081.95	1,179.32	
17		5	1,179.32	1,285.46	106.14	1,179.32	.00	
18		Totals		6,427.31	1,427.31	5,000.00		
19								
20		*Formulas in the amortization table:*						
21								
22		Year	Beginning	Total	Interest	Principal	Ending	
23			Balance	Payment	Paid	Paid	Balance	
24		1	=+D4	=$D$7	=+$D$5*C13	=+D13-E13	=+C13-F13	
25		2	=+G13	=$D$7	=+$D$5*C14	=+D14-E14	=+C14-F14	
26		3	=+G14	=$D$7	=+$D$5*C15	=+D15-E15	=+C15-F15	
27		4	=+G15	=$D$7	=+$D$5*C16	=+D16-E16	=+C16-F16	
28		5	=+G16	=$D$7	=+$D$5*C17	=+D17-E17	=+C17-F17	
29								
30		*Note:* Totals in the amortization table are calculated using the SUM formula.						
31								

SOURCE: Microsoft Excel

Of course, it is possible to rack up much larger debts. According to the Association of American Medical Colleges, medical students who borrowed to attend medical school and graduated in 2015 had an average student loan balance of $180,723. Ouch! In fact, it was reported that former Federal Reserve Chairman Ben Bernanke's son was on track to graduate with over $400,000 in student loans, although that included his undergraduate degree as well. How long will it take the average student to pay off her medical school loans?

Let's say she makes a monthly payment of $1,200, and the loan has an interest rate of 7 percent per year, or .5833 percent per month. See if you agree that it will take about 362 months, or about 30 years, to pay off the loan. Maybe MD really stands for "mucho debt"!

Concept Questions

6.4a What is a pure discount loan? An interest-only loan?

6.4b What does it mean to amortize a loan?

6.4c What is a balloon payment? How do you determine its value?

Summary and Conclusions   6.5

This chapter rounded out your understanding of fundamental concepts related to the time value of money and discounted cash flow valuation. Several important topics were covered:

1. There are two ways of calculating present and future values when there are multiple cash flows. Both approaches are straightforward extensions of our earlier analysis of single cash flows.

2. A series of constant cash flows that arrive or are paid at the end of each period is called an ordinary annuity, and we described some useful shortcuts for determining the present and future values of annuities.

3. Interest rates can be quoted in a variety of ways. For financial decisions, any rates being compared must first be converted to effective rates. The relationship between a quoted rate, such as an annual percentage rate (APR), and an effective annual rate (EAR) is given by:

$$EAR = [1 + (Quoted\ rate/m)]^m - 1$$

where m is the number of times during the year the money is compounded or, equivalently, the number of payments during the year.

4. Many loans are annuities. The process of providing for a loan to be paid off gradually is called amortizing the loan, and we discussed how amortization schedules are prepared and interpreted.

The principles developed in this chapter will figure prominently in the chapters to come. The reason for this is that most investments, whether they involve real assets or financial assets, can be analyzed using the discounted cash flow (DCF) approach. As a result, the DCF approach is broadly applicable and widely used in practice. For example, the next two chapters show how to value bonds and stocks using an extension of the techniques presented in this chapter. Before going on, therefore, you might want to do some of the problems that follow.

CONNECT TO FINANCE

 Do you use *Connect Finance* to practice what you learn? If you don't, you should—we can help you master the topics presented in this chapter. Log on to connect.mheducation.com to learn more!

Can you answer the following *Connect* Quiz questions?

Section 6.1 Two years ago, you opened an investment account and deposited $5,000. One year ago, you added another $2,000 to the account. Today, you are making a final deposit of $7,500. How much will you have in this account three years from today if you earn a 14 percent rate of return?

Section 6.2 A stream of equal payments that occur at the beginning of each month for one year is called a(n) _____.

Section 6.3 Your credit card charges interest of 1.2 percent per month. What is the annual percentage rate?

Section 6.4 What type of loan is repaid in a single lump sum?

CHAPTER REVIEW AND SELF-TEST PROBLEMS

6.1 **Present Values with Multiple Cash Flows** A first-round draft choice quarterback has been signed to a three-year, $25 million contract. The details provide for an immediate cash bonus of $2 million. The player is to receive $5 million in salary at the end of the first year, $8 million the next, and $10 million at the end of the last year. Assuming a 15 percent discount rate, is this package worth $25 million? If not, how much is it worth?

6.2 **Future Value with Multiple Cash Flows** You plan to make a series of deposits in an individual retirement account. You will deposit $1,000 today, $2,000 in two years, and $2,000 in five years. If you withdraw $1,500 in three years and $1,000 in seven years, assuming no withdrawal penalties, how much will you have after eight years if the interest rate is 7 percent? What is the present value of these cash flows?

6.3 **Annuity Present Value** You are looking into an investment that will pay you $12,000 per year for the next 10 years. If you require a 15 percent return, what is the most you would pay for this investment?

6.4 **APR versus EAR** The going rate on student loans is quoted as 8 percent APR. The terms of the loans call for monthly payments. What is the effective annual rate (EAR) on such a student loan?

6.5 **It's the Principal That Matters** Suppose you borrow $10,000. You are going to repay the loan by making equal annual payments for five years. The interest rate on the loan is 14 percent per year. Prepare an amortization schedule for the loan. How much interest will you pay over the life of the loan?

6.6 **Just a Little Bit Each Month** You've recently finished your MBA at the Darnit School. Naturally, you must purchase a new BMW immediately. The car costs about $36,000. The bank quotes an interest rate of 15 percent APR for a 72-month loan with a 10 percent down payment. You plan on trading the car in for a new one in two years. What will your monthly payment be? What is the effective interest rate on the loan? What will the loan balance be when you trade the car in?

ANSWERS TO CHAPTER REVIEW AND SELF-TEST PROBLEMS

6.1 Obviously, the package is not worth $25 million because the payments are spread out over three years. The bonus is paid today, so it's worth $2 million. The present values for the three subsequent salary payments are:

$$(\$5/1.15) + (8/1.15^2) + (10/1.15^3) = (\$5/1.15) + (8/1.3225) + (10/1.5209)$$
$$= \$16.9721 \text{ million}$$

The package is worth a total of $18.9721 million.

6.2 We will calculate the future values for each of the cash flows separately and then add them up. Notice that we treat the withdrawals as negative cash flows:

$$\$1,000 \times 1.07^8 = \quad \$1,000 \times 1.7182 = \quad \$\,1,718.19$$
$$2,000 \times 1.07^6 = \quad 2,000 \times 1.5007 = \quad 3,001.46$$
$$-1,500 \times 1.07^5 = -1,500 \times 1.4026 = -2,103.83$$
$$2,000 \times 1.07^3 = \quad 2,000 \times 1.2250 = \quad 2,450.09$$
$$-1,000 \times 1.07^1 = -1,000 \times 1.0700 = \underline{-1,070.00}$$

Total future value $= \$\,3,995.91$

To calculate the present value, we could discount each cash flow back to the present or we could discount back a single year at a time. However, because we already know that the future value in eight years is $3,995.91, the easy way to get the PV is just to discount this amount back eight years:

Present value = $3,995.91/1.07^8
= $3,995.91/1.7182
= $2,325.65

For practice, you can verify that this is what you get if you discount each cash flow back separately.

6.3   The most you would be willing to pay is the present value of $12,000 per year for 10 years at a 15 percent discount rate. The cash flows here are in ordinary annuity form, so the relevant present value factor is:

$$\text{Annuity present value factor} = (1 - \text{Present value factor})/r$$
$$= [1 - (1/1.15^{10})]/.15$$
$$= (1 - .2472)/.15$$
$$= 5.0188$$

The present value of the 10 cash flows is thus:

Present value = $12,000 × 5.0188
= $60,225

This is the most you would pay.

6.4   A rate of 8 percent APR with monthly payments is actually 8%/12 = .67% per month. The EAR is thus:

$$\text{EAR} = [1 + (.08/12)]^{12} - 1 = .0830, \text{ or } 8.30\%$$

6.5   We first need to calculate the annual payment. With a present value of $10,000, an interest rate of 14 percent, and a term of five years, the payment can be determined from:

$10,000 = Payment × {[1 − (1/1.14^5)]/.14}
= Payment × 3.4331

Therefore, the payment is $10,000/3.4331 = $2,912.84 (actually, it's $2,912.8355; this will create some small rounding errors in the following schedule). We can now prepare the amortization schedule as follows:

Year	Beginning Balance	Total Payment	Interest Paid	Principal Paid	Ending Balance
1	$10,000.00	$ 2,912.84	$1,400.00	$ 1,512.84	$8,487.16
2	8,487.16	2,912.84	1,188.20	1,724.63	6,762.53
3	6,762.53	2,912.84	946.75	1,966.08	4,796.45
4	4,796.45	2,912.84	671.50	2,241.33	2,555.12
5	2,555.12	2,912.84	357.72	2,555.12	0.00
Totals		$14,564.17	$4,564.17	$10,000.00	

182   **PART 3** Valuation of Future Cash Flows

6.6   The cash flows on the car loan are in annuity form, so we need to find only the payment. The interest rate is $15\%/12 = 1.25\%$ per month, and there are 72 months. The first thing we need is the annuity factor for 72 periods at 1.25 percent per period:

$$\text{Annuity present value factor} = (1 - \text{Present value factor})/r$$
$$= [1 - (1/1.0125^{72})]/.0125$$
$$= [1 - (1/2.4459)]/.0125$$
$$= (1 - .4088)/.0125$$
$$= 47.2925$$

The present value is the amount we finance. With a 10 percent down payment, we will be borrowing 90 percent of $36,000, or $32,400. To find the payment, we need to solve for C:

$$\$32,400 = C \times \text{Annuity present value factor}$$
$$= C \times 47.2925$$

Rearranging things a bit, we have:

$$C = \$32,400 \times (1/47.2925)$$
$$= \$32,400 \times .02115$$
$$= \$685.10$$

Your payment is just over $685 per month.

The actual interest rate on this loan is 1.25 percent per month. Based on our work in the chapter, we can calculate the effective annual rate as:

$$\text{EAR} = (1.0125)^{12} - 1 = .1608, \text{ or } 16.08\%$$

The effective rate is about one point higher than the quoted rate.

To determine the loan balance in two years, we could amortize the loan to see what the balance is at that time. This would be fairly tedious to do by hand. Using the information already determined in this problem, we can instead calculate the present value of the remaining payments. After two years, we have made 24 payments, so there are $72 - 24 = 48$ payments left. What is the present value of 48 monthly payments of $685.10 at 1.25 percent per month? The relevant annuity factor is:

$$\text{Annuity present value factor} = (1 - \text{Present value factor})/r$$
$$= [1 - (1/1.0125^{48})]/.0125$$
$$= [1 - (1/1.8154)]/.0125$$
$$= (1 - .5509)/.0125$$
$$= 35.9315$$

The present value is thus:

$$\text{Present value} = \$685.10 \times 35.9315 = \$24,616.60$$

You will owe about $24,617 on the loan in two years.

CONCEPTS REVIEW AND CRITICAL THINKING QUESTIONS

1.   **Annuity Factors** [LO1] There are four pieces to an annuity present value. What are they?

2.   **Annuity Period** [LO1] As you increase the length of time involved, what happens to the present value of an annuity? What happens to the future value?

3. **Interest Rates** [LO1] What happens to the future value of an annuity if you increase the rate r? What happens to the present value?

4. **Present Value** [LO1] What do you think about the Tri-State Megabucks lottery discussed in the chapter advertising a $500,000 prize when the lump sum option is $250,000? Is it deceptive advertising?

5. **Present Value** [LO1] If you were an athlete negotiating a contract, would you want a big signing bonus payable immediately and smaller payments in the future, or vice versa? How about looking at it from the team's perspective?

6. **Present Value** [LO1] Suppose two athletes each sign 10-year contracts for $80 million. In one case, we're told that the $80 million will be paid in 10 equal installments. In the other case, we're told that the $80 million will be paid in 10 installments, but the installments will increase by 5 percent per year. Who got the better deal?

7. **APR and EAR** [LO4] Should lending laws be changed to require lenders to report EARs instead of APRs? Why or why not?

8. **Time Value** [LO1] On subsidized Stafford loans, a common source of financial aid for college students, interest does not begin to accrue until repayment begins. Who receives a bigger subsidy, a freshman or a senior? Explain. In words, how would you go about valuing the subsidy on a subsidized Stafford loan?

9. **Time Value** [LO1] Eligibility for a subsidized Stafford loan is based on current financial need. However, both subsidized and unsubsidized Stafford loans are repaid out of future income. Given this, do you see a possible objection to having two types?

10. **Time Value** [LO1] A viatical settlement is a lump sum of money given to a terminally ill individual in exchange for his life insurance policy. When the insured person dies, the purchaser receives the payout from the life insurance policy. What factors determine the value of the viatical settlement? Do you think such settlements are ethical? Why or why not?

11. **Perpetuity Values** [LO1] What happens to the future value of a perpetuity if interest rates increase? What if interest rates decrease?

12. **Loans and Interest Rates** [LO4] In the chapter, we gave several examples of so-called payday loans. As you saw, the interest rates on these loans can be extremely high and are even called predatory by some. Do you think such high interest loans are ethical? Why or why not?

QUESTIONS AND PROBLEMS

1. **Present Value and Multiple Cash Flows** [LO1] McCann Co. has identified an investment project with the following cash flows. If the discount rate is 10 percent, what is the present value of these cash flows? What is the present value at 18 percent? At 24 percent?

BASIC
(Questions 1–28)

Year	Cash Flow
1	$ 530
2	690
3	875
4	1,090

2. **Present Value and Multiple Cash Flows** [LO1] Investment X offers to pay you $4,200 per year for eight years, whereas Investment Y offers to pay you $6,100 per year for five years. Which of these cash flow streams has the higher present value if the discount rate is 5 percent? If the discount rate is 15 percent?

3. **Future Value and Multiple Cash Flows** [LO1] Fuente, Inc., has identified an investment project with the following cash flows. If the discount rate is 8 percent, what is the future value of these cash flows in Year 4? What is the future value at a discount rate of 11 percent? At 24 percent?

Year	Cash Flow
1	$1,075
2	1,210
3	1,340
4	1,420

4. **Calculating Annuity Present Value** [LO1] An investment offers $4,350 per year for 15 years, with the first payment occurring one year from now. If the required return is 6 percent, what is the value of the investment? What would the value be if the payments occurred for 40 years? For 75 years? Forever?

5. **Calculating Annuity Cash Flows** [LO1] If you put up $41,000 today in exchange for a 5.1 percent, 15-year annuity, what will the annual cash flow be?

6. **Calculating Annuity Values** [LO1] Your company will generate $47,000 in annual revenue each year for the next seven years from a new information database. If the appropriate interest rate is 7.1 percent, what is the present value of the savings?

7. **Calculating Annuity Values** [LO1] If you deposit $4,500 at the end of each of the next 20 years into an account paying 9.7 percent interest, how much money will you have in the account in 20 years? How much will you have if you make deposits for 40 years?

8. **Calculating Annuity Values** [LO1] You want to have $60,000 in your savings account 12 years from now, and you're prepared to make equal annual deposits into the account at the end of each year. If the account pays 6.4 percent interest, what amount must you deposit each year?

9. **Calculating Annuity Values** [LO2] Prescott Bank offers you a five-year loan for $75,000 at an annual interest rate of 6.8 percent. What will your annual loan payment be?

10. **Calculating Perpetuity Values** [LO1] The Maybe Pay Life Insurance Co. is trying to sell you an investment policy that will pay you and your heirs $35,000 per year forever. If the required return on this investment is 4.7 percent, how much will you pay for the policy?

11. **Calculating Perpetuity Values** [LO1] In the previous problem, suppose a sales associate told you the policy costs $800,000. At what interest rate would this be a fair deal?

12. **Calculating EAR** [LO4] Find the EAR in each of the following cases:

Stated Rate (APR)	Number of Times Compounded	Effective Rate (EAR)
9%	Quarterly	
16	Monthly	
12	Daily	
11	Infinite	

13. **Calculating APR** [LO4] Find the APR, or stated rate, in each of the following cases:

Stated Rate (APR)	Number of Times Compounded	Effective Rate (EAR)
	Semiannually	11.1%
	Monthly	19.6
	Weekly	10.5
	Infinite	8.4

14. **Calculating EAR** [LO4] First National Bank charges 13.1 percent compounded monthly on its business loans. First United Bank charges 13.4 percent compounded semiannually. As a potential borrower, which bank would you go to for a new loan?

15. **Calculating APR** [LO4] Elliott Credit Corp. wants to earn an effective annual return on its consumer loans of 17.1 percent per year. The bank uses daily compounding on its loans. What interest rate is the bank required by law to report to potential borrowers? Explain why this rate is misleading to an uninformed borrower.

16. **Calculating Future Values** [LO1] What is the future value of $3,100 in 17 years assuming an interest rate of 8.4 percent compounded semiannually?

17. **Calculating Future Values** [LO1] Spartan Credit Bank is offering 8.1 percent compounded daily on its savings accounts. If you deposit $6,500 today, how much will you have in the account in 5 years? In 10 years? In 20 years?

18. **Calculating Present Values** [LO1] An investment will pay you $80,000 in 10 years. If the appropriate discount rate is 9 percent compounded daily, what is the present value?

19. **EAR versus APR** [LO4] Big Dom's Pawn Shop charges an interest rate of 27 percent per month on loans to its customers. Like all lenders, Big Dom must report an APR to consumers. What rate should the shop report? What is the effective annual rate?

20. **Calculating Loan Payments** [LO2, 4] You want to buy a new sports coupe for $84,500, and the finance office at the dealership has quoted you an APR of 5.2 percent for a 60-month loan to buy the car. What will your monthly payments be? What is the effective annual rate on this loan?

21. **Calculating Number of Periods** [LO3] One of your customers is delinquent on his accounts payable balance. You've mutually agreed to a repayment schedule of $450 per month. You will charge 1.3 percent per month interest on the overdue balance. If the current balance is $18,000, how long will it take for the account to be paid off?

22. **Calculating EAR** [LO4] Friendly's Quick Loans, Inc., offers you "three for four or I knock on your door." This means you get $3 today and repay $4 when you get your paycheck in one week (or else). What's the effective annual return Friendly's earns on this lending business? If you were brave enough to ask, what APR would Friendly's say you were paying?

23. **Valuing Perpetuities** [LO1] Live Forever Life Insurance Co. is selling a perpetuity contract that pays $1,250 monthly. The contract currently sells for $245,000. What is the monthly return on this investment vehicle? What is the APR? The effective annual return?

24. **Calculating Annuity Future Values** [LO1] You are planning to make monthly deposits of $475 into a retirement account that pays 10 percent interest compounded monthly. If your first deposit will be made one month from now, how large will your retirement account be in 30 years?

25. **Calculating Annuity Future Values** [LO1] In the previous problem, suppose you make $5,700 annual deposits into the same retirement account. How large will your account balance be in 30 years?

26. **Calculating Annuity Present Values** [LO1] Beginning three months from now, you want to be able to withdraw $2,500 each quarter from your bank account to cover college expenses over the next four years. If the account pays .57 percent interest per quarter, how much do you need to have in your bank account today to meet your expense needs over the next four years?

27. **Discounted Cash Flow Analysis** [LO1] If the appropriate discount rate for the following cash flows is 9 percent compounded quarterly, what is the present value of the cash flows?

Year	Cash Flow
1	$ 815
2	990
3	0
4	1,520

28. **Discounted Cash Flow Analysis** [LO1] If the appropriate discount rate for the following cash flows is 7.17 percent per year, what is the present value of the cash flows?

Year	Cash Flow
1	$2,480
2	0
3	3,920
4	2,170

INTERMEDIATE
(Questions 29–56)

29. **Simple Interest versus Compound Interest** [LO4] First Simple Bank pays 6.4 percent simple interest on its investment accounts. If First Complex Bank pays interest on its accounts compounded annually, what rate should the bank set if it wants to match First Simple Bank over an investment horizon of 10 years?

30. **Calculating EAR** [LO4] You are looking at an investment that has an effective annual rate of 11.6 percent. What is the effective semiannual return? The effective quarterly return? The effective monthly return?

31. **Calculating Interest Expense** [LO2] You receive a credit card application from Shady Banks Savings and Loan offering an introductory rate of 1.25 percent per year, compounded monthly for the first six months, increasing thereafter to 17.8 percent compounded monthly. Assuming you transfer the $8,000 balance from your existing credit card and make no subsequent payments, how much interest will you owe at the end of the first year?

32. **Calculating Annuities** [LO1] You are planning to save for retirement over the next 30 years. To do this, you will invest $750 per month in a stock account and $250 per month in a bond account. The return of the stock account is expected to be 10 percent, and the bond account will pay 6 percent. When you retire, you will combine your money into an account with a return of 5 percent. How much can you withdraw each month from your account assuming a 25-year withdrawal period?

33. **Calculating Future Values** [LO1] You have an investment that will pay you .67 percent per month. How much will you have per dollar invested in one year? In two years?

34. **Calculating Annuity Payments** [LO1] You want to be a millionaire when you retire in 40 years. How much do you have to save each month if you can earn an annual return of 9.7 percent? How much do you have to save each month if you wait 10 years before you begin your deposits? 20 years?

35. **Calculating Rates of Return** [LO2] Suppose an investment offers to triple your money in 12 months (don't believe it). What rate of return per quarter are you being offered?

36. **Comparing Cash Flow Streams** [LO1] You've just joined the investment bank- ✗
ing firm of Dewey, Cheatum, and Howe. They've offered you two different salary
arrangements. You can have $85,000 per year for the next two years, or you can have
$74,000 per year for the next two years, along with a $20,000 signing bonus today.
The bonus is paid immediately, and the salary is paid in equal amounts at the end
of each month. If the interest rate is 7 percent compounded monthly, which do you
prefer?

37. **Growing Annuity** [LO1] You have just won the lottery and will receive $1,500,000
in one year. You will receive payments for 30 years, and the payments will increase
by 2.7 percent per year. If the appropriate discount rate is 6.8 percent, what is the
present value of your winnings?

38. **Growing Annuity** [LO1] Your job pays you only once a year for all the work
you did over the previous 12 months. Today, December 31, you just received your
salary of $55,000 and you plan to spend all of it. However, you want to start saving
for retirement beginning next year. You have decided that one year from today you
will begin depositing 9 percent of your annual salary in an account that will earn
10 percent per year. Your salary will increase at 3 percent per year throughout your
career. How much money will you have on the date of your retirement 40 years
from today?

39. **Present Value and Interest Rates** [LO1] What is the relationship between the
value of an annuity and the level of interest rates? Suppose you just bought an annuity with 11 annual payments of $8,500 per year at the current interest rate of 10 per-
cent per year. What happens to the value of your investment if interest rates suddenly
drop to 5 percent? What if interest rates suddenly rise to 15 percent?

40. **Calculating the Number of Payments** [LO2] You're prepared to make monthly
payments of $175, beginning at the end of this month, into an account that pays
7 percent interest compounded monthly. How many payments will you have made
when your account balance reaches $15,000?

41. **Calculating Annuity Present Values** [LO2] You want to borrow $115,000 from
your local bank to buy a new sailboat. You can afford to make monthly payments of
$2,250, but no more. Assuming monthly compounding, what is the highest rate you
can afford on a 60-month APR loan?

42. **Calculating Loan Payments** [LO2] You need a 30-year, fixed-rate mortgage to
buy a new home for $235,000. Your mortgage bank will lend you the money at an
APR of 5.35 percent for this 360-month loan. However, you can afford monthly payments of only $925, so you offer to pay off any remaining loan balance at the end of
the loan in the form of a single balloon payment. How large will this balloon payment
have to be for you to keep your monthly payments at $925?

43. **Present and Future Values** [LO1] The present value of the following cash flow
stream is $7,500 when discounted at 9 percent annually. What is the value of the
missing cash flow?

Year	Cash Flow
1	$1,700
2	?
3	2,450
4	2,980

44. **Calculating Present Values** [LO1] You just won the TVM Lottery. You will receive $1 million today plus another 10 annual payments that increase by $375,000 per year. Thus, in one year, you receive $1.375 million. In two years, you get $1.75 million, and so on. If the appropriate interest rate is 6.5 percent, what is the value of your winnings today?

45. **EAR versus APR** [LO4] You have just purchased a new warehouse. To finance the purchase, you've arranged for a 30-year mortgage loan for 80 percent of the $3,400,000 purchase price. The monthly payment on this loan will be $16,500. What is the APR on this loan? The EAR?

46. **Present Value and Break-Even Interest** [LO1] Consider a firm with a contract to sell an asset for $145,000 four years from now. The asset costs $91,700 to produce today. Given a relevant discount rate of 11 percent per year, will the firm make a profit on this asset? At what rate does the firm just break even?

47. **Present Value and Multiple Cash Flows** [LO1] What is the value today of $4,400 per year, at a discount rate of 8.3 percent, if the first payment is received 6 years from today and the last payment is received 20 years from today?

48. **Variable Interest Rates** [LO1] A 15-year annuity pays $1,475 per month, and payments are made at the end of each month. If the interest rate is 9 percent compounded monthly for the first seven years, and 6 percent compounded monthly thereafter, what is the present value of the annuity?

49. **Comparing Cash Flow Streams** [LO1] You have your choice of two investment accounts. Investment A is a 13-year annuity that features end-of-month $1,250 payments and has an interest rate of 7.5 percent compounded monthly. Investment B is a 7 percent continuously compounded lump sum investment, also good for 13 years. How much money would you need to invest in Investment B today for it to be worth as much as Investment A 13 years from now?

50. **Calculating Present Value of a Perpetuity** [LO1] Given an interest rate of 5.3 percent per year, what is the value at date $t = 7$ of a perpetual stream of $6,400 payments that begins at date $t = 15$?

51. **Calculating EAR** [LO4] A local finance company quotes an interest rate of 17.1 percent on one-year loans. So, if you borrow $20,000, the interest for the year will be $3,420. Because you must repay a total of $23,420 in one year, the finance company requires you to pay $23,420/12, or $1,951.67, per month over the next 12 months. Is the interest rate on this loan 17.1 percent? What rate would legally have to be quoted? What is the effective annual rate?

52. **Calculating Present Values** [LO1] A five-year annuity of 10 $5,900 semiannual payments will begin 9 years from now, with the first payment coming 9.5 years from now. If the discount rate is 8 percent compounded monthly, what is the value of this annuity five years from now? What is the value three years from now? What is the current value of the annuity?

53. **Calculating Annuities Due** [LO1] Suppose you are going to receive $13,500 per year for five years. The appropriate interest rate is 6.8 percent.

  a. What is the present value of the payments if they are in the form of an ordinary annuity? What is the present value if the payments are an annuity due?

  b. Suppose you plan to invest the payments for five years. What is the future value if the payments are an ordinary annuity? What if the payments are an annuity due?

  c. Which has the highest present value, the ordinary annuity or the annuity due? Which has the highest future value? Will this always be true?

54. **Calculating Annuities Due** [LO1] You want to buy a new sports car from Muscle Motors for $57,500. The contract is in the form of a 60-month annuity due at an APR of 5.9 percent. What will your monthly payment be?

55. **Amortization with Equal Payments** [LO3] Prepare an amortization schedule for a five-year loan of $71,500. The interest rate is 7 percent per year, and the loan calls for equal annual payments. How much interest is paid in the third year? How much total interest is paid over the life of the loan?

56. **Amortization with Equal Principal Payments** [LO3] Rework Problem 55 assuming that the loan agreement calls for a principal reduction of $14,300 every year instead of equal annual payments.

57. **Calculating Annuity Values** [LO1] Bilbo Baggins wants to save money to meet three objectives. First, he would like to be able to retire 30 years from now with retirement income of $17,500 per month for 25 years, with the first payment received 30 years and 1 month from now. Second, he would like to purchase a cabin in Rivendell in 10 years at an estimated cost of $345,000. Third, after he passes on at the end of the 25 years of withdrawals, he would like to leave an inheritance of $2,000,000 to his nephew Frodo. He can afford to save $2,350 per month for the next 10 years. If he can earn an EAR of 10 percent before he retires and an EAR of 7 percent after he retires, how much will he have to save each month in Years 11 through 30?

CHALLENGE
(Questions 57–80)

58. **Calculating Annuity Values** [LO1] After deciding to buy a new car, you can either lease the car or purchase it on a three-year loan. The car you wish to buy costs $43,000. The dealer has a special leasing arrangement where you pay $4,300 today and $505 per month for the next three years. If you purchase the car, you will pay it off in monthly payments over the next three years at an APR of 6 percent. You believe you will be able to sell the car for $28,000 in three years. Should you buy or lease the car? What break-even resale price in three years would make you indifferent between buying and leasing?

59. **Calculating Annuity Values** [LO1] An All-Pro defensive lineman is in contract negotiations. The team has offered the following salary structure:

Time	Salary
0	$8,400,000
1	$4,700,000
2	$5,100,000
3	$5,700,000
4	$6,400,000
5	$7,100,000
6	$7,800,000

All salaries are to be paid in lump sums. The player has asked you as his agent to renegotiate the terms. He wants a $10 million signing bonus payable today and a contract value increase of $2 million. He also wants an equal salary paid every three months, with the first paycheck three months from now. If the interest rate is 4.8 percent compounded daily, what is the amount of his quarterly check? Assume 365 days in a year.

60. **Discount Interest Loans** [LO4] This question illustrates what is known as *discount interest*. Imagine you are discussing a loan with a somewhat unscrupulous lender. You want to borrow $25,000 for one year. The interest rate is 14.9 percent. You and

the lender agree that the interest on the loan will be .149 × $25,000 = $3,725. So the lender deducts this interest amount from the loan up front and gives you $21,275. In this case, we say that the discount is $3,725. What's wrong here?

61. **Calculating Annuity Values** [LO1] You are serving on a jury. A plaintiff is suing the city for injuries sustained after a freak street sweeper accident. In the trial, doctors testified that it will be five years before the plaintiff is able to return to work. The jury has already decided in favor of the plaintiff. You are the foreperson of the jury and propose that the jury give the plaintiff an award to cover the following: (a) The present value of two years' back pay. The plaintiff's annual salary for the last two years would have been $43,000 and $46,000, respectively. (b) The present value of five years' future salary. You assume the salary will be $51,000 per year. (c) $150,000 for pain and suffering. (d) $20,000 for court costs. Assume that the salary payments are equal amounts paid at the end of each month. If the interest rate you choose is an EAR of 6.5 percent, what is the size of the settlement? If you were the plaintiff, would you like to see a higher or lower interest rate?

62. **Calculating EAR with Points** [LO4] You are looking at a one-year loan of $10,000. The interest rate is quoted as 9.8 percent plus 2 points. A *point* on a loan is 1 percent (one percentage point) of the loan amount. Quotes similar to this one are common with home mortgages. The interest rate quotation in this example requires the borrower to pay 2 points to the lender up front and repay the loan later with 9.8 percent interest. What rate would you actually be paying here?

63. **Calculating EAR with Points** [LO4] The interest rate on a one-year loan is quoted as 12 percent plus 3 points (see the previous problem). What is the EAR? Is your answer affected by the loan amount?

64. **Calculating Interest Rates** [LO2] You are buying a house and will borrow $225,000 on a 30-year fixed rate mortgage with monthly payments to finance the purchase. Your loan officer has offered you a mortgage with an APR of 4.3 percent. Alternatively, she tells you that you can "buy down" the interest rate to 4.05 percent if you pay points up front on the loan. A point on a loan is 1 percent (one percentage point) of the loan value. How many points, at most, would you be willing to pay to buy down the interest rate?

65. **Calculating Interest Rates** [LO2] In the previous problem, suppose that you believe that you will only live in the house for eight years before selling the house and buying another house. This means that in eight years, you will pay off the remaining balance of the original mortgage. What is the maximum number of points that you would be willing to pay now?

66. **EAR versus APR** [LO4] Two banks in the area offer 30-year, $275,000 mortgages at 5.1 percent and charge a $4,300 loan application fee. However, the application fee charged by Insecurity Bank and Trust is refundable if the loan application is denied, whereas that charged by I.M. Greedy and Sons Mortgage Bank is not. The current disclosure law requires that any fees that will be refunded if the applicant is rejected be included in calculating the APR, but this is not required with nonrefundable fees (presumably because refundable fees are part of the loan rather than a fee). What are the EARs on these two loans? What are the APRs?

67. **Calculating EAR with Add-On Interest** [LO4] This problem illustrates a deceptive way of quoting interest rates called *add-on interest*. Imagine that you see an advertisement for Crazy Judy's Stereo City that reads something like this: "$1,000 Instant Credit! 17.3% Simple Interest! Three Years to Pay! Low, Low Monthly Payments!" You're not exactly sure what all this means and somebody has spilled ink over the APR on the loan contract, so you ask the manager for clarification.

Judy explains that if you borrow $1,000 for three years at 17.3 percent interest, in three years you will owe:

$$\$1,000 \times 1.173^3 = \$1,000 \times 1.61396 = \$1,613.96$$

Now, Judy recognizes that coming up with $1,613.96 all at once might be a strain, so she lets you make "low, low monthly payments" of $1,613.96/36 = $44.83 per month, even though this is extra bookkeeping work for her.

Is the interest rate on this loan 17.3 percent? Why or why not? What is the APR on this loan? What is the EAR? Why do you think this is called add-on interest?

68. **Growing Annuities** [LO1] You have successfully started and operated a company for the past 10 years. You have decided that it is time to sell your company and spend time on the beaches of Hawaii. A potential buyer is interested in your company, but he does not have the necessary capital to pay you a lump sum. Instead, he has offered $500,000 today and annuity payments for the balance. The first payment will be for $150,000 in three months. The payments will increase at 2 percent per quarter and a total of 25 quarterly payments will be made. If you require an EAR of 11 percent, how much are you being offered for your company?

69. **Calculating the Number of Periods** [LO2] Your Christmas ski vacation was great, but it unfortunately ran a bit over budget. All is not lost: You just received an offer in the mail to transfer your $15,000 balance from your current credit card, which charges an annual rate of 17.5 percent, to a new credit card charging a rate of 8.9 percent. How much faster could you pay the loan off by making your planned monthly payments of $250 with the new card? What if there was a fee of 2 percent charged on any balances transferred?

70. **Future Value and Multiple Cash Flows** [LO1] An insurance company is offering a new policy to its customers. Typically, the policy is bought by a parent or grandparent for a child at the child's birth. The purchaser (say, the parent) makes the following six payments to the insurance company:

First birthday:	$700
Second birthday:	$700
Third birthday:	$800
Fourth birthday:	$800
Fifth birthday:	$900
Sixth birthday:	$900

After the child's sixth birthday, no more payments are made. When the child reaches age 65, he or she receives $300,000. If the relevant interest rate is 10 percent for the first six years and 7 percent for all subsequent years, is the policy worth buying?

71. **Calculating a Balloon Payment** [LO2] You have just arranged for a $2,350,000 mortgage to finance the purchase of a large tract of land. The mortgage has an APR of 5.2 percent, and it calls for monthly payments over the next 30 years. However, the loan has an eight-year balloon payment, meaning that the loan must be paid off then. How big will the balloon payment be?

72. **Calculating Interest Rates** [LO4] A financial planning service offers a college savings program. The plan calls for you to make six annual payments of $15,000 each, with the first payment occurring today, your child's 12th birthday. Beginning

on your child's 18th birthday, the plan will provide $32,000 per year for four years. What return is this investment offering?

73. **Break-Even Investment Returns** [LO4] Your financial planner offers you two different investment plans. Plan X is an annual perpetuity of $35,000 per year. Plan Y is an annuity for 15 years and an annual payment of $47,000. Both plans will make their first payment one year from today. At what discount rate would you be indifferent between these two plans?

74. **Perpetual Cash Flows** [LO1] What is the value of an investment that pays $25,000 every *other* year forever, if the first payment occurs one year from today and the discount rate is 7 percent compounded daily? What is the value today if the first payment occurs four years from today?

75. **Ordinary Annuities and Annuities Due** [LO1] As discussed in the text, an annuity due is identical to an ordinary annuity except that the periodic payments occur at the beginning of each period instead of at the end of the period. Show that the relationship between the value of an ordinary annuity and the value of an otherwise equivalent annuity due is:

Annuity due value = Ordinary annuity value $\times (1 + r)$

Show this for both present and future values.

76. **Calculating Growing Annuities** [LO1] You have 45 years left until retirement and want to retire with $4 million. Your salary is paid annually, and you will receive $50,000 at the end of the current year. Your salary will increase at 3 percent per year, and you can earn an annual return of 9 percent on the money you invest. If you save a constant percentage of your salary, what percentage of your salary must you save each year?

77. **Calculating EAR** [LO4] A check-cashing store is in the business of making personal loans to walk-up customers. The store makes only one-week loans at 6.8 percent interest per week.

    a. What APR must the store report to its customers? What EAR are customers actually paying?

    b. Now suppose the store makes one-week loans at 6.8 percent discount interest per week (see Problem 60). What's the APR now? The EAR?

    c. The check-cashing store also makes one-month add-on interest loans at 6.8 percent discount interest per week. Thus if you borrow $100 for one month (four weeks), the interest will be ($100 $\times 1.068^4$) − 100 = $30.10. Because this is discount interest, your net loan proceeds today will be $69.90. You must then repay the store $100 at the end of the month. To help you out, though, the store lets you pay off this $100 in installments of $25 per week. What is the APR of this loan? What is the EAR?

78. **Present Value of a Growing Perpetuity** [LO1] What is the equation for the present value of a growing perpetuity with a payment of C one period from today if the payments grow by C each period?

79. **Rule of 72** [LO4] Earlier, we discussed the Rule of 72, a useful approximation for many interest rates and periods for the time it takes a lump sum to double in value. For a 10 percent interest rate, show that the "Rule of 73" is slightly better. For what rate is the Rule of 72 exact? (*Hint*: Use the Solver function in Excel.)

80. **Rule of 69.3** [LO4] A corollary to the Rule of 72 is the Rule of 69.3. The Rule of 69.3 is exactly correct except for rounding when interest rates are compounded continuously. Prove the Rule of 69.3 for continuously compounded interest.

EXCEL MASTER-IT! PROBLEM

This is a classic retirement problem. A friend is celebrating her birthday and wants to start saving for her anticipated retirement. She has the following years to retirement and retirement spending goals:

Years until retirement:	30
Amount to withdraw each year:	$90,000
Years to withdraw in retirement:	20
Interest rate:	8%

Because your friend is planning ahead, the first withdrawal will not take place until one year after she retires. She wants to make equal annual deposits into her account for her retirement fund.

a. If she starts making these deposits in one year and makes her last deposit on the day she retires, what amount must she deposit annually to be able to make the desired withdrawals at retirement?

b. Suppose your friend has just inherited a large sum of money. Rather than making equal annual payments, she has decided to make one lump sum deposit today to cover her retirement needs. What amount does she have to deposit today?

c. Suppose your friend's employer will contribute to the account each year as part of the company's profit sharing plan. In addition, your friend expects a distribution from a family trust 20 years from now. What amount must she deposit annually now to be able to make the desired withdrawals at retirement?

Employer's annual contribution:	$ 1,500
Years until trust fund distribution:	20
Amount of trust fund distribution:	$25,000

MINICASE

The MBA Decision

Ben Bates graduated from college six years ago with a finance undergraduate degree. Although he is satisfied with his current job, his goal is to become an investment banker. He feels that an MBA degree would allow him to achieve this goal. After examining schools, he has narrowed his choice to either Wilton University or Mount Perry College. Although internships are encouraged by both schools, to get class credit for the internship, no salary can be paid. Other than internships, neither school will allow its students to work while enrolled in its MBA program.

Ben currently works at the money management firm of Dewey and Louis. His annual salary at the firm is $53,000 per year, and his salary is expected to increase at 3 percent per year until retirement. He is currently 28 years old and expects to work for 38 more years. His current job includes a fully paid health insurance plan, and his current average tax rate is 26 percent. Ben has a savings account with enough money to cover the entire cost of his MBA program.

The Ritter College of Business at Wilton University is one of the top MBA programs in the country. The MBA degree requires two years of full-time enrollment at the university. The annual tuition is $58,000, payable at the beginning of each school year. Books and other supplies are estimated to cost $2,000 per year. Ben expects that after graduation from Wilton, he will receive a job offer for about $87,000 per year, with a $10,000 signing bonus. The salary at this job will increase at 4 percent per year. Because of the higher salary, his average income tax rate will increase to 31 percent.

The Bradley School of Business at Mount Perry College began its MBA program 16 years ago. The Bradley School is smaller and less well known than the Ritter College. Bradley offers an accelerated one-year program, with a tuition cost of $75,000 to be paid upon matriculation. Books and other supplies for the program are expected to cost $4,200. Ben thinks that he will receive an offer of $78,000 per year upon graduation, with an $8,000 signing bonus. The salary at this job will increase at 3.5 percent per year. His average tax rate at this level of income will be 29 percent.

Both schools offer a health insurance plan that will cost $3,000 per year, payable at the beginning of the year. Ben has also found that both schools offer graduate housing. His room and board expenses will decrease by $4,000 per year at either school he attends. The appropriate discount rate is 5.5 percent.

QUESTIONS

1. How does Ben's age affect his decision to get an MBA?

2. What other, perhaps nonquantifiable, factors affect Ben's decision to get an MBA?

3. Assuming all salaries are paid at the end of each year, what is the best option for Ben from a strictly financial standpoint?

4. Ben believes that the appropriate analysis is to calculate the future value of each option. How would you evaluate this statement?

5. What initial salary would Ben need to receive to make him indifferent between attending Wilton University and staying in his current position?

6. Suppose, instead of being able to pay cash for his MBA, Ben must borrow the money. The current borrowing rate is 5.4 percent. How would this affect his decision?

Interest Rates and Bond Valuation

7 Chapter

GENERALLY, WHEN AN INVESTMENT is made, you expect that you will get back more money in the future than you invested today. In December 2017, this wasn't the case for many bond investors. The yield on a 5-year German government bond was about negative .20 percent, and the yields on 2-year and 5-year Japanese government bonds were negative .14 percent and negative .09 percent, respectively. In fact, in 2016, the amount of debt worldwide that had a negative yield reached a record $13.4 trillion! And negative yields were not restricted to government bonds, as the yield on the chocolate maker Nestlé's bond was negative as well.

As you will see in this chapter, a bond's yield is an important determinant of a bond's price. In addition to showing you how to value a bond, we will talk about various bond features and the factors that affect bond yields.

Learning Objectives

After studying this chapter, you should be able to:

LO1 Define important bond features and types of bonds.

LO2 Explain bond values and yields and why they fluctuate.

LO3 Describe bond ratings and what they mean.

LO4 Outline the impact of inflation on interest rates.

LO5 Illustrate the term structure of interest rates and the determinants of bond yields.

©by_adri/iStockPhotoGettyImages

For updates on the latest happenings in finance, visit fundamentalsofcorporatefinance.blogspot.com.

Our goal in this chapter is to introduce you to bonds. We begin by showing how the techniques we developed in Chapters 5 and 6 can be applied to bond valuation. From there, we go on to discuss bond features and how bonds are bought and sold. One important thing we learn is that bond values depend, in large part, on interest rates. We therefore close the chapter with an examination of interest rates and their behavior.

7.1 Bonds and Bond Valuation

When a corporation or government wishes to borrow money from the public on a long-term basis, it usually does so by issuing or selling debt securities that are generically called *bonds*. In this section, we describe the various features of corporate bonds and some of the terminology associated with bonds. We then discuss the cash flows associated with a bond and how bonds can be valued using our discounted cash flow procedure.

BOND FEATURES AND PRICES

As we mentioned in our previous chapter, a bond is normally an interest-only loan, meaning that the borrower will pay the interest every period, but none of the principal will be repaid until the end of the loan. For example, suppose the Beck Corporation wants to borrow $1,000 for 30 years. The interest rate on similar debt issued by similar corporations is 12 percent. Beck will thus pay $.12 \times \$1,000 = \$120$ in interest every year for 30 years. At the end of 30 years, Beck will repay the $1,000. As this example suggests, a bond is a fairly simple financing arrangement. There is, however, a rich jargon associated with bonds, so we will use this example to define some of the more important terms.

In our example, the $120 regular interest payments that Beck promises to make are called the bond's **coupons**. Because the coupon is constant and paid every year, the type of bond we are describing is sometimes called a *level coupon bond*. The amount that will be repaid at the end of the loan is called the bond's **face value**, or **par value**. As in our example, this par value is usually $1,000 for corporate bonds, and a bond that sells for its par value is called a *par value bond*. Government bonds frequently have much larger face, or par, values. Finally, the annual coupon divided by the face value is called the **coupon rate** on the bond; in this case, because $120/1,000 = 12\%$, the bond has a 12 percent coupon rate.

The number of years until the face value is paid is called the bond's time to **maturity**. A corporate bond will frequently have a maturity of 30 years when it is originally issued, but this varies. Once the bond has been issued, the number of years to maturity declines as time goes by.

BOND VALUES AND YIELDS

As time passes, interest rates change in the marketplace. The cash flows from a bond, however, stay the same. As a result, the value of the bond will fluctuate. When interest rates rise, the present value of the bond's remaining cash flows declines, and the bond is worth less. When interest rates fall, the bond is worth more.

To determine the value of a bond at a particular point in time, we need to know the number of periods remaining until maturity, the face value, the coupon, and the market interest rate for bonds with similar features. This interest rate required in the market on a bond is called the bond's **yield to maturity (YTM)**. This rate is sometimes called the bond's *yield* for short. Given all this information, we can calculate the present value of the cash flows as an estimate of the bond's current market value.

For example, suppose the Xanth (pronounced "zanth") Co. were to issue a bond with 10 years to maturity. The Xanth bond has an annual coupon of $80. Similar bonds have a yield to maturity of 8 percent. Based on our preceding discussion, the Xanth bond will pay $80 per year for the next 10 years in coupon interest. In 10 years, Xanth will pay $1,000 to the owner of the bond. The cash flows from the bond are shown in Figure 7.1. What would this bond sell for?

As illustrated in Figure 7.1, the Xanth bond's cash flows have an annuity component (the coupons) and a lump sum (the face value paid at maturity). We thus estimate the market

coupon
The stated interest payment made on a bond.

face value
The principal amount of a bond that is repaid at the end of the term. Also called *par value*.

coupon rate
The annual coupon divided by the face value of a bond.

maturity
The specified date on which the principal amount of a bond is paid.

yield to maturity (YTM)
The rate required in the market on a bond.

FIGURE 7.1   **Cash Flows for Xanth Co. Bond**

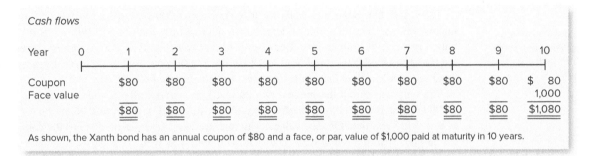

As shown, the Xanth bond has an annual coupon of $80 and a face, or par, value of $1,000 paid at maturity in 10 years.

value of the bond by calculating the present value of these two components separately and adding the results together. First, at the going rate of 8 percent, the present value of the $1,000 paid in 10 years is:

Present value = $1,000/1.08^{10} = $1,000/2.1589 = $463.19

Second, the bond offers $80 per year for 10 years; the present value of this annuity stream is:

$$\text{Annuity present value} = \$80 \times (1-1/1.08^{10})/.08$$
$$= \$80 \times (1-1/2.1589)/.08$$
$$= \$80 \times 6.7101$$
$$= \$536.81$$

We can now add the values for the two parts together to get the bond's value:

Total bond value = $463.19 + 536.81 = $1,000

This bond sells for exactly its face value. This is not a coincidence. The going interest rate in the market is 8 percent. Considered as an interest-only loan, what interest rate does this bond have? With an $80 coupon, this bond pays exactly 8 percent interest only when it sells for $1,000.

To illustrate what happens as interest rates change, suppose a year has gone by. The Xanth bond now has nine years to maturity. If the interest rate in the market has risen to 10 percent, what will the bond be worth? To find out, we repeat the present value calculations with 9 years instead of 10, and a 10 percent yield instead of an 8 percent yield. First, the present value of the $1,000 paid in nine years at 10 percent is:

Present value = $1,000/1.10^9 = $1,000/2.3579 = $424.10

Second, the bond now offers $80 per year for nine years; the present value of this annuity stream at 10 percent is:

$$\text{Annuity present value} = \$80 \times (1-1/1.10^9)/.10$$
$$= \$80 \times (1-1/2.3579)/.10$$
$$= \$80 \times 5.7590$$
$$= \$460.72$$

We can now add the values for the two parts together to get the bond's value:

Total bond value = $424.10 + 460.72 = $884.82

A good bond site to visit is **finance.yahoo.com/bonds**, which has loads of useful information.

Therefore, the bond should sell for about $885. In the vernacular, we say that this bond, with its 8 percent coupon, is priced to yield 10 percent at $885.

The Xanth Co. bond now sells for less than its $1,000 face value. Why? The market interest rate is 10 percent. Considered as an interest-only loan of $1,000, this bond pays only 8 percent, its coupon rate. Because this bond pays less than the going rate, investors are willing to lend only something less than the $1,000 promised repayment. Because the bond sells for less than face value, it is said to be a *discount bond*.

The only way to get the interest rate up to 10 percent is to lower the price to less than $1,000 so that the purchaser, in effect, has a built-in gain. For the Xanth bond, the price of $885 is $115 less than the face value, so an investor who purchases and keeps the bond will get $80 per year and will have a $115 gain at maturity as well. This gain compensates the lender for the below-market coupon rate.

Another way to see why the bond is discounted by $115 is to note that the $80 coupon is $20 below the coupon on a newly issued par value bond, based on current market conditions. The bond would be worth $1,000 only if it had a coupon of $100 per year. In a sense, an investor who buys and keeps the bond gives up $20 per year for nine years. At 10 percent, this annuity stream is worth:

$$\text{Annuity present value} = \$20 \times (1 - 1/1.10^9)/.10$$
$$= \$20 \times 5.7590$$
$$= \$115.18$$

This is the amount of the discount.

What would the Xanth bond sell for if interest rates had dropped by 2 percent instead of rising by 2 percent? As you might guess, the bond would sell for more than $1,000. Such a bond is said to sell at a *premium* and is called a *premium bond*.

This case is the opposite of that of a discount bond. The Xanth bond now has a coupon rate of 8 percent when the market rate is only 6 percent. Investors are willing to pay a premium to get this extra coupon amount. In this case, the relevant discount rate is 6 percent, and there are nine years remaining. The present value of the $1,000 face amount is:

$$\text{Present value} = \$1,000/1.06^9 = \$1,000/1.6895 = \$591.90$$

Online bond calculators are available at **personal .fidelity.com**; interest rate information is available at **money.cnn.com/data/bonds** and **www.bankrate.com**.

The present value of the coupon stream is:

$$\text{Annuity present value} = \$80 \times (1-1/1.06^9)/.06$$
$$= \$80 \times (1-1/1.6895)/.06$$
$$= \$80 \times 6.8017$$
$$= \$544.14$$

We can now add the values for the two parts together to get the bond's value:

$$\text{Total bond value} = \$591.90 + 544.14 = \$1,136.03$$

Total bond value is therefore about $136 in excess of par value. Once again, we can verify this amount by noting that the coupon is now $20 too high, based on current market conditions. The present value of $20 per year for nine years at 6 percent is:

$$\text{Annuity present value} = \$20 \times (1-1/1.06^9)/.06$$
$$= \$20 \times 6.8017$$
$$= \$136.03$$

This is just as we calculated.

Based on our examples, we can now write the general expression for the value of a bond. If a bond has (1) a face value of F paid at maturity, (2) a coupon of C paid per period, (3) t periods to maturity, and (4) a yield of r per period, its value is:

Bond value = $C \times [1 - 1/(1 + r)^t]/r$ + $F/(1 + r)^t$

Bond value =   Present value   +   Present value
               of the coupons   of the face amount

7.1

| **Semiannual Coupons** | **EXAMPLE 7.1** |

In practice, bonds issued in the United States usually make coupon payments twice a year. So, if an ordinary bond has a coupon rate of 14 percent, then the owner will get a total of $140 per year, but this $140 will come in two payments of $70 each. Suppose we are examining such a bond. The yield to maturity is quoted at 16 percent.

Bond yields are quoted like APRs; the quoted rate is equal to the actual rate per period multiplied by the number of periods. In this case, with a 16 percent quoted yield and semiannual payments, the true yield is 8 percent per six months. The bond matures in seven years. What is the bond's price? What is the effective annual yield on this bond?

Based on our discussion, we know the bond will sell at a discount because it has a coupon rate of 7 percent every six months when the market requires 8 percent every six months. So, if our answer exceeds $1,000, we know we have made a mistake.

To get the exact price, we first calculate the present value of the bond's face value of $1,000 paid in seven years. This seven-year period has 14 periods of six months each. At 8 percent per period, the value is:

Present value = $1,000/1.08^{14}$ = $1,000/2.9372$ = $340.46

The coupons can be viewed as a 14-period annuity of $70 per period. At an 8 percent discount rate, the present value of such an annuity is:

Annuity present value = $70 \times (1 - 1/1.08^{14})/.08$
= $70 \times (1 - .3405)/.08$
= 70×8.2442
= $577.10

The total present value gives us what the bond should sell for:

Total present value = $340.46 + 577.10 = $917.56

To calculate the effective yield on this bond, note that 8 percent every six months is equivalent to:

Effective annual rate = $(1 + .08)^2 - 1 = 16.64\%$

The effective yield is 16.64 percent.

As we have illustrated in this section, bond prices and interest rates always move in opposite directions. When interest rates rise, a bond's value, like any other present value, will decline. Similarly, when interest rates fall, bond values rise. Even if we are considering a bond that is riskless in the sense that the borrower is certain to make all the payments, there is still risk in owning a bond. We discuss this next.

Visit **investorguide.com** to learn more about bonds.

INTEREST RATE RISK

The risk that arises for bond owners from fluctuating interest rates is called *interest rate risk*. How much interest rate risk a bond has depends on how sensitive its price is to interest rate changes. This sensitivity directly depends on two things: The time to maturity and the coupon rate. As we will see momentarily, you should keep the following in mind when looking at a bond:

1. All other things being equal, the longer the time to maturity, the greater the interest rate risk.

2. All other things being equal, the lower the coupon rate, the greater the interest rate risk.

We illustrate the first of these two points in Figure 7.2. As shown, we compute and plot prices under different interest rate scenarios for 10 percent coupon bonds with maturities of 1 year and 30 years. Notice how the slope of the line connecting the prices is much steeper for the 30-year maturity than it is for the 1-year maturity. This steepness tells us that a relatively small change in interest rates will lead to a substantial change in the bond's value. In comparison, the 1-year bond's price is relatively insensitive to interest rate changes.

Intuitively, we can see that longer-term bonds have greater interest rate sensitivity because a large portion of a bond's value comes from the $1,000 face amount. The present value of this amount isn't greatly affected by a small change in interest rates if the

FIGURE 7.2

Interest Rate Risk and Time to Maturity

Value of a Bond with a 10 Percent Coupon Rate for Different Interest Rates and Maturities

	Time to Maturity	
Interest Rate	1 Year	30 Years
5%	$1,047.62	$1,768.62
10	1,000.00	1,000.00
15	956.52	671.70
20	916.67	502.11

amount is to be received in one year. Even a small change in the interest rate, however, once it is compounded for 30 years, can have a significant effect on the present value. As a result, the present value of the face amount will be much more volatile with a longer-term bond.

The other thing to know about interest rate risk is that, like most things in finance and economics, it increases at a decreasing rate. In other words, if we compared a 10-year bond to a 1-year bond, we would see that the 10-year bond has much greater interest rate risk. If you were to compare a 20-year bond to a 30-year bond, you would find that the 30-year bond has somewhat greater interest rate risk because it has a longer maturity, but the difference in the risk would be fairly small.

The reason that bonds with lower coupons have greater interest rate risk is essentially the same. As we discussed earlier, the value of a bond depends on the present value of its coupons and the present value of the face amount. If two bonds with different coupon rates have the same maturity, then the value of the one with the lower coupon is proportionately more dependent on the face amount to be received at maturity. As a result, all other things being equal, its value will fluctuate more as interest rates change. Put another way, the bond with the higher coupon has a larger cash flow early in its life, so its value is less sensitive to changes in the discount rate.

Bonds are rarely issued with maturities longer than 30 years. However, low interest rates in recent years have led to the issuance of much longer-term issues. In the 1990s, Walt Disney issued "Sleeping Beauty" bonds with a 100-year maturity. Similarly, BellSouth (now known as AT&T), Coca-Cola, and Dutch banking giant ABN AMRO all issued bonds with 100-year maturities. These companies evidently wanted to lock in the historical low interest rates for a *long* time. The current record holder for corporations looks to be Republic National Bank, which sold bonds with 1,000 years to maturity. Although somewhat rare, 100-year bond issues still occur, and recently they have even been issued by governments. For example, Belgium issued 100-year bonds in 2015, and Ireland issued 100-year bonds in 2016. The Irish bonds had a yield to maturity of only 2.35 percent when they were originally issued, something to keep in mind when we discuss the term structure of interest rates later in this chapter.

We can illustrate the effect of interest rate risk using the 100-year BellSouth (AT&T) issue. The following table provides some basic information about this issue, along with its prices on December 31, 1995, March 6, 2009, and December 29, 2017:

Maturity	Coupon Rate	Price on 12/31/95	Price on 3/6/09	Percentage Change in Price 1995–2009	Price on 12/29/17	Percentage Change in Price 2009–2017
2095	7.00%	$1,000.00	$803.43	−19.66%	$1,166.10	45.14%

Several things emerge from this table. First, interest rates apparently increased between December 31, 1995, and March 6, 2009 (why?). After that, they fell (why?). The bond's price first lost 19.66 percent and then gained 45.14 percent.

FINDING THE YIELD TO MATURITY: MORE TRIAL AND ERROR

Frequently, we will know a bond's price, coupon rate, and maturity date, but not its yield to maturity. For example, suppose we are interested in a six-year, 8 percent coupon bond with annual payments. A broker quotes a price of $955.14. What is the yield on this bond?

We've seen that the price of a bond can be written as the sum of its annuity and lump sum components. Knowing that there is an $80 coupon for six years and a $1,000 face value, we can say that the price is:

$$\$955.14 = \$80 \times [1 - 1/(1 + r)^6]/r + 1{,}000/(1 + r)^6$$

where r is the unknown discount rate, or yield to maturity. We have one equation here and one unknown, but we cannot solve it for r explicitly. The only way to find the answer is to use trial and error.

This problem is essentially identical to the one we examined in the last chapter when we tried to find the unknown interest rate on an annuity. Finding the rate (or yield) on a bond is even more complicated because of the $1,000 face amount.

We can speed up the trial-and-error process by using what we know about bond prices and yields. In this case, the bond has an $80 coupon and is selling at a discount. We know that the yield is greater than 8 percent. If we compute the price at 10 percent:

$$
\begin{aligned}
\text{Bond value} &= \$80 \times (1 - 1/1.10^6)/.10 + 1{,}000/1.10^6 \\
&= \$80 \times 4.3553 + 1{,}000/1.7716 \\
&= \$912.89
\end{aligned}
$$

Current market rates are available at **www.bankrate.com**.

current yield
A bond's annual coupon divided by its price.

At 10 percent, the value we calculate is lower than the actual price, so 10 percent is too high. The true yield must be somewhere between 8 and 10 percent. At this point, it's "plug and chug" to find the answer. You would probably want to try 9 percent next. If you did, you would see that this is in fact the bond's yield to maturity.

A bond's yield to maturity should not be confused with its **current yield**, which is a bond's annual coupon divided by its price. In the example we just worked, the bond's annual coupon was $80, and its price was $955.14. Given these numbers, we see that the current yield is $80/955.14 = 8.38 percent, which is less than the yield to maturity of 9 percent. The reason the current yield is too low is that it considers only the coupon portion of your return; it doesn't consider the built-in gain from the price discount. For a premium bond, the reverse is true, meaning that current yield would be higher because it ignores the built-in loss.

Our discussion of bond valuation is summarized in Table 7.1.

TABLE 7.1

Summary of Bond Valuation

I. Finding the Value of a Bond

Bond value = $C \times [1 - 1/(1 + r)^t]/r + F/(1 + r)^t$
where:
    C = Coupon paid each period
    r = Rate per period
    t = Number of periods
    F = Bond's face value

II. Finding the Yield on a Bond
Given a bond value, coupon, time to maturity, and face value, it is possible to find the implicit discount rate, or yield to maturity, by trial and error only. To do this, try different discount rates until the calculated bond value equals the given value (or let a financial calculator do it for you). Remember that increasing the rate *decreases* the bond value.

Current Events	EXAMPLE 7.2

A bond has a quoted price of $1,080.42. It has a face value of $1,000, a semiannual coupon of $30, and a maturity of five years. What is its current yield? What is its yield to maturity? Which is bigger? Why?

Notice that this bond makes semiannual payments of $30, so the annual payment is $60. The current yield is thus $60/1,080.42 = 5.55 percent. To calculate the yield to maturity, refer back to Example 7.1. In this case, the bond pays $30 every six months and has 10 six-month periods until maturity. So, we need to find r as follows:

$$\$1,080.42 = \$30 \times [1 - 1/(1 + r)^{10}]/r + 1,000/(1 + r)^{10}$$

After some trial and error, we find that r is equal to about 2.1 percent. But, the tricky part is that this 2.1 percent is the yield *per six months*. We have to double it to get the yield to maturity, so the yield to maturity is 4.2 percent, which is less than the current yield. The reason is that the current yield ignores the built-in loss of the premium between now and maturity.

Bond Yields	EXAMPLE 7.3

You're looking at two bonds identical in every way except for their coupons and, of course, their prices. Both have 12 years to maturity. The first bond has a 10 percent annual coupon rate and sells for $935.08. The second has a 12 percent annual coupon rate. What do you think it would sell for?

Because the two bonds are similar, they will be priced to yield about the same rate. We first need to calculate the yield on the 10 percent coupon bond. Proceeding as before, we know that the yield must be greater than 10 percent because the bond is selling at a discount. The bond has a fairly long maturity of 12 years. We've seen that long-term bond prices are relatively sensitive to interest rate changes, so the yield is probably close to 10 percent. A little trial and error reveals that the yield is actually 11 percent:

$$\text{Bond value} = \$100 \times (1 - 1/1.11^{12})/.11 + 1,000/1.11^{12}$$
$$= \$100 \times 6.4924 + 1,000/3.4985$$
$$= \$649.24 + 285.84$$
$$= \$935.08$$

With an 11 percent yield, the second bond will sell at a premium because of its $120 coupon. Its value is:

$$\text{Bond value} = \$120 \times (1 - 1/1.11^{12})/.11 + 1,000/1.11^{12}$$
$$= \$120 \times 6.4924 + 1,000/3.4985$$
$$= \$779.08 + 285.84$$
$$= \$1,064.92$$

CALCULATOR HINTS

How to Calculate Bond Prices and Yields Using a Financial Calculator

Many financial calculators have fairly sophisticated built-in bond valuation routines. However, these vary quite a lot in implementation, and not all financial calculators have them. As a result, we will illustrate a simple way to handle bond problems that will work on about any financial calculator.

204   **PART 3**   Valuation of Future Cash Flows

To begin, of course, we first remember to clear out the calculator! Returning to Example 7.3, we have two bonds to consider, both with 12 years to maturity. The first one sells for $935.08 and has a 10 percent annual coupon rate. To find its yield, we can do the following:

Notice that here we have entered both a future value of $1,000, representing the bond's face value, and a payment of 10 percent of $1,000, or $100, per year, representing the bond's annual coupon. Also, notice that we have a negative sign on the bond's price, which we have entered as the present value.

For the second bond, we now know that the relevant yield is 11 percent. It has a 12 percent annual coupon and 12 years to maturity, so what's the price? To answer, we enter the relevant values and solve for the present value of the bond's cash flows:

There is an important detail that comes up here. Suppose we have a bond with a price of $902.29, 10 years to maturity, and a coupon rate of 6 percent. As we mentioned earlier, most bonds actually make semiannual payments. Assuming that this is the case for the bond here, what's the bond's yield? To answer, we need to enter the relevant numbers like this:

Notice that we entered $30 as the payment because the bond actually makes payments of $30 every six months. Similarly, we entered 20 for N because there are actually 20 six-month periods. When we solve for the yield, we get 3.7 percent. The tricky thing to remember is that this is the yield *per six months*, so we have to double it to get the right answer: $2 \times 3.7 = 7.4$ percent, which would be the bond's reported yield.

SPREADSHEET STRATEGIES

How to Calculate Bond Prices and Yields Using a Spreadsheet

Most spreadsheets have fairly elaborate routines available for calculating bond values and yields; many of these routines involve details we have not discussed. Setting up a spreadsheet to calculate prices or yields is straightforward, as our next two spreadsheets show:

	A	B	C	D	E	F	G	H
1								
2		Using a spreadsheet to calculate bond values						
3								
4	Suppose we have a bond with 22 years to maturity, a coupon rate of 8 percent, and a yield to							
5	maturity of 9 percent. If the bond makes semiannual payments, what is its price today?							
6								
7	Settlement date:	1/1/00						
8	Maturity date:	1/1/22						
9	Annual coupon rate:	.08						
10	Yield to maturity:	.09						
11	Face value (% of par):	100						
12	Coupons per year:	2						
13	Bond price (% of par):	**90.49**						
14								
15	The formula entered in cell B13 is =PRICE(B7,B8,B9,B10,B11,B12); notice that face value and bond							
16	price are given as a percentage of face value.							

	A	B	C	D	E	F	G	H
1								
2		Using a spreadsheet to calculate bond yields						
3								
4	Suppose we have a bond with 22 years to maturity, a coupon rate of 8 percent, and a price of							
5	$960.17. If the bond makes semiannual payments, what is its yield to maturity?							
6								
7	Settlement date:	1/1/00						
8	Maturity date:	1/1/22						
9	Annual coupon rate:	.08						
10	Bond price (% of par):	96.017						
11	Face value (% of par):	100						
12	Coupons per year:	2						
13	Yield to maturity:	**.084**						
14								
15	The formula entered in cell B13 is =YIELD(B7,B8,B9,B10,B11,B12); notice that face value and bond							
16	price are entered as a percentage of face value.							
17								

In our spreadsheets, notice that we had to enter two dates: A settlement date and a maturity date. The settlement date is the date you actually pay for the bond, and the maturity date is the day the bond actually matures. In most of our problems, we don't explicitly have these dates, so we have to make them up. For example, because our bond has 22 years to maturity, we picked 1/1/2000 (January 1, 2000) as the settlement date and 1/1/2022 (January 1, 2022) as the maturity date. Any two dates would do as long as they are exactly 22 years apart, but these are particularly easy to work with. Finally, notice that we had to enter the coupon rate and yield to maturity in annual terms and then explicitly provide the number of coupon payments per year.

Concept Questions

7.1a   What are the cash flows associated with a bond?

7.1b   What is the general expression for the value of a bond?

7.1c   Is it true that the only risk associated with owning a bond is that the issuer will not make all the payments? Explain.

7.2   More about Bond Features

In this section, we continue our discussion of corporate debt by describing in some detail the basic terms and features that make up a typical long-term corporate bond. We discuss additional issues associated with long-term debt in subsequent sections.

Securities issued by corporations may be classified roughly as *equity securities* and *debt securities*. At the crudest level, a debt represents something that must be repaid; it is the result of borrowing money. When corporations borrow, they generally promise to make regularly scheduled interest payments and to repay the original amount borrowed (that is, the principal). The person or firm making the loan is called the *creditor* or *lender*. The corporation borrowing the money is called the *debtor* or *borrower*.

From a financial point of view, the main differences between debt and equity are the following:

1. Debt is not an ownership interest in the firm. Creditors generally do not have voting power.
2. The corporation's payment of interest on debt is considered a cost of doing business and is tax deductible (up to certain limits). Dividends paid to stockholders are *not* tax deductible.
3. Unpaid debt is a liability of the firm. If it is not paid, the creditors can legally claim the assets of the firm. This action can result in liquidation or reorganization, two of the possible consequences of bankruptcy. Thus, one of the costs of issuing debt is the possibility of financial failure. This possibility does not arise when equity is issued.

Information for bond investors
can be found at
www.investinginbonds.com.

IS IT DEBT OR EQUITY?

Sometimes it is unclear if a particular security is debt or equity. For example, suppose a corporation issues a perpetual bond with interest payable solely from corporate income if and only if earned. Whether this is really a debt is hard to say and is primarily a legal and semantic issue. Courts and taxing authorities would have the final say.

Corporations are adept at creating exotic, hybrid securities that have many features of equity but are treated as debt. Obviously, the distinction between debt and equity is important for tax purposes. So, one reason that corporations try to create a debt security that is really equity is to obtain the tax benefits of debt and the bankruptcy benefits of equity.

As a general rule, equity represents an ownership interest, and it is a residual claim. This means that equity holders are paid after debt holders. As a result of this, the risks and benefits associated with owning debt and equity are different. To give just one example, note that the maximum reward for owning a debt security is ultimately fixed by the amount of the loan, whereas there is no upper limit to the potential reward from owning an equity interest.

LONG-TERM DEBT: THE BASICS

Ultimately, all long-term debt securities are promises made by the issuing firm to pay principal when due and to make timely interest payments on the unpaid balance. Beyond this, a number of features distinguish these securities from one another. We discuss some of these features next.

The maturity of a long-term debt instrument is the length of time the debt remains outstanding with some unpaid balance. Debt securities can be *short-term* (with maturities of one year or less) or *long-term* (with maturities of more than one year).[1] Short-term debt is sometimes referred to as *unfunded debt.*[2]

Debt securities are typically called *notes*, *debentures*, or *bonds*. Strictly speaking, a bond is a secured debt. However, in common usage, the word *bond* refers to all kinds of secured and unsecured debt. We will continue to use the term generically to refer to long-term debt. Also, usually the only difference between a note and a bond is the original maturity. Issues with an original maturity of 10 years or less are often called notes. Longer-term issues are called bonds.

The two major forms of long-term debt are public-issue and privately placed. We concentrate on public-issue bonds. Most of what we say about them holds true for private-issue, long-term debt as well. The main difference between public-issue and privately placed debt is that the latter is directly placed with a lender and not offered to the public. Because this is a private transaction, the specific terms are up to the parties involved.

There are many other dimensions to long-term debt, including such things as security, call features, sinking funds, ratings, and protective covenants. The following table illustrates these features for a bond issued by technology giant Microsoft. If some of these terms are unfamiliar, have no fear. We will discuss them all presently.

Information about individual bonds can be found at **finra-markets.morningstar .com**.

Features of a Microsoft Bond		
Term		**Explanation**
Amount of Issue	$4.5 billion	The company issued $4.5 billion worth of bonds.
Date of Issue	8/8/2016	The bonds were sold on 8/8/2016.
Maturity	8/8/2046	The bonds mature on 8/8/2046.
Face value	$2,000	The denomination of the bonds is $2,000.
Annual coupon	3.700	Each bondholder will receive $74 per bond per year (3.700% of face value).
Offer price	99.515	The offer price will be 99.515% of the $2,000 face value, or $1,990, per bond.
Coupon payment dates	2/8, 8/8	Coupons of $74/2 = $37 will be paid on these dates.
Security	None	The bonds are not secured by specific assets.
Sinking fund	None	The bonds have no sinking fund.
Call provision	At any time	The bonds do not have a deferred call.
Call price	Treasury rate plus .25%	The bonds have a "make-whole" call price.
Rating	Moody's Aaa S&P AAA	The bonds have the highest possible credit rating.

Many of these features will be detailed in the bond indenture, so we discuss this first.

---

[1]There is no universally agreed-upon distinction between short-term and long-term debt. In addition, people often refer to *intermediate-term debt*, which has a maturity of more than 1 year and less than 3 to 5, or even 10, years.

[2]The word *funding* is part of the jargon of finance. It generally refers to the long term. A firm planning to "fund" its debt requirements may be replacing short-term debt with long-term debt.

THE INDENTURE

indenture
The written agreement between the corporation and the lender detailing the terms of the debt issue.

The **indenture** is the written agreement between the corporation (the borrower) and its creditors. It is sometimes referred to as the *deed of trust*.[3] Usually, a trustee (a bank, perhaps) is appointed by the corporation to represent the bondholders. The trust company must (1) make sure the terms of the indenture are obeyed, (2) manage the sinking fund (described in the following pages), and (3) represent the bondholders in default—that is, if the company defaults on its payments to them.

The bond indenture is a legal document. It can run several hundred pages and generally makes for tedious reading. It is an important document because it generally includes the following provisions:

1. The basic terms of the bonds.
2. The total amount of bonds issued.
3. A description of property used as security.
4. The repayment arrangements.
5. The call provisions.
6. Details of the protective covenants.

We discuss these features next.

Terms of a Bond   Corporate bonds usually have a face value (that is, a denomination) of $1,000, although par values of $2,000 like the Microsoft bond have become relatively common. Other par values also exist. For example, municipal bonds often have par values of $5,000, and Treasury bonds with par values of $10,000 or $100,000 are often sold. This *principal value* is stated on the bond certificate. So, if a corporation wanted to borrow $1 million, 1,000 bonds would have to be sold. The par value (that is, the initial accounting value) of a bond is almost always the same as the face value, and the terms are used interchangeably in practice.

Corporate bonds are usually in **registered form**. For example, the indenture might read as follows:

registered form
The form of bond issue in which the registrar of the company records ownership of each bond; payment is made directly to the owner of record.

> **Interest is payable semiannually on July 1 and January 1 of each year to the person in whose name the bond is registered at the close of business on June 15 or December 15, respectively.**

This means that the company has a registrar who will record the ownership of each bond and record any changes in ownership. The company will pay the interest and principal by check mailed directly to the address of the owner of record. A corporate bond may be registered and have attached "coupons." To obtain an interest payment, the owner must separate a coupon from the bond certificate and send it to the company registrar (the paying agent).

bearer form
The form of bond issue in which the bond is issued without record of the owner's name; payment is made to whomever holds the bond.

Alternatively, the bond could be in **bearer form**. This means that the certificate is the basic evidence of ownership, and the corporation will "pay the bearer." Ownership is not otherwise recorded, and, as with a registered bond with attached coupons, the holder of the bond certificate detaches the coupons and sends them to the company to receive payment.

There are two drawbacks to bearer bonds. First, they are difficult to recover if they are lost or stolen. Second, because the company does not know who owns its bonds, it cannot notify bondholders of important events. Bearer bonds were once the dominant type, but they are now much less common (in the United States) than registered bonds.

---

[3]The words *loan agreement* or *loan contract* are usually used for privately placed debt and term loans.

Security   Debt securities are classified according to the collateral and mortgages used to protect the bondholder.

Collateral is a general term that frequently means securities (for example, bonds and stocks) that are pledged as security for payment of debt. For example, collateral trust bonds often involve a pledge of common stock held by the corporation. However, the term *collateral* is commonly used to refer to any asset pledged on a debt.

Mortgage securities are secured by a mortgage on the real property of the borrower. The property involved is usually real estate—for example, land or buildings. The legal document that describes the mortgage is called a *mortgage trust indenture* or *trust deed.*

Sometimes mortgages are on specific property, such as a railroad car. More often, blanket mortgages are used. A *blanket mortgage* pledges all the real property owned by the company.[4]

Bonds frequently represent unsecured obligations of the company. A **debenture** is an unsecured bond, for which no specific pledge of property is made. The term **note** is generally used for such instruments if the maturity of the unsecured bond is less than 10 years when the bond is originally issued. Debenture holders have a claim only on property not otherwise pledged—in other words, the property that remains after mortgages and collateral trusts are taken into account. The Microsoft bonds in the table are an example of such an issue.

The terminology that we use here and elsewhere in this chapter is standard in the United States. Outside the United States, these same terms can have different meanings. For example, bonds issued by the British government ("gilts") are called treasury "stock." Also, in the United Kingdom, a debenture is a *secured* obligation.

At the current time, public bonds issued in the United States by industrial and financial companies are typically debentures. Most utility and railroad bonds are secured by a pledge of assets.

debenture
An unsecured debt, usually with a maturity of 10 years or more.

note
An unsecured debt, usually with a maturity under 10 years.

Seniority   In general terms, *seniority* indicates preference in position over other lenders, and debts are sometimes labeled as *senior* or *junior* to indicate seniority. Some debt is *subordinated*, as in, for example, a subordinated debenture.

In the event of default, holders of subordinated debt must give preference to other specified creditors. Usually, this means that the subordinated lenders will be paid off only after the specified creditors have been compensated. However, debt cannot be subordinated to equity.

The Securities Industry and Financial Markets Association (SIFMA) website is **www.sifma.org**.

Repayment   Bonds can be repaid at maturity, at which time the bondholder will receive the stated, or face, value of the bond; or they may be repaid in part or in entirety before maturity. Early repayment in some form is more typical and is often handled through a sinking fund.

A **sinking fund** is an account managed by the bond trustee for the purpose of repaying the bonds. The company makes annual payments to the trustee, who then uses the funds to retire a portion of the debt. The trustee does this by either buying up some of the bonds in the market or calling in a fraction of the outstanding bonds. This second option is discussed in the next section.

There are many different kinds of sinking fund arrangements, and the details are spelled out in the indenture. For example:

sinking fund
An account managed by the bond trustee for early bond redemption.

1. Some sinking funds start about 10 years after the initial issuance.
2. Some sinking funds establish equal payments over the life of the bond.

---

[4]Real property includes land and things "affixed thereto." It does not include cash or inventories.

3. Some high-quality bond issues establish payments to the sinking fund that are not sufficient to redeem the entire issue. As a consequence, there is the possibility of a large "balloon payment" at maturity.

call provision
An agreement giving the corporation the option to repurchase a bond at a specified price prior to maturity.

call premium
The amount by which the call price exceeds the par value of a bond.

deferred call provision
A call provision prohibiting the company from redeeming a bond prior to a certain date.

call-protected bond
A bond that, during a certain period, cannot be redeemed by the issuer.

The Call Provision   A **call provision** allows the company to repurchase or "call" part or all of the bond issue at stated prices over a specific period. Corporate bonds are usually callable.

Generally, the call price is above the bond's stated value (that is, the par value). The difference between the call price and the stated value is the **call premium**. The amount of the call premium may become smaller over time. One arrangement is to initially set the call premium equal to the annual coupon payment and then make it decline to zero as the call date moves closer to the time of maturity.

Call provisions are often not operative during the first part of a bond's life. This makes the call provision less of a worry for bondholders in the bond's early years. For example, a company might be prohibited from calling its bonds for the first 10 years. This is a **deferred call provision**. During this period of prohibition, the bond is said to be **call-protected**.

In recent years, a new type of call provision, a "make-whole" call, has become widespread in the corporate bond market. With such a feature, bondholders receive approximately what the bonds are worth if they are called. Because bondholders don't suffer a loss in the event of a call, they are "made whole."

To determine the make-whole call price, we calculate the present value of the remaining interest and principal payments at a rate specified in the indenture. For example, looking at our Microsoft issue, we see that the discount rate is "Treasury rate plus .25%." What this means is that we determine the discount rate by first finding a U.S. Treasury issue with the same maturity. We calculate the yield to maturity on the Treasury issue and then add on .25 percent to get the discount rate we use.

Notice that with a make-whole call provision, the call price is higher when interest rates are lower and vice versa (why?). Also notice that, as is common with a make-whole call, the Microsoft issue does not have a deferred call feature. Why might investors not be too concerned about the absence of this feature?

protective covenant
A part of the indenture limiting certain actions that might be taken during the term of the loan, usually to protect the lender's interest.

Protective Covenants   A **protective covenant** is that part of the indenture or loan agreement that limits certain actions a company might otherwise wish to take during the term of the loan. Protective covenants can be classified into two types: negative covenants and positive (or affirmative) covenants.

A *negative covenant* is a "thou shalt not" type of covenant. It limits or prohibits actions the company might take. Here are some typical examples:

1. The firm must limit the amount of dividends it pays according to some formula.
2. The firm cannot pledge any assets to other lenders.
3. The firm cannot merge with another firm.
4. The firm cannot sell or lease any major assets without approval by the lender.
5. The firm cannot issue additional long-term debt.

A *positive covenant* is a "thou shalt" type of covenant. It specifies an action the company agrees to take or a condition the company must abide by. Here are some examples:

1. The company must maintain its working capital at or above some specified minimum level.
2. The company must periodically furnish audited financial statements to the lender.
3. The firm must maintain any collateral or security in good condition.

Want detailed information about the amount and terms of the debt issued by a particular firm? Check out its latest financial statements by searching SEC filings at **www.sec.gov**

This is only a partial list of covenants; a particular indenture may feature many different ones.

Concept Questions

7.2a What are the distinguishing features of debt compared to equity?

7.2b What is the indenture? What are protective covenants? Give some examples.

7.2c What is a sinking fund?

Bond Ratings 7.3

Firms frequently pay to have their debt rated. The two leading bond-rating firms are Moody's and Standard & Poor's (S&P). The debt ratings are an assessment of the credit-worthiness of the corporate issuer. The definitions of creditworthiness used by Moody's and S&P are based on how likely the firm is to default and the protection creditors have in the event of a default.

It is important to recognize that bond ratings are concerned *only* with the possibility of default. Earlier, we discussed interest rate risk, which we defined as the risk of a change in the value of a bond resulting from a change in interest rates. Bond ratings do not address this issue. As a result, the price of a highly rated bond can still be quite volatile.

Bond ratings are constructed from information supplied by the corporation. The rating classes and some information concerning them are shown in the following table:

	Investment-Quality Bond Ratings				Low-Quality, Speculative, and/or "Junk" Bond Ratings					
	High Grade		Medium Grade		Low Grade			Very Low Grade		
Standard & Poor's	AAA	AA	A	BBB	BB	B	CCC	CC	C	D
Moody's	Aaa	Aa	A	Baa	Ba	B	Caa	Ca	C	

Moody's	S&P	
Aaa	AAA	Debt rated Aaa and AAA has the highest rating. Capacity to pay interest and principal is extremely strong.
Aa	AA	Debt rated Aa and AA has a very strong capacity to pay interest and repay principal. Together with the highest rating, this group comprises the high-grade bond class.
A	A	Debt rated A has a strong capacity to pay interest and repay principal, although it is somewhat more susceptible to the adverse effects of changes in circumstances and economic conditions than debt in high-rated categories.
Baa	BBB	Debt rated Baa and BBB is regarded as having an adequate capacity to pay interest and repay principal. Whereas it normally exhibits adequate protection parameters, adverse economic conditions or changing circumstances are more likely to lead to a weakened capacity to pay interest and repay principal for debt in this category than in higher-rated categories. These bonds are medium-grade obligations.
Ba; B Caa Ca C	BB; B CCC CC C	Debt rated in these categories is regarded, on balance, as predominantly speculative with respect to capacity to pay interest and repay principal in accordance with the terms of the obligation. BB and Ba indicate the lowest degree of speculation, and Ca, CC, and C the highest degree of speculation. Although such debt is likely to have some quality and protective characteristics, these are outweighed by large uncertainties or major risk exposures to adverse conditions. Issues rated C by Moody's are typically in default.
	D	Debt rated D is in default, and payment of interest and/or repayment of principal is in arrears.

NOTE: At times, both Moody's and S&P use adjustments (called notches) to these ratings. S&P uses plus and minus signs: A+ is the strongest A rating and A− the weakest. Moody's uses a 1, 2, or 3 designation, with 1 being the highest.

Want to know what criteria are commonly used to rate corporate and municipal bonds? Go to **www.standardandpoors .com, www.moodys.com**, or **www.fitchinv.com.**

The highest rating a firm's debt can have is AAA or Aaa, and such debt is judged to be the best quality and to have the lowest degree of risk. For example, the 100-year BellSouth issue we discussed earlier was originally rated AAA. This rating is not awarded very often: As of January 2018, only two nonfinancial U.S. companies, Johnson & Johnson and Microsoft, had AAA ratings. AA or Aa ratings indicate very good quality debt and are much more common.

A large part of corporate borrowing takes the form of low-grade, or "junk," bonds. If these low-grade corporate bonds are rated at all, they are rated below investment grade by the major rating agencies. Investment-grade bonds are bonds rated at least BBB by S&P or Baa by Moody's.

Rating agencies don't always agree. To illustrate, some bonds are known as "crossover" or "5B" bonds. The reason is that they are rated triple-B (or Baa) by one rating agency and double-B (or Ba) by another, a "split rating." For example, in February 2016, India-based textile and chemical company Standard Industries sold an issue of 10-year notes rated BBB– by S&P and Ba2 by Moody's.

A bond's credit rating can change as the issuer's financial strength improves or deteriorates. For example, in May 2016, Fitch Ratings cut the bond rating on retailer The Gap from BBB– to BB+, lowering the company's bond rating from investment grade to junk bond status. Bonds that drop into junk territory like this are called *fallen angels*. Fitch was concerned about the decline in same-store sales and gross margin at the company.

Credit ratings are important because defaults really do occur, and when they do, investors can lose heavily. For example, in 2000, AmeriServe Food Distribution, Inc., which supplied restaurants such as Burger King with everything from burgers to giveaway toys, defaulted on $200 million in junk bonds. After the default, the bonds traded at just 18 cents on the dollar, leaving investors with a loss of more than $160 million.

If you're nervous about the level of debt piled up by the U.S. government, don't go to **www.fiscal.treasury.gov** or to **www.usdebtclock .org/world-debt-clock.html**! Learn all about government bonds at **www.newyorkfed .org**.

Even worse in AmeriServe's case, the bonds had been issued only four months earlier, thereby making AmeriServe an NCAA champion. Although that might be a good thing for a college basketball team such as the University of Kentucky Wildcats, in the bond market it means "No Coupon At All," and it's not a good thing for investors.

Concept Questions

7.3a   What does a bond rating say about the risk of fluctuations in a bond's value resulting from interest rate changes?

7.3b   What is a junk bond?

7.4   Some Different Types of Bonds

Thus far we have considered only "plain vanilla" corporate bonds. In this section, we briefly look at bonds issued by governments and also at bonds with unusual features.

GOVERNMENT BONDS

The biggest borrower in the world—by a wide margin—is everybody's favorite family member, Uncle Sam. In early 2018, the total debt of the U.S. government was $20 *trillion*, or about $63,000 per citizen (and growing!). When the government wishes to borrow money for more than one year, it sells what are known as Treasury notes and bonds to the public (in fact, it does so every month). Currently, outstanding Treasury notes and bonds have original maturities ranging from 2 to 30 years.

Most U.S. Treasury issues are just ordinary coupon bonds. There are two important things to keep in mind. First, U.S. Treasury issues, unlike essentially all other bonds, have no default risk because (we hope) the Treasury can always come up with the money to make the payments. Second, Treasury issues are exempt from state income taxes (though not federal income taxes). In other words, the coupons you receive on a Treasury note or bond are taxed only at the federal level.

State and local governments also borrow money by selling notes and bonds. Such issues are called *municipal* notes and bonds, or just "munis." Unlike Treasury issues, munis have varying degrees of default risk, and, in fact, they are rated much like corporate issues. Also, they are almost always callable. The most intriguing thing about munis is that their coupons are exempt from federal income taxes (though not necessarily state income taxes). This makes them very attractive to high-income, high-tax bracket investors.

For information on municipal bonds, including prices, check out **emma.msrb.org**.

Because of the enormous tax break they receive, the yields on municipal bonds are much lower than the yields on taxable bonds. For example, in December 2017, long-term Aa-rated corporate bonds were yielding about 3.42 percent. At the same time, long-term Aa munis were yielding about 2.20 percent. Suppose an investor was in a 30 percent tax bracket. All else being the same, would this investor prefer a Aa corporate bond or a Aa municipal bond?

To answer, we need to compare the *aftertax* yields on the two bonds. Ignoring state and local taxes, the muni pays 2.20 percent on both a pretax and an aftertax basis. The corporate issue pays 3.42 percent before taxes, but it pays only $.0342 \times (1 - .30) = .0239$, or 2.39 percent, once we account for the 30 percent tax bite. Given this, the corporate bond has a better yield, but the difference is much smaller after we account for the tax bite.

Another good bond market site is **money.cnn.com/data /bonds**.

Taxable versus Municipal Bonds	**EXAMPLE 7.4**

Suppose taxable bonds are currently yielding 8 percent, while at the same time, munis of comparable risk and maturity are yielding 6 percent. Which is more attractive to an investor in a 40 percent bracket? What is the break-even tax rate? How do you interpret this rate?

For an investor in a 40 percent tax bracket, a taxable bond yields $8 \times (1 - .40) = 4.8$ percent after taxes, so the muni is much more attractive. The break-even tax rate is the tax rate at which an investor would be indifferent between a taxable and a nontaxable issue. If we let t^* stand for the break-even tax rate, then we can solve for it as follows:

$$.08 \times (1 - t^*) = .06$$
$$1 - t^* = .06/.08 = .75$$
$$t^* = .25$$

An investor in a 25 percent tax bracket would make 6 percent after taxes from either bond.

ZERO COUPON BONDS

A bond that pays no coupons at all must be offered at a price that is much lower than its stated value. Such bonds are called **zero coupon bonds**, or just *zeroes*.[5]

zero coupon bond
A bond that makes no coupon payments and is thus initially priced at a deep discount.

---

[5]A bond issued with a very low coupon rate (as opposed to a zero coupon rate) is an *original-issue discount* (*OID*) *bond*.

TABLE 7.2

Interest Expense for EIN's Zeroes

Year	Beginning Value	Ending Value	Implicit Interest Expense	Straight-Line Interest Expense
1	$508.35	$ 582.01	$ 73.66	$ 98.33
2	582.01	666.34	84.33	98.33
3	666.34	762.90	96.56	98.33
4	762.90	873.44	110.54	98.33
5	873.44	1,000.00	126.56	98.33
Total			$491.65	$491.65

Suppose the Eight-Inch Nails (EIN) Company issues a $1,000 face value, five-year zero coupon bond. The initial price is set at $508.35. Even though no interest payments are made on the bond, zero coupon bond calculations use semiannual periods to be consistent with coupon bond calculations. Using semiannual periods, it is straightforward to verify that, at this price, the bond yields about 14 percent to maturity. The total interest paid over the life of the bond is $1,000 − 508.35 = $491.65.

For tax purposes, the issuer of a zero coupon bond deducts interest every year even though no interest is actually paid. Similarly, the owner must pay taxes on interest accrued every year, even though no interest is actually received.

The way in which the yearly interest on a zero coupon bond is calculated is governed by tax law. Before 1982, corporations could calculate the interest deduction on a straight-line basis. For EIN, the annual interest deduction would have been $491.65/5 = $98.33 per year.

Under current tax law, the implicit interest is determined by amortizing the loan. We do this by first calculating the bond's value at the beginning of each year. For example, after one year, the bond will have four years until maturity, so it will be worth $1,000/1.07^8 = $582.01; the value in two years will be $1,000/1.07^6 = $666.34; and so on. The implicit interest each year is the change in the bond's value for the year. The values and interest expenses for the EIN bond are listed in Table 7.2.

Notice that under the old rules, zero coupon bonds were more attractive because the deductions for interest expense were larger in the early years (compare the implicit interest expense with the straight-line expense).

Under current tax law, EIN could deduct $73.66 in interest paid the first year and the owner of the bond would pay taxes on $73.66 in taxable income (even though no interest was actually received). This second tax feature makes taxable zero coupon bonds less attractive to individuals. They are still a very attractive investment for tax-exempt investors with long-term dollar-denominated liabilities, such as pension funds, because the future dollar value is known with relative certainty.

Some bonds are zero coupon bonds for only part of their lives. For example, General Motors has a debenture outstanding that matures on March 15, 2036. For the first 20 years of its life, no coupon payments will be made; but, after 20 years, it will begin paying coupons semiannually at a rate of 7.75 percent per year.

FLOATING-RATE BONDS

The conventional bonds we have talked about in this chapter have fixed-dollar obligations because the coupon rates are set as fixed percentages of the par values. Similarly, the principal amounts are set equal to the par values. Under these circumstances, the coupon payments and principal are completely fixed.

With *floating-rate bonds (floaters)*, the coupon payments are adjustable. The adjustments are tied to an interest rate index such as the Treasury bill interest rate or the 30-year Treasury bond rate.

The value of a floating-rate bond depends on exactly how the coupon payment adjustments are defined. In most cases, the coupon adjusts with a lag to some base rate. For example, suppose a coupon rate adjustment is made on June 1. The adjustment might be based on the simple average of Treasury bond yields during the previous three months. In addition, the majority of floaters have the following features:

1. The holder has the right to redeem the note at par on the coupon payment date after some specified amount of time. This is called a *put* provision, and it is discussed in the following section.

2. The coupon rate has a floor and a ceiling, meaning that the coupon is subject to a minimum and a maximum. In this case, the coupon rate is said to be "capped," and the upper and lower rates are sometimes called the *collar*.

A particularly interesting type of floating-rate bond is an *inflation-linked* bond. Such bonds have coupons that are adjusted according to the rate of inflation (the principal amount may be adjusted as well). The U.S. Treasury began issuing such bonds in January of 1997. The issues are sometimes called "TIPS," or Treasury Inflation-Protected Securities. Other countries, including Canada, Israel, and Britain, have issued similar securities.

Official information about U.S. inflation-indexed bonds is at **www.treasurydirect.gov**.

OTHER TYPES OF BONDS

Many bonds have unusual or exotic features. So-called catastrophe, or cat, bonds provide an interesting example. In May 2016, United Services Automobile Association (USAA), the company that specializes in insurance for military veterans, issued $250 million in cat bonds. These cat bonds covered U.S. storms, wildfires, meteor strikes, and solar flares. In the event of one of these triggering events, investors would lose some or all of their money.

The largest single cat bond issue to date is a series of six bonds sold by Merna Reinsurance in 2007 (reinsurance companies sell insurance to insurance companies). The six bond issues were to cover various catastrophes the company faced due to its reinsurance of State Farm. The six bonds totaled about $1.2 billion in par value. During 2016, about $7.1 billion in cat bonds were issued, and there was about $26.8 billion par value in cat bonds outstanding at the end of the year.

At this point, cat bonds probably seem pretty risky. It might be surprising to learn that since cat bonds were first issued in 1997, only four have not been paid in full. Because of Hurricane Katrina, cat bondholders lost $190 million. Cat bondholders also lost $300 million due to the 2011 tsunami in Japan. During 2011, two other cat bond issues, each worth $100 million, were triggered due to an unusually active tornado season.

Another possible bond feature is a *warrant*. A warrant gives the buyer of a bond the right to purchase shares of stock in the company at a fixed price. Such a right is very valuable if the stock price climbs substantially (a later chapter discusses this subject in greater depth). Because of the value of this feature, bonds with warrants are often issued at a very low coupon rate.

As these examples illustrate, bond features are really limited only by the imaginations of the parties involved. Unfortunately, there are far too many variations for us to cover in detail here. We close this discussion by mentioning a few of the more common types.

Income bonds are similar to conventional bonds, except that coupon payments depend on company income. Specifically, coupons are paid to bondholders only if the firm's income is sufficient. This would appear to be an attractive feature, but income bonds are not very common.

A *convertible bond* can be swapped for a fixed number of shares of stock anytime before maturity at the holder's option. Convertibles are relatively common, but the number has been decreasing in recent years.

A *put bond* allows the *holder* to force the issuer to buy back the bond at a stated price. For example, International Paper Co. has bonds outstanding that allow the holder to force International Paper to buy the bonds back at 100 percent of face value if certain "risk" events happen. One such event is a change in credit rating from investment grade to lower than investment grade by Moody's or S&P. The put feature is therefore just the reverse of the call provision.

The *reverse convertible* is a relatively new type of structured note. One type generally offers a high coupon rate, but the redemption at maturity can be paid in cash at par value or paid in shares of stock. For example, one recent General Motors (GM) reverse convertible had a coupon rate of 16 percent, which is a very high coupon rate in today's interest rate environment. However, at maturity, if GM's stock declined sufficiently, bondholders would receive a fixed number of GM shares that were worth less than par value. So, while the income portion of the bond return would be high, the potential loss in par value could easily erode the extra return.

Perhaps the most unusual bond (and certainly the most ghoulish) is the "death bond." Companies such as Stone Street Financial purchase life insurance policies from individuals who are expected to die within the next 10 years. They then sell bonds that are paid off from the life insurance proceeds received when the policyholders pass away. The return on the bonds to investors depends on how long the policyholders live. A major risk is that if medical treatment advances quickly, it will raise the life expectancy of the policyholders, thereby decreasing the return to the bondholder.

Structured notes are bonds that are based on stocks, bonds, commodities, or currencies. One particular type of structured note has a return based on a stock market index. At expiration, if the stock index has declined, the bond returns the principal. However, if the stock index has increased, the bond will return a portion of the stock index return, say 80 percent. Another type of structured note will return twice the stock index return, but with the potential for loss of principal.

A given bond may have many unusual features. Two of the most recent exotic bonds are *CoCo bonds*, which have a coupon payment, and *NoNo bonds*, which are zero coupon bonds. CoCo and NoNo bonds are contingent convertible, putable, callable, subordinated bonds. The contingent convertible clause is similar to the normal conversion feature, except the contingent feature must be met. For example, a contingent feature may require that the company stock trade at 110 percent of the conversion price for 20 out of the most recent 30 days. Valuing a bond of this sort can be quite complex, and the yield to maturity calculation is often meaningless.

SUKUK

You can find out more about sukuk at **www.sukuk.com**.

Worldwide demand for assets that comply with sharia, or Islamic law and cultural tradition, has grown dramatically. Assets, including deposits at Islamic financial institutions, totaled about $2.1 trillion in 2016, up from $1.3 trillion in 2011. One of the major differences between Western financial practices and sharia is that Islamic law does not permit charging or paying *riba*, or interest. Given our current discussion about bonds, this means that anyone following sharia cannot buy or issue conventional bonds.

To accommodate the restriction on interest payments, Islamic bonds, or *sukuk*, have been created. There are many possible structures to sukuk, such as partial ownership in a debt (sukuk al-murabaha) or an asset (sukuk al-ijara). In the case of a sukuk al-ijara, there is a binding promise to repurchase a certain asset by the issuer at maturity. Before the sukuk matures, rent is paid on the asset. While we have noted that traditional bonds can be relatively illiquid, most sukuk are bought and held to maturity. As a result, secondary markets in sukuk are extremely illiquid.

IN THEIR OWN WORDS ...

Edward I. Altman on Junk Bonds and Leveraged Loans

One of the most important developments in corporate finance over the last 40 years has been the reemergence of publicly owned and traded low-rated corporate debt. Originally offered to the public in the early 1900s to help finance some of our emerging growth industries, these high-yield, high-risk bonds (sometimes called "junk bonds") virtually disappeared after the rash of bond defaults during the Depression. Starting in the late 1970s, however, the junk bond market catapulted from being an insignificant element in the corporate fixed-income market to being one of the fastest-growing and most controversial types of financing mechanisms. Technically, high-yield bonds are bonds issued by companies whose rating given by one or more of the major rating agencies, i.e., Fitch, Moody's or Standard & Poor's, is below investment grade, e.g., below BBB− by S&P.

The term *junk* emanates from the dominant type of low-rated bond issues outstanding prior to 1977 when the "market" consisted almost exclusively of original-issue investment-grade bonds that fell from their lofty status to a higher-default risk, speculative-grade level. These so-called fallen angels amounted to about $8.5 billion in 1977. In 2016, fallen angels comprised about 12 percent of the $1.6 trillion publicly owned junk bond market. The balance are "original-issue," high-yield bonds.

The high-yield bond market in Europe, although in existence for decades, only began to grow significantly starting in 2009 from about €100 billion to about €500 billion at the end of 2016, and is now a fairly well diversified market, about 1/3 the size of the U.S. market.

Beginning in 1977, some speculative-grade issuers began to go directly to the public to raise debt capital for growth purposes. Early issuers of junk bonds were energy-related firms, cable TV companies, airlines, and assorted other industrial companies. The emerging growth company rationale coupled with relatively high returns to early investors helped legitimize this asset class and attract interest from the more established investment banks and asset managers in the mid-1980s. The pioneers in the high-yield market were Drexel Burnham Lambert, a boutique bank, and its junk bond "king," Michael Milken. I, personally, became interested in this new financing innovation in the early 1980s, when a major bank asked me to assess the market's potential.

By far the most important and controversial aspect of the early junk bond financings was its role in the corporate restructuring movement from 1985 to 1989. High-leverage transactions and acquisitions, such as leveraged buyouts (LBOs), which occur when a firm is taken private and the old shareholders are paid a premium to sell their shares, became numerous and threatening to many firms. Funds for this buyout were raised from traditional bank loans and high-yield bonds, plus equity. These leveraged recapitalizations helped to transform the face of corporate America, leading to a heated debate as to the economic and social consequences of firms' being bought by private-equity firms with debt-equity ratios of at least 6:1 in the restructured firm. Similar, but less emotional, comments accompanied a second LBO movement in 2004–2007, and even less so in the most recent heavy activity by private-equity firms in what is now (in 2017) an established and impressive market. The latter trend is not without some concerns, as the prices paid to buyout firms soared to above 10 times EBITA in 2015 and 2016, a very high multiple.

LBOs involved increasingly large companies, and the multi-billion dollar takeover became fairly common in the 1980s. The first mega-buyout was the huge $25+ billion RJR Nabisco LBO in 1989. LBOs were typically financed with about 60 percent senior bank and insurance company debt, about 25–30 percent subordinated public debt (usually junk bonds), and 10–15 percent equity. The junk bond segment is sometimes referred to as "mezzanine" financing because it lies between the "balcony" senior debt and the "basement" equity. In the most recent LBO binge, however, more than 30 percent of the financing has been equity but the transactions are, on average, much larger than in the late 1980s.

These restructurings resulted in huge fees to advisers and underwriters and large premiums (at least 30 to 40 percent in most cases) to the old shareholders who were bought out. They continued as long as the market was willing to buy these new debt offerings at what appeared to be a favorable risk–return trade-off. The bottom fell out of the market in the last six months of 1989 due to a number of factors, including a marked increase in defaults, government regulation against S&Ls holding junk bonds, and at least one highly publicized bankruptcy of a highly leveraged financial restructuring—Federated Department Stores. In addition, the leading underwriter, Drexel Burnham, went bankrupt and Milken was prosecuted and sent to jail. As a result, in the early 1990s, the financial market was questioning the very survival of the junk bond market. The answer as to its survival was a resounding "yes," as the amount of new issues soared to record annual levels of $40 billion in 1992, almost $80 billion in 1993, and in 1997 reached an impressive $119 billion. Coupled with plummeting default rates (under 2 percent each year in the 1993–97 period) and attractive returns in these years, the risk–return characteristics were extremely favorable. Despite legal and financial problems, Drexel's and Milken's positive legacy for pioneering the high-yield market is clear and important.

The junk bond market in the late 1990s was a quieter one compared to that of the 1980s, but, in terms of growth and returns, it was healthier than ever before. While the low default rates in 1992–1998 helped to fuel new investment funds and new issues, the market experienced its ups and downs in subsequent years. Indeed, default rates started to rise in 1999 and accelerated in 2000–2002. The latter year saw default rates reach record levels of over 12 percent as the economy slipped into a recession and investors suffered from the excesses of lending in the late 1990s.

Since the mid-1990s, a "sister" high-yield debt market developed in the private leveraged loan (LL) market. This low-quality (non-investment grade), higher-interest rate market grew enormously in the United States and Europe in the 2005–2007 period and was at least 30 percent larger than the high-yield bond market in 2008. Since the great financial crisis of 2008, the private LL market has once again become extremely popular and is a major source of funds in the private debt market. One of the main reasons for the recent growth and popularity of leveraged loans was that the issuing bank could, in most environments, easily sell these loans into structured finance vehicles called collateralized loan obligations (CLOs).

Private, leveraged loan debt facilities have registered lower default rates than high-yield bonds and higher recovery rates due to their senior status. They have continued to be a major source of corporate debt at levels exceeding $400 billion a year in the last five years, and with attractive risk–return trade-offs for major banks and the new and growing "shadow-banking" markets made up of non-bank lenders. I estimate that the shadow-banking market has perhaps more than $200 billion under management in 2017.

The market for leveraged financing rebounded quickly in 2003 and continued to prosper until the credit crisis of 2008–2009. With the "flight-to-quality" caused by the sub-prime mortgage market meltdown in the second half of 2007 and 2008, returns to investors in high-yield bonds and leveraged loans fell considerably, new issues dried up, and default rates increased from the unusually low-risk years that coincided with the leveraged excesses. Despite these highly volatile events and problems with liquidity, we were convinced that high-yield bonds, and their private debt companion, leveraged loans, would continue in the future to be a major source of corporate debt financing and a legitimate asset class for investors.

Indeed, the high yield bond market, as well as all risky bonds and common stocks, staged a remarkable recovery after the first quarter of 2009, and for the entire year 2009 the returns to high yield bond and leveraged loan investors were the highest in the almost 40 years of the modern era of leveraged finance markets. This amazing turnaround, despite near-record defaults in 2009, was remarkable in the speed and extent of the recovery, with returns of about 60 percent for high-yield bond investors. Impressive positive returns and record new issuance of highly leveraged financed projects and refinancing has continued almost unabated through 2016. And, the market was incredibly accepting of higher yielding bonds and loans, especially in the low interest rate environment of 2012–2016. But, we are now (2017) concerned about another bubble building as the current benign credit cycle, with low default rates and highly risky new issuance, continues for more than seven years since the last market downturn. Perhaps the next few years will be quite volatile with rising default rates and lower recoveries and returns. But, as always, the leveraged finance market will continue to exist and probably expand in the U.S., in Europe, and in other parts of the world.

Edward I. Altman is Max L. Heine Professor of Finance Emeritus and Director of Credit and Debt Markets Research at the NYU Salomon Center at the Stern School of Business. He is widely recognized as one of the world's leading experts on bankruptcy and credit analysis as well as the high-yield and distressed debt markets.

Concept Questions

7.4a   Why might an income bond be attractive to a corporation with volatile cash flows? Can you think of a reason why income bonds are not more popular?

7.4b   What do you think would be the effect of a put feature on a bond's coupon? How about a convertibility feature? Why?

7.5   Bond Markets

Excel Master It!

xlsx Excel Master
coverage online

Bonds are bought and sold in enormous quantities every day. You may be surprised to learn that the trading volume in bonds on a typical day is many, many times larger than the trading volume in stocks (by *trading volume* we mean the amount of money that changes hands). Here is a finance trivia question: What is the largest securities market in the world?

WORK THE WEB

Bond quotes have become more available with the rise of the Internet. One site where you can find current bond prices is finra-markets.morningstar.com. We went to the website and searched for bonds issued by Coca-Cola. Here is a look at part of what we found for one of the bonds:

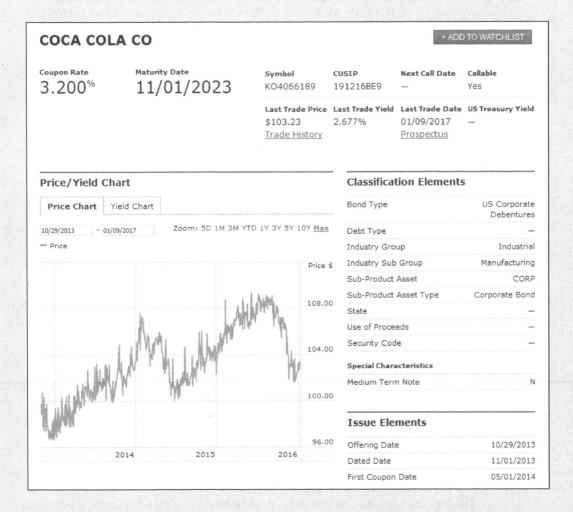

The bond has a coupon rate of 3.20 percent and matures on November 1, 2023. The last sale on this bond was at a price of 103.23 percent of par, which gives a yield to maturity of about 2.677 percent. Not only does the site provide the most recent price and yield information, but it also provides other important information about the bond, such as the credit rating, coupon date, call date, and call price. We'll leave it up to you to have a look at the page and the rest of the information available there.

Questions

1. Go to this website and find the bond shown above. What is the credit rating on this bond? What was the size of the bond issue? What were the yield to maturity and price when the bond was issued?

2. If you search for Chevron bonds (CVX), you will find bonds for several companies listed. Why do you think Chevron has bonds issued with different corporate names?

Most people would guess the New York Stock Exchange. In fact, the largest securities market in the world in terms of trading volume is the U.S. Treasury market.

HOW BONDS ARE BOUGHT AND SOLD

As we mentioned all the way back in Chapter 1, most trading in bonds takes place over the counter, or OTC. Recall that this means there is no particular place where buying and selling occur. Instead, dealers around the country (and around the world) stand ready to buy and sell. The various dealers are connected electronically.

One reason the bond markets are so big is that the number of bond issues far exceeds the number of stock issues. There are two reasons for this. First, a corporation would typically have only one common stock issue outstanding (there are exceptions to this that we discuss in our next chapter). A large corporation could easily have a dozen or more note and bond issues outstanding. Beyond this, federal, state, and local borrowing is enormous. For example, even a small city would usually have a wide variety of notes and bonds outstanding, representing money borrowed to pay for things like roads, sewers, and schools. When you think about how many small cities there are in the United States, you begin to get the picture!

Because the bond market is almost entirely OTC, it has historically had little or no transparency. A financial market is *transparent* if it is possible to easily observe its prices and trading volume. On the New York Stock Exchange, for example, it is possible to see the price and quantity for every single transaction. In contrast, in the bond market, it is often not possible to observe either. Transactions are privately negotiated between parties, and there is little or no centralized reporting of transactions.

Although the total volume of trading in bonds far exceeds that in stocks, only a small fraction of the total bond issues that exist actually trade on a given day. This fact, combined with the lack of transparency in the bond market, means that getting up-to-date prices on individual bonds can be difficult or impossible, particularly for smaller corporate or municipal issues. Instead, a variety of sources of estimated prices exist and are commonly used.

To learn more about TRACE, visit **www.finra.org**.

BOND PRICE REPORTING

In 2002, transparency in the corporate bond market began to improve dramatically. Under new regulations, corporate bond dealers are now required to report trade information through what is known as the Trade Reporting and Compliance Engine (TRACE). Our nearby *Work the Web* box shows you how to get bond quotes.

TRACE bond quotes are available at finra-markets.morningstar.com. As shown in Figure 7.3, the Financial Industry Regulatory Authority (FINRA) provides a daily snapshot from TRACE by reporting the most active issues. The information shown is largely self-explanatory. Notice that the price of the Microsoft bond dropped about 1.92 percentage points on this day. What do you think happened to the yield to maturity for this bond? Figure 7.3 focuses on the most active bonds with investment grade ratings, but the most active high-yield and convertible bonds are also available on the website.

The Federal Reserve Bank of St. Louis maintains dozens of online files containing macroeconomic data as well as rates on U.S. Treasury issues. Go to **fred.stlouisfed.org**

If you go to the website and click on a particular bond, you will get a lot of information about the bond, including the credit rating, the call schedule, original issue information, and trade information.

As we mentioned before, the U.S. Treasury market is the largest securities market in the world. As with bond markets in general, it is an OTC market, so there is limited transparency. Unlike the situation with bond markets in general, trading in Treasury issues,

FIGURE 7.3   **Sample TRACE Bond Quotations**

Most Active Investment Grade Bonds

Issuer Name	Symbol	Coupon	Maturity	Moody's/S&P/Fitch	High	Low	Last	Change	Yield%
COMCAST CORP NEW	CMCS4442549	3.300%	02/01/2027	//A-	101.35700	99.42200	99.63300	-0.484000	
TEVA PHARMACEUTICAL FIN NETH III B V	TEVA4384553	3.150%	10/01/2026	Baa2//BBB	94.39000	92.20800	92.22400	-1.096000	4.127938
MPLX LP	MPLX4403827	4.500%	07/15/2023	Baa3/BBB-/BBB-	102.83800	102.67100	102.68200	-0.442000	4.012035
COMCAST CORP NEW	CMCS4442550	3.000%	02/01/2024	//A-	100.04300	99.50700	99.55100	-0.492000	
BARCLAYS PLC	BCS4442016	4.950%	01/10/2047	Baa2//	102.77500	101.17600	101.17600	-1.438000	
ANHEUSER-BUSCH INBEV FIN INC	BUD4327588	4.900%	02/01/2046	A3/A-/BBB	108.92900	107.37500	107.83800	-1.034000	4.414289
MICROSOFT CORP	MSFT4389880	3.700%	08/08/2046	Aaa/AAA/AA+	95.82700	94.54000	94.68900	-1.918286	4.008024
ROYAL BK CDA	RY4297754	2.100%	10/14/2020	Aaa//AAA	99.83700	99.55300	99.73300	-0.035000	2.173974
ANHEUSER-BUSCH INBEV FIN INC	BUD4327481	3.650%	02/01/2026	A3/A-/BBB	103.01100	101.01600	101.07700	-0.598000	3.506954
ACTAVIS FDG SCS	ACT4218879	3.800%	03/15/2025	Baa3//BBB-	100.49600	99.55800	100.14200	-0.566000	3.778990

particularly recently issued ones, is very heavy. Each day, representative prices for outstanding Treasury issues are reported.

Figure 7.4 shows a portion of the daily Treasury note and bond listings from the website wsj.com. Examine the entry that begins "2/15/2036." Reading from left to right, the "2/15/2036" tells us that the bond's maturity is February 15, 2036. The next column is the coupon rate, which is 4.500 percent for this bond. Treasury bonds all make semiannual payments and have a minimum face value of $1,000, so this bond will pay $22.50 every six months until it matures.

The next two pieces of information are the **bid** and **asked prices**. In general, in any OTC or dealer market, the bid price represents what a dealer is willing to pay for a security, and the asked price (or "ask" price) is what a dealer is willing to take for it. The difference between the two prices is called the **bid-ask spread** (or just "spread"), and it represents the dealer's profit.

Treasury prices are quoted as a percentage of face value. The bid price, or what a dealer is willing to pay, on the 2/15/2036 bond is 128.0781. With a $1,000 face value, this quote represents $1,280.781. The asked price, or the price at which the dealer is willing to sell the bond, is 128.1406, or $1,281.406.

The next number quoted is the change in the asked price from the previous day, measured as a percentage of face value, so this issue's asked price increased by .7031 percent, or $7.031, in value from the previous day. Finally, the last number reported is the yield to maturity, based on the asked price. Notice that this is a premium bond because it sells for more than its face value. Not surprisingly, its yield to maturity (2.618 percent) is less than its coupon rate (4.50 percent).

The very last ordinary bond listed, the 11/15/2046, is often called the "bellwether" bond. This bond's yield is the one that is usually reported in the evening news. So, for example, when you hear that long-term interest rates rose, what is really being said is that the yield on this bond went up (and its price went down).

If you examine the yields on the various issues in Figure 7.4, you will clearly see that they vary by maturity. Why this occurs and what it might mean is one of the things we discuss in our next section. Government (referred to as "sovereign") bond yields also vary by country of origin. Nearby, we show the 10-year bond yields of several countries. The yields vary according to default risks and foreign exchange risks (to be discussed later in the text).

bid price
The price a dealer is willing to pay for a security.

asked price
The price a dealer is willing to take for a security.

bid–ask spread
The difference between the bid price and the asked price.

Current and historical Treasury yield information is available at **www.treasury.gov**.

FIGURE 7.4

Sample *Wall Street Journal* U.S. Treasury Note and Bond Prices

Source: Table recreated with data from wsj.com, January 9, 2017.

Treasury Notes and Bonds					
Maturity	**Coupon**	**Bid**	**Asked**	**Chg**	**Asked Yield**
11/15/2018	1.250	100.1484	100.1641	0.0391	1.160
4/15/2019	0.875	99.0703	99.0859	0.0625	1.286
4/30/2020	1.125	98.5938	98.6094	0.1016	1.558
8/15/2021	8.125	127.4844	127.5000	0.2344	1.857
7/31/2022	2.000	99.9609	99.9766	0.2266	2.004
2/28/2023	1.500	96.5703	96.5859	0.2500	2.096
5/15/2024	2.500	101.9375	101.9531	0.3125	2.210
8/15/2025	6.875	135.8438	135.8594	0.3438	2.262
8/15/2026	1.500	92.4766	92.4922	0.2969	2.380
8/15/2027	6.375	136.8281	136.8438	0.4688	2.414
8/15/2028	5.500	130.2891	130.3516	0.4531	2.473
11/15/2028	5.250	128.1563	128.2188	0.4453	2.485
2/15/2029	5.250	128.7578	128.8203	0.4609	2.478
8/15/2029	6.125	139.1875	139.2500	0.5391	2.478
5/15/2030	6.250	142.5781	142.6406	0.5938	2.478
2/15/2031	5.375	134.3438	134.4063	0.5625	2.470
2/15/2036	4.500	128.0781	128.1406	0.7031	2.618
2/15/2037	4.750	131.7891	131.8516	0.7500	2.688
5/15/2037	5.000	135.9531	136.0156	0.7656	2.690
5/15/2038	4.500	128.0625	128.1250	0.6875	2.749
2/15/2039	3.500	110.9844	111.0469	0.6406	2.824
8/15/2039	4.500	127.4922	127.5547	0.7344	2.839
2/15/2040	4.625	129.7188	129.7813	0.6953	2.855
11/15/2040	4.250	123.3438	123.4063	0.7422	2.885
2/15/2041	4.750	132.4688	132.5000	0.7578	2.872
2/15/2042	3.125	103.3516	103.3828	0.6484	2.934
2/15/2043	3.125	103.1406	103.1719	0.6250	2.950
5/15/2043	2.875	98.3594	98.3906	0.5625	2.963
2/15/2044	3.625	112.7266	112.7578	0.6484	2.939
2/15/2045	2.500	90.7578	90.7891	0.6016	2.987
11/15/2046	2.875	98.1172	98.1484	0.6719	2.969

SELECTED INTERNATIONAL GOVERNMENT 10-YEAR BOND YIELDS	
	Yield (%)
United States	2.41
United Kingdom	1.19
Japan	.04
Canada	2.04
Australia	2.63
Greece	4.03
Spain	1.55
Italy	2.00
India	7.32

SOURCE: Data pulled from www.bloomberg.com, December 30, 2017.

A NOTE ABOUT BOND PRICE QUOTES

If you buy a bond between coupon payment dates, the price you pay is usually more than the price you are quoted. The reason is that standard convention in the bond market is to quote prices net of "accrued interest," meaning that accrued interest is deducted to arrive at the quoted price. This quoted price is called the **clean price**. The price you actually pay, however, includes the accrued interest. This price is the **dirty price**, also known as the "full" or "invoice" price.

An example is the easiest way to understand these issues. Suppose you buy a bond with a 12 percent annual coupon, payable semiannually. You actually pay $1,080 for this bond, so $1,080 is the dirty, or invoice, price. Further, on the day you buy it, the next coupon is due in four months, so you are between coupon dates. Notice that the next coupon will be $60.

The accrued interest on a bond is calculated by taking the fraction of the coupon period that has passed, in this case two months out of six, and multiplying this fraction by the next coupon, $60. So, the accrued interest in this example is $2/6 \times \$60 = \$20$. The bond's quoted price (that is, its clean price) would be $1,080 − 20 = $1,060.[6]

> **clean price**
> The price of a bond net of accrued interest; this is the price that is typically quoted.

> **dirty price**
> The price of a bond including accrued interest, also known as the *full* or *invoice price*. This is the price the buyer actually pays.

Concept Questions

7.5a   Why do we say bond markets may have little or no transparency?
7.5b   In general, what are bid and ask prices?
7.5c   What is the difference between a bond's clean price and its dirty price?

Inflation and Interest Rates   7.6

So far, we haven't considered the role of inflation in our various discussions of interest rates, yields, and returns. Because this is an important consideration, we consider the impact of inflation next.

REAL VERSUS NOMINAL RATES

In examining interest rates, or any other financial market rates such as discount rates, bond yields, rates of return, and required returns, it is often necessary to distinguish between **real rates** and **nominal rates**. Nominal rates are called "nominal" because they have not been adjusted for inflation. Real rates are rates that have been adjusted for inflation.

To see the effect of inflation, suppose prices are currently rising by 5 percent per year. In other words, the rate of inflation is 5 percent. An investment is available that will be worth $115.50 in one year. It costs $100 today. Notice that with a present value of $100 and a future value in one year of $115.50, this investment has a 15.5 percent rate of return. In calculating this 15.5 percent return, we did not consider the effect of inflation, so this is the nominal return.

What is the impact of inflation here? To answer, suppose pizzas cost $5 apiece at the beginning of the year. With $100, we can buy 20 pizzas. Because the inflation rate is

> **real rates**
> Interest rates or rates of return that have been adjusted for inflation.

> **nominal rates**
> Interest rates or rates of return that have not been adjusted for inflation.

---

[6]The way accrued interest is calculated actually depends on the type of bond being quoted—for example, Treasury or corporate. The difference has to do with exactly how the fractional coupon period is calculated. In our example here, we implicitly treated the months as having exactly the same length (30 days each, 360 days in a year), which is consistent with the way corporate bonds are quoted. In contrast, for Treasury bonds, actual day counts are used.

5 percent, pizzas will cost 5 percent more, or $5.25, at the end of the year. If we take the investment, how many pizzas can we buy at the end of the year? Measured in pizzas, what is the rate of return on this investment?

Our $115.50 from the investment will buy us $115.50/$5.25 = 22 pizzas. This is up from 20 pizzas, so our pizza rate of return is 10 percent. What this illustrates is that even though the nominal return on our investment is 15.5 percent, our buying power goes up by only 10 percent because of inflation. Put another way, we are really only 10 percent richer. In this case, we say that the real return is 10 percent.

Alternatively, we can say that with 5 percent inflation, each of the $115.50 nominal dollars we get is worth 5 percent less in real terms, so the real dollar value of our investment in a year is:

$115.50/1.05 = $110

What we have done is to *deflate* the $115.50 by 5 percent. Because we give up $100 in current buying power to get the equivalent of $110, our real return is again 10 percent. Because we have removed the effect of future inflation here, this $110 is said to be measured in current dollars.

The difference between nominal and real rates is important and bears repeating:

> **The nominal rate on an investment is the percentage change in the number of dollars you have.**
>
> **The real rate on an investment is the percentage change in how much you can buy with your dollars—in other words, the percentage change in your buying power.**

THE FISHER EFFECT

Fisher effect
The relationship between nominal returns, real returns, and inflation.

Our discussion of real and nominal returns illustrates a relationship often called the **Fisher effect** (after the great economist Irving Fisher). Because investors are ultimately concerned with what they can buy with their money, they require compensation for inflation. Let R stand for the nominal rate and r stand for the real rate. The Fisher effect tells us that the relationship between nominal rates, real rates, and inflation can be written as:

$$1 + R = (1 + r) \times (1 + h)$$ **7.2**

where h is the inflation rate.

In the preceding example, the nominal rate was 15.50 percent and the inflation rate was 5 percent. What was the real rate? We can determine it by plugging in these numbers:

$$1 + .1550 = (1 + r) \times (1 + .05)$$
$$1 + r = 1.1550/1.05 = 1.10$$
$$r = .10, \text{ or } 10\%$$

This real rate is the same as we found before. If we take another look at the Fisher effect, we can rearrange things a little as follows:

$$1 + R = (1 + r) \times (1 + h)$$ **7.3**
$$R = r + h + r \times h$$

What this tells us is that the nominal rate has three components. First, there is the real rate on the investment, r. Next, there is the compensation for the decrease in the value of the money originally invested because of inflation, h. The third component represents compensation for the fact that the dollars earned on the investment are also worth less because of inflation.

This third component is usually small, so it is often dropped. The nominal rate is then approximately equal to the real rate plus the inflation rate:

$$R \approx r + h$$ **7.4**

The Fisher Effect   **EXAMPLE 7.5**

If investors require a 10 percent real rate of return, and the inflation rate is 8 percent, what must be the approximate nominal rate? The exact nominal rate?

The nominal rate is approximately equal to the sum of the real rate and the inflation rate: 10% + 8% = 18%. From the Fisher effect, we have:

$$1 + R = (1 + r) \times (1 + h)$$
$$= 1.10 \times 1.08$$
$$= 1.1880$$

Therefore, the nominal rate will actually be closer to 19 percent.

You would expect that investors would always require a positive real return since a primary purpose of investing is to be able to spend more in the future than you could today. This means that the only time investors would accept a negative yield on a bond would be if there was deflation, or negative inflation. Going back to our discussion at the beginning of the chapter about negative yields, while inflation rates were low at the time, they were not negative, so investors were willing to accept a negative real return. Why? After all, holding cash has a zero real return, which is better. One answer is that holding a huge amount of cash is both expensive and difficult to do, so investors were willing to accept a real return slightly below zero, at what amounts to a storage cost.

It is important to note that financial rates, such as interest rates, discount rates, and rates of return, are almost always quoted in nominal terms. To remind you of this, we will henceforth use the symbol R instead of r in most of our discussions about such rates.

INFLATION AND PRESENT VALUES

One question that often comes up is the effect of inflation on present value calculations. The basic principle is simple: Either discount nominal cash flows at a nominal rate or discount real cash flows at a real rate. As long as you are consistent, you will get the same answer.

To illustrate, suppose you want to withdraw money each year for the next three years, and you want each withdrawal to have $25,000 worth of purchasing power as measured in current dollars. If the inflation rate is 4 percent per year, then the withdrawals will have to increase by 4 percent each year to compensate. The withdrawals each year will thus be:

$$C_1 = \$25,000(1.04) = \$26,000$$
$$C_2 = \$25,000(1.04)^2 = \$27,040$$
$$C_3 = \$25,000(1.04)^3 = \$28,121.60$$

What is the present value of these cash flows if the appropriate nominal discount rate is 10 percent? This is a standard calculation, and the answer is:

$$PV = \$26,000/1.10 + \$27,040/1.10^2 + \$28,121.60/1.10^3 = \$67,111.65$$

Notice that we discounted the nominal cash flows at a nominal rate.

To calculate the present value using real cash flows, we need the real discount rate. Using the Fisher equation, the real discount rate is:

$$1 + R = (1 + r)(1 + h)$$
$$1 + .10 = (1 + r)(1 + .04)$$
$$r = .0577, \text{ or } 5.77\%$$

By design, the real cash flows are an annuity of $25,000 per year. So, the present value in real terms is:

$$PV = \$25,000[1 - (1/1.0577^3)]/.0577 = \$67,111.65$$

Thus, we get exactly the same answer (after allowing for a small rounding error in the real rate). Of course, you could also use the growing annuity equation we discussed in the previous chapter. The withdrawals are increasing at 4 percent per year; so using the growing annuity formula, the present value is:

$$PV = \$26,000 \left[\frac{1 - \left(\frac{1 + .04}{1 + .10} \right)^3}{.10 - .04} \right] = \$26,000(2.58122) = \$67,111.65$$

This is exactly the same present value we calculated before.

Concept Questions

7.6a   What is the difference between a nominal and a real return? Which is more important to a typical investor?

7.6b   What is the Fisher effect?

7.7 Determinants of Bond Yields

We are now in a position to discuss the determinants of a bond's yield. As we will see, the yield on any particular bond reflects a variety of factors, some common to all bonds and some specific to the issue under consideration.

THE TERM STRUCTURE OF INTEREST RATES

At any point in time, short-term and long-term interest rates will generally be different. Sometimes short-term rates are higher, sometimes lower. Figure 7.5 gives us a long-range perspective on this by showing over two centuries of short- and long-term interest rates. As shown, through time, the difference between short- and long-term rates has ranged from essentially zero to up to several percentage points, both positive and negative.

The relationship between short- and long-term interest rates is known as the **term structure of interest rates**. To be a little more precise, the term structure of interest rates tells us what *nominal* interest rates are on *default-free, pure discount* bonds of all maturities. These rates are, in essence, "pure" interest rates because they involve no risk of default and a single, lump sum future payment. In other words, the term structure tells us the pure time value of money for different lengths of time.

When long-term rates are higher than short-term rates, we say that the term structure is upward sloping; when short-term rates are higher, we say it is downward sloping. The term structure can also be "humped." When this occurs, it is usually because rates increase at first, but then begin to decline as we look at longer- and longer-term rates. The most

term structure of interest rates
The relationship between nominal interest rates on default-free, pure discount securities and time to maturity; that is, the pure time value of money.

FIGURE 7.5   **U.S. Interest Rates: 1800–2016**

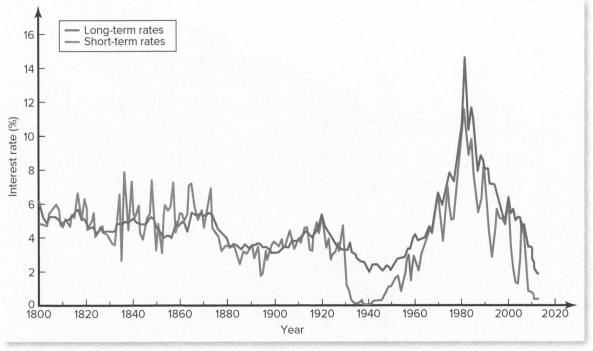

SOURCE: Siegel, Jeremy J., *Stocks for the Long Run*, 4th edition. New York: McGraw-Hill, 2008, updated by the authors.

common shape of the term structure, particularly in modern times, is upward sloping; but the degree of steepness has varied quite a bit.

What determines the shape of the term structure? There are three basic components. The first two are the ones we discussed in our previous section: the real rate of interest and the rate of inflation. The real rate of interest is the compensation investors demand for forgoing the use of their money. You can think of it as the pure time value of money after adjusting for the effects of inflation.

The real rate of interest is the basic component underlying every interest rate, regardless of the time to maturity. When the real rate is high, all interest rates will tend to be higher, and vice versa. Thus, the real rate doesn't really determine the shape of the term structure; instead, it mostly influences the overall level of interest rates.

In contrast, the prospect of future inflation strongly influences the shape of the term structure. Investors thinking about lending money for various lengths of time recognize that future inflation erodes the value of the dollars that will be returned. As a result, investors demand compensation for this loss in the form of higher nominal rates. This extra compensation is called the **inflation premium**.

If investors believe the rate of inflation will be higher in the future, then long-term nominal interest rates will tend to be higher than short-term rates. Thus, an upward-sloping term structure may reflect anticipated increases in inflation. Similarly, a downward-sloping term structure probably reflects the belief that inflation will be falling in the future.

The third, and last, component of the term structure has to do with interest rate risk. As we discussed earlier in the chapter, longer-term bonds have much greater risk of loss resulting from changes in interest rates than do shorter-term bonds. Investors recognize this risk, and they demand extra compensation in the form of higher rates for bearing it. This extra compensation is called the **interest rate risk premium**. The longer the term to maturity, the greater the interest rate risk, so the interest rate risk premium increases with

inflation premium
The portion of a nominal interest rate that represents compensation for expected future inflation.

interest rate risk premium
The compensation investors demand for bearing interest rate risk.

FIGURE 7.6

The Term Structure of Interest Rates

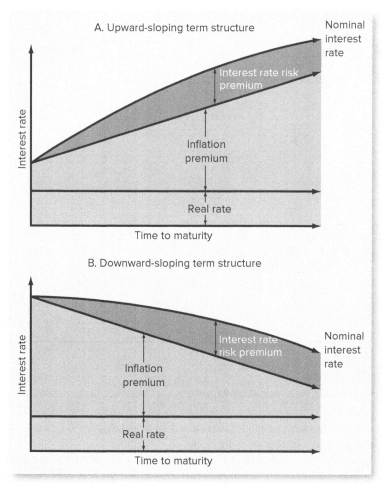

maturity. However, as we discussed earlier, interest rate risk increases at a decreasing rate, so the interest rate risk premium does as well.[7]

Putting the pieces together, we see that the term structure reflects the combined effect of the real rate of interest, the inflation premium, and the interest rate risk premium. Figure 7.6 shows how these can interact to produce an upward-sloping term structure (in Part A of Figure 7.6) or a downward-sloping term structure (in Part B).

In Part A of Figure 7.6, notice how the rate of inflation is expected to rise gradually. At the same time, the interest rate risk premium increases at a decreasing rate, so the combined effect is to produce a pronounced upward-sloping term structure. In Part B of Figure 7.6, the rate of inflation is expected to fall in the future, and the expected decline is enough to offset the interest rate risk premium and produce a downward-sloping term structure. Notice that if the rate of inflation was expected to decline by only a small amount, we could still get an upward-sloping term structure because of the interest rate risk premium.

We assumed in drawing Figure 7.6 that the real rate would remain the same. Actually, expected future real rates could be larger or smaller than the current real rate. Also, for simplicity, we used straight lines to show expected future inflation rates as rising or declining, but they do not necessarily have to look like this. They could, for example, rise and then fall, leading to a humped yield curve.

---

[7]In days of old, the interest rate risk premium was called a "liquidity" premium. Today, the term *liquidity premium* has an altogether different meaning, which we explore in our next section. Also, the interest rate risk premium is sometimes called a *maturity risk premium*. Our terminology is consistent with the modern view of the term structure.

FIGURE 7.7 · The Treasury Yield Curve: December 29, 2017

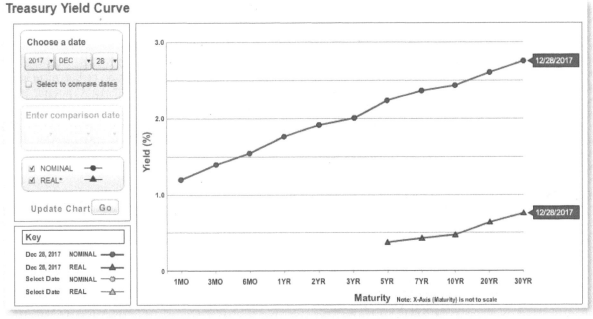

SOURCE: www.treasury.gov, December 29, 2017.

BOND YIELDS AND THE YIELD CURVE: PUTTING IT ALL TOGETHER

Going back to Figure 7.4, recall that we saw that the yields on Treasury notes and bonds of different maturities are not the same. Each day, in addition to the Treasury prices and yields shown in Figure 7.4, the U.S. Treasury provides a plot of Treasury yields relative to maturity. This plot is called the **Treasury yield curve** (or just the yield curve). Figure 7.7 shows the yield curve as of December 29, 2017. Note, the yield curve available on the U.S. Treasury website will display both the nominal and real yield curves.

As you probably now suspect, the shape of the yield curve reflects the term structure of interest rates. In fact, the Treasury yield curve and the term structure of interest rates are almost the same thing. The only difference is that the term structure is based on pure discount bonds, whereas the yield curve is based on coupon bond yields. As a result, Treasury yields depend on the three components that underlie the term structure—the real rate, expected future inflation, and the interest rate risk premium.

Treasury notes and bonds have three important features that we need to remind you of: They are default-free, they are taxable, and they are highly liquid. This is not true of bonds in general, so we need to examine what additional factors come into play when we look at bonds issued by corporations or municipalities.

The first thing to consider is credit risk—that is, the possibility of default. Investors recognize that issuers other than the Treasury may or may not make all the promised payments on a bond, so they demand a higher yield as compensation for this risk. This extra compensation is called the **default risk premium**. Earlier in the chapter, we saw how bonds were rated based on their credit risk. What you will find if you start looking at bonds of different ratings is that lower-rated bonds have higher yields.

An important thing to recognize about a bond's yield is that it is calculated assuming that all the promised payments will be made. As a result, it is really a promised yield, and it may or may not be what you will earn. In particular, if the issuer defaults, your actual yield will be lower—probably much lower. This fact is particularly important when it comes to junk bonds. Thanks

Treasury yield curve
A plot of the yields on Treasury notes and bonds relative to maturity.

Online yield curve information is available at **www.bloomberg.com /markets**.

default risk premium
The portion of a nominal interest rate or bond yield that represents compensation for the possibility of default.

To see how the yield curve has changed over time, check out the "living yield curve" at **stockcharts.com /freecharts/yieldcurve.php**.

to a clever bit of marketing, such bonds are now commonly called high-yield bonds, which has a much nicer ring to it; but now you recognize that these are really high *promised* yield bonds.

Next, recall that we discussed earlier how municipal bonds are free from most taxes and, as a result, have much lower yields than taxable bonds. Investors demand the extra yield on a taxable bond as compensation for the unfavorable tax treatment. This extra compensation is the **taxability premium**.

Finally, bonds have varying degrees of liquidity. As we discussed earlier, there are an enormous number of bond issues, most of which do not trade regularly. As a result, if you wanted to sell quickly, you would probably not get as good a price as you could otherwise. Investors prefer liquid assets to illiquid ones, so they demand a **liquidity premium** on top of all the other premiums we have discussed. As a result, all else being the same, less liquid bonds will have higher yields than more liquid bonds.

taxability premium
The portion of a nominal interest rate or bond yield that represents compensation for unfavorable tax status.

liquidity premium
The portion of a nominal interest rate or bond yield that represents compensation for lack of liquidity.

CONCLUSION

If we combine all of the things we have discussed regarding bond yields, we find that bond yields represent the combined effect of no fewer than six things. The first is the real rate of interest. On top of the real rate are five premiums representing compensation for (1) expected future inflation, (2) interest rate risk, (3) default risk, (4) taxability, and (5) lack of liquidity. As a result, determining the appropriate yield on a bond requires careful analysis of each of these effects.

Concept Questions

7.7a   What is the term structure of interest rates? What determines its shape?
7.7b   What is the Treasury yield curve?
7.7c   What six components make up a bond's yield?

7.8 Summary and Conclusions

This chapter has explored bonds, bond yields, and interest rates:

1. Determining bond prices and yields is an application of basic discounted cash flow principles.
2. Bond values move in the direction opposite that of interest rates, leading to potential gains or losses for bond investors.
3. Bonds have a variety of features spelled out in a document called the indenture.
4. Bonds are rated based on their default risk. Some bonds, such as Treasury bonds, have no risk of default, whereas so-called junk bonds have substantial default risk.
5. A wide variety of bonds exist, many of which contain exotic or unusual features.
6. Almost all bond trading is OTC, with little or no market transparency in many cases. As a result, bond price and volume information can be difficult to find for some types of bonds.
7. Bond yields and interest rates reflect the effect of six different things: the real interest rate and five premiums that investors demand as compensation for inflation, interest rate risk, default risk, taxability, and lack of liquidity.

In closing, we note that bonds are a vital source of financing to governments and corporations of all types. Bond prices and yields are a rich subject, and our one chapter, necessarily, touches on only the most important concepts and ideas. There is a great deal more we could say, but, instead, we will move on to stocks in our next chapter.

CONNECT TO FINANCE

 Do you use *Connect Finance* to practice what you learned? If you don't, you should—we can help you master the topics presented in this chapter. Log on to connect.mheducation.com to learn more!

Can you answer the following *Connect* Quiz questions?

Section 7.1   An 8 percent, semiannual coupon bond has a face value of $1,000 and a current market value of $1,030. What is the current yield?

Section 7.3   The 10-year bonds issued by KP Enterprises were rated as BBB and Baa last year. This year, the bonds are rated as CC and Ca. What term best applies to these bonds today?

Section 7.4   What type of bonds is most apt to have a "collar"?

Section 7.6   Kate wants to earn a 4 percent real rate of return. To do this, what nominal rate must she earn if the inflation rate is 3.6 percent?

Section 7.7   The term structure of interest rates is based on what type of bonds?

CHAPTER REVIEW AND SELF-TEST PROBLEMS

7.1   Bond Values   A Microgates Industries bond has a 10 percent coupon rate and a $1,000 face value. Interest is paid semiannually, and the bond has 20 years to maturity. If investors require a 12 percent yield, what is the bond's value? What is the effective annual yield on the bond?

7.2   Bond Yields   A Macrohard Corp. bond carries an 8 percent coupon, paid semiannually. The par value is $1,000, and the bond matures in six years. If the bond currently sells for $911.37, what is its yield to maturity? What is the effective annual yield?

ANSWERS TO CHAPTER REVIEW AND SELF-TEST PROBLEMS

7.1   Because the bond has a 10 percent coupon yield and investors require a 12 percent return, we know that the bond must sell at a discount. Notice that, because the bond pays interest semiannually, the coupons amount to $100/2 = $50 every six months. The required yield is 12%/2 = 6% every six months. Finally, the bond matures in 20 years, so there are a total of 40 six-month periods.

The bond's value is thus equal to the present value of $50 every six months for the next 40 six-month periods plus the present value of the $1,000 face amount:

$$\text{Bond value} = \$50 \times [(1 - 1/1.06^{40})/.06] + 1,000/1.06^{40}$$
$$= \$50 \times 15.0463 + 1,000/10.2857$$
$$= \$849.54$$

Notice that we discounted the $1,000 back 40 periods at 6 percent per period, rather than 20 years at 12 percent. The reason is that the effective annual yield on the bond is $1.06^2 - 1 = .1236$, or 12.36%, not 12 percent. We thus could have used 12.36 percent per year for 20 years when we calculated the present value of the $1,000 face amount, and the answer would have been the same.

7.2 The present value of the bond's cash flows is its current price, $911.37. The coupon is $40 every six months for 12 periods. The face value is $1,000. So the bond's yield is the unknown discount rate in the following:

$$\$911.37 = \$40 \times [1 - 1/(1 + r)^{12}]/r + 1{,}000/(1 + r)^{12}$$

The bond sells at a discount. Because the coupon rate is 8 percent, the yield must be something in excess of that.

If we were to solve this by trial and error, we might try 12 percent (or 6 percent per six months):

$$\text{Bond value} = \$40 \times (1 - 1/1.06^{12})/.06 + 1{,}000/1.06^{12}$$

$$= \$832.32$$

This is less than the actual value, so our discount rate is too high. We now know that the yield is somewhere between 8 and 12 percent. With further trial and error (or a little machine assistance), the yield works out to be 10 percent, or 5 percent every six months.

By convention, the bond's yield to maturity would be quoted as $2 \times 5\% = 10\%$. The effective yield is thus $1.05^2 - 1 = .1025$, or 10.25%.

CONCEPTS REVIEW AND CRITICAL THINKING QUESTIONS

1. **Treasury Bonds** [LO1] Is it true that a U.S. Treasury security is risk-free?

2. **Interest Rate Risk** [LO2] Which has greater interest rate risk, a 30-year Treasury bond or a 30-year BB corporate bond?

3. **Treasury Pricing** [LO1] With regard to bid and ask prices on a Treasury bond, is it possible for the bid price to be higher? Why or why not?

4. **Yield to Maturity** [LO2] Treasury bid and ask quotes are sometimes given in terms of yields, so there would be a bid yield and an ask yield. Which do you think would be larger? Explain.

5. **Call Provisions** [LO1] A company is contemplating a long-term bond issue. It is debating whether to include a call provision. What are the benefits to the company from including a call provision? What are the costs? How do these answers change for a put provision?

6. **Coupon Rate** [LO1] How does a bond issuer decide on the appropriate coupon rate to set on its bonds? Explain the difference between the coupon rate and the required return on a bond.

7. **Real and Nominal Returns** [LO4] Are there any circumstances under which an investor might be more concerned about the nominal return on an investment than the real return?

8. **Bond Ratings** [LO3] Companies pay rating agencies such as Moody's and S&P to rate their bonds, and the costs can be substantial. However, companies are not required to have their bonds rated; doing so is strictly voluntary. Why do you think they do it?

9. **Bond Ratings** [LO3] Often, junk bonds are not rated. Why?

10. **Term Structure** [LO5] What is the difference between the term structure of interest rates and the yield curve?

11. **Crossover Bonds** [LO3] Looking back at the crossover bonds we discussed in the chapter, why do you think split ratings such as these occur?

12. **Municipal Bonds** [LO1] Why is it that municipal bonds are not taxed at the federal level, but are taxable across state lines? Why are U.S. Treasury bonds not taxable at the state level? (You may need to dust off the history books for this one.)

13. **Bond Market** [LO1] What does the lack of transparency in the bond market imply for bond investors?

14. **Rating Agencies** [LO3] A controversy erupted regarding bond-rating agencies when some agencies began to provide unsolicited bond ratings. Why do you think this is controversial?

15. **Bonds as Equity** [LO1] The 100-year bonds we discussed in the chapter have something in common with junk bonds. Critics charge that, in both cases, the issuers are really selling equity in disguise. What are the issues here? Why would a company want to sell "equity in disguise"?

QUESTIONS AND PROBLEMS

1. **Interpreting Bond Yields** [LO1] Is the yield to maturity on a bond the same thing as the required return? Is YTM the same thing as the coupon rate? Suppose today a 10 percent coupon bond sells at par. Two years from now, the required return on the same bond is 8 percent. What is the coupon rate on the bond then? The YTM?

BASIC
(Questions 1–17)

2. **Interpreting Bond Yields** [LO2] Suppose you buy a 7 percent coupon, 20-year bond today when it's first issued. If interest rates suddenly rise to 15 percent, what happens to the value of your bond? Why?

3. **Valuing Bonds** [LO2] Even though most corporate bonds in the United States make coupon payments semiannually, bonds issued elsewhere often have annual coupon payments. Suppose a German company issues a bond with a par value of €1,000, 23 years to maturity, and a coupon rate of 3.8 percent paid annually. If the yield to maturity is 4.7 percent, what is the current price of the bond?

4. **Bond Yields** [LO2] A Japanese company has a bond outstanding that sells for 105.43 percent of its ¥100,000 par value. The bond has a coupon rate of 3.4 percent paid annually and matures in 16 years. What is the yield to maturity of this bond?

5. **Coupon Rates** [LO2] Gabriele Enterprises has bonds on the market making annual payments, with eight years to maturity, a par value of $1,000, and selling for $948. At this price, the bonds yield 5.1 percent. What must the coupon rate be on the bonds?

6. **Bond Prices** [LO2] Weismann Co. issued 15-year bonds a year ago at a coupon rate of 4.9 percent. The bonds make semiannual payments and have a par value of $1,000. If the YTM on these bonds is 4.5 percent, what is the current bond price?

7. **Bond Yields** [LO2] West Corp. issued 25-year bonds two years ago at a coupon rate of 5.3 percent. The bonds make semiannual payments. If these bonds currently sell for 105 percent of par value, what is the YTM?

8. **Coupon Rates** [LO2] McConnell Corporation has bonds on the market with 14.5 years to maturity, a YTM of 5.3 percent, a par value of $1,000, and a current price of $1,045. The bonds make semiannual payments. What must the coupon rate be on these bonds?

9. **Zero Coupon Bonds** [LO2] You find a zero coupon bond with a par value of $10,000 and 17 years to maturity. If the yield to maturity on this bond is 4.2 percent, what is the price of the bond? Assume semiannual compounding periods.

10. **Valuing Bonds** [LO2] Yan Yan Corp. has a $2,000 par value bond outstanding with a coupon rate of 4.4 percent paid semiannually and 13 years to maturity. The yield to maturity of the bond is 4.8 percent. What is the price of the bond?

11. **Valuing Bonds** [LO2] Union Local School District has a bond outstanding with a coupon rate of 2.8 percent paid semiannually and 16 years to maturity. The yield to maturity on this bond is 3.4 percent, and the bond has a par value of $5,000. What is the price of the bond?

12. **Calculating Real Rates of Return** [LO4] If Treasury bills are currently paying 4.7 percent and the inflation rate is 2.2 percent, what is the approximate real rate of interest? The exact real rate?

13. **Inflation and Nominal Returns** [LO4] Suppose the real rate is 2.1 percent and the inflation rate is 3.4 percent. What rate would you expect to see on a Treasury bill?

14. **Nominal and Real Returns** [LO4] An investment offers a total return of 12.3 percent over the coming year. Janice Yellen thinks the total real return on this investment will be only 8 percent. What does Janice believe the inflation rate will be over the next year?

15. **Nominal versus Real Returns** [LO4] Say you own an asset that had a total return last year of 11.65 percent. If the inflation rate last year was 2.75 percent, what was your real return?

16. **Using Treasury Quotes** [LO2] Locate the Treasury issue in Figure 7.4 maturing in May 2038. What is its coupon rate? What is its bid price? What was the *previous* day's asked price? Assume a par value of $10,000.

17. **Using Treasury Quotes** [LO2] Locate the Treasury bond in Figure 7.4 maturing in February 2040. Is this a premium or a discount bond? What is its current yield? What is its yield to maturity? What is the bid-ask spread in dollars? Assume a par value of $10,000.

INTERMEDIATE
(Questions 18–31)

18. **Bond Price Movements** [LO2] Bond X is a premium bond making semiannual payments. The bond pays a coupon rate of 7.4 percent, has a YTM of 6.8 percent, and has 13 years to maturity. Bond Y is a discount bond making semiannual payments. This bond pays a coupon rate of 6.8 percent, has a YTM of 7.4 percent, and also has 13 years to maturity. What is the price of each bond today? If interest rates remain unchanged, what do you expect the price of these bonds to be one year from now? In three years? In eight years? In 12 years? In 13 years? What's going on here? Illustrate your answers by graphing bond prices versus time to maturity.

19. **Interest Rate Risk** [LO2] Both Bond Sam and Bond Dave have 7.3 percent coupons, make semiannual payments, and are priced at par value. Bond Sam has three years to maturity, whereas Bond Dave has 20 years to maturity. If interest rates suddenly rise by 2 percent, what is the percentage change in the price of Bond Sam? Of Bond Dave? If rates were to suddenly fall by 2 percent instead, what would the percentage change in the price of Bond Sam be then? Of Bond Dave? Illustrate your answers by graphing bond prices versus YTM. What does this problem tell you about the interest rate risk of longer-term bonds?

20. **Interest Rate Risk** [LO2] Bond J has a coupon rate of 3 percent. Bond K has a coupon rate of 9 percent. Both bonds have 14 years to maturity, make semiannual payments, and have a YTM of 6 percent. If interest rates suddenly rise by 2 percent, what is the percentage price change of these bonds? What if rates suddenly fall by 2 percent instead? What does this problem tell you about the interest rate risk of lower-coupon bonds?

21. **Bond Yields** [LO2] Workman Software has 6.4 percent coupon bonds on the market with 18 years to maturity. The bonds make semiannual payments and currently sell for 94.31 percent of par. What is the current yield on the bonds? The YTM? The effective annual yield?

22. **Bond Yields** [LO2] Chamberlain Co. wants to issue new 20-year bonds for some much-needed expansion projects. The company currently has 6 percent coupon bonds on the market that sell for $1,083, make semiannual payments, and mature in 20 years. What coupon rate should the company set on its new bonds if it wants them to sell at par?

23. **Accrued Interest** [LO2] You purchase a bond with an invoice price of $948. The bond has a coupon rate of 5.9 percent, and there are four months to the next semiannual coupon date. What is the clean price of the bond?

24. **Accrued Interest** [LO2] You purchase a bond with a coupon rate of 5.3 percent and a clean price of $951. If the next semiannual coupon payment is due in two months, what is the invoice price?

25. **Finding the Bond Maturity** [LO2] Excey Corp. has 8 percent coupon bonds making annual payments with a YTM of 7.2 percent. The current yield on these bonds is 7.55 percent. How many years do these bonds have left until they mature?

26. **Using Bond Quotes** [LO2] Suppose the following bond quotes for IOU Corporation appear in the financial page of today's newspaper. Assume the bond has a face value of $2,000 and the current date is April 19, 2018. What is the yield to maturity of the bond? What is the current yield?

Company (Ticker)	Coupon	Maturity	Last Price	Last Yield	EST Vol (000s)
IOU (IOU)	5.7	Apr 19, 2034	108.96	??	1,827

27. **Bond Prices versus Yields** [LO2]

    a. What is the relationship between the price of a bond and its YTM?

    b. Explain why some bonds sell at a premium over par value while other bonds sell at a discount. What do you know about the relationship between the coupon rate and the YTM for premium bonds? What about for discount bonds? For bonds selling at par value?

    c. What is the relationship between the current yield and YTM for premium bonds? For discount bonds? For bonds selling at par value?

28. **Interest on Zeroes** [LO2] Imagination Dragons Corporation needs to raise funds to finance a plant expansion, and it has decided to issue 25-year zero coupon bonds with a par value of $1,000 each to raise the money. The required return on the bonds will be 4.9 percent. Assume semiannual compounding periods.

    a. What will these bonds sell for at issuance?

    b. Using the IRS amortization rule, what interest deduction can the company take on these bonds in the first year? In the last year?

    c. Repeat part (b) using the straight-line method for the interest deduction.

    d. Based on your answers in (b) and (c), which interest deduction method would the company prefer? Why?

29. **Zero Coupon Bonds** [LO2] Suppose your company needs to raise $53 million and you want to issue 20-year bonds for this purpose. Assume the required return on your bond issue will be 5.3 percent, and you're evaluating two issue alternatives: a semiannual coupon bond with a coupon rate of 5.3 percent, and a zero coupon bond. Your company's tax rate is 21 percent. Both bonds will have a par value of $1,000.

    a. How many of the coupon bonds would you need to issue to raise the $53 million? How many of the zeroes would you need to issue?

b. In 20 years, what will your company's repayment be if you issue the coupon bonds? What if you issue the zeroes?

c. Based on your answers in (a) and (b), why would you ever want to issue the zeroes? To answer, calculate the firm's aftertax cash flows for the first year under the two different scenarios. Assume the IRS amortization rules apply for the zero coupon bonds.

30. **Finding the Maturity** [LO2] You've just found a 10 percent coupon bond on the market that sells for par value. What is the maturity on this bond?

31. **Real Cash Flows** [LO4] You want to have $2.5 million in real dollars in an account when you retire in 40 years. The nominal return on your investment is 10.3 percent and the inflation rate is 3.7 percent. What real amount must you deposit each year to achieve your goal?

CHALLENGE
(Questions 32–38)

32. **Components of Bond Returns** [LO2] Bond P is a premium bond with a coupon rate of 9 percent. Bond D has a coupon rate of 5 percent and is currently selling at a discount. Both bonds make annual payments, have a YTM of 7 percent, and have 10 years to maturity. What is the current yield for Bond P? For Bond D? If interest rates remain unchanged, what is the expected capital gains yield over the next year for Bond P? For Bond D? Explain your answers and the interrelationships among the various types of yields.

33. **Holding Period Yield** [LO2] The YTM on a bond is the interest rate you earn on your investment if interest rates don't change. If you actually sell the bond before it matures, your realized return is known as the *holding period yield* (HPY).

a. Suppose that today you buy a bond with an annual coupon rate of 7 percent for $1,060. The bond has 21 years to maturity. What rate of return do you expect to earn on your investment? Assume a par value of $1,000.

b. Two years from now, the YTM on your bond has declined by 1 percent, and you decide to sell. What price will your bond sell for? What is the HPY on your investment? Compare this yield to the YTM when you first bought the bond. Why are they different?

34. **Valuing Bonds** [LO2] Jallouk Corporation has two different bonds currently outstanding. Bond M has a face value of $20,000 and matures in 20 years. The bond makes no payments for the first six years, then pays $900 every six months over the subsequent eight years, and finally pays $1,300 every six months over the last six years. Bond N also has a face value of $20,000 and a maturity of 20 years; it makes no coupon payments over the life of the bond. If the required return on both these bonds is 5.4 percent compounded semiannually, what is the current price of Bond M? Of Bond N?

35. **Valuing the Call Feature** [LO2] At one point, certain U.S. Treasury bonds were callable. Consider the prices in the following three Treasury issues as of May 15, 2017:

5/15/2023	6.500	106.31250	106.37500	−.31250	5.28
5/15/2023	8.250	103.43750	103.50000	−.09375	5.24
5/15/2023	12.000	134.78125	134.96875	−.46875	5.32

The bond in the middle is callable in February 2018. What is the implied value of the call feature? Assume a par value of $1,000. (*Hint*: Is there a way to combine the two noncallable issues to create an issue that has the same coupon as the callable bond?)

36. Treasury Bonds [LO2] The following Treasury bond quote appeared in *The Wall Street Journal* on May 11, 2004:

5/15/2009	9.125	100.09375	100.12500	0	−2.15

Why would anyone buy this Treasury bond with a negative yield to maturity? How is this possible?

37. Real Cash Flows [LO4] When Marilyn Monroe died, ex-husband Joe DiMaggio vowed to place fresh flowers on her grave every Sunday as long as he lived. The week after she died in 1962, a bunch of fresh flowers that the former baseball player thought appropriate for the star cost about $7. Based on actuarial tables, "Joltin' Joe" could expect to live for 30 years after the actress died. Assume that the EAR is 6.4 percent. Also, assume that the price of the flowers will increase at 3.7 percent per year, when expressed as an EAR. Assuming that each year has exactly 52 weeks, what is the present value of this commitment? Joe began purchasing flowers the week after Marilyn died.

38. Real Cash Flows [LO4] You are planning to save for retirement over the next 30 years. To save for retirement, you will invest $800 per month in a stock account in real dollars and $400 per month in a bond account in real dollars. The effective annual return of the stock account is expected to be 11 percent, and the bond account will earn 7 percent. When you retire, you will combine your money into an account with an effective return of 9 percent. The returns are stated in nominal terms. The inflation rate over this period is expected to be 4 percent. How much can you withdraw each month from your account in real terms assuming a 25-year withdrawal period? What is the nominal dollar amount of your last withdrawal?

EXCEL MASTER IT! PROBLEM

Companies often buy bonds to meet a future liability or cash outlay. Such an investment is called a dedicated portfolio because the proceeds of the portfolio are dedicated to the future liability. In such a case, the portfolio is subject to reinvestment risk. Reinvestment risk occurs because the company will be reinvesting the coupon payments it receives. If the YTM on similar bonds falls, these coupon payments will be reinvested at a lower interest rate, which will result in a portfolio value that is lower than desired at maturity. Of course, if interest rates increase, the portfolio value at maturity will be higher than needed.

Suppose Ice Cubes, Inc., has the following liability due in five years. The company is going to buy five-year bonds today to meet the future obligation. The liability and current YTM are below.

Amount of liability:	$100,000,000
Current YTM:	8%

a. At the current YTM, what is the face value of the bonds the company has to purchase today to meet its future obligation? Assume that the bonds in the relevant range will have the same coupon rate as the current YTM and these bonds make semiannual coupon payments.

b. Assume that the interest rates remain constant for the next five years. Thus, when the company reinvests the coupon payments, it will reinvest at the current YTM. What is the value of the portfolio in five years?

238   **PART 3**   Valuation of Future Cash Flows

c. Assume that immediately after the company purchases the bonds, interest rates either rise or fall by 1 percent. What is the value of the portfolio in five years under these circumstances?

One way to eliminate reinvestment risk is called *immunization*. Rather than buying bonds with the same maturity as the liability, the company instead buys bonds with the same duration as the liability. If you think about the dedicated portfolio, if the interest rate falls, the future value of the reinvested coupon payments decreases. However, as interest rates fall, the price of the bond increases. These effects offset each other in an immunized portfolio.

Another advantage of using duration to immunize a portfolio is that the duration of a portfolio is the weighted average of the duration of the assets in the portfolio. In other words, to find the duration of a portfolio, you take the weight of each asset multiplied by its duration and then sum the results.

d. What is the duration of the liability for Ice Cubes, Inc.?

e. Suppose the two bonds shown below are the only bonds available to immunize the liability. What face amount of each bond will the company need to purchase to immunize the portfolio?

	Bond A	Bond B
Settlement:	1/1/2000	1/1/2000
Maturity:	1/1/2003	1/1/2008
Coupon rate:	7.00%	8.00%
YTM:	7.50%	9.00%
Coupons per year:	2	2

MINICASE

Financing S&S Air's Expansion Plans with a Bond Issue

Mark Sexton and Todd Story, the owners of S&S Air, have decided to expand their operations. They instructed their newly hired financial analyst, Chris Guthrie, to enlist an underwriter to help sell $35 million in new 10-year bonds to finance construction. Chris has entered into discussions with Renata Harper, an underwriter from the firm of Raines and Warren, about which bond features S&S Air should consider and what coupon rate the issue will likely have.

Although Chris is aware of the bond features, he is uncertain about the costs and benefits of some features, so he isn't sure how each feature would affect the coupon rate of the bond issue. You are Renata's assistant, and she has asked you to prepare a memo to Chris describing the effect of each of the following bond features on the coupon rate of the bond. She would also like you to list any advantages or disadvantages of each feature.

QUESTIONS

1. The security of the bond—that is, whether the bond has collateral.

2. The seniority of the bond.

3. The presence of a sinking fund.

4. A call provision with specified call dates and call prices.

5. A deferred call accompanying the call provision.

6. A make-whole call provision.

7. Any positive covenants. Also, discuss several possible positive covenants S&S Air might consider.

8. Any negative covenants. Also, discuss several possible negative covenants S&S Air might consider.

9. A conversion feature (note that S&S Air is not a publicly traded company).

10. A floating-rate coupon.

Stock Valuation

WHEN THE STOCK MARKET CLOSED on December 29, 2017, the common stock of video game retailer GameStop was going for $17.95 per share. On that same day, stock in industrial giant General Electric closed at $17.45, while stock in data center and technology company Switch, Inc., closed at $18.19. Because the stock prices of these three companies were so similar, you might expect that they would be offering similar dividends to their stockholders, but you would be wrong. In fact, GameStop's annual dividend was $1.52 per share, General Electric's was $.48 per share, and Switch was paying no dividend at all!

As we will see in this chapter, the dividends currently being paid are one of the primary factors we look at when attempting to value common stocks. However, it is obvious from looking at Micron Technology that current dividends are not the end of the story. This chapter explores dividends, stock values, and the connection between the two.

Learning Objectives

After studying this chapter, you should be able to:

LO1 Explain how stock prices depend on future dividends and dividend growth.

LO2 Show how to value stocks using multiples.

LO3 Lay out the different ways corporate directors are elected to office.

LO4 Define how the stock markets work.

©by_adri/iStockPhoto/GettyImages

For updates on the latest happenings in finance, visit fundamentalsofcorporatefinance.blogspot.com.

In our previous chapter, we introduced you to bonds and bond valuation. In this chapter, we turn to the other major source of financing for corporations: Common and preferred stock. We first describe the cash flows associated with a share of stock and then go on to develop a famous result, the dividend growth model. From there, we move on to examine various important features of common and preferred stock, focusing on shareholder rights. We close the chapter with a discussion of how shares of stock are traded and how stock prices and other important information are reported in the financial press.

8.1 Common Stock Valuation

A share of common stock is more difficult to value in practice than a bond for at least three reasons. First, with common stock, not even the promised cash flows are known in advance. Second, the life of the investment is essentially forever because common stock has no maturity. Third, there is no way to easily observe the rate of return that the market requires. Nonetheless, as we will see, there are cases in which we can come up with the present value of the future cash flows for a share of stock and thus determine its value.

CASH FLOWS

Imagine that you are considering buying a share of stock today. You plan to sell the stock in one year. You somehow know that the stock will be worth $70 at that time. You predict that the stock will also pay a $10 per share dividend at the end of the year. If you require a 25 percent return on your investment, what is the most you would pay for the stock? In other words, what is the present value of the $10 dividend along with the $70 ending value at 25 percent?

If you buy the stock today and sell it at the end of the year, you will have a total of $80 in cash. At 25 percent:

Present value = ($10 + 70)/1.25 = $64

Therefore, $64 is the value you would assign to the stock today.

More generally, let P_0 be the current price of the stock, and assign P_1 to be the price in one period. If D_1 is the cash dividend paid at the end of the period, then:

$$P_0 = (D_1 + P_1)/(1 + R)$$ [8.1]

where R is the required return in the market on this investment.

Notice that we really haven't said much so far. If we wanted to determine the value of a share of stock today (P_0), we would first have to come up with the value in one year (P_1). This is even harder to do, so we've only made the problem more complicated.

What is the price in one period, P_1? We don't know in general. Instead, suppose we somehow knew the price in two periods, P_2. Given a predicted dividend in two periods, D_2, the stock price in one period would be:

$$P_1 = (D_2 + P_2)/(1 + R)$$

If we were to substitute this expression for P_1 into our expression for P_0, we would have:

$$P_0 = \frac{D_1 + P_1}{1 + R} = \frac{D_1 + \dfrac{D_2 + P_2}{1 + R}}{1 + R}$$

$$= \frac{D_1}{(1 + R)^1} + \frac{D_2}{(1 + R)^2} + \frac{P_2}{(1 + R)^2}$$

Now we need to get a price in two periods. We don't know this either, so we can procrastinate again and write:

$$P_2 = (D_3 + P_3)/(1 + R)$$

If we substitute this back in for P_2, we have:

$$P_0 = \frac{D_1}{(1+R)^1} + \frac{D_2}{(1+R)^2} + \frac{P_2}{(1+R)^2}$$

$$= \frac{D_1}{(1+R)^1} + \frac{D_2}{(1+R)^2} + \frac{\dfrac{D_3 + P_3}{1+R}}{(1+R)^2}$$

$$= \frac{D_1}{(1+R)^1} + \frac{D_2}{(1+R)^2} + \frac{D_3}{(1+R)^3} + \frac{P_3}{(1+R)^3}$$

You should start to notice that we can push the problem of coming up with the stock price off into the future forever. Note that no matter what the stock price is, the present value is essentially zero if we push the sale of the stock far enough away.[1] What we are eventually left with is the result that the current price of the stock can be written as the present value of the dividends beginning in one period and extending out forever:

$$P_0 = \frac{D_1}{(1+R)^1} + \frac{D_2}{(1+R)^2} + \frac{D_3}{(1+R)^3} + \frac{D_4}{(1+R)^4} + \frac{D_5}{(1+R)^5} + \cdots$$

We have illustrated here that the price of the stock today is equal to the present value of all of the future dividends. How many future dividends are there? In principle, there can be an infinite number. This means that we still can't compute a value for the stock because we would have to forecast an infinite number of dividends and then discount them all. In the next section, we consider some special cases in which we can get around this problem.

---

[1] The only assumption we make about the stock price is that it is a finite number no matter how far away we push it. It can be extremely large, just not infinitely so. Because no one has ever observed an infinite stock price, this assumption is plausible.

Growth Stocks   EXAMPLE 8.1

You might be wondering about shares of stock in companies such as Alphabet that currently pay no dividends. Small, growing companies frequently plow back everything and pay no dividends. Are such shares worth nothing? It depends. When we say that the value of the stock is equal to the present value of the future dividends, we don't rule out the possibility that some number of those dividends are zero. They just can't *all* be zero.

Imagine a company that has a provision in its corporate charter that prohibits the paying of dividends now or ever. The corporation never borrows any money, never pays out any money to stockholders in any form whatsoever, and never sells any assets. Such a corporation couldn't really exist because the IRS wouldn't like it, and the stockholders could always vote to amend the charter if they wanted to. If it did exist, however, what would the stock be worth?

The stock would be worth absolutely nothing. Such a company would be a financial "black hole." Money goes in, but nothing valuable ever comes out. Because nobody would ever get any return on this investment, the investment would have no value. This example is a little absurd, but it illustrates that when we speak of companies that don't pay dividends, what we really mean is that they are not *currently* paying dividends.

SOME SPECIAL CASES

In a few useful special circumstances, we can come up with a value for the stock. What we have to do is make some simplifying assumptions about the pattern of future dividends. The three cases we consider are the following: (1) The dividend has a zero growth rate, (2) the dividend grows at a constant rate, and (3) the dividend grows at a constant rate after some length of time. We consider each of these separately.

Zero Growth   The case of zero growth is one we've already seen. A share of common stock in a company with a constant dividend is much like a share of preferred stock. From Chapter 6 (see Example 6.7), we know that the dividend on a share of preferred stock has zero growth and is constant through time. For a zero-growth share of common stock, this implies that:

$$D_1 = D_2 = D_3 = D = \text{constant}$$

So, the value of the stock is:

$$P_0 = \frac{D}{(1 + R)^1} + \frac{D}{(1 + R)^2} + \frac{D}{(1 + R)^3} + \frac{D}{(1 + R)^4} + \frac{D}{(1 + R)^5} + \cdots$$

Because the dividend is always the same, the stock can be viewed as an ordinary perpetuity with a cash flow equal to D every period. The per-share value is given by:

$$P_0 = D/R \tag{8.2}$$

where R is the required return.

For example, suppose the Paradise Prototyping Company has a policy of paying a $10 per share dividend every year. If this policy is to be continued indefinitely, what is the value of a share of stock if the required return is 20 percent? The stock in this case amounts to an ordinary perpetuity, so the stock is worth $10/.20 = $50 per share.

Constant Growth   Suppose we know that the dividend for some company always grows at a steady rate. Call this growth rate g. If we let D_0 be the dividend just paid, then the next dividend, D_1, is:

$$D_1 = D_0 \times (1 + g)$$

The dividend in two periods is:

$$
\begin{aligned}
D_2 &= D_1 \times (1 + g) \\
&= [D_0 \times (1 + g)] \times (1 + g) \\
&= D_0 \times (1 + g)^2
\end{aligned}
$$

We could repeat this process to come up with the dividend at any point in the future. In general, from our discussion of compound growth in Chapter 6, we know that the dividend t periods into the future, D_t, is given by:

$$D_t = D_0 \times (1 + g)^t$$

As we have previously seen, an asset with cash flows that grow at a constant rate forever is called a *growing perpetuity*.

The assumption of steady dividend growth might strike you as peculiar. Why would the dividend grow at a constant rate? The reason is that, for many companies, steady growth in dividends is an explicit goal. For example, in 2016, Procter & Gamble, the Cincinnati-based maker of personal care and household products, increased its dividend by 1 percent to $2.68 per share; this increase was notable because it was the 60th in a row. The subject of dividend growth falls under the general heading of dividend policy, so we will defer further discussion of it to a later chapter.

| **Dividend Growth** | **EXAMPLE 8.2** |

The Hedless Corporation has just paid a dividend of $3 per share. The dividend of this company grows at a steady rate of 8 percent per year. Based on this information, what will the dividend be in five years?

Here we have a $3 current amount that grows at 8 percent per year for five years. The future amount is thus:

$3 \times 1.08^5 = \$3 \times 1.4693 = \$4.41$

The dividend will increase by $1.41 over the coming five years.

If the dividend grows at a steady rate, then we have replaced the problem of forecasting an infinite number of future dividends with the problem of coming up with a single growth rate, a considerable simplification. In this case, if we take D_0 to be the dividend just paid and g to be the constant growth rate, the value of a share of stock can be written as:

$$P_0 = \frac{D_1}{(1+R)^1} + \frac{D_2}{(1+R)^2} + \frac{D_3}{(1+R)^3} + \cdots$$
$$= \frac{D_0(1+g)^1}{(1+R)^1} + \frac{D_0(1+g)^2}{(1+R)^2} + \frac{D_0(1+g)^3}{(1+R)^3} + \cdots$$

As long as the growth rate, g, is less than the discount rate, r, the present value of this series of cash flows can be written as:

$$P_0 = \frac{D_0 \times (1+g)}{R-g} = \frac{D_1}{R-g}$$

8.3

This elegant result goes by a lot of different names. We will call it the **dividend growth model**. By any name, it is easy to use. To illustrate, suppose D_0 is $2.30, R is 13 percent, and g is 5 percent. The price per share in this case is:

$P_0 = D_0 \times (1+g)/(R-g)$
$= \$2.30 \times 1.05/(.13 - .05)$
$= \$2.415/.08$
$= \$30.19$

dividend growth model
A model that determines the current price of a stock as its dividend next period divided by the discount rate less the dividend growth rate.

We can actually use the dividend growth model to get the stock price at any point in time, not just today. In general, the price of the stock as of Time t is:

$$P_t = \frac{D_t \times (1+g)}{R-g} = \frac{D_{t+1}}{R-g}$$

8.4

In our example, suppose we are interested in the price of the stock in five years, P_5. We first need the dividend at Time 5, D_5. Because the dividend just paid is $2.30 and the growth rate is 5 percent per year, D_5 is:

$D_5 = \$2.30 \times 1.05^5 = \$2.30 \times 1.2763 = \$2.935$

From the dividend growth model, we get the price of the stock in five years:

$$P_5 = \frac{D_5 \times (1+g)}{R-g} = \frac{\$2.935 \times 1.05}{.13 - .05} = \frac{\$3.0822}{.08} = \$38.53$$

EXAMPLE 8.3	**Gordon Growth Company**

The next dividend for the Gordon Growth Company will be $4 per share. Investors require a 16 percent return on companies such as Gordon. Gordon's dividend increases by 6 percent every year. Based on the dividend growth model, what is the value of Gordon's stock today? What is the value in four years?

The only tricky thing here is that the next dividend, D_1, is given as $4, so we won't multiply this by $(1 + g)$. With this in mind, the price per share is given by:

$$P_0 = D_1/(R - g)$$
$$= \$4/(.16 - .06)$$
$$= \$4/.10$$
$$= \$40$$

Because we already have the dividend in one year, we know that the dividend in four years is equal to $D_1 \times (1 + g)^3 = \$4 \times 1.06^3 = \$4.764$. So, the price in four years is:

$$P_4 = D_4 \times (1 + g)/(R - g)$$
$$= \$4.764 \times 1.06/(.16 - .06)$$
$$= \$5.05/.10$$
$$= \$50.50$$

Notice in this example that P_4 is equal to $P_0 \times (1 + g)^4$.

$$P_4 = \$50.50 = \$40 \times 1.06^4 = P_0 \times (1 + g)^4$$

To see why this is so, notice first that:

$$P_4 = D_5/(R - g)$$

However, D_5 is just equal to $D_1 \times (1 + g)^4$, so we can write P_4 as:

$$P_4 = D_1 \times (1 + g)^4/(R - g)$$
$$= [D_1/(R - g)] \times (1 + g)^4$$
$$= P_0 \times (1 + g)^4$$

This last example illustrates that the dividend growth model makes the implicit assumption that the stock price will grow at the same constant rate as the dividend. This really isn't too surprising. What it tells us is that if the cash flows on an investment grow at a constant rate through time, so does the value of that investment.

You might wonder what would happen with the dividend growth model if the growth rate, g, were greater than the discount rate, R. It looks like we would get a negative stock price because $R - g$ would be less than zero. This is not what would happen.

Instead, if the constant growth rate exceeds the discount rate, then the stock price is infinitely large. Why? If the growth rate is bigger than the discount rate, the present value of the dividends keeps getting bigger. Essentially the same is true if the growth rate and the discount rate are equal. In both cases, the simplification that allows us to replace the infinite stream of dividends with the dividend growth model is "illegal," so the answers we get from the dividend growth model are nonsense unless the growth rate is less than the discount rate.

Finally, the expression we came up with for the constant growth case will work for any growing perpetuity, not just dividends on common stock. As we saw in Chapter 6, if C_1 is the next cash flow on a growing perpetuity, then the present value of the cash flows is given by:

Present value $= C_1/(R - g) = C_0(1 + g)/(R - g)$

Notice that this expression looks like the result for an ordinary perpetuity except that we have $R - g$ on the bottom instead of just R.

Nonconstant Growth The next case we consider is nonconstant growth. The main reason to consider this case is to allow for "supernormal" growth rates over some finite length of time. As we discussed earlier, the growth rate cannot exceed the required return indefinitely, but it certainly could do so for some number of years. To avoid the problem of having to forecast and discount an infinite number of dividends, we will require that the dividends start growing at a constant rate sometime in the future.

For a simple example of nonconstant growth, consider the case of a company that is currently not paying dividends. You predict that, in five years, the company will pay a dividend for the first time. The dividend will be \$.50 per share. You expect that this dividend will then grow at a rate of 10 percent per year indefinitely. The required return on companies such as this one is 20 percent. What is the price of the stock today?

To see what the stock is worth today, we first find out what it will be worth once dividends are paid. We can then calculate the present value of that future price to get today's price. The first dividend will be paid in five years, and the dividend will grow steadily from then on. Using the dividend growth model, we can say that the price in four years will be:

$$P_4 = D_4 \times (1 + g)/(R - g)$$
$$= D_5/(R - g)$$
$$= \$.50/(.20 - .10)$$
$$= \$5$$

If the stock will be worth \$5 in four years, then we can get the current value by discounting this price back four years at 20 percent:

$$P_0 = \$5/1.20^4 = \$5/2.0736 = \$2.41$$

The stock is worth \$2.41 today.

The problem of nonconstant growth is only slightly more complicated if the dividends are not zero for the first several years. For example, suppose you have come up with the following dividend forecasts for the next three years:

Year	Expected Dividend
1	\$1.00
2	\$2.00
3	\$2.50

After the third year, the dividend will grow at a constant rate of 5 percent per year. The required return is 10 percent. What is the value of the stock today?

In dealing with nonconstant growth, a time line can be helpful. Figure 8.1 illustrates a time line for this problem. The important thing to notice is when constant growth starts. As we've shown, for this problem, constant growth starts at Time 3. This means we can use our constant growth model to determine the stock price at Time 3, P_3. By far the most common mistake in this situation is to incorrectly identify the start of the constant growth phase and, as a result, calculate the future stock price at the wrong time.

As always, the value of the stock is the present value of all the future dividends. To calculate this present value, we first have to compute the present value of the stock price three years down the road, just as we did before. We then have to add in the present

FIGURE 8.1

Nonconstant Growth

value of the dividends that will be paid between now and then. So, the price in three years is:

$$P_3 = D_3 \times (1 + g)/(R - g)$$
$$= \$2.50 \times 1.05/(.10 - .05)$$
$$= \$52.50$$

We can now calculate the total value of the stock as the present value of the first three dividends plus the present value of the price at Time 3, P_3:

$$P_0 = \frac{D_1}{(1 + R)^1} + \frac{D_2}{(1 + R)^2} + \frac{D_3}{(1 + R)^3} + \frac{P_3}{(1 + R)^3}$$
$$= \frac{\$1}{1.10} + \frac{2}{1.10^2} + \frac{2.50}{1.10^3} + \frac{52.50}{1.10^3}$$
$$= \$.91 + 1.65 + 1.88 + 39.44$$
$$= \$43.88$$

The value of the stock today is thus $43.88.

EXAMPLE 8.4	Supernormal Growth

Chain Reaction, Inc., has been growing at a phenomenal rate of 30 percent per year because of its rapid expansion and explosive sales. You believe this growth rate will last for three more years and will then drop to 10 percent per year. If the growth rate then remains at 10 percent indefinitely, what is the total value of the stock? Total dividends just paid were $5 million, and the required return is 20 percent.

Chain Reaction's situation is an example of supernormal growth. It is unlikely that a 30 percent growth rate can be sustained for any extended time. To value the equity in this company, we first need to calculate the total dividends over the supernormal growth period:

Year	Total Dividends (in millions)
1	$5.00 × 1.3 = $ 6.500
2	6.50 × 1.3 = 8.450
3	8.45 × 1.3 = 10.985

The price at Time 3 can be calculated as:

$$P_3 = D_3 \times (1 + g)/(R - g)$$

where g is the long-run growth rate. So, we have:

$$P_3 = \$10.985 \times 1.10/(.20 - .10) = \$120.835$$

To determine the value today, we need the present value of this amount plus the present value of the total dividends:

$$P_0 = \frac{D_1}{(1+R)^1} + \frac{D_2}{(1+R)^2} + \frac{D_3}{(1+R)^3} + \frac{P_3}{(1+R)^3}$$

$$= \frac{\$6.50}{1.20} + \frac{8.45}{1.20^2} + \frac{10.985}{1.20^3} + \frac{120.835}{1.20^3}$$

$$= \$5.42 + 5.87 + 6.36 + 69.93$$

$$= \$87.57$$

The total value of the stock today is thus $87.57 million. If there were, for example, 20 million shares, then the stock would be worth $87.57/20 = $4.38 per share.

Two-Stage Growth   The last case we consider is a special case of nonconstant growth: Two-stage growth. Here, the idea is that the dividend will grow at a rate of g_1 for t years and then grow at a rate of g_2 thereafter, forever. In this case, the value of the stock can be written as:

$$P_0 = \frac{D_1}{R - g_1} \times \left[1 - \left(\frac{1 + g_1}{1 + R}\right)^t\right] + \frac{P_t}{(1 + R)^t} \qquad \textbf{8.5}$$

Notice that the first term in our expression is the present value of a growing annuity, which we discussed in Chapter 6. In this first stage, g_1 can be greater than R. The second part is the present value of the stock price once the second stage begins at Time t.

We can calculate P_t as follows:

$$P_t = \frac{D_{t+1}}{R - g_2} = \frac{D_0 \times (1 + g_1)^t \times (1 + g_2)}{R - g_2} \qquad \textbf{8.6}$$

In this calculation, we need the dividend at Time $t + 1$, D_{t+1}, to get the stock price at Time t, P_t. Notice that to get the dividend at Time $t + 1$, we grew the current dividend, D_0, at rate g_1 for t periods and then grew it one period at rate g_2. Also, in this second stage, g_2 must be less than R.

Two-Stage Growth   **EXAMPLE 8.5**

The Highfield Company's dividend is expected to grow at 20 percent for the next five years. After that, the growth is expected to be 4 percent forever. If the required return is 10 percent, what's the value of the stock? The dividend just paid was $2.

There is a fair amount of computation here, but it is mostly just "plug and chug" with a calculator. We can start by calculating the stock price five years from now, P_5:

$$P_5 = \frac{D_6}{R - g_2} = \frac{D_0 \times (1 + g_1)^5 \times (1 + g_2)}{R - g_2}$$

$$= \frac{\$2 \times (1 + .20)^5 \times (1 + .04)}{.10 - .04} = \frac{\$5.18}{.06}$$

$$= \$86.26$$

We then plug this result into our two-stage growth formula to get the price today:

$$P_0 = \frac{D_1}{R - g_1} \times \left[1 - \left(\frac{1 + g_1}{1 + R}\right)^t\right] + \frac{P_t}{(1 + R)^t}$$

$$= \frac{\$2 \times (1 + .20)}{.10 - .20} \times \left[1 - \left(\frac{1 + .20}{1 + .10}\right)^5\right] + \frac{\$86.26}{(1 + .10)^5}$$

$$= \$66.64$$

> Notice that we were given $D_0 = \$2$ here, so we had to grow it by 20 percent for one period to get D_1. Notice also that g_1 is bigger than R in this problem, but that fact does not cause a problem.

COMPONENTS OF THE REQUIRED RETURN

Thus far, we have taken the required return, or discount rate, R, as given. We will have quite a bit to say about this subject in Chapters 12 and 13. For now, we want to examine the implications of the dividend growth model for this required return. Earlier, we calculated P_0 as:

$$P_0 = D_1/(R - g)$$

If we rearrange this to solve for R, we get:

$$R - g = D_1/P_0$$
$$R = D_1/P_0 + g$$

8.7

dividend yield
A stock's expected cash dividend divided by its current price.

This tells us that the total return, R, has two components. The first of these, D_1/P_0, is called the **dividend yield**. Because this is calculated as the expected cash dividend divided by the current price, it is conceptually similar to the current yield on a bond.

capital gains yield
The dividend growth rate, or the rate at which the value of an investment grows.

The second part of the total return is the growth rate, g. We know that the dividend growth rate is also the rate at which the stock price grows (see Example 8.3). This growth rate can be interpreted as the **capital gains yield**—that is, the rate at which the value of the investment grows.[2]

To illustrate the components of the required return, suppose we observe a stock selling for $20 per share. The next dividend will be $1 per share. You think that the dividend will grow by 10 percent per year more or less indefinitely. What return does this stock offer if this is correct?

The dividend growth model calculates total return as:

$$R = \text{Dividend yield} + \text{Capital gains yield}$$
$$R = \qquad D_1/P_0 \qquad + \qquad g$$

In this case, total return works out to be:

$$R = \$1/20 + 10\%$$
$$= 5\% + 10\%$$
$$= 15\%$$

This stock has an expected return of 15 percent.

We can verify this answer by calculating the price in one year, P_1, using 15 percent as the required return. Based on the dividend growth model, this price is:

$$P_1 = D_1 \times (1 + g)/(R - g)$$
$$= \$1 \times 1.10/(.15 - .10)$$
$$= \$1.10/.05$$
$$= \$22$$

---

[2]Here and elsewhere, we use the term *capital gains* a little loosely. For the record, a capital gain (or loss) is, strictly speaking, something defined by the IRS. For our purposes, it would be more accurate (but less common) to use the term *price appreciation* instead of *capital gain*.

Notice that this $22 is $20 × 1.1, so the stock price has grown by 10 percent, as it should. If you pay $20 for the stock today, you will get a $1 dividend at the end of the year, and you will have a $22 − 20 = $2 gain. Your dividend yield is thus $1/20 = 5%. Your capital gains yield is $2/20 = 10%, so your total return is 5% + 10% = 15%.

To get a feel for actual numbers in this context, consider that, according to the December 2016 Value Line *Investment Survey,* Procter & Gamble's dividends were expected to grow by 5 percent over the next 5 or so years, compared to a historical growth rate of 7.5 percent over the preceding 5 years and 9.5 percent over the preceding 10 years. In 2017, the projected dividend for the coming year was given as $2.85. The stock price at that time was about $85 per share. What is the return investors require on P&G? Here, the dividend yield is 3.35 percent and the capital gains yield is 5 percent, giving a total required return of 8.35 percent on P&G stock.

STOCK VALUATION USING MULTIPLES

An obvious problem with our dividend-based approach to stock valuation is that many companies don't pay dividends. What do we do in such cases? A common approach is to make use of the PE ratio, which we defined in Chapter 3 as the ratio of a stock's price per share to its earnings per share (EPS) over the previous year. The idea here is to have some sort of benchmark or reference PE ratio, which we then multiply by earnings to come up with a price:

Price at Time $t = P_t$ = Benchmark PE ratio × EPS$_t$ [8.8]

The benchmark PE ratio could come from one of several possible sources. It could be based on similar companies (perhaps an industry average or median), or it could be based on a company's own historical values. For example, suppose we are trying to value Inactivision, Inc., a video game developer known for its hit *Slack Ops* series. Inactivision does not pay dividends, but after studying the industry, you feel that a PE ratio of 20 is appropriate for a company like this one. Total earnings over the four most recent quarters combined are $2 per share, so you think the stock should sell for 20 × $2 = $40. You might view this stock as an attractive purchase if it is going for less than $40, but not attractive if it sells for more than $40.

Security analysts spend a lot of time forecasting future earnings, particularly for the coming year. A PE ratio that is based on estimated future earnings is called a *forward* PE ratio. For example, suppose you felt that Inactivision's earnings for the coming year were going to be $2.50, reflecting the growing popularity of the company's *World of Slackcraft* massively multiplayer online role-playing game (MMORPG). In this case, if the current stock price is $40, the forward PE ratio is $40/$2.50 = 16.

Finally, notice that your benchmark PE of 20 applies to earnings over the previous year. If earnings over the coming year turn out to be $2.50, then the stock price one year from today should be 20 × $2.50 = $50. Forecast prices such as this one are often called *target* prices.

Often we will be interested in valuing newer companies that both don't pay dividends and are not yet profitable, meaning that earnings are negative. What do we do then? One answer is to use the price-sales ratio, which we also introduced in Chapter 3. As the name suggests, this ratio is the price per share on the stock divided by sales per share. You use this ratio just like you use the PE ratio, except you use sales per share instead of earnings per share. As with PE ratios, price-sales ratios vary depending on company age and industry. Typical values are in the .8–2.0 range, but they can be much higher for younger, faster-growing companies.

For future reference, our discussion of stock valuation techniques is summarized in Table 8.1.

TABLE 8.1

Summary of Stock Valuation

I. The General Case

In general, the price today of a share of stock, P_0, is the present value of all of its future dividends, $D_1, D_2, D_3, \ldots$:

$$P_0 = \frac{D_1}{(1+R)^1} + \frac{D_2}{(1+R)^2} + \frac{D_3}{(1+R)^3} + \cdots$$

where R is the required return.

II. Constant Growth Case

If the dividend grows at a steady rate, g, then the price can be written as:

$$P_0 = \frac{D_1}{R-g}$$

This result is called the *dividend growth model.*

III. Nonconstant Growth

If the dividend grows steadily after t periods, then the price can be written as:

$$P_0 = \frac{D_1}{(1+R)^1} + \frac{D_2}{(1+R)^2} + \cdots + \frac{D_t}{(1+R)^t} + \frac{P_t}{(1+R)^t}$$

where

$$P_t = \frac{D_t \times (1+g)}{(R-g)}$$

IV. Two-Stage Growth

If the dividend grows at rate g_1 for t periods and then grows at rate g_2 thereafter, then the price can be written as:

$$P_0 = \frac{D_1}{R-g_1} \times \left[1 - \left(\frac{1+g_1}{1+R}\right)^t\right] + \frac{P_t}{(1+R)^t}$$

where

$$P_t = \frac{D_{t+1}}{R-g_2} = \frac{D_0 \times (1+g_1)^t \times (1+g_2)}{R-g_2}$$

V. Valuation Using Multiples

For stocks that don't pay dividends (or have erratic dividend growth rates), we can value them using the PE ratio and/or the price-sales ratio:

P_t = Benchmark PE ratio $\times$ EPS_t

P_t = Benchmark price-sales ratio $\times$ Sales per share$_t$

VI. The Required Return

The required return, R, can be written as the sum of two things:

$R = D_1/P_0 + g$

where D_1/P_0 is the *dividend yield* and g is the *capital gains yield* (which is the same thing as the growth rate in dividends for the steady growth case).

Concept Questions

8.1a   What are the relevant cash flows for valuing a share of common stock?

8.1b   Does the value of a share of stock depend on how long you expect to keep it?

8.1c   What is the value of a share of stock when the dividend grows at a constant rate?

Some Features of Common and Preferred Stocks

8.2

In discussing common stock features, we focus on shareholder rights and dividend payments. For preferred stock, we explain what *preferred* means, and we also debate whether preferred stock is really debt or equity.

COMMON STOCK FEATURES

The term **common stock** means different things to different people, but it is usually applied to stock that has no special preference either in receiving dividends or in bankruptcy.

common stock
Equity without priority for dividends or in bankruptcy.

Shareholder Rights   The conceptual structure of the corporation assumes that shareholders elect directors who, in turn, hire managers to carry out their directives. Shareholders, therefore, control the corporation through the right to elect the directors. Generally, only shareholders have this right.

Directors are elected each year at an annual meeting. Although there are exceptions (discussed next), the general idea is "one share, one vote" (*not* one share*holder*, one vote). Corporate democracy is thus very different from our political democracy. With corporate democracy, the "golden rule" prevails absolutely.[3]

Directors are elected at an annual shareholders' meeting by a vote of the holders of a majority of shares who are present and entitled to vote. However, the exact mechanism for electing directors differs across companies. The most important difference is whether shares must be voted cumulatively or voted straight.

To illustrate the two different voting procedures, imagine that a corporation has two shareholders: Smith with 20 shares and Jones with 80 shares. Both want to be a director. Jones does not want Smith to be a director, however. We assume there are a total of four directors to be elected.

The effect of **cumulative voting** is to permit minority participation.[4] If cumulative voting is permitted, the total number of votes that each shareholder may cast is determined first. This is usually calculated as the number of shares (owned or controlled) multiplied by the number of directors to be elected.

cumulative voting
A procedure in which a shareholder may cast all votes for one member of the board of directors.

With cumulative voting, the directors are elected all at once. In our example, this means that the top four vote getters will be the new directors. A shareholder can distribute votes however he or she wishes.

Will Smith get a seat on the board? If we ignore the possibility of a five-way tie, then the answer is yes. Smith will cast $20 \times 4 = 80$ votes, and Jones will cast $80 \times 4 = 320$ votes. If Smith gives all his votes to himself, he is assured of a directorship. The reason is that Jones can't divide 320 votes among four candidates in such a way as to give all of them more than 80 votes, so Smith will finish fourth at worst.

In general, if there are N directors up for election, then $1/(N + 1)$ percent of the stock plus one share will guarantee you a seat. In our current example, this is $1/(4 + 1) = .20$, or 20%. So the more seats that are up for election at one time, the easier (and cheaper) it is to win one.

straight voting
A procedure in which a shareholder may cast all votes for each member of the board of directors.

With **straight voting**, the directors are elected one at a time. Each time, Smith can cast 20 votes and Jones can cast 80. As a consequence, Jones will elect all of the candidates. The

---

[3]The golden rule: Whosoever has the gold makes the rules.

[4]By *minority participation*, we mean participation by shareholders with relatively small amounts of stock.

only way to guarantee a seat is to own 50 percent plus one share. This also guarantees that you will win every seat, so it's really all or nothing.

EXAMPLE 8.6	Buying the Election

Stock in JRJ Corporation sells for $20 per share and features cumulative voting. There are 10,000 shares outstanding. If three directors are up for election, how much does it cost to ensure yourself a seat on the board?

The question here is how many shares of stock it will take to get a seat. The answer is 2,501, so the cost is 2,501 × $20 = $50,020. Why 2,501? Because there is no way the remaining 7,499 votes can be divided among three people to give all of them more than 2,501 votes. For example, suppose two people receive 2,502 votes and the first two seats. A third person can receive at most 10,000 − 2,502 − 2,502 − 2,501 = 2,495, so the third seat is yours.

Many companies have staggered elections for directors. With staggered elections, only a fraction of the directorships (often one-third) are up for election at a particular time. If only two directors are up for election at any one time, it will take $1/(2 + 1) = .3333$, or 33.33% of the stock plus one share to guarantee a seat. Staggered boards are often called *classified* boards because directors are placed into different classes with terms that expire at different times. In recent years, corporations have come under pressure to declassify their boards, meaning that all directors would stand for election every year, and many have done so.

Overall, staggering has two basic effects:

1. Staggering makes it more difficult for a minority to elect a director because there are fewer directors to be elected at one time.

2. Staggering makes takeover attempts less likely to be successful because it makes it more difficult to vote in a majority of new directors.

We should note that staggering may serve a beneficial purpose. It provides "institutional memory"—that is, continuity on the board of directors. This may be important for corporations with significant long-range plans and projects.

proxy
A grant of authority by a shareholder allowing another individual to vote his or her shares.

Proxy Voting   A **proxy** is the grant of authority by a shareholder to someone else to vote his or her shares. For convenience, much of the voting in large public corporations is actually done by proxy.

As we have seen, with straight voting, each share of stock has one vote. The owner of 10,000 shares has 10,000 votes. Large companies have hundreds of thousands or even millions of shareholders. Shareholders can come to the annual meeting and vote in person, or they can transfer their right to vote to another party.

Obviously, management always tries to get as many proxies as possible transferred to it. If shareholders are not satisfied with management, an "outside" group of shareholders can try to obtain votes via proxy. They can vote by proxy in an attempt to replace management by electing enough directors. The resulting battle is called a *proxy fight*.

Classes of Stock   Some firms have more than one class of common stock. Often the classes are created with unequal voting rights. The Ford Motor Company, for example, has Class B common stock, which is not publicly traded (it is held by Ford family interests and trusts). This class has 40 percent of the voting power, even though it represents less than 10 percent of the total number of shares outstanding.

There are many other cases of corporations with different classes of stock. For example, at one time, General Motors had its "GM Classic" shares (the original) and two additional classes, Class E ("GME") and Class H ("GMH"). These classes were created to help pay for two large acquisitions, Electronic Data Systems and Hughes Aircraft. Another good example is Alphabet, the web search company, which became publicly owned in 2004. Alphabet originally had two classes of common stock, A and B. The Class A shares are held by the public, and each share has one vote. The Class B shares are held by company insiders, and each Class B share has 10 votes. Then, in 2014, the company had a stock split of its Class B shares, creating Class C shares, which have no vote at all. As a result, Alphabet's founders and managers control the company. Facebook joined Alphabet when it created its own nonvoting Class C shares in 2016.

Historically, the New York Stock Exchange did not allow companies to create classes of publicly traded common stock with unequal voting rights. Exceptions (like Ford) appear to have been made. In addition, many non-NYSE companies have dual classes of common stock.

A primary reason for creating dual or multiple classes of stock has to do with control of the firm. If such stock exists, management of a firm can raise equity capital by issuing nonvoting or limited-voting stock while maintaining control.

The subject of unequal voting rights is controversial in the United States, and the idea of one share, one vote has a strong following and a long history. Interestingly, shares with unequal voting rights are quite common in the United Kingdom and elsewhere around the world.

Other Rights   The value of a share of common stock in a corporation is directly related to the general rights of shareholders. In addition to the right to vote for directors, shareholders usually have the following rights:

1. The right to share proportionally in dividends paid.
2. The right to share proportionally in assets remaining after liabilities have been paid in a liquidation.
3. The right to vote on stockholder matters of great importance, such as a merger. Voting is usually done at the annual meeting or a special meeting.

In addition, stockholders sometimes have the right to share proportionally in any new stock sold. This is called the *preemptive right*.

Essentially, a preemptive right means that a company that wishes to sell stock must first offer it to the existing stockholders before offering it to the general public. The purpose is to give stockholders the opportunity to protect their proportionate ownership in the corporation.

Dividends   A distinctive feature of corporations is that they have shares of stock on which they are authorized by law to pay dividends to their shareholders. **Dividends** paid to shareholders represent a return on the capital directly or indirectly contributed to the corporation by the shareholders. The payment of dividends is at the discretion of the board of directors.

dividends
Payments by a corporation to shareholders, made in either cash or stock.

Some important characteristics of dividends include the following:

1. Unless a dividend is declared by the board of directors of a corporation, it is not a liability of the corporation. A corporation cannot default on an undeclared dividend. As a consequence, corporations cannot become bankrupt because of nonpayment of dividends. The amount of the dividend and even whether it is paid are decisions based on the business judgment of the board of directors.

2. The payment of dividends by the corporation is not a business expense. Dividends are not deductible for corporate tax purposes. In short, dividends are paid out of the corporation's aftertax profits.

3. Dividends received by individual shareholders are taxable. In 2018, the tax rate was 15 to 20 percent. However, corporations that own stock in other corporations are permitted to exclude 50 percent of the dividend amounts they receive and are taxed on only the remaining 50 percent (the 50 percent exclusion was reduced from 70 percent by the Tax Cuts and Jobs Act of 2017).[5]

PREFERRED STOCK FEATURES

preferred stock
Stock with dividend priority over common stock, normally with a fixed dividend rate, sometimes without voting rights.

Preferred stock differs from common stock because it has preference over common stock in the payment of dividends and in the distribution of corporation assets in the event of liquidation. *Preference* means only that the holders of the preferred shares must receive a dividend (in the case of an ongoing firm) before holders of common shares are entitled to anything.

Preferred stock is a form of equity from a legal and tax standpoint. It is important to note that holders of preferred stock sometimes have no voting privileges.

Stated Value
Preferred shares have a stated liquidating value, usually $100 per share. The cash dividend is described in terms of dollars per share. For example, General Motors "$5 preferred" easily translates into a dividend yield of 5 percent of stated value.

Cumulative and Noncumulative Dividends
A preferred dividend is *not* like interest on a bond. The board of directors may decide not to pay the dividends on preferred shares, and their decision may have nothing to do with the current net income of the corporation.

Dividends payable on preferred stock are either *cumulative* or *noncumulative*; most are cumulative. If preferred dividends are cumulative and are not paid in a particular year, they will be carried forward as an *arrearage*. Usually, both the accumulated (past) preferred dividends and the current preferred dividends must be paid before the common shareholders can receive anything.

Unpaid preferred dividends are *not* debts of the firm. Directors elected by the common shareholders can defer preferred dividends indefinitely. In such cases, common shareholders must also forgo dividends. In addition, holders of preferred shares are often granted voting and other rights if preferred dividends have not been paid for some time. For example, at one point, USAir (now part of American Airlines) had failed to pay dividends on one of its preferred stock issues for six quarters. As a consequence, the holders of the shares were allowed to nominate two people to represent their interests on the airline's board. Because preferred stockholders receive no interest on the accumulated dividends, some have argued that firms have an incentive to delay paying preferred dividends; but, as we have seen, this may mean sharing control with preferred stockholders.

Is Preferred Stock Really Debt?
A good case can be made that preferred stock is really debt in disguise, a kind of equity bond. Preferred shareholders receive a stated dividend only; and if the corporation is liquidated, preferred shareholders get a stated value. Often, preferred stocks carry credit ratings much like those of bonds. Furthermore,

---

[5]For the record, the 70 percent exclusion applies when the recipient owns less than 20 percent of the outstanding stock in a corporation. If a corporation owns more than 20 percent but less than 80 percent, the exclusion is 80 percent. If more than 80 percent is owned, the corporation can file a single "consolidated" return and the exclusion is effectively 100 percent.

preferred stock is sometimes convertible into common stock, and preferred stocks are often callable.

In addition, many issues of preferred stock have obligatory sinking funds. The existence of such a sinking fund effectively creates a final maturity because it means that the entire issue will ultimately be retired. For these reasons, preferred stock seems to be a lot like debt. For tax purposes, preferred dividends are treated like common stock dividends.

In the 1990s, firms began to sell securities that looked a lot like preferred stocks but were treated as debt for tax purposes. The new securities were given interesting acronyms like TOPrS (trust-originated preferred securities, or toppers), MIPS (monthly income preferred securities), and QUIPS (quarterly income preferred securities), among others. Because of various specific features, these instruments can be counted as debt for tax purposes, making the interest payments tax deductible (up to certain limits). Payments made to investors in these instruments are treated as interest for personal income taxes. Until 2003, interest payments and dividends were taxed at the same marginal tax rate. When the tax rate on dividend payments was reduced, these instruments were not included, so individuals must still pay their higher income tax rate on dividend payments received from these instruments.

Concept Questions

8.2a What is a proxy?
8.2b What rights do stockholders have?
8.2c Why is preferred stock called *preferred*?

The Stock Markets

8.3

Back in Chapter 1, we briefly mentioned that shares of stock are bought and sold on various stock exchanges, the two most important of which are the New York Stock Exchange and NASDAQ. From our earlier discussion, recall that the stock market consists of a **primary market** and a **secondary market**. In the primary, or new issue, market, shares of stock are first brought to the market and sold to investors. In the secondary market, existing shares are traded among investors.

In the primary market, companies sell securities to raise money. We will discuss this process in detail in a later chapter. We focus mainly on secondary market activity in this section. We conclude with a discussion of how stock prices are quoted in the financial press.

DEALERS AND BROKERS

Because most securities transactions involve dealers and brokers, it is important to understand exactly what is meant by the terms *dealer* and *broker*. A **dealer** maintains an inventory and stands ready to buy and sell at any time. In contrast, a **broker** brings buyers and sellers together but does not maintain an inventory. When we speak of used car dealers and real estate brokers, we recognize that the used car dealer maintains an inventory, whereas the real estate broker does not.

In the securities markets, a dealer stands ready to buy securities from investors wishing to sell them and sell securities to investors wishing to buy them. Recall from our previous chapter that the price the dealer is willing to pay is called the *bid price*. The price at which the dealer will sell is called the *ask price* (sometimes called the asked, offered, or offering price). The difference between the bid and ask prices is called the *spread,* and it is the basic source of dealer profits.

Excel Master It!
Excel Master coverage online

primary market
The market in which new securities are originally sold to investors.

secondary market
The market in which previously issued securities are traded among investors.

dealer
An agent who buys and sells securities from inventory.

broker
An agent who arranges security transactions among investors.

How big is the bid-ask spread on your favorite stock? Check out the latest quotes at **www.bloomberg.com**.

Dealers exist in all areas of the economy, not just the stock markets. For example, your local college bookstore is probably both a primary and a secondary market textbook dealer. If you buy a new book, this is a primary market transaction. If you buy a used book, this is a secondary market transaction, and you pay the store's ask price. If you sell the book back, you receive the store's bid price (often half of the ask price). The bookstore's spread is the difference between the two prices.

In contrast, a securities broker arranges transactions between investors, matching investors wishing to buy securities with investors wishing to sell securities. The distinctive characteristic of security brokers is that they do not buy or sell securities for their own accounts. Facilitating trades by others is their business.

ORGANIZATION OF THE NYSE

The New York Stock Exchange, or NYSE, popularly known as the Big Board, celebrated its bicentennial a few years ago. It has occupied its current location on Wall Street since the turn of the twentieth century. Measured in terms of the total value of shares listed, it is the largest stock market in the world.

members
As of 2006, a member is the owner of a trading license on the NYSE.

Members The NYSE has 1,366 exchange **members**. Prior to 2006, the exchange members were said to own "seats" on the exchange, and collectively the members of the exchange were also the owners. For this and other reasons, seats were valuable and were bought and sold fairly regularly. Seat prices reached a record $4 million in 2005.

In 2006, all of this changed when the NYSE became a publicly owned corporation. Naturally, its stock was listed on the NYSE. Now, instead of purchasing seats, exchange members must purchase trading licenses, the number of which is still limited to 1,366. In 2017, a license would set you back a cool $40,000—per year. Having a license entitles you to buy and sell securities on the floor of the exchange. Different members play different roles in this regard.

On April 4, 2007, the NYSE grew even larger when it merged with Euronext to form NYSE Euronext. Euronext was a stock exchange in Amsterdam, with subsidiaries in Belgium, France, Portugal, and the United Kingdom. With the merger, NYSE Euronext became the world's "first global exchange." Further expansion occurred in 2008 when NYSE Euronext merged with the American Stock Exchange. Then, in November 2013, the acquisition of the NYSE by the Intercontinental Exchange (ICE) was completed. ICE, which was founded in May 2000, was originally a commodities exchange, but its rapid growth gave it the necessary $8.2 billion for the acquisition of the NYSE.

As we briefly describe how the NYSE operates, keep in mind that other markets owned by NYSE Euronext and ICE may function differently. What makes the NYSE somewhat unique is that it is a *hybrid market*. In a hybrid market, trading takes place both electronically and face-to-face.

designated market makers (DMMs)
NYSE members who act as dealers in particular stocks. Formerly known as "specialists."

floor brokers
NYSE members who execute customer buy and sell orders.

supplemental liquidity providers (SLPs)
Investment firms that are active participants in stocks assigned to them. Their job is to make a one-sided market (i.e., offering to either buy or sell). They trade purely for their own accounts.

With electronic trading, orders to buy and orders to sell are submitted to the exchange. Orders are compared by a computer and whenever there is a match, the orders are executed with no human intervention. Most trades on the NYSE occur this way. For orders that are not handled electronically, the NYSE relies on its license holders. There are three different types of license holders, **designated market makers (DMMs)**, **floor brokers**, and **supplemental liquidity providers (SLPs)**, and we now discuss the role played by each.

The DMMs, formerly known as "specialists," act as dealers in particular stocks. Typically, each stock on the NYSE is assigned to a single DMM. As a dealer, a DMM maintains a two-sided market, meaning that the DMM continually posts and updates bid and ask prices. By doing so, the DMM ensures that there is always a buyer or seller available, thereby promoting market liquidity.

The job of a floor broker is to execute trades for customers, with an emphasis on getting the best price possible. Floor brokers are generally employees of large brokerage firms such as Merrill Lynch, the wealth management division of Bank of America. The interaction between floor brokers and DMMs is the key to nonelectronic trading on the NYSE. We discuss this interaction in detail in just a moment.

The SLPs are essentially investment firms that agree to be active participants in stocks assigned to them. Their job is to regularly make a one-sided market (i.e., offering to either buy or sell). They trade purely for their own accounts (using their own money), so they do not represent customers. They are given a small rebate on their buys and sells, thereby encouraging them to be more aggressive. The NYSE's goal is to generate as much liquidity as possible, which makes it easier for ordinary investors to quickly buy and sell at prevailing prices. Unlike DMMs and floor brokers, SLPs do not operate on the floor of the stock exchange.

In recent years, floor brokers have become less important on the exchange floor because of the efficient Pillar system, which allows orders to be transmitted electronically directly to the DMM. Additionally, the NYSE has an electronic platform called Arca, which accounts for a substantial percentage of all trading on the NYSE, particularly for smaller orders. The average time for a trade on the NYSE Arca is less than 1 second.

Finally, a small number of NYSE members are floor traders who independently trade for their own accounts. Floor traders try to anticipate temporary price fluctuations and profit from them by buying low and selling high. In recent decades, the number of floor traders has declined substantially, suggesting that it has become increasingly difficult to profit from short-term trading on the exchange floor.

Operations   Now that we have a basic idea of how the NYSE is organized and who the major players are, we turn to the question of how trading actually takes place. Fundamentally, the business of the NYSE is to attract and process **order flow**. The term *order flow* refers to the flow of customer orders to buy and sell stocks. The customers of the NYSE are the millions of individual investors and tens of thousands of institutional investors who place their orders to buy and sell shares in NYSE-listed companies. The NYSE has been quite successful in attracting order flow. Currently, it is not unusual for well over a billion shares to change hands in a single day.

order flow
The flow of customer orders to buy and sell securities.

Floor Activity   It is quite likely that you have seen footage of the NYSE trading floor on television. If so, you would have seen a big room, about the size of a basketball gym. This big room is called, technically, "the Big Room." There are a few other, smaller rooms that you normally don't see, one of which is called "the Garage," because that is what it was before it was taken over for trading.

On the floor of the exchange are a number of stations, each with a roughly figure-eight shape. These stations have multiple counters with numerous terminal screens above and on the sides. People operate behind and in front of the counters in relatively stationary positions.

Other people move around on the exchange floor, frequently returning to the many telephones positioned along the exchange walls. In all, you may be reminded of worker ants moving around an ant colony. It is natural to wonder, "What are all those people doing down there (and why are so many wearing funny-looking coats)?"

Take a virtual field trip to the New York Stock Exchange at **www.nyse.com**.

As an overview of exchange floor activity, here is a quick look at what goes on. Each of the counters is a **DMM's post**. DMMs normally operate in front of their posts to monitor and manage trading in the stocks assigned to them. Clerical employees working for the DMMs operate behind the counter. Moving from the many workstations lining the walls of the exchange out to the exchange floor and back again are swarms of floor brokers, receiving customer orders, walking out to DMMs' posts where the orders can be executed, and returning to confirm order executions and receive new customer orders.

DMM's post
A fixed place on the exchange floor where the DMM operates.

To better understand activity on the NYSE trading floor, imagine yourself as a floor broker. Your phone clerk has just handed you an order to sell 20,000 shares of Walmart for a customer of the brokerage company that employs you. The customer wants to sell the stock at the best possible price as soon as possible. You immediately walk (running violates exchange rules) to the DMM's post where Walmart stock is traded.

As you approach the DMM's post where Walmart is traded, you check the terminal screen for information on the current market price. The screen reveals that the last executed trade was at $60.10 and that the DMM is bidding $60 per share. You could immediately sell to the DMM at $60, but that would be too easy.

Instead, as the customer's representative, you are obligated to get the best possible price. It is your job to "work" the order, and your job depends on providing satisfactory order execution service. So, you look around for another broker who represents a customer who wants to buy Walmart stock. Luckily, you quickly find another broker at the DMM's post with an order to buy 20,000 shares. Noticing that the DMM is asking $60.10 per share, you both agree to execute your orders with each other at a price of $60.05. This price is exactly halfway between the DMM's bid and ask prices, and it saves each of your customers $.05 × 20,000 = $1,000 as compared to dealing at the posted prices.

For a very actively traded stock, there may be many buyers and sellers around the DMM's post, and most of the trading will be done directly between brokers. This is called trading in the "crowd." In such cases, the DMM's responsibility is to maintain order and to make sure that all buyers and sellers receive a fair price. In other words, the DMM essentially functions as a referee.

More often, there will be no crowd at the DMM's post. Going back to our Walmart example, suppose you are unable to quickly find another broker with an order to buy 20,000 shares. Because you have an order to sell immediately, you may have no choice but to sell to the DMM at the bid price of $60. In this case, the need to execute an order quickly takes priority, and the DMM provides the liquidity necessary to allow immediate order execution.

Finally, note that colored coats are worn by many of the people on the floor of the exchange. The color of the coat indicates the person's job or position. Clerks, runners, visitors, exchange officials, and so on wear particular colors to identify themselves. Also, things can get a little hectic on a busy day, with the result that good clothing doesn't last long; the cheap coats offer some protection.

NASDAQ OPERATIONS

In terms of total dollar volume of trading, the second largest stock market in the United States is NASDAQ (say "Naz-dak"). The somewhat odd name originally was an acronym for the National Association of Securities Dealers Automated Quotations system, but NASDAQ is now a name in its own right.

Introduced in 1971, the NASDAQ market is a computer network of securities dealers and others that disseminates timely security price quotes to computer screens worldwide. NASDAQ dealers act as market makers for securities listed on the NASDAQ. As market makers, NASDAQ dealers post bid and ask prices at which they accept sell and buy orders, respectively. With each price quote, they also post the number of shares that they obligate themselves to trade at their quoted prices.

Like NYSE DMMs, NASDAQ market makers trade on an inventory basis—that is, using their inventory as a buffer to absorb buy and sell order imbalances. Unlike the NYSE specialist system, NASDAQ features multiple market makers for actively traded stocks. There are two key differences between the NYSE and NASDAQ:

1. NASDAQ is a computer network and has no physical location where trading takes place.
2. NASDAQ has a multiple market maker system rather than a DMM system.

Traditionally, a securities market largely characterized by dealers who buy and sell securities for their own inventories is called an **over-the-counter (OTC) market**. Consequently, NASDAQ is often referred to as an OTC market. In their efforts to promote a

over-the-counter (OTC) market
Securities market in which trading is almost exclusively done through dealers who buy and sell for their own inventories.

distinct image, NASDAQ officials prefer that the term OTC not be used when referring to the NASDAQ market. Nevertheless, old habits die hard, and many people still refer to NASDAQ as an OTC market.

The NASDAQ network operates with three levels of information access. Level 1 is designed to provide a timely, accurate source of price quotations. These prices are freely available over the Internet.

Level 2 allows users to view price quotes from all NASDAQ market makers. In particular, this level allows access to inside quotes. Inside quotes are the highest bid quotes and the lowest asked quotes for a NASDAQ-listed security. Level 2 is now available on the web, sometimes for a small fee. Level 3 is for the use of market makers only. This access level allows NASDAQ dealers to enter or change their price quote information. See our nearby *Work the Web* box for an example of inside quotes.

NASDAQ is actually made up of three separate markets: The NASDAQ Global Select Market, the NASDAQ Global Market, and the NASDAQ Capital Market. As the market for NASDAQ's larger and more actively traded securities, the Global Select Market lists about 1,600 companies (as of early 2017), including some of the best-known companies in the world, such as Microsoft and Intel. Global Market companies are somewhat smaller in size, and NASDAQ lists about 810 of these. Finally, the smallest companies listed on NASDAQ are in the NASDAQ Capital Market; about 820 are currently listed. Of course, as Capital Market companies become more established, they may move up to the Global Market or Global Select Market.

inside quotes
The highest bid quotes and the lowest ask quotes for a security.

NASDAQ (**www.nasdaq.com**) has a great website; check it out!

WORK THE WEB

You can actually watch trading taking place on the web by visiting www.batstrading.com. The BATS Exchange is somewhat unique in that the "order book," meaning the list of all buy and sell orders, is public in real time. As shown below, we have captured a sample of the order book for Intel (INTC). On the top in blue are sell orders (asks); buy orders (bids) are in green on the bottom. All orders are "limit" orders, which means the customer has specified the most he or she will pay (for buy orders) or the least he or she will accept (for sell orders). The inside quotes (the highest bid, or buy, and the lowest ask, or sell) in the market are in the middle of the quotes.

INTC			Orders Accepted	Total Volume
INTEL CORP COM			238,440	905,015
TOP OF BOOK			LAST 10 TRADES	
Shares	Price	Time	Price	Shares
1,900	**36.8000**	13:51:33	36.7500	100
2,302	36.7900	13:51:33	36.7500	200
2,201	36.7800	13:51:33	36.7500	100
2,723	36.7700	13:50:56	36.7500	100
982	36.7600	13:50:56	36.7500	100
801	**36.7500**	13:50:56	36.7500	100
2,274	36.7400	13:50:56	36.7500	100
2,262	36.7300	13:50:56	36.7500	100
2,561	36.7200	13:50:56	36.7500	100
2,602	36.7100	13:50:47	36.7550	66

If you visit the site, you can see trading take place as orders are entered and executed. Notice that on this particular day, about 905,000 shares of Intel had traded on BATS. At that time, the inside quotes for Intel were 801 shares bid at $36.75 and 982 shares offered at $36.76. This is not the entire order book for Intel, as there are more buy orders below $36.75 and more sell orders above $36.76.

260   **PART 3**   Valuation of Future Cash Flows

Questions

1. Go to www.bats.com/us/equities and look up the order book for Microsoft (MSFT). What are the inside quotes for Microsoft?
2. Go to www.bats.com/us/equities. The website shows the 25 most active stocks. Looking down through this list, what are the bid-ask spreads for these stocks?

---

electronic communications networks (ECNs)
A website that allows investors to trade directly with each other.

ECNs   In a very important development in the late 1990s, the NASDAQ system was opened to so-called **electronic communications networks (ECNs)**. ECNs are basically websites that allow investors to trade directly with one another. Investor buy and sell orders placed on ECNs are transmitted to the NASDAQ and displayed along with market maker bid and ask prices. As a result, the ECNs open up the NASDAQ by essentially allowing individual investors, not just market makers, to enter orders. As a result, the ECNs act to increase liquidity and competition.

Of course, the NYSE and the NASDAQ are not the only places stocks are traded. See our nearby *Work the Web* box for a discussion of somewhat wilder markets.

You can get real-time stock quotes on the web. See **finance.yahoo.com** for details.

STOCK MARKET REPORTING

In recent years, the reporting of stock prices and related information has increasingly moved from traditional print media, such as *The Wall Street Journal*, to various websites. Yahoo! Finance (finance.yahoo.com) is a good example. We went there and requested a stock quote on wholesale club Costco, which is listed on the NASDAQ. Here is a portion of what we found:

Costco Wholesale Corporation (COST)
NasdaqGS - NasdaqGS Real Time Price. Currency in USD   ☆ Add to watchlist

160.63 -1.03 (-0.64%)
As of 1:49PM EST. Market open.

| Summary | Conversations | Statistics | Profile | Financials | Options | Holders | Historical Data | Analysts |

Previous Close	161.66	Market Cap	70.56B
Open	161.47	Beta	0.90
Bid	160.33 x 100	PE Ratio (TTM)	29.31
Ask	160.41 x 200	EPS (TTM)	5.48
Day's Range	160.35 - 162.35	Earnings Date	Mar 2, 2017
52 Week Range	138.57 - 169.59	Dividend & Yield	1.80 (1.12%)
Volume	686,350	Ex-Dividend Date	N/A
Avg. Volume	2,289,400	1y Target Est	173.12

WORK THE WEB

Where do companies trade when they can't (or don't want to) meet the listing requirements of the larger stock markets? Mostly, they trade on the OTCQX®, OTCQB®, and OTC Pink® marketplaces operated by OTC Markets Group. The OTCQX® marketplace includes qualitative and quantitative standards and the OTCQB® marketplace imposes some requirements as well, though these requirements are less restrictive than those enforced by the larger stock markets. OTC Pink® is called the "Open Marketplace" because there are no filing or financial requirements.

A small portion of companies also continue to trade on the Over-the-Counter Bulletin Board, or OTCBB, operated by the Financial Industry Regulatory Authority, known as FINRA. The OTCBB began as an electronic bulletin board that was created to facilitate OTC trading in non-listed stocks. It has effectively been replaced by OTC Markets Group's OTCQB® marketplace as the primary marketplace for these types of companies. Like the OTCQX® and OTCQB®, the OTCBB imposes some requirements, though they are not as restrictive as the larger markets. For example, OTCBB only requires that listed firms file financial statements with the SEC (or other relevant agency).

Trading at any of the OTC Markets Group marketplaces, as well as the OTCBB, is conducted under a dealer-driven framework. So, aside from the minimal requirements for inclusion on these marketplaces, all that is necessary for a particular security to begin trading is a registered broker-dealer willing (and approved) to quote and make a market in the security. Investors can trade OTCQX®, OTCQB®, and OTC Pink® securities in a manner similar to the trading in an exchange-listed stock. Given the ease of trading, these marketplaces (OTCQX®, in particular) are attractive to foreign firms that file with regulators in their home countries, but do not have interest in filing with U.S. regulators. These markets are also an option for companies that have been delisted from the larger markets either by choice or for failure to maintain their listing requirements.

Stocks traded on these markets often have very low prices and are frequently referred to as *penny stocks*, *microcaps*, or even *nanocaps*. Relatively few brokers do any research on these companies, so information is often spread through word of mouth or the Internet (not the most reliable of sources). To get a feel for what trading looks like, we captured a typical screen from the OTCBB website (http://finra -markets.morningstar.com/MarketData/EquityOptions/default.jsp):

OOTC Equity

| Most Actives | % Gainers | % Losers | Exchange by | OOTC ▼ |

Symbol		Last	Chg	Chg %	Vol (mil) ▼
MLCG	▲	0.0003	0.0000	0.0000	307.3956
TPAC	▲	0.0006	0.0001	20.0000	220.4887
GAWK	▲	0.0002	0.0000	0.0000	157.7228
ICNM	▲	0.0002	0.0001	100.0000	136.8407
GDGI	▲	0.0002	0.0001	100.0000	128.5851
SNMN	▲	0.0017	0.0010	142.8571	121.8124
SDVI	▼	0.0012	-0.0003	-20.0000	105.6642
KGET	▼	0.0001	-0.0001	-25.0000	103.3502
FWDG	▲	0.0001	0.0000	0.0000	99.8849
ASTI	▲	0.0019	0.0002	11.7647	94.4509

First, take a look at the returns. SNM Global Holdings (SNMN) had an intraday return on this day of 142.86 percent. That's not something you see very often. Of course, the big return was generated by a whopping price increase of $.0010 per share. A stock listed on the OTCBB is often the most actively traded stock on any particular day. For example, by the end of this particular day, Bank of America was the most active stock on the NYSE, trading about 81.3 million shares. In contrast, Alumifuel Power Corp. traded about 480 million shares. But, at an average price of, say, $.0001 per share, the total dollar volume in Alumifuel was all of $48,000. In contrast, trades in Bank of America amounted to about $1.88 billion.

All in all, the OTC markets can be pretty wild places to trade. Low stock prices allow for huge percentage returns on small stock price movements. Be advised that attempts at manipulation and fraud are possible. Also, stocks on these markets are often thinly traded, meaning there is little volume. It is not unusual for a stock listed on any of these markets to have no trades on a given day. Even two or three days in a row without a trade in a particular stock is not uncommon.

262   **PART 3**   Valuation of Future Cash Flows

You can get real-time stock quotes on the web. See **finance.yahoo.com** for details.

Most of this information is self-explanatory. The price $160.63 is the real-time price of the last trade. Availability of real-time prices for free is a relatively new development. The reported change is from the previous day's closing price. The opening price is the first trade of the day. We see the bid and ask prices of $160.33 and $160.41, respectively, along with the market "depth," which is the number of shares sought at the bid price and offered at the ask price. The "1y Target Est" is the average estimated stock price one year ahead based on estimates from security analysts who follow the stock.

We also have the range of prices for this day, followed by the range over the previous 52 weeks. Volume is the number of shares traded today, followed by average daily volume over the last three months. In the second column, Market Cap is number of shares outstanding (from the most recent quarterly financial statements) multiplied by the current price per share. The PE ratio was discussed in Chapter 3. The earnings per share (EPS) used in the calculation is "TTM," meaning "trailing twelve months." Finally, we have the dividend on the stock, which is actually the most recent quarterly dividend multiplied by 4, and the dividend yield. Notice that the yield is the reported dividend divided by the stock price: $1.80/$160.63 = .0112, or 1.12%.

Concept Questions

8.3a   What is the difference between a securities broker and a securities dealer?

8.3b   Which is bigger, the bid price or the ask price? Why?

8.3c   How does NASDAQ differ from the NYSE?

8.4 Summary and Conclusions

This chapter has covered the basics of stocks and stock valuation:

1. The cash flows from owning a share of stock come in the form of future dividends. We saw that in certain special cases it is possible to calculate the present value of all the future dividends and come up with a value for the stock.

2. As the owner of shares of common stock in a corporation, you have various rights, including the right to vote to elect corporate directors. Voting in corporate elections can be either cumulative or straight. Most voting is actually done by proxy, and a proxy battle breaks out when competing sides try to gain enough votes to elect their candidates for the board.

3. In addition to common stock, some corporations have issued preferred stock. The name stems from the fact that preferred stockholders must be paid first, before common stockholders can receive anything. Preferred stock has a fixed dividend.

4. The two biggest stock markets in the United States are the NYSE and the NASDAQ. We discussed the organization and operation of these two markets, and we saw how stock price information is reported.

This chapter completes Part 3 of our book. By now, you should have a good grasp of what we mean by *present value*. You should also be familiar with how to calculate present values, loan payments, and so on. In Part 4, we cover capital budgeting decisions. As you will see, the techniques you learned in Chapters 5–8 form the basis for our approach to evaluating business investment decisions.

CONNECT TO FINANCE

 For more practice, you should be using *Connect Finance*. Log on to connect.mheducation.com to get started!

Can you answer the following *Connect* Quiz questions?

Section 8.1 A stock is selling for $11.90 a share given a market return of 14 percent and a capital gains yield of 5 percent. What was the amount of the last annual dividend that was paid?

Section 8.2 An 8 percent preferred stock sells for $54 a share. What is the rate of return?

Section 8.3 What kind of market is the NYSE?

CHAPTER REVIEW AND SELF-TEST PROBLEMS

8.1 **Dividend Growth and Stock Valuation** The Brigapenski Co. has just paid a cash dividend of $2 per share. Investors require a 16 percent return from investments such as this. If the dividend is expected to grow at a steady 8 percent per year, what is the current value of the stock? What will the stock be worth in five years?

8.2 **More Dividend Growth and Stock Valuation** In Self-Test Problem 8.1, what would the stock sell for today if the dividend was expected to grow at 20 percent per year for the next three years and then settle down to 8 percent per year indefinitely?

ANSWERS TO CHAPTER REVIEW AND SELF-TEST PROBLEMS

8.1 The last dividend, D_0, was $2. The dividend is expected to grow steadily at 8 percent. The required return is 16 percent. Based on the dividend growth model, we can say that the current price is:

$$P_0 = D_1/(R - g) = D_0 \times (1 + g)/(R - g)$$
$$= \$2 \times 1.08/(.16 - .08)$$
$$= \$2.16/.08$$
$$= \$27$$

We could calculate the price in five years by calculating the dividend in five years and then using the growth model again. Alternatively, we could recognize that the stock price will increase by 8 percent per year and calculate the future price directly. We'll do both. First, the dividend in five years will be:

$$D_5 = D_0 \times (1 + g)^5$$
$$= \$2 \times 1.08^5$$
$$= \$2.9387$$

The price in five years would therefore be:

$$P_5 = D_5 \times (1 + g)/(R - g)$$
$$= \$2.9387 \times 1.08/.08$$
$$= \$3.1738/.08$$
$$= \$39.67$$

Once we understand the dividend model, however, it's easier to notice that:

$$P_5 = P_0 \times (1 + g)^5$$
$$= \$27 \times 1.08^5$$
$$= \$27 \times 1.4693$$
$$= \$39.67$$

Notice that both approaches yield the same price in five years.

8.2   In this scenario, we have supernormal growth for the next three years. We'll need to calculate the dividends during the rapid growth period and the stock price in three years. The dividends are:

$$D_1 = \$2.00 \times 1.20 = \$2.400$$
$$D_2 = \$2.40 \times 1.20 = \$2.880$$
$$D_3 = \$2.88 \times 1.20 = \$3.456$$

After three years, the growth rate falls to 8 percent indefinitely. The price at that time, P_3, is thus:

$$P_3 = D_3 \times (1 + g)/(R - g)$$
$$= \$3.456 \times 1.08/(.16 - .08)$$
$$= \$3.7325/.08$$
$$= \$46.656$$

To complete the calculation of the stock's present value, we have to determine the present value of the three dividends and the future price:

$$P_0 = \frac{D_1}{(1 + R)^1} + \frac{D_2}{(1 + R)^2} + \frac{D_3}{(1 + R)^3} + \frac{P_3}{(1 + R)^3}$$
$$= \frac{\$2.40}{1.16} + \frac{2.88}{1.16^2} + \frac{3.456}{1.16^3} + \frac{46.656}{1.16^3}$$
$$= \$2.07 + 2.14 + 2.21 + 29.89$$
$$= \$36.31$$

CONCEPTS REVIEW AND CRITICAL THINKING QUESTIONS

1. **Stock Valuation** [LO1] Why does the value of a share of stock depend on dividends?

2. **Stock Valuation** [LO1] A substantial percentage of the companies listed on the NYSE and NASDAQ don't pay dividends, but investors are nonetheless willing to buy shares in them. How is this possible given your answer to the previous question?

3. **Dividend Policy** [LO1] Referring to the previous questions, under what circumstances might a company choose not to pay dividends?

4. **Dividend Growth Model** [LO1] Under what two assumptions can we use the dividend growth model presented in the chapter to determine the value of a share of stock? Comment on the reasonableness of these assumptions.

5. **Common versus Preferred Stock** [LO1] Suppose a company has a preferred stock issue and a common stock issue. Both have just paid a $2 dividend. Which do you think will have a higher price, a share of the preferred or a share of the common?

6. **Dividend Growth Model** [LO1] Based on the dividend growth model, what are the two components of the total return on a share of stock? Which do you think is typically larger?

7. **Growth Rate** [LO1] In the context of the dividend growth model, is it true that the growth rate in dividends and the growth rate in the price of the stock are identical?

8. **Voting Rights** [LO3] When it comes to voting in elections, what are the differences between U.S. political democracy and U.S. corporate democracy?

9. **Corporate Ethics** [LO3] Is it unfair or unethical for corporations to create classes of stock with unequal voting rights?

10. **Voting Rights** [LO3] Some companies, such as Alphabet, have created classes of stock with no voting rights at all. Why would investors buy such stock?

11. **Stock Valuation** [LO1] Evaluate the following statement: Managers should not focus on the current stock value because doing so will lead to an overemphasis on short-term profits at the expense of long-term profits.

12. **Two-Stage Dividend Growth Model** [LO1] One of the assumptions of the two-stage growth model is that the dividends drop immediately from the high growth rate to the perpetual growth rate. What do you think about this assumption? What happens if this assumption is violated?

13. **Voting Rights** [LO3] In the chapter, we mentioned that many companies have been under pressure to declassify their boards of directors. Why would investors want a board to be declassified? What are the advantages of a classified board?

14. **Price Ratio Valuation** [LO2] What are the difficulties in using the PE ratio to value stock?

QUESTIONS AND PROBLEMS

1. **Stock Values** [LO1] The Jackson-Timberlake Wardrobe Co. just paid a dividend of $2.15 per share on its stock. The dividends are expected to grow at a constant rate of 4 percent per year indefinitely. If investors require a return of 10.5 percent on the company's stock, what is the current price? What will the price be in three years? In 15 years?

BASIC
(Questions 1–13)

2. **Stock Values** [LO1] The next dividend payment by Savitz, Inc., will be $2.34 per share. The dividends are anticipated to maintain a growth rate of 4.5 percent forever. If the stock currently sells for $37 per share, what is the required return?

3. **Stock Values** [LO1] For the company in the previous problem, what is the dividend yield? What is the expected capital gains yield?

4. **Stock Values** [LO1] Hudson Corporation will pay a dividend of $3.28 per share next year. The company pledges to increase its dividend by 3.75 percent per year indefinitely. If you require a return of 10 percent on your investment, how much will you pay for the company's stock today?

5. **Stock Valuation** [LO1] Grateful Eight Co. is expected to maintain a constant 3.7 percent growth rate in its dividends indefinitely. If the company has a dividend yield of 5.6 percent, what is the required return on the company's stock?

6. **Stock Valuation** [LO1] Suppose you know that a company's stock currently sells for $74 per share and the required return on the stock is 10.6 percent. You also know that the total return on the stock is evenly divided between a capital gains yield and a dividend yield. If it's the company's policy to always maintain a constant growth rate in its dividends, what is the current dividend per share?

7. **Stock Valuation** [LO1] Burnett Corp. pays a constant $8.25 dividend on its stock. The company will maintain this dividend for the next 13 years and will then cease paying dividends forever. If the required return on this stock is 11.2 percent, what is the current share price?

8. **Valuing Preferred Stock** [LO1] Bedekar, Inc., has an issue of preferred stock outstanding that pays a $3.40 dividend every year in perpetuity. If this issue currently sells for $91 per share, what is the required return?

9. **Stock Valuation and Required Return** [LO1] Red, Inc., Yellow Corp., and Blue Company each will pay a dividend of $3.65 next year. The growth rate in dividends for all three companies is 4 percent. The required return for each company's stock is 8 percent, 11 percent, and 14 percent, respectively. What is the stock price for each company? What do you conclude about the relationship between the required return and the stock price?

10. **Voting Rights** [LO3] After successfully completing your corporate finance class, you feel the next challenge ahead is to serve on the board of directors of Schenkel Enterprises. Unfortunately, you will be the only person voting for you. If the company has 650,000 shares outstanding, and the stock currently sells for $43, how much will it cost you to buy a seat if the company uses straight voting?

11. **Voting Rights** [LO3] In the previous problem, assume that the company uses cumulative voting, and there are four seats in the current election. How much will it cost you to buy a seat now?

12. **Stock Valuation and PE** [LO2] The Perfect Rose Co. has earnings of $3.18 per share. The benchmark PE for the company is 18. What stock price would you consider appropriate? What if the benchmark PE were 21?

13. **Stock Valuation and PS** [LO2] TwitterMe, Inc., is a new company and currently has negative earnings. The company's sales are $2.1 million and there are 130,000 shares outstanding. If the benchmark price-sales ratio is 4.3, what is your estimate of an appropriate stock price? What if the price-sales ratio were 3.6?

INTERMEDIATE
(Questions 14–31)

14. **Stock Valuation** [LO1] Moody Farms just paid a dividend of $2.65 on its stock. The growth rate in dividends is expected to be a constant 3.8 percent per year indefinitely. Investors require a return of 15 percent for the first three years, a return of 13 percent for the next three years, and a return of 11 percent thereafter. What is the current share price?

15. **Nonconstant Growth** [LO1] Metallica Bearings, Inc., is a young start-up company. No dividends will be paid on the stock over the next nine years because the firm needs to plow back its earnings to fuel growth. The company will pay a dividend of $17 per share 10 years from today and will increase the dividend by 3.9 percent per year thereafter. If the required return on this stock is 12.5 percent, what is the current share price?

16. **Nonconstant Dividends** [LO1] Maurer, Inc., has an odd dividend policy. The company has just paid a dividend of $2.75 per share and has announced that it will increase the dividend by $4.50 per share for each of the next five years and then never pay another dividend. If you require a return of 11 percent on the company's stock, how much will you pay for a share today?

17. **Nonconstant Dividends** [LO1] Lohn Corporation is expected to pay the following dividends over the next four years: $13, $9, $6, and $2.75. Afterward, the company pledges to maintain a constant 5 percent growth rate in dividends forever. If the required return on the stock is 10.75 percent, what is the current share price?

18. **Supernormal Growth** [LO1] Synovec Co. is growing quickly. Dividends are expected to grow at a rate of 30 percent for the next three years, with the growth rate falling off to a constant 4 percent thereafter. If the required return is 11 percent, and the company just paid a dividend of $2.45, what is the current share price?

19. **Supernormal Growth** [LO1] Mobray Corp. is experiencing rapid growth. Dividends are expected to grow at 25 percent per year during the next three years, 15 percent over the following year, and then 6 percent per year indefinitely. The required return on this stock is 10 percent, and the stock currently sells for $79 per share. What is the projected dividend for the coming year?

20. **Negative Growth** [LO1] Antiques R Us is a mature manufacturing firm. The company just paid a dividend of $9.80, but management expects to reduce the payout by 4 percent per year indefinitely. If you require a return of 9.5 percent on this stock, what will you pay for a share today?

21. **Finding the Dividend** [LO1] Mannix Corporation stock currently sells for $57 per share. The market requires a return of 11 percent on the firm's stock. If the company maintains a constant 3.75 percent growth rate in dividends, what was the most recent dividend per share paid on the stock?

22. **Valuing Preferred Stock** [LO1] E-Eyes.com just issued some new preferred stock. The issue will pay an annual dividend of $20 in perpetuity, beginning 20 years from now. If the market requires a return of 5.65 percent on this investment, how much does a share of preferred stock cost today?

23. **Using Stock Quotes** [LO4] You have found the following stock quote for RJW Enterprises, Inc., in the financial pages of today's newspaper. What was the closing price for this stock that appeared in *yesterday's* paper? If the company currently has 25 million shares of stock outstanding, what was net income for the most recent four quarters?

52-WEEK							
HI	LO	STOCK (DIV)	YLD %	PE	VOL 100s	CLOSE	NET CHG
84.13	53.17	RJW 1.75	2.35	19	17652	??	−.23

24. **Two-Stage Dividend Growth Model** [LO1] A7X Corp. just paid a dividend of $1.55 per share. The dividends are expected to grow at 21 percent for the next eight years and then level off to a growth rate of 3.5 percent indefinitely. If the required return is 12 percent, what is the price of the stock today?

25. **Two-Stage Dividend Growth Model** [LO1] Navel County Choppers, Inc., is experiencing rapid growth. The company expects dividends to grow at 18 percent per year for the next 11 years before leveling off at 4 percent into perpetuity. The required return on the company's stock is 10 percent. If the dividend per share just paid was $1.94, what is the stock price?

26. **Stock Valuation and PE** [LO2] Domergue Corp. currently has an EPS of $3.76, and the benchmark PE for the company is 21. Earnings are expected to grow at 5.1 percent per year.

   a. What is your estimate of the current stock price?

   b. What is the target stock price in one year?

   c. Assuming the company pays no dividends, what is the implied return on the company's stock over the next year? What does this tell you about the implicit stock return using PE valuation?

27. **Stock Valuation and PE** [LO2] You have found the following historical information for the Daniela Company over the past four years:

	Year 1	Year 2	Year 3	Year 4
Stock price	$49.18	$53.18	$58.14	$56.32
EPS	2.35	2.47	2.78	3.04

Earnings are expected to grow at 11 percent for the next year. Using the company's historical average PE as a benchmark, what is the target stock price one year from today?

28. **Stock Valuation and PE** [LO2] In the previous problem, we assumed that the stock had a single stock price for the year. However, if you look at stock prices over any year, you will find a high and low stock price for the year. Instead of a single benchmark PE ratio, we now have a high and low PE ratio for each year. We can use these ratios to calculate a high and a low stock price for the next year. Suppose we have the following information on a particular company over the past four years:

	Year 1	Year 2	Year 3	Year 4
High price	$27.43	$26.32	$30.42	$37.01
Low price	19.86	20.18	25.65	26.41
EPS	1.35	1.58	1.51	1.85

Earnings are projected to grow at 9 percent over the next year. What are your high and low target stock prices over the next year?

29. **Stock Valuation and PE** [LO2] RAK, Inc., currently has an EPS of $2.45 and an earnings growth rate of 8 percent. If the benchmark PE ratio is 23, what is the target share price five years from now?

30. **PE and Terminal Stock Price** [LO2] In practice, a common way to value a share of stock when a company pays dividends is to value the dividends over the next five years or so, then find the "terminal" stock price using a benchmark PE ratio. Suppose a company just paid a dividend of $1.36. The dividends are expected to grow at 13 percent over the next five years. In five years, the estimated payout ratio is 40 percent and the benchmark PE ratio is 19. What is the target stock price in five years? What is the stock price today assuming a required return of 11 percent on this stock?

31. **Stock Valuation and PE** [LO2] Perine, Inc., has balance sheet equity of $6.8 million. At the same time, the income statement shows net income of $815,000. The company paid dividends of $285,000 and has 245,000 shares of stock outstanding. If the benchmark PE ratio is 16, what is the target stock price in one year?

CHALLENGE
(Questions 32–38)

32. **Capital Gains versus Income** [LO1] Consider four different stocks, all of which have a required return of 13 percent and a most recent dividend of $3.75 per share. Stocks W, X, and Y are expected to maintain constant growth rates in dividends for the foreseeable future of 10 percent, 0 percent, and −5 percent per year, respectively. Stock Z is a growth stock that will increase its dividend by 20 percent for the next two years and then maintain a constant 5 percent growth rate thereafter. What is the dividend yield for each of these four stocks? What is the expected capital gains yield? Discuss the relationship among the various returns that you find for each of these stocks.

33. **Stock Valuation** [LO1] Most corporations pay quarterly dividends on their common stock rather than annual dividends. Barring any unusual circumstances during

the year, the board raises, lowers, or maintains the current dividend once a year and then pays this dividend out in equal quarterly installments to its shareholders.

a. Suppose a company currently pays an annual dividend of $3.40 on its common stock in a single annual installment, and management plans on raising this dividend by 3.8 percent per year indefinitely. If the required return on this stock is 10.5 percent, what is the current share price?

b. Now suppose the company in (a) actually pays its annual dividend in equal quarterly installments; thus, the company has just paid a dividend of $.85 per share, as it has for the previous three quarters. What is your value for the current share price now? (*Hint*: Find the equivalent annual end-of-year dividend for each year.) Comment on whether you think this model of stock valuation is appropriate.

34. **Nonconstant Growth** [LO1] Storico Co. just paid a dividend of $3.15 per share. The company will increase its dividend by 20 percent next year and then reduce its dividend growth rate by 5 percentage points per year until it reaches the industry average of 5 percent dividend growth, after which the company will keep a constant growth rate forever. If the required return on the company's stock is 12 percent, what will a share of stock sell for today?

35. **Nonconstant Growth** [LO1] This one's a little harder. Suppose the current share price for the firm in the previous problem is $54.50 and all the dividend information remains the same. What required return must investors be demanding on the company's stock? (*Hint*: Set up the valuation formula with all the relevant cash flows, and use trial and error to find the unknown rate of return.)

36. **Constant Dividend Growth Model** [LO1] Assume a stock has dividends that grow at a constant rate forever. If you value the stock using the constant dividend growth model, how many years worth of dividends constitute one-half of the stock's current price?

37. **Two-Stage Dividend Growth** [LO1] Regarding the two-stage dividend growth model in the chapter, show that the price of a share of stock today can be written as follows:

$$P_0 = \frac{D_0 \times (1 + g_1)}{R - g_1} \times \left[1 - \left(\frac{1 + g_1}{1 + R} \right)^t \right] + \left(\frac{1 + g_1}{1 + R} \right)^t \times \frac{D_0 \times (1 + g_2)}{R - g_2}$$

Can you provide an intuitive interpretation of this expression?

38. **Two-Stage Dividend Growth** [LO1] The chapter shows that in the two-stage dividend growth model, the growth rate in the first stage, g_1, can be greater than or less than the discount rate, R. Can they be exactly equal? (*Hint*: Yes, but what does the expression for the value of the stock look like?)

EXCEL MASTER IT! PROBLEM

In practice, the use of the dividend discount model is refined from the method we presented in the textbook. Many analysts will estimate the dividend for the next 5 years and then estimate a perpetual growth rate at some point in the future, typically 10 years. Rather than have the dividend growth fall dramatically from the fast growth period to the perpetual growth period, linear interpolation is applied. That is, the dividend growth is projected to fall by an equal amount each year. For example, if the fast growth period is 15 percent for the next 5 years and the dividends are expected to fall to a 5 percent perpetual growth rate 5 years later, the dividend growth rate would decline by 2 percent each year.

Suppose you find the following information about a particular stock:

Current dividend: $3.95
5-year dividend growth rate: 9.5%
Perpetual growth rate: 4%
Required return: 11%

a. Assume that the perpetual growth rate begins 10 years from now and use linear interpolation between the high growth rate and perpetual growth rate. Construct a table that shows the dividend growth rate and dividend each year. What is the stock price at Year 10? What is the stock price today?

b. How sensitive is the current stock price to changes in the perpetual growth rate? Graph the current stock price against the perpetual growth rate in 10 years to find out.

Instead of applying the constant dividend growth model to find the stock price in the future, analysts will often combine the dividend discount method with price ratio valuation, often with the PE ratio. Remember that the PE ratio is the price per share divided by the earnings per share. So, if we know the PE ratio, the dividend, and the payout ratio, we can solve for the stock price. To illustrate, suppose we also have the following information about the company:

Payout ratio: 25%
PE ratio at constant growth rate: 15

c. Use the PE ratio to calculate the stock price when the company reaches a perpetual growth rate in dividends. Now find the value of the stock today using the present value of the dividends during the nonconstant growth period and the price you calculated using the PE ratio.

d. How sensitive is the current stock price to changes in the PE ratio when the stock reaches the perpetual growth rate? Graph the current stock price against the PE ratio in 10 years to find out.

MINICASE

Stock Valuation at Ragan, Inc.

Ragan, Inc., was founded nine years ago by brother and sister Carrington and Genevieve Ragan. The company manufactures and installs commercial heating, ventilation, and cooling (HVAC) units. Ragan, Inc., has experienced rapid growth because of a proprietary technology that increases the energy efficiency of its units. The company is equally owned by Carrington and Genevieve. The original partnership agreement between the siblings gave each 50,000 shares of stock. In the event either wished to sell stock, the shares first had to be offered to the other at a discounted price.

Although neither sibling wants to sell, they have decided they should value their holdings in the company. To get started,

they have gathered the information about their main competitors in the table below.

Expert HVAC Corporation's negative earnings per share were the result of an accounting write-off last year. Without the write-off, earnings per share for the company would have been $1.10. The ROE for Expert HVAC is based on net income excluding the write-off.

Last year, Ragan, Inc., had an EPS of $3.15 and paid a dividend to Carrington and Genevieve of $45,000 each. The company also had a return on equity of 17 percent. The siblings believe that 14 percent is an appropriate required return for the company.

Ragan, Inc., Competitors					
	EPS	DPS	Stock Price	ROE	R
Arctic Cooling, Inc.	$1.30	$.16	$25.34	8.50%	10.00%
National Heating & Cooling	1.95	.23	29.85	10.50	13.00
Expert HVAC Corp.	−.37	.14	22.13	9.78	12.00
Industry Average	$ .96	$.18	$25.77	9.59%	11.67%

QUESTIONS

1. Assuming the company continues its current growth rate, what is the value per share of the company's stock?

2. To verify their calculations, Carrington and Genevieve have hired Josh Schlessman as a consultant. Josh was previously an equity analyst and covered the HVAC industry. Josh has examined the company's financial statements, as well as examining its competitors' financials. Although Ragan, Inc., currently has a technological advantage, his research indicates that other companies are investigating methods to improve efficiency. Given this, Josh believes that the company's technological advantage will last only for the next five years. After that period, the company's growth will likely slow to the industry growth average. Additionally, Josh believes that the required return used by the company is too high. He believes the industry average required return is more appropriate. Under this growth rate assumption, what is your estimate of the stock price?

3. What is the industry average price-earnings ratio? What is the price-earnings ratio for Ragan, Inc.? Is this the relationship you would expect between the two ratios? Why?

4. Carrington and Genevieve are unsure how to interpret the price-earnings ratio. After some head scratching, they've come up with the following expression for the price-earnings ratio:

$$\frac{P_0}{E_1} = \frac{1 - b}{R - (\text{ROE} \times b)}$$

Beginning with the constant dividend growth model, verify this result. What does this expression imply about the relationship between the dividend payout ratio, the required return on the stock, and the company's ROE?

5. Assume the company's growth rate slows to the industry average in five years. What future return on equity does this imply, assuming a constant payout ratio?

6. After discussing the stock value with Josh, Carrington and Genevieve agree that they would like to increase the value of the company stock. Like many small business owners, they want to retain control of the company, so they do not want to sell stock to outside investors. They also feel that the company's debt is at a manageable level and do not want to borrow more money. How can they increase the price of the stock? Are there any conditions under which this strategy would *not* increase the stock price?

Capital Budgeting

Chapter

9 | Net Present Value and Other Investment Criteria

ALTHOUGH KNOWN AS Apple's largest supplier, Foxconn does have other buyers. In December 2016, Foxconn announced a joint venture with Sharp to build an $8.8 billion plant in China. The new plant would be a Gen-10.5 facility used to manufacture large-screen LCDs. And while the price tag of the new LCD plant may seem large, it wasn't even the biggest project announced by Foxconn that year. Earlier, Foxconn announced that it was looking to invest $10 billion to build a new plant to manufacture iPhones in India.

Foxconn's new plants are examples of capital budgeting decisions. Decisions such as these, with price tags well over $1 billion, are obviously major undertakings, and the risks and rewards must be carefully weighed. In this chapter, we discuss the basic tools used in making such decisions.

In Chapter 1, we saw that increasing the value of the stock in a company is the goal of financial management. Thus, what we need to know is how to tell whether a particular investment will achieve that or not. This chapter considers a variety of techniques that are used in practice for this purpose. More important, it shows how many of these techniques can be misleading, and it explains why the net present value approach is the right one.

Learning Objectives

After studying this chapter, you should be able to:

LO1 Show the reasons why the net present value criterion is the best way to evaluate proposed investments.

LO2 Discuss the payback rule and some of its shortcomings.

LO3 Discuss the discounted payback rule and some of its shortcomings.

LO4 Explain accounting rates of return and some of the problems with them.

LO5 Present the internal rate of return criterion and its strengths and weaknesses.

LO6 Calculate the modified internal rate of return.

LO7 Illustrate the profitability index and its relation to net present value.

©by_adri/iStockPhotoGettyImages

In Chapter 1, we identified the three key areas of concern to the financial manager. The first of these involved the question: What fixed assets should we buy? We called this the *capital budgeting decision*. In this chapter, we begin to deal with the issues that arise in answering this question.

The process of allocating or budgeting capital is usually more involved than deciding whether to buy a particular fixed asset. We frequently face broader issues, like whether we should launch a new product or enter a new market. Decisions such as these determine the nature of a firm's operations and products for years to come, primarily because fixed asset investments are generally long-lived and not easily reversed once they are made.

The most fundamental decision a business must make concerns its product line. What services will we offer or what will we sell? In what markets will we compete? What new products will we introduce? The answer to any of these questions will require that the firm commit its scarce and valuable capital to certain types of assets. As a result, all of these strategic issues fall under the general heading of capital budgeting. The process of capital budgeting could be given a more descriptive (not to mention impressive) name: *Strategic asset allocation.*

For the reasons we have discussed, the capital budgeting question is probably the most important issue in corporate finance. How a firm chooses to finance its operations (the capital structure question) and how a firm manages its short-term operating activities (the working capital question) are certainly issues of concern, but the fixed assets define the business of the firm. Airlines, for example, are airlines because they operate airplanes, regardless of how they finance them.

Any firm possesses a huge number of possible investments. Each possible investment is an option available to the firm. Some options are valuable and some are not. The essence of successful financial management, of course, is learning to identify which ones are which. With this in mind, our goal in this chapter is to introduce you to the techniques used to analyze potential business ventures to decide which are worth undertaking.

We present and compare a number of different procedures used in practice. Our primary goal is to acquaint you with the advantages and disadvantages of the various approaches. As we will see, the most important concept in this area is the idea of net present value. We consider this next.

Net Present Value

9.1

In Chapter 1, we argued that the goal of financial management is to create value for the stockholders. The financial manager must examine a potential investment in light of its likely effect on the price of the firm's shares. In this section, we describe a widely used procedure for doing this: The net present value approach.

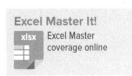

Excel Master It!

xlsx Excel Master coverage online

THE BASIC IDEA

An investment is worth undertaking if it creates value for its owners. In the most general sense, we create value by identifying an investment worth more in the marketplace than it costs us to acquire. How can something be worth more than it costs? It's a case of the whole being worth more than the cost of the parts.

For example, suppose you buy a run-down house for $25,000 and spend another $25,000 on painters, plumbers, and so on to get it fixed up. Your total investment is $50,000. When the work is completed, you place the house back on the market and find that it's worth $60,000. The market value ($60,000) exceeds the cost ($50,000) by $10,000. What you have done here is to act as a manager to bring together some fixed assets (a house), some labor (plumbers, carpenters, and others), and some materials (carpeting, paint, and so on). The net result is that you have created $10,000 in value. Put another way, this $10,000 is the *value added* by management.

With our house example, it turned out *after the fact* that $10,000 in value had been created. Things worked out nicely. The real challenge, of course, would have been to somehow identify *ahead of time* whether investing the necessary $50,000 was a good idea in the first place. This is what capital budgeting is all about—namely, trying to determine whether a proposed investment or project will be worth more, once it is in place, than it costs.

For reasons that will be obvious in a moment, the difference between an investment's market value and its cost is called the **net present value** of the investment, abbreviated **NPV**. In other words, net present value is a measure of how much value is created or added today by undertaking an investment. Given our goal of creating value for the stockholders, the capital budgeting process can be viewed as a search for investments with positive net present values.

With our run-down house, you can probably imagine how we would go about making the capital budgeting decision. We would first look at what comparable, fixed-up properties were selling for in the market. We would then get estimates of the cost of buying a particular property and bringing it to market. At this point, we would have an estimated total cost and an estimated market value. If the difference was positive, then this investment would be worth undertaking because it would have a positive estimated net present value. There is risk, of course, because there is no guarantee that our estimates will turn out to be correct.

As our example illustrates, investment decisions are greatly simplified when there is a market for assets similar to the investment we are considering. Capital budgeting becomes much more difficult when we cannot observe the market price for at least roughly comparable investments. The reason is that we then face the problem of estimating the value of an investment using only indirect market information. Unfortunately, this is precisely the situation the financial manager usually encounters. We examine this issue next.

ESTIMATING NET PRESENT VALUE

Imagine we are thinking of starting a business to produce and sell a new product—say, organic fertilizer. We can estimate the start-up costs with reasonable accuracy because we know what we will need to buy to begin production. Would this be a good investment? Based on our discussion, you know that the answer depends on whether the value of the new business exceeds the cost of starting it. In other words, does this investment have a positive NPV?

This problem is much more difficult than our "fixer upper" house example because entire fertilizer companies are not routinely bought and sold in the marketplace, so it is essentially impossible to observe the market value of a similar investment. As a result, we must somehow estimate this value by other means.

Based on our work in Chapters 5 and 6, you may be able to guess how we will go about estimating the value of our fertilizer business. We will first try to estimate the future cash flows we expect the new business to produce. We will then apply our basic discounted cash flow procedure to estimate the present value of those cash flows. Once we have this estimate, we will then estimate NPV as the difference between the present value of the future cash flows and the cost of the investment. As we mentioned in Chapter 5, this procedure is often called **discounted cash flow (DCF) valuation**.

To see how we might go about estimating NPV, suppose we believe the cash revenues from our fertilizer business will be $20,000 per year, assuming everything goes as expected. Cash costs (including taxes) will be $14,000 per year. We will wind down the business in eight years. The plant, property, and equipment will be worth $2,000 as salvage at that time. The project costs $30,000 to launch. We use a 15 percent discount rate on new projects such as this one. Is this a good investment? If there are 1,000 shares of stock outstanding, what will be the effect on the price per share of taking this investment?

net present value (NPV)
The difference between an investment's market value and its cost.

discounted cash flow (DCF) valuation
The process of valuing an investment by discounting its future cash flows.

FIGURE 9.1

From a purely mechanical perspective, we need to calculate the present value of the future cash flows at 15 percent. The net cash inflow will be $20,000 cash income less $14,000 in costs per year for eight years. These cash flows are illustrated in Figure 9.1. As Figure 9.1 suggests, we effectively have an eight-year annuity of $20,000 − 14,000 = $6,000 per year, along with a single lump sum inflow of $2,000 in eight years. Calculating the present value of the future cash flows comes down to the same type of problem we considered in Chapter 6. The total present value is:

$$Present\ value = \$6,000 \times [1 - (1/1.15^8)]/.15 + (2,000/1.15^8)$$
$$= (\$6,000 \times 4.4873) + (2,000/3.0590)$$
$$= \$26,924 + 654$$
$$= \$27,578$$

When we compare this to the $30,000 estimated cost, we see that the NPV is:

$$NPV = -\$30,000 + 27,578 = -\$2,422$$

Therefore, this is *not* a good investment. Based on our estimates, taking it would *decrease* the total value of the stock by $2,422. With 1,000 shares outstanding, our best estimate of the impact of taking this project is a loss of value of $2,422/1,000 = $2.42 per share.

Our fertilizer example illustrates how NPV estimates can be used to determine whether an investment is desirable. From our example, notice that if the NPV is negative, the effect on share value will be unfavorable. If the NPV were positive, the effect would be favorable. As a consequence, all we need to know about a particular proposal for the purpose of making an accept–reject decision is whether the NPV is positive or negative.

Given that the goal of financial management is to increase share value, our discussion in this section leads us to the *net present value rule*:

> **An investment should be accepted if the net present value is positive and rejected if it is negative.**

In the unlikely event that the net present value turned out to be exactly zero, we would be indifferent between taking the investment and not taking it.

Two comments about our example are in order. First and foremost, it is not the rather mechanical process of discounting the cash flows that is important. Once we have the cash flows and the appropriate discount rate, the required calculations are fairly straightforward. The task of coming up with the cash flows and the discount rate is much more challenging. We will have much more to say about this in the next several chapters. For the remainder of this chapter, we take it as a given that we have estimates of the cash revenues and costs and, where needed, an appropriate discount rate.

The second thing to keep in mind about our example is that the −$2,422 NPV is an estimate. Like any estimate, it can be high or low. The only way to find out the true NPV would be to place the investment up for sale and see what we could get for it. We generally won't be doing this, so it is important that our estimates be reliable. Once again, we will say more about this later. For the rest of this chapter, we will assume the estimates are accurate.

EXAMPLE 9.1   **Using the NPV Rule**

Suppose we are asked to decide whether a new consumer product should be launched. Based on projected sales and costs, we expect that the cash flows over the five-year life of the project will be $2,000 in the first two years, $4,000 in the next two, and $5,000 in the last year. It will cost about $10,000 to begin production. We use a 10 percent discount rate to evaluate new products. What should we do here?

Given the cash flows and discount rate, we can calculate the total value of the product by discounting the cash flows back to the present:

$$\text{Present value} = (\$2,000/1.1) + (2,000/1.1^2) + (4,000/1.1^3)$$
$$+ (4,000/1.1^4) + (5,000/1.1^5)$$
$$= \$1,818 + 1,653 + 3,005 + 2,732 + 3,105$$
$$= \$12,313$$

The present value of the expected cash flows is $12,313, but the cost of getting those cash flows is only $10,000, so the NPV is $12,313 − 10,000 = $2,313. This is positive; so, based on the net present value rule, we should take on the project.

As we have seen in this section, estimating NPV is one way of assessing the profitability of a proposed investment. It is certainly not the only way profitability is assessed, and we now turn to some alternatives. As we will see, when compared to NPV, each of the alternative ways of assessing profitability that we will examine is flawed in some key way; so NPV is the preferred approach in principle, if not always in practice.

SPREADSHEET STRATEGIES

Calculating NPVs with a Spreadsheet

Spreadsheets are commonly used to calculate NPVs. Examining the use of spreadsheets in this context also allows us to issue an important warning. Let's rework Example 9.1:

You can get a freeware NPV calculator at **www.wheatworks.com**

	A	B	C	D	E	F	G	H
1								
2			Using a spreadsheet to calculate net present values					
3								
4	From Example 9.1, the project's cost is $10,000. The cash flows are $2,000 per year for the first							
5	two years, $4,000 per year for the next two, and $5,000 in the last year. The discount rate is							
6	10 percent; what's the NPV?							
7								
8		Year	Cash Flow					
9		0	−$10,000		Discount rate =		10%	
10		1	2,000					
11		2	2,000		NPV =	$2,102.72	(*wrong* answer)	
12		3	4,000		NPV =	$2,312.99	(*right* answer)	
13		4	4,000					
14		5	5,000					
15		.						
16	The formula entered in cell F11 is =NPV(F9, C9:C14). This gives the wrong answer because the							
17	NPV function actually calculates present values, not *net* present values.							
18								
19	The formula entered in cell F12 is =NPV(F9, C10:C14) + C9. This gives the right answer because the							
20	NPV function is used to calculate the present value of the cash flows and then the initial cost is							
21	subtracted to calculate the answer. Notice that we added cell C9 because it is already negative.							

SOURCE: Microsoft Excel

In our spreadsheet example, notice that we have provided two answers. By comparing the answers to that found in Example 9.1, we see that the first answer is wrong even though we used the spreadsheet's NPV formula. What happened is that the "NPV" function in our spreadsheet is actually a PV function; unfortunately, one of the original spreadsheet programs many years ago got the definition wrong, and subsequent spreadsheets have copied it! Our second answer shows how to use the formula properly.

The example here illustrates the danger of blindly using calculators or computers without understanding what is going on; we shudder to think of how many capital budgeting decisions in the real world are based on incorrect use of this particular function. We will see another example of something that can go wrong with a spreadsheet later in the chapter.

Concept Questions

9.1a   What is the net present value rule?

9.1b   If we say an investment has an NPV of $1,000, what exactly do we mean?

The Payback Rule

9.2

Excel Master It!
Excel Master
coverage online

It is common in practice to talk of the payback on a proposed investment. Loosely, the *payback* is the length of time it takes to recover our initial investment or "get our bait back." Because this idea is widely understood and used, we will examine it in some detail.

DEFINING THE RULE

We can illustrate how to calculate a payback with an example. Figure 9.2 shows the cash flows from a proposed investment. How many years do we have to wait until the accumulated cash flows from this investment equal or exceed the cost of the investment? As Figure 9.2 indicates, the initial investment is $50,000. After the first year, the firm has recovered $30,000, leaving $20,000. The cash flow in the second year is exactly $20,000, so this investment "pays for itself" in exactly two years. Put another way, the **payback period** is two years. If we require a payback of, say, three years or less, then this investment is acceptable. This illustrates the *payback period rule*:

payback period
The amount of time required for an investment to generate cash flows sufficient to recover its initial cost.

> **Based on the payback rule, an investment is acceptable if its calculated payback period is less than some prespecified number of years.**

In our example, the payback works out to be exactly two years. This won't usually happen, of course. When the numbers don't work out exactly, it is customary to work with fractional years. For example, suppose the initial investment is $60,000, and the cash flows are $20,000 in the first year and $90,000 in the second. The cash flows over the first two years

FIGURE 9.2

Net Project Cash Flows

Year	0	1	2	3	4
	−$50,000	$30,000	$20,000	$10,000	$5,000

are $110,000, so the project obviously pays back sometime in the second year. After the first year, the project has paid back $20,000, leaving $40,000 to be recovered. To figure out the fractional year, note that this $40,000 is $40,000/$90,000 = 4/9 of the second year's cash flow. Assuming that the $90,000 cash flow is received uniformly throughout the year, the payback would be $1\frac{4}{9}$ years.

EXAMPLE 9.2	Calculating Payback

Here are the projected cash flows from a proposed investment:

Year	Cash Flow
1	$100
2	200
3	500

This project costs $500. What is the payback period for this investment?

The initial cost is $500. After the first two years, the cash flows total $300. After the third year, the total cash flow is $800, so the project pays back sometime between the end of Year 2 and the end of Year 3. Because the accumulated cash flows for the first two years are $300, we need to recover $200 in the third year. The third-year cash flow is $500, so we will have to wait $200/$500 = .4 years to do this. The payback period is thus 2.4 years, or about two years and five months.

Now that we know how to calculate the payback period on an investment, using the payback period rule for making decisions is straightforward. A particular cutoff time is selected—say, two years—and all investment projects that have payback periods of two years or less are accepted, whereas any that pay off in more than two years are rejected.

Table 9.1 illustrates cash flows for five different projects. The figures shown as the Year 0 cash flows are the costs of the investments. We examine these to indicate some peculiarities that can, in principle, arise with payback periods.

The payback for the first project, A, is easily calculated. The sum of the cash flows for the first two years is $70, leaving us with $100 − 70 = $30 to go. Because the cash flow in the third year is $50, the payback occurs sometime in that year. When we compare the $30 we need to the $50 that will be coming in, we get $30/$50 = .6; so, payback will occur 60 percent of the way into the year. The payback period is thus 2.6 years.

Project B's payback is also easy to calculate: It *never* pays back because the cash flows never total up to the original investment. Project C has a payback of exactly four years because it supplies the $130 that B is missing in Year 4. Project D is a little strange. Because of the negative cash flow in Year 3, you can easily verify that it has two different payback periods, two years and four years. Which of these is correct? Both of them; the way the

TABLE 9.1

Expected Cash Flows for Projects A through E

Year	A	B	C	D	E
0	−$100	−$200	−$200	−$200	−$ 50
1	30	40	40	100	100
2	40	20	20	100	−50,000,000
3	50	10	10	−200	
4	60		130	200	

payback period is calculated doesn't guarantee a single answer. Finally, Project E is obviously unrealistic, but it does pay back in six months, thereby illustrating the point that a rapid payback does not guarantee a good investment.

ANALYZING THE RULE

When compared to the NPV rule, the payback period rule has some rather severe shortcomings. First, we calculate the payback period by adding up the future cash flows. There is no discounting involved, so the time value of money is completely ignored. The payback rule also fails to consider any risk differences. The payback would be calculated the same way for both very risky and very safe projects.

Perhaps the biggest problem with the payback period rule is coming up with the right cutoff period: We don't really have an objective basis for choosing a particular number. Put another way, there is no economic rationale for looking at payback in the first place, so we have no guide for how to pick the cutoff. As a result, we end up using a number that is arbitrarily chosen.

Suppose we have somehow decided on an appropriate payback period of two years or less. As we have seen, the payback period rule ignores the time value of money for the first two years. More seriously, cash flows after the second year are ignored entirely. To see this, consider the two investments, Long and Short, in Table 9.2. Both projects cost $250. Based on our discussion, the payback on Long is $2 + (\$50/\$100) = 2.5$ years, and the payback on Short is $1 + (\$150/\$200) = 1.75$ years. With a cutoff of two years, Short is acceptable and Long is not.

Is the payback period rule guiding us to the right decisions? Maybe not. Suppose we require a 15 percent return on this type of investment. We can calculate the NPV for these two investments as:

$$\text{NPV(Short)} = -\$250 + (100/1.15) + (200/1.15^2) = -\$11.81$$
$$\text{NPV(Long)} = -\$250 + (100 \times \{[1 - (1/1.15^4)]/.15\}) = \$35.50$$

Now we have a problem. The NPV of the shorter-term investment is actually negative, meaning that taking it diminishes the value of the shareholders' equity. The opposite is true for the longer-term investment—it increases share value.

Our example illustrates two primary shortcomings of the payback period rule. First, by ignoring time value, we may be led to take investments (like Short) that actually are worth less than they cost. Second, by ignoring cash flows beyond the cutoff, we may be led to reject profitable longer-term investments (like Long). More generally, using a payback period rule will tend to bias us toward shorter-term investments.

REDEEMING QUALITIES OF THE RULE

Despite its shortcomings, the payback period rule is often used by large and sophisticated companies when they are making relatively minor decisions. There are several reasons for this. The primary reason is that many decisions do not warrant detailed analysis because

Year	Long	Short
0	−$250	−$250
1	100	100
2	100	200
3	100	0
4	100	0

TABLE 9.2

Investment Projected Cash Flows

the cost of the analysis would exceed the possible loss from a mistake. As a practical matter, it can be said that an investment that pays back rapidly and has benefits extending beyond the cutoff period probably has a positive NPV.

Small investment decisions are made by the hundreds every day in large organizations. Moreover, they are made at all levels. As a result, it would not be uncommon for a corporation to require, for example, a two-year payback on all investments of less than $10,000. Investments larger than this would be subjected to greater scrutiny. The requirement of a two-year payback is not perfect for reasons we have seen, but it does exercise some control over expenditures and limits possible losses.

In addition to its simplicity, the payback rule has two other positive features. First, because it is biased toward short-term projects, it is biased toward liquidity. In other words, a payback rule tends to favor investments that free up cash for other uses quickly. This could be important for a small business; it would be less so for a large corporation. Second, the cash flows that are expected to occur later in a project's life are probably more uncertain. Arguably, a payback period rule adjusts for the extra riskiness of later cash flows, but it does so in a rather draconian fashion—by ignoring them altogether.

We should note here that some of the apparent simplicity of the payback rule is an illusion. The reason is that we still must come up with the cash flows first, and, as we discussed earlier, this is not at all easy to do. It would probably be more accurate to say that the *concept* of a payback period is both intuitive and easy to understand.

SUMMARY OF THE RULE

To summarize, the payback period is a kind of "break-even" measure. Because time value is ignored, you can think of the payback period as the length of time it takes to break even in an accounting sense, but not in an economic sense. The biggest drawback to the payback period rule is that it doesn't ask the right question. The relevant issue is the impact an investment will have on the value of the stock, not how long it takes to recover the initial investment.

Nevertheless, because it is so simple, companies often use it as a screen for dealing with the myriad minor investment decisions they have to make. There is certainly nothing wrong with this practice. As with any simple rule of thumb, there will be some errors in using it; but it wouldn't have survived all this time if it weren't useful. Now that you understand the rule, you can be on the alert for circumstances under which it might lead to problems. To help you remember, the following table lists the pros and cons of the payback period rule:

Advantages and Disadvantages of the Payback Period Rule	
Advantages	**Disadvantages**
1. Easy to understand.	1. Ignores the time value of money.
2. Adjusts for uncertainty of later cash flows.	2. Requires an arbitrary cutoff point.
3. Biased toward liquidity.	3. Ignores cash flows beyond the cutoff date.
	4. Biased against long-term projects, such as research and development, and new projects.

Concept Questions

9.2a   In words, what is the payback period? The payback period rule?

9.2b   Why do we say that the payback period is, in a sense, an accounting break-even measure?

The Discounted Payback

9.3

We saw that one shortcoming of the payback period rule was that it ignored time value. A variation of the payback period, the discounted payback period, fixes this particular problem. The **discounted payback period** is the length of time until the sum of the discounted cash flows is equal to the initial investment. The *discounted payback rule* is therefore:

Excel Master It!
Excel Master
coverage online

> Based on the discounted payback rule, an investment is acceptable if its discounted payback is less than some prespecified number of years.

discounted payback period
The length of time required for an investment's discounted cash flows to equal its initial cost.

To see how we might calculate the discounted payback period, suppose we require a 12.5 percent return on new investments. We have an investment that costs $300 and has cash flows of $100 per year for five years. To get the discounted payback, we have to discount each cash flow at 12.5 percent and then start adding them. We do this in Table 9.3. In Table 9.3, we have both the discounted and the undiscounted cash flows. Looking at the accumulated cash flows, we see that the regular payback is almost exactly three years (look for the highlighted figure in Year 3). The discounted cash flows total $301 only after four years, so the discounted payback is four years, as shown.[1]

How do we interpret the discounted payback? Recall that the ordinary payback is the time it takes to break even in an accounting sense. Because it includes the time value of money, the discounted payback is the time it takes to break even in an economic or financial sense. Loosely speaking, in our example, we get our money back, along with the interest we could have earned elsewhere, in four years.

Figure 9.3 illustrates this idea by comparing the *future* value of the $300 investment at 12.5 percent to the *future* value of the $100 annual cash flows at 12.5 percent. Notice that the two lines cross at exactly four years. This tells us that the value of the project's cash flows catches up and then passes the original investment in four years.

Table 9.3 and Figure 9.3 illustrate another interesting feature of the discounted payback period. If a project ever pays back on a discounted basis, then it must have a positive NPV.[2] This is true because, by definition, the NPV is zero when the sum of the discounted cash flows equals the initial investment. For example, the present value of all the cash flows in

	Cash Flow		Accumulated Cash Flow	
Year	Undiscounted	Discounted	Undiscounted	Discounted
1	$100	$89	$100	$ 89
2	100	79	200	168
3	100	70	300	238
4	100	62	400	301
5	100	55	500	356

TABLE 9.3

Ordinary and Discounted Payback

---

[1]In this case, the discounted payback is an even number of years. This won't ordinarily happen, of course. Calculating a fractional year for the discounted payback period is more involved than it is for the ordinary payback, and it is not commonly done.

[2]This argument assumes the cash flows, other than the first, are all positive. If they are not, then these statements are not necessarily correct. Also, there may be more than one discounted payback.

FIGURE 9.3

Future Value of Project Cash Flows

Future Value at 12.5%		
Year	$100 Annuity (Projected Cash Flow)	$300 Lump Sum (Projected Investment)
0	$ 0	$300
1	100	338
2	213	380
3	339	427
4	481	481
5	642	541

Table 9.3 is $356. The cost of the project was $300, so the NPV is obviously $56. This $56 is the value of the cash flow that occurs *after* the discounted payback (see the last line in Table 9.3). In general, if we use a discounted payback rule, we won't accidentally take any projects with a negative estimated NPV.

Based on our example, the discounted payback would seem to have much to recommend it. You may be surprised to find out that it is rarely used in practice. Why? Probably because it really isn't any simpler to use than NPV. To calculate a discounted payback, you have to discount cash flows, add them up, and compare them to the cost, just as you do with NPV. So, unlike an ordinary payback, the discounted payback is not especially simple to calculate.

A discounted payback period rule has a couple of other significant drawbacks. The biggest one is that the cutoff still has to be arbitrarily set, and cash flows beyond that point are ignored.[3] As a result, a project with a positive NPV may be found unacceptable because the cutoff is too short. Also, just because one project has a shorter discounted payback than another does not mean it has a larger NPV.

All things considered, the discounted payback is a compromise between a regular payback and NPV that lacks the simplicity of the first and the conceptual rigor of the second. Nonetheless, if we need to assess the time it will take to recover the investment required by a project, then the discounted payback is better than the ordinary payback because it

---

[3]If the cutoff were forever, then the discounted payback rule would be the same as the NPV rule. It would also be the same as the profitability index rule considered in a later section.

considers time value. In other words, the discounted payback recognizes that we could have invested the money elsewhere and earned a return on it. The ordinary payback does not take this into account. The advantages and disadvantages of the discounted payback rule are summarized in the following table:

Advantages and Disadvantages of the Discounted Payback Period Rule	
Advantages	**Disadvantages**
1. Includes time value of money.	1. May reject positive NPV investments.
2. Easy to understand.	2. Requires an arbitrary cutoff point.
3. Does not accept negative estimated NPV investments.	3. Ignores cash flows beyond the cutoff date.
4. Biased toward liquidity.	4. Biased against long-term projects, such as research and development, and new projects.

Calculating Discounted Payback

EXAMPLE 9.3

Consider an investment that costs $400 and pays $100 per year forever. We use a 20 percent discount rate on this type of investment. What is the ordinary payback? What is the discounted payback? What is the NPV?

The NPV and ordinary payback are easy to calculate in this case because the investment is a perpetuity. The present value of the cash flows is $100/.2 = $500, so the NPV is $500 − 400 = $100. The ordinary payback is obviously four years.

To get the discounted payback, we need to find the number of years such that a $100 annuity has a present value of $400 at 20 percent. In other words, the present value annuity factor is $400/$100 = 4, and the interest rate is 20 percent per period; so what's the number of periods? If we solve for the number of periods, we find that the answer is a little less than nine years, so this is the discounted payback.

Concept Questions

9.3a In words, what is the discounted payback period? Why do we say it is, in a sense, a financial or economic break-even measure?

9.3b What advantage(s) does the discounted payback have over the ordinary payback?

The Average Accounting Return

9.4

Another attractive, but flawed, approach to making capital budgeting decisions involves the **average accounting return (AAR)**. There are many different definitions of the AAR. However, in one form or another, the AAR is always defined as:

$$\frac{\text{Some measure of average accounting profit}}{\text{Some measure of average accounting value}}$$

The specific definition we will use is:

$$\frac{\text{Average net income}}{\text{Average book value}}$$

To see how we might calculate this number, suppose we are deciding whether to open a store in a new shopping mall. The required investment in improvements is $500,000.

Excel Master It!
Excel Master coverage online

average accounting return (AAR)
An investment's average net income divided by its average book value.

TABLE 9.4

Projected Yearly Revenue and Costs for Average Accounting Return

	Year 1	Year 2	Year 3	Year 4	Year 5
Revenue	$433,333	$450,000	$266,667	$200,000	$133,333
Expenses	200,000	150,000	100,000	100,000	100,000
Earnings before depreciation	$233,333	$300,000	$166,667	$100,000	$ 33,333
Depreciation	100,000	100,000	100,000	100,000	100,000
Earnings before taxes	$133,333	$200,000	$ 66,667	$ 0	− $ 66,667
Taxes (25%)	33,333	50,000	16,667	0	− 16,667
Net income	$100,000	$150,000	$ 50,000	$ 0	−$ 50,000

$$\text{Average net income} = \frac{\$100,000 + 150,000 + 50,000 + 0 - 50,000}{5} = \$50,000$$

$$\text{Average book value} = \frac{\$500,000 + 0}{2} = \$250,000$$

The store would have a five-year life because everything reverts to the mall owners after that time. The required investment would be 100 percent depreciated (straight-line) over five years, so the depreciation would be $500,000/5 = $100,000 per year. The tax rate is 25 percent. Table 9.4 contains the projected revenues and expenses. Net income in each year, based on these figures, is also shown.

To calculate the average book value for this investment, we note that we started out with a book value of $500,000 (the initial cost) and ended up at $0. The average book value during the life of the investment is ($500,000 + 0)/2 = $250,000. As long as we use straight-line depreciation, the average investment will always be one-half of the initial investment.[4]

Looking at Table 9.4, we see that net income is $100,000 in the first year, $150,000 in the second year, $50,000 in the third year, $0 in Year 4, and −$50,000 in Year 5. The average net income, then, is:

[$100,000 + 150,000 + 50,000 + 0 + (−50,000)]/5 = $50,000

The average accounting return is:

$$\text{AAR} = \frac{\text{Average net income}}{\text{Average book value}} = \frac{\$50,000}{\$250,000} = .20, \text{ or } 20\%$$

If the firm has a target AAR of less than 20 percent, then this investment is acceptable; otherwise, it is not. The *average accounting return rule* is:

> **Based on the average accounting return rule, a project is acceptable if its average accounting return exceeds a target average accounting return.**

As we will now see, the use of this rule has a number of problems.

You should recognize the chief drawback to the AAR immediately. Above all else, the AAR is not a rate of return in any meaningful economic sense. Instead, it is the ratio of

---

[4]We could, of course, calculate the average of the six book values directly. In thousands, we would have ($500 + 400 + 300 + 200 + 100 + 0)/6 = $250.

two accounting numbers, and it is not comparable to the returns offered, for example, in financial markets.[5]

One of the reasons the AAR is not a true rate of return is that it ignores time value. When we average figures that occur at different times, we are treating the near future and the more distant future in the same way. There was no discounting involved when we computed the average net income, for example.

The second problem with the AAR is similar to the problem we had with the payback period rule concerning the lack of an objective cutoff period. Because a calculated AAR is really not comparable to a market return, the target AAR must somehow be specified. There is no generally agreed-upon way to do this. One way of doing it is to calculate the AAR for the firm as a whole and use this as a benchmark, but there are lots of other ways as well.

The third, and perhaps worst, flaw in the AAR is that it doesn't even look at the right things. Instead of cash flow and market value, it uses net income and book value. These are both poor substitutes. As a result, an AAR doesn't tell us what we really want to know—which is, What effect will taking this investment have on share price?

Does the AAR have any redeeming features? About the only one is that it almost always can be computed. The reason is that accounting information will almost always be available, both for the project under consideration and for the firm as a whole. We hasten to add that once the accounting information is available, we can always convert it to cash flows, so even this is not a particularly important fact. The AAR is summarized in the following table:

Advantages and Disadvantages of the Average Accounting Return	
Advantages	**Disadvantages**
1. Easy to calculate. 2. Needed information will usually be available.	1. Not a true rate of return; time value of money is ignored. 2. Uses an arbitrary benchmark cutoff rate. 3. Based on accounting (book) values, not cash flows and market values.

Concept Questions

9.4a   What is an average accounting rate of return (AAR)?

9.4b   What are the weaknesses of the AAR rule?

The Internal Rate of Return   9.5

We now come to the most important alternative to NPV, the **internal rate of return**, universally known as the **IRR**. As we will see, the IRR is closely related to NPV. With the IRR, we try to find a single rate of return that summarizes the merits of a project. Furthermore, we want this rate to be an "internal" rate in the sense that it depends only on the cash flows of a particular investment, not on rates offered elsewhere.

To illustrate the idea behind the IRR, consider a project that costs $100 today and pays $110 in one year. Suppose you were asked, "What is the return on this investment?" What would you say? It seems both natural and obvious to say that the return is 10 percent

Excel Master It!
Excel Master coverage online

internal rate of return (IRR)
The discount rate that makes the NPV of an investment zero.

---

[5]The AAR is closely related to the return on assets (ROA) discussed in Chapter 3. In practice, the AAR is sometimes computed by first calculating the ROA for each year and then averaging the results. This produces a number that is similar, but not identical, to the one we computed.

because, for every dollar we put in, we get $1.10 back. In fact, as we will see in a moment, 10 percent is the internal rate of return, or IRR, on this investment.

Is this project with its 10 percent IRR a good investment? Once again, it would seem apparent that this is a good investment only if our required return is less than 10 percent. This intuition is also correct and illustrates the *IRR rule*:

> **Based on the IRR rule, an investment is acceptable if the IRR exceeds the required return. It should be rejected otherwise.**

Imagine that we want to calculate the NPV for our simple investment. At a discount rate of R, the NPV is:

$$NPV = -\$100 + [110/(1 + R)]$$

Now, suppose we don't know the discount rate. This presents a problem, but we can still ask how high the discount rate would have to be before this project would be deemed unacceptable. We know that we are indifferent between taking and not taking this investment when its NPV is just equal to zero. In other words, this investment is *economically* a break-even proposition when the NPV is zero because value is neither created nor destroyed. To find the break-even discount rate, we set NPV equal to zero and solve for R:

$$NPV = 0 = -\$100 + [110/(1 + R)]$$
$$\$100 = \$110/(1 + R)$$
$$1 + R = \$110/\$100 = 1.1$$
$$R = .10, \text{ or } 10\%$$

This 10 percent is what we already have called the return on this investment. What we have now illustrated is that the internal rate of return on an investment (or just "return" for short) is the discount rate that makes the NPV equal to zero. This is an important observation, so it bears repeating:

> **The IRR on an investment is the required return that results in a zero NPV when it is used as the discount rate.**

The fact that the IRR is the discount rate that makes the NPV equal to zero is important because it tells us how to calculate the returns on more complicated investments. As we have seen, finding the IRR turns out to be relatively easy for a single-period investment. Suppose you were now looking at an investment with the cash flows shown in Figure 9.4. As illustrated, this investment costs $100 and has a cash flow of $60 per year for two years, so it's only slightly more complicated than our single-period example. If you were asked for the return on this investment, what would you say? There doesn't seem to be any obvious answer (at least not to us). Based on what we now know, we can set the NPV equal to zero and solve for the discount rate:

$$NPV = 0 = -\$100 + [60/(1 + IRR)] + [60/(1 + IRR)^2]$$

FIGURE 9.4

Project Cash Flows

Discount Rate	NPV
0%	$20.00
5	11.56
10	4.13
15	− 2.46
20	− 8.33

TABLE 9.5

NPV at Different Discount Rates

Unfortunately, the only way to find the IRR in general is by trial and error, either by hand or by calculator. This is precisely the same problem that came up in Chapter 5, when we found the unknown rate for an annuity, and in Chapter 7, when we found the yield to maturity on a bond. In fact, we now see that in both of those cases, we were finding an IRR.

In this particular case, the cash flows form a two-period, $60 annuity. To find the unknown rate, we can try some different rates until we get the answer. If we were to start with a 0 percent rate, the NPV would obviously be $120 − 100 = $20. At a 10 percent discount rate, we would have:

$$NPV = -\$100 + (60/1.1) + (60/1.1^2) = \$4.13$$

Now, we're getting close. We can summarize these and some other possibilities as shown in Table 9.5. From our calculations, the NPV appears to be zero with a discount rate between 10 percent and 15 percent, so the IRR is somewhere in that range. With a little more effort, we can find that the IRR is about 13.1 percent.[6] So, if our required return were less than 13.1 percent, we would take this investment. If our required return exceeded 13.1 percent, we would reject it.

By now, you have probably noticed that the IRR rule and the NPV rule appear to be quite similar. In fact, the IRR is sometimes called the *discounted cash flow*, or *DCF*, *return*. The easiest way to illustrate the relationship between NPV and IRR is to plot the numbers we calculated for Table 9.5. We put the different NPVs on the vertical axis, or *y*-axis, and the discount rates on the horizontal axis, or *x*-axis. If we had a very large number of points, the resulting picture would be a smooth curve called a **net present value profile**. Figure 9.5 illustrates the NPV profile for this project. Beginning with a 0 percent discount

net present value profile
A graphical representation of the relationship between an investment's NPVs and various discount rates.

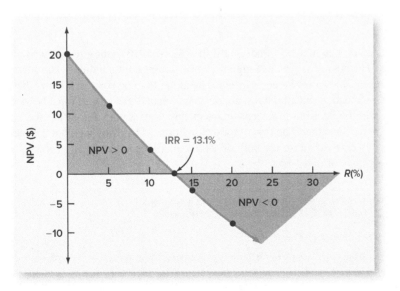

FIGURE 9.5

An NPV Profile

---

[6]With a lot more effort (or a personal computer), we can find that the IRR is approximately (to 9 decimal places) 13.066238629 percent—not that anybody would ever want this many decimal places!

288   **PART 4**   Capital Budgeting

rate, we have $20 plotted directly on the *y*-axis. As the discount rate increases, the NPV declines smoothly. Where will the curve cut through the *x*-axis? This will occur where the NPV is just equal to zero, so it will happen right at the IRR of 13.1 percent.

In our example, the NPV rule and the IRR rule lead to identical accept–reject decisions. We will accept an investment using the IRR rule if the required return is less than 13.1 percent. As Figure 9.5 illustrates, the NPV is positive at any discount rate less than 13.1 percent, so we would accept the investment using the NPV rule as well. The two rules give equivalent results in this case.

EXAMPLE 9.4	Calculating the IRR

A project has a total up-front cost of $435.44. The cash flows are $100 in the first year, $200 in the second year, and $300 in the third year. What's the IRR? If we require an 18 percent return, should we take this investment?

We'll describe the NPV profile and find the IRR by calculating some NPVs at different discount rates. You should check our answers for practice. Beginning with 0 percent, we have:

Discount Rate	NPV
0%	$164.56
5	100.36
10	46.15
15	.00
20	− 39.61

The NPV is zero at 15 percent, so 15 percent is the IRR. If we require an 18 percent return, then we should not take the investment. The reason is that the NPV is negative at 18 percent (verify that it is −$24.47). The IRR rule tells us the same thing in this case. We shouldn't take this investment because its 15 percent return is below our required 18 percent return.

At this point, you may be wondering if the IRR and NPV rules always lead to identical decisions. The answer is yes, as long as two very important conditions are met. First, the project's cash flows must be *conventional*, meaning that the first cash flow (the initial investment) is negative and all the rest are positive. Second, the project must be *independent*, meaning that the decision to accept or reject this project does not affect the decision to accept or reject any other. The first of these conditions is typically met, but the second often is not. In any case, when one or both of these conditions are not met, problems can arise. We discuss some of these next.

SPREADSHEET STRATEGIES

Calculating IRRs with a Spreadsheet

Because IRRs are so tedious to calculate by hand, financial calculators and especially spreadsheets are generally used. The procedures used by various financial calculators are too different for us to illustrate here, so we will focus on using a spreadsheet (financial calculators are covered in Appendix D). As the following example illustrates, using a spreadsheet is easy.

	A	B	C	D	E	F	G	H
1								
2			Using a spreadsheet to calculate internal rates of return					
3								
4	Suppose we have a four-year project that costs $500. The cash flows over the four-year life will be							
5	$100, $200, $300, and $400. What is the IRR?							
6								
7		Year	Cash Flow					
8		0	–$500					
9		1	100		IRR =	27.3%		
10		2	200					
11		3	300					
12		4	400					
13								
14								
15	The formula entered in cell F9 is =IRR(C8:C12). Notice that the Year 0 cash flow has a negative							
16	sign representing the initial cost of the project.							
17								

SOURCE: Microsoft Excel

PROBLEMS WITH THE IRR

The problems with the IRR come about when the cash flows are not conventional or when we are trying to compare two or more investments to see which is best. In the first case, surprisingly, the simple question "What's the return?" can become difficult to answer. In the second case, the IRR can be a misleading guide.

Nonconventional Cash Flows   Suppose we have a strip-mining project that requires a $60 investment. Our cash flow in the first year will be $155. In the second year, the mine will be depleted, but we will have to spend $100 to restore the terrain. As Figure 9.6 illustrates, both the first and third cash flows are negative.

To find the IRR on this project, we can calculate the NPV at various rates:

Discount Rate	NPV
0%	–$5.00
10	– 1.74
20	– .28
30	.06
40	– .31

The NPV appears to be behaving in a peculiar fashion here. First, as the discount rate increases from 0 percent to 30 percent, the NPV starts out negative and becomes positive. This seems backward because the NPV is rising as the discount rate rises. It then starts getting smaller and becomes negative again. What's the IRR? To find out, we draw the NPV profile as shown in Figure 9.7.

In Figure 9.7, notice that the NPV is zero when the discount rate is 25 percent, so this is the IRR. Or is it? The NPV is also zero at $33\frac{1}{3}$ percent. Which of these is correct? The answer is both or neither; more precisely, there is no unambiguously correct answer.

FIGURE 9.6

Project Cash Flows

FIGURE 9.7

NPV Profile

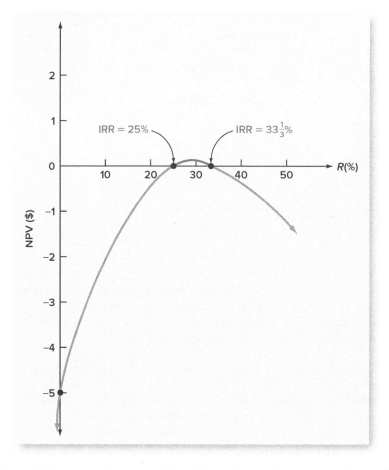

**multiple rates
of return**

The possibility that more than one discount rate will make the NPV of an investment zero.

This is the **multiple rates of return** problem. Many financial computer packages (including a best seller for personal computers) aren't aware of this problem and just report the first IRR that is found. Others report only the smallest positive IRR, even though this answer is no better than any other.

In our current example, the IRR rule breaks down completely. Suppose our required return is 10 percent. Should we take this investment? Both IRRs are greater than 10 percent, so, by the IRR rule, maybe we should. As Figure 9.7 shows, the NPV is negative at any discount rate less than 25 percent, so this is not a good investment. When should we take it? Looking at Figure 9.7 one last time, we see that the NPV is positive only if our required return is between 25 percent and $33\frac{1}{3}$ percent.

Nonconventional cash flows can occur in a variety of ways. For example, Northeast Utilities, owner of the Connecticut-located Millstone nuclear power plant, had to shut down the plant's three reactors in November 1995. The reactors were expected to be back online in January 1997. By some estimates, the cost of the shutdown would run about $334 million. In fact, all nuclear plants eventually have to be shut down forever, and the costs associated with decommissioning a plant are enormous, creating large negative cash flows at the end of the project's life. The four companies in Germany that operate nuclear power plants have set aside $45 billion to decommission nuclear plants in that country.

The moral of the story is that when the cash flows aren't conventional, strange things can start to happen to the IRR. This is not anything to get upset about because the NPV rule, as always, works just fine. This illustrates the fact that, oddly enough, the obvious question—What's the rate of return?—may not always have a good answer.

What's the IRR?		**EXAMPLE 9.5**

You are looking at an investment that requires you to invest $51 today. You'll get $100 in one year, but you must pay out $50 in two years. What is the IRR on this investment?

You're on the alert now for the nonconventional cash flow problem, so you probably wouldn't be surprised to see more than one IRR. If you start looking for an IRR by trial and error, it will take you a long time. The reason is that there is no IRR. The NPV is negative at every discount rate, so we shouldn't take this investment under any circumstances. What's the return on this investment? Your guess is as good as ours.

"I Think; Therefore, I Know How Many IRRs There Can Be."		**EXAMPLE 9.6**

We've seen that it's possible to get more than one IRR. If you wanted to make sure that you had found all of the possible IRRs, how could you do it? The answer comes from the great mathematician, philosopher, and financial analyst Descartes (of "I think; therefore, I am" fame). Descartes' Rule of Sign says that the maximum number of IRRs that there can be is equal to the number of times that the cash flows change sign from positive to negative and/or negative to positive.[7]

In our example with the 25 percent and $33\frac{1}{3}$ percent IRRs, could there be yet another IRR? The cash flows flip from negative to positive, then back to negative, for a total of two sign changes. Therefore, according to Descartes' rule, the maximum number of IRRs is two, and we don't need to look for any more. Note that the actual number of IRRs can be less than the maximum (see Example 9.5).

Mutually Exclusive Investments   Even if there is a single IRR, another problem can arise concerning **mutually exclusive investment decisions**. If two investments, X and Y, are mutually exclusive, then taking one of them means that we cannot take the other. Two projects that are not mutually exclusive are said to be independent. For example, if we own one corner lot, then we can build a gas station or an apartment building, but not both. These are mutually exclusive alternatives.

Thus far, we have asked whether a given investment is worth undertaking. A related question comes up often: Given two or more mutually exclusive investments, which one is the best? The answer is simple enough: The best one is the one with the largest NPV. Can we also say that the best one has the highest return? As we show, the answer is no.

To illustrate the problem with the IRR rule and mutually exclusive investments, consider the following cash flows from two mutually exclusive investments:

mutually exclusive investment decisions
A situation in which taking one investment prevents the taking of another.

Year	Investment A	Investment B
0	−$100	−$100
1	50	20
2	40	40
3	40	50
4	30	60

---

[7]To be more precise, the number of IRRs that are bigger than −100 percent is equal to the number of sign changes, or it differs from the number of sign changes by an even number. Thus, for example, if there are five sign changes, there are five IRRs, three IRRs, or one IRR. If there are two sign changes, there are either two IRRs or no IRRs.

The IRR for A is 24 percent, and the IRR for B is 21 percent. Because these investments are mutually exclusive, we can take only one of them. Simple intuition suggests that Investment A is better because of its higher return. Unfortunately, simple intuition is not always correct.

To see why Investment A is not necessarily the better of the two investments, we've calculated the NPV of these investments for different required returns:

Discount Rate	NPV(A)	NPV(B)
0%	$60.00	$70.00
5	43.13	47.88
10	29.06	29.79
15	17.18	14.82
20	7.06	2.31
25	− 1.63	− 8.22

The IRR for A (24 percent) is larger than the IRR for B (21 percent). However, if you compare the NPVs, you'll see that which investment has the higher NPV depends on our required return. B has greater total cash flow, but it pays back more slowly than A. As a result, it has a higher NPV at lower discount rates.

In our example, the NPV and IRR rankings conflict for some discount rates. If our required return is 10 percent, for instance, then B has the higher NPV and is the better of the two even though A has the higher return. If our required return is 15 percent, then there is no ranking conflict: A is better.

The conflict between the IRR and NPV for mutually exclusive investments can be illustrated by plotting the investments' NPV profiles as we have done in Figure 9.8. In Figure 9.8, notice that the NPV profiles cross at about 11.1 percent. Notice also that at any discount rate less than 11.1 percent, the NPV for B is higher. In this range, taking B benefits us more than taking A, even though A's IRR is higher. At any rate greater than 11.1 percent, Investment A has the greater NPV.

FIGURE 9.8

NPV Profiles for Mutually Exclusive Investments

This example illustrates that when we have mutually exclusive projects, we shouldn't rank them based on their returns. More generally, anytime we are comparing investments to determine which is best, looking at IRRs can be misleading. Instead, we need to look at the relative NPVs to avoid the possibility of choosing incorrectly. Remember, we're ultimately interested in creating value for the shareholders, so the option with the higher NPV is preferred, regardless of the relative returns.

If this seems counterintuitive, think of it this way. Suppose you have two investments. One has a 10 percent return and makes you $100 richer immediately. The other has a 20 percent return and makes you $50 richer immediately. Which one do you like better? We would rather have $100 than $50, regardless of the returns, so we like the first one better.

Calculating the Crossover Rate	EXAMPLE 9.7

In Figure 9.8, the NPV profiles cross at about 11 percent. How can we determine just what this crossover point is? The *crossover rate*, by definition, is the discount rate that makes the NPVs of two projects equal. To illustrate, suppose we have the following two mutually exclusive investments:

Year	Investment A	Investment B
0	−$400	−$500
1	250	320
2	280	340

What's the crossover rate?

To find the crossover, first consider moving out of Investment A and into Investment B. If you make the move, you'll have to invest an extra $100 (= $500 − 400). For this $100 investment, you'll get an extra $70 (= $320 − 250) in the first year and an extra $60 (= $340 − 280) in the second year. Is this a good move? In other words, is it worth investing the extra $100?

Based on our discussion, the NPV of the switch, NPV(B − A), is:

$$\text{NPV(B − A)} = -\$100 + [70/(1 + R)] + [60/(1 + R)^2]$$

We can calculate the return on this investment by setting the NPV equal to zero and solving for the IRR:

$$\text{NPV(B − A)} = 0 = -\$100 + [70/(1 + IRR)] + [60/(1 + IRR)^2]$$

If you go through this calculation, you will find the IRR is exactly 20 percent. What this tells us is that at a 20 percent discount rate, we are indifferent between the two investments because the NPV of the difference in their cash flows is zero. As a consequence, the two investments have the same value, so this 20 percent is the crossover rate. Check to see that the NPV at 20 percent is $2.78 for both investments.

In general, you can find the crossover rate by taking the difference in the cash flows and calculating the IRR using the difference. It doesn't make any difference which one you subtract from which. To see this, find the IRR for (A − B); you'll see it's the same number. Also, for practice, you might want to find the exact crossover in Figure 9.8. (*Hint:* It's 11.0704 percent.)

Investing or Financing?   Consider the following two independent investments:

Year	Investment A	Investment B
0	−$100	$100
1	130	− 130

FIGURE 9.9   **NPV Profile for Investing and Financing Investments**

The company initially pays out cash with Investment A and initially receives cash for Investment B. While most projects are more like Investment A, projects like Investment B also occur. For example, consider a corporation conducting a seminar where the participants pay in advance. Because large expenses are frequently incurred at the seminar date, cash inflows precede cash outflows.

For these two projects, suppose the required return for each investment project is 12 percent. According to the IRR decision rule, which, if either, project should we accept? If you calculate the IRRs, you will find that they are 30 percent for both projects.

According to the IRR decision rule, we should accept both projects. However, if we calculate the NPV of B at 12 percent, we get:

$$\$100 - \frac{\$130}{1.12} = -\$16.07$$

In this case, the NPV and IRR decision rules disagree. To see what's going on, Figure 9.9 shows the NPV profile for each project. As you can see, the NPV profile for B is upward sloping. The project should be accepted if the required return is *greater* than 30 percent.

When a project has cash flows like Investment B's, the IRR is really a rate that you are paying, not receiving. For this reason, we say that the project has *financing type* cash flows, whereas Investment A has *investing type* cash flows. You should take a project with financing-type cash flows only if it is an inexpensive source of financing, meaning that its IRR is *lower* than your required return.

REDEEMING QUALITIES OF THE IRR

Despite its flaws, the IRR is very popular in practice—more so than even the NPV. It probably survives because it fills a need that the NPV does not. In analyzing investments, people in general, and financial analysts in particular, seem to prefer talking about rates of return rather than dollar values.

In a similar vein, the IRR also appears to provide a simple way of communicating information about a proposal. One manager might say to another, "Remodeling the clerical wing has a 20 percent return." This may somehow seem simpler than saying, "At a 10 percent discount rate, the net present value is $4,000."

Finally, under certain circumstances, the IRR may have a practical advantage over the NPV. We can't estimate the NPV unless we know the appropriate discount rate, but we can still estimate the IRR. Suppose we didn't know the required return on an investment, but we found, for example, that it had a 40 percent return. We would probably be inclined to take it because it would be unlikely that the required return would be that high. The advantages and disadvantages of the IRR are summarized as follows:

Advantages and Disadvantages of the Internal Rate of Return	
Advantages	**Disadvantages**
1. Closely related to NPV, often leading to identical decisions.	1. May result in multiple answers or not deal with nonconventional cash flows.
2. Easy to understand and communicate.	2. May lead to incorrect decisions in comparisons of mutually exclusive investments.

THE MODIFIED INTERNAL RATE OF RETURN (MIRR)

To address some of the problems that can crop up with the standard IRR, it is often proposed that a modified version be used. As we will see, there are several different ways of calculating a modified IRR, or MIRR, but the basic idea is to modify the cash flows first and then calculate an IRR using the modified cash flows.

To illustrate, let's go back to the cash flows in Figure 9.6: −$60, +$155, and −$100. As we saw, there are two IRRs, 25 percent and $33\frac{1}{3}$ percent. We next illustrate three different MIRRs, all of which have the property that only one answer will result, thereby eliminating the multiple IRR problem.

Method #1: The Discounting Approach With the discounting approach, the idea is to discount all negative cash flows back to the present at the required return and add them to the initial cost. Then, calculate the IRR. Because only the first modified cash flow is negative, there will be only one IRR. The discount rate used might be the required return, or it might be some other externally supplied rate. We will use the project's required return.

If the required return on the project is 20 percent, then the modified cash flows look like this:

$$\text{Time 0:} \quad -\$60 + \frac{-\$100}{1.20^2} = -\$129.44$$
$$\text{Time 1:} \quad +\$155$$
$$\text{Time 2:} \quad +\$0$$

If you calculate the MIRR now, you should get 19.74 percent.

Method #2: The Reinvestment Approach With the reinvestment approach, we compound *all* cash flows (positive and negative) except the first out to the end of the project's life and then calculate the IRR. In a sense, we are "reinvesting" the cash flows and not taking them out of the project until the very end. The rate we use could be the required return on the project, or it could be a separately specified "reinvestment rate." We will use the project's required return. When we do, here are the modified cash flows:

$$\text{Time 0:} \quad -\$60$$
$$\text{Time 1:} \quad +0$$
$$\text{Time 2:} \quad -\$100 + (\$155 \times 1.2) = \$86$$

The MIRR on this set of cash flows is 19.72 percent, or a little lower than we got using the discounting approach.

Method #3: The Combination Approach   As the name suggests, the combination approach blends our first two methods. Negative cash flows are discounted back to the present, and positive cash flows are compounded to the end of the project. In practice, different discount or compounding rates might be used, but we will again stick with the project's required return.

With the combination approach, the modified cash flows are as follows:

Time 0: $-\$60 + \dfrac{-\$100}{1.20^2} = -\$129.44$

Time 1: $+0$

Time 2: $\$155 \times 1.2 = \$186$

See if you don't agree that the MIRR is 19.87 percent, the highest of the three.

MIRR or IRR: Which Is Better?   MIRRs are controversial. At one extreme are those who claim that MIRRs are superior to IRRs, period. For example, by design, they clearly don't suffer from the multiple rate of return problem.

At the other end, detractors say that MIRR should stand for "meaningless internal rate of return." As our example makes clear, one problem with MIRRs is that there are different ways of calculating them, and there is no clear reason to say one of our three methods is better than any other. The differences are small with our simple cash flows, but they could be much larger for a more complex project. Further, it's not clear how to interpret an MIRR. It may look like a rate of return, but it's a rate of return on a modified set of cash flows, not the project's actual cash flows.

We're not going to take sides. However, notice that calculating an MIRR requires discounting, compounding, or both, which leads to two obvious observations. First, if we have the relevant discount rate, why not calculate the NPV and be done with it? Second, because an MIRR depends on an externally supplied discount (or compounding) rate, the answer you get is not truly an "internal" rate of return, which, by definition, depends on only the project's cash flows.

We *will* take a stand on one issue that frequently comes up in this context. The value of a project does not depend on what the firm does with the cash flows generated by that project. A firm might use a project's cash flows to fund other projects, to pay dividends, or to buy an executive jet. It doesn't matter: How the cash flows are spent in the future does not affect their value today. As a result, there is generally no need to consider reinvestment of interim cash flows.

Concept Questions

9.5a   Under what circumstances will the IRR and NPV rules lead to the same accept-reject decisions? When might they conflict?

9.5b   Is it generally true that an advantage of the IRR rule over the NPV rule is that we don't need to know the required return to use the IRR rule?

9.6 The Profitability Index

Excel Master It!
Excel Master coverage online

Another tool used to evaluate projects is called the **profitability index (PI)** or benefit-cost ratio. This index is defined as the present value of the future cash flows divided by the initial investment. So, if a project costs $200 and the present value of its future cash flows is $220, the profitability index value would be $220/$200 = 1.1. Notice that the NPV for this investment is $20, so it is a desirable investment.

More generally, if a project has a positive NPV, then the present value of the future cash flows must be bigger than the initial investment. The profitability index will be bigger than 1 for a positive NPV investment and less than 1 for a negative NPV investment.

How do we interpret the profitability index? In our example, the PI was 1.1. This tells us that, per dollar invested, $1.10 in value or $.10 in NPV results. The profitability index measures "bang for the buck"—that is, the value created per dollar invested. For this reason, it is often proposed as a measure of performance for government or other not-for-profit investments. Also, when capital is scarce, it may make sense to allocate it to projects with the highest PIs. We will return to this issue in a later chapter.

The PI is obviously similar to the NPV. However, consider an investment that costs $5 and has a $10 present value and an investment that costs $100 with a $150 present value. The first of these investments has an NPV of $5 and a PI of 2. The second has an NPV of $50 and a PI of 1.5. If these are mutually exclusive investments, then the second one is preferred even though it has a lower PI. This ranking problem is similar to the IRR ranking problem we saw in the previous section. In all, there seems to be little reason to rely on the PI instead of the NPV. Our discussion of the PI is summarized as follows:

profitability index (PI)
The present value of an investment's future cash flows divided by its initial cost. Also called the benefit-cost ratio.

Advantages and Disadvantages of the Profitability Index	
Advantages	**Disadvantages**
1. Closely related to NPV, generally leading to identical decisions.	1. May lead to incorrect decisions in comparisons of mutually exclusive investments.
2. Easy to understand and communicate.	
3. May be useful when available investment funds are limited.	

Concept Questions

9.6a   What does the profitability index measure?
9.6b   How would you state the profitability index rule?

The Practice of Capital Budgeting   9.7

Given that NPV seems to be telling us directly what we want to know, you might be wondering why there are so many other procedures and why alternative procedures are commonly used. Recall that we are trying to make an investment decision and that we are frequently operating under considerable uncertainty about the future. We can only *estimate* the NPV of an investment in this case. The resulting estimate can be very "soft," meaning that the true NPV might be quite different.

Because the true NPV is unknown, the astute financial manager seeks clues to help in assessing whether the estimated NPV is reliable. For this reason, firms would typically use multiple criteria for evaluating a proposal. For example, suppose we have an investment with a positive estimated NPV. Based on our experience with other projects, this one appears to have a short payback and a very high AAR. In this case, the different indicators seem to agree that it's "all systems go." Put another way, the payback and the AAR are consistent with the conclusion that the NPV is positive.

On the other hand, suppose we had a positive estimated NPV, a long payback, and a low AAR. This could still be a good investment, but it looks like we need to be much more careful in making the decision because we are getting conflicting signals. If the estimated

NPV is based on projections in which we have little confidence, then further analysis is probably in order. We will consider how to evaluate NPV estimates in more detail in the next two chapters.

Large firms often have huge capital budgets. For example, for 2017, ExxonMobil announced that it expected to have about $22 billion in capital outlays during the year, down from its record $42.5 billion in 2013. About the same time, competitor Chevron announced that it would decrease its capital budgeting for 2017 to $19.8 billion, down from $26.6 billion in 2016. Other companies with large capital spending budgets included Walmart, which projected capital spending of about $11 billion for 2017, and Apple, which projected capital spending of about $16 billion for 2017.

According to information released by the Census Bureau in 2017, capital investment for the economy as a whole was $1.401 trillion in 2013, $1.507 trillion in 2014, and $1.545 trillion in 2015. The total for the three years therefore exceeded $4.4 trillion! Given the sums at stake, it is not too surprising that careful analysis of capital expenditures is something at which successful businesses seek to become adept.

There have been a number of surveys conducted asking firms what types of investment criteria they actually use. Table 9.6 summarizes the results of several of these. Panel A of the table is a historical comparison looking at the primary capital budgeting techniques used by large firms through time. In 1959, only 19 percent of the firms surveyed used either IRR or NPV, and 68 percent used either payback periods or accounting returns. It is clear that by the 1980s, IRR and NPV had become the dominant criteria.

Panel B of Table 9.6 summarizes the results of a 1999 survey of chief financial officers (CFOs) at both large and small firms in the United States. A total of 392 CFOs responded. What is shown is the percentage of CFOs who always or almost always used

TABLE 9.6   **Capital Budgeting Techniques in Practice**

A. Historical Comparison of the Primary Use of Various Capital Budgeting Techniques							
	1959	1964	1970	1975	1977	1979	1981
Payback period	34%	24%	12%	15%	9%	10%	5%
Average accounting return (AAR)	34	30	26	10	25	14	11
Internal rate of return (IRR)	19	38	57	37	54	60	65
Net present value (NPV)	—	—	—	26	10	14	17
IRR or NPV	19	38	57	63	64	74	82

B. Percentage of CFOs Who Always or Almost Always Used a Given Technique in 1999				
Capital Budgeting Technique	Percentage Always or Almost Always Using	Average Score [Scale is 4 (always) to 0 (never)]		
		Overall	Large Firms	Small Firms
Internal rate of return	76%	3.09	3.41	2.87
Net present value	75	3.08	3.42	2.83
Payback period	57	2.53	2.25	2.72
Discounted payback period	29	1.56	1.55	1.58
Accounting rate of return	20	1.34	1.25	1.41
Profitability index	12	.83	.75	.88

SOURCES: Graham, J. R., and Harvey, C. R., "The Theory and Practice of Corporate Finance: Evidence from the Field," Journal of Financial Economics, May–June 2001, 187–243; Moore, J. S, and Reichert, A. K., "An Analysis of the Financial Management Techniques Currently Employed by Large U.S. Corporations," Journal of Business Finance and Accounting, Winter 1983, 623–45; and Stanley, M. T., and Block, S. R., "A Survey of Multinational Capital Budgeting," The Financial Review, March 1984, 36–51.

the various capital budgeting techniques we describe in this chapter. Not surprisingly, IRR and NPV were the two most widely used techniques, particularly at larger firms. However, over half of the respondents always, or almost always, used the payback criterion as well. In fact, among smaller firms, payback was used just about as much as NPV and IRR. Less commonly used were discounted payback, accounting rates of return, and the profitability index. For future reference, the various criteria we have discussed are summarized in Table 9.7.

TABLE 9.7

Summary of Investment Criteria

I.	**Discounted Cash Flow Criteria**
	A. *Net present value (NPV)*: The NPV of an investment is the difference between its market value and its cost. The NPV rule is to take a project if its NPV is positive. NPV is frequently estimated by calculating the present value of the future cash flows (to estimate market value) and then subtracting the cost. NPV has no serious flaws; it is the preferred decision criterion.
	B. *Internal rate of return (IRR)*: The IRR is the discount rate that makes the estimated NPV of an investment equal to zero; it is sometimes called the *discounted cash flow (DCF) return*. The IRR rule is to take a project when its IRR exceeds the required return. IRR is closely related to NPV, and it leads to exactly the same decisions as NPV for conventional, independent projects. When project cash flows are not conventional, there may be no IRR or there may be more than one. More seriously, the IRR cannot be used to rank mutually exclusive projects; the project with the highest IRR is not necessarily the preferred investment.
	C. *Modified internal rate of return (MIRR)*: The MIRR is a modification to the IRR. A project's cash flows are modified by (1) discounting the negative cash flows back to the present; (2) compounding cash flows to the end of the project's life; or (3) combining (1) and (2). An IRR is then computed on the modified cash flows. MIRRs are guaranteed to avoid the multiple rate of return problem, but it is unclear how to interpret them; and they are not truly "internal" because they depend on externally supplied discounting or compounding rates.
	D. *Profitability index (PI)*: The PI, also called the *benefit-cost ratio*, is the ratio of present value to cost. The PI rule is to take an investment if the index exceeds 1. The PI measures the present value of an investment per dollar invested. It is quite similar to NPV; but, like IRR, it cannot be used to rank mutually exclusive projects. However, it is sometimes used to rank projects when a firm has more positive NPV investments than it can currently finance.
II.	**Payback Criteria**
	A. *Payback period*: The payback period is the length of time until the sum of an investment's cash flows equals its cost. The payback period rule is to take a project if its payback is less than some cutoff. The payback period is a flawed criterion, primarily because it ignores risk, the time value of money, and cash flows beyond the cutoff point.
	B. *Discounted payback period*: The discounted payback period is the length of time until the sum of an investment's discounted cash flows equals its cost. The discounted payback period rule is to take an investment if the discounted payback is less than some cutoff. The discounted payback rule is flawed, primarily because it ignores cash flows after the cutoff.
III.	**Accounting Criterion**
	A. *Average accounting return (AAR)*: The AAR is a measure of accounting profit relative to book value. It is not related to the IRR, but it is similar to the accounting return on assets (ROA) measure in Chapter 3. The AAR rule is to take an investment if its AAR exceeds a benchmark AAR. The AAR is seriously flawed for a variety of reasons, and it has little to recommend it.

300   **PART 4**   Capital Budgeting

> ## Concept Questions
>
> **9.7a**   What are the most commonly used capital budgeting procedures?
> **9.7b**   If NPV is conceptually the best procedure for capital budgeting, why do you think multiple measures are used in practice?

9.8 Summary and Conclusions

This chapter has covered the different criteria used to evaluate proposed investments. The seven criteria, in the order we discussed them, are these:

1. Net present value (NPV).
2. Payback period.
3. Discounted payback period.
4. Average accounting return (AAR).
5. Internal rate of return (IRR).
6. Modified internal rate of return (MIRR).
7. Profitability index (PI).

We illustrated how to calculate each of these and discussed the interpretation of the results. We also described the advantages and disadvantages of each of them. Ultimately a good capital budgeting criterion must tell us two things. First, is a particular project a good investment? Second, if we have more than one good project, but we can take only one of them, which one should we take? The main point of this chapter is that only the NPV criterion can always provide the correct answer to both questions.

For this reason, NPV is one of the two or three most important concepts in finance, and we will refer to it many times in the chapters ahead. When we do, keep two things in mind: (1) NPV is always the difference between the market value of an asset or project and its cost and (2) the financial manager acts in the shareholders' best interests by identifying and taking positive NPV projects.

Finally, we noted that NPVs can't normally be observed in the market; instead, they must be estimated. Because there is always the possibility of a poor estimate, financial managers use multiple criteria for examining projects. The other criteria provide additional information about whether a project truly has a positive NPV.

CONNECT TO FINANCE

 If you are using *Connect Finance* in your course, get online to take a Practice Test, check out study tools, and find out where you need additional practice.

Can you answer the following *Connect* Quiz questions?

Section 9.1   The net present value rule states that you should accept a project if its net present value _____.

Section 9.2   A drawback of the payback method of project analysis is _____.

Section 9.3 The discounted payback period for a project will be _____ the payback period for the project given a positive, nonzero discount rate.

Section 9.4 What is an advantage of the average accounting return method of project analysis?

Section 9.6 What is a benefit-cost ratio?

Section 9.7 What method of analysis tends to be least utilized by CFOs, according to the survey conducted in 1999 as presented in your textbook?

CHAPTER REVIEW AND SELF-TEST PROBLEMS

9.1 **Investment Criteria** This problem will give you some practice calculating NPVs and paybacks. A proposed overseas expansion has the following cash flows:

Year	Cash Flow
0	−$200
1	50
2	60
3	70
4	200

Calculate the payback, the discounted payback, and the NPV at a required return of 10 percent.

9.2 **Mutually Exclusive Investments** Consider the following two mutually exclusive investments. Calculate the IRR for each and the crossover rate. Under what circumstances will the IRR and NPV criteria rank the two projects differently?

Year	Investment A	Investment B
0	−$75	−$75
1	20	60
2	40	50
3	70	15

9.3 **Average Accounting Return** You are looking at a three-year project with a projected net income of $2,000 in Year 1, $4,000 in Year 2, and $6,000 in Year 3. The cost is $12,000, which will be depreciated straight-line to zero over the three-year life of the project. What is the average accounting return (AAR)?

ANSWERS TO CHAPTER REVIEW AND SELF-TEST PROBLEMS

9.1 In the following table, we have listed the cash flow, cumulative cash flow, discounted cash flow (at 10 percent), and cumulative discounted cash flow for the proposed project.

	Cash Flow		Accumulated Cash Flow	
Year	Undiscounted	Discounted	Undiscounted	Discounted
1	$ 50	$ 45.45	$ 50	$ 45.45
2	60	49.59	110	95.04
3	70	52.59	180	147.63
4	200	136.60	380	284.24

Recall that the initial investment was $200. When we compare this to accumulated undiscounted cash flows, we see that payback occurs between Years 3 and 4. The cash flows for the first three years are $180 total, so, going into the fourth year, we are short by $20. The total cash flow in Year 4 is $200, so the payback is 3 + ($20/200) = 3.10 years.

Looking at the accumulated discounted cash flows, we see that the discounted payback occurs between Years 3 and 4. The sum of the discounted cash flows is $284.24, so the NPV is $84.24. Notice that this is the present value of the cash flows that occur after the discounted payback.

9.2 To calculate the IRR, we might try some guesses, as in the following table:

Discount Rate	NPV(A)	NPV(B)
0%	$55.00	$50.00
10	28.83	32.14
20	9.95	18.40
30	− 4.09	7.57
40	− 14.80	− 1.17

Several things are immediately apparent from our guesses. First, the IRR for A must be between 20 percent and 30 percent (why?). With some more effort, we find that it's 26.79 percent. For B, the IRR must be a little less than 40 percent (again, why?); it works out to be 38.54 percent. Also, notice that at rates between 0 percent and 10 percent, the NPVs are very close, indicating that the crossover is in that vicinity.

To find the crossover exactly, we can compute the IRR on the difference in the cash flows. If we take the cash flows from A minus the cash flows from B, the resulting cash flows are:

Year	A − B
0	$ 0
1	− 40
2	− 10
3	55

These cash flows look a little odd; but the sign changes only once, so we can find an IRR. With some trial and error, you'll see that the NPV is zero at a discount rate of 5.42 percent, so this is the crossover rate.

The IRR for B is higher. However, as we've seen, A has the larger NPV for any discount rate less than 5.42 percent, so the NPV and IRR rankings will conflict in that range. Remember, if there's a conflict, we will go with the higher NPV. Our decision rule is thus simple: Take A if the required return is less than 5.42 percent, take B if the required return is between 5.42 percent and 38.54 percent (the IRR on B), and take neither if the required return is more than 38.54 percent.

9.3 Here we need to calculate the ratio of average net income to average book value to get the AAR. Average net income is:

Average net income = ($2,000 + 4,000 + 6,000)/3 = $4,000

Average book value is:

Average book value = $12,000/2 = $6,000

So the average accounting return is:

AAR = $4,000/6,000 = .6667, or 66.67%

This is an impressive return. Remember, however, that it isn't really a rate of return like an interest rate or an IRR, so the size doesn't tell us a lot. In particular, our money is probably not going to grow at a rate of 66.67 percent per year, sorry to say.

CONCEPTS REVIEW AND CRITICAL THINKING QUESTIONS

1. **Payback Period and Net Present Value** [LO1, 2] If a project with conventional cash flows has a payback period less than the project's life, can you definitively state the algebraic sign of the NPV? Why or why not? If you know that the discounted payback period is less than the project's life, what can you say about the NPV? Explain.

2. **Net Present Value** [LO1] Suppose a project has conventional cash flows and a positive NPV. What do you know about its payback? Its discounted payback? Its profitability index? Its IRR? Explain.

3. **Payback Period** [LO2] Concerning payback:
   a. Describe how the payback period is calculated, and describe the information this measure provides about a sequence of cash flows. What is the payback criterion decision rule?
   b. What are the problems associated with using the payback period to evaluate cash flows?
   c. What are the advantages of using the payback period to evaluate cash flows? Are there any circumstances under which using payback might be appropriate? Explain.

4. **Discounted Payback** [LO3] Concerning discounted payback:
   a. Describe how the discounted payback period is calculated, and describe the information this measure provides about a sequence of cash flows. What is the discounted payback criterion decision rule?
   b. What are the problems associated with using the discounted payback period to evaluate cash flows?
   c. What conceptual advantage does the discounted payback method have over the regular payback method? Can the discounted payback ever be longer than the regular payback? Explain.

5. **Average Accounting Return** [LO4] Concerning AAR:
   a. Describe how the average accounting return is usually calculated, and describe the information this measure provides about a sequence of cash flows. What is the AAR criterion decision rule?
   b. What are the problems associated with using the AAR to evaluate a project's cash flows? What underlying feature of AAR is most troubling to you from a financial perspective? Does the AAR have any redeeming qualities?

6. **Net Present Value** [LO1] Concerning NPV:

    a. Describe how NPV is calculated, and describe the information this measure provides about a sequence of cash flows. What is the NPV criterion decision rule?

    b. Why is NPV considered a superior method of evaluating the cash flows from a project? Suppose the NPV for a project's cash flows is computed to be $2,500. What does this number represent with respect to the firm's shareholders?

7. **Internal Rate of Return** [LO5] Concerning IRR:

    a. Describe how the IRR is calculated, and describe the information this measure provides about a sequence of cash flows. What is the IRR criterion decision rule?

    b. What is the relationship between IRR and NPV? Are there any situations in which you might prefer one method over the other? Explain.

    c. Despite its shortcomings in some situations, why do most financial managers use IRR along with NPV when evaluating projects? Can you think of a situation in which IRR might be a more appropriate measure to use than NPV? Explain.

8. **Profitability Index** [LO7] Concerning the profitability index:

    a. Describe how the profitability index is calculated, and describe the information this measure provides about a sequence of cash flows. What is the profitability index decision rule?

    b. What is the relationship between the profitability index and NPV? Are there any situations in which you might prefer one method over the other? Explain.

9. **Payback and Internal Rate of Return** [LO2, 5] A project has perpetual cash flows of C per period, a cost of I, and a required return of R. What is the relationship between the project's payback and its IRR? What implications does your answer have for long-lived projects with relatively constant cash flows?

10. **International Investment Projects** [LO1] In 2016, automobile manufacturer BMW completed its $1 billion investment to increase production at its South Carolina plant by 50 percent. BMW apparently felt that it would be better able to compete and create value with U.S-based facilities. Other companies such as Fuji Film and Swiss chemical company Lonza have reached similar conclusions and taken similar actions. What are some of the reasons that foreign manufacturers of products as diverse as automobiles, film, and chemicals might arrive at this same conclusion?

11. **Capital Budgeting Problems** [LO1] What difficulties might come up in actual applications of the various criteria we discussed in this chapter? Which one would be the easiest to implement in actual applications? The most difficult?

12. **Capital Budgeting in Not-for-Profit Entities** [LO1] Are the capital budgeting criteria we discussed applicable to not-for-profit corporations? How should such entities make capital budgeting decisions? What about the U.S. government? Should it evaluate spending proposals using these techniques?

13. **Modified Internal Rate of Return** [LO6] One of the less flattering interpretations of the acronym MIRR is "meaningless internal rate of return." Why do you think this term is applied to MIRR?

14. **Net Present Value** [LO1] It is sometimes stated that "the net present value approach assumes reinvestment of the intermediate cash flows at the required return." Is this claim correct? To answer, suppose you calculate the NPV of a project in the usual way. Next, suppose you do the following:

    a. Calculate the future value (as of the end of the project) of all the cash flows other than the initial outlay assuming they are reinvested at the required return, producing a single future value figure for the project.

b. Calculate the NPV of the project using the single future value calculated in the previous step and the initial outlay. It is easy to verify that you will get the same NPV as in your original calculation only if you use the required return as the reinvestment rate in the previous step.

15. **Internal Rate of Return** [LO5] It is sometimes stated that "the internal rate of return approach assumes reinvestment of the intermediate cash flows at the internal rate of return." Is this claim correct? To answer, suppose you calculate the IRR of a project in the usual way. Next, suppose you do the following:

a. Calculate the future value (as of the end of the project) of all the cash flows other than the initial outlay assuming they are reinvested at the IRR, producing a single future value figure for the project.

b. Calculate the IRR of the project using the single future value calculated in the previous step and the initial outlay. It is easy to verify that you will get the same IRR as in your original calculation only if you use the IRR as the reinvestment rate in the previous step.

QUESTIONS AND PROBLEMS

1. **Calculating Payback** [LO2] What is the payback period for the following set of cash flows?

Year	Cash Flow
0	−$8,300
1	2,100
2	3,000
3	2,300
4	1,700

BASIC
(Questions 1–19)

2. **Calculating Payback** [LO2] An investment project provides cash inflows of $745 per year for eight years. What is the project payback period if the initial cost is $1,700? What if the initial cost is $3,300? What if it is $6,100?

3. **Calculating Payback** [LO2] Bronco, Inc., imposes a payback cutoff of three years for its international investment projects. If the company has the following two projects available, should it accept either of them?

Year	Cash Flow (A)	Cash Flow (B)
0	−$35,000	−$ 45,000
1	12,000	11,000
2	17,000	13,000
3	14,000	16,000
4	9,000	255,000

4. **Calculating Discounted Payback** [LO3] An investment project has annual cash inflows of $2,800, $3,700, $5,100, and $4,300, for the next four years, respectively. The discount rate is 11 percent. What is the discounted payback period for these cash flows if the initial cost is $5,200? What if the initial cost is $6,400? What if it is $10,400?

5. **Calculating Discounted Payback** [LO3] An investment project costs $17,000 and has annual cash flows of $4,700 for six years. What is the discounted payback period if the discount rate is zero percent? What if the discount rate is 5 percent? If it is 19 percent?

6. Calculating AAR [LO4] You're trying to determine whether to expand your business by building a new manufacturing plant. The plant has an installation cost of $13.5 million, which will be depreciated straight-line to zero over its four-year life. If the plant has projected net income of $1,570,000, $1,684,200, $1,716,300, and $1,097,400 over these four years, respectively, what is the project's average accounting return (AAR)?

7. Calculating IRR [LO5] A firm evaluates all of its projects by applying the IRR rule. If the required return is 14 percent, should the firm accept the following project?

Year	Cash Flow
0	−$34,000
1	15,000
2	17,000
3	13,000

8. Calculating NPV [LO1] For the cash flows in the previous problem, suppose the firm uses the NPV decision rule. At a required return of 11 percent, should the firm accept this project? What if the required return is 24 percent?

9. Calculating NPV and IRR [LO1, 5] A project that provides annual cash flows of $11,700 for nine years costs $63,000 today. Is this a good project if the required return is 8 percent? What if it's 20 percent? At what discount rate would you be indifferent between accepting the project and rejecting it?

10. Calculating IRR [LO5] What is the IRR of the following set of cash flows?

Year	Cash Flow
0	−$15,400
1	7,300
2	9,100
3	5,900

11. Calculating NPV [LO1] For the cash flows in the previous problem, what is the NPV at a discount rate of zero percent? What if the discount rate is 10 percent? If it is 20 percent? If it is 30 percent?

12. NPV versus IRR [LO1, 5] Bruin, Inc., has identified the following two mutually exclusive projects:

Year	Cash Flow (A)	Cash Flow (B)
0	−$37,500	−$37,500
1	17,300	5,700
2	16,200	12,900
3	13,800	16,300
4	7,600	27,500

a. What is the IRR for each of these projects? Using the IRR decision rule, which project should the company accept? Is this decision necessarily correct?

b. If the required return is 11 percent, what is the NPV for each of these projects? Which project will the company choose if it applies the NPV decision rule?

c. Over what range of discount rates would the company choose Project A? Project B? At what discount rate would the company be indifferent between these two projects? Explain.

13. **NPV versus IRR** [LO1, 5] Consider the following two mutually exclusive projects:

Year	Cash Flow (X)	Cash Flow (Y)
0	−$23,000	−$23,000
1	10,490	12,000
2	10,900	9,360
3	10,500	10,400

Sketch the NPV profiles for X and Y over a range of discount rates from zero to 25 percent. What is the crossover rate for these two projects?

14. **Problems with IRR** [LO5] Light Sweet Petroleum, Inc., is trying to evaluate a generation project with the following cash flows:

Year	Cash Flow
0	−$48,000,000
1	71,000,000
2	− 13,000,000

a. If the company requires a return of 12 percent on its investments, should it accept this project? Why?

b. Compute the IRR for this project. How many IRRs are there? Using the IRR decision rule, should the company accept the project? What's going on here?

15. **Calculating Profitability Index** [LO7] What is the profitability index for the following set of cash flows if the relevant discount rate is 10 percent? What if the discount rate is 15 percent? If it is 22 percent?

Year	Cash Flow
0	−$16,700
1	9,700
2	7,800
3	4,300

16. **Problems with Profitability Index** [LO1, 7] The Sloan Corporation is trying to choose between the following two mutually exclusive design projects:

Year	Cash Flow (I)	Cash Flow (II)
0	−$63,000	−$15,500
1	28,900	7,900
2	28,900	7,900
3	28,900	7,900

a. If the required return is 10 percent and the company applies the profitability index decision rule, which project should the firm accept?

b. If the company applies the NPV decision rule, which project should it take?

c. Explain why your answers in (a) and (b) are different.

17. **Comparing Investment Criteria** [LO1, 2, 3, 5, 7] Consider the following two mutually exclusive projects:

Year	Cash Flow (A)	Cash Flow (B)
0	−$364,000	−$52,000
1	46,000	25,000
2	68,000	22,000
3	68,000	21,500
4	458,000	17,500

Whichever project you choose, if any, you require a return of 11 percent on your investment.

   a. If you apply the payback criterion, which investment will you choose? Why?
   b. If you apply the discounted payback criterion, which investment will you choose? Why?
   c. If you apply the NPV criterion, which investment will you choose? Why?
   d. If you apply the IRR criterion, which investment will you choose? Why?
   e. If you apply the profitability index criterion, which investment will you choose? Why?
   f. Based on your answers in (a) through (e), which project will you finally choose? Why?

18. **NPV and Discount Rates** [LO1] An investment has an installed cost of $527,630. The cash flows over the four-year life of the investment are projected to be $212,200, $243,800, $203,500, and $167,410, respectively. If the discount rate is zero, what is the NPV? If the discount rate is infinite, what is the NPV? At what discount rate is the NPV just equal to zero? Sketch the NPV profile for this investment based on these three points.

19. **MIRR** [LO6] Solo Corp. is evaluating a project with the following cash flows:

Year	Cash Flow
0	−$47,000
1	16,900
2	20,300
3	25,800
4	19,600
5	− 9,500

The company uses an interest rate of 10 percent on all of its projects. Calculate the MIRR of the project using all three methods.

INTERMEDIATE
(Questions 20–22)

20. **MIRR** [LO6] Suppose the company in the previous problem uses a discount rate of 11 percent and a reinvestment rate of 8 percent on all of its projects. Calculate the MIRR of the project using all three methods using these interest rates.

21. **NPV and the Profitability Index** [LO1, 7] If we define the NPV index as the ratio of NPV to cost, what is the relationship between this index and the profitability index?

22. **Cash Flow Intuition** [LO1, 2] A project has an initial cost of I, a required return of R, and pays C annually for N years.

   a. Find C in terms of I and N such that the project has a payback period just equal to its life.

b. Find C in terms of I, N, and R such that this is a profitable project according to the NPV decision rule.

c. Find C in terms of I, N, and R such that the project has a benefit-cost ratio of 2.

23. **Payback and NPV** [LO1, 2] An investment under consideration has a payback of seven years and a cost of $685,000. If the required return is 11 percent, what is the worst-case NPV? The best-case NPV? Explain. Assume the cash flows are conventional.

CHALLENGE
(Questions 23–28)

24. **Multiple IRRs** [LO5] This problem is useful for testing the ability of financial calculators and spreadsheets. Consider the following cash flows. How many different IRRs are there? (*Hint*: Search between 20 percent and 70 percent.) When should we take this project?

Year	Cash Flow
0	−$ 3,024
1	17,172
2	− 36,420
3	34,200
4	− 12,000

25. **NPV Valuation** [LO1] The Yurdone Corporation wants to set up a private cemetery business. According to the CFO, Barry M. Deep, business is "looking up." As a result, the cemetery project will provide a net cash inflow of $145,000 for the firm during the first year, and the cash flows are projected to grow at a rate of 4 percent per year forever. The project requires an initial investment of $1,900,000.

a. If the company requires an 11 percent return on such undertakings, should the cemetery business be started?

b. The company is somewhat unsure about the assumption of a growth rate of 4 percent in its cash flows. At what constant growth rate would the company just break even if it still required a return of 11 percent on investment?

26. **Problems with IRR** [LO5] A project has the following cash flows:

Year	Cash Flow
0	$59,000
1	− 34,000
2	− 39,000

What is the IRR for this project? If the required return is 12 percent, should the firm accept the project? What is the NPV of this project? What is the NPV of the project if the required return is 0 percent? 24 percent? What is going on here? Sketch the NPV profile to help you with your answer.

27. **Problems with IRR** [LO5] McKeekin Corp. has a project with the following cash flows:

Year	Cash Flow
0	$25,000
1	− 11,000
2	7,000

What is the IRR of the project? What is happening here?

310 **PART 4** Capital Budgeting

28. **NPV and IRR** [LO1, 5] Anderson International Limited is evaluating a project in Erewhon. The project will create the following cash flows:

Year	Cash Flow
0	−$1,275,000
1	435,000
2	505,000
3	415,000
4	345,000

All cash flows will occur in Erewhon and are expressed in dollars. In an attempt to improve its economy, the Erewhonian government has declared that all cash flows created by a foreign company are "blocked" and must be reinvested with the government for one year. The reinvestment rate for these funds is 4 percent. If Anderson uses a required return of 11 percent on this project, what are the NPV and IRR of the project? Is the IRR you calculated the MIRR of the project? Why or why not?

EXCEL MASTER IT! PROBLEM

As you have already seen, Excel does not have a function to calculate the payback period, so you will create your own. Below, the cash flows for a project are shown. You need to calculate the payback period using two different methods.

a. Calculate the payback period in a table. The first three columns of the table will be the year, the cash flow for that year, and the cumulative cash flow. The fourth column will show the whole year for the payback. In other words, if the payback period is three-plus years, this column will have a 3, otherwise it will be a 0. The next column will calculate the fractional part of the payback period, or else it will display 0. The last column will add the previous two columns and display the final payback period calculation. You should also have a cell that displays the final payback period by itself and a cell that returns the correct accept or reject decision based on the payback criteria.

b. Write a nested IF statement that calculates the payback period using only the project cash flow column. The IF statement should return a value of "Never" if the project has no payback period. In contrast to the example we showed previously, the nested IF function should test for the payback period starting with shorter payback periods and working toward longer payback periods. Another cell should display the correct accept or reject decision based on the payback criteria.

t	Cash Flow
0	−$250,000
1	41,000
2	48,000
3	63,000
4	79,000
5	88,000
6	64,000
7	41,000
Required payback:	5

MINICASE

Bullock Gold Mining

Seth Bullock, the owner of Bullock Gold Mining, is evaluating a new gold mine in South Dakota. Dan Dority, the company's geologist, has just finished his analysis of the mine site. He has estimated that the mine would be productive for eight years, after which the gold would be completely mined. Dan has taken an estimate of the gold deposits to Alma Garrett, the company's financial officer. Alma has been asked by Seth to perform an analysis of the new mine and present her recommendation on whether the company should open the new mine.

Alma has used the estimates provided by Dan to determine the revenues that could be expected from the mine. She has also projected the expense of opening the mine and the annual operating expenses. If the company opens the mine, it will cost $635 million today, and it will have a cash outflow of $45 million nine years from today in costs associated with closing the mine and reclaiming the area surrounding it. The expected cash flows each year from the mine are shown in the table. Bullock Mining has a required return of 12 percent on all of its gold mines.

Year	Cash Flow
0	−$635,000,000
1	89,000,000
2	105,000,000
3	130,000,000
4	173,000,000
5	205,000,000
6	155,000,000
7	145,000,000
8	122,000,000
9	− 45,000,000

QUESTIONS

1. Construct a spreadsheet to calculate the payback period, internal rate of return, modified internal rate of return, and net present value of the proposed mine.

2. Based on your analysis, should the company open the mine?

3. Bonus question: Most spreadsheets do not have a built-in formula to calculate the payback period. Write a VBA script that calculates the payback period for a project.

Chapter

10 | Making Capital Investment Decisions

IS THERE GREEN IN GREEN? General Electric (GE) thinks so. Through its "Ecomagination" program, the company planned to double research and development spending on green products. By 2015, GE had invested over $13 billion in its Ecomagination program, and currently about one-half of the company's R&D budget is spent on green projects. As an example, GE's Evolution® Series Locomotive required over $600 million in development, but it allows railroads to move one ton of freight more than 480 miles with a single gallon of fuel. GE's green initiative seems to be paying off. Revenue from green products has totaled more than $230 billion since its launch in 2005, with $36 billion in 2015 alone. Even further, revenues from Ecomagination products were growing at twice the rate of the rest of the company's revenues. The company's internal commitment to green was increased when it announced its goal to decrease greenhouse gas emissions and water consumption by an additional 20 percent by 2020.

As you no doubt recognize from your study of the previous chapter, GE's decision to develop and market green technology represents a capital budgeting decision. In this chapter, we further investigate such decisions, how they are made, and how to look at them objectively.

This chapter follows up on our previous one by delving more deeply into capital budgeting. We have two main tasks. First, recall that in the last chapter, we saw that cash flow estimates are the critical input in a net present value analysis, but we didn't say much about where these cash flows come from; so we will now examine this question in some detail. Our second goal is to learn how to critically examine NPV estimates, and, in particular, how to evaluate the sensitivity of NPV estimates to assumptions made about the uncertain future.

Learning Objectives

After studying this chapter, you should be able to:

LO1 Determine the relevant cash flows for a proposed project.

LO2 Evaluate whether a project is acceptable.

LO3 Explain how to set a bid price for a project.

LO4 Evaluate the equivalent annual cost of a project.

For updates on the latest happenings in finance, visit fundamentalsofcorporatefinance.blogspot.com.

So far, we've covered various parts of the capital budgeting decision. Our task in this chapter is to start bringing these pieces together. In particular, we will show you how to "spread the numbers" for a proposed investment or project and, based on those numbers, make an initial assessment about whether the project should be undertaken.

In the discussion that follows, we focus on the process of setting up a discounted cash flow analysis. From the last chapter, we know that the projected future cash flows are the key element in such an evaluation. Accordingly, we emphasize working with financial and accounting information to come up with these figures.

In evaluating a proposed investment, we pay special attention to deciding what information is relevant to the decision at hand and what information is not. As we will see, it is easy to overlook important pieces of the capital budgeting puzzle.

We will wait until the next chapter to describe in detail how to go about evaluating the results of our discounted cash flow analysis. Also, where needed, we will assume that we know the relevant required return, or discount rate. We continue to defer in-depth discussion of this subject to Part 5.

Project Cash Flows: A First Look

10.1

The effect of taking a project is to change the firm's overall cash flows today and in the future. To evaluate a proposed investment, we must consider these changes in the firm's cash flows and then decide whether they add value to the firm. The first (and most important) step, therefore, is to decide which cash flows are relevant.

RELEVANT CASH FLOWS

What is a relevant cash flow for a project? The general principle is simple enough: A relevant cash flow for a project is a change in the firm's overall future cash flow that comes about as a direct consequence of the decision to take that project. Because the relevant cash flows are defined in terms of changes in, or increments to, the firm's existing cash flow, they are called the **incremental cash flows** associated with the project.

The concept of incremental cash flow is central to our analysis, so we will state a general definition and refer back to it as needed:

> The incremental cash flows for project evaluation consist of *any and all* changes in the firm's future cash flows that are a direct consequence of taking the project.

incremental cash flows
The difference between a firm's future cash flows with a project and those without the project.

This definition of incremental cash flows has an obvious and important corollary: Any cash flow that exists regardless of *whether or not* a project is undertaken is *not* relevant.

THE STAND-ALONE PRINCIPLE

In practice, it would be cumbersome to actually calculate the future total cash flows to the firm with and without a project, especially for a large firm. Fortunately, it is not really necessary to do so. Once we identify the effect of undertaking the proposed project on the firm's cash flows, we need focus only on the project's resulting incremental cash flows. This is called the **stand-alone principle**.

What the stand-alone principle says is that once we have determined the incremental cash flows from undertaking a project, we can view that project as a kind of "minifirm" with its own future revenues and costs, its own assets, and, of course, its own cash flows. We will then be primarily interested in comparing the cash flows from this minifirm to the cost of acquiring it. An important consequence of this approach is that we will be evaluating the proposed project purely on its own merits, in isolation from any other activities or projects.

stand-alone principle
The assumption that evaluation of a project may be based on the project's incremental cash flows.

> **Concept Questions**
>
> **10.1a**   What are the relevant incremental cash flows for project evaluation?
> **10.1b**   What is the stand-alone principle?

10.2   Incremental Cash Flows

We are concerned here with only cash flows that are incremental and that result from a project. Looking back at our general definition, we might think it would be easy enough to decide whether a cash flow is incremental. Even so, in a few situations it is easy to make mistakes. In this section, we describe some common pitfalls and how to avoid them.

SUNK COSTS

sunk cost
A cost that has already been incurred and cannot be removed and therefore should not be considered in an investment decision.

A **sunk cost**, by definition, is a cost we have already paid or have already incurred the liability to pay. Such a cost cannot be changed by the decision today to accept or reject a project. Put another way, the firm will have to pay this cost no matter what. Based on our general definition of incremental cash flow, such a cost is clearly irrelevant to the decision at hand. So, we will always be careful to exclude sunk costs from our analysis.

That a sunk cost is irrelevant seems obvious given our discussion. Nonetheless, it's easy to fall prey to the fallacy that a sunk cost should be associated with a project. Suppose General Milk Company hires a financial consultant to help evaluate whether a line of chocolate milk should be launched. When the consultant turns in the report, General Milk objects to the analysis because the consultant did not include the hefty consulting fee as a cost of the chocolate milk project.

Who is correct? By now, we know that the consulting fee is a sunk cost: It must be paid whether or not the chocolate milk line is actually launched (this is an attractive feature of the consulting business).

OPPORTUNITY COSTS

opportunity cost
The most valuable alternative that is given up if a particular investment is undertaken.

When we think of costs, we normally think of out-of-pocket costs—namely those that require us to actually spend some amount of cash. An **opportunity cost** is slightly different; it requires us to give up a benefit. A common situation arises in which a firm already owns some of the assets a proposed project will be using. For example, we might be thinking of converting an old rustic cotton mill we bought years ago for $100,000 into upmarket condominiums.

If we undertake this project, there will be no direct cash outflow associated with buying the old mill because we already own it. For purposes of evaluating the condo project, should we then treat the mill as "free"? The answer is no. The mill is a valuable resource used by the project. If we didn't use it here, we could do something else with it. Like what? The obvious answer is that, at a minimum, we could sell it. Using the mill for the condo complex has an opportunity cost: We give up the valuable opportunity to do something else with the mill.[1]

There is another issue here. Once we agree that the use of the mill has an opportunity cost, how much should we charge the condo project for this use? Given that we paid $100,000, it might seem that we should charge this amount to the condo project. Is this correct? The answer is no, and the reason is based on our discussion concerning sunk costs.

The fact that we paid $100,000 some years ago is irrelevant. That cost is sunk. At a minimum, the opportunity cost that we charge the project is what the mill would sell for today

---

[1]Economists sometimes use the acronym TANSTAAFL, which is short for "There ain't no such thing as a free lunch," to describe the fact that only very rarely is something truly free.

(net of any selling costs) because this is the amount we give up by using the mill instead of selling it.[2]

SIDE EFFECTS

Remember that the incremental cash flows for a project include all the resulting changes in the *firm's* future cash flows. It would not be unusual for a project to have side, or spillover, effects, both good and bad. For example, in 2017, the time between the theatrical release of a feature film and the release of the DVD had shrunk to 17 weeks compared to 29 weeks in 1998, although several studios have shorter times. This shortened release time was blamed for at least part of the decline in movie theater box office receipts. Of course, retailers cheered the move because it was credited with increasing DVD sales. A negative impact on the cash flows of an existing product from the introduction of a new product is called **erosion**.[3] In this case, the cash flows from the new line should be adjusted downward to reflect lost profits on other lines.

erosion
The cash flows of a new project that come at the expense of a firm's existing projects.

In accounting for erosion, it is important to recognize that any sales lost as a result of launching a new product might be lost anyway because of future competition. Erosion is relevant only when the sales would not otherwise be lost.

Side effects show up in a lot of different ways. For example, one of The Walt Disney Company's concerns when it built Euro Disney (now known as Disneyland Paris) was that the new park would drain visitors from the Florida park, a popular vacation destination for Europeans.

There are beneficial spillover effects, of course. For example, you might think that Hewlett-Packard would have been concerned when the price of a printer that sold for $500 to $600 in 1994 declined to below $100 by 2017, but such was not the case. HP realized that the big money is in the consumables that printer owners buy to keep their printers going, such as ink-jet cartridges, laser toner cartridges, and special paper. The profit margins for these products are substantial.

NET WORKING CAPITAL

Normally a project will require that the firm invest in net working capital in addition to long-term assets. For example, a project will generally need some amount of cash on hand to pay any expenses that arise. In addition, a project will need an initial investment in inventories and accounts receivable (to cover credit sales). Some of the financing for this will be in the form of amounts owed to suppliers (accounts payable), but the firm will have to supply the balance. This balance represents the investment in net working capital.

It's easy to overlook an important feature of net working capital in capital budgeting. As a project winds down, inventories are sold, receivables are collected, bills are paid, and cash balances can be drawn down. These activities free up the net working capital originally invested. So the firm's investment in project net working capital closely resembles a loan. The firm supplies working capital at the beginning and recovers it toward the end.

FINANCING COSTS

In analyzing a proposed investment, we will *not* include interest paid or any other financing costs such as dividends or principal repaid because we are interested in the cash flow generated by the assets of the project. As we mentioned in Chapter 2, interest paid, for example, is a component of cash flow to creditors, not cash flow from assets.

---

[2]If the asset in question is unique, then the opportunity cost might be higher because there might be other valuable projects we could undertake that would use it. However, if the asset in question is of a type that is routinely bought and sold (a used car, perhaps), then the opportunity cost is always the going price in the market because that is the cost of buying another similar asset.

[3]More colorfully, erosion is sometimes called *piracy* or *cannibalism*.

More generally, our goal in project evaluation is to compare the cash flow from a project to the cost of acquiring that project in order to estimate NPV. The particular mixture of debt and equity a firm actually chooses to use in financing a project is a managerial variable and primarily determines how project cash flow is divided between owners and creditors. This is not to say that financing arrangements are unimportant. They are just something to be analyzed separately. We will cover this in later chapters.

OTHER ISSUES

There are some other things to watch out for. First, we are interested only in measuring cash flow. Moreover, we are interested in measuring it when it actually occurs, not when it accrues in an accounting sense. Second, we are always interested in *aftertax* cash flow because taxes are definitely a cash outflow. In fact, whenever we write *incremental cash flows*, we mean aftertax incremental cash flows. Remember, aftertax cash flow and accounting profit, or net income, are entirely different things.

Concept Questions

10.2a   What is a sunk cost? An opportunity cost?

10.2b   Explain what erosion is and why it is relevant.

10.2c   Explain why interest paid is an irrelevant cash flow for project evaluation.

10.3 Pro Forma Financial Statements and Project Cash Flows

Excel Master It!

Excel Master coverage online

The first thing we need when we begin evaluating a proposed investment is a set of pro forma, or projected, financial statements. Given these, we can develop the projected cash flows from the project. Once we have the cash flows, we can estimate the value of the project using the techniques we described in the previous chapter.

GETTING STARTED: PRO FORMA FINANCIAL STATEMENTS

pro forma financial statements
Financial statements projecting future years' operations.

Pro forma financial statements are a convenient and easily understood means of summarizing much of the relevant information for a project. To prepare these statements, we will need estimates of quantities such as unit sales, the selling price per unit, the variable cost per unit, and total fixed costs. We will also need to know the total investment required, including any investment in net working capital.

To illustrate, suppose we think we can sell 50,000 cans of shark attractant per year at a price of $4 per can. It costs us about $2.50 per can to make the attractant, and a new product such as this one typically has only a three-year life (perhaps because the customer base dwindles rapidly). We require a 20 percent return on new products.

Fixed costs for the project, including such things as rent on the production facility, will run $17,430 per year.[4] Further, we will need to invest a total of $90,000 in manufacturing equipment. For simplicity, we will assume that this $90,000 will be 100 percent depreciated over the three-year life of the project.[5] Furthermore, the cost of removing the equipment will roughly equal its actual value in three years, so it will be essentially worthless on

---

[4]By *fixed cost*, we literally mean a cash outflow that will occur regardless of the level of sales. This should not be confused with some sort of accounting period charge.

[5]We will also assume that a full year's depreciation can be taken in the first year.

Sales (50,000 units at $4/unit)	$200,000
Variable costs ($2.50/unit)	125,000
Fixed costs	17,430
Depreciation ($90,000/3)	30,000
EBIT	$ 27,570
Taxes (21%)	5,790
Net income	$ 21,780

TABLE 10.1

Projected Income Statement, Shark Attractant Project

	Year			
	0	1	2	3
Net working capital	$ 20,000	$20,000	$20,000	$20,000
Net fixed assets	90,000	60,000	30,000	0
Total investment	$110,000	$80,000	$50,000	$20,000

TABLE 10.2

Projected Capital Requirements, Shark Attractant Project

a market value basis as well. Finally, the project will require an initial $20,000 investment in net working capital, and the tax rate is 21 percent.

In Table 10.1, we organize these initial projections by first preparing the pro forma income statement. Once again, notice that we have *not* deducted any interest expense. This will always be so. As we described earlier, interest paid is a financing expense, not a component of operating cash flow.

We can also prepare a series of abbreviated balance sheets that show the capital requirements for the project as we've done in Table 10.2. Here we have net working capital of $20,000 in each year. Fixed assets are $90,000 at the start of the project's life (Year 0), and they decline by the $30,000 in depreciation each year, ending up at zero. Notice that the total investment given here for future years is the total book, or accounting, value—not market value.

At this point, we need to start converting this accounting information into cash flows. We consider how to do this next.

PROJECT CASH FLOWS

To develop the cash flows from a project, we need to recall (from Chapter 2) that cash flow from assets has three components: Operating cash flow, capital spending, and changes in net working capital. To evaluate a project, or minifirm, we need to estimate each of these.

Once we have estimates of the components of cash flow, we will calculate cash flow for our minifirm just as we did in Chapter 2 for an entire firm:

Project cash flow = Project operating cash flow

- Project change in net working capital

- Project capital spending

We consider these components next.

Project Operating Cash Flow   To determine the operating cash flow associated with a project, we first need to recall the definition of operating cash flow:

Operating cash flow = Earnings before interest and taxes

+ Depreciation

- Taxes

TABLE 10.3

Projected Income
Statement,
Abbreviated, Shark
Attractant Project

Sales	$200,000
Variable costs	125,000
Fixed costs	17,430
Depreciation	30,000
EBIT	$ 27,570
Taxes (21%)	5,790
Net income	$ 21,780

TABLE 10.4

Projected Operating
Cash Flow, Shark
Attractant Project

EBIT	$27,570
Depreciation	+ 30,000
Taxes	− 5,790
Operating cash flow	$51,780

TABLE 10.5

Projected Total Cash
Flows, Shark Attractant
Project

	Year			
	0	1	2	3
Operating cash flow		$51,780	$51,780	$51,780
Changes in NWC	−$ 20,000			+ 20,000
Capital spending	− 90,000			
Total project cash flow	−$110,000	$51,780	$51,780	$71,780

To illustrate the calculation of operating cash flow, we will use the projected information from the shark attractant project. For ease of reference, Table 10.3 repeats the income statement in more abbreviated form.

Given the income statement in Table 10.3, calculating the operating cash flow is straightforward. As we see in Table 10.4, projected operating cash flow for the shark attractant project is $51,780.

Project Net Working Capital and Capital Spending We next need to take care of the fixed asset and net working capital requirements. Based on our balance sheets, we know that the firm must spend $90,000 up front for fixed assets and invest an additional $20,000 in net working capital. The immediate outflow is a total of $110,000. At the end of the project's life, the fixed assets will be worthless, but the firm will recover the $20,000 that was tied up in working capital.[6] This will lead to a $20,000 *inflow* in the last year.

On a purely mechanical level, notice that whenever we have an investment in net working capital, that same investment has to be recovered; in other words, the same number needs to appear at some time in the future with the opposite sign.

PROJECTED TOTAL CASH FLOW AND VALUE

Given the information we've accumulated, we can finish the preliminary cash flow analysis as illustrated in Table 10.5.

---

[6]In reality, the firm would probably recover something less than 100 percent of this amount because of bad debts, inventory loss, and so on. If we wanted to, we could just assume that, for example, only 90 percent was recovered and proceed from there.

Now that we have cash flow projections, we are ready to apply the various criteria we discussed in the last chapter. First, the NPV at the 20 percent required return is:

$$NPV = -\$110{,}000 + 51{,}780/1.2 + 51{,}780/1.2^2 + 71{,}780/1.2^3$$
$$= \$10{,}648$$

Based on these projections, the project creates over \$10,000 in value and should be accepted. Also, the return on this investment obviously exceeds 20 percent (because the NPV is positive at 20 percent). After some trial and error, we find that the IRR works out to be about 25.8 percent.

In addition, if required, we could calculate the payback and the average accounting return, or AAR. Inspection of the cash flows shows that the payback on this project is a little over two years (verify that it's about 2.1 years).[7]

From the last chapter, we know that the AAR is average net income divided by average book value. The net income each year is \$21,780. The average (in thousands) of the four book values (from Table 10.2) for total investment is (\$110 + 80 + 50 + 20)/4 = \$65. So the AAR is \$21,780/\$65,000 = .3351, or 33.51 percent.[8] We've already seen that the return on this investment (the IRR) is about 26 percent. The fact that the AAR is larger illustrates again why the AAR cannot be meaningfully interpreted as the return on a project.

Concept Questions

10.3a   What is the definition of project operating cash flow? How does this differ from net income?

10.3b   For the shark attractant project, why did we add back the firm's net working capital investment in the final year?

More about Project Cash Flow   10.4

In this section, we take a closer look at some aspects of project cash flow. In particular, we discuss project net working capital in more detail. We then examine current tax laws regarding depreciation. Finally, we work through a more involved example of the capital investment decision.

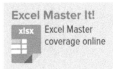

Excel Master It!
Excel Master coverage online

A CLOSER LOOK AT NET WORKING CAPITAL

In calculating operating cash flow, we did not explicitly consider the fact that some of our sales might be on credit. Also, we may not have actually paid some of the costs shown. In either case, the cash flow in question would not yet have occurred. We show here that these possibilities are not a problem as long as we don't forget to include changes in net working capital in our analysis. This discussion emphasizes the importance and the effect of doing so.

---

[7]We're guilty of a minor inconsistency here. When we calculated the NPV and the IRR, we assumed that all the cash flows occurred at end of year. When we calculated the payback, we assumed that the cash flows occurred uniformly throughout the year.

[8]Notice that the average total book value is not the initial total of \$110,000 divided by 2. The reason is that the \$20,000 in working capital doesn't "depreciate."

Suppose that during a particular year of a project we have the following simplified income statement:

Sales	$500
Costs	310
Net income	$190

Depreciation and taxes are zero. No fixed assets are purchased during the year. Also, to illustrate a point, we assume that the only components of net working capital are accounts receivable and payable. The beginning and ending amounts for these accounts are as follows:

	Beginning of Year	End of Year	Change
Accounts receivable	$880	$910	+$30
Accounts payable	550	605	+ 55
Net working capital	$330	$305	−$25

Based on this information, what is total cash flow for the year? We can first just mechanically apply what we have been discussing to come up with the answer. Operating cash flow in this particular case is the same as EBIT because there are no taxes or depreciation; thus, it equals $190. Also, notice that net working capital actually *declined* by $25. This just means that $25 was freed up during the year. There was no capital spending, so the total cash flow for the year is:

$$\text{Total cash flow} = \text{Operating cash flow} - \text{Change in NWC} - \text{Capital spending}$$
$$= \$190 - (-25) - 0$$
$$= \$215$$

Now, we know that this $215 total cash flow has to be "dollars in" less "dollars out" for the year. We could therefore ask a different question: What were cash revenues for the year? Also, what were cash costs?

To determine cash revenues, we need to look more closely at net working capital. During the year, we had sales of $500. However, accounts receivable rose by $30 over the same time period. What does this mean? The $30 increase tells us that sales exceeded collections by $30. In other words, we haven't yet received the cash from $30 of the $500 in sales. As a result, our cash inflow is $500 − 30 = $470. In general, cash income is sales minus the increase in accounts receivable.

Cash outflows can be similarly determined. We show costs of $310 on the income statement, but accounts payable increased by $55 during the year. This means that we have not yet paid $55 of the $310, so cash costs for the period are just $310 − 55 = $255. In other words, in this case, cash costs equal costs less the increase in accounts payable.[9]

Putting this information together, we calculate that cash inflows less cash outflows are $470 − 255 = $215, just as we had before. Notice that:

$$\text{Cash flow} = \text{Cash inflow} - \text{Cash outflow}$$
$$= (\$500 - 30) - (310 - 55)$$
$$= (\$500 - 310) - (30 - 55)$$
$$= \text{Operating cash flow} - \text{Change in NWC}$$
$$= \$190 - (-25)$$
$$= \$215$$

---

[9]If there were other accounts, we might have to make some further adjustments. For example, a net increase in inventory would be a cash outflow.

IN THEIR OWN WORDS ...

Samuel Weaver on Capital Budgeting at The Hershey Company

The capital program at The Hershey Company and most Fortune 500 or Fortune 1,000 companies involves a three-phase approach: Planning or budgeting, evaluation, and postcompletion reviews.

The first phase involves identification of likely projects at strategic planning time. These are selected to support the strategic objectives of the corporation. This identification is generally broad in scope with minimal financial evaluation attached. Projects are classified as new product, cost savings, capacity expansion, etc. As the planning process focuses more closely on the short-term plans (or budgets), major capital expenditures are discussed more rigorously. Project costs are more closely honed, and specific projects may be reconsidered.

Each project is then individually reviewed and authorized. Planning, developing, and refining cash flows underlie capital analysis at Hershey. Once the cash flows have been determined, the application of capital evaluation techniques such as those using net present value, internal rate of return, and payback period is routine. Presentation of the results is enhanced using sensitivity analysis, which plays a major role for management in assessing the critical assumptions and resulting impact.

The final phase relates to postcompletion reviews in which the original forecasts of the project's performance are compared to actual results and/or revised expectations.

Capital expenditure analysis is only as good as the assumptions that underlie the project. The old cliché of GIGO (garbage in, garbage out) applies in this case. Incremental cash flows primarily result from incremental sales or margin improvements (cost savings). For the most part, a range of incremental cash flows can be identified from marketing research or engineering studies. However, for a number of projects, correctly discerning the implications and the relevant cash flows is analytically challenging. For example, when a new product is introduced and is expected to generate millions of dollars' worth of sales, the appropriate analysis focuses on the incremental sales after accounting for cannibalization of existing products.

One of the problems that we face at Hershey deals with the application of net present value, NPV, versus internal rate of return, IRR. NPV offers us the correct investment indication when dealing with mutually exclusive alternatives. However, decision makers at all levels sometimes find it difficult to comprehend the result. Specifically, an NPV of, say, $535,000 needs to be interpreted. It is not enough to know that the NPV is positive or even that it is more positive than an alternative. Decision makers seek to determine a level of "comfort" regarding how profitable the investment is by relating it to other standards.

Although the IRR may provide a misleading indication of which project to select, the result is provided in a way that can be interpreted by all parties. The resulting IRR can be mentally compared to expected inflation, current borrowing rates, the cost of capital, an equity portfolio's return, and so on. An IRR of, say, 18 percent is readily interpretable by management. Perhaps this ease of understanding is why surveys indicate that many Fortune 500 or Fortune 1,000 companies use the IRR method (in conjunction with NPV) as a primary evaluation technique.

In addition to the NPV versus IRR problem, there are a limited number of projects for which traditional capital expenditure analysis is difficult to apply because the cash flows can't be determined. When new computer equipment is purchased, an office building is renovated, or a parking lot is repaved, it is essentially impossible to identify the cash flows, so the use of traditional evaluation techniques is limited. These types of "capital expenditure" decisions are made using other techniques that hinge on management's judgment.

Samuel Weaver, Ph.D., is the former director, financial planning and analysis, for Hershey. He is a certified management accountant and certified financial manager. His position combined the theoretical with the pragmatic and involved the analysis of many different facets of finance in addition to capital expenditure analysis.

More generally, this example illustrates that including net working capital changes in our calculations has the effect of adjusting for the discrepancy between accounting sales and costs and actual cash receipts and payments.

Cash Collections and Costs	**EXAMPLE 10.1**

For the year just completed, the Combat Wombat Telestat Co. (CWT) reports sales of $998 and costs of $734. You have collected the following beginning and ending balance sheet information:

	Beginning	Ending
Accounts receivable	$100	$110
Inventory	100	80
Accounts payable	100	70
Net working capital	$100	$120

Based on these figures, what are cash inflows? Cash outflows? What happened to each account? What is net cash flow?

Sales were $998, but receivables rose by $10. So cash collections were $10 less than sales, or $988. Costs were $734, but inventories fell by $20. This means that we didn't replace $20 worth of inventory, so costs are actually overstated by this amount. Also, payables fell by $30. This means that, on a net basis, we actually paid our suppliers $30 more than we received from them, resulting in a $30 understatement of costs. Adjusting for these events, we calculate that cash costs are $734 − 20 + 30 = $744. Net cash flow is $988 − 744 = $244.

Finally, notice that net working capital increased by $20 overall. We can check our answer by noting that the original accounting sales less costs (= $998 − 734) are $264. In addition, CWT spent $20 on net working capital, so the net result is a cash flow of $264 − 20 = $244, as we calculated.

DEPRECIATION

As we note elsewhere, accounting depreciation is a noncash deduction. As a result, depreciation has cash flow consequences only because it influences the tax bill. The way that depreciation is computed for tax purposes is the relevant method for capital investment decisions. Not surprisingly, the procedures are governed by tax law. We now discuss some specifics of the depreciation system enacted by the Tax Reform Act of 1986. This system is a modification of the **accelerated cost recovery system (ACRS)** instituted in 1981.

accelerated cost recovery system (ACRS)
A depreciation method under U.S. tax law allowing for the accelerated write-off of property under various classifications.

Modified ACRS Depreciation (MACRS)   Calculating depreciation is normally mechanical. Although there are a number of *ifs*, *ands*, and *buts* involved, the basic idea under MACRS is that every asset is assigned to a particular class. An asset's class establishes its life for tax purposes. Once an asset's tax life is determined, the depreciation for each year is computed by multiplying the cost of the asset by a fixed percentage.[10] The expected salvage value (what we think the asset will be worth when we dispose of it) and the expected economic life (how long we expect the asset to be in service) are not explicitly considered in the calculation of depreciation.

Some typical depreciation classes are given in Table 10.6, and associated percentages (as specified by the IRS) are shown in Table 10.7.[11]

A nonresidential real property, such as an office building, is depreciated over 31.5 years using straight-line depreciation. A residential real property, such as an apartment building, is depreciated straight-line over 27.5 years. Remember that land cannot be depreciated.[12]

---

[10]Under certain circumstances, the cost of the asset may be adjusted before computing depreciation. The result is called the *depreciable basis*, and depreciation is calculated using this number instead of the actual cost.

[11]For the curious, these depreciation percentages are derived from a double-declining balance scheme with a switch to straight-line when the latter becomes advantageous. Further, there is a half-year convention, meaning that all assets are assumed to be placed in service midway through the tax year. This convention is maintained unless more than 40 percent of an asset's cost is incurred in the final quarter. In this case, a midquarter convention is used. The odd-looking rounding is courtesy of the IRS.

[12]There are, however, depletion allowances for firms in extraction-type lines of business (such as mining). These are somewhat similar to depreciation allowances.

Class	Examples
Three-year	Equipment used in research
Five-year	Autos, computers
Seven-year	Most industrial equipment

TABLE 10.6

Modified ACRS Property Classes

	Property Class		
Year	Three-Year	Five-Year	Seven-Year
1	33.33%	20.00%	14.29%
2	44.45	32.00	24.49
3	14.81	19.20	17.49
4	7.41	11.52	12.49
5		11.52	8.93
6		5.76	8.92
7			8.93
8			4.46

TABLE 10.7

Modified ACRS Depreciation Allowances

To illustrate how depreciation is calculated, we consider an automobile costing \$12,000. Autos are normally classified as five-year property. Looking at Table 10.7, we see that the relevant figure for the first year of a five-year asset is 20 percent.[13] The depreciation in the first year is thus \$12,000 × .20 = \$2,400. The relevant percentage in the second year is 32 percent, so the depreciation in the second year is \$12,000 × .32 = \$3,840, and so on. We can summarize these calculations as follows:

Year	MACRS Percentage	Depreciation		
1	20.00%	.2000 × \$12,000 =		\$ 2,400.00
2	32.00	.3200 × 12,000 =		3,840.00
3	19.20	.1920 × 12,000 =		2,304.00
4	11.52	.1152 × 12,000 =		1,382.40
5	11.52	.1152 × 12,000 =		1,382.40
6	5.76	.0576 × 12,000 =		691.20
	100.00%			\$12,000.00

Notice that the MACRS percentages sum up to 100 percent. As a result, we write off 100 percent of the cost of the asset, or \$12,000 in this case.

Bonus Depreciation   For a number of years prior to 2018, various tax rules and regulations were enacted that allowed "bonus" depreciation. Based on the Protecting Americans from Tax Hikes (PATH) Act of 2015, the size of the bonus in 2017 was 50%. What this means is that a firm can take a depreciation deduction of 50% of the cost on an eligible asset in the first year and then depreciate the remaining 50% using the MACRS schedules as we have just described. Significantly, in late 2017, Congress passed the Tax Cuts and Jobs Act, which increased the bonus depreciation to 100% for 2018, lasting until the end of 2022. After that it, drops by 20% per year until it reaches zero after 2026. The implication is that most firms will not use the MACRS schedules until 2023 unless they wish to (taking the bonus depreciation is optional). Of course, future legislation may change things.

Book Value versus Market Value   In calculating depreciation under current tax law, the economic life and future market value of the asset are not an issue. As a result, the

---

[13]It may appear odd that five-year property is depreciated over six years. The tax accounting reason is that it is assumed we have the asset for only six months in the first year and, consequently, six months in the last year. As a result, there are five 12-month periods, but we have some depreciation in each of six different tax years.

TABLE 10.8

MACRS Book Values

Year	Beginning Book Value	Depreciation	Ending Book Value
1	$12,000.00	$2,400.00	$9,600.00
2	9,600.00	3,840.00	5,760.00
3	5,760.00	2,304.00	3,456.00
4	3,456.00	1,382.40	2,073.60
5	2,073.60	1,382.40	691.20
6	691.20	691.20	.00

book value of an asset can differ substantially from its actual market value. For example, with our $12,000 car, book value after the first year is $12,000 less the first year's depreciation of $2,400, or $9,600. The remaining book values are summarized in Table 10.8. After six years, the book value of the car is zero.

Suppose we wanted to sell the car after five years. Based on historical averages, it would be worth, say, 25 percent of the purchase price, or .25 × $12,000 = $3,000. If we actually sold it for this, then we would have to pay taxes at the ordinary income tax rate on the difference between the sale price of $3,000 and the book value of $691.20. For a corporation in the 21 percent bracket, the tax liability would be .21 × $2,308.80 = $484.85.[14]

The reason taxes must be paid in this case is that the difference between market value and book value is "excess" depreciation, and it must be "recaptured" when the asset is sold. What this means is that, as it turns out, we overdepreciated the asset by $3,000 − 691.20 = $2,308.80. Because we deducted $2,308.80 too much in depreciation, we paid $484.85 too little in taxes, and we have to make up the difference.

Notice that this is *not* a tax on a capital gain. As a general (albeit rough) rule, a capital gain occurs only if the market price exceeds the original cost. However, what is and what is not a capital gain is ultimately up to taxing authorities, and the specific rules can be complex. We will ignore capital gains taxes for the most part.

Finally, if the book value exceeds the market value, then the difference is treated as a loss for tax purposes. For example, if we sell the car after two years for $4,000, then the book value exceeds the market value by $1,760. In this case, a tax savings of .21 × $1,760 = $369.60 occurs.

---

[14]The rules are different and more complicated with real property. Essentially, in this case, only the difference between the actual book value and the book value that would have existed if straight-line depreciation had been used is recaptured. Anything above the straight-line book value is considered a capital gain.

EXAMPLE 10.2   **MACRS Depreciation**

The Staple Supply Co. has just purchased a new computerized information system with an installed cost of $160,000. The computer is treated as five-year property. What are the yearly depreciation allowances? Based on historical experience, we think that the system will be worth only $10,000 when Staple gets rid of it in four years. What are the tax consequences of the sale? What is the total aftertax cash flow from the sale?

The yearly depreciation allowances are calculated by multiplying $160,000 by the five-year percentages found in Table 10.7:

Year	MACRS Percentage	Depreciation		Ending Book Value
1	20.00%	.2000 × $160,000 =	$ 32,000	$128,000
2	32.00	.3200 × 160,000 =	51,200	76,800
3	19.20	.1920 × 160,000 =	30,720	46,080
4	11.52	.1152 × 160,000 =	18,432	27,648
5	11.52	.1152 × 160,000 =	18,432	9,216
6	5.76	.0576 × 160,000 =	9,216	0
	100.00%		$160,000	

Notice that we have also computed the book value of the system as of the end of each year. The book value at the end of Year 4 is $27,648. If Staple sells the system for $10,000 at that time, it will have a loss of $17,648 (the difference) for tax purposes. This loss, of course, is like depreciation because it isn't a cash expense.

What really happens? Two things. First, Staple gets $10,000 from the buyer. Second, it saves .21 × $17,648 = $3,706 in taxes. So, the total aftertax cash flow from the sale is a $13,706 cash inflow.

AN EXAMPLE: THE MAJESTIC MULCH AND COMPOST COMPANY (MMCC)

At this point, we want to go through a somewhat more involved capital budgeting analysis. Keep in mind as you read that the basic approach here is exactly the same as that in the shark attractant example used earlier. We have just added some real-world detail (and a lot more numbers).

MMCC is investigating the feasibility of a new line of power mulching tools aimed at the growing number of home composters. Based on exploratory conversations with buyers for large garden shops, MMCC projects unit sales as follows:

Year	Unit Sales
1	3,000
2	5,000
3	6,000
4	6,500
5	6,000
6	5,000
7	4,000
8	3,000

The new power mulcher will sell for $120 per unit to start. When the competition catches up after three years, however, MMCC anticipates that the price will drop to $110.

The power mulcher project will require $20,000 in net working capital at the start. Subsequently, total net working capital at the end of each year will be about 15 percent of sales for that year. The variable cost per unit is $60, and total fixed costs are $25,000 per year.

It will cost about $800,000 to buy the equipment necessary to begin production. This investment is primarily in industrial equipment, which qualifies as seven-year MACRS property. We assume there is no bonus depreciation, so we apply MACRS to the entire cost. The equipment will actually be worth about 20 percent of its cost in eight years, or .20 × $800,000 = $160,000. The relevant tax rate is 21 percent, and the required return is 15 percent. Based on this information, should MMCC proceed?

Operating Cash Flows   There is a lot of information here that we need to organize. The first thing we can do is calculate projected sales. Sales in the first year are projected at 3,000 units at $120 apiece, or $360,000 total. The remaining figures are shown in Table 10.9.

Next, we compute the depreciation on the $800,000 investment in Table 10.10 (remember, there is no bonus depreciation in this case). With this information, we can prepare the pro forma income statements, as shown in Table 10.11. From here, computing the operating cash flows is straightforward. The results are shown in the first part of Table 10.13.

TABLE 10.9

**Projected Revenues,
Power Mulcher Project**

Year	Unit Price	Unit Sales	Revenues
1	$120	3,000	$360,000
2	120	5,000	600,000
3	120	6,000	720,000
4	110	6,500	715,000
5	110	6,000	660,000
6	110	5,000	550,000
7	110	4,000	440,000
8	110	3,000	330,000

TABLE 10.10

**Annual Depreciation,
Power Mulcher Project**

Year	MACRS Percentage	Depreciation	Ending Book Value
1	14.29%	.1429 × $800,000 = $114,320	$685,680
2	24.49	.2449 × 800,000 = 195,920	489,760
3	17.49	.1749 × 800,000 = 139,920	349,840
4	12.49	.1249 × 800,000 = 99,920	249,920
5	8.93	.0893 × 800,000 = 71,440	178,480
6	8.92	.0892 × 800,000 = 71,360	107,120
7	8.93	.0893 × 800,000 = 71,440	35,680
8	4.46	.0446 × 800,000 = 35,680	0
	100.00%	$800,000	

TABLE 10.11 Projected Income Statements, Power Mulcher Project

	Year							
	1	2	3	4	5	6	7	8
Unit price	$ 120	$ 120	$ 120	$ 110	$ 110	$ 110	$ 110	$ 110
Unit sales	3,000	5,000	6,000	6,500	6,000	5,000	4,000	3,000
Revenues	$360,000	$600,000	$720,000	$715,000	$660,000	$550,000	$440,000	$330,000
Variable costs	180,000	300,000	360,000	390,000	360,000	300,000	240,000	180,000
Fixed costs	25,000	25,000	25,000	25,000	25,000	25,000	25,000	25,000
Depreciation	114,320	195,920	139,920	99,920	71,440	71,360	71,440	35,680
EBIT	$ 40,680	$ 79,080	$195,080	$200,080	$203,560	$153,640	$103,560	$ 89,320
Taxes (21%)	8,543	16,607	40,967	42,017	42,748	32,264	21,748	18,757
Net income	$ 32,137	$ 62,473	$154,113	$158,063	$160,812	$121,376	$ 81,812	$ 70,563

Change in NWC   Now that we have the operating cash flows, we need to determine the changes in NWC. By assumption, net working capital requirements change as sales change. In each year, MMCC will generally either add to or recover some of its project net working capital. Recalling that NWC starts out at $20,000 and then rises to 15 percent of sales, we can calculate the amount of NWC for each year as shown in Table 10.12.

As illustrated, during the first year, net working capital grows from $20,000 to .15 × $360,000 = $54,000. The increase in net working capital for the year is thus $54,000 − 20,000 = $34,000. The remaining figures are calculated in the same way.

Year	Revenues	Net Working Capital	Cash Flow
0		$ 20,000	−$20,000
1	$360,000	54,000	− 34,000
2	600,000	90,000	− 36,000
3	720,000	108,000	− 18,000
4	715,000	107,250	750
5	660,000	99,000	8,250
6	550,000	82,500	16,500
7	440,000	66,000	16,500
8	330,000	49,500	16,500

TABLE 10.12

Changes in Net Working Capital, Power Mulcher Project

TABLE 10.13   Projected Cash Flows, Power Mulcher Project

					Year				
	0	1	2	3	4	5	6	7	8
I. Operating Cash Flow									
EBIT		$ 40,680	$ 79,080	$195,080	$200,080	$203,560	$153,640	$103,560	$ 89,320
Depreciation		114,320	195,920	139,920	99,920	71,440	71,360	71,440	35,680
Taxes		− 8,543	− 16,607	− 40,967	− 42,017	− 42,748	− 32,264	− 21,748	− 18,757
Operating cash flow		$146,457	$258,393	$294,033	$257,983	$232,252	$192,736	$153,252	$106,243
II. Net Working Capital									
Initial NWC	−$ 20,000								
Change in NWC		−$ 34,000	−$ 36,000	−$ 18,000	$ 750	$ 8,250	$ 16,500	$ 16,500	$ 16,500
NWC recovery									49,500
Total change in NWC	−$ 20,000	−$ 34,000	−$ 36,000	−$ 18,000	$ 750	$ 8,250	$ 16,500	$ 16,500	$ 66,000
III. Capital Spending									
Initial outlay	−$800,000								
Aftertax salvage									$126,400
Capital spending	−$800,000								$126,400

Remember that an increase in net working capital is a cash outflow, so we use a negative sign in this table to indicate an additional investment that the firm makes in net working capital. A positive sign represents net working capital returning to the firm. For example, $16,500 in NWC flows back to the firm in Year 6. Over the project's life, net working capital builds to a peak of $108,000 and declines from there as sales begin to drop off.

We show the result for changes in net working capital in the second part of Table 10.13. Notice that at the end of the project's life, there is $49,500 in net working capital still to be recovered. Therefore, in the last year, the project returns $16,500 of NWC during the year and then returns the remaining $49,500 at the end of the year, for a total of $66,000.

TABLE 10.14   Projected Total Cash Flows, Power Mulcher Project

	Year								
	0	1	2	3	4	5	6	7	8
Operating cash flow		$146,457	$258,393	$ 294,033	$257,983	$232,252	$192,736	$153,252	$ 106,243
Change in NWC	–$ 20,000	– 34,000	– 36,000	– 18,000	750	8,250	16,500	16,500	66,000
Capital spending	– 800,000								126,400
Total project cash flow	–$820,000	$112,457	$222,393	$276,033	$258,733	$240,502	$209,236	$169,752	$298,643
Cumulative cash flow	–$820,000	–$707,543	–$485,150	–$209,116	–$ 49,617	$290,119	$499,355	$669,107	$967,750
Discounted cash flow @ 15%	– 820,000	97,789	168,161	181,496	147,932	119,572	90,458	63,816	97,627

Net present value (15%) = $146,852

Internal rate of return   = 19.86%

Payback   = 3.81 years

Capital Spending   Finally, we have to account for the long-term capital invested in the project. In this case, MMCC invests $800,000 at Year 0. By assumption, this equipment will be worth $160,000 at the end of the project. It will have a book value of zero at that time. As we discussed earlier, this $160,000 excess of market value over book value is taxable, so the aftertax proceeds will be $160,000 × (1 − .21) = $126,400. These figures are shown in the third part of Table 10.13.

Total Cash Flow and Value   We now have all the cash flow pieces, and we put them together in Table 10.14. If you notice, the project cash flows each year are the same as the cash flow from assets that we calculated in Chapter 3. In addition to the total project cash flows, we have calculated the cumulative cash flows and the discounted cash flows. At this point, it's essentially plug-and-chug to calculate the net present value, internal rate of return, and payback.

If we sum the discounted flows and the initial investment, the net present value (at 15 percent) works out to be $146,852. This is positive, so, based on these preliminary projections, the power mulcher project is acceptable. The internal, or DCF, rate of return is greater than 15 percent because the NPV is positive. It works out to be 19.86 percent, again indicating that the project is acceptable.

Looking at the cumulative cash flows, we can see that the project is paid back between three and four years because the table shows that the cumulative cash flow becomes positive at that time. As indicated, the fractional year works out to be $209,116/$258,733 = .81, so the payback is 3.81 years. We can't say whether or not this is good because we don't have a benchmark for MMCC. This is the usual problem with payback periods.

Conclusion   ˙This completes our preliminary DCF analysis. Where do we go from here? If we have a great deal of confidence in our projections, there is no further analysis to be done. MMCC should begin production and marketing immediately. It is unlikely that this will be the case. It is important to remember that the result of our analysis is an estimate of NPV, and we will usually have less than complete confidence in our projections. This means we have more work to do. In particular, we will almost surely want to spend some time evaluating the quality of our estimates. We will take up this subject in the next chapter. For now, we look at some alternative definitions of operating cash flow, and we illustrate some different cases that arise in capital budgeting.

> **Concept Questions**
>
> **10.4a** Why is it important to consider changes in net working capital in developing cash flows? What is the effect of doing so?
>
> **10.4b** How is depreciation calculated for fixed assets under current tax law? What effects do expected salvage value and estimated economic life have on the calculated depreciation deduction?

Alternative Definitions of Operating Cash Flow

10.5

The analysis we went through in the previous section is quite general and can be adapted to almost any capital investment problem. In the next section, we illustrate some particularly useful variations. Before we do so, we need to discuss the fact that there are different definitions of project operating cash flow that are commonly used, both in practice and in finance texts.

As we will see, the different approaches to operating cash flow that exist all measure the same thing. If they are used correctly, they all produce the same answer, and one is not necessarily any better or more useful than another. Unfortunately, the fact that alternative definitions are used does sometimes lead to confusion. For this reason, we examine several of these variations next to see how they are related.

In the discussion that follows, keep in mind that when we speak of cash flow, we literally mean dollars in less dollars out. This is all we are concerned with. Different definitions of operating cash flow amount to different ways of manipulating basic information about sales, costs, depreciation, and taxes to get at cash flow.

For a particular project and year under consideration, suppose we have the following estimates:

Sales = \$1,500
Costs = \$700
Depreciation = \$600

With these estimates, notice that EBIT is:

$$EBIT = Sales - Costs - Depreciation$$
$$= \$1,500 - 700 - 600$$
$$= \$200$$

Once again, we assume that no interest is paid, so the tax bill is:

$$Taxes = EBIT \times T_c$$
$$= \$200 \times .21 = \$42$$

where T_c, the corporate tax rate, is 21 percent.

When we put all of this together, we see that project operating cash flow, OCF, is:

$$OCF = EBIT + Depreciation - Taxes$$
$$= \$200 + 600 - 42 = \$758$$

There are some other ways to determine OCF that could be (and are) used. We consider these next.

THE BOTTOM-UP APPROACH

Because we are ignoring any financing expenses, such as interest, in our calculations of project OCF, we can write project net income as:

$$Project\ net\ income = EBIT - Taxes$$
$$= \$200 - 42$$
$$= \$158$$

If we add the depreciation to both sides, we arrive at a slightly different and very common expression for OCF:

OCF = Net income + Depreciation
$$= \$158 + 600$$
$$= \$758$$

This is the *bottom-up* approach. Here, we start with the accountant's bottom line (net income) and add back any noncash deductions such as depreciation. It is crucial to remember that this definition of operating cash flow as net income plus depreciation is correct only if there is no interest expense subtracted in the calculation of net income.

Applying this approach to the shark attractant project (see Section 10.3), net income was $21,780 and depreciation was $30,000, so the bottom-up calculation is:

$$OCF = \$21,780 + 30,000 = \$51,780$$

This is exactly the same OCF we had previously.

THE TOP-DOWN APPROACH

Perhaps the most obvious way to calculate OCF is:

OCF = Sales − Costs − Taxes
$$= \$1,500 - 700 - 42 = \$758$$

This is the *top-down* approach, the second variation on the basic OCF definition. Here, we start at the top of the income statement with sales and work our way down to net cash flow by subtracting costs, taxes, and other expenses. Along the way, we leave out any strictly noncash items such as depreciation.

For the shark attractant project, the operating cash flow can be readily calculated using the top-down approach. With sales of $200,000, total costs (fixed plus variable) of $142,430, and a tax bill of $5,790, the OCF is:

$$OCF = \$200,000 - 142,430 - 5,790 = \$51,780$$

This is as we had before.

THE TAX SHIELD APPROACH

The third variation on our basic definition of OCF is the *tax shield* approach. This approach will be useful for some problems we consider in the next section. The tax shield definition of OCF is:

OCF = (Sales − Costs) × (1 − T_c) + Depreciation × T_c

where T_c is again the corporate tax rate. Assuming that $T_c = 21\%$, the OCF works out to be:

$$OCF = (\$1,500 - 700) \times .79 + 600 \times .21$$
$$= \$632 + 126$$
$$= \$758$$

This is as we had before.

This approach views OCF as having two components. The first part is what the project's cash flow would be if there were no depreciation expense. In this case, this would-have-been cash flow is $632.

The second part of OCF in this approach is the depreciation deduction multiplied by the tax rate. This is called the **depreciation tax shield**. We know that depreciation is a noncash expense. The only cash flow effect of deducting depreciation is to reduce our taxes, a benefit to us. At the current 21 percent corporate tax rate, every dollar in depreciation expense saves us 21 cents in taxes. So, in our example, the $600 depreciation deduction saves us $600 × .21 = $126 in taxes.

For the shark attractant project we considered earlier in the chapter, the depreciation tax shield would be $30,000 × .21 = $6,300. The aftertax value for sales less costs would be ($200,000 − 142,430) × (1 − .21) = $45,480. Adding these together yields the value of OCF:

OCF = $45,480 + 6,300 = $51,780

This calculation verifies that the tax shield approach is completely equivalent to the approach we used before.

depreciation tax shield
The tax saving that results from the depreciation deduction, calculated as depreciation multiplied by the corporate tax rate.

CONCLUSION

Now that we've seen that all of these approaches are the same, you're probably wondering why everybody doesn't just agree on one of them. One reason, as we will see in the next section, is that different approaches are useful in different circumstances. The best approach to use is whichever one happens to be the most convenient for the problem at hand.

Concept Questions

10.5a   What are the top-down and bottom-up definitions of operating cash flow?

10.5b   What is meant by the term *depreciation tax shield*?

Some Special Cases of Discounted Cash Flow Analysis

10.6

To finish our chapter, we look at three common cases involving discounted cash flow analysis. The first case involves investments that are primarily aimed at improving efficiency and thereby cutting costs. The second case we consider comes up when a firm is involved in submitting competitive bids. The third and final case arises in choosing between equipment options with different economic lives.

We could consider many other special cases, but these three are particularly important because problems similar to these are so common. Also, they illustrate some diverse applications of cash flow analysis and DCF valuation.

Excel Master It!

Excel Master coverage online

EVALUATING COST-CUTTING PROPOSALS

One decision we frequently face is whether to upgrade existing facilities to make them more cost-effective. The issue is whether the cost savings are large enough to justify the necessary capital expenditure.

For example, suppose we are considering automating some part of an existing production process. The necessary equipment costs $80,000 to buy and install. The automation will save $22,000 per year (before taxes) by reducing labor and material costs. For simplicity, assume that the equipment has a five-year life and is depreciated to zero on a straight-line basis over that period. It will actually be worth $20,000 in five years. Should we automate? The tax rate is 21 percent, and the discount rate is 10 percent.

As always, the first step in making such a decision is to identify the relevant incremental cash flows. First, determining the relevant capital spending is easy enough. The initial cost is $80,000. The aftertax salvage value is $20,000 × (1 − .21) = $15,800 because the book value will be zero in five years. Second, there are no working capital consequences here, so we don't need to worry about changes in net working capital.

Operating cash flows are the third component to consider. Buying the new equipment affects our operating cash flows in two ways. First, we save $22,000 before taxes every year. In other words, the firm's operating income increases by $22,000, so this is the relevant incremental project operating income.

Second (and it's easy to overlook this), we have an additional depreciation deduction. In this case, the depreciation is $80,000/5 = $16,000 per year.

Because the project has an operating income of $22,000 (the annual pretax cost saving) and a depreciation deduction of $16,000, taking the project will increase the firm's EBIT by $22,000 − 16,000 = $6,000, so this is the project's EBIT.

Finally, because EBIT is rising for the firm, taxes will increase. This increase in taxes will be $6,000 × .21 = $1,260. With this information, we can compute operating cash flow in the usual way:

EBIT	$ 6,000
+ Depreciation	16,000
− Taxes	1,260
Operating cash flow	$20,740

So, our aftertax operating cash flow is $20,740.

It might be somewhat more enlightening to calculate operating cash flow using a different approach. What is actually going on here is very simple. First, the cost savings increase our pretax income by $22,000. We have to pay taxes on this amount, so our tax bill increases by .21 × $22,000 = $4,620. In other words, the $22,000 pretax saving amounts to $22,000 × (1 − .21) = $17,380 after taxes.

Second, the extra $16,000 in depreciation isn't really a cash outflow, but it does reduce our taxes by $16,000 × .21 = $3,360. The sum of these two components is $17,380 + 3,360 = $20,740, as we had before. Notice that the $3,360 is the depreciation tax shield we discussed earlier, and we have effectively used the tax shield approach here.

We can now finish our analysis. Based on our discussion, here are the relevant cash flows:

	Year					
	0	**1**	**2**	**3**	**4**	**5**
Operating cash flow		$20,740	$20,740	$20,740	$20,740	$20,740
Capital spending	−$80,000					15,800
Total cash flow	−$80,000	$20,740	$20,740	$20,740	$20,740	$36,540

At 10 percent, it's straightforward to verify that the NPV here is $8,431, so we should go ahead and automate.

To Buy or Not to Buy	EXAMPLE 10.3

We are considering the purchase of a $200,000 computer-based inventory management system. It will be depreciated straight-line to zero over its four-year life. It will be worth $30,000 at the end of that time. The system will save us $60,000 before taxes in inventory-related costs. The relevant tax rate is 21 percent. Because the new setup is more efficient than our existing one, we will be able to carry less total inventory and thus free up $45,000 in net working capital. What is the NPV at 16 percent? What is the DCF return (the IRR) on this investment?

We can first calculate the operating cash flow. The aftertax cost savings are $60,000 × (1 − .21) = $47,400. The depreciation is $200,000/4 = $50,000 per year, so the depreciation tax shield is $50,000 × .21 = $10,500. Operating cash flow is $47,400 + 10,500 = $57,900 per year.

The capital spending involves $200,000 up front to buy the system. The aftertax salvage is $30,000 × (1 − .21) = $23,700. Finally, and this is the somewhat tricky part, the initial investment in net working capital is a $45,000 *inflow* because the system frees up working capital. Furthermore, we will have to put this back in at the end of the project's life. What this really means is simple: While the system is in operation, we have $45,000 to use elsewhere.

To finish our analysis, we can compute the total cash flows:

	Year				
	0	1	2	3	4
Operating cash flow		$57,900	$57,900	$57,900	$57,900
Change in NWC	$ 45,000				− 45,000
Capital spending	− 200,000				23,700
Total cash flow	−$155,000	$57,900	$57,900	$57,900	$36,600

At 16 percent, the NPV is −$4,749, so the investment is not attractive. After some trial and error, we find that the NPV is zero when the discount rate is 14.36 percent, so the IRR on this investment is about 14.4 percent.

SETTING THE BID PRICE

Early on, we used discounted cash flow analysis to evaluate a proposed new product. A somewhat different (and common) scenario arises when we must submit a competitive bid to win a job. Under such circumstances, the winner is whoever submits the lowest bid.

There is an old joke concerning this process: The low bidder is whoever makes the biggest mistake. This is called the winner's curse. In other words, if you win, there is a good chance you underbid. In this section, we look at how to go about setting the bid price to avoid the winner's curse. The procedure we describe is useful anytime we have to set a price on a product or service.

To illustrate how to go about setting a bid price, imagine we are in the business of buying stripped-down truck platforms and then modifying them to customer specifications for resale. A local distributor has requested bids for five specially modified trucks each year for the next four years, for a total of 20 trucks in all.

We need to decide what price per truck to bid. The goal of our analysis is to determine the lowest price we can profitably charge. This maximizes our chances of being awarded the contract while guarding against the winner's curse.

Suppose we can buy the truck platforms for $10,000 each. The facilities we need can be leased for $24,000 per year. The labor and material cost to do the modification works out to be about $4,000 per truck. Total cost per year will thus be $24,000 + 5 × (10,000 + 4,000) = $94,000.

We will need to invest $60,000 in new equipment. This equipment will be depreciated straight-line to a zero salvage value over the four years. It will be worth about $5,000 at the end of that time. We will also need to invest $40,000 in raw materials inventory and other working capital items. The relevant tax rate is 21 percent. What price per truck should we bid if we require a 20 percent return on our investment?

We start by looking at the capital spending and net working capital investment. We have to spend $60,000 today for new equipment. The aftertax salvage value is $5,000 × (1 − .21) = $3,950. Furthermore, we have to invest $40,000 today in working capital. We will get this back in four years.

We can't determine the operating cash flow just yet because we don't know the sales price. If we draw a time line, here is what we have so far:

	Year				
	0	1	2	3	4
Operating cash flow		+OCF	+OCF	+OCF	+OCF
Change in NWC	−$ 40,000				$40,000
Capital spending	− 60,000				3,950
Total cash flow	−$100,000	+OCF	+OCF	+OCF	+OCF + $43,950

With this in mind, note that the key observation is the following: The lowest possible price we can profitably charge will result in a zero NPV at 20 percent. At that price, we earn exactly 20 percent on our investment.

Given this observation, we first need to determine what the operating cash flow must be for the NPV to equal zero. To do this, we calculate the present value of the $43,050 non-operating cash flow from the last year and subtract it from the $100,000 initial investment:

$100,000 − 43,950/1.20^4 = $100,000 − 21,195 = $78,805$

Once we have done this, our time line is as follows:

	Year				
	0	1	2	3	4
Total cash flow	−$78,805	+OCF	+OCF	+OCF	+OCF

As the time line suggests, the operating cash flow is now an unknown ordinary annuity amount. The four-year annuity factor for 20 percent is 2.58873, so we have:

$NPV = 0 = −$78,805 + OCF × 2.58873$

This implies that:

$OCF = $78,805/2.58873 = $30,442$

So the operating cash flow needs to be $30,442 each year.

We're not quite finished. The final problem is to find out what sales price results in an operating cash flow of $30,442. The easiest way to do this is to recall that operating cash flow can be written as net income plus depreciation (the bottom-up definition). The depreciation here is $60,000/4 = $15,000. Given this, we can determine what net income must be:

Operating cash flow = Net income + Depreciation
$30,442 = Net income + $15,000
Net income = $15,442

From here, we work our way backward up the income statement. If net income is $15,442, then our income statement is as follows:

Sales	?
Costs	$94,000
Depreciation	15,000
Taxes (21%)	?
Net income	$15,442

We can solve for sales by noting that:

$$\text{Net income} = (\text{Sales} - \text{Costs} - \text{Depreciation}) \times (1 - T_C)$$
$$\$15,442 = (\text{Sales} - \$94,000 - \$15,000) \times (1 - .21)$$
$$\text{Sales} = \$15,442/.79 + 94,000 + 15,000$$
$$= \$128,546$$

Sales per year must be $128,546. Because the contract calls for five trucks per year, the sales price has to be $128,546/5 = $25,709. If we round this up a bit, it looks as though we need to bid about $26,000 per truck. At this price, were we to get the contract, our return would be just over 20 percent.

EVALUATING EQUIPMENT OPTIONS WITH DIFFERENT LIVES

The final problem we consider involves choosing among different possible systems, equipment setups, or procedures. Our goal is to choose the most cost-effective alternative. The approach we consider here is necessary only when two special circumstances exist. First, the possibilities under evaluation have different economic lives. Second, and just as important, we will need whatever we buy more or less indefinitely. As a result, when it wears out, we will buy another one.

We can illustrate this problem with a simple example. Imagine we are in the business of manufacturing stamped metal subassemblies. Whenever a stamping mechanism wears out, we have to replace it with a new one to stay in business. We are considering which of two stamping mechanisms to buy.

Machine A costs $100 to buy and $10 per year to operate. It wears out and must be replaced every two years. Machine B costs $140 to buy and $8 per year to operate. It lasts for three years and must then be replaced. Ignoring taxes, which one should we choose if we use a 10 percent discount rate?

In comparing the two machines, we notice that the first is cheaper to buy, but it costs more to operate and it wears out more quickly. How can we evaluate these trade-offs? We can start by computing the present value of the costs for each:

Machine A: PV = −$100 + −10/1.1 + −10/1.1² = −$117.36
Machine B: PV = −$140 + −8/1.1 + −8/1.1² + −8/1.1³ = −$159.89

Notice that *all* the numbers here are costs, so they all have negative signs. If we stopped here, it might appear that A is more attractive because the PV of the costs is less. However, all we have really discovered so far is that A effectively provides two years' worth of stamping service for $117.36, whereas B effectively provides three years' worth for $159.89. These costs are not directly comparable because of the difference in service periods.

We need to somehow work out a cost per year for these two alternatives. To do this, we ask: What amount, paid each year over the life of the machine, has the same PV of costs? This amount is called the **equivalent annual cost (EAC)**.

Calculating the EAC involves finding an unknown payment amount. For example, for Machine A, we need to find a two-year ordinary annuity with a PV of −$117.36 at 10 percent. Going back to Chapter 6, we know that the two-year annuity factor is:

$$\text{Annuity factor} = (1 - 1/1.10^2)/.10 = 1.7355$$

For Machine A, then, we have:

$$\text{PV of costs} = -\$117.36 = \text{EAC} \times 1.7355$$
$$\text{EAC} = -\$117.36/1.7355$$
$$= -\$67.62$$

For Machine B, the life is three years, so we first need the three-year annuity factor:

$$\text{Annuity factor} = (1 - 1/1.10^3)/.10 = 2.4869$$

We calculate the EAC for B just as we did for A:

$$\text{PV of costs} = -\$159.89 = \text{EAC} \times 2.4869$$
$$\text{EAC} = -\$159.89/2.4869$$
$$= -\$64.30$$

Based on this analysis, we should purchase B because it effectively costs $64.30 per year versus $67.62 for A. In other words, all things considered, B is cheaper. In this case, the longer life and lower operating cost are more than enough to offset the higher initial purchase price.

equivalent annual cost (EAC)
The present value of a project's costs calculated on an annual basis.

EXAMPLE 10.4	**Equivalent Annual Costs**

This extended example illustrates what happens to the EAC when we consider taxes. You are evaluating two different pollution control options. A filtration system will cost $1.1 million to install and $60,000 annually, before taxes, to operate. It will have to be completely replaced every five years. A precipitation system will cost $1.9 million to install but only $10,000 per year to operate. The precipitation equipment has an effective operating life of eight years. Straight-line depreciation is used throughout, and neither system has any salvage value. Which option should we select if we use a 12 percent discount rate? The tax rate is 21 percent.

We need to consider the EACs for the two systems because they have different service lives and will be replaced as they wear out. The relevant information can be summarized as follows:

	Filtration System	Precipitation System
Aftertax operating cost	−$ 47,400	−$ 7,900
Depreciation tax shield	46,200	49,875
Operating cash flow	−$ 1,200	$ 41,975
Economic life	5 years	8 years
Annuity factor (12%)	3.6048	4.9676
Present value of operating cash flow	−$ 4,326	$ 208,517
Capital spending	− 1,100,000	− 1,900,000
Total PV of costs	−$1,104,326	−$1,691,483

Notice that the operating cash flow is actually positive in the second case because of the large depreciation tax shield. This can occur whenever the operating cost is small relative to the purchase price.

To decide which system to purchase, we compute the EACs for both using the appropriate annuity factors:

Filtration system: $-\$1{,}104{,}326 = \text{EAC} \times 3.6048$
$$\text{EAC} = -\$306{,}351$$
Precipitation system: $-\$1{,}691{,}483 = \text{EAC} \times 4.9676$
$$\text{EAC} = -\$340{,}500$$

The filtration system is the cheaper of the two, so we select it. In this case, the longer life and smaller operating cost of the precipitation system are insufficient to offset its higher initial cost.

Concept Questions

10.6a In setting a bid price, we used a zero NPV as our benchmark. Explain why this is appropriate.

10.6b Under what circumstances do we have to worry about unequal economic lives? How do you interpret the EAC?

Summary and Conclusions   10.7

This chapter has described how to put together a discounted cash flow analysis. In it, we covered:

1. The identification of relevant project cash flows: We discussed project cash flows and described how to handle some issues that often come up, including sunk costs, opportunity costs, financing costs, net working capital, and erosion.

2. Preparing and using pro forma, or projected, financial statements: We showed how information from such financial statements is useful in coming up with projected cash flows, and we also looked at some alternative definitions of operating cash flow.

3. The role of net working capital and depreciation in determining project cash flows: We saw that including the change in net working capital was important in cash flow analysis because it adjusted for the discrepancy between accounting revenues and costs and cash revenues and costs. We also went over the calculation of depreciation expense under current tax law.

4. Some special cases encountered in using discounted cash flow analysis: Here we looked at three special issues. First, we evaluated cost-cutting investments. Next, we examined how to go about setting a bid price. Finally, we looked at unequal lives problem.

The discounted cash flow analysis we've covered here is a standard tool in the business world. It is a very powerful tool, so care should be taken in its use. The most important thing is to identify the cash flows in a way that makes economic sense. This chapter gives you a good start in learning how to do this.

CONNECT TO FINANCE

 Connect Finance offers you plenty of opportunities to practice mastering these concepts. Log on to connect.mheducation.com to learn more. If you like what you see, ask your professor about using *Connect Finance*!

Can you answer the following *Connect* Quiz questions?

Section 10.1 The analysis of a project based on the project's relevant cash flows is referred to as the _____.

Section 10.2 What should NOT be included as an incremental cash flow for a proposed project?

Section 10.3 A project has projected sales of $62,000, costs of $48,000, depreciation expense of $6,200, and a tax rate of 21 percent. What is the operating cash flow for this project?

Section 10.4 An asset costs $24,000 and is classified as three-year MACRS property. What is the depreciation expense in Year 2?

Section 10.5 A firm has sales for the year of $92,000, costs of $46,000, and taxes of $21,000. What is the operating cash flow for the year?

Section 10.6 What rate of return will a firm earn if it accepts a project with a sales price per unit set equal to the bid price?

CHAPTER REVIEW AND SELF-TEST PROBLEMS

10.1 **Capital Budgeting for Project X** Based on the following information for Project X, should we undertake the venture? To answer, first prepare a pro forma income statement for each year. Next calculate operating cash flow. Finish the problem by determining total cash flow and then calculating NPV assuming a 28 percent required return. Use a 21 percent tax rate throughout. For help, look back at our shark attractant and power mulcher examples.

Project X involves a new type of graphite composite in-line skate wheel. We think we can sell 6,000 units per year at a price of $1,000 each. Variable costs will run about $400 per unit, and the product should have a four-year life.

Fixed costs for the project will run $450,000 per year. Further, we will need to invest a total of $1,250,000 in manufacturing equipment. This equipment is seven-year MACRS property for tax purposes. In four years, the equipment will be worth about half of what we paid for it. We will have to invest $1,150,000 in net working capital at the start. After that, net working capital requirements will be 25 percent of sales.

10.2 **Calculating Operating Cash Flow** Mont Blanc Livestock Pens, Inc., has projected a sales volume of $1,650 for the second year of a proposed expansion project. Costs normally run 60 percent of sales, or about $990 in this case. The depreciation expense will be $100, and the tax rate is 21 percent. What is the operating cash flow? Calculate your answer using all of the approaches (including the top-down, bottom-up, and tax shield approaches) described in the chapter.

10.3 **Spending Money to Save Money?** For help on this one, refer back to the computerized inventory management system in Example 10.3. Here, we're contemplating a new automatic surveillance system to replace our current contract security system. It will cost $450,000 to get the new system. The cost will be depreciated straight-line to zero over the system's four-year expected life. The system is expected to be worth $250,000 at the end of four years after removal costs.

We think the new system will save us $125,000 per year, before taxes, in contract security costs. The tax rate is 21 percent. What are the NPV and IRR for buying the new system? The required return is 17 percent.

ANSWERS TO CHAPTER REVIEW AND SELF-TEST PROBLEMS

10.1 To develop the pro forma income statements, we need to calculate the depreciation for each of the four years. The relevant MACRS percentages, depreciation allowances, and book values for the first four years are shown here:

Year	MACRS Percentage	Depreciation	Ending Book Value
1	14.29%	.1429 × $1,250,000 = $178,625	$1,071,375
2	24.49	.2449 × 1,250,000 = 306,125	765,250
3	17.49	.1749 × 1,250,000 = 218,625	546,625
4	12.49	.1249 × 1,250,000 = 156,125	390,500

The projected income statements, therefore, are as follows:

	Year			
	1	**2**	**3**	**4**
Sales	$6,000,000	$6,000,000	$6,000,000	$6,000,000
Variable costs	2,400,000	2,400,000	2,400,000	2,400,000
Fixed costs	450,000	450,000	450,000	450,000
Depreciation	178,625	306,125	218,625	156,125
EBIT	$2,971,375	$2,843,875	$2,931,375	$2,993,875
Taxes (21%)	623,989	597,214	615,589	628,714
Net income	$2,347,386	$2,246,661	$2,315,786	$2,365,161

Based on this information, here are the operating cash flows:

	Year			
	1	**2**	**3**	**4**
EBIT	$2,971,375	$2,843,875	$2,931,375	$2,993,875
Depreciation	178,625	306,125	218,625	156,125
Taxes	623,989	597,214	615,589	628,714
Operating cash flow	$2,526,011	$2,552,786	$2,534,411	$2,521,286

We now have to worry about the nonoperating cash flows. Net working capital starts out at $1,150,000 and then rises to 25 percent of sales, or $1,500,000. This is a $350,000 change in net working capital.

Finally, we have to invest $1,250,000 to get started. In four years, the book value of this investment will be $390,500, compared to an estimated market value of $625,000 (half of the cost). The aftertax salvage is thus $625,000 − .21 × ($625,000 − 390,500) = $575,755.

When we combine all this information, the projected cash flows for Project X are as follows:

	Year				
	0	1	2	3	4
Operating cash flow		$2,526,011	$2,552,786	$2,534,411	$2,521,286
Change in NWC	−$1,150,000	− 350,000			1,500,000
Capital spending	− 1,250,000				575,755
Total cash flow	−$2,400,000	$2,176,011	$2,552,786	$2,534,411	$4,597,041

With these cash flows, the NPV at 28 percent is:

$$NPV = -\$2,400,000 + 2,176,011/1.28 + 2,552,786/1.28^2$$
$$+2,534,411/1.28^3 + 4,597,041/1.28^4$$
$$= \$3,779,139$$

So, this project appears to be quite profitable.

10.2 First, we can calculate the project's EBIT, its tax bill, and its net income:

$$EBIT = Sales - Costs - Depreciation$$
$$= \$1,650 - 990 - 100 = \$560$$
$$Taxes = \$560 \times .21 = \$118$$
$$Net\ income = \$560 - 118 = \$442$$

With these numbers, operating cash flow is:

$$OCF = EBIT + Depreciation - Taxes$$
$$= \$560 + 100 - 118$$
$$= \$542$$

Using the other OCF definitions, we have:

$$Bottom\text{-}up\ OCF = Net\ income + Depreciation$$
$$= \$442 + 100$$
$$= \$542$$

$$Top\text{-}down\ OCF = Sales - Costs - Taxes$$
$$= \$1,650 - 990 - 118$$
$$= \$542$$

$$Tax\ shield\ OCF = (Sales - Costs) \times (1 - .21) + Depreciation \times .21$$
$$= (\$1,650 - 990) \times .79 + 100 \times .21$$
$$= \$542$$

As expected, all of these definitions produce exactly the same answer.

10.3 The $125,000 pretax saving amounts to $(1 - .21) \times \$125,000 = \$98,750$ after taxes. The annual depreciation of $\$450,000/4 = \$112,500$ generates a tax shield of $.21 \times \$112,500 = \$23,625$ each year. Putting these together, we calculate that the operating cash flow is $\$98,750 + 23,625 = \$122,375$. Because the book value is zero in four years, the aftertax salvage value is $(1 - .21) \times \$250,000 = \$197,500$. There are no working capital consequences, so here are the cash flows:

		Year			
	0	**1**	**2**	**3**	**4**
Operating cash flow		$122,375	$122,375	$122,375	$122,375
Capital spending	−$450,000				165,000
Total cash flow	−$450,000	$122,375	$122,375	$122,375	$287,375

You can verify that the NPV at 17 percent is −$26,244, and the return on the new surveillance system is only about 14.40 percent. The project does not appear to be profitable.

CONCEPTS REVIEW AND CRITICAL THINKING QUESTIONS

1. **Opportunity Cost** [LO1] In the context of capital budgeting, what is an opportunity cost?

2. **Depreciation** [LO1] Given the choice, would a firm prefer to use MACRS depreciation or straight-line depreciation? Why?

3. **Net Working Capital** [LO1] In our capital budgeting examples, we assumed that a firm would recover all of the working capital it invested in a project. Is this a reasonable assumption? When might it not be valid?

4. **Stand-Alone Principle** [LO1] Suppose a financial manager is quoted as saying, "Our firm uses the stand-alone principle. Because we treat projects like minifirms in our evaluation process, we include financing costs because they are relevant at the firm level." Critically evaluate this statement.

5. **Equivalent Annual Cost** [LO4] When is EAC analysis appropriate for comparing two or more projects? Why is this method used? Are there any implicit assumptions required by this method that you find troubling? Explain.

6. **Cash Flow and Depreciation** [LO1] "When evaluating projects, we're concerned with only the relevant incremental aftertax cash flows. Therefore, because depreciation is a noncash expense, we should ignore its effects when evaluating projects." Critically evaluate this statement.

7. **Capital Budgeting Considerations** [LO1] A major college textbook publisher has an existing finance textbook. The publisher is debating whether to produce an "essentialized" version, meaning a shorter (and lower-priced) book. What are some of the considerations that should come into play?

To answer the next three questions, refer to the following example. In 2003, Porsche unveiled its new sports utility vehicle (SUV), the Cayenne. With a price tag of over $40,000, the Cayenne went from zero to 62 mph in 9.7 seconds. Porsche's decision to enter the SUV market was a response to the runaway success of other high-priced SUVs such as the Mercedes-Benz M-class. Vehicles in this class had generated years of high profits. The Cayenne certainly spiced up the market, and Porsche subsequently introduced the Cayenne Turbo S, which goes from zero to 60 mph in 3.8 seconds and has a top speed of 176 mph. The price tag for the Cayenne Turbo S in 2018? About $130,000!

Some analysts questioned Porsche's entry into the luxury SUV market. The analysts were concerned not only that Porsche was a late entry into the market, but also that the introduction of the Cayenne would damage Porsche's reputation as a maker of high-performance automobiles.

8. **Erosion** [LO1] In evaluating the Cayenne, would you use the term *erosion* to describe the possible damage to Porsche's reputation?

9. **Capital Budgeting** [LO1] Porsche was one of the last manufacturers to enter the sports utility vehicle market. Why would one company decide to proceed with a product when other companies, at least initially, decide not to enter the market?

10. **Capital Budgeting** [LO1] In evaluating the Cayenne, what do you think Porsche needs to assume regarding the substantial profit margins that exist in this market? Is it likely they will be maintained as the market becomes more competitive, or will Porsche be able to maintain the profit margin because of its image and the performance of the Cayenne?

QUESTIONS AND PROBLEMS

BASIC
(Questions 1–20)

1. **Relevant Cash Flows** [LO1] Parker & Stone, Inc., is looking at setting up a new manufacturing plant in South Park to produce garden tools. The company bought some land six years ago for $3.6 million in anticipation of using it as a warehouse and distribution site, but the company has since decided to rent these facilities from a competitor instead. If the land were sold today, the company would net $4.1 million. The company wants to build its new manufacturing plant on this land; the plant will cost $18.1 million to build, and the site requires $950,000 worth of grading before it is suitable for construction. What is the proper cash flow amount to use as the initial investment in fixed assets when evaluating this project? Why?

2. **Relevant Cash Flows** [LO1] Winnebagel Corp. currently sells 20,000 motor homes per year at $97,000 each and 14,000 luxury motor coaches per year at $145,000 each. The company wants to introduce a new portable camper to fill out its product line; it hopes to sell 30,000 of these campers per year at $21,000 each. An independent consultant has determined that if the company introduces the new campers, it should boost the sales of its existing motor homes by 2,700 units per year and reduce the sales of its motor coaches by 1,300 units per year. What is the amount to use as the annual sales figure when evaluating this project? Why?

3. **Calculating Projected Net Income** [LO1] A proposed new investment has projected sales of $585,000. Variable costs are 44 percent of sales, and fixed costs are $187,000; depreciation is $51,000. Prepare a pro forma income statement assuming a tax rate of 21 percent. What is the projected net income?

4. **Calculating OCF** [LO1] Consider the following income statement:

Sales	$747,300
Costs	582,600
Depreciation	89,300
EBIT	?
Taxes (22%)	?
Net income	?

Fill in the missing numbers and then calculate the OCF. What is the depreciation tax shield?

5. **OCF from Several Approaches** [LO1] A proposed new project has projected sales of $175,000, costs of $93,000, and depreciation of $24,800. The tax rate is 23 percent. Calculate operating cash flow using the four different approaches described in the chapter and verify that the answer is the same in each case.

6. **Calculating Depreciation** [LO1] A piece of newly purchased industrial equipment costs $1,375,000 and is classified as seven-year property under MACRS. Calculate the annual depreciation allowances and end-of-the-year book values for this equipment.

7. **Calculating Salvage Value** [LO1] Consider an asset that costs $680,000 and is depreciated straight-line to zero over its eight-year tax life. The asset is to be used in a five-year project; at the end of the project, the asset can be sold for $143,000. If the relevant tax rate is 21 percent, what is the aftertax cash flow from the sale of this asset?

8. **Calculating Salvage Value** [LO1] An asset used in a four-year project falls in the five-year MACRS class for tax purposes. The asset has an acquisition cost of $5,100,000 and will be sold for $1,600,000 at the end of the project. If the tax rate is 21 percent, what is the aftertax salvage value of the asset?

9. **Calculating Project OCF** [LO1] Quad Enterprises is considering a new three-year expansion project that requires an initial fixed asset investment of $2.32 million. The fixed asset will be depreciated straight-line to zero over its three-year tax life, after which time it will be worthless. The project is estimated to generate $1.735 million in annual sales, with costs of $650,000. If the tax rate is 21 percent, what is the OCF for this project?

10. **Calculating Project NPV** [LO1] In the previous problem, suppose the required return on the project is 12 percent. What is the project's NPV?

11. **Calculating Project Cash Flow from Assets** [LO1] In the previous problem, suppose the project requires an initial investment in net working capital of $250,000, and the fixed asset will have a market value of $180,000 at the end of the project. What is the project's Year 0 net cash flow? Year 1? Year 2? Year 3? What is the new NPV?

12. **NPV and MACRS** [LO1] In the previous problem, suppose the fixed asset actually falls into the three-year MACRS class. All the other facts are the same. What is the project's Year 1 net cash flow now? Year 2? Year 3? What is the new NPV?

13. **NPV and Bonus Depreciation** [LO1] In the previous problem, suppose the fixed asset actually qualifies for 100 percent bonus depreciation in the first year. All the other facts are the same. What is the project's Year 1 net cash flow now? Year 2? Year 3? What is the new NPV?

14. **Project Evaluation** [LO1] Dog Up! Franks is looking at a new sausage system with an installed cost of $460,000. This cost will be depreciated straight-line to zero over the project's five-year life, at the end of which the sausage system can be scrapped for $55,000. The sausage system will save the firm $155,000 per year in pretax operating costs, and the system requires an initial investment in net working capital of $29,000. If the tax rate is 21 percent and the discount rate is 10 percent, what is the NPV of this project?

15. **NPV and Bonus Depreciation** [LO1] In the previous problem, suppose the fixed asset actually qualifies for 100 percent bonus depreciation in the first year. What is the new NPV?

16. **Project Evaluation** [LO1] Your firm is contemplating the purchase of a new $485,000 computer-based order entry system. The system will be depreciated straight-line to zero over its five-year life. It will be worth $35,000 at the end of that time. You will save $140,000 before taxes per year in order processing costs, and you will be able to reduce working capital by $60,000 (this is a one-time reduction). If the tax rate is 24 percent, what is the IRR for this project?

17. **Project Evaluation** [LO2] In the previous problem, suppose your required return on the project is 11 percent and your pretax cost savings are $150,000 per year. Will you accept the project? What if the pretax cost savings are $100,000 per year? At

what level of pretax cost savings would you be indifferent between accepting the project and not accepting it?

18. **Calculating EAC** [LO4] A five-year project has an initial fixed asset investment of $315,000, an initial NWC investment of $25,000, and an annual OCF of −$35,000. The fixed asset is fully depreciated over the life of the project and has no salvage value. If the required return is 11 percent, what is this project's equivalent annual cost, or EAC?

19. **Calculating EAC** [LO4] You are evaluating two different silicon wafer milling machines. The Techron I costs $245,000, has a three-year life, and has pretax operating costs of $63,000 per year. The Techron II costs $420,000, has a five-year life, and has pretax operating costs of $35,000 per year. For both milling machines, use straight-line depreciation to zero over the project's life and assume a salvage value of $40,000. If your tax rate is 22 percent and your discount rate is 10 percent, compute the EAC for both machines. Which do you prefer? Why?

20. **Calculating a Bid Price** [LO3] Martin Enterprises needs someone to supply it with 125,000 cartons of machine screws per year to support its manufacturing needs over the next five years, and you've decided to bid on the contract. It will cost you $910,000 to install the equipment necessary to start production; you'll depreciate this cost straight-line to zero over the project's life. You estimate that, in five years, this equipment can be salvaged for $85,000. Your fixed production costs will be $485,000 per year, and your variable production costs should be $17.35 per carton. You also need an initial investment in net working capital of $90,000. If your tax rate is 21 percent and you require a return of 12 percent on your investment, what bid price should you submit?

INTERMEDIATE
(Questions 21–33)

21. **Cost-Cutting Proposals** [LO2] Masters Machine Shop is considering a four-year project to improve its production efficiency. Buying a new machine press for $385,000 is estimated to result in $145,000 in annual pretax cost savings. The press falls in the MACRS five-year class, and it will have a salvage value at the end of the project of $45,000. The press also requires an initial investment in spare parts inventory of $20,000, along with an additional $3,100 in inventory for each succeeding year of the project. If the shop's tax rate is 22 percent and its discount rate is 9 percent, should the company buy and install the machine press?

22. **NPV and Bonus Depreciation** [LO1] Eggz, Inc., is considering the purchase of new equipment that will allow the company to collect loose hen feathers for sale. The equipment will cost $425,000 and will be eligible for 100 percent bonus depreciation. The equipment can be sold for $25,000 at the end of the project in 5 years. Sales would be $275,000 per year, with annual fixed costs of $47,000 and variable costs equal to 35 percent of sales. The project would require an investment of $25,000 in NWC that would be returned at the end of the project. The tax rate is 22 percent and the required return is 9 percent. What is the project's NPV?

23. **Comparing Mutually Exclusive Projects** [LO1] Letang Industrial Systems Company (LISC) is trying to decide between two different conveyor belt systems. System A costs $265,000, has a four-year life, and requires $73,000 in pretax annual operating costs. System B costs $345,000, has a six-year life, and requires $67,000 in pretax annual operating costs. Both systems are to be depreciated straight-line to zero over their lives and will have zero salvage value. Whichever project is chosen, it will *not* be replaced when it wears out. If the tax rate is 21 percent and the discount rate is 8 percent, which project should the firm choose?

24. **Comparing Mutually Exclusive Projects** [LO4] Suppose in the previous problem that the company always needs a conveyor belt system; when one wears out, it must be replaced. Which project should the firm choose now?

25. **Calculating a Bid Price** [LO3] Consider a project to supply 100 million postage stamps per year to the U.S. Postal Service for the next five years. You have an idle parcel of land available that cost $750,000 five years ago; if the land were sold today, it would net you $1,125,000 aftertax. The land can be sold for $1,295,000 after taxes in five years. You will need to install $5.1 million in new manufacturing plant and equipment to actually produce the stamps; this plant and equipment will be depreciated straight-line to zero over the project's five-year life. The equipment can be sold for $450,000 at the end of the project. You will also need $425,000 in initial net working capital for the project, and an additional investment of $50,000 in every year thereafter. Your production costs are .38 cents per stamp, and you have fixed costs of $1.1 million per year. If your tax rate is 23 percent and your required return on this project is 10 percent, what bid price should you submit on the contract?

26. **Interpreting a Bid Price** [LO3] In the previous problem, suppose you were going to use a three-year MACRS depreciation schedule for your manufacturing equipment and you could keep working capital investments down to only $25,000 per year. How would this new information affect your calculated bid price? What if you used 100 bonus depreciation?

27. **Comparing Mutually Exclusive Projects** [LO4] Vandelay Industries is considering the purchase of a new machine for the production of latex. Machine A costs $2,900,000 and will last for six years. Variable costs are 35 percent of sales, and fixed costs are $210,000 per year. Machine B costs $5,800,000 and will last for nine years. Variable costs for this machine are 30 percent of sales and fixed costs are $245,000 per year. The sales for each machine will be $13 million per year. The required return is 10 percent, and the tax rate is 24 percent. Both machines will be depreciated on a straight-line basis. If the company plans to replace the machine when it wears out on a perpetual basis, which machine should it choose?

28. **Equivalent Annual Cost** [LO4] Light-emitting diode (LED) light bulbs have become required in recent years, but do they make financial sense? Suppose a typical 60-watt incandescent light bulb costs $.45 and lasts for 1,000 hours. A 7-watt LED, which provides the same light, costs $2.25 and lasts for 40,000 hours. A kilowatt-hour of electricity costs $.121, which is about the national average. A kilowatt-hour is 1,000 watts for 1 hour. If you require a 10 percent return and use a light fixture 500 hours per year, what is the equivalent annual cost of each lightbulb?

29. **Break-Even Cost** [LO2] The previous problem suggests that using LEDs instead of incandescent bulbs is a no-brainer. However, electricity costs actually vary quite a bit depending on location and user type (you can get information on your rates from your local power company). An industrial user in West Virginia might pay $.04 per kilowatt-hour whereas a residential user in Hawaii might pay $.25. What's the break-even cost per kilowatt-hour in Problem 25?

30. **Break-Even Replacement** [LO2] The previous two problems suggest that using LEDs is a good idea from a purely financial perspective unless you live in an area where power is relatively inexpensive, but there is another wrinkle. Suppose you have a residence with a lot of incandescent bulbs that are used on average 500 hours a year. The average bulb will be about halfway through its life, so it will have 500 hours remaining (and you can't tell which bulbs are older or newer). At what cost per kilowatt-hour does it make sense to replace your incandescent bulbs today?

31. **Issues in Capital Budgeting** [LO1] Before LEDs became a popular replacement for incandescent light bulbs, compact fluorescent lamps (CFLs) were hailed as the new generation of lighting. However, CFLs had even more wrinkles. In no particular order:

    1. Incandescent bulbs generate a lot more heat than CFLs.

2. CFL prices will probably decline relative to incandescent bulbs.

3. CFLs unavoidably contain small amounts of mercury, a significant environmental hazard, and special precautions must be taken in disposing of burned-out units (and also in cleaning up a broken lamp). Currently, there is no agreed-upon way to recycle a CFL. Incandescent bulbs pose no disposal/breakage hazards.

4. Depending on a light's location (or the number of lights), there can be a nontrivial cost to change bulbs (i.e., labor cost in a business).

5. Coal-fired power generation accounts for a substantial portion of the mercury emissions in the U.S., though the emissions will drop sharply in the relatively near future.

6. Power generation accounts for a substantial portion of CO_2 emissions in the U.S.

7. CFLs are more energy and material intensive to manufacture. On-site mercury contamination and worker safety are issues.

8. If you install a CFL in a permanent lighting fixture in a building, you will probably move long before the CFL burns out.

9. Even as CFLs began to replace incandescent light bulbs, LEDs were in the latter stages of development. At the time, LEDs were much more expensive than CFLs, but costs were coming down. LEDs last much longer than CFLs and use even less power. Plus, LEDs don't contain mercury.

Qualitatively, how would these issues affect your position in the CFL versus incandescent light bulb debate? Some countries banned incandescent bulbs. Does your analysis suggest such a move was wise? Are there other regulations short of an outright ban that make sense to you?

32. **Replacement Decisions** [LO2] Your small remodeling business has two work vehicles. One is a small passenger car used for job site visits and for other general business purposes. The other is a heavy truck used to haul equipment. The car gets 25 miles per gallon (mpg). The truck gets 10 mpg. You want to improve gas mileage to save money, and you have enough money to upgrade one vehicle. The upgrade cost will be the same for both vehicles. An upgraded car will get 40 mpg; an upgraded truck will get 12.5 mpg. The cost of gasoline is $2.65 per gallon. Assuming an upgrade is a good idea in the first place, which one should you upgrade? Both vehicles are driven 12,000 miles per year.

33. **Replacement Decisions** [LO2] In the previous problem, suppose you drive the truck x miles per year. How many miles would you have to drive the car before upgrading the car would be the better choice? *Hint:* Look at the relative gas savings.

CHALLENGE
(Questions 34–40)

34. **Calculating Project NPV** [LO1] You have been hired as a consultant for Pristine Urban-Tech Zither, Inc. (PUTZ), manufacturers of fine zithers. The market for zithers is growing quickly. The company bought some land three years ago for $1.9 million in anticipation of using it as a toxic waste dump site but has recently hired another company to handle all toxic materials. Based on a recent appraisal, the company believes it could sell the land for $2.1 million on an aftertax basis. In four years, the land could be sold for $2.3 million after taxes. The company also hired a marketing firm to analyze the zither market, at a cost of $175,000. An excerpt of the marketing report is as follows:

The zither industry will have a rapid expansion in the next four years. With the brand name recognition that PUTZ brings to bear, we feel that the company will be able to sell 5,100, 5,800, 6,400, and 4,700 units each year for the next four years, respectively.

Again, capitalizing on the name recognition of PUTZ, we feel that a premium price of $425 can be charged for each zither. Because zithers appear to be a fad, we feel at the end of the four-year period, sales should be discontinued.

PUTZ believes that fixed costs for the project will be $345,000 per year, and variable costs are 15 percent of sales. The equipment necessary for production will cost $2.65 million and will be depreciated according to a three-year MACRS schedule. At the end of the project, the equipment can be scrapped for $395,000. Net working capital of $125,000 will be required immediately. PUTZ has a tax rate of 22 percent, and the required return on the project is 13 percent. What is the NPV of the project?

35. **NPV and Bonus Depreciation** [LO1] In the previous problem, suppose the fixed asset actually qualifies for 100 percent bonus depreciation in the first year. What is the new NPV?

36. **Project Evaluation** [LO1] Aria Acoustics, Inc. (AAI), projects unit sales for a new seven-octave voice emulation implant as follows:

Year	Unit Sales
1	73,000
2	86,000
3	105,000
4	97,000
5	67,000

Production of the implants will require $1,500,000 in net working capital to start and additional net working capital investments each year equal to 15 percent of the projected sales increase for the following year. Total fixed costs are $3,200,000 per year, variable production costs are $255 per unit, and the units are priced at $375 each. The equipment needed to begin production has an installed cost of $16,500,000. Because the implants are intended for professional singers, this equipment is considered industrial machinery and thus qualifies as seven-year MACRS property. In five years, this equipment can be sold for about 20 percent of its acquisition cost. The tax rate is 21 percent and the required return is 18 percent. Based on these preliminary project estimates, what is the NPV of the project? What is the IRR?

37. **Calculating Required Savings** [LO2] A proposed cost-saving device has an installed cost of $735,000. The device will be used in a five-year project but is classified as three-year MACRS property for tax purposes. The required initial net working capital investment is $55,000, the tax rate is 22 percent, and the project discount rate is 9 percent. The device has an estimated Year 5 salvage value of $85,000. What level of pretax cost savings do we require for this project to be profitable?

38. **Financial Break-Even Analysis** [LO2] To solve the bid price problem presented in the text, we set the project NPV equal to zero and found the required price using the definition of OCF. Thus the bid price represents a financial break-even level for the project. This type of analysis can be extended to many other types of problems.

   a. In Problem 20, assume that the price per carton is $26 and find the project NPV. What does your answer tell you about your bid price? What do you know about the number of cartons you can sell and still break even? How about your level of costs?

   b. Solve Problem 20 again with the price still at $26, but find the quantity of cartons per year that you can supply and still break even. *Hint*: It's less than 125,000.

c. Repeat (b) with a price of $26 and a quantity of 125,000 cartons per year, and find the highest level of fixed costs you could afford and still break even. *Hint*: It's more than $485,000.

39. Calculating a Bid Price [LO3] Your company has been approached to bid on a contract to sell 4,800 voice recognition (VR) computer keyboards per year for four years. Due to technological improvements, beyond that time they will be outdated and no sales will be possible. The equipment necessary for the production will cost $3.1 million and will be depreciated on a straight-line basis to a zero salvage value. Production will require an investment in net working capital of $395,000 to be returned at the end of the project, and the equipment can be sold for $305,000 at the end of production. Fixed costs are $570,000 per year, and variable costs are $75 per unit. In addition to the contract, you feel your company can sell 11,400, 13,500, 17,900, and 10,400 additional units to companies in other countries over the next four years, respectively, at a price of $170. This price is fixed. The tax rate is 23 percent, and the required return is 10 percent. Additionally, the president of the company will undertake the project only if it has an NPV of $100,000. What bid price should you set for the contract?

40. Replacement Decisions [LO2] Suppose we are thinking about replacing an old computer with a new one. The old one cost us $1,560,000; the new one will cost $1,872,000. The new machine will be depreciated straight-line to zero over its five-year life. It will probably be worth about $360,000 after five years.

The old computer is being depreciated at a rate of $312,000 per year. It will be completely written off in three years. If we don't replace it now, we will have to replace it in two years. We can sell it now for $504,000; in two years, it will probably be worth $144,000. The new machine will save us $348,000 per year in operating costs. The tax rate is 22 percent, and the discount rate is 12 percent.

a. Suppose we recognize that if we don't replace the computer now, we will be replacing it in two years. Should we replace it now or should we wait? *Hint*: What we effectively have here is a decision either to "invest" in the old computer (by not selling it) or to invest in the new one. Notice that the two investments have unequal lives.

b. Suppose we consider only whether we should replace the old computer now without worrying about what's going to happen in two years. What are the relevant cash flows? Should we replace it or not? *Hint*: Consider the net change in the firm's aftertax cash flows if we do the replacement.

EXCEL MASTER IT! PROBLEM

For this Master It! assignment, refer to the Conch Republic Electronics minicase below. For your convenience, we have entered the relevant values in the case such as the price and variable cost. For this project, answer the following questions:

a. What is the profitability index of the project?

b. What is the IRR of the project?

c. What is the NPV of the project?

d. At what price would Conch Republic Electronics be indifferent to accepting the project?

e. At what level of variable costs per unit would Conch Republic Electronics be indifferent to accepting the project?

MINICASE

Conch Republic Electronics, Part 1

Conch Republic Electronics is a midsized electronics manu-facturer located in Key West, Florida. The company president is Shelley Couts, who inherited the company. When it was founded over 70 years ago, the company originally repaired radios and other household appliances. Over the years, the company expanded into manufacturing and is now a reputable manufacturer of various electronic items. Jay McCanless, a recent MBA graduate, has been hired by the company's finance department.

One of the major revenue-producing items manufactured by Conch Republic is a smartphone. Conch Republic currently has one smartphone model on the market, and sales have been excellent. The smartphone is a unique item in that it comes in a variety of tropical colors and is preprogrammed to play Jimmy Buffett music. However, as with any electronic item, technology changes rapidly, and the current smartphone has limited features in comparison with newer models. Conch Republic spent $750,000 to develop a prototype for a new smartphone that has all the features of the existing smartphone but adds new features such as WiFi tethering. The company has spent a further $200,000 for a marketing study to determine the expected sales figures for the new smartphone.

Conch Republic can manufacture the new smartphones for $220 each in variable costs. Fixed costs for the operation are estimated to run $6.4 million per year. The estimated sales volume is 155,000, 165,000, 125,000, 95,000, and 75,000 per year for the next five years, respectively. The unit price of the new smartphone will be $535. The necessary equipment can be purchased for $43.5 million and will be depreciated on a seven-year MACRS schedule. It is believed the value of the equipment in five years will be $6.5 million.

As previously stated, Conch Republic currently manufactures a smartphone. Production of the existing model is expected to be terminated in two years. If Conch Republic does not introduce the new smartphone, sales will be 95,000 units and 65,000 units for the next two years, respectively. The price of the existing smartphone is $385 per unit, with variable costs of $145 each and fixed costs of $4.3 million per year. If Conch Republic does introduce the new smartphone, sales of the existing smartphone will fall by 30,000 units per year, and the price of the existing units will have to be lowered to $215 each. Net working capital for the smartphones will be 20 percent of sales and will occur with the timing of the cash flows for the year; for example, there is no initial outlay for NWC, but changes in NWC will first occur in Year 1 with the first year's sales. Conch Republic has a 21 percent corporate tax rate and a required return of 12 percent.

Shelley has asked Jay to prepare a report that answers the following questions.

QUESTIONS

1. What is the payback period of the project?
2. What is the profitability index of the project?
3. What is the IRR of the project?
4. What is the NPV of the project?

Chapter

11 Project Analysis and Evaluation

IN THE SUMMER OF 2016, the movie *Ben-Hur*, starring Jack Huston and Morgan Freeman, thundered into theaters with the slogan, "First to finish. Last to die." But what died was the film's box office. One critic called it "a dull, clunking return to one of cinema's great warhorses." Others were even more harsh, saying the movie was "a digitalized eyesore hobbled in every department by staggering incompetence."

Looking at the numbers, *Ben-Hur*'s losses were epic. After production, distribution, and marketing costs, movie maker MGM and its partners were estimated to have lost as much as $120 million on the film. In fact, about 4 out of 10 movies lose money at the box office, though DVD sales often help the final tally. Of course, there are movies that do quite well. Also in 2016, the Twentieth Century Fox production *Deadpool* raked in about $782 million worldwide at a production cost of $58 million.

Obviously, MGM didn't *plan* to lose $120 million on *Ben-Hur*, but it happened. As this particular box office bomb shows, projects don't always go as companies think they will. This chapter explores how this can happen and what companies can do to analyze and possibly avoid these situations.

Learning Objectives

After studying this chapter, you should be able to:

LO1 Perform and interpret a sensitivity analysis for a proposed investment.

LO2 Perform and interpret a scenario analysis for a proposed investment.

LO3 Determine and interpret cash, accounting, and financial break-even points.

LO4 Explain how the degree of operating leverage can affect the cash flows of a project.

LO5 Discuss how capital rationing affects the ability of a company to accept projects.

For updates on the latest happenings in finance, visit fundamentalsofcorporatefinance.blogspot.com.

In the previous chapter, we discussed how to identify and organize the relevant cash flows for capital investment decisions. Our primary interest there was in coming up with a preliminary estimate of the net present value for a proposed project. In this chapter, we focus on assessing the reliability of such an estimate and on some additional considerations in project analysis.

We begin by discussing the need for an evaluation of cash flow and NPV estimates. We go on to develop some useful tools for such an evaluation. We also examine additional complications and concerns that can arise in project evaluation.

Evaluating NPV Estimates   11.1

As we discussed in Chapter 9, an investment has a positive net present value if its market value exceeds its cost. Such an investment is desirable because it creates value for its owner. The primary problem in identifying such opportunities is that most of the time we can't actually observe the relevant market value. Instead, we estimate it. Having done so, it is only natural to wonder whether our estimates are at least close to the true values. We consider this question next.

THE BASIC PROBLEM

Suppose we are working on a preliminary discounted cash flow analysis along the lines we described in the previous chapter. We carefully identify the relevant cash flows, avoiding such things as sunk costs, and we remember to consider working capital requirements. We add back any depreciation; we account for possible erosion; and we pay attention to opportunity costs. Finally, we double-check our calculations; when all is said and done, the bottom line is that the estimated NPV is positive.

Now what? Do we stop here and move on to the next proposal? Probably not. The fact that the estimated NPV is positive is definitely a good sign; but, more than anything, this tells us that we need to take a closer look.

If you think about it, there are two circumstances under which a DCF analysis could lead us to conclude that a project has a positive NPV. The first possibility is that the project really does have a positive NPV. That's the good news. The bad news is the second possibility: A project may appear to have a positive NPV because our estimate is inaccurate.

Notice that we could also err in the opposite way. If we conclude that a project has a negative NPV when the true NPV is positive, we lose a valuable opportunity.

PROJECTED VERSUS ACTUAL CASH FLOWS

There is a somewhat subtle point we need to make here. When we say something like, "The projected cash flow in Year 4 is $700," what exactly do we mean? Does this mean that we think the cash flow will actually be $700? Not really. It could happen, of course, but we would be surprised to see it turn out exactly that way. The reason is that the $700 projection is based on only what we know today. Almost anything could happen between now and then to change that cash flow.

Loosely speaking, we really mean that if we took all the possible cash flows that could occur in four years and averaged them, the result would be $700. So, we don't really expect a projected cash flow to be exactly right in any one case. What we do expect is that if we evaluate a large number of projects, our projections will be right on average.

FORECASTING RISK

The key inputs into a discounted cash flow (DCF) analysis are projected future cash flows. If the projections are seriously in error, then we have a classic GIGO (garbage in, garbage out) system. In such a case, no matter how carefully we arrange the numbers and manipulate them, the resulting answer can still be grossly misleading. This is the danger in using a relatively sophisticated technique like DCF. It is sometimes easy to get caught up in number crunching and forget the underlying nuts-and-bolts economic reality.

The possibility that we will make a bad decision because of errors in the projected cash flows is called **forecasting risk** (or *estimation risk*). Because of forecasting risk, there is the danger that we will think a project has a positive NPV when it really does not. How is this possible? It happens if we are overly optimistic about the future, and, as a result, our projected cash flows don't realistically reflect the possible future cash flows.

Forecasting risk can take many forms. For example, Microsoft spent several billion dollars developing and bringing the Xbox One game console to market. Technologically more sophisticated than its competition, the Xbox One was the best way to play against competitors over the Internet and included other features, such as the Kinect motion detector. However, Microsoft sold only four million Xboxes in the first four months of sales, which was at the low end of Microsoft's expected range and noticeably fewer than the 6.6 million Sony PS4s sold. Since the Xbox was arguably the best available game console at the time, why didn't it sell better? A major reason given by analysts was that the Xbox cost $100 more than the PS4.

So far, we have not explicitly considered what to do about the possibility of errors in our forecasts; so one of our goals in this chapter is to develop some tools that are useful in identifying areas where potential errors exist and where they might be especially damaging. In one form or another, we will be trying to assess the economic "reasonableness" of our estimates. We will also be wondering how much damage will be done by errors in those estimates.

forecasting risk
The possibility that errors in projected cash flows will lead to incorrect decisions. Also known as *estimation risk*.

SOURCES OF VALUE

The first line of defense against forecasting risk is to ask, "What is it about this investment that leads to a positive NPV?" We should be able to point to something specific as the source of value. For example, if the proposal under consideration involves a new product, then we might ask questions such as the following: Are we certain that our new product is significantly better than that of the competition? Can we truly manufacture at lower cost, or distribute more effectively, or identify undeveloped market niches, or gain control of a market?

These are just a few of the potential sources of value. There are many others. For example, in 2004, Google announced a new, free email service: Gmail. Why? Free email service is widely available from big hitters like Microsoft and Yahoo! and, obviously, it's free! The answer is that Google's email service is integrated with its acclaimed search engine, thereby giving it an edge. Also, offering email lets Google expand its lucrative keyword-based advertising delivery. So, Google's source of value is leveraging its proprietary web search and ad delivery technologies.

A key factor to keep in mind is the degree of competition in the market. A basic principle of economics is that positive NPV investments will be rare in a highly competitive environment. Therefore, proposals that appear to show significant value in the face of stiff competition are particularly troublesome, and the likely reaction of the competition to any innovations must be closely examined.

To give an example, in 2008, demand for flat-screen LCD televisions was high, prices were high, and profit margins were fat for retailers. But, also in 2008, manufacturers of the screens, such as Samsung and Sony, were projected to pour several billion dollars into new production facilities. Anyone thinking of entering this highly profitable market would have done well to reflect on what the supply (and profit margin) situation would look like in just a few years. And, in fact, the high prices did not last. By 2017, television sets that had been selling for well over $1,000 only a few years before were selling for around $300–$400. And, it is likely that the new 4K television sets will experience a similar price drop in the next few years.

It is also necessary to think about *potential* competition. For example, suppose home improvement retailer Lowe's identifies an area that is underserved and is thinking about opening a store. If the store is successful, what will happen? The answer is that Home Depot (or another competitor) will likely also build a store, thereby driving down volume and profits. So, we always need to keep in mind that success attracts imitators and competitors.

The point to remember is that positive NPV investments are probably not all that common, and the number of positive NPV projects is almost certainly limited for any given firm. If we can't articulate some sound economic basis for thinking ahead of time that we have found something special, then the conclusion that our project has a positive NPV should be viewed with some suspicion.

Concept Questions

11.1a   What is forecasting risk? Why is it a concern for the financial manager?

11.1b   What are some potential sources of value in a new project?

Scenario and Other What-If Analyses   11.2

Our basic approach to evaluating cash flow and NPV estimates involves asking what-if questions. Accordingly, we discuss some organized ways of going about a what-if analysis. Our goal in performing such an analysis is to assess the degree of forecasting risk and to identify the most critical components of the success or failure of an investment.

Excel Master It!

Excel Master coverage online

GETTING STARTED

We are investigating a new project. Naturally, the first thing we do is estimate NPV based on our projected cash flows. We will call this initial set of projections the *base case*. Now, we recognize the possibility of error in these cash flow projections. After completing the base case, we wish to investigate how different assumptions about the future will impact our estimates.

One way to organize this investigation is to put upper and lower bounds on the various components of the project. For example, suppose we forecast sales at 100 units per year. We know this estimate may be high or low, but we are relatively certain it is not off by more than 10 units in either direction. In this situation, we would pick a lower bound of 90 and an upper bound of 110. We go on to assign such bounds to any other cash flow components we are unsure about.

When we pick these upper and lower bounds, we are not ruling out the possibility that the actual values could be outside this range. What we are saying, again loosely speaking, is that it is unlikely that the true average (as opposed to our estimated average) of the possible values is outside this range.

An example is useful to illustrate the idea here. The project under consideration costs $200,000, has a five-year life, and has no salvage value. Depreciation is straight-line to zero. The required return is 12 percent, and the tax rate is 21 percent. In addition, we have compiled the following information:

	Base Case	Lower Bound	Upper Bound
Unit sales	6,000	5,500	6,500
Price per unit	$ 80	$ 75	$ 85
Variable costs per unit	$ 60	$ 58	$ 62
Fixed costs per year	$50,000	$45,000	$55,000

With this information, we can calculate the base-case NPV by first calculating net income:

Sales	$480,000
Variable costs	360,000
Fixed costs	50,000
Depreciation	40,000
EBIT	$ 30,000
Taxes (21%)	6,300
Net income	$ 23,700

Operating cash flow is $30,000 + 40,000 − 6,300 = $63,700 per year. At 12 percent, the five-year annuity factor is 3.6048, so the base-case NPV is:

$$\text{Base-case NPV} = -\$200,000 + 63,700 \times 3.6048$$
$$= \$29,624$$

The project looks good so far.

SCENARIO ANALYSIS

scenario analysis
The determination of what happens to NPV estimates when we ask what-if questions.

The basic form of what-if analysis is called **scenario analysis**. What we do is investigate the changes in our NPV estimates that result from asking questions like: What if unit sales realistically should be projected at 5,500 units instead of 6,000?

Once we start looking at alternative scenarios, we might find that most of the plausible ones result in positive NPVs. In this case, we have some confidence in proceeding with the project. If a substantial percentage of the scenarios look bad, the degree of forecasting risk is high and further investigation is in order.

We can consider a number of possible scenarios. A good place to start is with the worst-case scenario. This will tell us the minimum NPV of the project. If this turns out to be positive, we will be in good shape. While we are at it, we will go ahead and determine the other extreme, the best case. This puts an upper bound on our NPV.

To get the worst case, we assign the least favorable value to each item. This means *low* values for items like units sold and price per unit and *high* values for costs. We do the reverse for the best case. For our project, these values would be the following:

	Worst Case	Best Case
Unit sales	5,500	6,500
Price per unit	$ 75	$ 85
Variable costs per unit	$ 62	$ 58
Fixed costs per year	$55,000	$45,000

With this information, we can calculate the net income and cash flows under each scenario (check these for yourself):

Scenario	Net Income	Cash Flow	Net Present Value	IRR
Base case	$23,700	$63,700	$ 29,624	17.8%
Worst case*	−18,565	21,435	−122,732	−17.7
Best case	71,495	111,495	201,915	47.9

*We assume a tax credit is created in our worst-case scenario.

What we learn is that under the worst scenario, the cash flow is still positive at $21,435. That's good news. The bad news is that the return is −17.7 percent in this case, and the NPV is −$122,732. Because the project costs $200,000, we stand to lose more than half of the original investment under the worst possible scenario. The best case offers an attractive 47.9 percent return.

The terms *best case* and *worst case* are commonly used, and we will stick with them; but they are somewhat misleading. The absolutely best thing that could happen would be something absurdly unlikely, such as launching a new diet soda and subsequently learning that our (patented) formulation also just happens to cure the common cold. Similarly, the true worst case would involve some incredibly remote possibility of total disaster. We're not claiming that these things don't happen; once in a while they do. Some products, such as personal computers, succeed beyond the wildest expectations; and some turn out to be absolute catastrophes. For example, in April 2010, BP's Gulf of Mexico oil rig *Deepwater Horizon* caught fire and sank following an explosion, leading to a massive oil spill. The leak was finally stopped in July after releasing over 200 million gallons of crude oil into the Gulf. When everything was included, BP's costs associated with the disaster were about $62 billion, not including opportunity costs such as lost government contracts. Nonetheless, our point is that in assessing the reasonableness of an NPV estimate, we need to stick to cases that are reasonably likely to occur.

Instead of *best* and *worst*, then, it is probably more accurate to use the words *optimistic* and *pessimistic*. In broad terms, if we were thinking about a reasonable range for, say, unit sales, then what we call the best case would correspond to something near the upper end of that range. The worst case would correspond to the lower end.

Not all companies complete (or at least publish) all three estimates. For example, Almaden Minerals, Ltd., made a press release with information concerning its Elk Gold Project in British Columbia. Here is a table of the possible outcomes given by the company:

Project Summary	Base Case	$1,200 Case	Unit
Assumed gold price	1,000	1,200	$US/tr.oz
Tonnes per day treated	500	1,000	tpd
Life	7	9	years
Total tonnes treated	1.1	2.6	MT
Grade	4.14	3.89	g/t
Waste: Ore ratio	16.4	30.1	
Plant recovery	92	92	%
Ounces Au produced	139,198	297,239	tr.oz
Initial capital expense	9.91	17.50	$CADM
Working and preproduction capital	2.27	9.60	$CADM
Waste mining	2.42	1.90	$CAD/tonne waste
Ore mining	8.38	5.87	$CAD/tonne ore
Processing	20.68	14.74	$CAD/tonne ore
Administration and overheads	2.07	1.27	$CAD/tonne ore
Total operating cost	70.30	78.91	$CAD/tonne ore
Pretax NPV @ 8%	28.7	67.9	$CADM
Pretax IRR	51%	39%	
Max exposure	13.66	33.53	$CADM
Payback, years from start production	1.85	3.30	years
Ratio, gross earnings: max exposure	5.02	6.00	
Ratio, NPV: max exposure	2.10	2.03	

As you can see, the NPV is projected at C$28.7 million in the base case and C$67.9 million in the best ($1,200 price) case. Unfortunately, Almaden did not release a worst-case analysis, but we hope the company also examined this possibility.

As we have mentioned, there are an unlimited number of different scenarios that we could examine. At a minimum, we might want to investigate two intermediate cases by going halfway between the base amounts and the extreme amounts. This would give us five scenarios in all, including the base case.

Beyond this point, it is hard to know when to stop. As we generate more and more possibilities, we run the risk of experiencing "paralysis of analysis." The difficulty is that no matter how many scenarios we run, all we can learn are possibilities—some good and some bad. Beyond that, we don't get any guidance as to what to do. Scenario analysis is useful in telling us what can happen and in helping us gauge the potential for disaster, but it does not tell us whether to take a project.

Unfortunately, in practice, even the worst-case scenarios may not be low enough. Two recent examples show what we mean. The Eurotunnel, or Chunnel, may be one of the new wonders of the world. The tunnel under the English Channel connects England to France and covers 24 miles. It took 8,000 workers eight years to remove 9.8 million cubic yards of rock. When the tunnel was finally built, it cost $17.9 billion, or slightly more than twice the original estimate of $8.8 billion. And things got worse. Forecasts called for 16.8 million passengers in the first year, but only 4 million actually used it. Revenue estimates for 2003 were $2.88 billion, but actual revenue was only about one-third of that. The major problems faced by the Eurotunnel were increased competition from ferry services, which dropped their prices, and the rise of low-cost airlines. In 2006, things got so bad that the company operating the Eurotunnel was forced into negotiations with creditors to chop its $11.1 billion debt in half to avoid bankruptcy. The debt reduction appeared to help. In 2007, the Eurotunnel reported its first profit of €1 million ($1.6 million). By 2013, the Chunnel had a profit of €101 million ($138 million). Sales for the year were €1.09 billion ($1.49 billion), the first year its sales exceeded €1 billion, and for the first time it transported more than 10 million passengers in a year. And, by 2016, the Chunnel's profit reached €535 million ($700 million).

Another example is the Samsung Note 7 cell phone, which caught fire with consumers when it was introduced in August 2016. Unfortunately, the phones subsequently began to actually catch fire, causing the Federal Aviation Administration to ban them from flights, even in a checked bag. In early September, Samsung recalled 2.5 million Note 7s. The company halted all further production and sales in early October, which caused Samsung's market capitalization to drop about $17 billion. The company was expected to eventually write off about $5 billion, a "Note-able" loss.

SENSITIVITY ANALYSIS

sensitivity analysis
Investigation of what happens to NPV when only one variable is changed.

Sensitivity analysis is a variation on scenario analysis that is useful in pinpointing the areas where forecasting risk is especially severe. The basic idea with a sensitivity analysis is to freeze all of the variables except one and then see how sensitive our estimate of NPV is to changes in that one variable. If our NPV estimate turns out to be very sensitive to relatively small changes in the projected value of some component of project cash flow, then the forecasting risk associated with that variable is high.

To illustrate how sensitivity analysis works, we go back to our base case for every item except unit sales. We can then calculate cash flow and NPV using the largest and smallest unit sales figures.

Scenario	Unit Sales	Cash Flow	Net Present Value	IRR
Base case	6,000	$63,700	$29,624	17.8%
Worst case	5,500	55,800	1,147	12.2
Best case	6,500	71,600	58,102	23.2

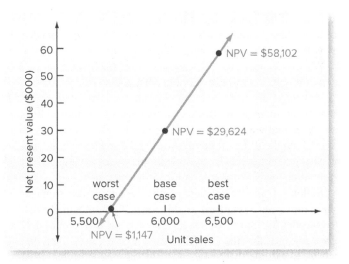

FIGURE 11.1

Sensitivity Analysis for Unit Sales

For comparison, we now freeze everything except fixed costs and repeat the analysis:

Scenario	Fixed Costs	Cash Flow	Net Present Value	IRR
Base case	$50,000	$63,700	$29,624	17.8%
Worst case	55,000	59,750	15,385	15.1
Best case	45,000	67,650	43,863	20.5

What we see here is that given our ranges, the estimated NPV of this project is more sensitive to changes in projected unit sales than it is to changes in projected fixed costs. In fact, under the worst case for fixed costs, the NPV is still positive.

The results of our sensitivity analysis for unit sales can be illustrated graphically as in Figure 11.1. Here we place NPV on the vertical axis and unit sales on the horizontal axis. When we plot the combinations of unit sales versus NPV, we see that all possible combinations fall on a straight line. The steeper the resulting line is, the greater the sensitivity of the estimated NPV to changes in the projected value of the variable being investigated.

Sensitivity analysis can produce results that vary dramatically depending on the assumptions. For example, Bard Ventures Ltd. announced its projections for a molybdenum mine in British Columbia. At a cost of capital of 10 percent and an average molybdenum price of $19 per ton, the NPV of the new mine would be $112 million with an IRR of 12.4 percent. At a high price of $30 per ton, the NPV would be $1.152 billion, and the IRR would be 32.0 percent.

As we have illustrated, sensitivity analysis is useful in pinpointing which variables deserve the most attention. If we find that our estimated NPV is especially sensitive to changes in a variable that is difficult to forecast (such as unit sales), then the degree of forecasting risk is high. We might decide that further market research would be a good idea in this case.

Because sensitivity analysis is a form of scenario analysis, it suffers from the same drawbacks. Sensitivity analysis is useful for pointing out where forecasting errors will do the most damage, but it does not tell us what to do about possible errors.

SIMULATION ANALYSIS

Scenario analysis and sensitivity analysis are widely used. With scenario analysis, we let all the different variables change, but we let them take on only a few values. With sensitivity analysis, we let only one variable change, but we let it take on many values. If we combine the two approaches, the result is a crude form of **simulation analysis**.

simulation analysis
A combination of scenario and sensitivity analysis.

If we want to let all the items vary at the same time, we have to consider a very large number of scenarios, and computer assistance is almost certainly needed. In the simplest case, we start with unit sales and assume that any value in our 5,500 to 6,500 range is equally likely. We start by randomly picking one value (or by instructing a computer to do so). We then randomly pick a price, a variable cost, and so on.

Once we have values for all the relevant components, we calculate an NPV. We repeat this sequence as many times as we desire, probably several thousand times. The result is many NPV estimates that we summarize by calculating the average value and some measure of how spread out the different possibilities are. For example, it would be of some interest to know what percentage of the possible scenarios result in negative estimated NPVs.

Because simulation analysis (or simulation) is an extended form of scenario analysis, it has the same problems. Once we have the results, no simple decision rule tells us what to do. Also, we have described a relatively simple form of simulation. To really do it right, we would have to consider the interrelationships between the different cash flow components. Furthermore, we assumed that the possible values were equally likely to occur. It is probably more realistic to assume that values near the base case are more likely than extreme values, but coming up with the probabilities is difficult, to say the least.

For these reasons, the use of simulation is somewhat limited in practice. However, recent advances in computer software and hardware (and user sophistication) lead us to believe it may become more common in the future, particularly for large-scale projects.

Concept Questions

11.2a   What are scenario, sensitivity, and simulation analysis?
11.2b   What are the drawbacks to the various types of what-if analysis?

11.3 Break-Even Analysis

It will frequently turn out that the crucial variable for a project is sales volume. If we are thinking of creating a new product or entering a new market, for example, the hardest thing to forecast accurately is how much we can sell. For this reason, sales volume is usually analyzed more closely than other variables.

Break-even analysis is a popular and commonly used tool for analyzing the relationship between sales volume and profitability. There are a variety of different break-even measures, and we have already seen several types. For example, we discussed (in Chapter 9) how the payback period can be interpreted as the length of time until a project breaks even, ignoring time value.

All break-even measures have a similar goal. Loosely speaking, we will always be asking, "How bad do sales have to get before we actually begin to lose money?" Implicitly, we will also be asking, "Is it likely that things will get that bad?" To get started on this subject, we first discuss fixed and variable costs.

FIXED AND VARIABLE COSTS

In discussing break-even, the difference between fixed and variable costs becomes very important. As a result, we need to be a little more explicit about the difference than we have been so far.

variable costs
Costs that change when the quantity of output changes.

Variable Costs   By definition, **variable costs** change as the quantity of output changes, and they are zero when production is zero. For example, direct labor costs and raw

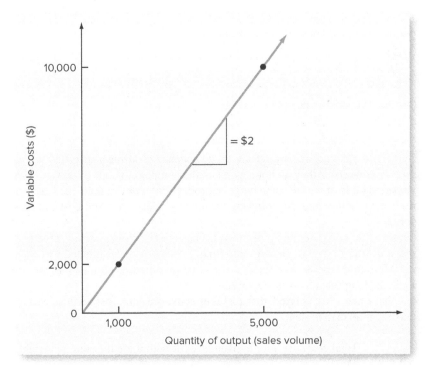

FIGURE 11.2

**Output Level and
Variable Costs**

material costs are usually considered variable. This makes sense because if we shut down operations tomorrow, there will be no future costs for labor or raw materials.

We will assume that variable costs are a constant amount per unit of output. This means that total variable cost is equal to the cost per unit multiplied by the number of units. In other words, the relationship between total variable cost (VC), cost per unit of output (v), and total quantity of output (Q) can be written as:

Total variable cost = Total quantity of output × Cost per unit of output

$$VC = Q \times v$$

For example, suppose variable costs (v) are $2 per unit. If total output (Q) is 1,000 units, what will total variable costs (VC) be?

$$
\begin{aligned}
VC &= Q \times v \\
&= 1{,}000 \times \$2 \\
&= \$2{,}000
\end{aligned}
$$

Similarly, if Q is 5,000 units, then VC will be $5,000 \times \$2 = \$10,000$. Figure 11.2 illustrates the relationship between output level and variable costs in this case. In Figure 11.2, notice that increasing output by one unit results in variable costs rising by $2, so "the rise over the run" (the slope of the line) is given by $2/1 = $2.

Variable Costs   **EXAMPLE 11.1**

The Blume Corporation is a manufacturer of pencils. It has received an order for 5,000 pencils, and the company has to decide whether to accept the order. From recent experience, the company knows that each pencil requires 5 cents in raw materials and 50 cents in direct labor costs. These variable costs are expected to continue to apply in the future. What will Blume's total variable costs be if it accepts the order?

360   PART 4   Capital Budgeting

In this case, the cost per unit is 50 cents in labor plus 5 cents in material for a total of 55 cents per unit. At 5,000 units of output, we have:

$$VC = Q \times v$$
$$= 5,000 \times \$.55$$
$$= \$2,750$$

Therefore, total variable costs will be $2,750.

---

fixed costs
Costs that do not change when the quantity of output changes during a particular time period.

Fixed Costs   Fixed costs, by definition, do not change during a specified time period. So, unlike variable costs, they do not depend on the amount of goods or services produced during a period (at least within some range of production). For example, the lease payment on a production facility and the company president's salary are fixed costs, at least over some period.

Naturally, fixed costs are not fixed forever. They are fixed only during some particular time, say, a quarter or a year. Beyond that time, leases can be terminated and executives "retired." More to the point, any fixed cost can be modified or eliminated given enough time; so, in the long run, all costs are variable.

Notice that when a cost is fixed, that cost is effectively a sunk cost because we are going to have to pay it no matter what.

Total Costs   Total costs (TC) for a given level of output are the sum of variable costs (VC) and fixed costs (FC):

$$TC = VC + FC$$
$$= v \times Q + FC$$

So, for example, if we have variable costs of $3 per unit and fixed costs of $8,000 per year, our total cost is:

$$TC = \$3 \times Q + \$8,000$$

If we produce 6,000 units, our total production cost will be $3 × 6,000 + $8,000 = $26,000. At other production levels, we have the following:

Quantity Produced	Total Variable Costs	Fixed Costs	Total Costs
0	$ 0	$8,000	$ 8,000
1,000	3,000	8,000	11,000
5,000	15,000	8,000	23,000
10,000	30,000	8,000	38,000

marginal cost
The change in costs that occurs when there is a small change in output. Also called *incremental cost.*

By plotting these points in Figure 11.3, we see that the relationship between quantity produced and total costs is given by a straight line. In Figure 11.3, notice that total costs equal fixed costs when sales are zero. Beyond that point, every one-unit increase in production leads to a $3 increase in total costs, so the slope of the line is 3. In other words, the **marginal**, or **incremental**, **cost** of producing one more unit is $3.

EXAMPLE 11.2	Average Cost versus Marginal Cost

Suppose the Blume Corporation has a variable cost per pencil of 55 cents. The lease payment on the production facility runs $5,000 per month. If Blume produces 100,000 pencils per year, what are the total costs of production? What is the average cost per pencil?

The fixed costs are $5,000 per month, or $60,000 per year. The variable cost is $.55 per pencil. So the total cost for the year, assuming that Blume produces 100,000 pencils, is:

$$\text{Total cost} = v \times Q + FC$$
$$= \$.55 \times 100,000 + \$60,000$$
$$= \$115,000$$

The average cost per pencil is $115,000/100,000 = $1.15.

Now suppose that Blume has received a special, one-shot order for 5,000 pencils. Blume has sufficient capacity to manufacture the 5,000 pencils on top of the 100,000 already produced, so no additional fixed costs will be incurred. Also, there will be no effect on existing orders. If Blume can get 75 cents per pencil for this order, should the order be accepted?

What this boils down to is a simple proposition. It costs 55 cents to make another pencil. Anything Blume can get for this pencil in excess of the 55-cent incremental cost contributes in a positive way toward covering fixed costs. The 75-cent **marginal**, or **incremental**, **revenue** exceeds the 55-cent marginal cost, so Blume should take the order.

The fixed cost of $60,000 is irrelevant to this decision because it is effectively sunk, at least for the current period. In the same way, the fact that the average cost is $1.15 is irrelevant because this average reflects the fixed cost. As long as producing the extra 5,000 pencils truly does not cost anything beyond the 55 cents per pencil, then Blume should accept any price above 55 cents.

marginal revenue
The change in revenue that occurs when there is a small change in output. Also called *incremental revenue*.

ACCOUNTING BREAK-EVEN

The most widely used measure of break-even is **accounting break-even**. The accounting break-even point is the sales level that results in a zero project net income.

To determine a project's accounting break-even, we start off with some common sense. Suppose we retail one-petabyte computer disks for $5 apiece. We can buy disks from a wholesale supplier for $3 apiece. We have accounting expenses of $600 in fixed costs and $300 in depreciation. How many disks do we have to sell to break even—that is, for net income to be zero?

accounting break-even
The sales level that results in zero project net income.

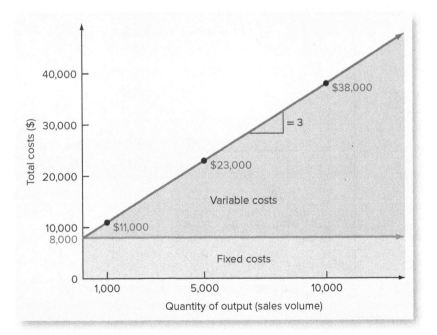

FIGURE 11.3

Output Level and Total Costs

362 **PART 4** Capital Budgeting

For every disk we sell, we pick up $5 − 3 = $2 toward covering our other expenses (this $2 difference between the selling price and the variable cost is often called the *contribution margin per unit*). We have to cover a total of $600 + 300 = $900 in accounting expenses, so we obviously need to sell $900/$2 = 450 disks. We can check this by noting that at a sales level of 450 units, our revenues are $5 × 450 = $2,250 and our variable costs are $3 × 450 = $1,350. Here is the income statement:

Sales	$2,250
Variable costs	1,350
Fixed costs	600
Depreciation	300
EBIT	$ 0
Taxes (21%)	0
Net income	$ 0

Remember, because we are discussing a proposed new project, we do not consider any interest expense in calculating net income or cash flow from the project. Also, notice that we include depreciation in calculating expenses here, even though depreciation is not a cash outflow. That is why we call it an accounting break-even. Finally, notice that when net income is zero, so are pretax income and, of course, taxes. In accounting terms, our revenues are equal to our costs, so there is no profit to tax.

Figure 11.4 presents another way to see what is happening. This figure looks a lot like Figure 11.3 except that we add a line for revenues. As indicated, total revenues are zero when output is zero. Beyond that, each unit sold brings in another $5, so the slope of the revenue line is 5.

From our preceding discussion, we know that we break even when revenues are equal to total costs. The line for revenues and the line for total costs cross right where output is at

FIGURE 11.4

Accounting Break-Even

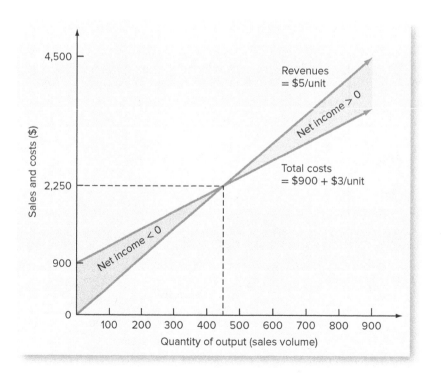

450 units. As illustrated, at any level of output below 450, our accounting profit is negative, and at any level above 450, we have a positive net income.

ACCOUNTING BREAK-EVEN: A CLOSER LOOK

In our numerical example, notice that the break-even level is equal to the sum of fixed costs and depreciation, divided by price per unit less variable costs per unit. This is always true. To see why, we recall all of the following variables:

P = Selling price per unit
v = Variable cost per unit
Q = Total units sold
S = Total sales = $P \times Q$
VC = Total variable costs = $v \times Q$
FC = Fixed costs
D = Depreciation
T_C = Tax rate

Project net income is given by:

$$\text{Net income} = (\text{Sales} - \text{Variable costs} - \text{Fixed costs} - \text{Depreciation}) \times (1 - T_C)$$
$$= (S - VC - FC - D) \times (1 - T_C)$$

From here, it is not difficult to calculate the break-even point. If we set this net income equal to zero, we get:

$$\text{Net income} \overset{\text{SET}}{=} 0 = (S - VC - FC - D) \times \left(1 - T_C\right)$$

Divide both sides by $(1 - T_C)$ to get:

$$S - VC - FC - D = 0$$

As we have seen, this says that when net income is zero, so is pretax income. If we recall that $S = P \times Q$ and VC = $v \times Q$, then we can rearrange the equation to solve for the break-even level:

$$S - VC = FC + D$$
$$P \times Q - v \times Q = FC + D$$
$$(P - v) \times Q = FC + D$$
$$\boldsymbol{Q = (FC + D)/(P - v)}$$

11.1

This is the same result we described earlier.

USES FOR THE ACCOUNTING BREAK-EVEN

Why would anyone be interested in knowing the accounting break-even point? To illustrate how it can be useful, suppose we are a small specialty ice cream manufacturer with a strictly local distribution. We are thinking about expanding into new markets. Based on the estimated cash flows, we find that the expansion has a positive NPV.

Going back to our discussion of forecasting risk, we know that it is likely that what will make or break our expansion is sales volume. The reason is that, in this case at least, we probably have a fairly good idea of what we can charge for the ice cream. Further, we know relevant production and distribution costs reasonably well because we are already in the business. What we do not know with any real precision is how much ice cream we can sell.

Given the costs and selling price, we can immediately calculate the break-even point. Once we have done so, we might find that we need to get 30 percent of the market just to break even. If we think that this is unlikely to occur, because, for example, we have only 10 percent of our current market, then we know our forecast is questionable and there is a real possibility that the true NPV is negative. On the other hand, we might find that we already have firm commitments from buyers for about the break-even amount, so we are almost certain we can sell more. In this case, the forecasting risk is much lower, and we have greater confidence in our estimates.

There are several other reasons why knowing the accounting break-even can be useful. First, as we will discuss in more detail later, accounting break-even and payback period are similar measures. Like payback period, accounting break-even is relatively easy to calculate and explain.

Second, managers are often concerned with the contribution a project will make to the firm's total accounting earnings. A project that does not break even in an accounting sense actually reduces total earnings.

Third, a project that just breaks even on an accounting basis loses money in a financial or opportunity cost sense. This is true because we could have earned more by investing elsewhere. Such a project does not lose money in an out-of-pocket sense. As described in the following sections, we get back exactly what we put in. For noneconomic reasons, opportunity losses may be easier to live with than out-of-pocket losses.

Concept Questions

11.3a How are fixed costs similar to sunk costs?

11.3b What is net income at the accounting break-even point? What about taxes?

11.3c Why might a financial manager be interested in the accounting break-even point?

11.4 Operating Cash Flow, Sales Volume, and Break-Even

Excel Master It!

Excel Master coverage online

Accounting break-even is one tool that is useful for project analysis. Ultimately, we are more interested in cash flow than accounting income. So, for example, if sales volume is the critical variable, then we need to know more about the relationship between sales volume and cash flow than just the accounting break-even.

Our goal in this section is to illustrate the relationship between operating cash flow and sales volume. We also discuss some other break-even measures. To simplify matters somewhat, we will ignore the effect of taxes. We start off by looking at the relationship between accounting break-even and cash flow.

ACCOUNTING BREAK-EVEN AND CASH FLOW

Now that we know how to find the accounting break-even, it is natural to wonder what happens with cash flow. To illustrate, suppose the Wettway Sailboat Corporation is considering whether to launch its new Margo-class sailboat. The selling price will be $40,000 per boat. The variable costs will be about half that, or $20,000 per boat, and fixed costs will be $500,000 per year.

The Base Case   The total investment needed to undertake the project is $3,500,000. This amount will be depreciated straight-line to zero over the five-year life of the equipment.

The salvage value is zero, and there are no working capital consequences. Wettway has a 20 percent required return on new projects.

Based on market surveys and historical experience, Wettway projects total sales for the five years at 425 boats, or about 85 boats per year. Ignoring taxes, should this project be launched?

To begin, ignoring taxes, the operating cash flow at 85 boats per year is:

$$
\begin{aligned}
\text{Operating cash flow} &= \text{EBIT} + \text{Depreciation} - \text{Taxes} \\
&= (S - \text{VC} - \text{FC} - D) + D - 0 \\
&= 85 \times (\$40,000 - 20,000) - \$500,000 \\
&= \$1,200,000 \text{ per year}
\end{aligned}
$$

At 20 percent, the five-year annuity factor is 2.9906, so the NPV is:

$$
\begin{aligned}
\text{NPV} &= -\$3,500,000 + \$1,200,000 \times 2.9906 \\
&= -\$3,500,000 + 3,588,735 \\
&= \$88,735
\end{aligned}
$$

In the absence of additional information, the project should be launched.

Calculating the Break-Even Level   To begin looking a little closer at this project, you might ask a series of questions. For example, how many new boats does Wettway need to sell for the project to break even on an accounting basis? If Wettway does break even, what will be the annual cash flow from the project? What will be the return on the investment in this case?

Before fixed costs and depreciation are considered, Wettway generates $40,000 - 20,000 = $20,000 per boat (this is revenue less variable cost). Depreciation is $3,500,000/5 = $700,000 per year. Fixed costs and depreciation together total $1.2 million, so Wettway needs to sell $(FC + D)/(P - v) = $1.2 million/$20,000 = 60 boats per year to break even on an accounting basis. This is 25 boats less than projected sales; so, assuming that Wettway is confident its projection is accurate to within, say, 15 boats, it appears unlikely that the new investment will fail to at least break even on an accounting basis.

To calculate Wettway's cash flow in this case, we note that if 60 boats are sold, net income will be exactly zero. Recalling from the previous chapter that operating cash flow for a project can be written as net income plus depreciation (the bottom-up definition), we can see that the operating cash flow is equal to the depreciation, or $700,000 in this case. The internal rate of return is exactly zero (why?).

Payback and Break-Even   As our example illustrates, whenever a project breaks even on an accounting basis, the cash flow for that period will equal the depreciation. This result makes perfect accounting sense. For example, suppose we invest $100,000 in a five-year project. The depreciation is straight-line to a zero salvage, or $20,000 per year. If the project exactly breaks even every period, then the cash flow will be $20,000 per period.

The sum of the cash flows for the life of this project is $5 \times \$20,000 = \$100,000$, the original investment. What this shows is that a project's payback period is exactly equal to its life if the project breaks even every period. Similarly, a project that does better than break even has a payback that is shorter than the life of the project and has a positive rate of return.

The bad news is that a project that just breaks even on an accounting basis has a negative NPV and a zero return. For our sailboat project, the fact that Wettway will almost surely break even on an accounting basis is partially comforting because it means that the firm's "downside" risk (its potential loss) is limited, but we still don't know if the project is truly profitable. More work is needed.

366 PART 4 Capital Budgeting

SALES VOLUME AND OPERATING CASH FLOW

At this point, we can generalize our example and introduce some other break-even measures. From our discussion in the previous section, we know that, ignoring taxes, a project's operating cash flow, OCF, can be written as EBIT plus depreciation:

$$\textbf{OCF} = [(P - v) \times Q - \text{FC} - D] + D$$
$$= \textbf{(}P - v\textbf{)} \times \textbf{Q} - \textbf{FC}$$

11.2

For the Wettway sailboat project, the general relationship (in thousands of dollars) between operating cash flow and sales volume is:

$$\text{OCF} = (P - v) \times Q - \text{FC}$$
$$= (\$40 - 20) \times Q - 500$$
$$= -\$500 + \$20 \times Q$$

What this tells us is that the relationship between operating cash flow and sales volume is given by a straight line with a slope of $20 and a y-intercept of −$500. If we calculate some different values, we get:

Quantity Sold	Operating Cash Flow
0	−$ 500
15	− 200
30	100
50	500
75	1,000

These points are plotted in Figure 11.5, where we have indicated three different break-even points. We discuss these next.

CASH FLOW, ACCOUNTING, AND FINANCIAL BREAK-EVEN POINTS

We know from the preceding discussion that the relationship between operating cash flow and sales volume (ignoring taxes) is:

$$\text{OCF} = (P - v) \times Q - \text{FC}$$

If we rearrange this and solve for Q, we get:

$$\textbf{Q} = \textbf{(FC} + \textbf{OCF)}/\textbf{(}P - v\textbf{)}$$

11.3

FIGURE 11.5

Operating Cash Flow and Sales Volume

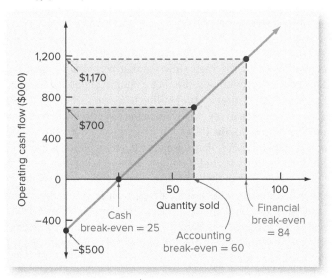

This tells us what sales volume (Q) is necessary to achieve any given OCF, so this result is more general than the accounting break-even. We use it to find the various break-even points in Figure 11.5.

Accounting Break-Even Revisited   Looking at Figure 11.5, suppose operating cash flow is equal to depreciation (D). Recall that this situation corresponds to our break-even point on an accounting basis. To find the sales volume, we substitute the $700 depreciation amount for OCF in our general expression:

$$Q = (FC + OCF)/(P - v)$$
$$= (\$500 + 700)/\$20$$
$$= 60$$

This is the same quantity we had before.

Cash Break-Even   We have seen that a project that breaks even on an accounting basis has a net income of zero, but it still has a positive cash flow. At some sales level below the accounting break-even, the operating cash flow actually goes negative. This is a particularly unpleasant occurrence. If it happens, we actually have to supply additional cash to the project to keep it afloat.

To calculate the **cash break-even** (the point where operating cash flow is equal to zero), we put in a zero for OCF:

$$Q = (FC + 0)/(P - v)$$
$$= \$500/\$20$$
$$= 25$$

cash break-even
The sales level that results in a zero operating cash flow.

Wettway must therefore sell 25 boats to cover the $500 in fixed costs. As we show in Figure 11.5, this point occurs right where the operating cash flow line crosses the horizontal axis.

Notice that a project that just breaks even on a cash flow basis can cover its own fixed operating costs, but that is all. It never pays back anything, so the original investment is a complete loss (the IRR is −100 percent).

Financial Break-Even   The last case we consider is that of **financial break-even**, the sales level that results in a zero NPV. To the financial manager, this is the most interesting case. What we do is first determine what operating cash flow has to be for the NPV to be zero. We then use this amount to determine the sales volume.

financial break-even
The sales level that results in a zero NPV.

To illustrate, recall that Wettway requires a 20 percent return on its $3,500 (in thousands) investment. How many sailboats does Wettway have to sell to break even once we account for the 20 percent per year opportunity cost?

The sailboat project has a five-year life. The project has a zero NPV when the present value of the operating cash flows equals the $3,500 investment. Because the cash flow is the same each year, we can solve for the unknown amount by viewing it as an ordinary annuity. The five-year annuity factor at 20 percent is 2.9906, and the OCF can be determined as follows:

$$\$3,500 = OCF \times 2.9906$$
$$OCF = \$3,500/2.9906$$
$$= \$1,170$$

Wettway needs an operating cash flow of $1,170 each year to break even. We can now plug this OCF into the equation for sales volume:

$$Q = (\$500 + 1,170)/\$20$$
$$= 83.5$$

So, Wettway needs to sell about 84 boats per year. This is not good news.

As indicated in Figure 11.5, the financial break-even is substantially higher than the accounting break-even. This will often be the case. Moreover, what we have discovered is that the sailboat project has a substantial degree of forecasting risk. We project sales of 85 boats per year, but it takes 84 just to earn the required return.

Conclusion Overall, it seems unlikely that the Wettway sailboat project would fail to break even on an accounting basis. However, there appears to be a very good chance that the true NPV is negative. This illustrates the danger in looking at just the accounting break-even.

What should Wettway do? Is the new project all wet? The decision at this point is essentially a managerial issue—a judgment call. The crucial questions are these:

1. How much confidence do we have in our projections?
2. How important is the project to the future of the company?
3. How badly will the company be hurt if sales turn out to be low? What options are available to the company in this case?

We will consider questions such as these in a later section. For future reference, our discussion of the different break-even measures is summarized in Table 11.1.

TABLE 11.1

Summary of Break-Even Measures

I.	**The General Break-Even Expression**

Ignoring taxes, the relation between operating cash flow (OCF) and quantity of output or sales volume (Q) is:

$$Q = \frac{FC + OCF}{P - v}$$

where

   FC = Total fixed costs
   P = Price per unit
   v = Variable cost per unit

As shown next, this relation can be used to determine the accounting, cash, and financial break-even points.

II.	**The Accounting Break-Even Point**

Accounting break-even occurs when net income is zero. Operating cash flow is equal to depreciation when net income is zero, so the accounting break-even point is:

$$Q = \frac{FC + D}{P - v}$$

A project that always just breaks even on an accounting basis has a payback exactly equal to its life, a negative NPV, and an IRR of zero.

III.	**The Cash Break-Even Point**

Cash break-even occurs when operating cash flow is zero. The cash break-even point is:

$$Q = \frac{FC}{P - v}$$

A project that always just breaks even on a cash basis never pays back, has an NPV that is negative and equal to the initial outlay, and has an IRR of −100 percent.

IV.	**The Financial Break-Even Point**

Financial break-even occurs when the NPV of the project is zero. The financial break-even point is:

$$Q = \frac{FC + OCF^*}{P - v}$$

where OCF* is the level of OCF that results in a zero NPV. A project that breaks even on a financial basis has a discounted payback equal to its life, a zero NPV, and an IRR just equal to the required return.

Operating Leverage

11.5

We have discussed how to calculate and interpret various measures of break-even for a proposed project. What we have not explicitly discussed is what determines these points and how they might be changed. We now turn to this subject.[1]

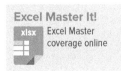

THE BASIC IDEA

Operating leverage is the degree to which a project or firm is committed to fixed production costs. A firm with low operating leverage will have low fixed costs compared to a firm with high operating leverage. Generally speaking, projects with a relatively heavy investment in plant and equipment will have a relatively high degree of operating leverage. Such projects are said to be *capital intensive*.

operating leverage
The degree to which a firm or project relies on fixed costs.

Anytime we are thinking about a new venture, there will normally be alternative ways of producing and delivering the product. For example, Wettway Sailboat Corporation can purchase the necessary equipment and build all of the components for its sailboats in-house. Alternatively, some of the work could be farmed out to other firms. The first option involves a greater investment in plant and equipment, greater fixed costs and depreciation, and, as a result, a higher degree of operating leverage.

IMPLICATIONS OF OPERATING LEVERAGE

Regardless of how it is measured, operating leverage has important implications for project evaluation. Fixed costs act like a lever in the sense that a small percentage change in operating revenue can be magnified into a large percentage change in operating cash flow and NPV. This explains why we call it operating "leverage."

The higher the degree of operating leverage, the greater is the potential danger from forecasting risk. The reason is that relatively small errors in forecasting sales volume can get magnified, or "levered up," into large errors in cash flow projections.

From a managerial perspective, one way of coping with highly uncertain projects is to keep the degree of operating leverage as low as possible. This will generally have the effect of keeping the break-even point (however measured) at its minimum level. We will illustrate this point in a bit, but first we need to discuss how to measure operating leverage.

MEASURING OPERATING LEVERAGE

One way of measuring operating leverage is to ask: If quantity sold rises by 5 percent, what will be the percentage change in operating cash flow? In other words, the **degree of operating leverage (DOL)** is defined such that:

Percentage change in OCF = DOL × Percentage change in Q

degree of operating leverage (DOL)
The percentage change in operating cash flow relative to the percentage change in quantity sold.

[1]The assumption of no taxes still holds. To see the effect of taxes on break-even and DOL, see Problems 25 and 26.

Based on the relationship between OCF and Q, DOL can be written as:[2]

DOL = 1 + FC/OCF   ⑪·④

The ratio FC/OCF measures fixed costs as a percentage of total operating cash flow. Notice that zero fixed costs would result in a DOL of 1, implying that percentage changes in quantity sold would show up one for one in operating cash flow. In other words, no magnification, or leverage, effect would exist.

To illustrate this measure of operating leverage, we go back to the Wettway sailboat project. Fixed costs were $500 and $(P - v)$ was $20, so OCF was:

$$OCF = -\$500 + \$20 \times Q$$

Suppose Q is currently 50 boats. At this level of output, OCF is $-\$500 + 1,000 = \$500$.

If Q rises by 1 unit to 51, then the percentage change in Q is $(51 - 50)/50 = .02$, or 2%. OCF rises to $520, a change of $P - v = \$20$. The percentage change in OCF is $(\$520 - 500)/\$500 = .04$, or 4%. So a 2 percent increase in the number of boats sold leads to a 4 percent increase in operating cash flow. The degree of operating leverage must be exactly 2.00. We can check this by noting that:

$$\begin{aligned} DOL &= 1 + FC/OCF \\ &= 1 + \$500/\$500 \\ &= 2 \end{aligned}$$

This verifies our previous calculations.

Our formulation of DOL depends on the current output level, Q. However, it can handle changes from the current level of any size, not just one unit. For example, suppose Q rises from 50 to 75, a 50 percent increase. With DOL equal to 2, operating cash flow should increase by 100 percent, or exactly double. Does it? The answer is yes, because, at a Q of 75, OCF is:

$$OCF = -\$500 + \$20 \times 75 = \$1,000$$

Notice that operating leverage declines as output (Q) rises. For example, at an output level of 75, we have:

$$\begin{aligned} DOL &= 1 + \$500/\$1,000 \\ &= 1.50 \end{aligned}$$

The reason DOL declines is that fixed costs, considered as a percentage of operating cash flow, get smaller and smaller, so the leverage effect diminishes.

---

[2]To see this, note that if Q goes up by one unit, OCF will go up by $(P - v)$. In this case, the percentage change in Q is $1/Q$, and the percentage change in OCF is $(P - v)/OCF$. Given this, we have:

$$Percentage\ change\ in\ OCF = DOL \times Percentage\ change\ in\ Q$$
$$(P - v)/OCF = DOL \times 1/Q$$
$$DOL = (P - v) \times Q/OCF$$

Also, based on our definitions of OCF:

$$OCF + FC = (P - v) \times Q$$

Thus, DOL can be written as:

$$\begin{aligned} DOL &= (OCF + FC)/OCF \\ &= 1 + FC/OCF \end{aligned}$$

| **Operating Leverage** | **EXAMPLE 11.3** |

The Sasha Corp. currently sells gourmet dog food for $1.20 per can. The variable cost is 80 cents per can, and the packaging and marketing operations have fixed costs of $360,000 per year. Depreciation is $60,000 per year. What is the accounting break-even? Ignoring taxes, what will be the increase in operating cash flow if the quantity sold rises to 10 percent above the break-even point?

The accounting break-even is $420,000/$.40 = 1,050,000 cans. As we know, the operating cash flow is equal to the $60,000 depreciation at this level of production, so the degree of operating leverage is:

$$DOL = 1 + FC/OCF$$
$$= 1 + \$360,000/\$60,000$$
$$= 7$$

Given this, a 10 percent increase in the number of cans of dog food sold will increase operating cash flow by a substantial 70 percent.

To check this answer, we note that if sales rise by 10 percent, then the quantity sold will rise to 1,050,000 × 1.1 = 1,155,000. Ignoring taxes, the operating cash flow will be 1,155,000 × $.40 − $360,000 = $102,000. Compared to the $60,000 cash flow we had, this is exactly 70 percent more: $102,000/$60,000 = 1.70.

OPERATING LEVERAGE AND BREAK-EVEN

We illustrate why operating leverage is an important consideration by examining the Wettway sailboat project under an alternative scenario. At a Q of 85 boats, the degree of operating leverage for the sailboat project under the original scenario is:

$$DOL = 1 + FC/OCF$$
$$= 1 + \$500/\$1,200$$
$$= 1.42$$

Also, recall that the NPV at a sales level of 85 boats was $88,735, and the accounting break-even was 60 boats.

An option available to Wettway is to subcontract production of the boat hull assemblies. If the company does this, the necessary investment falls to $3,200,000 and the fixed operating costs fall to $180,000. Variable costs will rise to $25,000 per boat because subcontracting is more expensive than producing in-house. Ignoring taxes, evaluate this option.

For practice, see if you don't agree with the following:

NPV at 20% (85 units) = $74,720
Accounting break-even = 55 boats
Degree of operating leverage = 1.16

What has happened? This option results in a slightly lower estimated net present value, and the accounting break-even point falls to 55 boats from 60 boats.

Given that this alternative has the lower NPV, is there any reason to consider it further? Maybe there is. The degree of operating leverage is substantially lower in the second case. If Wettway is worried about the possibility of an overly optimistic projection, then it might prefer to subcontract.

There is another reason why Wettway might consider the second arrangement. If sales turn out to be better than expected, the company still has the option of starting to produce in-house at a later date. As a practical matter, it is much easier to increase operating leverage (by purchasing equipment) than to decrease it (by selling off equipment). As we discuss in a later chapter, one of the drawbacks to discounted cash flow analysis is that it is difficult to explicitly include options of this sort in the analysis, even though they may be quite important.

Concept Questions
11.5a What is operating leverage?
11.5b How is operating leverage measured?
11.5c What are the implications of operating leverage for the financial manager?

11.6   Capital Rationing

capital rationing
The situation that exists if a firm has positive NPV projects but cannot find the necessary financing.

Capital rationing is said to exist when we have profitable (positive NPV) investments available but we can't get the funds needed to undertake them. For example, as division managers for a large corporation, we might identify $5 million in excellent projects but find that, for whatever reason, we can spend only $2 million. Now what? Unfortunately, for reasons we will discuss, there may be no truly satisfactory answer.

SOFT RATIONING

soft rationing
The situation that occurs when units in a business are allocated a certain amount of financing for capital budgeting.

The situation we have just described is called **soft rationing**. This occurs when, for example, different units in a business are allocated some fixed amount of money each year for capital spending. Such an allocation is primarily a means of controlling and keeping track of overall spending. The important thing to note about soft rationing is that the corporation as a whole isn't short of capital; more can be raised on ordinary terms if management so desires.

If we face soft rationing, the first thing to do is to try to get a larger allocation. Failing that, one common suggestion is to generate as large a net present value as possible within the existing budget. This amounts to choosing projects with the largest benefit-cost ratio (profitability index).

Strictly speaking, this is the correct thing to do only if the soft rationing is a one-time event—that is, it won't exist next year. If the soft rationing is a chronic problem, then something is amiss. The reason goes all the way back to Chapter 1. Ongoing soft rationing means we are constantly bypassing positive NPV investments. This contradicts the goal of our firm. If we are not trying to maximize value, then the question of which projects to take becomes ambiguous because we no longer have an objective goal in the first place.

HARD RATIONING

hard rationing
The situation that occurs when a business cannot raise financing for a project under any circumstances.

With **hard rationing**, a business cannot raise capital for a project under any circumstances. For large, healthy corporations, this situation probably does not occur very often. This is fortunate because, with hard rationing, our DCF analysis breaks down, and the best course of action is ambiguous.

The reason DCF analysis breaks down has to do with the required return. Suppose we say our required return is 20 percent. Implicitly, we are saying we will take a project with a return that exceeds this. However, if we face hard rationing, then we are not going to take a new project no matter what the return on that project is, so the whole concept of a required return is ambiguous. About the only interpretation we can give this situation is that the required return is so large that no project has a positive NPV in the first place.

Hard rationing can occur when a company experiences financial distress, meaning that bankruptcy is a possibility. Also, a firm may not be able to raise capital without violating a preexisting contractual agreement. We discuss these situations in greater detail in a later chapter.

Concept Questions

11.6a   What is capital rationing? What types are there?
11.6b   What problems does capital rationing create for discounted cash flow analysis?

Summary and Conclusions   11.7

In this chapter, we looked at some ways of evaluating the results of a discounted cash flow analysis; we also touched on some of the problems that can come up in practice:

1. Net present value estimates depend on projected future cash flows. If there are errors in those projections, then our estimated NPVs can be misleading. We called this possibility *forecasting risk*.

2. Scenario and sensitivity analysis are useful tools for identifying which variables are critical to the success of a project and where forecasting problems can do the most damage.

3. Break-even analysis in its various forms is a particularly common type of scenario analysis that is useful for identifying critical levels of sales.

4. Operating leverage is a key determinant of break-even levels. It reflects the degree to which a project or a firm is committed to fixed costs. The degree of operating leverage tells us the sensitivity of operating cash flow to changes in sales volume.

5. Projects usually have future managerial options associated with them. These options may be important, but standard discounted cash flow analysis tends to ignore them.

6. Capital rationing occurs when apparently profitable projects cannot be funded. Standard discounted cash flow analysis is troublesome in this case because NPV is not necessarily the appropriate criterion.

The most important thing to carry away from reading this chapter is that estimated NPVs or returns should not be taken at face value. They depend critically on projected cash flows. If there is room for significant disagreement about those projected cash flows, the results from the analysis have to be taken with a grain of salt.

Despite the problems we have discussed, discounted cash flow analysis is still *the* way of attacking problems because it forces us to ask the right questions. What we have learned in this chapter is that knowing the questions to ask does not guarantee we will get all the answers.

CONNECT TO FINANCE

 Do you use *Connect Finance* to practice what you learned? If you don't, you should—we can help you master the topics presented in this chapter. Log on to connect.mheducation.com to learn more!

374   **PART 4**   Capital Budgeting

Can you answer the following *Connect* Quiz questions?

Section 11.1 The potential for believing that a project has a positive net present value when it does not is referred to as _____.

Section 11.2 Marcos Entertainment expects to sell 84,000 theater tickets at $12 each during the coming year. What is the worst-case sales revenue if all estimates are accurate to within a ±3 percent range?

Section 11.3 Delta Tool has projected sales of 8,500 units at a sales price per unit of $9,400. Fixed costs are estimated at $5.2 million, and estimated variable costs per unit are $8,300. What is the amount of the total costs if the firm temporarily stops production?

Section 11.4 What is true for a project if that project is operating at its financial break-even point?

Section 11.5 A capital-intensive project is one that has a _____.

Section 11.6 Pavloki, Inc., has three proposed projects with positive net present values. These projects and their net present values are: Project A—NPV $46,300; Project B—NPV $31,900; Project C—NPV $6,400. If the firm is faced with hard rationing, which of the projects will it accept?

CHAPTER REVIEW AND SELF-TEST PROBLEMS

Use the following base-case information to work the self-test problems:

A project under consideration costs $750,000, has a five-year life, and has no salvage value. Depreciation is straight-line to zero. The required return is 17 percent, and the tax rate is 21 percent. Sales are projected at 500 units per year. Price per unit is $2,500, variable cost per unit is $1,500, and fixed costs are $200,000 per year.

11.1 Scenario Analysis Suppose you think that the unit sales, price, variable cost, and fixed cost projections given here are accurate to within 5 percent. What are the upper and lower bounds for these projections? What is the base-case NPV? What are the best- and worst-case scenario NPVs?

11.2 Break-Even Analysis Given the base-case projections in the previous problem, what are the cash, accounting, and financial break-even sales levels for this project? Ignore taxes in answering.

ANSWERS TO CHAPTER REVIEW AND SELF-TEST PROBLEMS

11.1 We can summarize the relevant information as follows:

	Base Case	Lower Bound	Upper Bound
Unit sales	500	475	525
Price per unit	$ 2,500	$ 2,375	$ 2,625
Variable cost per unit	$ 1,500	$ 1,425	$ 1,575
Fixed cost per year	$200,000	$190,000	$210,000

Depreciation is $150,000 per year; knowing this, we can calculate the cash flows under each scenario. Remember that we assign high costs and low prices and volume for the worst case and just the opposite for the best case:

Scenario	Unit Sales	Unit Price	Unit Variable Cost	Fixed Costs	Cash Flow
Base case	500	$2,500	$1,500	$200,000	$268,500
Best case	525	2,625	1,425	190,000	379,100
Worst case	475	2,375	1,575	210,000	165,800

At 17 percent, the five-year annuity factor is 3.19935, so the NPVs are:

$$\text{Base-case NPV} = -\$750,000 + 3.19935 \times \$268,500$$
$$= \$109,024$$
$$\text{Best-case NPV} = -\$750,000 + 3.19935 \times \$379,100$$
$$= \$462,872$$
$$\text{Worst-case NPV} = -\$750,000 + 3.19935 \times \$165,800$$
$$= -\$219,548$$

11.2 In this case, we have $200,000 in cash fixed costs to cover. Each unit contributes $2,500 − 1,500 = $1,000 toward covering fixed costs. The cash break-even is thus $200,000/$1,000 = 200 units. We have another $150,000 in depreciation, so the accounting break-even is ($200,000 + 150,000)/$1,000 = 350 units.

To get the financial break-even, we need to find the OCF such that the project has a zero NPV. As we have seen, the five-year annuity factor is 3.19935 and the project costs $750,000, so the OCF must be such that:

$$\$750,000 = \text{OCF} \times 3.19935$$

So, for the project to break even on a financial basis, the project's cash flow must be $750,000/3.19935, or $234,423 per year. If we add this to the $200,000 in cash fixed costs, we get a total of $434,423 that we have to cover. At $1,000 per unit, we need to sell $434,423/$1,000 = 435 units.

CONCEPTS REVIEW AND CRITICAL THINKING QUESTIONS

1. **Forecasting Risk** [LO1] What is forecasting risk? In general, would the degree of forecasting risk be greater for a new product or a cost-cutting proposal? Why?

2. **Sensitivity Analysis and Scenario Analysis** [LO1, 2] What is the essential difference between sensitivity analysis and scenario analysis?

3. **Marginal Cash Flows** [LO3] A co-worker claims that looking at all this marginal this and incremental that is just a bunch of nonsense, saying, "Listen, if our average revenue doesn't exceed our average cost, then we will have a negative cash flow, and we will go broke!" How do you respond?

4. **Operating Leverage** [LO4] At one time at least, many Japanese companies had a "no-layoff" policy (for that matter, so did IBM). What are the implications of such a policy for the degree of operating leverage a company faces?

5. **Operating Leverage** [LO4] Airlines offer an example of an industry in which the degree of operating leverage is fairly high. Why?

6. **Break-Even** [LO3] As a shareholder of a firm that is contemplating a new project, would you be more concerned with the accounting break-even point, the cash break-even point, or the financial break-even point? Why?

7. **Break-Even** [LO3] Assume a firm is considering a new project that requires an initial investment and has equal sales and costs over its life. Will the project reach the accounting, cash, or financial break-even point first? Which will it reach next? Last? Will this ordering always apply?

8. **Capital Rationing** [LO5] How do soft rationing and hard rationing differ? What are the implications if a firm is experiencing soft rationing? Hard rationing?

9. **Capital Rationing** [LO5] Going all the way back to Chapter 1, recall that we saw that partnerships and proprietorships can face difficulties when it comes to raising capital. In the context of this chapter, the implication is that small businesses will generally face what problem?

10. **Scenario Analysis** [LO2] You are at work when a co-worker excitedly comes to your desk and shows you the scenario analysis that he has just completed for a potential new project. All three scenarios show a positive NPV. He states, "We have to take this project!" What is your initial reaction regarding this new project. Do you believe the results of the scenario analysis?

QUESTIONS AND PROBLEMS

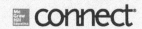

BASIC
(Questions 1–15)

1. **Calculating Costs and Break-Even** [LO3] Night Shades, Inc. (NSI), manufactures biotech sunglasses. The variable materials cost is $11.13 per unit, and the variable labor cost is $7.29 per unit.

    a. What is the variable cost per unit?

    b. Suppose the company incurs fixed costs of $875,000 during a year in which total production is 190,000 units. What are the total costs for the year?

    c. If the selling price is $44.99 per unit, does the company break even on a cash basis? If depreciation is $435,000 per year, what is the accounting break-even point?

2. **Computing Average Cost** [LO3] K-Too Everwear Corporation can manufacture mountain climbing shoes for $33.18 per pair in variable raw material costs and $24.36 per pair in variable labor expense. The shoes sell for $170 per pair. Last year, production was 145,000 pairs. Fixed costs were $1,750,000. What were total production costs? What is the marginal cost per pair? What is the average cost? If the company is considering a one-time order for an extra 5,000 pairs, what is the minimum acceptable total revenue from the order? Explain.

3. **Scenario Analysis** [LO2] Sloan Transmissions, Inc., has the following estimates for its new gear assembly project: Price = $1,440 per unit; variable costs = $460 per unit; fixed costs = $3.9 million; quantity = 85,000 units. Suppose the company believes all of its estimates are accurate only to within ±15 percent. What values should the company use for the four variables given here when it performs its best-case scenario analysis? What about the worst-case scenario?

4. **Sensitivity Analysis** [LO1] For the company in the previous problem, suppose management is most concerned about the impact of its price estimate on the project's profitability. How could you address this concern? Describe how you would calculate your answer. What values would you use for the other forecast variables?

5. **Sensitivity Analysis and Break-Even** [LO1, 3] We are evaluating a project that costs $786,000, has an eight-year life, and has no salvage value. Assume that depreciation is straight-line to zero over the life of the project. Sales are projected at 65,000 units per year. Price per unit is $48, variable cost per unit is $25, and fixed costs are $725,000 per year. The tax rate is 22 percent, and we require a return of 10 percent on this project.

    a. Calculate the accounting break-even point. What is the degree of operating leverage at the accounting break-even point?

    b. Calculate the base-case cash flow and NPV. What is the sensitivity of NPV to changes in the quantity sold? Explain what your answer tells you about a 500-unit decrease in the quantity sold.

    c. What is the sensitivity of OCF to changes in the variable cost figure? Explain what your answer tells you about a $1 decrease in estimated variable costs.

6. **Scenario Analysis** [LO2] In the previous problem, suppose the projections given for price, quantity, variable costs, and fixed costs are all accurate to within ±10 percent. Calculate the best-case and worst-case NPV figures.

7. **Calculating Break-Even** [LO3] In each of the following cases, calculate the accounting break-even and the cash break-even points. Ignore any tax effects in calculating the cash break-even.

Unit Price	Unit Variable Cost	Fixed Costs	Depreciation
$2,980	$2,135	$8,100,000	$3,100,000
46	41	185,000	183,000
9	3	2,770	1,050

8. **Calculating Break-Even** [LO3] In each of the following cases, find the unknown variable:

Accounting Break-Even	Unit Price	Unit Variable Cost	Fixed Costs	Depreciation
125,736	$39	$30	$ 820,000	?
165,000	?	27	2,320,000	$975,000
21,430	92	?	237,000	128,700

9. **Calculating Break-Even** [LO3] A project has the following estimated data: Price = $62 per unit; variable costs = $28 per unit; fixed costs = $27,300; required return = 12 percent; initial investment = $34,800; life = four years. Ignoring the effect of taxes, what is the accounting break-even quantity? The cash break-even quantity? The financial break-even quantity? What is the degree of operating leverage at the financial break-even level of output?

10. **Using Break-Even Analysis** [LO3] Consider a project with the following data: Accounting break-even quantity = 13,700 units; cash break-even quantity = 9,600 units; life = five years; fixed costs = $185,000; variable costs = $23 per unit; required return = 12 percent. Ignoring the effect of taxes, find the financial break-even quantity.

11. **Calculating Operating Leverage** [LO4] At an output level of 45,000 units, you calculate that the degree of operating leverage is 2.79. If output rises to 48,000 units, what will the percentage change in operating cash flow be? Will the new level of operating leverage be higher or lower? Explain.

12. **Leverage** [LO4] In the previous problem, suppose fixed costs are $175,000. What is the operating cash flow at 43,000 units? The degree of operating leverage?

13. **Operating Cash Flow and Leverage** [LO4] A proposed project has fixed costs of $89,000 per year. The operating cash flow at 10,400 units is $127,400. Ignoring the effect of taxes, what is the degree of operating leverage? If units sold rise from 10,400 to 11,100, what will be the increase in operating cash flow? What is the new degree of operating leverage?

14. **Cash Flow and Leverage** [LO4] At an output level of 17,500 units, you have calculated that the degree of operating leverage is 3.26. The operating cash flow is $78,000 in this case. Ignoring the effect of taxes, what are fixed costs? What will the operating cash flow be if output rises to 18,500 units? If output falls to 16,500 units?

15. **Leverage** [LO4] In the previous problem, what will be the new degree of operating leverage in each case?

INTERMEDIATE
(Questions 16–24)

16. **Break-Even Intuition** [LO3] Consider a project with a required return of R percent that costs $\$I$ and will last for N years. The project uses straight-line depreciation to zero over the N-year life; there is no salvage value or net working capital requirements.

   a. At the accounting break-even level of output, what is the IRR of this project? The payback period? The NPV?

   b. At the cash break-even level of output, what is the IRR of this project? The payback period? The NPV?

   c. At the financial break-even level of output, what is the IRR of this project? The payback period? The NPV?

17. **Sensitivity Analysis** [LO1] Consider a four-year project with the following information: Initial fixed asset investment = $575,000; straight-line depreciation to zero over the four-year life; zero salvage value; price = $29; variable costs = $19; fixed costs = $235,000; quantity sold = 76,000 units; tax rate = 21 percent. How sensitive is OCF to changes in quantity sold?

18. **Operating Leverage** [LO4] In the previous problem, what is the degree of operating leverage at the given level of output? What is the degree of operating leverage at the accounting break-even level of output?

19. **Project Analysis** [LO1, 2, 3, 4] You are considering a new product launch. The project will cost $1,950,000, have a four-year life, and have no salvage value; depreciation is straight-line to zero. Sales are projected at 210 units per year; price per unit will be $17,500, variable cost per unit will be $10,600, and fixed costs will be $560,000 per year. The required return on the project is 12 percent, and the relevant tax rate is 21 percent.

   a. Based on your experience, you think the unit sales, variable cost, and fixed cost projections given here are probably accurate to within ±10 percent. What are the upper and lower bounds for these projections? What is the base-case NPV? What are the best-case and worst-case scenarios?

   b. Evaluate the sensitivity of your base-case NPV to changes in fixed costs.

   c. What is the cash break-even level of output for this project (ignoring taxes)?

   d. What is the accounting break-even level of output for this project? What is the degree of operating leverage at the accounting break-even point? How do you interpret this number?

20. **Project Analysis** [LO1, 2] McGilla Golf has decided to sell a new line of golf clubs. The clubs will sell for $845 per set and have a variable cost of $405 per set. The company has spent $150,000 for a marketing study that determined the company will sell 60,000 sets per year for seven years. The marketing study also determined that the company will lose sales of 10,000 sets of its high-priced clubs. The high-priced clubs sell at $1,175 and have variable costs of $620. The company will also increase sales of its cheap clubs by 12,000 sets. The cheap clubs sell for $435 and have variable costs of $200 per set. The fixed costs each year will be $9.75 million. The company has also spent $1 million on research and development for the new clubs. The plant and equipment required will cost $37.1 million and will be depreciated on a straight-line basis. The new clubs will also require an increase in net working

capital of $1.7 million that will be returned at the end of the project. The tax rate is 25 percent, and the cost of capital is 10 percent. Calculate the payback period, the NPV, and the IRR.

21. **Scenario Analysis** [LO2] In the previous problem, you feel that the values are accurate to within only ±10 percent. What are the best-case and worst-case NPVs? *Hint*: The price and variable costs for the two existing sets of clubs are known with certainty; only the sales gained or lost are uncertain.

22. **Sensitivity Analysis** [LO1] In Problem 20, McGilla Golf would like to know the sensitivity of NPV to changes in the price of the new clubs and the quantity of new clubs sold. What is the sensitivity of the NPV to each of these variables?

23. **Break-Even Analysis** [LO3] Hybrid cars are touted as a "green" alternative; however, the financial aspects of hybrid ownership are not as clear. Consider the 2016 Toyota Camry Hybrid LE, which had a list price of $5,500 (including tax consequences) more than the comparable Volkswagen Touareg VR6. Additionally, the annual ownership costs (other than fuel) for the hybrid were expected to be $350 more than the traditional sedan. The EPA mileage estimate was 39 mpg for the hybrid and 30 mpg for the traditional sedan.

    a. Assume that gasoline costs $2.85 per gallon and you plan to keep either car for six years. How many miles per year would you need to drive to make the decision to buy the hybrid worthwhile, ignoring the time value of money?

    b. If you drive 15,000 miles per year and keep either car for six years, what price per gallon would make the decision to buy the hybrid worthwhile, ignoring the time value of money?

    c. Rework parts (a) and (b) assuming the appropriate interest rate is 10 percent and all cash flows occur at the end of the year.

    d. What assumption did the analysis in the previous parts make about the resale value of each car?

24. **Break-Even Analysis** [LO3] In an effort to capture the large jet market, Airbus invested $13 billion developing its A380, which is capable of carrying 800 passengers. The plane had a list price of $280 million. In discussing the plane, Airbus stated that the company would break even when 249 A380s were sold.

    a. Assuming the break-even sales figure given is the accounting break-even, what is the cash flow per plane?

    b. Airbus promised its shareholders a 20 percent rate of return on the investment. If sales of the plane continue in perpetuity, how many planes must the company sell per year to deliver on this promise?

    c. Suppose instead that the sales of the A380 last for only 10 years. How many planes must Airbus sell per year to deliver the same rate of return?

25. **Break-Even and Taxes** [LO3] This problem concerns the effect of taxes on the various break-even measures.   **CHALLENGE**
    (Questions 25–30)

    a. Show that, when we consider taxes, the general relationship between operating cash flow, OCF, and sales volume, Q, can be written as:

$$Q = \frac{FC + \dfrac{OCF - T_c \times D}{1 - T_c}}{P - v}$$

    b. Use the expression in part (a) to find the cash, accounting, and financial break-even points for the Wettway sailboat example in the chapter. Assume a 21 percent tax rate.

380   **PART 4**   Capital Budgeting

    c. In part (b), the accounting break-even should be the same as before. Why? Verify this algebraically.

26. **Operating Leverage and Taxes** [LO4] Show that if we consider the effect of taxes, the degree of operating leverage can be written as:

$$DOL = 1 + [FC \times (1 - T_C) - T_C \times D]/OCF$$

Notice that this reduces to our previous result if $T_C = 0$. Can you interpret this in words?

27. **Scenario Analysis** [LO2] Consider a project to supply Detroit with 30,000 tons of machine screws annually for automobile production. You will need an initial $4.3 million investment in threading equipment to get the project started; the project will last for five years. The accounting department estimates that annual fixed costs will be $1.025 million and that variable costs should be $190 per ton; accounting will depreciate the initial fixed asset investment straight-line to zero over the five-year project life. It also estimates a salvage value of $400,000 after dismantling costs. The marketing department estimates that the automakers will let the contract at a selling price of $290 per ton. The engineering department estimates you will need an initial net working capital investment of $410,000. You require a return of 13 percent and face a tax rate of 22 percent on this project.

    a. What is the estimated OCF for this project? The NPV? Should you pursue this project?

    b. Suppose you believe that the accounting department's initial cost and salvage value projections are accurate only to within ±15 percent; the marketing department's price estimate is accurate only to within ±10 percent; and the engineering department's net working capital estimate is accurate only to within ±5 percent. What is your worst-case scenario for this project? Your best-case scenario? Do you still want to pursue the project?

28. **Sensitivity Analysis** [LO1] In Problem 27, suppose you're confident about your own projections, but you're a little unsure about Detroit's actual machine screw requirement. What is the sensitivity of the project OCF to changes in the quantity supplied? What about the sensitivity of NPV to changes in quantity supplied? Given the sensitivity number you calculated, is there some minimum level of output below which you wouldn't want to operate? Why?

29. **Break-Even Analysis** [LO3] Use the results of Problem 25 to find the accounting, cash, and financial break-even quantities for the company in Problem 27.

30. **Operating Leverage** [LO4] Use the results of Problem 26 to find the degree of operating leverage for the company in Problem 27 at the base-case output level of 30,000 tons. How does this number compare to the sensitivity figure you found in Problem 28? Verify that either approach will give you the same OCF figure at any new quantity level.

EXCEL MASTER IT! PROBLEM

Harper Industries is examining a new project to manufacture cell phones. The company has examined several alternatives for the manufacturing process. With Process I, the company would manufacture the cell phone entirely in-house. This would require the highest initial cost and fixed costs. Process II would involve subcontracting the manufacture of the electronics. While this choice would reduce the initial cost and fixed costs, it would result in higher variable costs. Finally, Process III would subcontract all production, with Harper Industries only completing the final assembly and testing. Below you are given the information for each of the options available to the company.

	Process I	Process II	Process III
Initial cost:	$75,000,000	$55,000,000	$36,000,000
Life (years):	7		
Units:	450,000		
Price per unit:	$ 345		
VC per unit:	$ 85	$ 137	$ 182
Fixed costs:	$81,000,000	$63,000,000	$48,000,000
Required return:	13%		
Tax rate:	21%		

a. Calculate the NPV for each of the three manufacturing processes available to the company.

b. What are the accounting break-even, cash break-even, and financial break-even points for each manufacturing process?

c. What is the DOL for each manufacturing process? Graph the DOL for each manufacturing process on the same graph for different unit sales.

MINICASE

Conch Republic Electronics, Part 2

Shelley Couts, the owner of Conch Republic Electronics, has received the capital budgeting analysis from Jay McCanless for the new smartphone the company is considering. Shelley is pleased with the results, but she still has concerns about the new smartphone. Conch Republic has used a small market research firm for the past 20 years, but recently the founder of that firm has retired. Because of this, Shelley is not convinced the sales projections presented by the market research firm are entirely accurate. Additionally, because of rapid changes in technology, she is concerned that a competitor may enter the market. This would likely force Conch Republic to lower the sales price of its new smartphone. For these reasons, she

has asked Jay to analyze how changes in the price of the new smartphone and changes in the quantity sold will affect the NPV of the project.

Shelley has asked Jay to prepare a memo answering the following questions.

QUESTIONS

1. How sensitive is the NPV to changes in the price of the new smartphone?

2. How sensitive is the NPV to changes in the quantity sold of the new smartphone?

Risk and Return

Chapter 12 | Some Lessons from Capital Market History

WITH THE S&P 500 UP about 12 percent and the NASDAQ index up about 9 percent in 2016, stock market performance overall was mixed for the year. The S&P 500 return was about average, while the NASDAQ return was below average. However, investors in AK Steel had to be thrilled with the 359 percent gain in that stock, and investors in United States Steel had to feel pleased with its 332 percent gain. Of course, not all stocks increased during the year. Stock in pharmaceutical company Endo International fell 73 percent during the year, and stock in First Solar fell 51 percent.

These examples show that there were tremendous potential profits to be made during 2016, but there was also the risk of losing money—lots of it. So what should you, as a stock market investor, expect when you invest your own money? In this chapter, we study almost nine decades of market history to find out.

Learning Objectives

After studying this chapter, you should be able to:

LO1 Calculate the return on an investment.

LO2 Discuss the historical returns on various important types of investments.

LO3 Discuss the historical risks on various important types of investments.

LO4 Explain the implications of market efficiency.

For updates on the latest happenings in finance, visit fundamentalsofcorporatefinance.blogspot.com.

Thus far, we haven't had much to say about what determines the required return on an investment. In one sense, the answer is simple: The required return depends on the risk of the investment. The greater the risk, the greater is the required return.

Having said this, we are left with a somewhat more difficult problem. How can we measure the amount of risk present in an investment? Put another way, what does it mean to say that one investment is riskier than another? Obviously, we need to define what we mean by *risk* if we are going to answer these questions. This is our task in this chapter and the next.

From the last several chapters, we know that one of the responsibilities of the financial manager is to assess the value of proposed real asset investments. In doing this, it is important that we first look at what financial investments have to offer. At a minimum, the return we require from a proposed nonfinancial investment must be greater than what we can get by buying financial assets of similar risk.

Our goal in this chapter is to provide a perspective on what capital market history can tell us about risk and return. The most important thing to get out of this chapter is a feel for the numbers. What is a high return? What is a low return? More generally, what returns should we expect from financial assets, and what are the risks of such investments? This perspective is essential for understanding how to analyze and value risky investment projects.

We start our discussion of risk and return by describing the historical experience of investors in U.S. financial markets. In 1931, for example, the stock market lost 44 percent of its value. Just two years later, the stock market gained 54 percent. In more recent memory, the market lost about 25 percent of its value on October 19, 1987, alone. What lessons, if any, can financial managers learn from such shifts in the stock market? We will explore almost a century of market history to find out.

Not everyone agrees on the value of studying history. On the one hand, there is philosopher George Santayana's famous comment: "Those who do not remember the past are condemned to repeat it."* On the other hand, there is industrialist Henry Ford's equally famous comment: "History is more or less bunk."† Nonetheless, perhaps everyone would agree with Mark Twain's observation: "October. This is one of the peculiarly dangerous months to speculate in stocks. The others are July, January, September, April, November, May, March, June, December, August, and February."‡

Two central lessons emerge from our study of market history. First, there is a reward for bearing risk. Second, the greater is the potential reward, the greater is the risk. To illustrate these facts about market returns, we devote much of this chapter to reporting the statistics and numbers that make up the modern capital market history of the United States. In the next chapter, these facts provide the foundation for our study of how financial markets put a price on risk.

Returns

12.1

We wish to discuss historical returns on different types of financial assets. The first thing we need to do, then, is to briefly discuss how to calculate the return from investing.

DOLLAR RETURNS

If you buy an asset of any sort, your gain (or loss) from that investment is called the *return on your investment*. This return will usually have two components. First, you may receive some cash directly while you own the investment. This is called the *income component* of your return. Second, the value of the asset you purchase will often change. In this case, you have a capital gain or capital loss on your investment.[1]

How did the market do today? Find out at **finance.yahoo.com**.

To illustrate, suppose the Video Concept Company has several thousand shares of stock outstanding. You purchased some of these shares of stock in the company at the beginning of the year. It is now year-end, and you want to determine how well you have done on your investment.

First, over the year, a company may pay cash dividends to its shareholders. As a stockholder in Video Concept Company, you are a part owner of the company. If the company is profitable, it may choose to distribute some of its profits to shareholders (we discuss the details of dividend policy in a later chapter). So, as the owner of some stock, you will receive some cash. This cash is the income component from owning the stock.

In addition to the dividend, the other part of your return is the capital gain or capital loss on the stock. This part arises from changes in the value of your investment. For example, consider the cash flows illustrated in Figure 12.1. At the beginning of the year, the stock was selling for $37 per share. If you had bought 100 shares, you would have had a total outlay of $3,700. Suppose that, over the year, the stock paid a dividend of $1.85 per share. By the end of the year, then, you would have received income of:

Dividend = $1.85 × 100 = $185

---

*Source: George Santayana, Philosopher (1863–1952)

†Source: Henry Ford, Industrialist (1863–1947)

‡Source: Mark Twain (1835–1910)

[1]As we mentioned in an earlier chapter, strictly speaking, what is and what is not a capital gain (or loss) is determined by the IRS. We use the terms loosely.

FIGURE 12.1

Dollar Returns

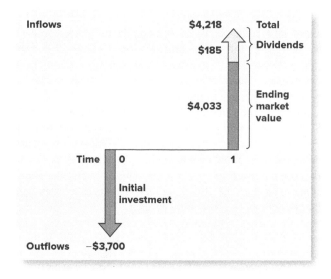

Also, the value of the stock has risen to $40.33 per share by the end of the year. Your 100 shares are now worth $4,033, so you have a capital gain of:

Capital gain = ($40.33 − 37) × 100 = $333

On the other hand, if the price had dropped to, say, $34.78, you would have a capital loss of:

Capital loss = ($34.78 − 37) × 100 = −$222

Notice that a capital loss is the same thing as a negative capital gain.

The total dollar return on your investment is the sum of the dividend and the capital gain:

Total dollar return = Dividend income + Capital gain (or loss)

In our first example, the total dollar return is given by:

Total dollar return = $185 + 333 = $518

Notice that if you sold the stock at the end of the year, the total amount of cash you would have would equal your initial investment plus the total return. In the preceding example, then:

Total cash if stock is sold = Initial investment + Total return
                              = $3,700 + 518
                              = $4,218

As a check, notice that this is the same as the proceeds from the sale of the stock plus the dividends:

Proceeds from stock sale + Dividends = $40.33 × 100 + 185
                                       = $4,033 + 185
                                       = $4,218

Suppose you hold on to your Video Concept stock and don't sell it at the end of the year. Should you still consider the capital gain as part of your return? Isn't this only a "paper" gain and not really a cash flow if you don't sell the stock?

The answer to the first question is a strong yes, and the answer to the second is an equally strong no. The capital gain is every bit as much a part of your return as the dividend, and you should certainly count it as part of your return. That you actually decided to keep the stock and not sell (you don't "realize" the gain) is irrelevant because you could have converted it to cash if you had wanted to. Whether you choose to do so or not is up to you.

After all, if you insisted on converting your gain to cash, you could always sell the stock at year-end and immediately reinvest by buying the stock back. There is no net difference between doing this and just not selling (assuming, of course, that there are no tax consequences from selling the stock). Again, the point is that your decision to actually cash out and buy sodas (or whatever) or to reinvest by not selling doesn't affect the return you earn.

PERCENTAGE RETURNS

It is usually more convenient to summarize information about returns in percentage terms, rather than dollar terms, because that way your return doesn't depend on how much you actually invest. The question we want to answer is this: How much do we get for each dollar we invest?

To answer this question, let P_t be the price of the stock at the beginning of the year and let D_{t+1} be the dividend paid on the stock during the year. Consider the cash flows in Figure 12.2. These are the same as those in Figure 12.1, except that we have now expressed everything on a per-share basis.

In our example, the price at the beginning of the year was $37 per share and the dividend paid during the year on each share was $1.85. As we discussed in Chapter 8, expressing the dividend as a percentage of the beginning stock price results in the dividend yield:

Dividend yield $= D_{t+1}/P_t$

$= \$1.85/\$37 = .05$, or 5%

This says that for each dollar we invest, we get five cents in dividends.

The second component of our percentage return is the capital gains yield. Recall (from Chapter 8) that this is calculated as the change in the price during the year (the capital gain) divided by the beginning price:

Capital gains yield $= (P_{t+1} - P_t)/P_t$

$= (\$40.33 - 37)/\$37$

$= \$3.33/\$37$

$= .09$, or 9%

So, per dollar invested, we get nine cents in capital gains.

FIGURE 12.2

Percentage Returns

Putting it together, per dollar invested, we get 5 cents in dividends and 9 cents in capital gains; so we get a total of 14 cents. Our percentage return is 14 cents on the dollar, or 14 percent.

To check this, notice that we invested $3,700 and ended up with $4,218. By what percentage did our $3,700 increase? As we saw, we picked up $4,218 − 3,700 = $518. This is a $518/$3,700 = 14% increase.

EXAMPLE 12.1	**Calculating Returns**

Suppose you buy some stock at the beginning of the year for $25 per share. At the end of the year, the price is $35 per share. During the year, you receive a $2 dividend per share. This is the situation illustrated in Figure 12.3. What is the dividend yield? The capital gains yield? The percentage return? If your total investment was $1,000, how much do you have at the end of the year?

Your $2 dividend per share works out to a dividend yield of:

$$\text{Dividend yield} = D_{t+1}/P_t$$
$$= \$2/\$25 = .08, \text{ or } 8\%$$

The per-share capital gain is $10, so the capital gains yield is:

$$\text{Capital gains yield} = (P_{t+1} - P_t)/P_t$$
$$= (\$35 - 25)/\$25$$
$$= \$10/\$25$$
$$= .40, \text{ or } 40\%$$

The total percentage return is 48 percent.

If you had invested $1,000, you would have $1,480 at the end of the year, representing a 48 percent increase. To check this, note that your $1,000 would have bought you $1,000/$25 = 40 shares. Your 40 shares would then have paid you a total of 40 × $2 = $80 in cash dividends. Your $10 per-share gain would give you a total capital gain of $10 × 40 = $400. Add these together, and you get the $480 increase.

FIGURE 12.3 **Cash Flow—An Investment Example**

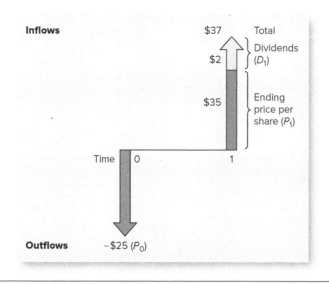

To give another example, stock in entertainment company Time Warner began 2016 at $70.65 per share. Time Warner paid dividends of $1.61 during 2016, and the stock price at the end of the year was $93.85. What was the return on Time Warner for the year? For practice, see if you agree that the answer is 35.12 percent. Of course, negative returns occur as well. For example, again in 2016, the stock price of shoe giant Nike was $62.50 per share at the beginning of the year and dividends of $.66 were paid. The stock ended the year at $50.83 per share. Verify that the loss was 17.62 percent for the year.

Concept Questions

12.1a   What are the two parts of total return?

12.1b   Why are unrealized capital gains or losses included in the calculation of returns?

12.1c   What is the difference between a dollar return and a percentage return? Why are percentage returns more convenient?

The Historical Record

12.2

Excel Master It!

Excel Master coverage online

Roger Ibbotson and Rex Sinquefield conducted a famous set of studies dealing with rates of return in U.S. financial markets.[2] They presented year-to-year historical rates of return on five important types of financial investments. The returns can be interpreted as what you would have earned if you had held portfolios of the following:

1. *Large-company stocks:* This common stock portfolio is based on the Standard & Poor's (S&P) 500 index, which contains 500 of the largest companies (in terms of total market value of outstanding stock) in the United States.
2. *Small-company stocks:* This is a portfolio composed of the stock corresponding to the smallest 20 percent of the companies listed on the New York Stock Exchange, again as measured by market value of outstanding stock.
3. *Long-term corporate bonds:* This is based on high-quality bonds with 20 years to maturity.
4. *Long-term U.S. government bonds:* This is based on U.S. government bonds with 20 years to maturity.
5. *U.S. Treasury bills:* This is based on Treasury bills (T-bills for short) with a one-month maturity.

These returns are not adjusted for inflation or taxes; they are nominal, pretax returns.

In addition to the year-to-year returns on these financial instruments, the year-to-year percentage change in the consumer price index (CPI) is also computed. This is a commonly used measure of inflation, so we can calculate real returns using this as the inflation rate.

For more about market history, visit **www.globalfinancialdata.com**.

A FIRST LOOK

Before looking closely at the different portfolio returns, we take a look at the big picture. Figure 12.4 shows what happened to $1 invested in these different portfolios at the end of 1925. The growth in value for each of the different portfolios over the 91-year period ending in 2016 is given separately (the long-term corporate bonds are omitted). Notice that to get everything on a single graph, some modification in scaling is used. As is commonly

[2]R. G. Ibbotson and R. A. Sinquefield, *Stocks, Bonds, Bills, and Inflation* [SBBI] (Charlottesville, VA: Financial Analysis Research Foundation, 1982).

388   **PART 5**   Risk and Return

FIGURE 12.4   **A $1 Investment in Different Types of Portfolios: 1926–2016 (Year-End 1925 = $1)**

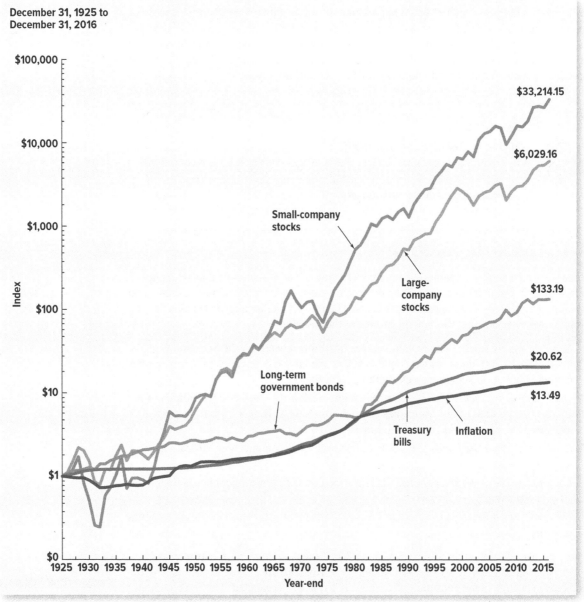

SOURCE: Morningstar, 2017, author calculations.

Go to
bigcharts.marketwatch.com
to see both intraday and long-term charts.

done with financial series, the vertical axis is scaled so that equal distances measure equal percentage (as opposed to dollar) changes in values.[3]

Looking at Figure 12.4, we see that the "small-cap" (short for small-capitalization) investment did the best overall. Every dollar invested grew to a remarkable $33,214.15 over the 91 years. The large-company common stock portfolio did less well; a dollar invested in it grew to $6,029.16.

_____

[3]In other words, the scale is logarithmic.

At the other end, the T-bill portfolio grew to only $20.62. This is even less impressive when we consider the inflation over the period in question. As illustrated, the increase in the price level was such that $13.49 was needed at the end of the period just to replace the original $1.

Given the historical record, why would anybody buy anything other than small-cap stocks? If you look closely at Figure 12.4, you will probably see the answer. The T-bill and long-term government bond portfolios grew more slowly than did the stock portfolios, but they also grew much more steadily. The small stocks ended up on top; but as you can see, they grew quite erratically at times. For example, the small stocks were the worst performers for about the first 10 years and had a smaller return than long-term government bonds for over 15 years.

A CLOSER LOOK

To illustrate the variability of the different investments, Figures 12.5 through 12.8 plot the year-to-year percentage returns in the form of vertical bars drawn from the horizontal

FIGURE 12.5

Year-by-Year Total Returns on Large-Company Common Stocks

SOURCE: Morningstar, 2017

FIGURE 12.6

Year-by-Year Total Returns on Small-Company Stocks

SOURCE: Morningstar, 2017

FIGURE 12.7

Year-by-Year Total Returns on Bonds and Bills

SOURCE: Morningstar, 2017

axis. The height of the bar tells us the return for the particular year. For example, looking at the long-term government bonds (Figure 12.7), we see that the largest historical return (44.28 percent) occurred in 1982. This was a good year for bonds. In comparing these charts, notice the differences in the vertical axis scales. With these differences in mind, you can see how predictably the Treasury bills (Figure 12.7) behaved compared to the small-company stocks (Figure 12.6).

The returns shown in these bar graphs are sometimes very large. Looking at the graphs, for example, we see that the largest single-year return is a remarkable 142.87 percent for the small-cap stocks in 1933. In the same year, the large-company stocks returned "only" 52.95 percent. In contrast, the largest Treasury bill return was 14.60 percent in 1981. For future reference, the actual year-to-year returns for the large-company stocks, long-term government bonds, Treasury bills, and the CPI are shown in Table 12.1.

IN THEIR OWN WORDS ...

Roger Ibbotson on Capital Market History

The financial markets are the most carefully documented human phenomena in history. Every day, almost 2,000 NYSE stocks are traded, and at least 8,000 more stocks are listed on other U.S. exchanges and trading venues. Bonds, commodities, futures, and options also provide a wealth of data. These data are available across a wide spectrum of electronic media, including newswires, websites, and market data platforms like Bloomberg. A record actually exists of almost every transaction, providing not only a real-time database but also a historical record extending back, in many cases, more than a century.

The global market adds another dimension to this wealth of data. Over 2,500 stocks trade on Japanese stock markets while the London Exchange reports on over 2,000 domestic and foreign issues a day. Altogether, more than 20 billion shares trade globally on a typical day.

The data generated by these transactions are quantifiable, quickly analyzed and disseminated, and are easily accessible. Because of this, finance has increasingly come to resemble one of the exact sciences. The use of financial market data ranges from the simple, such as using the S&P 500 index to compare the performance of a portfolio, to the incredibly complex. For example, only a few decades ago, the bond market was the most staid province on Wall Street. Today, it attracts swarms of traders seeking to exploit arbitrage opportunities—small temporary mispricings—using real-time data and computers to analyze them.

Financial market data are the foundation for the extensive empirical understanding we now have of the financial markets. The following is a list of some of the principal findings of such research:

- Trading is more automated and its cost is lower than ever.
- Risky securities, such as stocks, have higher average returns than riskless securities, such as Treasury bills.
- Stocks of small companies have higher average returns than those of larger companies.
- More liquid stocks have higher valuations, but lower returns than less liquid stocks.
- The cost of capital for a company, project, or division can be estimated using data from the markets.

Because phenomena in the financial markets are so well measured, finance is the most readily quantifiable branch of economics. Researchers are able to do more extensive empirical research than in any other economic field, and the research can be quickly translated into action in the marketplace.

Roger Ibbotson is Professor in the Practice of Management at the Yale School of Management. He is also chairman of Zebra Capital, an equity investment manager. He is the founder of Ibbotson Associates, now part of Morningstar, Inc., a major supplier of financial data and analysis. An outstanding scholar, he is best known for his original estimates of the historical rates of return realized by investors in different markets.

FIGURE 12.8

Year-by-Year Inflation

SOURCE: Morningstar, 2017

392   **PART 5**   Risk and Return

TABLE 12.1   Year-to-Year Total Returns: 1926–2016

Year	Large-Company Stocks	Long-Term Government Bonds	U.S. Treasury Bills	Consumer Price Index	Year	Large-Company Stocks	Long-Term Government Bonds	U.S. Treasury Bills	Consumer Price Index
1926	13.75%	5.69%	3.30%	−1.12%	1972	18.99%	2.39%	4.23%	3.41%
1927	35.70	6.58	3.15	−2.26	1973	−14.69	3.30	7.29	8.71
1928	45.08	1.15	4.05	−1.16	1974	−26.47	4.00	7.99	12.34
1929	−8.80	4.39	4.47	.58	1975	37.23	5.52	5.87	6.94
1930	−25.13	4.47	2.27	−6.40	1976	23.93	15.56	5.07	4.86
1931	−43.60	−2.15	1.15	−9.32	1977	−7.16	.38	5.45	6.70
1932	−8.75	8.51	.88	−10.27	1978	6.57	−1.26	7.64	9.02
1933	52.95	1.92	.52	.76	1979	18.61	−2.76	10.56	13.29
1934	−2.31	7.59	.27	1.52	1980	32.50	−2.48	12.10	12.52
1935	46.79	4.20	.17	2.99	1981	−4.92	4.04	14.60	8.92
1936	32.49	5.13	.17	1.45	1982	21.55	44.28	10.94	3.83
1937	−35.45	1.44	.27	2.86	1983	22.56	1.29	8.99	3.79
1938	31.63	4.21	.06	−2.78	1984	6.27	15.29	9.90	3.95
1939	−1.43	3.84	.04	.00	1985	31.73	32.27	7.71	3.80
1940	−10.36	5.70	.04	.71	1986	18.67	22.39	6.09	1.10
1941	−12.02	.47	.14	9.93	1987	5.25	−3.03	5.88	4.43
1942	20.75	1.80	.34	9.03	1988	16.61	6.84	6.94	4.42
1943	25.38	2.01	.38	2.96	1989	31.69	18.54	8.44	4.65
1944	19.49	2.27	.38	2.30	1990	−3.10	7.74	7.69	6.11
1945	36.21	5.29	.38	2.25	1991	30.46	19.36	5.43	3.06
1946	−8.42	.54	.38	18.13	1992	7.62	7.34	3.48	2.90
1947	5.05	−1.02	.62	8.84	1993	10.08	13.06	3.03	2.75
1948	4.99	2.66	1.06	2.99	1994	1.32	−7.32	4.39	2.67
1949	17.81	4.58	1.12	−2.07	1995	37.58	25.94	5.61	2.54
1950	30.05	−.98	1.22	5.93	1996	22.96	.13	5.14	3.32
1951	23.79	−.20	1.56	6.00	1997	33.36	12.02	5.19	1.70
1952	18.39	2.43	1.75	.75	1998	28.58	14.45	4.86	1.61
1953	−1.07	2.28	1.87	.75	1999	21.04	−7.51	4.80	2.68
1954	52.23	3.08	.93	−.74	2000	−9.10	17.22	5.98	3.39
1955	31.62	−.73	1.80	.37	2001	−11.89	5.51	3.33	1.55
1956	6.91	−1.72	2.66	2.99	2002	−22.10	15.15	1.61	2.38
1957	−10.50	6.82	3.28	2.90	2003	28.89	2.01	.94	1.88
1958	43.57	−1.72	1.71	1.76	2004	10.88	8.12	1.14	3.26
1959	12.01	−2.02	3.48	1.73	2005	4.91	6.89	2.79	3.42
1960	.47	11.21	2.81	1.36	2006	15.79	.28	4.97	2.54
1961	26.84	2.20	2.40	.67	2007	5.49	10.85	4.52	4.08
1962	−8.75	5.72	2.82	1.33	2008	−37.00	41.78	1.24	.09
1963	22.70	1.79	3.23	1.64	2009	26.46	−25.61	.15	2.72
1964	16.43	3.71	3.62	.97	2010	15.06	7.73	.14	1.50
1965	12.38	.93	4.06	1.92	2011	2.11	35.75	.06	2.96
1966	−10.06	5.12	4.94	3.46	2012	16.00	1.80	.08	1.74
1967	23.98	−2.86	4.39	3.04	2013	32.39	−14.69	.05	1.50
1968	11.03	2.25	5.49	4.72	2014	13.69	24.74	.03	.75
1969	−8.43	−5.63	6.90	6.20	2015	1.41	−.64	.04	.74
1970	3.94	18.92	6.50	5.57	2016	11.98	1.76	.21	2.11
1971	14.30	11.24	4.36	3.27					

SOURCE: Authors' calculation based on data obtained from *Global Financial Data* and other sources.

Concept Questions

12.2a With 20/20 hindsight, what do you say was the best investment for the period from 1926 through 1935?

12.2b Why doesn't everyone just buy small stocks as investments?

12.2c What was the smallest return observed over the 91 years for each of these investments? Approximately when did it occur?

12.2d About how many times did large-company stocks return more than 30 percent? How many times did they return less than −20 percent?

12.2e What was the longest "winning streak" (years without a negative return) for large-company stocks? For long-term government bonds?

12.2f How often did the T-bill portfolio have a negative return?

Average Returns: The First Lesson   12.3

As you've probably begun to notice, the history of capital market returns is too complicated to be of much use in its undigested form. We need to begin summarizing all these numbers. Accordingly, we discuss how to go about condensing the detailed data. We start out by calculating average returns.

Excel Master It!
Excel Master coverage online

CALCULATING AVERAGE RETURNS

The obvious way to calculate the average returns on the different investments in Table 12.1 is to add up the yearly returns and divide by 91. The result is the historical average of the individual values.

For example, if you add up the returns for the large-company stocks in Figure 12.5 for the 91 years, you will get about 10.88. The average annual return is 10.88/91 = .120, or 12.0%. You interpret this 12.0 percent just like any other average. If you were to pick a year at random from the 91-year history and you had to guess what the return in that year was, the best guess would be 12.0 percent.

AVERAGE RETURNS: THE HISTORICAL RECORD

Table 12.2 shows the average returns for the investments we have discussed. As shown, in a typical year, the small-company stocks increased in value by 16.6 percent. Notice also how much larger the returns are for stocks, compared to the returns on bonds.

These averages are, of course, nominal because we haven't worried about inflation. Notice that the average inflation rate was 3.0 percent per year over this 91-year span. The nominal return on U.S. Treasury bills was 3.4 percent per year. The average real return on

TABLE 12.2

Average Annual Returns: 1926–2016

Investment	Average Return
Large-company stocks	12.0%
Small-company stocks	16.6
Long-term corporate bonds	6.3
Long-term government bonds	6.0
U.S. Treasury bills	3.4
Inflation	3.0

SOURCE: Morningstar, 2017, author calculations.

Treasury bills was approximately .4 percent per year; so the real return on T-bills has been quite low historically.

At the other extreme, small stocks had an average real return of about $16.6\% - 3.0 = 13.6\%$, which is relatively large. If you remember the Rule of 72 (Chapter 5), then you know that a quick back-of-the-envelope calculation tells us that 13.6 percent real growth doubles your buying power about every five years. Notice also that the real value of the large-company stock portfolio increased by about 9 percent in a typical year.

RISK PREMIUMS

Now that we have computed some average returns, it seems logical to see how they compare with each other. One such comparison involves government-issued securities. These are free of much of the variability we see in, for example, the stock market.

The government borrows money by issuing bonds in different forms. The ones we will focus on are the Treasury bills. These have the shortest time to maturity of the different government bonds. Because the government can always raise taxes to pay its bills, the debt represented by T-bills is virtually free of any default risk over its short life. We will call the rate of return on such debt the *risk-free return*, and we will use it as a kind of benchmark.

A particularly interesting comparison involves the virtually risk-free return on T-bills and the very risky return on common stocks. The difference between these two returns can be interpreted as a measure of the *excess return* on the average risky asset (assuming that the stock of a large U.S. corporation has about average risk compared to all risky assets).

risk premium
The excess return required from an investment in a risky asset over that required from a risk-free investment.

We call this the "excess" return because it is the additional return we earn by moving from a relatively risk-free investment to a risky one. Because it can be interpreted as a reward for bearing risk, we will call it a **risk premium**.

Using Table 12.2, we can calculate the risk premiums for the different investments; these are shown in Table 12.3. We report only the nominal risk premiums because there is only a slight difference between the historical nominal and real risk premiums.

The risk premium on T-bills is shown as zero in the table because we have assumed that they are riskless.

THE FIRST LESSON

Looking at Table 12.3, we see that the average risk premium earned by a typical large-company stock is $12.0\% - 3.4 = 8.6\%$. This is a significant reward. The fact that it exists historically is an important observation, and it is the basis for our first lesson: Risky assets, on average, earn a risk premium. Put another way, there is a reward for bearing risk.

Why is this so? Why, for example, is the risk premium for small stocks so much larger than the risk premium for large stocks? More generally, what determines the relative sizes of the risk premiums for the different assets? The answers to these questions are at the heart of modern finance, and the next chapter is devoted to them. For now, we can find part of the answer by looking at the historical variability of the returns on these different investments. So, to get started, we now turn our attention to measuring variability in returns.

TABLE 12.3

Average Annual Returns and Risk Premiums: 1926–2016

Investment	Average Return	Risk Premium
Large-company stocks	12.0%	8.6%
Small-company stocks	16.6	13.2
Long-term corporate bonds	6.3	2.9
Long-term government bonds	6.0	2.6
U.S. Treasury bills	3.4	0.0

SOURCE: Morningstar, 2017, author calculations.

> ## Concept Questions
>
> **12.3a** What do we mean by *excess return* and *risk premium*?
>
> **12.3b** What was the real (as opposed to nominal) risk premium on the common stock portfolio?
>
> **12.3c** What was the nominal risk premium on corporate bonds? The real risk premium?
>
> **12.3d** What is the first lesson from capital market history?

The Variability of Returns: The Second Lesson   12.4

We have already seen that the year-to-year returns on common stocks tend to be more volatile than the returns on, say, long-term government bonds. We now discuss measuring this variability of stock returns so we can begin examining the subject of risk.

Excel Master It!

Excel Master coverage online

FREQUENCY DISTRIBUTIONS AND VARIABILITY

To get started, we can draw a *frequency distribution* for the common stock returns like the one in Figure 12.9. What we have done here is to count the number of times the annual return on the common stock portfolio falls within each 10 percent range. For example, in Figure 12.9, the height of 17 times in the range of 10 to 20 percent means that 17 of the 91 annual returns were in that range.

What we need to do now is to actually measure the spread in returns. We know, for example, that the return on small stocks in a typical year was 16.6 percent. We now want

FIGURE 12.9   **Frequency Distribution of Returns on Large-Company Stocks: 1926–2016**

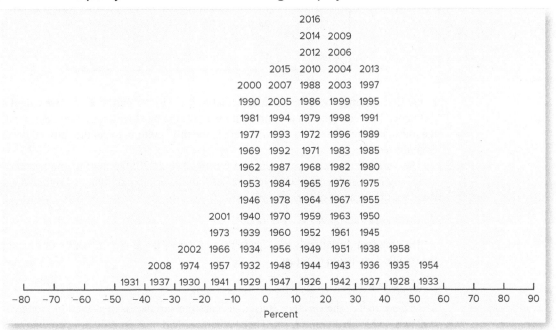

SOURCE: Morningstar, 2017, author calculations.

variance
The average squared difference between the actual return and the average return.

standard deviation
The positive square root of the variance.

For an easy-to-read review of basic stats, check out **www.robertniles.com/stats/**.

to know how much the actual return deviates from this average in a typical year. In other words, we need a measure of the volatility of the return. The **variance** and its square root, the **standard deviation**, are the most commonly used measures of volatility. We describe how to calculate them next.

THE HISTORICAL VARIANCE AND STANDARD DEVIATION

The variance essentially measures the average squared difference between the actual returns and the average return. The bigger this number is, the more the actual returns tend to differ from the average return. Also, the larger the variance or standard deviation is, the more spread out the returns will be.

The way we will calculate the variance and standard deviation will depend on the specific situation. In this chapter, we are looking at historical returns; so the procedure we describe here is the correct one for calculating the *historical* variance and standard deviation. If we were examining projected future returns, then the procedure would be different. We describe this procedure in the next chapter.

To illustrate how we calculate the historical variance, suppose a particular investment had returns of 10 percent, 12 percent, 3 percent, and −9 percent over the last four years. The average return is (.10 + .12 + .03 − .09)/4 = .04, or 4%. Notice that the return is never actually equal to 4 percent. Instead, the first return deviates from the average by .10 − .04 = .06, the second return deviates from the average by .12 − .04 = .08, and so on. To compute the variance, we square each of these deviations, add them, and divide the result by the number of returns less 1, or 3 in this case. Most of this information is summarized in the following table:

	(1) Actual Return	(2) Average Return	(3) Deviation (1) − (2)	(4) Squared Deviation
	.10	.04	.06	.0036
	.12	.04	.08	.0064
	.03	.04	−.01	.0001
	−.09	.04	−.13	.0169
Totals	.16		.00	.0270

In the first column, we write the four actual returns. In the third column, we calculate the difference between the actual returns and the average by subtracting 4 percent. Finally, in the fourth column, we square the numbers in the third column to get the squared deviations from the average.

The variance can now be calculated by dividing .0270, the sum of the squared deviations, by the number of returns less 1. Let Var(R), or σ^2 (read this as "sigma squared"), stand for the variance of the return:

$$\text{Var}(R) = \sigma^2 = .027/(4 - 1) = .009$$

The standard deviation is the square root of the variance. So, if SD(R), or σ, stands for the standard deviation of return:

$$\text{SD}(R) = \sigma = \sqrt{.009} = .09487$$

The square root of the variance is used because the variance is measured in "squared" percentages and is hard to interpret. The standard deviation is an ordinary percentage, so the answer could be written as 9.487 percent.

In the preceding table, notice that the sum of the deviations is equal to zero. This will always be the case, and it provides a good way to check your work. In general, if we have T historical returns, where T is some number, we can write the historical variance as:

$$\text{Var}(R) = \frac{1}{T-1}[(R_1 - \overline{R})^2 + \cdots + (R_T - \overline{R})^2]$$

 12.3

This formula tells us to do what we just did: Take each of the T individual returns $(R_1, R_2, \ldots)$ and subtract the average return, $\overline{R}$; square the results, and add them; and finally, divide this total by the number of returns less 1, $(T - 1)$. The standard deviation is always the square root of $\text{Var}(R)$. Standard deviations are a widely used measure of volatility. Our nearby *Work the Web* box gives a real-world example.

Calculating the Variance and Standard Deviation   EXAMPLE 12.2

Suppose the Supertech Company and the Hyperdrive Company have experienced the following returns in the last four years:

Year	Supertech Return	Hyperdrive Return
2014	−.20	.05
2015	.50	.09
2016	.30	−.12
2017	.10	.20

What are the average returns? The variances? The standard deviations? Which investment was more volatile?

To calculate the average returns, we add the returns and divide by 4. The results are:

Supertech average return = $\overline{R}$ = .70/4 = .175
Hyperdrive average return = $\overline{R}$ = .22/4 = .055

To calculate the variance for Supertech, we can summarize the relevant calculations as follows:

Year	(1) Actual Return	(2) Average Return	(3) Deviation (1) − (2)	(4) Squared Deviation
2014	−.20	.175	−.375	.140625
2015	.50	.175	.325	.105625
2016	.30	.175	.125	.015625
2017	.10	.175	−.075	.005625
Totals	.70		.000	.267500

Because there are four years of returns, we calculate the variance by dividing .2675 by $(4 − 1) = 3$:

	Supertech	Hyperdrive
Variance (σ^2)	.2675/3 = .0892	.0529/3 = .0176
Standard deviation (σ)	$\sqrt{.0892}$ = .2986	$\sqrt{.0176}$ = .1328

For practice, verify that you get the same answer as we do for Hyperdrive. Notice that the standard deviation for Supertech, 29.86 percent, is a little more than twice Hyperdrive's 13.28 percent; Supertech is the more volatile investment.

THE HISTORICAL RECORD

Figure 12.10 summarizes much of our discussion of capital market history so far. It displays average returns, standard deviations, and frequency distributions of annual returns on a common scale. In Figure 12.10, for example, notice that the standard deviation for the small-stock portfolio (31.9 percent per year) is more than 10 times larger than the T-bill portfolio's standard deviation (3.1 percent per year). We will return to these figures momentarily.

WORK THE WEB

Standard deviations are widely reported for mutual funds. For example, the Fidelity Magellan Fund was one of the better-known mutual funds in the United States at the time this was written. How volatile is it? To find out, we went to www.morningstar.com, entered the ticker symbol FMAGX, and clicked the "Ratings & Risk" link. Here is what we found:

MPT Statistics FMAGX

3-Year | 5-Year | 10-Year | 15-Year

3-Year Trailing	Index	R-Squared	Beta	Alpha	Treynor Ratio	Currency
vs. Best-Fit Index						
FMAGX	Russell 3000 Growth TR USD	95.66	0.99	-0.42	—	USD
vs. Standard Index						
FMAGX	S&P 500 TR USD	92.53	1.04	-1.36	7.26	USD
Category: LG	S&P 500 TR USD	83.21	1.02	-3.04	5.47	USD

12/31/2016

Volatility Measures FMAGX

3-Year | 5-Year | 10-Year | 15-Year

3-Year Trailing	Standard Deviation	Return	Sharpe Ratio	Sortino Ratio	Bear Market Percentile Rank
FMAGX	11.63	7.70	0.68	1.21	—
S&P 500 TR USD	10.74	8.87	0.83	1.51	—
Category: LG	12.12	5.70	0.51	0.89	—

12/31/2016

The standard deviation for the Fidelity Magellan Fund is 11.63 percent. When you consider that the average stock has a standard deviation of about 50 percent, this seems like a low number. The reason for the low standard deviation has to do with the power of diversification, a topic we discuss in the next chapter. The return column is the average return, so over the last three years, investors in the Magellan Fund gained 7.70 percent per year. Also, under the Volatility Measures section, you will see the Sharpe ratio. The Sharpe ratio is calculated as the risk premium of the asset divided by the standard deviation. As such, it is a measure of return relative to the level of risk taken (as measured by standard deviation). The "beta" for the Fidelity Magellan Fund is .99. We will have more to say about this number—lots more—in the next chapter.

Questions

1. *Go to the Morningstar website at www.morningstar.com. What does the Sortino ratio measure? What does the Bear Market Percentile Rank measure?*
2. *Get a quote for the Fidelity Magellan Fund at Morningstar. What are the five sectors that have the highest percentage investment for this fund? What are the five stocks with the highest percentage investment?*

Chapter 12   Some Lessons from Capital Market History   **399**

FIGURE 12.10   Historical Returns, Standard Deviations, and Frequency Distributions: 1926–2016

Series	Average Return	Standard Deviation	Frequency Distribution
Large-company stocks	12.0%	19.9%	
Small-company stocks	16.6	31.9	*
Long-term corporate bonds	6.3	8.4	
Long-term government bonds	6.0	9.9	
Intermediate-term government bonds	5.3	5.6	
U.S. Treasury bills	3.4	3.1	
Inflation	3.0	4.1	

*The 1933 small-company stocks total return was 142.9 percent.
SOURCE: Morningstar, 2017, author calculations.

NORMAL DISTRIBUTION

For many different random events in nature, a particular frequency distribution, the **normal distribution** (or *bell curve*), is useful for describing the probability of ending up in a given range. For example, the idea behind "grading on a curve" comes from the fact that exam score distributions often resemble a bell curve.

Figure 12.11 illustrates a normal distribution and its distinctive bell shape. As you can see, this distribution has a much cleaner appearance than the actual return distributions illustrated in Figure 12.10. Even so, like the normal distribution, the actual distributions do appear to be at least roughly mound-shaped and symmetric. When this is true, the normal distribution is often a very good approximation.

Also, keep in mind that the distributions in Figure 12.10 are based on only 91 yearly observations, whereas Figure 12.11 is, in principle, based on an infinite number. So,

normal distribution
A symmetric, bell-shaped frequency distribution that is completely defined by its mean and standard deviation.

FIGURE 12.11

The Normal Distribution

NOTE: Illustrated returns are based on the historical return and standard deviation for a portfolio of large-company common stocks.

if we had been able to observe returns for, say, 1,000 years, we might have filled in a lot of the irregularities and ended up with a much smoother picture in Figure 12.10. For our purposes, it is enough to observe that the returns are at least roughly normally distributed.

The usefulness of the normal distribution stems from the fact that it is completely described by the average and the standard deviation. If you have these two numbers, then there is nothing else to know. For example, with a normal distribution, the probability that we will end up within one standard deviation of the average is about 2/3. The probability that we will end up within two standard deviations is about 95 percent. Finally, the probability of being more than three standard deviations away from the average is less than 1 percent. These ranges and the probabilities are illustrated in Figure 12.11.

To see why this is useful, recall from Figure 12.10 that the standard deviation of returns on the large-company stocks is 19.9 percent. The average return is 12.0 percent. So, assuming that the frequency distribution is at least approximately normal, the probability that the return in a given year is in the range of −7.9 to 31.9 percent (12.0 percent plus or minus one standard deviation, 19.9 percent) is about 2/3. This range is illustrated in Figure 12.11. In other words, there is about one chance in three that the return will be *outside* this range. This literally tells you that, if you buy stocks in large companies, you should expect to be outside this range in one year out of every three. This reinforces our earlier observations about stock market volatility. However, there is only a 5 percent chance (approximately) that we would end up outside the range of −27.8 to 51.8 percent (12.0% plus or minus 2 × 19.9%). These points are also illustrated in Figure 12.11.

THE SECOND LESSON

Our observations concerning the year-to-year variability in returns are the basis for our second lesson from capital market history. On average, bearing risk is handsomely rewarded; but in a given year, there is a significant chance of a dramatic change in value. Our second lesson is this: The greater the potential reward, the greater is the risk.

2008: A YEAR TO REMEMBER

To reinforce our point concerning stock market volatility, consider that just a few short years ago, 2008 entered the record books as one of the worst years for stock market investors in

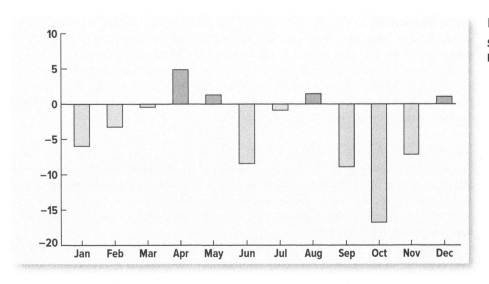

FIGURE 12.12

**S&P 500 Monthly
Returns: 2008**

U.S. history. How bad was it? As shown in several exhibits in the chapter (e.g., Table 12.1), the widely followed S&P 500 index plunged 37 percent. Of the 500 stocks in the index, 485 were down for the year.

Over the period 1926–2016, only the year 1931 had a lower return than 2008 (−44 percent versus −37 percent). Making matters worse, the downdraft continued with a further decline of 8.43 percent in January 2009. In all, from November 2007 (when the decline began) through March 2009 (when it ended), the S&P 500 lost 50 percent of its value.

Figure 12.12 shows the month-by-month performance of the S&P 500 during 2008. As indicated, returns were negative in 8 of the 12 months. Most of the damage occurred in the fall, with investors losing almost 17 percent in October alone. Small stocks fared no better. They also fell 37 percent for the year (with a 21 percent drop in October), their worst performance since losing 58 percent in 1937.

As Figure 12.12 suggests, stock prices were highly volatile during the year. Oddly, the S&P had 126 up days and 126 down days (remember the markets are closed weekends and holidays). Of course, the down days were much worse on average. To see how extraordinary volatility was in 2008, consider that there were 18 days during which the value of the S&P changed by more than 5 percent. There were only 17 such moves between 1956 and 2007!

The drop in stock prices was a global phenomenon, and many of the world's major markets were off by much more than the S&P. China, India, and Russia, for example, all experienced declines of more than 50 percent. Tiny Iceland saw share prices drop by more than 90 percent for the year. Trading on the Icelandic exchange was temporarily suspended on October 9. In what has to be a modern record for a single day, stocks fell by 76 percent when trading resumed on October 14.

Were there any bright spots in 2008 for U.S. investors? The answer is yes because, as stocks tanked, bonds soared, particularly U.S. Treasury bonds. In fact, long-term Treasuries gained 40 percent, while shorter-term Treasury bonds were up 13 percent. Long-term corporate bonds did less well, but still managed to finish in positive territory, up 9 percent. These returns were especially impressive considering that the rate of inflation, as measured by the CPI, was essentially zero.

Of course, stock prices can be volatile in both directions. From March 2009 through February 2011, a period of about 700 days, the S&P 500 doubled in value. This climb was the fastest doubling since 1936 when the S&P did it in just 500 days. So, what lessons should investors take away from this very recent, and very turbulent, bit of capital market history? First, and most obviously, stocks have significant risk! But there is a second, equally important lesson. Depending on the mix, a diversified portfolio of stocks and bonds might have suffered in 2008, but the losses would have been much smaller than those experienced by an all-stock portfolio. In other words, diversification matters, a point we will examine in detail in our next chapter.

USING CAPITAL MARKET HISTORY

Based on the discussion in this section, you should begin to have an idea of the risks and rewards from investing. For example, in early 2017, Treasury bills were paying about .4 percent. Suppose we had an investment that we thought had about the same risk as a portfolio of large-firm common stocks. At a minimum, what return would this investment have to offer for us to be interested?

From Table 12.3, we see that the risk premium on large-company stocks has been 8.6 percent historically, so a reasonable estimate of our required return would be this premium plus the T-bill rate, .4% + 8.6 = 9%. This may strike you as being high; but if we were thinking of starting a new business, then the risks of doing so might resemble those of investing in small-company stocks. In this case, the historical risk premium is 13.2 percent, so, at a minimum, we might require as much as 13.6 percent from such an investment.

We will discuss the relationship between risk and required return in more detail in the next chapter. For now, you should notice that a projected internal rate of return, or IRR, on a risky investment in the 10 to 20 percent range isn't particularly outstanding. It depends on the level of risk. This, too, is an important lesson from capital market history.

EXAMPLE 12.3	**Investing in Growth Stocks**

The term *growth stock* is frequently used as a euphemism for small-company stock. Are such investments suitable for "widows and orphans"? Before answering, you should consider the historical volatility. For example, from the historical record, what is the approximate probability that you will actually lose more than 15 percent of your money in a single year if you buy a portfolio of stocks of such companies?

Looking back at Figure 12.10, we see that the average return on small-company stocks is 16.6 percent and the standard deviation is 31.9 percent. Assuming the returns are approximately normal, there is about a 1/3 probability that you will experience a return outside the range of −15.3 to 48.5 percent (16.6% ± 31.9%).

Because the normal distribution is symmetric, the odds of being above or below this range are equal. There is a 1/6 chance (half of 1/3) that you will lose more than −15.3 percent. You should expect this to happen once in every six years, on average. Such investments can be *very* volatile, and they are not well suited for those who cannot afford the risk.

MORE ON THE STOCK MARKET RISK PREMIUM

As we have discussed, the historical stock market risk premium has been substantial. In fact, based on standard economic models, it has been argued that the historical risk premium is *too* big and is an overestimate of what is likely to happen in the future.

Of course, any time we use the past to predict the future, there is the danger that the past period we observe isn't representative of what the future will hold. For example, in

FIGURE 12.13   **Stock Market Risk Premiums for 17 Countries: 1900–2005**

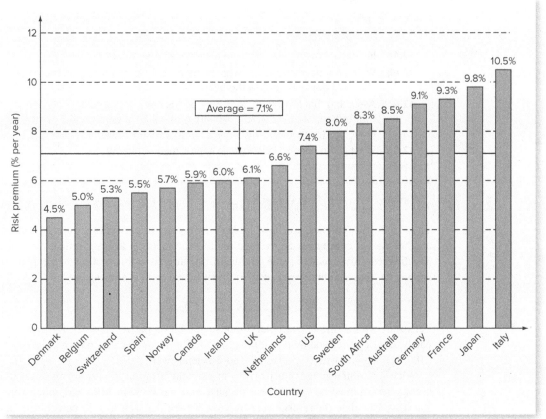

SOURCE: Based on Dimson, Elroy et al., "The Worldwide Equity Premium: A Smaller Puzzle," in *Handbook of the Equity Risk Premium*, Rajnish Mehra, ed., Amsterdam: Elsevier, 2007.

this chapter, we studied the period 1926–2016. Perhaps investors got lucky over this period and earned particularly high returns. Data from earlier years is available, though it is not of the same quality. With that caveat in mind, researchers have traced returns back to 1802, and the risk premiums seen in the pre-1926 era are perhaps a little smaller, but not dramatically so.

Another possibility is that the U.S. stock market experience was unusually good. Investors in at least some other major countries did not do as well because their financial markets were nearly or completely wiped out because of revolution, war, and/or hyperinflation. A recent study addresses this issue by examining data from 1900–2005 for 17 countries.

Figure 12.13 shows the historical average stock market risk premium for all 17 countries over the 106-year period. Looking at the numbers, the U.S. risk premium is the 8th highest at 7.4 percent (which differs from our earlier estimate because of the differing time periods examined). The overall average risk premium is 7.1 percent. These numbers make it clear that U.S. investors did well, but not exceptionally so relative to investors in many other countries.

So, is the U.S. stock market risk premium estimated from 1926–2016 too high? The evidence seems to suggest that the answer is "maybe a little." One thing we haven't stressed so far is that even with 106 years of data, the average risk premium is still not measured with great precision. From a statistical standpoint, the standard error associated with the U.S.

estimated risk premium of 7.4 percent is about 2 percent.[4] Even a one standard error range covers 5.4 to 9.4 percent.

Concept Questions

12.4a In words, how do we calculate a variance? A standard deviation?

12.4b With a normal distribution, what is the probability of ending up more than one standard deviation below the average?

12.4c Assuming that long-term corporate bonds have an approximately normal distribution, what is the approximate probability of earning 14.7 percent or more in a given year? With T-bills, roughly what is this probability?

12.4d What is the second lesson from capital market history?

12.5 More about Average Returns

Excel Master It!

xlsx Excel Master coverage online

Thus far in this chapter, we have looked closely at simple average returns. But there is another way of computing an average return. The fact that average returns are calculated two different ways leads to some confusion, so our goal in this section is to explain the two approaches and also the circumstances under which each is appropriate.

ARITHMETIC VERSUS GEOMETRIC AVERAGES

Let's start with a simple example. Suppose you buy a particular stock for $100. Unfortunately, the first year you own it, it falls to $50. The second year you own it, it rises back to $100, leaving you where you started (no dividends were paid).

What was your average return on this investment? Common sense seems to say that your average return must be exactly zero because you started with $100 and ended with $100. But if we calculate the returns year-by-year, we see that you lost 50 percent the first year (you lost half of your money). The second year, you made 100 percent (you doubled your money). Your average return over the two years was $(-50\% + 100)/2 = 25\%$!

geometric average return

The average compound return earned per year over a multiyear period.

Which is correct, 0 percent or 25 percent? Both are correct: They just answer different questions. The 0 percent is called the **geometric average return**. The 25 percent is called the **arithmetic average return**. The geometric average return answers the question, "What was your average compound return per year over a particular period?" The arithmetic average return answers the question, "What was your return in an average year over a particular period?"

arithmetic average return

The return earned in an average year over a multiyear period.

Notice that, in previous sections, the average returns we calculated were all arithmetic averages and we already know how to calculate them. What we need to do now is (1) learn how to calculate geometric averages and (2) learn the circumstances under which one average is more meaningful than the other.

CALCULATING GEOMETRIC AVERAGE RETURNS

First, to illustrate how we calculate a geometric average return, suppose a particular investment had annual returns of 10 percent, 12 percent, 3 percent, and −9 percent over the last four years. The geometric average return over this four-year period is calculated as $(1.10 \times 1.12 \times 1.03 \times .91)^{1/4} - 1 = .0366$, or 3.66%. In contrast, the average arithmetic return we have been calculating is $(.10 + .12 + .03 - .09)/4 = .04$, or 4.0%.

---

[4]Recall from basic "sadistics" that the standard error of a sample mean is the sample standard deviation divided by the square root of the sample size. In our case, the standard deviation over the 1900–2005 period was 19.6 percent, so the standard error is $.196/\sqrt{106} = .019$.

IN THEIR OWN WORDS ...

Jeremy J. Siegel on Stocks for the Long Run

The most fascinating characteristic about the data on real financial market returns that I collected is the stability of the long-run real equity returns. The compound annual (geometric) real return on U.S. stocks averaged 6.7% per year from 1802 through 2013, and this return had remained remarkably stable over long-term periods. From 1802 through 1871, the real return averaged 6.7%; from 1871, when the Cowles Foundation data became available, through 1925, the real return on stocks averaged 6.6% per year; and since 1925, which the well-known Ibbotson data cover, the real return has averaged 6.7%. Despite the fact that the price level has increased over ten times since the end of the Second World War, real stock returns have still averaged 6.8%.

The long-run stability of real returns on stocks is strongly indicative of *mean reversion of equity return*. Mean reversion means that stock returns can be very volatile in the short run, but show a remarkable stability in the long run. When my research was first published, there was much skepticism of the mean reversion properties of equity market returns, but now this concept is widely accepted for stocks. If mean reversion prevails, portfolios geared for the long term should have a greater share of equities than short-term portfolios. This conclusion has long been the "conventional" wisdom on investing, but it does not follow if stock returns follow a random walk, a concept widely accepted by academics in the 1970s and 1980s.

When my data first appeared, there was also much discussion of "survivorship bias," the fact that the U.S. stock returns are unusually good because the U.S. was the most successful capitalist country. But three British researchers, Elroy Dimson, Paul Marsh, and Michael Staunton, surveyed stock returns in 16 countries since the beginning of the 20th century and wrote up their results in a book entitled *Triumph of the Optimists*. The authors concluded that U.S. stock returns do not give a distorted picture of the superiority of stocks over bonds worldwide.

Jeremy J. Siegel is the Russell E. Palmer Professor of Finance at The Wharton School of the University of Pennsylvania and author of Stocks for the Long Run and The Future for Investors. His research covers macroeconomics and monetary policy, financial market returns, and long-term economic trends.

In general, if we have T years of returns, the geometric average return over these T years is calculated using this formula:

Geometric average return $= [(1 + R_1) \times (1 + R_2) \times \ldots \times (1 + R_T)]^{1/T} - 1$

This formula tells us that four steps are required:

1. Take each of the T annual returns $R_1, R_2, \ldots, R_T$ and add 1 to each (after converting them to decimals!).
2. Multiply the numbers from Step 1 together.
3. Take the result from Step 2 and raise it to the power of $1/T$.
4. Finally, subtract 1 from the result of Step 3. The result is the geometric average return.

Calculating the Geometric Average Return	EXAMPLE 12.4

Calculate the geometric average return for S&P 500 large-cap stocks for the first five years in Table 12.1, 1926–1930.

First, convert percentages to decimal returns, add 1, and then calculate their product:

S&P 500 Returns	Product
13.75	1.1375
35.70	×1.3570
45.08	×1.4508
−8.80	× .9120
−25.13	× .7487
	1.5291

Notice that the number 1.5291 is what our investment is worth after five years if we started with a $1 investment. The geometric average return is then calculated as follows:

Geometric average return = $1.5291^{1/5} - 1 = .0887$, or 8.87%

The geometric average return is about 8.87 percent in this example. Here is a tip: If you are using a financial calculator, you can enter $1 as the present value, $1.5291 as the future value, and 5 as the number of periods. Then, solve for the unknown rate. You should get the same answer we did.

One thing you may have noticed in our examples thus far is that the geometric average returns seem to be smaller. This will always be true (as long as the returns are not all identical, in which case the two "averages" would be the same). To illustrate, Table 12.4 shows the arithmetic averages and standard deviations from Figure 12.10, along with the geometric average returns.

As shown in Table 12.4, the geometric averages are all smaller (before rounding), but the magnitude of the difference varies quite a bit. The reason is that the difference is greater for more volatile investments. In fact, there is a useful approximation. Assuming all the numbers are expressed in decimals (as opposed to percentages), the geometric average return is approximately equal to the arithmetic average return minus half the variance. For example, looking at the large-company stocks, the arithmetic average is .120 and the standard deviation is .199, implying that the variance is .040. The approximate geometric average is thus $.120 - .040/2 = .100$, which is the same as the actual value in this case.

EXAMPLE 12.5	More Geometric Averages

Take a look back at Figure 12.4. There, we showed the value of a $1 investment after 91 years. Use the value for the large-company stock investment to check the geometric average in Table 12.4.

In Figure 12.4, the large-company investment grew to $6,029.16 over 91 years. The geometric average return is thus

Geometric average return = $6,029.16^{1/91} - 1 = .1000$, or 10.0%

This 10.0% is the value shown in Table 12.4. For practice, check some of the other numbers in Table 12.4 the same way.

TABLE 12.4

Geometric versus Arithmetic Average Returns: 1926–2016

| Series | Average Return | | Standard Deviation |
	Geometric	Arithmetic	
Large-company stocks	10.0%	12.0%	19.9%
Small-company stocks	12.0	16.6	31.9
Long-term corporate bonds	6.0	6.3	8.4
Long-term government bonds	5.5	6.0	9.9
Intermediate-term government bonds	5.3	5.3	5.6
U.S. Treasury bills	3.4	3.4	3.1
Inflation	2.9	3.0	4.1

SOURCE: Morningstar, 2017, author calculations.

ARITHMETIC AVERAGE RETURN OR GEOMETRIC AVERAGE RETURN?

When we look at historical returns, the difference between the geometric and arithmetic average returns isn't too hard to understand. To put it slightly differently, the geometric average tells you what you actually earned per year on average, compounded annually. The arithmetic average tells you what you earned in a typical year. You should use whichever one answers the question you want answered.

A somewhat trickier question concerns which average return to use when forecasting future wealth levels, and there's a lot of confusion on this point among analysts and financial planners. First, let's get one thing straight: If you *know* the true arithmetic average return, then this is what you should use in your forecast. For example, if you know the arithmetic return is 10 percent, then your best guess of the value of a $1,000 investment in 10 years is the future value of $1,000 at 10 percent for 10 years, or $2,593.74.

The problem we face is that we usually have only *estimates* of the arithmetic and geometric returns, and estimates have errors. In this case, the arithmetic average return is probably too high for longer periods and the geometric average is probably too low for shorter periods. You should regard long-run projected wealth levels calculated using arithmetic averages as optimistic. Short-run projected wealth levels calculated using geometric averages are probably pessimistic.

The good news is that there is a simple way of combining the two averages, which we will call *Blume's formula*.[5] Suppose we have calculated geometric and arithmetic return averages from N years of data, and we wish to use these averages to form a T-year average return forecast, $R(T)$, where T is less than N. Here's how we do it:

$$R(T) = \frac{T-1}{N-1} \times \textit{Geometric average} + \frac{N-T}{N-1} \times \textit{Arithmetic average}$$

12.5

For example, suppose that, from 25 years of annual returns data, we calculate an arithmetic average return of 12 percent and a geometric average return of 9 percent. From these averages, we wish to make 1-year, 5-year, and 10-year average return forecasts. These three average return forecasts are calculated as follows:

$$R(1) = \frac{1-1}{24} \times 9\% + \frac{25-1}{24} \times 12\% = 12\%$$

$$R(5) = \frac{5-1}{24} \times 9\% + \frac{25-5}{24} \times 12\% = 11.5\%$$

$$R(10) = \frac{10-1}{24} \times 9\% + \frac{25-10}{24} \times 12\% = 10.875\%$$

We see that 1-year, 5-year, and 10-year forecasts are 12 percent, 11.5 percent, and 10.875 percent, respectively.

As a practical matter, Blume's formula says that if you are using averages calculated over a long period (such as the 91 years we use) to forecast up to a decade or so into the future, then you should use the arithmetic average. If you are forecasting a few decades into the future (as you might do for retirement planning), then you should split the difference between the arithmetic and geometric average returns. Finally, if for some reason you are doing very long forecasts covering many decades, use the geometric average.

This concludes our discussion of geometric versus arithmetic averages. One last note: In the future, when we say "average return," we mean arithmetic unless we explicitly say otherwise.

---

[5]This elegant result is due to Marshall Blume ("Unbiased Estimates of Long-Run Expected Rates of Return," *Journal of the American Statistical Association,* September 1974, pp. 634–38).

> **Concept Questions**
>
> **12.5a** If you want to forecast what the stock market is going to do over the next year, should you use an arithmetic or geometric average?
>
> **12.5b** If you want to forecast what the stock market is going to do over the next century, should you use an arithmetic or geometric average?

12.6 Capital Market Efficiency

Capital market history suggests that the market values of stocks and bonds can fluctuate widely from year to year. Why does this occur? At least part of the answer is that prices change because new information arrives, and investors reassess asset values based on that information.

The behavior of market prices has been extensively studied. A question that has received particular attention is whether prices adjust quickly and correctly when new information arrives. A market is said to be "efficient" if this is the case. To be more precise, in an **efficient capital market**, current market prices fully reflect available information. By this we mean that, based on available information, there is no reason to believe that the current price is too low or too high.

efficient capital market
A market in which security prices reflect available information.

The concept of market efficiency is a rich one, and much has been written about it. A full discussion of the subject goes beyond the scope of our study of corporate finance. Because the concept figures so prominently in studies of market history, we briefly describe the key points here.

PRICE BEHAVIOR IN AN EFFICIENT MARKET

To illustrate how prices behave in an efficient market, suppose the F-Stop Camera Corporation (FCC) has, through years of secret research and development, developed a camera with an autofocusing system whose speed will double that of the autofocusing systems now available. FCC's capital budgeting analysis suggests that launching the new camera will be a highly profitable move; in other words, the NPV appears to be positive and substantial. The key assumption thus far is that FCC has not released any information about the new system; the fact of its existence is "inside" information only.

Now consider a share of stock in FCC. In an efficient market, its price reflects what is known about FCC's current operations and profitability, and it reflects the market opinion about FCC's potential for future growth and profits. The value of the new autofocusing system is not reflected because the market is unaware of the system's existence.

If the market agrees with FCC's assessment of the value of the new project, FCC's stock price will rise when the decision to launch is made public. For example, assume the announcement is made in a press release on Wednesday morning. In an efficient market, the price of shares in FCC will adjust quickly to this new information. Investors should not be able to buy the stock on Wednesday afternoon and make a profit on Thursday. This would imply that it took the stock market a full day to realize the implication of the FCC press release. If the market is efficient, the price of shares of FCC stock on Wednesday afternoon will already reflect the information contained in the Wednesday morning press release.

Figure 12.14 presents three possible stock price adjustments for FCC. In Figure 12.14, Day 0 represents the announcement day. As illustrated, before the announcement, FCC's stock sells for $140 per share. The NPV per share of the new system is, say, $40, so the new price will be $180 once the value of the new project is fully reflected.

FIGURE 12.14

Reaction of Stock Price to New Information in Efficient and Inefficient Markets

Efficient market reaction: The price instantaneously adjusts to and fully reflects new information; there is no tendency for subsequent increases and decreases to occur.
Delayed reaction: The price partially adjusts to the new information; eight days elapse before the price completely reflects the new information.
Overreaction: The price overadjusts to the new information; it overshoots the new price and subsequently corrects.

The solid line in Figure 12.14 represents the path taken by the stock price in an efficient market. In this case, the price adjusts immediately to the new information and no further changes in the price of the stock take place. The broken line in Figure 12.14 depicts a delayed reaction. Here it takes the market eight days or so to fully absorb the information. Finally, the dotted line illustrates an overreaction and subsequent adjustment to the correct price.

The broken line and the dotted line in Figure 12.14 illustrate paths that the stock price might take in an inefficient market. If, for example, stock prices don't adjust immediately to new information (the broken line), then buying stock immediately following the release of new information and then selling it several days later would be a positive NPV activity because the price is too low for several days after the announcement.

THE EFFICIENT MARKETS HYPOTHESIS

The **efficient markets hypothesis (EMH)** asserts that well-organized capital markets, such as the NYSE, are efficient markets, at least as a practical matter. In other words, an advocate of the EMH might argue that although inefficiencies may exist, they are relatively small and uncommon.

efficient markets hypothesis (EMH)
The hypothesis that actual capital markets, such as the NYSE, are efficient.

If a market is efficient, then there is a very important implication for market participants: All investments in that market are zero NPV investments. The reason is not complicated. If prices are neither too low nor too high, then the difference between the market value of an investment and its cost is zero; hence, the NPV is zero. As a result, in an efficient market, investors get exactly what they pay for when they buy securities, and firms receive exactly what their stocks and bonds are worth when they sell them.

What makes a market efficient is competition among investors. Many individuals spend their entire lives trying to find mispriced stocks. For any given stock, they study what has

Look under the "Contents" link at **www.investorhome.com** for more info on the EMH.

happened in the past to the stock price and the stock's dividends. They learn, to the extent possible, what a company's earnings have been, how much the company owes to creditors, what taxes it pays, what businesses it is in, what new investments are planned, how sensitive it is to changes in the economy, and so on.

Not only is there a great deal to know about any particular company, but there is also a powerful incentive for knowing it—namely, the profit motive. If you know more about some company than other investors in the marketplace, you can profit from that knowledge by investing in the company's stock if you have good news and by selling it if you have bad news.

The logical consequence of all this information gathering and analysis is that mispriced stocks will become fewer and fewer. In other words, because of competition among investors, the market will become increasingly efficient. A kind of equilibrium comes into being with which there is just enough mispricing around for those who are best at identifying it to make a living at it. For most other investors, the activity of information gathering and analysis will not pay.[6]

SOME COMMON MISCONCEPTIONS ABOUT THE EMH

No other idea in finance has attracted as much attention as that of efficient markets, and not all of the attention has been flattering. Rather than rehash the arguments here, we will be content to observe that some markets are more efficient than others. For example, financial markets on the whole are probably much more efficient than real asset markets.

Having said this, we can also say that much of the criticism of the EMH is misguided because it is based on a misunderstanding of what the hypothesis says and what it doesn't say. For example, when the notion of market efficiency was first publicized and debated in the popular financial press, it was often characterized by words to the effect that "throwing darts at the financial page will produce a portfolio that can be expected to do as well as any managed by professional security analysts."[7]

Confusion over statements of this sort has often led to a failure to understand the implications of market efficiency. For example, sometimes it is wrongly argued that market efficiency means that it doesn't matter how you invest your money because the efficiency of the market will protect you from making a mistake. However, a random dart thrower might wind up with all of the darts sticking into one or two high-risk stocks that deal in genetic engineering. Would you really want all of your money in two such stocks?

A contest run by *The Wall Street Journal* provides a good example of the controversy surrounding market efficiency. Each month, the *Journal* asked four professional money managers to pick one stock each. At the same time, it threw four darts at the stock page to select a comparison group. In the 147 five-and one-half month contests from July 1990 to September 2002, the pros won 90 times.

The fact that the pros are ahead of the darts by 90 to 57 suggests that markets are not efficient. Or does it? One problem is that the darts naturally tend to select stocks of average risk. The pros are playing to win and naturally select riskier stocks, or so it is argued. If this is true, then, on average, we *expect* the pros to win. Furthermore, the pros' picks are

---

[6]The idea behind the EMH can be illustrated by the following short story: A student was walking down the hall with her finance professor when they both saw a $20 bill on the ground. As the student bent down to pick it up, the professor shook his head slowly and, with a look of disappointment on his face, said patiently to the student, "Don't bother. If it were really there, someone else would have picked it up already." The moral of the story reflects the logic of the efficient markets hypothesis: If you think you have found a pattern in stock prices or a simple device for picking winners, you probably have not.

[7]Malkiel, B. G., *A Random Walk Down Wall Street,* revised and updated ed. New York: Norton, 2016.

IN THEIR OWN WORDS ...

Richard Roll on Market Efficiency

The concept of an efficient market is a special application of the "no free lunch" principle. In an efficient financial market, costless trading policies will not generate "excess" returns. After adjusting for the riskiness of the policy, the trader's return will be no larger than the return of a randomly selected portfolio, at least on average.

This is often thought to imply something about the amount of "information" reflected in asset prices. However, it really doesn't mean that prices reflect all information nor even that they reflect publicly available information. Instead it means that the connection between unreflected information and prices is too subtle and tenuous to be easily or costlessly detected.

Relevant information is difficult and expensive to uncover and evaluate. Thus, if costless trading policies are ineffective, there must exist some traders who make a living by "beating the market." They cover their costs (including the opportunity cost of their time) by trading. The existence of such traders is actually a necessary precondition for markets to become efficient. Without such professional traders, prices would fail to reflect everything that is cheap and easy to evaluate.

Efficient market prices should approximate a random walk, meaning that they will appear to fluctuate more or less randomly. Prices can fluctuate nonrandomly to the extent that their departure from randomness is expensive to discern. Also, observed price series can depart from apparent randomness due to changes in preferences and expectations, but this is really a technicality and does not imply a free lunch relative to current investor sentiments.

Richard Roll is Linde Institute Professor of Finance at the California Institute of Technology. He is a preeminent financial researcher, and he has written extensively in almost every area of modern finance. He is particularly well known for his insightful analyses and great creativity in understanding empirical phenomena.

announced to the public at the start. This publicity may boost the prices of the shares involved somewhat, leading to a partially self-fulfilling prophecy. Unfortunately, the *Journal* discontinued the contest in 2002, so this test of market efficiency is no longer ongoing.

More than anything else, what efficiency implies is that the price a firm will obtain when it sells a share of its stock is a "fair" price in the sense that it reflects the value of that stock given the information available about the firm. Shareholders do not have to worry that they are paying too much for a stock with a low dividend or some other sort of characteristic because the market has already incorporated that characteristic into the price. We sometimes say that the information has been "priced out."

The concept of efficient markets can be explained further by replying to a frequent objection. It is sometimes argued that the market cannot be efficient because stock prices fluctuate from day to day. If the prices are right, the argument goes, then why do they change so much and so often? From our discussion of the market, we can see that these price movements are in no way inconsistent with efficiency. Investors are bombarded with information every day. The fact that prices fluctuate is, at least in part, a reflection of that information flow. In fact, the absence of price movements in a world that changes as rapidly as ours would suggest inefficiency.

THE FORMS OF MARKET EFFICIENCY

It is common to distinguish between three forms of market efficiency. Depending on the degree of efficiency, we say that markets are either *weak form efficient*, *semistrong form efficient*, or *strong form efficient*. The difference between these forms relates to what information is reflected in prices.

We start with the extreme case. If the market is strong form efficient, then *all* information of *every* kind is reflected in stock prices. In such a market, there is no such thing as inside information. Therefore, in our FCC example, we apparently were assuming that the market was not strong form efficient.

Casual observation, particularly in recent years, suggests that inside information does exist, and it can be valuable to possess. Whether it is lawful or ethical to use that information is another issue. In any event, we conclude that private information about a particular stock may exist and may not be currently reflected in the price of the stock. For example, prior knowledge of a takeover attempt could be very valuable.

The second form of efficiency, semistrong form efficiency, is the most controversial. If a market is semistrong form efficient, then all *public* information is reflected in the stock price. The reason this form is controversial is that it implies that a security analyst who tries to identify mispriced stocks using, for example, financial statement information, is wasting time because that information is already reflected in the current price.

The third form of efficiency, weak form efficiency, suggests that, at a minimum, the current price of a stock reflects the stock's own past prices. In other words, studying past prices in an attempt to identify mispriced securities is futile if the market is weak form efficient. Although this form of efficiency might seem rather mild, it implies that searching for patterns in historical prices that will be useful in identifying mispriced stocks will not work (although this practice is quite common).

What does capital market history say about market efficiency? Here again, there is great controversy. At the risk of going out on a limb, we can say that the evidence seems to tell us three things. First, prices appear to respond rapidly to new information, and the response is at least not grossly different from what we would expect in an efficient market. Second, the future of market prices, particularly in the short run, is difficult to predict based on publicly available information. Third, if mispriced stocks exist, then there is no obvious means of identifying them. Put another way, simpleminded schemes based on public information will probably not be successful.

Concept Questions	
12.6a	What is an efficient market?
12.6b	What are the forms of market efficiency?

12.7 Summary and Conclusions

This chapter has explored the subject of capital market history. Such history is useful because it tells us what to expect in the way of returns from risky assets. We summarized our study of market history with two key lessons:

1. Risky assets, on average, earn a risk premium. There is a reward for bearing risk.

2. The greater the potential reward from a risky investment, the greater is the risk.

These lessons have significant implications for the financial manager. We will consider these implications in the chapters ahead.

We also discussed the concept of market efficiency. In an efficient market, prices adjust quickly and correctly to new information. Consequently, asset prices in efficient markets are rarely too high or too low. How efficient capital markets (such as the NYSE) are is a matter of debate; but, at a minimum, they are probably much more efficient than most real asset markets.

CONNECT TO FINANCE

 If you are using *Connect Finance* in your course, get online to take a Practice Test, check out study tools, and find out where you need additional practice. Log on to connect.mheducation.com to learn more!

Can you answer the following *Connect* Quiz questions?

Section 12.1 Chase Bank pays an annual dividend of $1.05 per share on its common stock. One year ago, this stock sold for $48 per share. Today, the stock is priced to sell at $31 per share. What is the capital gains yield?

Section 12.3 The risk premium is computed as the excess return that a security earns over and above the rate for what?

Section 12.4 How are risk and reward related?

Section 12.5 A stock produced annual rates of return of 11 percent, –17 percent, 2 percent, and 14 percent over the past four years, respectively. What is the geometric average return for this period?

Section 12.6 Corporate insiders cannot benefit financially from the inside information they possess in what type of market?

CHAPTER REVIEW AND SELF-TEST PROBLEMS

12.1 Recent Return History Use Table 12.1 to calculate the average return over the years 1996 through 2000 for large-company stocks, long-term government bonds, and Treasury bills.

12.2 More Recent Return History Calculate the standard deviation for each security type using information from Problem 12.1. Which of the investments was the most volatile over this period?

ANSWERS TO CHAPTER REVIEW AND SELF-TEST PROBLEMS

12.1 We calculate the averages as follows:

	Actual Returns		
Year	Large-Company Stocks	Long-Term Government Bonds	Treasury Bills
1996	.2296	.0013	.0514
1997	.3336	.1202	.0519
1998	.2858	.1445	.0486
1999	.2104	–.0751	.0480
2000	–.0910	.1722	.0598
Average	.1937	.0726	.0519

12.2 We first need to calculate the deviations from the average returns. Using the averages from Problem 12.1, we get the following values:

	Deviations from Average Returns		
Year	Large-Company Stocks	Long-Term Government Bonds	Treasury Bills
1996	.0359	−.0713	−.0005
1997	.1399	.0476	.0000
1998	.0921	.0719	−.0033
1999	.0167	−.1477	−.0039
2000	−.2847	.0996	.0079
Total	.0000	.0000	.0000

We square these deviations and calculate the variances and standard deviations:

	Squared Deviations from Average Returns		
Year	Large-Company Stocks	Long-Term Government Bonds	Treasury Bills
1996	.0012902	.0050865	.0000003
1997	.0195776	.0022639	.0000000
1998	.0084861	.0051667	.0000112
1999	.0002796	.0218212	.0000155
2000	.0810427	.0099162	.0000618
Variance	.0276691	.0110636	.0000222
Std dev	.1663402	.1051838	.0047104

To calculate the variances, we added the squared deviations and divided by 4, the number of returns less 1. Notice that the stocks had much more volatility than the bonds, with a much larger average return. For large-company stocks, this was a particularly good period: The average return was 19.37 percent.

CONCEPTS REVIEW AND CRITICAL THINKING QUESTIONS

1. **Investment Selection** [LO4] Given that AK Steel was up by about 359 percent for 2016, why didn't all investors hold this stock?

2. **Investment Selection** [LO4] Given that Endo International was down by 73 percent for 2016, why did some investors hold the stock? Why didn't they sell out before the price declined so sharply?

3. **Risk and Return** [LO2, 3] We have seen that over long periods, stock investments have tended to substantially outperform bond investments. However, it is common to observe investors with long horizons holding portfolios composed entirely of bonds. Are such investors irrational?

4. **Market Efficiency Implications** [LO4] Explain why a characteristic of an efficient market is that investments in that market have zero NPVs.

5. **Efficient Markets Hypothesis** [LO4] A stock market analyst is able to identify mispriced stocks by comparing the average price for the last 10 days to the average price for the last 60 days. If this is true, what do you know about the market?

6. **Semistrong Efficiency** [LO4] If a market is semistrong form efficient, is it also weak form efficient? Explain.

7. **Efficient Markets Hypothesis** [LO4] What are the implications of the efficient markets hypothesis for investors who buy and sell stocks in an attempt to "beat the market"?

8. **Stocks versus Gambling** [LO4] Critically evaluate the following statement: Playing the stock market is like gambling. Such speculative investing has no social value other than the pleasure people get from this form of gambling.

9. **Efficient Markets Hypothesis** [LO4] Several celebrated investors and stock pickers frequently mentioned in the financial press have recorded huge returns on their investments over the past two decades. Is the success of these particular investors an invalidation of the EMH? Explain.

10. **Efficient Markets Hypothesis** [LO4] For each of the following scenarios, discuss whether profit opportunities exist from trading in the stock of the firm under the conditions that (1) the market is not weak form efficient, (2) the market is weak form but not semistrong form efficient, (3) the market is semistrong form but not strong form efficient, and (4) the market is strong form efficient.

    a. The stock price has risen steadily each day for the past 30 days.

    b. The financial statements for a company were released three days ago, and you believe you've uncovered some anomalies in the company's inventory and cost control reporting techniques that are causing the firm's true liquidity strength to be understated.

    c. You observe that the senior managers of a company have been buying a lot of the company's stock on the open market over the past week.

QUESTIONS AND PROBLEMS

1. **Calculating Returns** [LO1] Suppose a stock had an initial price of $65 per share, paid a dividend of $1.45 per share during the year, and had an ending share price of $71. Compute the percentage total return.

2. **Calculating Yields** [LO1] In Problem 1, what was the dividend yield? The capital gains yield?

3. **Return Calculations** [LO1] Rework Problems 1 and 2 assuming the ending share price is $58.

4. **Calculating Returns** [LO1] Suppose you bought a bond with an annual coupon of 7 percent one year ago for $1,010. The bond sells for $985 today.

    a. Assuming a $1,000 face value, what was your total dollar return on this investment over the past year?

    b. What was your total nominal rate of return on this investment over the past year?

    c. If the inflation rate last year was 3 percent, what was your total real rate of return on this investment?

5. **Nominal versus Real Returns** [LO2] What was the average annual return on large-company stocks from 1926 through 2016:

    a. In nominal terms?

    b. In real terms?

BASIC
(Questions 1–12)

6. **Bond Returns** [LO2] What is the historical real return on long-term government bonds? On long-term corporate bonds?

7. **Calculating Returns and Variability** [LO1] Using the following returns, calculate the arithmetic average returns, the variances, and the standard deviations for X and Y.

	Returns	
Year	X	Y
1	12%	25%
2	28	34
3	9	13
4	−7	−27
5	10	14

8. **Risk Premiums** [LO2, 3] Refer to Table 12.1 in the text and look at the period from 1970 through 1975.

   a. Calculate the arithmetic average returns for large-company stocks and T-bills over this period.

   b. Calculate the standard deviation of the returns for large-company stocks and T-bills over this period.

   c. Calculate the observed risk premium in each year for the large-company stocks versus the T-bills. What was the average risk premium over this period? What was the standard deviation of the risk premium over this period?

   d. Is it possible for the risk premium to be negative before an investment is undertaken? Can the risk premium be negative after the fact? Explain.

9. **Calculating Returns and Variability** [LO1] You've observed the following returns on Crash-n-Burn Computer's stock over the past five years: 8 percent, −15 percent, 19 percent, 31 percent, and 21 percent.

   a. What was the arithmetic average return on the company's stock over this five-year period?

   b. What was the variance of the company's returns over this period? The standard deviation?

10. **Calculating Real Returns and Risk Premiums** [LO1] For Problem 9, suppose the average inflation rate over this period was 3.1 percent and the average T-bill rate over the period was 3.9 percent.

    a. What was the average real return on the company's stock?

    b. What was the average nominal risk premium on the company's stock?

11. **Calculating Real Rates** [LO1] Given the information in Problem 10, what was the average real risk-free rate over this time period? What was the average real risk premium?

12. **Effects of Inflation** [LO2] Look at Table 12.1 and Figure 12.7 in the text. When were T-bill rates at their highest over the period from 1926 through 2016? Why do you think they were so high during this period? What relationship underlies your answer?

INTERMEDIATE
(Questions 13–22)

13. **Calculating Investment Returns** [LO1] You bought one of Great White Shark Repellant Co.'s 5.8 percent coupon bonds one year ago for $1,030. These bonds make annual payments and mature 14 years from now. Suppose you decide to sell your bonds today, when the required return on the bonds is 5.1 percent. If the inflation rate was 3.9 percent over the past year, what was your total real return on investment?

14. **Calculating Returns and Variability** [LO1] You find a certain stock that had returns of 9 percent, −16 percent, 18 percent, and 14 percent for four of the last five years. If the average return of the stock over this period was 10.3 percent, what was the stock's return for the missing year? What is the standard deviation of the stock's return?

15. **Arithmetic and Geometric Returns** [LO1] A stock has had returns of 8 percent, 26 percent, 14 percent, −17 percent, 31 percent, and −1 percent over the last six years. What are the arithmetic and geometric average returns for the stock?

16. **Arithmetic and Geometric Returns** [LO1] A stock has had the following year-end prices and dividends:

Year	Price	Dividend
1	$63.40	—
2	70.20	$.85
3	79.18	.95
4	75.32	1.03
5	84.18	1.11
6	98.62	1.20

What are the arithmetic and geometric average returns for the stock?

17. **Using Return Distributions** [LO3] Suppose the returns on long-term corporate bonds are normally distributed. Based on the historical record, what is the approximate probability that your return on these bonds will be less than −2.1 percent in a given year? What range of returns would you expect to see 95 percent of the time? What range would you expect to see 99 percent of the time?

18. **Using Return Distributions** [LO3] Assuming that the returns from holding small-company stocks are normally distributed, what is the approximate probability that your money will double in value in a single year? What about triple in value?

19. **Distributions** [LO3] In Problem 18, what is the probability that the return is less than −100 percent (think)? What are the implications for the distribution of returns?

20. **Blume's Formula** [LO1] Over a 40-year period, an asset had an arithmetic return of 11.2 percent and a geometric return of 9.4 percent. Using Blume's formula, what is your best estimate of the future annual returns over 5 years? 10 years? 20 years?

21. **Blume's Formula** [LO1, 2] Assume that the historical return on large-company stocks is a predictor of the future returns. What return would you estimate for large-company stocks over the next year? The next 10 years? 20 years? 40 years?

22. **Calculating Returns** [LO2, 3] Refer to Table 12.1 in the text and look at the period from 1973 through 1980:

   a. Calculate the average return for Treasury bills and the average annual inflation rate (consumer price index) for this period.

   b. Calculate the standard deviation of Treasury bill returns and inflation over this period.

   c. Calculate the real return for each year. What is the average real return for Treasury bills?

   d. Many people consider Treasury bills risk-free. What do these calculations tell you about the potential risks of Treasury bills?

418   **PART 5**   Risk and Return

CHALLENGE
(Questions 23–24)

23. **Using Probability Distributions** [LO3] Suppose the returns on large-company stocks are normally distributed. Based on the historical record, use the NORMDIST function in Excel® to determine the probability that in any given year you will lose money by investing in common stock.

24. **Using Probability Distributions** [LO3] Suppose the returns on long-term corporate bonds and T-bills are normally distributed. Based on the historical record, use the NORMDIST function in Excel® to answer the following questions:

   a. What is the probability that in any given year, the return on long-term corporate bonds will be greater than 10 percent? Less than 0 percent?

   b. What is the probability that in any given year, the return on T-bills will be greater than 10 percent? Less than 0 percent?

   c. In 1979, the return on long-term government bonds was −2.76 percent. How likely is it that such a low return will recur at some point in the future? T-bills had a return of 10.56 percent in this same year. How likely is it that such a high return on T-bills will recur at some point in the future?

EXCEL MASTER IT! PROBLEM

As we have seen, over the 1926–2016 period, small company stocks had the highest return and the highest risk, while U.S. Treasury bills had the lowest return and the lowest risk. While we certainly hope you have a 91-year holding period, likely your investment will be for fewer years. One way risk and return is examined over a shorter investment period is by using rolling returns and standard deviations. Suppose you have a series of annual returns and you want to calculate a three-year rolling average return. You would calculate the first rolling average at Year 3 using the returns for the first three years. The next rolling average would be calculated using the returns from Years 2, 3, and 4.

   a. Using the annual returns for large company stocks and Treasury bills, and inflation, calculate both the 5- and 10-year rolling average return and standard deviation.

   b. Over how many 5-year periods did Treasury bills outperform large company stocks? How many 10-year periods?

   c. Over how many 5-year periods did Treasury bills have a larger standard deviation than large company stocks? Over how many 10-year periods?

   d. Graph the rolling 5-year and 10-year average returns for large company stocks and Treasury bills.

   e. What conclusions do you draw from the above results?

MINICASE

A Job at S&S Air

You recently graduated from college, and your job search led you to S&S Air. Because you felt the company's business was taking off, you accepted a job offer. The first day on the job, while you are finishing your employment paperwork, Chris Guthrie, who works in Finance, stops by to inform you about the company's 401(k) plan.

A 401(k) plan is a retirement plan offered by many companies. Such plans are tax-deferred savings vehicles, meaning that any deposits you make into the plan are deducted from your current pretax income, so no current taxes are paid on the money. For example, assume your salary will be $50,000 per year. If you contribute $3,000 to the 401(k) plan, you will pay taxes on only $47,000 in income. There are also no taxes paid on any capital gains or income while you are invested in the plan, but you do pay taxes when you withdraw money at retirement. As is fairly common, the company also has a 5 percent match. This means that the company will match your contribution up to 5 percent of your salary, but you must contribute to get the match.

The 401(k) plan has several options for investments, most of which are mutual funds. A mutual fund is a portfolio of assets. When you purchase shares in a mutual fund, you are actually purchasing partial ownership of the fund's assets. The return of the fund is the weighted average of the return of the assets owned by the fund, minus any expenses. The largest expense is typically the management fee, paid to the fund manager. The management fee is compensation for the manager, who makes all of the investment decisions for the fund.

S&S Air uses Bledsoe Financial Services as its 401(k) plan administrator. Here are the investment options offered for employees:

Company Stock One option in the 401(k) plan is stock in S&S Air. The company is currently privately held. However, when you interviewed with the owners, Mark Sexton and Todd Story, they informed you the company stock was expected to go public in the next three to four years. Until then, a company stock price is simply set each year by the board of directors.

Bledsoe S&P 500 Index Fund This mutual fund tracks the S&P 500. Stocks in the fund are weighted exactly the same as the S&P 500. This means the fund return is approximately the return on the S&P 500, minus expenses. Because an index fund purchases assets based on the composition of the index it is following, the fund manager is not required to research stocks and make investment decisions. The result is that the fund expenses are usually low. The Bledsoe S&P 500 Index Fund charges expenses of .15 percent of assets per year.

Bledsoe Small-Cap Fund This fund primarily invests in small-capitalization stocks. As such, the returns of the fund are more volatile. The fund can also invest 10 percent of its assets in companies based outside the United States. This fund charges 1.70 percent in expenses.

Bledsoe Large-Company Stock Fund This fund invests primarily in large-capitalization stocks of companies based in the United States. The fund is managed by Evan Bledsoe and has outperformed the market in six of the last eight years. The fund charges 1.50 percent in expenses.

Bledsoe Bond Fund This fund invests in long-term corporate bonds issued by U.S.-domiciled companies. The fund is restricted to investments in bonds with an investment-grade credit rating. This fund charges 1.40 percent in expenses.

Bledsoe Money Market Fund This fund invests in short-term, high credit-quality debt instruments, which include Treasury bills. As such, the return on the money market fund is only slightly higher than the return on Treasury bills. Because of the credit quality and short-term nature of the investments, there is only a very slight risk of a negative return. The fund charges .60 percent in expenses.

QUESTIONS

1. What advantages do the mutual funds offer compared to the company stock?

2. Assume that you invest 5 percent of your salary and receive the full 5 percent match from S&S Air. What EAR do you earn from the match? What conclusions do you draw about matching plans?

3. Assume you decide you should invest at least part of your money in large-capitalization stocks of companies based in the United States. What are the advantages and disadvantages of choosing the Bledsoe Large-Company Stock Fund compared to the Bledsoe S&P 500 Index Fund?

4. The returns on the Bledsoe Small-Cap Fund are the most volatile of all the mutual funds offered in the 401(k) plan. Why would you ever want to invest in this fund? When you examine the expenses of the mutual funds, you will notice that this fund also has the highest expenses. Does this affect your decision to invest in this fund?

5. A measure of risk-adjusted performance that is often used is the Sharpe ratio. The Sharpe ratio is calculated as the risk premium of an asset divided by its standard deviation. The standard deviation and return of the funds over the past 10 years are listed in the following table. Calculate the Sharpe ratio for each of these funds. Assume that the expected return and standard deviation of the company stock will be 17 percent and 70 percent, respectively. Calculate the Sharpe ratio for the company stock. How appropriate is the Sharpe ratio for these assets? When would you use the Sharpe ratio?

	10-Year Annual Return	Standard Deviation
Bledsoe S&P 500 Index Fund	6.88%	10.75%
Bledsoe Small-Cap Fund	9.29	12.81
Bledsoe Large-Company Stock Fund	3.56	10.99
Bledsoe Bond Fund	5.27	7.12

6. What portfolio allocation would you choose? Why? Explain your thinking carefully.

Chapter

13 | Return, Risk, and the Security Market Line

IN JANUARY 2017, Constellation Brands, Volkswagen, and Chipotle all made major announcements. Constellation Brands, best-known as the importer of Modelo and Corona beers, announced that its sales were up 10 percent from the previous year and that profits had exceeded analysts' estimates. German auto maker Volkswagen announced that it had agreed in principle to pay a $4.3 billion fine to settle a U.S. Justice Department probe into the company's diesel engine emissions scandal. For Chipotle, the company announced that its fourth quarter profit would be 50 to 58 cents per share, well below analysts' estimates of 96 cents. You might expect that these three cases represent good news for Constellation Brands and bad news for Volkswagen and Chipotle, and usually you would be right. But here, Constellation Brands's stock price dropped about 7 percent, Volkswagen's stock jumped by about 3.4 percent, and Chipotle's stock price rose about 5 percent.

So we see that stock price reactions do not always match what we might expect based on news. So when is good news really good news? The answer is fundamental to understanding risk and return, and—the good news is—this chapter explores it in some detail.

Learning Objectives

After studying this chapter, you should be able to:

LO1 Show how to calculate expected returns, variance, and standard deviation.

LO2 Discuss the impact of diversification.

LO3 Summarize the systematic risk principle.

LO4 Describe the security market line and the risk–return trade-off.

For updates on the latest happenings in finance, visit fundamentalsofcorporatefinance.blogspot.com.

In our last chapter, we learned some important lessons from capital market history. Most important, we learned that there is a reward, on average, for bearing risk. We called this reward a *risk premium*. The second lesson is that this risk premium is larger for riskier investments. This chapter explores the economic and managerial implications of this basic idea.

Thus far, we have concentrated mainly on the return behavior of a few large portfolios. We need to expand our consideration to include individual assets. Specifically, we have two tasks to accomplish. First, we have to define risk and discuss how to measure it. We then must quantify the relationship between an asset's risk and its required return.

When we examine the risks associated with individual assets, we find there are two types of risk: Systematic and unsystematic. This distinction is crucial because, as we will see, systematic risk affects almost all assets in the economy, at least to some degree, whereas unsystematic risk affects at most a small number of assets. We then develop the principle of diversification, which shows that highly diversified portfolios will tend to have almost no unsystematic risk.

The principle of diversification has an important implication: To a diversified investor, only systematic risk matters. It follows that in deciding whether to buy a particular individual asset, a diversified investor will be concerned only with that asset's systematic risk. This is a key observation, and it allows us to say a great deal about the risks and returns on individual assets. In particular, it is the basis for a famous relationship between risk and return called the *security market line*, or the SML. To develop the SML, we introduce the equally famous "beta" coefficient, one of the centerpieces of modern finance. Beta and the SML are key concepts because they supply us with at least part of the answer to the question of how to determine the required return on an investment.

Expected Returns and Variances

13.1

In our previous chapter, we discussed how to calculate average returns and variances using historical data. We now begin to discuss how to analyze returns and variances when the information we have concerns future possible returns and their probabilities.

Excel Master It!

Excel Master coverage online

EXPECTED RETURN

We start with a straightforward case. Consider a single period of time—say a year. We have two stocks, L and U, which have the following characteristics: Stock L is expected to have a return of 25 percent in the coming year. Stock U is expected to have a return of 20 percent for the same period.

In a situation like this, if all investors agreed on the expected returns, why would anyone want to hold Stock U? After all, why invest in one stock when the expectation is that another will do better? Clearly, the answer must depend on the risk of the two investments. The return on Stock L, although it is *expected* to be 25 percent, could actually turn out to be higher or lower.

For example, suppose the economy booms. In this case, we think Stock L will have a 70 percent return. If the economy enters a recession, we think the return will be −20 percent. In this case, we say that there are two *states of the economy*, which means that these are the only two possible situations. This setup is oversimplified, of course, but it allows us to illustrate some key ideas without a lot of computation.

Suppose we think a boom and a recession are equally likely to happen, for a 50–50 chance of each. Table 13.1 illustrates the basic information we have described and some additional information about Stock U. Notice that Stock U earns 30 percent if there is a recession and 10 percent if there is a boom.

Obviously, if you buy one of these stocks, say Stock U, what you earn in any particular year depends on what the economy does during that year. However, suppose the probabilities stay the same through time. If you hold Stock U for a number of years, you'll earn 30 percent about half the time and 10 percent the other half. In this case, we say that your **expected return** on Stock U, E(R_U), is 20 percent:

$$E(R_U) = .50 \times 30\% + .50 \times 10\% = 20\%$$

In other words, you should expect to earn 20 percent from this stock, on average.

expected return
The return on a risky asset expected in the future.

State of Economy	Probability of State of Economy	Rate of Return If State Occurs	
		Stock L	Stock U
Recession	.50	−20%	30%
Boom	.50	70	10
	1.00		

TABLE 13.1

States of the Economy and Stock Returns

TABLE 13.2

Calculation of Expected Return

(1) State of Economy	(2) Probability of State of Economy	Stock L		Stock U	
		(3) Rate of Return If State Occurs	(4) Product (2) × (3)	(5) Rate of Return If State Occurs	(6) Product (2) × (5)
Recession	.50	−.20	−.10	.30	.15
Boom	.50	.70	.35	.10	.05
	1.00		$E(R_L)$ = .25, or 25%		$E(R_U)$ = .20, or 20%

For Stock L, the probabilities are the same, but the possible returns are different. Here, we lose 20 percent half the time, and we gain 70 percent the other half. The expected return on L, $E(R_L)$, is 25 percent:

$$E(R_L) = .50 \times -20\% + .50 \times 70\% = 25\%$$

Table 13.2 illustrates these calculations.

In our previous chapter, we defined the risk premium as the difference between the return on a risky investment and that on a risk-free investment, and we calculated the historical risk premiums on some different investments. Using our projected returns, we can calculate the *projected*, or *expected*, *risk premium* as the difference between the expected return on a risky investment and the certain return on a risk-free investment.

For example, suppose risk-free investments are currently offering 8 percent. We will say that the risk-free rate, which we label as R_f, is 8 percent. Given this, what is the projected risk premium on Stock U? On Stock L? Because the expected return on Stock U, $E(R_U)$, is 20 percent, the projected risk premium is:

Risk premium = Expected return − Risk-free rate   **13.1**

$$= E(R_U) - R_f$$
$$= 20\% - 8$$
$$= 12\%$$

Similarly, the risk premium on Stock L is $25\% - 8 = 17\%$.

In general, the expected return on a security or other asset is equal to the sum of the possible returns multiplied by their probabilities. So, if we had 100 possible returns, we would multiply each one by its probability and sum the results. The result would be the expected return. The risk premium would then be the difference between this expected return and the risk-free rate.

EXAMPLE 13.1   **Unequal Probabilities**

Look again at Tables 13.1 and 13.2. Suppose you think a boom will occur only 20 percent of the time instead of 50 percent. What are the expected returns on Stocks U and L in this case? If the risk-free rate is 10 percent, what are the risk premiums?

The first thing to notice is that a recession must occur 80 percent of the time (1 − .20 = .80) because there are only two possibilities. With this in mind, we see that Stock U has a 30 percent return in 80 percent of the years and a 10 percent return in 20 percent of the years. To calculate the expected return, we again just multiply the possibilities by the probabilities and add up the results:

$$E(R_U) = .80 \times 30\% + .20 \times 10\% = 26\%$$

Table 13.3 summarizes the calculations for both stocks. Notice that the expected return on L is −2 percent.

(1) State of Economy	(2) Probability of State of Economy	Stock L		Stock U	
		(3) Rate of Return If State Occurs	(4) Product (2) × (3)	(5) Rate of Return If State Occurs	(6) Product (2) × (5)
Recession	.80	−.20	−.16	.30	.24
Boom	.20	.70	.14	.10	.02
			$E(R_L)$ = −.02, or −2%		$E(R_U)$ = .26 =, or 26%

TABLE 13.3

Calculation of Expected Return

The risk premium for Stock U is 26% − 10 = 16% in this case. The risk premium for Stock L is: −2% − 10 = −12%. This is a little odd; but, for reasons we discuss later, it is not impossible.

CALCULATING THE VARIANCE

To calculate the variances of the returns on our two stocks, we first determine the squared deviations from the expected return. We then multiply each possible squared deviation by its probability. We add these, and the result is the variance. The standard deviation, as always, is the square root of the variance.

To illustrate, let us return to the Stock U we originally discussed, which has an expected return of $E(R_U) = 20\%$. In a given year, it will actually return either 30 percent or 10 percent. The possible deviations are 30% − 20% = 10% and 10% − 20% = −10%. In this case, the variance is:

$$\text{Variance} = \sigma^2 = .50 \times .10^2 + .50 \times (-.10)^2 = .01$$

The standard deviation is the square root of this:

$$\text{Standard deviation} = \sigma = \sqrt{.01} = .10, \text{ or } 10\%$$

Table 13.4 summarizes these calculations for both stocks. Notice that Stock L has a much larger variance.

When we put the expected return and variability information for our two stocks together, we have the following:

	Stock L	Stock U
Expected return, $E(R)$	25%	20%
Variance, σ^2	.2025	.0100
Standard deviation, σ	45%	10%

Stock L has a higher expected return, but U has less risk. You could get a 70 percent return on your investment in L, but you could also lose 20 percent. Notice that an investment in U will always pay at least 10 percent.

Which of these two stocks should you buy? We can't really say; it depends on your personal preferences. We can be reasonably sure that some investors would prefer L to U and some would prefer U to L.

You've probably noticed that the way we have calculated expected returns and variances here is somewhat different from the way we did it in the last chapter. The reason is that, in Chapter 12, we were examining actual historical returns, so we estimated the average return and the variance based on some actual events. Here, we have projected *future* returns and their associated probabilities, so this is the information with which we must work.

TABLE 13.4

Calculation of Variance

(1) State of Economy	(2) Probability of State of Economy	(3) Return Deviation from Expected Return	(4) Squared Return Deviation from Expected Return	(5) Product (2) × (4)
Stock L				
Recession	.50	$-.20 - .25 = -.45$	$-.45^2 = .2025$	.10125
Boom	.50	$.70 - .25 = .45$	$.45^2 = .2025$	.10125
				$\sigma_L^2 = .20250$
Stock U				
Recession	.50	$.30 - .20 = .10$	$.10^2 = .01$	.005
Boom	.50	$.10 - .20 = -.10$	$-.10^2 = .01$	.005
				$\sigma_U^2 = .010$

EXAMPLE 13.2   More Unequal Probabilities

Going back to Example 13.1, what are the variances on the two stocks once we have unequal probabilities? The standard deviations?

We can summarize the needed calculations as follows:

(1) State of Economy	(2) Probability of State of Economy	(3) Return Deviation from Expected Return	(4) Squared Return Deviation from Expected Return	(5) Product (2) × (4)
Stock L				
Recession	.80	$-.20 - (-.02) = -.18$	.0324	.02592
Boom	.20	$.70 - (-.02) = .72$	.5184	.10368
				$\sigma_L^2 = .12960$
Stock U				
Recession	.80	$.30 - .26 = .04$	.0016	.00128
Boom	.20	$.10 - .26 = -.16$	.0256	.00512
				$\sigma_U^2 = .00640$

Based on these calculations, the standard deviation for L is $\sigma_L = \sqrt{.1296} = .36$, or 36%. The standard deviation for U is much smaller: $\sigma_U = \sqrt{.0064} = .08$, or 8%.

Concept Questions

13.1a   How do we calculate the expected return on a security?

13.1b   In words, how do we calculate the variance of the expected return?

13.2 Portfolios

Excel Master It!

Excel Master coverage online

Thus far in this chapter, we have concentrated on individual assets considered separately. However, most investors actually hold a **portfolio** of assets. All we mean by this is that investors tend to own more than just a single stock, bond, or other asset. Given this, portfolio return and portfolio risk are of obvious relevance. Accordingly, we now discuss portfolio expected returns and variances.

(1) State of Economy	(2) Probability of State of Economy	(3) Portfolio Return If State Occurs	(4) Product (2) × (3)
Recession	.50	.50 × −20% + .50 × 30% = 5%	.025
Boom	.50	.50 × 70% + .50 × 10% = 40%	.200
			E(R_p) = .225, or 22.5%

TABLE 13.5

Expected Return on an Equally Weighted Portfolio of Stock L and Stock U

PORTFOLIO WEIGHTS

There are many equivalent ways of describing a portfolio. The most convenient approach is to list the percentage of the total portfolio's value that is invested in each portfolio asset. We call these percentages the **portfolio weights**.

For example, if we have $50 in one asset and $150 in another, our total portfolio is worth $200. The percentage of our portfolio in the first asset is $50/$200 = .25. The percentage of our portfolio in the second asset is $150/$200, or .75. Our portfolio weights are .25 and .75. Notice that the weights have to sum to 1.00 because all of our money is invested somewhere.[1]

PORTFOLIO EXPECTED RETURNS

Let's go back to Stocks L and U. You put half your money in each. The portfolio weights are obviously .50 and .50. What is the pattern of returns on this portfolio? The expected return?

To answer these questions, suppose the economy actually enters a recession. In this case, half your money (the half in L) loses 20 percent. The other half (the half in U) gains 30 percent. Your portfolio return, R_p, in a recession is:

$$R_p = .50 \times -20\% + .50 \times 30\% = 5\%$$

Table 13.5 summarizes the remaining calculations. Notice that when a boom occurs, your portfolio will return 40 percent:

$$R_p = .50 \times 70\% + .50 \times 10\% = 40\%$$

As indicated in Table 13.5, the expected return on your portfolio, E(R_p), is 22.5 percent.

We can save ourselves some work by calculating the expected return more directly. Given these portfolio weights, we could have reasoned that we expect half of our money to earn 25 percent (the half in L) and half of our money to earn 20 percent (the half in U). Our portfolio expected return is thus:

$$
\begin{aligned}
\mathrm{E}\!\left(R_p\right) &= .50 \times \mathrm{E}\!\left(R_L\right) + .50 \times \mathrm{E}\!\left(R_U\right) \\
&= .50 \times 25\% + .50 \times 20\% \\
&= 22.5\%
\end{aligned}
$$

This is the same portfolio expected return we calculated previously.

This method of calculating the expected return on a portfolio works no matter how many assets there are in the portfolio. Suppose we had n assets in our portfolio, where n is any number. If we let x_i stand for the percentage of our money in Asset i, then the expected return would be:

$$E(R_p) = x_1 \times E(R_1) + x_2 \times E(R_2) + \cdots + x_n \times E(R_n)$$

Want more information about investing? Visit **www.thestreet.com**.

---

[1]Some of it could be in cash, of course, but we would then just consider the cash to be one of the portfolio assets.

426   **PART 5**   Risk and Return

This says that the expected return on a portfolio is a straightforward combination of the expected returns on the assets in that portfolio. This seems somewhat obvious; but, as we will examine next, the obvious approach is not always the right one.

EXAMPLE 13.3	Portfolio Expected Return

Suppose we have the following projections for three stocks:

State of Economy	Probability of State of Economy	Returns If State Occurs		
		Stock A	Stock B	Stock C
Boom	.40	10%	15%	20%
Bust	.60	8	4	0

We want to calculate portfolio expected returns in two cases. First, what would be the expected return on a portfolio with equal amounts invested in each of the three stocks? Second, what would be the expected return if half of the portfolio were in A, with the remainder equally divided between B and C?

Based on what we've learned from our earlier discussions, we can determine that the expected returns on the individual stocks are (check these for practice):

$E(R_A) = 8.8\%$
$E(R_B) = 8.4\%$
$E(R_C) = 8.0\%$

If a portfolio has equal investments in each asset, the portfolio weights are all the same. Such a portfolio is said to be *equally weighted*. Because there are three stocks in this case, the weights are all equal to 1/3. The portfolio expected return is thus:

$E(R_P) = (1/3) \times 8.8\% + (1/3) \times 8.4\% + (1/3) \times 8\% = 8.4\%$

In the second case, verify that the portfolio expected return is 8.5 percent.

PORTFOLIO VARIANCE

From our earlier discussion, the expected return on a portfolio that contains equal investments in Stocks U and L is 22.5 percent. What is the standard deviation of return on this portfolio? Simple intuition might suggest that because half of the money has a standard deviation of 45 percent and the other half has a standard deviation of 10 percent, the portfolio's standard deviation might be calculated as:

$\sigma_P = .50 \times 45\% + .50 \times 10\% = 27.5\%$

Unfortunately, this approach is completely incorrect!

Let's see what the standard deviation really is. Table 13.6 summarizes the relevant calculations. As we see, the portfolio's variance is about .031, and its standard deviation is less than we thought—it's only 17.5 percent. What is illustrated here is that the variance on a portfolio is not generally a simple combination of the variances of the assets in the portfolio.

We can illustrate this point a little more dramatically by considering a slightly different set of portfolio weights. Suppose we put 2/11 (about 18 percent) in L and the other 9/11 (about 82 percent) in U. If a recession occurs, this portfolio will have a return of:

$R_P = (2/11) \times -20\% + (9/11) \times 30\% = 20.91\%$

(1) State of Economy	(2) Probability of State of Economy	(3) Portfolio Return If State Occurs	(4) Squared Deviation from Expected Return	(5) Product (2) × (4)
Recession	.50	5%	$(.05 - .225)^2 = .030625$	.0153125
Boom	.50	40	$(.40 - .225)^2 = .030625$	.0153125
			$\sigma_P^2 = .030625$	
			$\sigma_P = \sqrt{.030625} = .175$, or 17.5%	

TABLE 13.6

Variance on an Equally Weighted Portfolio of Stock L and Stock U

If a boom occurs, this portfolio will have a return of:

$$R_P = (2/11) \times 70\% + (9/11) \times 10\% = 20.91\%$$

Notice that the return is the same no matter what happens. No further calculations are needed: This portfolio has a zero variance. Apparently, combining assets into portfolios can substantially alter the risks faced by the investor. This is a crucial observation, and we will begin to explore its implications in the next section.

Portfolio Variance and Standard Deviation   **EXAMPLE 13.4**

In Example 13.3, what are the standard deviations on the two portfolios? To answer, we first have to calculate the portfolio returns in the two states. We will work with the second portfolio, which has 50 percent in Stock A and 25 percent in each of Stocks B and C. The relevant calculations can be summarized as follows:

State of Economy	Probability of State of Economy	Rate of Return If State Occurs			
		Stock A	Stock B	Stock C	Portfolio
Boom	.40	10%	15%	20%	13.75%
Bust	.60	8	4	0	5.00

The portfolio return when the economy booms is calculated as:

$$E(R_P) = .50 \times 10\% + .25 \times 15\% + .25 \times 20\% = 13.75\%$$

The return when the economy goes bust is calculated the same way. The expected return on the portfolio is 8.5 percent. The variance is thus:

$$\sigma_P^2 = .40 \times (.1375 - .085)^2 + .60 \times (.05 - .085)^2$$

$$= .0018375$$

The standard deviation is about 4.3 percent. For our equally weighted portfolio, check to see that the standard deviation is about 5.4 percent.

Concept Questions

13.2a What is a portfolio weight?

13.2b How do we calculate the expected return on a portfolio?

13.2c Is there a simple relationship between the standard deviation on a portfolio and the standard deviations of the assets in the portfolio?

13.3 Announcements, Surprises, and Expected Returns

Now that we know how to construct portfolios and evaluate their returns, we begin to describe more carefully the risks and returns associated with individual securities. Thus far, we have measured volatility by looking at the difference between the actual return on an asset or portfolio, R, and the expected return, E(R). We now look at why those deviations exist.

EXPECTED AND UNEXPECTED RETURNS

To begin, for concreteness, we consider the return on the stock of a company called Flyers. What will determine this stock's return in, say, the coming year?

The return on any stock traded in a financial market is composed of two parts. First, the normal, or expected, return from the stock is the part of the return that shareholders in the market predict or expect. This return depends on the information shareholders have that bears on the stock, and it is based on the market's understanding today of the important factors that will influence the stock in the coming year.

The second part of the return on the stock is the uncertain, or risky, part. This is the portion that comes from unexpected information revealed within the year. A list of all possible sources of such information would be endless, but here are a few examples:

- News about Flyers research.
- Government figures released on gross domestic product (GDP).
- The results from the latest arms control talks.
- The news that Flyers sales figures are higher than expected.
- A sudden, unexpected drop in interest rates.

Based on this discussion, one way to express the return on Flyers stock in the coming year would be:

Total return = Expected return + Unexpected return

$$R = E(R) + U$$

[13.3]

where R stands for the actual total return in the year, E(R) stands for the expected part of the return, and U stands for the unexpected part of the return. What this says is that the actual return, R, differs from the expected return, E(R), because of surprises that occur during the year. In any given year, the unexpected return will be positive or negative; but, through time, the average value of U will be zero. This means that on average, the actual return equals the expected return.

ANNOUNCEMENTS AND NEWS

We need to be careful when we talk about the effect of news items on the return. For example, suppose Flyers's business is such that the company prospers when GDP grows at a relatively high rate and suffers when GDP is relatively stagnant. In this case, in deciding what return to expect this year from owning stock in Flyers, shareholders either implicitly or explicitly must think about what GDP is likely to be for the year.

When the government actually announces GDP figures for the year, what will happen to the value of Flyers's stock? Obviously, the answer depends on what figure is released. More to the point, however, the impact depends on how much of that figure is *new* information.

At the beginning of the year, market participants will have some idea or forecast of what the yearly GDP will be. To the extent that shareholders have predicted GDP, that prediction will already be factored into the expected part of the return on the stock, E(R). On the other hand, if the announced GDP is a surprise, the effect will be part of U, the unanticipated portion of the return. As an example, suppose shareholders in the market had forecast that the GDP increase this year would be .5 percent. If the actual announcement this year is exactly .5 percent, the same as the forecast, then the shareholders don't really learn anything, and the announcement isn't news. There will be no impact on the stock price as a result. This is like receiving confirmation of something you suspected all along; it doesn't reveal anything new.

A common way of saying that an announcement isn't news is to say that the market has already "discounted" the announcement. The use of the word *discount* here is different from the use of the term in computing present values, but the spirit is the same. When we discount a dollar in the future, we say it is worth less to us because of the time value of money. When we discount an announcement or a news item, we say that it has less of an impact on the price because the market already knew much of it.

Going back to Flyers, suppose the government announces that the actual GDP increase during the year has been 1.5 percent. Now shareholders have learned something—namely, that the increase is one percentage point higher than they had forecast. This difference between the actual result and the forecast, one percentage point in this example, is sometimes called the *innovation* or the *surprise*.

This distinction explains why what seems to be good news can actually be bad news (and vice versa). Going back to the companies we discussed in our chapter opener, even though Constellation Brands beat sales and profit estimates, investors were concerned about slowing beer sales and the potential for tariffs on the company's imports. For Chipotle, earnings were below estimates and same-store sales had declined, but the decline was lower than previous quarters, indicating a possible reversal in falling sales caused by a previous foodborne contamination problem. An additional cause of the decreased earnings—an increase in the price of avocados—was not expected to continue.

In the case of Volkswagen, even though its $4.3 billion settlement seems negative, it actually was a positive for investors. The Justice Department probe had centered on "dieselgate," a reference to excess emissions from diesel engines in Volkswagen vehicles. Volkswagen had programmed certain models to activate controls that worked only during emissions tests, allowing the cars to meet the emissions standards for NO_x. During normal operations, the cars emitted as much as 40 times more NO_x than under testing conditions. Even though the settlement was large, investors had been worried that the probe would drag on much longer and that the fine would be much higher.

To summarize, an announcement can be broken into two parts: the anticipated, or expected, part and the surprise, or innovation:

Announcement = Expected part + Surprise

The expected part of any announcement is the part of the information that the market uses to form the expectation, E(R), of the return on the stock. The surprise is the news that influences the unanticipated return on the stock, U.

Our discussion of market efficiency in the previous chapter bears on this discussion. We are assuming that relevant information known today is already reflected in the expected return. This is identical to saying that the current price reflects relevant publicly available information. We are implicitly assuming that markets are at least reasonably efficient in the semistrong form.

Henceforth, when we speak of news, we will mean the surprise part of an announcement and not the portion that the market has expected and therefore already discounted.

> **Concept Questions**
>
> **13.3a** What are the two basic parts of a return?
> **13.3b** Under what conditions will a company's announcement have no effect on common stock prices?

13.4 Risk: Systematic and Unsystematic

The unanticipated part of the return, that portion resulting from surprises, is the true risk of any investment. After all, if we always receive exactly what we expect, then the investment is perfectly predictable and, by definition, risk-free. In other words, the risk of owning an asset comes from surprises—unanticipated events.

There are important differences, though, among various sources of risk. Returning to our example in the previous section, look back at the list of news stories that could impact the return on Flyers's stock. Some of these stories are directed specifically at Flyers, and some are more general. Which of the news items are of specific importance to Flyers?

Announcements about interest rates or GDP are clearly important for nearly all companies, whereas news about Flyers's president, its research, or its sales is of specific interest to Flyers. We will distinguish between these two types of events because, as we will see, they have different implications.

SYSTEMATIC AND UNSYSTEMATIC RISK

systematic risk
A risk that influences a large number of assets. Also called *market risk.*

unsystematic risk
A risk that affects at most a small number of assets. Also called *unique* or *asset-specific risk.*

The first type of surprise—the one that affects many assets—we will label **systematic risk**. A systematic risk is one that influences a large number of assets, each to a greater or lesser extent. Because systematic risks have marketwide effects, they are sometimes called *market risks.*

The second type of surprise we will call **unsystematic risk**. An unsystematic risk is one that affects a single asset or a small group of assets. Because these risks are unique to individual companies or assets, they are sometimes called *unique* or *asset-specific risks.* We will use these terms interchangeably.

As we have seen, uncertainties about general economic conditions (such as GDP, interest rates, or inflation) are examples of systematic risks. These conditions affect nearly all companies to some degree. An unanticipated increase, or surprise, in inflation, for example, affects wages and the costs of the supplies that companies buy; it affects the value of the assets that companies own; and it affects the prices at which companies sell their products. Forces such as these, to which all companies are susceptible, are the essence of systematic risk.

In contrast, the announcement of an oil strike by a company will primarily affect that company and, perhaps, a few others (such as primary competitors and suppliers). It is unlikely to have much of an effect on the world oil market, or on the affairs of companies not in the oil business, so this is an unsystematic event.

SYSTEMATIC AND UNSYSTEMATIC COMPONENTS OF RETURN

The distinction between a systematic risk and an unsystematic risk is never really as exact as we make it out to be. Even the most narrow and peculiar bit of news about a company ripples through the economy. This is true because every enterprise, no matter how tiny, is a part of the economy. It's like the tale of a kingdom that was lost because one horse lost a shoe. This is mostly hairsplitting. Some risks are clearly much more general than others. We'll see some evidence on this point in just a moment.

The distinction between the types of risk allows us to break down the surprise portion, U, of the return on the Flyers stock into two parts. Earlier, we had the actual return broken down into its expected and surprise components:

$$R = E(R) + U$$

We now recognize that the total surprise component for Flyers, U, has a systematic and an unsystematic component, so:

$R = E(R) +$ Systematic portion $+$ Unsystematic portion

Because it is traditional, we will use the Greek letter epsilon, ϵ, to stand for the unsystematic portion. Because systematic risks are often called market risks, we will use the letter m to stand for the systematic part of the surprise. With these symbols, we can rewrite the formula for the total return:

$$R = E(R) + U$$
$$= E(R) + m + \epsilon$$

The important thing about the way we have broken down the total surprise, U, is that the unsystematic portion, ϵ, is more or less unique to Flyers. For this reason, it is unrelated to the unsystematic portion of the return on most other assets. To see why this is important, we need to return to the subject of portfolio risk.

Concept Questions

13.4a What are the two basic types of risk?
13.4b What is the distinction between the two types of risk?

Diversification and Portfolio Risk

13.5

We've seen earlier that portfolio risks can, in principle, be quite different from the risks of the assets that make up the portfolio. We now look more closely at the riskiness of an individual asset versus the risk of a portfolio of many different assets. We will once again examine some market history to get an idea of what happens with actual investments in U.S. capital markets.

Excel Master It!
Excel Master
coverage online

THE EFFECT OF DIVERSIFICATION: ANOTHER LESSON FROM MARKET HISTORY

In our previous chapter, we saw that the standard deviation of the annual return on a portfolio of 500 large common stocks has historically been about 20 percent per year. Does this mean that the standard deviation of the annual return on a typical stock in that group of 500 is about 20 percent? As you might suspect by now, the answer is no. This is an extremely important observation.

To illustrate the relationship between portfolio size and portfolio risk, Table 13.7 illustrates typical average annual standard deviations for equally weighted portfolios that contain different numbers of randomly selected NYSE securities.

In Column 2 of Table 13.7, we see that the standard deviation for a "portfolio" of one security is about 49 percent. What this means is that if you randomly selected a single NYSE stock and put all your money into it, your standard deviation of return would typically be a substantial 49 percent per year. If you were to randomly select two stocks and invest

For more about risk and diversification, visit **www .investopedia.com/university**.

TABLE 13.7

Standard Deviations of Annual Portfolio Returns

(1) Number of Stocks in Portfolio	(2) Average Standard Deviation of Annual Portfolio Returns	(3) Ratio of Portfolio Standard Deviation to Standard Deviation of a Single Stock
1	49.24%	1.00
2	37.36	.76
4	29.69	.60
6	26.64	.54
8	24.98	.51
10	23.93	.49
20	21.68	.44
30	20.87	.42
40	20.46	.42
50	20.20	.41
100	19.69	.40
200	19.42	.39
300	19.34	.39
400	19.29	.39
500	19.27	.39
1,000	19.21	.39

SOURCE: These figures are from Table 1 in Statman, M., "How Many Stocks Make a Diversified Portfolio?" *Journal of Financial and Quantitative Analysis* 22, September 1987, 353–63. They were derived from Elton, E. J. and Gruber, M. J., "Risk Reduction and Portfolio Size: An Analytical Solution," *Journal of Business* 50, October 1977, 415–37.

half your money in each, your standard deviation would be about 37 percent on average, and so on.

The important thing to notice in Table 13.7 is that the standard deviation declines as the number of securities is increased. By the time we have 100 randomly chosen stocks, the portfolio's standard deviation has declined by about 60 percent, from 49 percent to about 20 percent. With 500 securities, the standard deviation is 19.27 percent, similar to the 20 percent we saw in our previous chapter for the large common stock portfolio. The small difference exists because the portfolio securities and time periods examined are not identical.

THE PRINCIPLE OF DIVERSIFICATION

Figure 13.1 illustrates the point we've been discussing. What we have plotted is the standard deviation of return versus the number of stocks in the portfolio. Notice in Figure 13.1 that the benefit in terms of risk reduction from adding securities drops off as we add more and more. By the time we have 10 securities, most of the effect is already realized; and by the time we get to 30 or so, there is little remaining benefit.

Figure 13.1 illustrates two key points. First, some of the riskiness associated with individual assets can be eliminated by forming portfolios. The process of spreading an investment across assets (and thereby forming a portfolio) is called *diversification*. The **principle of diversification** tells us that spreading an investment across many assets will eliminate some of the risk. The blue shaded area in Figure 13.1, labeled "diversifiable risk," is the part that can be eliminated by diversification.

The second point is equally important. There is a minimum level of risk that cannot be eliminated by diversifying. This minimum level is labeled "nondiversifiable risk" in

principle of diversification

Spreading an investment across a number of assets will eliminate some, but not all, of the risk.

FIGURE 13.1

Portfolio Diversification

Figure 13.1. Taken together, these two points are another important lesson from capital market history: Diversification reduces risk, but only up to a point. Put another way, some risk is diversifiable and some is not.

To give a recent example of the impact of diversification, the S&P 500, which is a widely followed stock market index of 500 large, well-known U.S. stocks, was up about 12 percent in 2016. As we saw in our previous chapter, this gain represents an average year for a portfolio of large-cap stocks. The biggest individual winners for the year were Nvidia (up a whopping 224 percent), ONEOK (up 147 percent), and Freeport-McMoRan (up 95 percent). But not all 500 stocks were up: The losers included TripAdvisor (down 46 percent), Perrigo (down 42 percent), and Vertex Pharmaceuticals (down 41 percent). Again, the lesson is clear: Diversification reduces exposure to extreme outcomes, both good and bad.

DIVERSIFICATION AND UNSYSTEMATIC RISK

From our discussion of portfolio risk, we know that some of the risk associated with individual assets can be diversified away and some cannot. We are left with an obvious question: Why is this so? It turns out that the answer hinges on the distinction we made earlier between systematic and unsystematic risk.

By definition, an unsystematic risk is one that is particular to a single asset or, at most, a small group. For example, if the asset under consideration is stock in a single company, the discovery of positive NPV projects such as successful new products and innovative cost savings will tend to increase the value of the stock. Unanticipated lawsuits, industrial accidents, strikes, and similar events will tend to decrease future cash flows and thereby reduce share values.

Here is the important observation: If we held only a single stock, the value of our investment would fluctuate because of company-specific events. If we hold a large portfolio, on the other hand, some of the stocks in the portfolio will go up in value because of positive company-specific events and some will go down in value because of negative events. The net effect on the overall value of the portfolio will be relatively small because these effects will tend to cancel each other out.

Now we see why some of the variability associated with individual assets is eliminated by diversification. When we combine assets into portfolios, the unique, or unsystematic, events—both positive and negative—tend to "wash out" once we have more than just a few assets.

This is an important point that bears repeating:

> **Unsystematic risk is essentially eliminated by diversification, so a portfolio with many assets has almost no unsystematic risk.**

In fact, the terms *diversifiable risk* and *unsystematic risk* are often used interchangeably.

DIVERSIFICATION AND SYSTEMATIC RISK

We've seen that unsystematic risk can be eliminated by diversifying. What about systematic risk? Can it also be eliminated by diversification? The answer is no because, by definition, a systematic risk affects almost all assets to some degree. As a result, no matter how many assets we put into a portfolio, the systematic risk doesn't go away. For obvious reasons, the terms *systematic risk* and *nondiversifiable risk* are used interchangeably.

Because we have introduced so many different terms, it is useful to summarize our discussion before moving on. What we have seen is that the total risk of an investment, as measured by the standard deviation of its return, can be written as:

Total risk = Systematic risk + Unsystematic risk   **13.6**

Systematic risk is also called *nondiversifiable risk* or *market risk*. Unsystematic risk is also called *diversifiable risk*, *unique risk*, or *asset-specific risk*. For a well-diversified portfolio, the unsystematic risk is negligible. For such a portfolio, essentially all of the risk is systematic.

Concept Questions

13.5a What happens to the standard deviation of return for a portfolio if we increase the number of securities in the portfolio?

13.5b What is the principle of diversification?

13.5c Why is some risk diversifiable? Why is some risk not diversifiable?

13.5d Why can't systematic risk be diversified away?

13.6 Systematic Risk and Beta

Excel Master It!

Excel Master coverage online

The question that we now begin to address is this: What determines the size of the risk premium on a risky asset? Put another way, why do some assets have a larger risk premium than other assets? The answer to these questions, as we discuss next, is also based on the distinction between systematic and unsystematic risk.

THE SYSTEMATIC RISK PRINCIPLE

Thus far, we've seen that the total risk associated with an asset can be decomposed into two components: Systematic and unsystematic risk. We have also seen that unsystematic risk can be essentially eliminated by diversification. The systematic risk present in an asset, on the other hand, cannot be eliminated by diversification.

Based on our study of capital market history, we know that there is a reward, on average, for bearing risk. We now need to be more precise about what we mean by risk. The **systematic risk principle** states that the reward for bearing risk depends only on the systematic risk of an investment. The underlying rationale for this principle is straightforward: Because unsystematic risk can be eliminated at virtually no cost (by diversifying), there is no reward for bearing it. Put another way, the market does not reward risks that are borne unnecessarily.

The systematic risk principle has a remarkable and very important implication:

systematic risk principle
The expected return on a risky asset depends only on that asset's systematic risk.

> **The expected return on an asset depends only on that asset's systematic risk.**

There is an obvious corollary to this principle: No matter how much total risk an asset has, only the systematic portion is relevant in determining the expected return (and the risk premium) on that asset.

For more about beta, see **www.investools.com** and **money.msn.com**.

MEASURING SYSTEMATIC RISK

Because systematic risk is the crucial determinant of an asset's expected return, we need some way of measuring the level of systematic risk for different investments. The specific measure we will use is called the **beta coefficient**, for which we will use the Greek symbol β. A beta coefficient, or beta for short, tells us how much systematic risk a particular asset has relative to an average asset. By definition, an average asset has a beta of 1.0 relative to itself. An asset with a beta of .50, therefore, has half as much systematic risk as an average asset; an asset with a beta of 2.0 has twice as much.

Table 13.8 contains the estimated beta coefficients for the stocks of some well-known companies. The range of betas in Table 13.8 is typical for stocks of large U.S. corporations. Betas outside this range occur, but they are less common.

The important thing to remember is that the expected return, and thus the risk premium, of an asset depends only on its systematic risk. Because assets with larger betas have greater systematic risks, they will have greater expected returns. From Table 13.8, an investor who buys stock in Coca-Cola, with a beta of .74, should expect to earn less, on average, than an investor who buys stock in Apple, with a beta of about 1.44.

beta coefficient
The amount of systematic risk present in a particular risky asset relative to that in an average asset.

	Beta Coefficient (β)
Johnson & Johnson	.67
Coca-Cola	.74
Twitter	.85
Pfizer	.99
Tesla	1.19
Ford	1.29
Apple	1.44
CBS Corporation	1.71

TABLE 13.8

Beta Coefficients for Selected Companies

SOURCE: Yahoo! Finance, 2017.

One cautionary note is in order: Not all betas are created equal. Different providers use somewhat different methods for estimating betas, and significant differences sometimes occur. As a result, it is a good idea to look at several sources. See our nearby *Work the Web* box for more about beta.

WORK THE WEB

You can find beta estimates at many sites on the web. One of the best is finance.yahoo.com. Here is a snapshot of the "Statistics" screen for Sears Holdings (SHLD), parent of Sears and K-Mart stores:

Stock Price History	
Beta	1.44
52-Week Change [3]	-52.89%
S&P500 52-Week Change [3]	20.11%
52 Week High [3]	19.12
52 Week Low [3]	8.00

Management Effectiveness	
Return on Assets (ttm)	-8.07%
Return on Equity (ttm)	N/A

Balance Sheet	
Total Cash (mrq)	258M
Total Cash Per Share (mrq)	2.41
Total Debt (mrq)	4.46B
Total Debt/Equity (mrq)	N/A
Current Ratio (mrq)	1.04
Book Value Per Share (mrq)	-22.12

The reported beta for Sears is 1.44, which means that Sears has about one and one-half times the systematic risk of a typical stock. You would expect that the company is very risky and, looking at the other numbers, we agree. Sears's ROA is negative 8.07 percent, which indicates the company lost money over the past year, but the ROE is not reported. Why? If you look at the book value per share, it is negative. In this case, the larger the loss, the larger the ROE! That's not good. Given this, Sears appears to be a good candidate for a high beta.

Questions

1. As we mentioned, the book value per share of stock for Sears is negative. What is the current book value per share reported on this website?
2. What growth rate are analysts projecting for Sears? How does this growth rate compare to the industry?

Total Risk versus Beta

EXAMPLE 13.5

Consider the following information about two securities. Which has greater total risk? Which has greater systematic risk? Greater unsystematic risk? Which asset will have a higher risk premium?

	Standard Deviation	Beta
Security A	40%	.50
Security B	20	1.50

From our discussion in this section, Security A has greater total risk, but it has substantially less systematic risk. Because total risk is the sum of systematic and unsystematic risk, Security A must have greater unsystematic risk. Finally, from the systematic risk principle, Security B will have a higher risk premium and a greater expected return, despite the fact that it has less total risk.

PORTFOLIO BETAS

Earlier, we saw that the riskiness of a portfolio has no simple relationship to the risks of the assets in the portfolio. A portfolio beta, however, can be calculated, just like a portfolio expected return. For example, looking again at Table 13.8, suppose you put half of your money in Apple and half in Coca-Cola. What would the beta of this combination be? Because Apple has a beta of 1.44 and Coca-Cola has a beta of .74, the portfolio's beta, β_p, would be:

$$\beta_P = .50 \times \beta_{Apple} + .50 \times \beta_{Coca\text{-}Cola}$$
$$= .50 \times 1.44 + .50 \times .74$$
$$= 1.09$$

In general, if we had many assets in a portfolio, we would multiply each asset's beta by its portfolio weight and then add the results to get the portfolio's beta.

Portfolio Betas

EXAMPLE 13.6

Suppose we had the following investments:

Security	Amount Invested	Expected Return	Beta
Stock A	$1,000	8%	.80
Stock B	2,000	12	.95
Stock C	3,000	15	1.10
Stock D	4,000	18	1.40

What is the expected return on this portfolio? What is the beta of this portfolio? Does this portfolio have more or less systematic risk than an average asset?

To answer, we first have to calculate the portfolio weights. Notice that the total amount invested is $10,000. Of this, $1,000/10,000 = 10% is invested in Stock A. Similarly, 20 percent is invested in Stock B, 30 percent is invested in Stock C, and 40 percent is invested in Stock D. The expected return, $E(R_p)$, is:

$$E(R_p) = .10 \times E(R_A) + .20 \times E(R_B) + .30 \times E(R_C) + .40 \times E(R_D)$$
$$= .10 \times 8\% + .20 \times 12\% + .30 \times 15\% + .40 \times 18\%$$
$$= 14.9\%$$

Similarly, the portfolio beta, β_p, is:

$$\beta_P = .10 \times \beta_A + .20 \times \beta_B + .30 \times \beta_C + .40 \times \beta_D$$
$$= .10 \times .80 + .20 \times .95 + .30 \times 1.10 + .40 \times 1.40$$
$$= 1.16$$

This portfolio has an expected return of 14.9 percent and a beta of 1.16. Because the beta is larger than 1, this portfolio has greater systematic risk than an average asset.

Betas are easy to find on the web. Try **finance.yahoo.com** and **money.cnn.com**.

Concept Questions

13.6a What is the systematic risk principle?

13.6b What does a beta coefficient measure?

13.6c True or false: The expected return on a risky asset depends on that asset's total risk. Explain.

13.6d How do you calculate a portfolio beta?

13.7 The Security Market Line

We're now in a position to see how risk is rewarded in the marketplace. To begin, suppose that Asset A has an expected return of $E(R_A) = 20\%$ and a beta of $\beta_A = 1.6$. Furthermore, suppose that the risk-free rate is $R_f = 8\%$. Notice that a risk-free asset, by definition, has no systematic risk (or unsystematic risk), so a risk-free asset has a beta of zero.

BETA AND THE RISK PREMIUM

Consider a portfolio made up of Asset A and a risk-free asset. We can calculate some different possible portfolio expected returns and betas by varying the percentages invested in these two assets. For example, if 25 percent of the portfolio is invested in Asset A, then the expected return is:

$$E(R_P) = .25 \times E(R_A) + (1 - .25) \times R_f$$
$$= .25 \times 20\% + .75 \times 8\%$$
$$= 11\%$$

Similarly, the beta on the portfolio, β_P, would be:

$$\beta_P = .25 \times \beta_A + (1 - .25) \times 0$$
$$= .25 \times 1.6$$
$$= .40$$

Notice that because the weights have to add up to 1, the percentage invested in the risk-free asset is equal to 1 minus the percentage invested in Asset A.

One thing that you might wonder about is whether it is possible for the percentage invested in Asset A to exceed 100 percent. The answer is yes. This can happen if the investor borrows at the risk-free rate. For example, suppose an investor has $100 and borrows an additional $50 at 8 percent, the risk-free rate. The total investment in Asset A would be $150, or 150 percent of the investor's wealth. The expected return in this case would be:

$$
\begin{aligned}
E(R_p) &= 1.50 \times E(R_A) + (1 - 1.50) \times R_f \\
&= 1.50 \times 20\% - .50 \times 8\% \\
&= 26\%
\end{aligned}
$$

The beta on the portfolio would be:

$$
\begin{aligned}
\beta_p &= 1.50 \times \beta_A + (1 - 1.50) \times 0 \\
&= 1.50 \times 1.6 \\
&= 2.4
\end{aligned}
$$

We can calculate some other possibilities, as follows:

Percentage of Portfolio in Asset A	Portfolio Expected Return	Portfolio Beta
0%	8%	.0
25	11	.4
50	14	.8
75	17	1.2
100	20	1.6
125	23	2.0
150	26	2.4

In Figure 13.2A, these portfolio expected returns are plotted against the portfolio betas. Notice that all the combinations fall on a straight line.

The Reward-to-Risk Ratio   What is the slope of the straight line in Figure 13.2A? As always, the slope of a straight line is equal to "the rise over the run." In this case, as we move out of the risk-free asset into Asset A, the beta increases from zero to 1.6

FIGURE 13.2A

Portfolio Expected Returns and Betas for Asset A

(a "run" of 1.6). At the same time, the expected return goes from 8 percent to 20 percent, a "rise" of 12 percent. The slope of the line is thus $12\%/1.6 = 7.5\%$.

Notice that the slope of our line is the risk premium on Asset A, $E(R_A) - R_f$, divided by Asset A's beta, β_A:

$$
\begin{aligned}
\text{Slope} &= \frac{E(R_A) - R_f}{\beta_A} \\
&= \frac{.20 - .08}{1.6} = .075, \text{ or } 7.5\%
\end{aligned}
$$

What this tells us is that Asset A offers a *reward-to-risk* ratio of 7.5 percent.[2] In other words, Asset A has a risk premium of 7.5 percent per "unit" of systematic risk.

The Basic Argument   Now suppose we consider a second asset, Asset B. This asset has a beta of 1.2 and an expected return of 16 percent. Which investment is better, Asset A or Asset B? You might think that, once again, we really cannot say—some investors might prefer A; some investors might prefer B. Actually, we can say: A is better because, as we will demonstrate, B offers inadequate compensation for its level of systematic risk, at least, relative to A.

To begin, we calculate different combinations of expected returns and betas for portfolios of Asset B and a risk-free asset, just as we did for Asset A. For example, if we put 25 percent in Asset B and the remaining 75 percent in the risk-free asset, the portfolio's expected return will be:

$$
\begin{aligned}
E(R_p) &= .25 \times E(R_B) + (1 - .25) \times R_f \\
&= .25 \times 16\% + .75 \times 8\% \\
&= 10\%
\end{aligned}
$$

Similarly, the beta on the portfolio, β_p, will be:

$$
\begin{aligned}
\beta_p &= .25 \times \beta_B + (1 - .25) \times 0 \\
&= .25 \times 1.2 \\
&= .30
\end{aligned}
$$

Some other possibilities are as follows:

Percentage of Portfolio in Asset B	Portfolio Expected Return	Portfolio Beta
0%	8%	.0
25	10	.3
50	12	.6
75	14	.9
100	16	1.2
125	18	1.5
150	20	1.8

When we plot these combinations of portfolio expected returns and portfolio betas in Figure 13.2B, we get a straight line as we did for Asset A.

---

[2]This ratio is sometimes called the *Treynor index*, after one of its originators.

FIGURE 13.2B

Portfolio Expected Returns and Betas for Asset B

FIGURE 13.2C

Portfolio Expected Returns and Betas for Both Assets

The key thing to notice is that when we compare the results for Assets A and B, as in Figure 13.2C, the line describing the combinations of expected returns and betas for Asset A is higher than the one for Asset B. This tells us that for any given level of systematic risk (as measured by β), some combination of Asset A and the risk-free asset always offers a larger return. This is why we were able to state that Asset A is a better investment than Asset B.

Another way of seeing that A offers a superior return for its level of risk is to note that the slope of our line for Asset B is:

$$\text{Slope} = \frac{E\left(R_B\right) - R_f}{\beta_B}$$

$$= \frac{.16 - .08}{1.2} = .0667, \text{ or } 6.67\%$$

Asset B has a reward-to-risk ratio of 6.67 percent, which is less than the 7.5 percent offered by Asset A.

The Fundamental Result The situation we have described for Assets A and B could not persist in a well-organized, active market, because investors would be attracted to Asset A and away from Asset B. As a result, Asset A's price would rise and Asset B's price would fall. Because prices and returns move in opposite directions, A's expected return would decline and B's would rise.

This buying and selling would continue until the two assets plotted on exactly the same line, which means they would offer the same reward for bearing risk. In other words, in an active, competitive market, we must have the situation that:

$$\frac{E(R_A) - R_f}{\beta_A} = \frac{E(R_B) - R_f}{\beta_B}$$

This is the fundamental relationship between risk and return.

Our basic argument can be extended to more than just two assets. In fact, no matter how many assets we have, we will always reach the same conclusion:

The reward-to-risk ratio must be the same for all the assets in the market.

This result is really not so surprising. What it says is that, for example, if one asset has twice as much systematic risk as another asset, its risk premium will be twice as large.

Because all of the assets in the market must have the same reward-to-risk ratio, they all must plot on the same line. This argument is illustrated in Figure 13.3. As shown, Assets A and B plot directly on the line and have the same reward-to-risk ratio. If an asset plotted above the line, such as C in Figure 13.3, its price would rise and its expected return would fall until it plotted exactly on the line. Similarly, if an asset plotted below the line, such as D in Figure 13.3, its expected return would rise until it too plotted directly on the line. As an aside, it is common to refer to the vertical distance between an asset's expected return and the SML as the asset's "alpha."

FIGURE 13.3

Expected Returns and Systematic Risk

The fundamental relationship between beta and expected return is that all assets must have the same reward-to-risk ratio, $[E(R_i) - R_f]/\beta_i$. This means that they would all plot on the same straight line. Assets A and B are examples of this behavior. Asset C's expected return is too high; Asset D's is too low.

The arguments we have presented apply to active, competitive, well-functioning markets. The financial markets, such as the NYSE, best meet these criteria. Other markets, such as real asset markets, may or may not meet these criteria. For this reason, these concepts are most useful in examining financial markets. We will focus on such markets here. As we discuss in a later section, the information about risk and return gleaned from financial markets is crucial in evaluating the investments that a corporation makes in real assets.

| **Buy Low, Sell High** | **EXAMPLE 13.7** |

An asset is said to be *overvalued* if its price is too high given its expected return and risk. Suppose you observe the following situation:

Security	Beta	Expected Return
SWMS Co.	1.3	14%
Insec Co.	.8	10

The risk-free rate is currently 6 percent. Is one of the two securities overvalued relative to the other?

    To answer, we compute the reward-to-risk ratio for both. For SWMS, this ratio is (14% − 6)/1.3 = 6.15%. For Insec, this ratio is 5 percent. What we conclude is that Insec offers an insufficient expected return for its level of risk, at least relative to SWMS. Because its expected return is too low, its price is too high. In other words, Insec is overvalued relative to SWMS, and we would expect to see its price fall relative to SWMS's. Notice that we could also say SWMS is undervalued relative to Insec.

THE SECURITY MARKET LINE

The line that results when we plot expected returns and beta coefficients is obviously of some importance, so it's time we gave it a name. This line, which we use to describe the relationship between systematic risk and expected return in financial markets, is usually called the **security market line (SML)**. After NPV, the SML is arguably the most important concept in modern finance.

Market Portfolios   It will be very useful to know the equation of the SML. There are many different ways we could write it, but one way is particularly common. Suppose we consider a portfolio made up of all of the assets in the market. Such a portfolio is called a market portfolio, and we will express the expected return on this market portfolio as $E(R_M)$.

    Because all the assets in the market must plot on the SML, so must a market portfolio made up of those assets. To determine where it plots on the SML, we need to know the beta of the market portfolio, β_M. Because this portfolio is representative of all of the assets in the market, it must have average systematic risk. In other words, it has a beta of 1. We could express the slope of the SML as:

$$\text{SML slope} = \frac{E(R_M) - R_f}{\beta_M} = \frac{E(R_M) - R_f}{1} = E(R_M) - R_f$$

The term $E(R_M) - R_f$ is often called the **market risk premium** because it is the risk premium on a market portfolio.

The Capital Asset Pricing Model   To finish up, if we let $E(R_i)$ and β_i stand for the expected return and beta, respectively, on any asset in the market, then we know that asset

security market line (SML)
A positively sloped straight line displaying the relationship between expected return and beta.

market risk premium
The slope of the SML, which is the difference between the expected return on a market portfolio and the risk-free rate.

must plot on the SML. As a result, we know that its reward-to-risk ratio is the same as the overall market's:

$$\frac{E(R_i) - R_f}{\beta_i} = E(R_M) - R_f$$

If we rearrange this, then we can write the equation for the SML as:

$$E(R_i) = R_f + [E(R_M) - R_f] \times \beta_i$$

13.7

capital asset pricing model (CAPM)
The equation of the SML showing the relationship between expected return and beta.

This result is the famous **capital asset pricing model (CAPM)**.

The CAPM shows that the expected return for a particular asset depends on three things:

1. *The pure time value of money*: As measured by the risk-free rate, R_f, this is the reward for merely waiting for your money, without taking any risk.

2. *The reward for bearing systematic risk*: As measured by the market risk premium, $E(R_M) - R_f$, this component is the reward the market offers for bearing an average amount of systematic risk in addition to waiting.

3. *The amount of systematic risk*: As measured by β_i, this is the amount of systematic risk present in a particular asset or portfolio, relative to that in an average asset.

By the way, the CAPM works for portfolios of assets just as it does for individual assets. In an earlier section, we saw how to calculate a portfolio's β. To find the expected return on a portfolio, we use this β in the CAPM equation.

Figure 13.4 summarizes our discussion of the SML and the CAPM. As before, we plot expected return against beta. Now we recognize that, based on the CAPM, the slope of the SML is equal to the market risk premium, $E(R_M) - R_f$.

This concludes our presentation of concepts related to the risk–return trade-off. For future reference, Table 13.9 summarizes the various concepts in the order in which we discussed them.

FIGURE 13.4

The Security Market Line (SML)

The slope of the security market line is equal to the market risk premium—that is, the reward for bearing an average amount of systematic risk. The equation describing the SML can be written:

$$E(R_i) = R_f + [E(R_M) - R_f] \times \beta_i$$

which is the capital asset pricing model (CAPM).

Risk and Return

EXAMPLE 13.8

Suppose the risk-free rate is 4 percent, the market risk premium is 8.6 percent, and a particular stock has a beta of 1.3. Based on the CAPM, what is the expected return on this stock? What would the expected return be if the beta were to double?

With a beta of 1.3, the risk premium for the stock is 1.3 × 8.6%, or 11.18 percent. The risk-free rate is 4 percent, so the expected return is 15.18 percent. If the beta were to double to 2.6, the risk premium would double to 22.36 percent, so the expected return would be 26.36 percent.

TABLE 13.9

Summary of Risk and Return

I.	Total Risk
	The *total risk* of an investment is measured by the variance or, more commonly, the standard deviation of its return.
II.	Total Return
	The *total return* on an investment has two components: The expected return and the unexpected return. The unexpected return comes about because of unanticipated events. The risk from investing stems from the possibility of an unanticipated event.
III.	Systematic and Unsystematic Risks
	Systematic risks (also called *market risks*) are unanticipated events that affect almost all assets to some degree because the effects are economy-wide. *Unsystematic risks* are unanticipated events that affect single assets or small groups of assets. Unsystematic risks are also called *unique* or *asset-specific risks*.
IV.	The Effect of Diversification
	Some, but not all, of the risk associated with a risky investment can be eliminated by diversification. The reason is that unsystematic risks, which are unique to individual assets, tend to wash out in a large portfolio, but systematic risks, which affect all of the assets in a portfolio to some extent, do not.
V.	The Systematic Risk Principle and Beta
	Because unsystematic risk can be freely eliminated by diversification, the *systematic risk principle* states that the reward for bearing risk depends only on the level of systematic risk. The level of systematic risk in a particular asset, relative to the average, is given by the beta of that asset.
VI.	The Reward-to-Risk Ratio and the Security Market Line
	The *reward-to-risk ratio* for Asset i is the ratio of its risk premium, $E(R_i) - R_f$, to its beta, β_i: $$\frac{E(R_i) - R_f}{\beta_i}$$ In a well-functioning market, this ratio is the same for every asset. As a result, when asset expected returns are plotted against asset betas, all assets plot on the same straight line, called the *security market line* (SML).
VII.	The Capital Asset Pricing Model
	From the SML, the expected return on Asset i can be written: $$E(R_i) = R_f + [E(R_M) - R_f] \times \beta_i$$ This is the *capital asset pricing model* (CAPM). The expected return on a risky asset has three components. The first is the pure time value of money (R_f), the second is the market risk premium $[E(R_M) - R_f]$, and the third is the beta for that asset (β_i).

Concept Questions

13.7a What is the fundamental relationship between risk and return in well-functioning markets?

13.7b What is the security market line? Why must all assets plot directly on the SML in a well-functioning market?

13.7c What is the capital asset pricing model (CAPM)? What does it tell us about the required return on a risky investment?

13.8 The SML and the Cost of Capital: A Preview

Our goal in studying risk and return is twofold. First, risk is an extremely important consideration in almost all business decisions, so we want to discuss what risk is and how it is rewarded in the market. Our second purpose is to learn what determines the appropriate discount rate for future cash flows. We briefly discuss this second subject now; we will discuss it in more detail in a subsequent chapter.

THE BASIC IDEA

The security market line tells us the reward for bearing risk in financial markets. At an absolute minimum, any new investment our firm undertakes must offer an expected return that is no worse than what the financial markets offer for the same risk. The reason for this is that our shareholders can always invest for themselves in the financial markets.

The only way we benefit our shareholders is by finding investments with expected returns that are superior to what the financial markets offer for the same risk. Such an investment will have a positive NPV. So, if we ask, "What is the appropriate discount rate?" the answer is that we should use the expected return offered in financial markets on investments with the same systematic risk.

In other words, to determine whether an investment has a positive NPV, we essentially compare the expected return on that new investment to what the financial market offers on an investment with the same beta. This is why the SML is so important: It tells us the "going rate" for bearing risk in the economy.

THE COST OF CAPITAL

cost of capital
The minimum required return on a new investment.

The appropriate discount rate on a new project is the minimum expected rate of return an investment must offer to be attractive. This minimum required return is often called the **cost of capital** associated with the investment. It is called this because the required return is what the firm must earn on its capital investment in a project just to break even. It can be interpreted as the opportunity cost associated with the firm's capital investment.

Notice that when we say an investment is attractive if its expected return exceeds what is offered in financial markets for investments of the same risk, we are effectively using the internal rate of return (IRR) criterion that we developed and discussed in Chapter 9. The only difference is that now we have a much better idea of what determines the required return on an investment. This understanding will be critical when we discuss cost of capital and capital structure in Part 6 of our book.

Concept Questions

13.8a   If an investment has a positive NPV, would it plot above or below the SML? Why?

13.8b   What is meant by the term *cost of capital*?

Summary and Conclusions   13.9

This chapter has covered the essentials of risk. Along the way, we have introduced a number of definitions and concepts. The most important of these is the security market line, or SML. The SML is important because it tells us the reward offered in financial markets for bearing risk. Once we know this, we have a benchmark against which we can compare the returns expected from real asset investments to determine if they are desirable.

Because we have covered quite a bit of ground, it's useful to summarize the basic economic logic underlying the SML as follows:

1. Based on capital market history, there is a reward for bearing risk. This reward is the risk premium on an asset.

2. The total risk associated with an asset has two parts: Systematic risk and unsystematic risk. Unsystematic risk can be freely eliminated by diversification (this is the principle of diversification), so only systematic risk is rewarded. As a result, the risk premium on an asset is determined by its systematic risk. This is the systematic risk principle.

3. An asset's systematic risk, relative to the average, can be measured by its beta coefficient, β_i. The risk premium on an asset is then given by its beta coefficient multiplied by the market risk premium, $[E(R_M) - R_f] \times \beta_i$.

4. The expected return on an asset, $E(R_i)$, is equal to the risk-free rate, R_f, plus the risk premium:

$$E(R_i) = R_f + [E(R_M) - R_f] \times \beta_i$$

This is the equation of the SML, and it is often called the capital asset pricing model (CAPM).

This chapter completes our discussion of risk and return. Now that we have a better understanding of what determines a firm's cost of capital for an investment, the next several chapters will examine more closely how firms raise the long-term capital needed for investment.

CONNECT TO FINANCE

Connect Finance offers you plenty of opportunities to practice mastering these concepts. Log on to connect.mheducation.com to learn more. If you like what you see, ask your professor about using *Connect Finance*!

Can you answer the following *Connect* Quiz questions?

Section 13.1 A stock is expected to earn 15 percent in a boom economy and 7 percent in a normal economy. There is a 35 percent chance the economy will boom and a 65 percent chance the economy will be normal. What is the standard deviation of these returns?

Section 13.5 Which type of risk can be eliminated through diversification?

Section 13.6 Beta is a measure of what?

Section 13.7 The slope of the security market line is equal to what?

Section 13.8 Where would a negative net present value project appear on a security market line graph?

CHAPTER REVIEW AND SELF-TEST PROBLEMS

13.1 Expected Return and Standard Deviation This problem will give you some practice calculating measures of prospective portfolio performance. There are two assets and three states of the economy:

State of Economy	Probability of State of Economy	Rate of Return If State Occurs	
		Stock A	Stock B
Recession	.20	−.15	.20
Normal	.50	.20	.30
Boom	.30	.60	.40

What are the expected returns and standard deviations for these two stocks?

13.2 Portfolio Risk and Return Using the information in the previous problem, suppose you have $20,000 total. If you put $15,000 in Stock A and the remainder in Stock B, what will be the expected return and standard deviation of your portfolio?

13.3 Risk and Return Suppose you observe the following situation:

Security	Beta	Expected Return
Cooley, Inc.	1.8	22.00%
Moyer Co.	1.6	20.44

If the risk-free rate is 7 percent, are these securities correctly priced? What would the risk-free rate have to be if they are correctly priced?

13.4 CAPM Suppose the risk-free rate is 8 percent. The expected return on the market is 16 percent. If a particular stock has a beta of .7, what is its expected return based on the CAPM? If another stock has an expected return of 24 percent, what must its beta be?

ANSWERS TO CHAPTER REVIEW AND SELF-TEST PROBLEMS

13.1 The expected returns are just the possible returns multiplied by the associated probabilities:

$$E(R_A) = (.20 \times -.15) + (.50 \times .20) + (.30 \times .60) = .25, \text{ or } 25\%$$
$$E(R_B) = (.20 \times .20) + (.50 \times .30) + (.30 \times .40) = .31, \text{ or } 31\%$$

The variances are given by the sums of the squared deviations from the expected returns multiplied by their probabilities:

$$\sigma_A^2 = .20 \times (-.15 - .25)^2 + .50 \times (.20 - .25)^2 + .30 \times (.60 - .25)^2$$
$$= (.20 \times -.40^2) + (.50 \times -.05^2) + (.30 \times .35^2)$$
$$= (.20 \times .16) + (.50 \times .0025) + (.30 \times .1225)$$
$$= .0700$$

$$\sigma_B^2 = .20 \times (.20 - .31)^2 + .50 \times (.30 - .31)^2 + .30 \times (.40 - .31)^2$$
$$= (.20 \times -.11^2) + (.50 \times -.01^2) + (.30 \times .09^2)$$
$$= (.20 \times .0121) + (.50 \times .0001) + (.30 \times .0081)$$
$$= .0049$$

The standard deviations are thus:

$$\sigma_A = \sqrt{.0700} = .2646, \text{ or } 26.46\%$$
$$\sigma_B = \sqrt{.0049} = .07, \text{ or } 7\%$$

13.2 The portfolio weights are $15,000/$20,000 = .75 and $5,000/$20,000 = .25. The expected return is thus:

$$E(R_p) = .75 \times E(R_A) + .25 \times E(R_B)$$
$$= (.75 \times .25) + (.25 \times .31)$$
$$= .265, \text{ or } 26.5\%$$

Alternatively, we could calculate the portfolio's return in each of the states:

State of Economy	Probability of State of Economy	Portfolio Return If State Occurs
Recession	.20	$(.75 \times -.15) + (.25 \times .20) = -.0625$
Normal	.50	$(.75 \times .20) + (.25 \times .30) = .2250$
Boom	.30	$(.75 \times .60) + (.25 \times .40) = .5500$

The portfolio's expected return is:

$$E(R_p) = (.20 \times -.0625) + (.50 \times .2250) + (.30 \times .5500) = .265, \text{ or } 26.5\%$$

This is the same as we had before.
The portfolio's variance is:

$$\sigma_P^2 = .20 \times (-.0625 - .265)^2 + .50 \times (.225 - .265)^2$$
$$+ .30 \times (.55 - .265)^2$$
$$= .0466$$

So the standard deviation is $\sqrt{.0466} = .2159$, or 21.59%.

13.3 If we compute the reward-to-risk ratios, we get $(.22 - .07)/1.8 = .0833$, or 8.33% for Cooley versus 8.4% for Moyer. Relative to that of Cooley, Moyer's expected return is too high, so its price is too low. If they are correctly priced, then they must offer the same reward-to-risk ratio. The risk-free rate would have to be such that:

$$(.22 - R_f)/1.8 = (.2044 - R_f)/1.6$$

With a little algebra, we find that the risk-free rate must be 8 percent:

$$.2\% - R_f = (.2044 - R_f)(1.8/1.6)$$
$$.22 - .2044 \times 1.125 = R_f - R_f \times 1.125$$
$$R_f = .08, \text{ or } 8\%$$

13.4 Because the expected return on the market is 16 percent, the market risk premium is .16 − .08 = .08, or 8%. The first stock has a beta of .7, so its expected return is .08 + .7 × .08 = .136, or 13.6%.

For the second stock, notice that the risk premium is .24% − .08 = .16, or 16%. Because this is twice as large as the market risk premium, the beta must be exactly equal to 2. We can verify this using the CAPM:

$$E(R_i) = R_f + [E(R_M) − R_f] × \beta_i$$
$$.24 = .08 + (.16 − .08) × \beta_i$$
$$\beta_i = .16/.08$$
$$= 2.0$$

CONCEPTS REVIEW AND CRITICAL THINKING QUESTIONS

1. **Diversifiable and Nondiversifiable Risks** [LO3] In broad terms, why are some risks diversifiable? Why are some risks nondiversifiable? Does it follow that an investor can control the level of unsystematic risk in a portfolio, but not the level of systematic risk?

2. **Information and Market Returns** [LO3] Suppose the government announces that, based on a just-completed survey, the growth rate in the economy is likely to be 2 percent in the coming year, as compared to 5 percent for the past year. Will security prices increase, decrease, or stay the same following this announcement? Does it make any difference whether the 2 percent figure was anticipated by the market? Explain.

3. **Systematic versus Unsystematic Risk** [LO3] Classify the following events as mostly systematic or mostly unsystematic. Is the distinction clear in every case?
   a. Short-term interest rates increase unexpectedly.
   b. The interest rate a company pays on its short-term debt borrowing is increased by its bank.
   c. Oil prices unexpectedly decline.
   d. An oil tanker ruptures, creating a large oil spill.
   e. A manufacturer loses a multimillion-dollar product liability suit.
   f. A Supreme Court decision substantially broadens producer liability for injuries suffered by product users.

4. **Systematic versus Unsystematic Risk** [LO3] Indicate whether the following events might cause stocks in general to change price, and whether they might cause Big Widget Corp.'s stock to change price:
   a. The government announces that inflation unexpectedly jumped by 2 percent last month.
   b. Big Widget's quarterly earnings report, just issued, generally fell in line with analysts' expectations.
   c. The government reports that economic growth last year was at 3 percent, which generally agreed with most economists' forecasts.
   d. The directors of Big Widget die in a plane crash.
   e. Congress approves changes to the tax code that will increase the top marginal corporate tax rate. The legislation had been debated for the previous six months.

5. **Expected Portfolio Returns** [LO1] If a portfolio has a positive investment in every asset, can the expected return on the portfolio be greater than that on every asset in the portfolio? Can it be less than that on every asset in the portfolio? If you answer yes to one or both of these questions, give an example to support your answer.

6. **Diversification** [LO2] True or false: The most important characteristic in determining the expected return of a well-diversified portfolio is the variance of the individual assets in the portfolio. Explain.

7. **Portfolio Risk** [LO2] If a portfolio has a positive investment in every asset, can the standard deviation on the portfolio be less than that on every asset in the portfolio? What about the portfolio beta?

8. **Beta and CAPM** [LO4] Is it possible that a risky asset could have a beta of zero? Explain. Based on the CAPM, what is the expected return on such an asset? Is it possible that a risky asset could have a negative beta? What does the CAPM predict about the expected return on such an asset? Can you give an explanation for your answer?

9. **Alpha** [LO4] In our discussion of the SML, we defined alpha. What does alpha measure? What alpha would you like to see on your investments?

10. **Alpha** [LO4] Common advice on Wall Street is "Keep your alpha high and your beta low." Why?

11. **Corporate Downsizing** [LO1] In recent years, it has been common for companies to experience significant stock price changes in reaction to announcements of massive layoffs. Critics charge that such events encourage companies to fire long-time employees and that Wall Street is cheering them on. Do you agree or disagree?

12. **Earnings and Stock Returns** [LO1] As indicated by a number of examples in this chapter, earnings announcements by companies are closely followed by, and frequently result in, share price revisions. Two issues should come to mind. First, earnings announcements concern past periods. If the market values stocks based on expectations of the future, why are numbers summarizing past performance relevant? Second, these announcements concern accounting earnings. Going back to Chapter 2, such earnings may have little to do with cash flow—so, again, why are they relevant?

QUESTIONS AND PROBLEMS

1. **Determining Portfolio Weights** [LO1] What are the portfolio weights for a portfolio that has 115 shares of Stock A that sell for $43 per share and 180 shares of Stock B that sell for $19 per share?

2. **Portfolio Expected Return** [LO1] You own a portfolio that has $3,480 invested in Stock A and $7,430 invested in Stock B. If the expected returns on these stocks are 8 percent and 11 percent, respectively, what is the expected return on the portfolio?

3. **Portfolio Expected Return** [LO1] You own a portfolio that is invested 35 percent in Stock X, 20 percent in Stock Y, and 45 percent in Stock Z. The expected returns on these three stocks are 9 percent, 15 percent, and 12 percent, respectively. What is the expected return on the portfolio?

4. **Portfolio Expected Return** [LO1] You have $10,000 to invest in a stock portfolio. Your choices are Stock X with an expected return of 12.1 percent and Stock Y with

BASIC
(Questions 1–19)

an expected return of 9.8 percent. If your goal is to create a portfolio with an expected return of 10.85 percent, how much money will you invest in Stock X? In Stock Y?

5. **Calculating Expected Return** [LO1] Based on the following information, calculate the expected return:

State of Economy	Probability of State of Economy	Portfolio Return If State Occurs
Recession	.20	−.08
Boom	.80	.15

6. **Calculating Expected Return** [LO1] Based on the following information, calculate the expected return:

State of Economy	Probability of State of Economy	Portfolio Return If State Occurs
Recession	.10	−.15
Normal	.60	.09
Boom	.30	.23

7. **Calculating Returns and Standard Deviations** [LO1] Based on the following information, calculate the expected return and standard deviation for Stock A and Stock B:

State of Economy	Probability of State of Economy	Rate of Return If State Occurs	
		Stock A	Stock B
Recession	.10	.04	−.17
Normal	.60	.09	.12
Boom	.30	.17	.27

8. **Calculating Expected Returns** [LO1] A portfolio is invested 25 percent in Stock G, 55 percent in Stock J, and 20 percent in Stock K. The expected returns on these stocks are 11 percent, 9 percent, and 15 percent, respectively. What is the portfolio's expected return? How do you interpret your answer?

9. **Returns and Variances** [LO1] Consider the following information:

State of Economy	Probability of State of Economy	Rate of Return If State Occurs		
		Stock A	Stock B	Stock C
Boom	.75	.08	.17	.24
Bust	.25	.11	−.05	−.08

   a. What is the expected return on an equally weighted portfolio of these three stocks?

   b. What is the variance of a portfolio invested 20 percent each in A and B and 60 percent in C?

10. **Returns and Standard Deviations** [LO1] Consider the following information:

State of Economy	Probability of State of Economy	Rate of Return If State Occurs		
		Stock A	Stock B	Stock C
Boom	.10	.35	.40	.27
Good	.60	.16	.17	.08
Poor	.25	−.01	−.03	−.04
Bust	.05	−.12	−.18	−.09

a. Your portfolio is invested 30 percent each in A and C, and 40 percent in B. What is the expected return of the portfolio?

b. What is the variance of this portfolio? The standard deviation?

11. **Calculating Portfolio Betas** [LO4] You own a stock portfolio invested 20 percent in Stock Q, 30 percent in Stock R, 35 percent in Stock S, and 15 percent in Stock T. The betas for these four stocks are .79, 1.23, 1.13, and 1.36, respectively. What is the portfolio beta?

12. **Calculating Portfolio Betas** [LO4] You own a portfolio equally invested in a risk-free asset and two stocks. If one of the stocks has a beta of 1.17 and the total portfolio is equally as risky as the market, what must the beta be for the other stock in your portfolio?

13. **Using CAPM** [LO4] A stock has a beta of 1.15, the expected return on the market is 10.3 percent, and the risk-free rate is 3.1 percent. What must the expected return on this stock be?

14. **Using CAPM** [LO4] A stock has an expected return of 10.2 percent, the risk-free rate is 3.9 percent, and the market risk premium is 7.2 percent. What must the beta of this stock be?

15. **Using CAPM** [LO4] A stock has an expected return of 10.45 percent, its beta is .93, and the risk-free rate is 3.6 percent. What must the expected return on the market be?

16. **Using CAPM** [LO4] A stock has an expected return of 11.85 percent, its beta is 1.24, and the expected return on the market is 10.2 percent. What must the risk-free rate be?

17. **Using the SML** [LO4] Asset W has an expected return of 11.8 percent and a beta of 1.10. If the risk-free rate is 3.3 percent, complete the following table for portfolios of Asset W and a risk-free asset. Illustrate the relationship between portfolio expected return and portfolio beta by plotting the expected returns against the betas. What is the slope of the line that results?

Percentage of Portfolio in Asset W	Portfolio Expected Return	Portfolio Beta
0%		
25		
50		
75		
100		
125		
150		

18. **Reward-to-Risk Ratios** [LO4] Stock Y has a beta of 1.2 and an expected return of 11.1 percent. Stock Z has a beta of .80 and an expected return of 7.85 percent. If the risk-free rate is 2.4 percent and the market risk premium is 7.2 percent, are these stocks correctly priced?

19. **Reward-to-Risk Ratios** [LO4] In the previous problem, what would the risk-free rate have to be for the two stocks to be correctly priced?

20. **Using CAPM** [LO4] A stock has a beta of 1.12 and an expected return of 10.8 percent. A risk-free asset currently earns 2.7 percent.

INTERMEDIATE
(Questions 20–24)

a. What is the expected return on a portfolio that is equally invested in the two assets?

b. If a portfolio of the two assets has a beta of .92, what are the portfolio weights?

    c. If a portfolio of the two assets has an expected return of 9 percent, what is its beta?

    d. If a portfolio of the two assets has a beta of 2.24, what are the portfolio weights? How do you interpret the weights for the two assets in this case? Explain.

21. Portfolio Returns [LO2] Using information from the previous chapter on capital market history, determine the return on a portfolio that is equally invested in large-company stocks and long-term government bonds. What is the return on a portfolio that is equally invested in small-company stocks and Treasury bills?

22. CAPM [LO4] Using the CAPM, show that the ratio of the risk premiums on two assets is equal to the ratio of their betas.

23. Portfolio Returns and Deviations [LO2] Consider the following information about three stocks:

State of Economy	Probability of State of Economy	Rate of Return If State Occurs		
		Stock A	Stock B	Stock C
Boom	.25	.21	.33	.55
Normal	.60	.17	.11	.09
Bust	.15	.00	−.21	−.45

    a. If your portfolio is invested 40 percent each in A and B and 20 percent in C, what is the portfolio expected return? The variance? The standard deviation?

    b. If the expected T-bill rate is 3.80 percent, what is the expected risk premium on the portfolio?

    c. If the expected inflation rate is 3.30 percent, what are the approximate and exact expected real returns on the portfolio? What are the approximate and exact expected real risk premiums on the portfolio?

24. Analyzing a Portfolio [LO2, 4] You want to create a portfolio equally as risky as the market, and you have $1,000,000 to invest. Given this information, fill in the rest of the following table:

Asset	Investment	Beta
Stock A	$165,000	.80
Stock B	$350,000	1.09
Stock C		1.27
Risk-free asset		

CHALLENGE
(Questions 25–28)

25. Analyzing a Portfolio [LO2, 4] You have $100,000 to invest in a portfolio containing Stock X and Stock Y. Your goal is to create a portfolio that has an expected return of 12.7 percent. If Stock X has an expected return of 11.4 percent and a beta of 1.25, and Stock Y has an expected return of 8.68 percent and a beta of .85, how much money will you invest in Stock Y? How do you interpret your answer? What is the beta of your portfolio?

26. Systematic versus Unsystematic Risk [LO3] Consider the following information about Stocks I and II:

State of Economy	Probability of State of Economy	Rate of Return If State Occurs	
		Stock I	Stock II
Recession	.15	.03	−.23
Normal	.70	.20	.09
Irrational exuberance	.15	.08	.43

The market risk premium is 7 percent, and the risk-free rate is 3.5 percent. Which stock has the most systematic risk? Which one has the most unsystematic risk? Which stock is "riskier"? Explain.

27. **SML [LO4]** Suppose you observe the following situation:

Security	Beta	Expected Return
Pete Corp.	1.25	.1323
Repete Co.	.87	.0967

Assume these securities are correctly priced. Based on the CAPM, what is the expected return on the market? What is the risk-free rate?

28. **SML [LO4]** Suppose you observe the following situation:

	Probability of	Return If State Occurs	
State of Economy	State of Economy	Stock A	Stock B
Bust	.15	−.08	−.10
Normal	.60	.11	.09
Boom	.25	.30	.27

a. Calculate the expected return on each stock.

b. Assuming the capital asset pricing model holds and Stock A's beta is greater than Stock B's beta by .35, what is the expected market risk premium?

EXCEL MASTER IT! PROBLEM

The CAPM is one of the most thoroughly researched models in financial economics. When beta is estimated in practice, a variation of CAPM called the market model is often used. To derive the market model, we start with the CAPM:

$$E(R_i) = R_f + \beta[E(R_M) - R_f]$$

Since CAPM is an equation, we can subtract the risk-free rate from both sides, which gives us:

$$E(R_i) - R_f = \beta[E(R_M) - R_f]$$

This equation is deterministic, by which we mean it is exact. In a regression, we realize that there is some indeterminate error. We need to formally recognize this in the equation by adding epsilon, ε, which represents this error:

$$E(R_i) - R_f = \beta[E(R_M) - R_f] + \varepsilon$$

Finally, think of the above equation in a regression. Since there is no intercept in the equation, the intercept is zero. However, when we estimate the regression equation, we can add an intercept term, which we will call alpha:

$$E(R_i) - R_f = \alpha_i + \beta[E(R_M) - R_f] + \varepsilon$$

This equation is often called the "market" model, though it is not the only equation with that name, which is a source of confusion. The intercept term is known as Jensen's alpha, and it represents the "excess" return. If CAPM holds exactly, this intercept should be zero.

If you think of alpha in terms of the SML, then if the alpha is positive, the stock plots above the SML, and if alpha is negative, the stock plots below the SML.

a. You want to estimate the market model for an individual stock and a mutual fund. First, go to finance.yahoo.com and download the adjusted prices for the last 61 months for an individual stock, a mutual fund, and the S&P 500. Next, go to the St. Louis Federal Reserve website at www.stlouisfed.org. You should find the FRED® database there. Look for the 1-Month Treasury Constant Maturity Rate and download this data. This series will be the proxy for the risk-free rate. When using this rate, you should be aware that this interest rate is the annualized interest rate. Since we are using monthly stock returns, you will need to adjust the 1-month T-bill rate. For the stock and mutual fund you select, estimate the beta and alpha using the market model. When you estimate the regression model, find the box that says "Residuals" and check this box when you do each regression. Because you are saving the residuals, you may want to save the regression output in a new worksheet.

1. Are the alpha and beta for each regression statistically different from zero?
2. How do you interpret the alpha and beta for the stock and the mutual fund?
3. Which of the two regression estimates has the highest R-squared? Is this what you would have expected? Why?

b. In part (a), you asked Excel to return the residuals of the regression, which is the epsilon in the regression equation. If you remember back to basic statistics, the residuals are the distance from each observation to the regression line. In this context, the residuals are the part of the monthly return that is not explained by the market model estimate. The residuals can be used to calculate the appraisal ratio, which is the alpha divided by the standard deviation of the residuals.

1. What do you think the appraisal ratio is intended to measure?
2. Calculate the appraisal ratios for the stock and the mutual fund. Which has a better appraisal ratio?
3. Often, the appraisal ratio is used to evaluate the performance of mutual fund managers. Why do you think the appraisal ratio is used more often for mutual funds, which are portfolios, than for individual stocks?

MINICASE

The Beta for Colgate-Palmolive

Joey Moss, a recent finance graduate, has just begun his job with the investment firm of Covili and Wyatt. Paul Covili, one of the firm's founders, has been talking to Joey about the firm's investment portfolio.

As with any investment, Paul is concerned about the risk of the investment as well as the potential return. More specifically, because the company holds a diversified portfolio, Paul is concerned about the systematic risk of current and potential investments. One such position the company currently holds is stock in Colgate-Palmolive (CL). Colgate-Palmolive is the well-known manufacturer of consumer products under brand names such as Colgate, Palmolive, Softsoap, Irish Spring, Ajax, and others.

Covili and Wyatt currently uses a commercial data vendor for information about its positions. Because of this, Paul is

unsure exactly how the numbers provided are calculated. The data provider considers its methods proprietary, and it will not disclose how stock betas and other information are calculated. Paul is uncomfortable with not knowing exactly how these numbers are being computed and also believes that it could be less expensive to calculate the necessary statistics in-house. To explore this question, Paul has asked Joey to do the following assignments.

QUESTIONS

1. Go to finance.yahoo.com and download the ending monthly stock prices for Colgate-Palmolive for the last 60 months. Use the adjusted closing price, which adjusts for dividend payments and stock splits. Next, download the ending value of the S&P 500 index over the same

period. For the historical risk-free rate, go to the St. Louis Federal Reserve website (www.stlouisfed.org) and find the three-month Treasury bill secondary market rate. Download this file. What are the monthly returns, average monthly returns, and standard deviations for Colgate-Palmolive stock, the three-month Treasury bill, and the S&P 500 for this period?

2. Beta is often estimated by linear regression. A model commonly used is called the *market model*, which is:

$$R_t - R_{ft} = \alpha_i + \beta_i [R_{Mt} - R_{ft}] + \varepsilon_t$$

In this regression, R_t is the return on the stock and R_{ft} is the risk-free rate for the same period. R_{Mt} is the return on a stock market index such as the S&P 500 index; α_i is the regression intercept; β_i is the slope (and the stock's estimated beta); and ε_t represents the residuals for the regression. What do you think is the motivation for this particular regression? The intercept, α, is often called *Jensen's alpha*. What does it measure? If an asset has a positive Jensen's alpha, where would it plot with respect to the SML? What is the financial interpretation of the residuals in the regression?

3. Use the market model to estimate the beta for Colgate-Palmolive using the last 36 months of returns (the regression procedure in Excel is one easy way to do this). Plot the monthly returns on Colgate-Palmolive against the index and also show the fitted line.

4. When the beta of a stock is calculated using monthly returns, there is a debate over the number of months that should be used in the calculation. Rework the previous questions using the last 60 months of returns. How does this answer compare to what you calculated previously? What are some arguments for and against using shorter versus longer periods? Also, you've used monthly data, which is a common choice. You could have used daily, weekly, quarterly, or even annual data. What do you think are the issues here?

5. Compare your beta for Colgate-Palmolive to the beta you find on finance.yahoo.com. How similar are they? Why might they be different?

Cost of Capital and Long-Term Financial Policy

Part 6 Cost of Capital and Long-Term Financial Policy

14 | Cost of Capital

WITH OVER 112,000 EMPLOYEES ON FIVE CONTINENTS, Germany-based BASF is a major international company. The company operates in a variety of industries, including agriculture, oil and gas, chemicals, and plastics. In an attempt to increase value, BASF launched Vision 2020, a comprehensive plan that included all functions within the company and challenged and encouraged all employees to act in an entrepreneurial manner. The major financial component of the strategy was that the company expected to earn its weighted average cost of capital, or WACC, plus a premium. So, what exactly is the WACC?

The WACC is the minimum return a company needs to earn to satisfy all of its investors, including stockholders, bondholders, and preferred stockholders. In 2017, for example, BASF pegged its cost of capital at 10 percent, the same WACC that it used during 2016, but down slightly from the 11 percent used in 2015. In this chapter, we learn how to compute a firm's cost of capital and find out what it means to the firm and its investors. We will also learn when to use the firm's cost of capital, and, perhaps more important, when not to use it.

Learning Objectives

After studying this chapter, you should be able to:

LO1 Determine a firm's cost of equity capital.

LO2 Determine a firm's cost of debt.

LO3 Determine a firm's overall cost of capital and how to use it to value a company.

LO4 Explain how to correctly include flotation costs in capital budgeting projects.

LO5 Describe some of the pitfalls associated with a firm's overall cost of capital and what to do about them.

©by_adri/iStockPhotoGettyImages

For updates on the latest happenings in finance, visit fundamentalsofcorporatefinance.blogspot.com.

Suppose you have just become the president of a large company, and the first decision you face is whether to go ahead with a plan to renovate the company's warehouse distribution system. The plan will cost the company $50 million, and it is expected to save $12 million per year after taxes over the next six years.

This is a familiar problem in capital budgeting. To address it, you would determine the relevant cash flows, discount them, and, if the net present value is positive, take on the project; if the NPV is negative, you would scrap it. So far, so good; but what should you use as the discount rate?

From our discussion of risk and return, you know that the correct discount rate depends on the riskiness of the project to renovate the warehouse distribution system. In particular, the new project will have a positive NPV only if its return exceeds what the financial markets offer on investments of similar risk. We called this minimum required return the *cost of capital* associated with the project.[1]

To make the right decision as president, you must examine what the capital markets have to offer and use this information to arrive at an estimate of the project's cost of capital. Our primary purpose in this chapter is to describe how to go about doing this. There are a variety of approaches to this task, and a number of conceptual and practical issues arise.

One of the most important concepts we develop is that of the *weighted average cost of capital* (WACC). This is the cost of capital for the firm as a whole, and it can be interpreted as the required return on the overall firm. In discussing the WACC, we will recognize the fact that a firm will normally raise capital in a variety of forms and that these different forms of capital may have different costs associated with them.

We also recognize in this chapter that taxes are an important consideration in determining the required return on an investment: We are always interested in valuing the aftertax cash flows from a project. We will therefore discuss how to incorporate taxes explicitly into our estimates of the cost of capital.

The Cost of Capital: Some Preliminaries   14.1

In Chapter 13, we developed the security market line, or SML, and used it to explore the relationship between the expected return on a security and its systematic risk. In our examination of the risky returns from buying securities, we took the viewpoint of, for example, a shareholder in the firm. This helped us to better understand the alternatives available to an investor in the capital markets.

In this chapter, we turn things around a bit and look more closely at the other side of the problem, which is how these returns and securities look from the viewpoint of the companies that issue them. The important fact to note is that the return an investor in a security receives is the cost of that security to the company that issued it.

REQUIRED RETURN VERSUS COST OF CAPITAL

When we say that the required return on an investment is, say, 10 percent, we usually mean that the investment will have a positive NPV only if its return exceeds 10 percent. Another way of interpreting the required return is to observe that the firm must earn 10 percent on the investment to compensate its investors for the use of the capital needed to finance the project. This is why we could also say that 10 percent is the cost of capital associated with the investment.

To illustrate the point further, imagine that we are evaluating a risk-free project. In this case, how to determine the required return is obvious: We look at the capital markets and observe the current rate offered by risk-free investments, and we use this rate to discount the project's cash flows. Thus, the cost of capital for a risk-free investment is the risk-free rate.

If a project is risky, then, assuming that all the other information is unchanged, the required return is obviously higher. In other words, the cost of capital for this project, if it is risky, is greater than the risk-free rate, and the appropriate discount rate would exceed the risk-free rate.

We will henceforth use the terms *required return*, *appropriate discount rate*, and *cost of capital* more or less interchangeably because, as the discussion in this section suggests,

---

[1]The term *cost of money* is also used.

they all mean essentially the same thing. The key fact to grasp is that the cost of capital associated with an investment depends on the risk of that investment. This is one of the most important lessons in corporate finance, so it bears repeating:

> **The cost of capital depends primarily on the use of the funds, not the source.**

It is a common error to forget this crucial point and fall into the trap of thinking that the cost of capital for an investment depends primarily on how and where the capital is raised.

FINANCIAL POLICY AND COST OF CAPITAL

We know that the particular mixture of debt and equity a firm chooses to employ—its capital structure—is a managerial variable. In this chapter, we will take the firm's financial policy as given. In particular, we will assume that the firm has a fixed debt-equity ratio that it maintains. This ratio reflects the firm's *target* capital structure. How a firm might choose that ratio is the subject of a later chapter.

From the preceding discussion, we know that a firm's overall cost of capital will reflect the required return on the firm's assets as a whole. Given that a firm uses both debt and equity capital, this overall cost of capital will be a mixture of the returns needed to compensate its creditors and those needed to compensate its stockholders. In other words, a firm's cost of capital will reflect both its cost of debt capital and its cost of equity capital. We discuss these costs separately in the sections that follow.

Concept Questions

14.1a   What is the primary determinant of the cost of capital for an investment?

14.1b   What is the relationship between the required return on an investment and the cost of capital associated with that investment?

14.2 The Cost of Equity

cost of equity
The return that equity investors require on their investment in the firm.

To open our discussion of cost of capital, we begin with the most difficult question: What is the firm's overall **cost of equity**? The reason this is a difficult question is that there is no way of directly observing the return that the firm's equity investors require on their investment. Instead, we must somehow estimate it. This section discusses two approaches to determining the cost of equity: The dividend growth model approach and the security market line (SML) approach.

THE DIVIDEND GROWTH MODEL APPROACH

The easiest way to estimate the cost of equity capital is to use the dividend growth model we developed in Chapter 8. Recall that, under the assumption that the firm's dividend will grow at a constant rate, g, the price per share of the stock, P_0, can be written as:

$$P_0 = \frac{D_0 \times (1 + g)}{R_E - g} = \frac{D_1}{R_E - g}$$

where D_0 is the dividend just paid and D_1 is the next period's projected dividend. Notice that we have used the symbol R_E (the E stands for equity) for the required return on the stock.

As we discussed in Chapter 8, we can rearrange this to solve for R_E as follows:

$$R_E = D_1/P_0 + g$$

Because R_E is the return that the shareholders require on the stock, it can be interpreted as the firm's cost of equity capital.

Implementing the Approach   To estimate R_E using the dividend growth model approach, we obviously need three pieces of information: P_0, D_0, and g.[2] Of these, for a publicly traded, dividend-paying company, the first two can be observed directly, so they are easily obtained. Only the third component, the expected growth rate for dividends, must be estimated.

To illustrate how we estimate R_E, suppose Greater States Public Service, a large public utility, paid a dividend of $4 per share last year. The stock currently sells for $60 per share. You estimate that the dividend will grow steadily at a rate of 6 percent per year into the indefinite future. What is the cost of equity capital for Greater States?

Using the dividend growth model, we can calculate that the expected dividend for the coming year, D_1, is:

$$
\begin{aligned}
D_1 &= D_0 \times (1 + g) \\
&= \$4 \times 1.06 \\
&= \$4.24
\end{aligned}
$$

Given this, the cost of equity, R_E, is:

$$
\begin{aligned}
R_E &= D_1/P_0 + g \\
&= \$4.24/\$60 + .06 \\
&= .1307, \text{ or } 13.07\%
\end{aligned}
$$

The cost of equity is 13.07 percent.

Estimating g   To use the dividend growth model, we must come up with an estimate for g, the growth rate. There are essentially two ways of doing this: (1) Use historical growth rates or (2) use analysts' forecasts of future growth rates. Analysts' forecasts are available from a variety of sources. Naturally, different sources will have different estimates, so one approach might be to obtain multiple estimates and then average them.

Alternatively, we might observe dividends for the previous, say, five years, calculate the year-to-year growth rates, and average them. For example, suppose we observe the following for some company:

Year	Dividend
2013	$1.10
2014	1.20
2015	1.35
2016	1.40
2017	1.55

Growth estimates can be found at **www.zacks.com.**

We can calculate the percentage change in the dividend for each year as follows:

Year	Dividend	Dollar Change	Percentage Change
2013	$1.10	—	—
2014	1.20	$.10	9.09%
2015	1.35	.15	12.50
2016	1.40	.05	3.70
2017	1.55	.15	10.71

---

[2]Notice that if we have D_0 and g, we can simply calculate D_1 by multiplying D_0 by $(1 + g)$.

Notice that we calculated the change in the dividend on a year-to-year basis and then expressed the change as a percentage. In 2014 for example, the dividend rose from $1.10 to $1.20, an increase of $.10. This represents a $.10/$1.10 = .0909, or 9.09% increase.

If we average the four growth rates, the result is (.0909 + .1250 + .0370 + .1071)/4 = .09, or 9%, so we could use this as an estimate for the expected growth rate, g. Notice that this 9 percent growth rate we have calculated is a simple, or arithmetic, average. Going back to Chapter 12, we also could calculate a geometric growth rate. Here, the dividend grows from $1.10 to $1.55 over a four-year period. What's the compound, or geometric, growth rate? See if you don't agree that it's 8.95 percent; you can view this as a simple time value of money problem where $1.10 is the present value and $1.55 is the future value.

As usual, the geometric average (8.95 percent) is lower than the arithmetic average (9 percent), but the difference here is not likely to be of any practical significance. In general, if the dividend has grown at a relatively steady rate, as we assume when we use this approach, then it can't make much difference which way we calculate the average dividend growth rate.

Advantages and Disadvantages of the Approach   The primary advantage of the dividend growth model approach is its simplicity. It is both easy to understand and easy to use. There are a number of associated practical problems and disadvantages.

First and foremost, the dividend growth model is obviously applicable only to companies that pay dividends. This means that the approach is useless in many cases. Furthermore, even for companies that pay dividends, the key underlying assumption is that the dividend grows at a constant rate. As our previous example illustrates, this will never be *exactly* the case. More generally, the model is really applicable only to cases in which reasonably steady growth is likely to occur.

A second problem is that the estimated cost of equity is very sensitive to the estimated growth rate. For a given stock price, an upward revision of g by just one percentage point, for example, increases the estimated cost of equity by at least a full percentage point. Because D_1 will probably be revised upward as well, the increase will actually be somewhat larger than that.

Finally, this approach really does not explicitly consider risk. Unlike the SML approach (which we consider next), there is no direct adjustment for the riskiness of the investment. For example, there is no allowance for the degree of certainty or uncertainty surrounding the estimated growth rate for dividends. As a result, it is difficult to say whether or not the estimated return is commensurate with the level of risk.[3]

THE SML APPROACH

In Chapter 13, we discussed the security market line, or SML. Our primary conclusion was that the required or expected return on a risky investment depends on three things:

1. The risk-free rate, R_f.
2. The market risk premium, $E(R_M) - R_f$.
3. The systematic risk of the asset relative to average, which we called its beta coefficient, β.

Using the SML, we can write the expected return on the company's equity, $E(R_E)$, as:

$$E(R_E) = R_f + \beta_E \times [E(R_M) - R_f]$$

where β_E is the estimated beta. To make the SML approach consistent with the dividend growth model, we will drop the Es denoting expectations and henceforth write the required return from the SML, R_E, as:

$$R_E = R_f + \beta_E \times (R_M - R_f)$$

14.2

---

[3]There is an implicit adjustment for risk because the current stock price is used. All other things being equal, the higher the risk, the lower is the stock price. Further, the lower the stock price, the greater is the cost of equity, again assuming all the other information is the same.

Implementing the Approach   To use the SML approach, we need a risk-free rate, R_f, an estimate of the market risk premium, $R_M - R_f$, and an estimate of the relevant beta, β_E. In Chapter 12, we saw that one estimate of the market risk premium (based on large common stocks) is about 7 percent. U.S. Treasury bills are paying about .40 percent as this chapter is being written, so we will use this as our risk-free rate. Beta coefficients for publicly traded companies are widely available.[4]

Betas and T-bill rates both can be found at **www.bloomberg.com**.

To illustrate, in Chapter 13, we saw that Tesla had an estimated beta of 1.19 (Table 13.8). We could estimate Tesla's cost of equity as:

$$
\begin{aligned}
R_{Tesla} &= R_f + \beta_{Tesla} \times (R_M - R_f) \\
&= .0040 + 1.19 \times .07 \\
&= .0873, \text{ or } 8.73\%
\end{aligned}
$$

Using the SML approach, we calculate that Tesla's cost of equity is about 8.73 percent.

Advantages and Disadvantages of the Approach   The SML approach has two primary advantages. First, it explicitly adjusts for risk. Second, it is applicable to companies other than just those with steady dividend growth. It may be useful in a wider variety of circumstances.

There are drawbacks, of course. The SML approach requires that two things be estimated: The market risk premium and the beta coefficient. To the extent that our estimates are poor, the resulting cost of equity will be inaccurate. For example, our estimate of the market risk premium, 7 percent, is based on about 100 years of returns on particular stock portfolios and markets. Using different time periods or different stocks and markets could result in very different estimates.

Finally, as with the dividend growth model, we essentially rely on the past to predict the future when we use the SML approach. Economic conditions can change quickly; so as always, the past may not be a good guide to the future. In the best of all worlds, both approaches (the dividend growth model and the SML) are applicable and the two result in similar answers. If this happens, we might have some confidence in our estimates. We might also wish to compare the results to those for other similar companies as a reality check.

---

[4]We can also estimate beta coefficients directly by using historical data. For a discussion of how to do this, see Chapters 10, 11, and 13 in S. A. Ross, R. W. Westerfield, J. J. Jaffe, and B. D. Jordan, *Corporate Finance*, 11th ed. (New York: McGraw-Hill, 2016).

The Cost of Equity	**EXAMPLE 14.1**

Suppose stock in Alpha Air Freight has a beta of 1.2. The market risk premium is 7 percent, and the risk-free rate is 6 percent. Alpha's last dividend was $2 per share, and the dividend is expected to grow at 8 percent indefinitely. The stock currently sells for $30. What is Alpha's cost of equity capital?

We can start off by using the SML. Doing this, we find that the expected return on the common stock of Alpha Air Freight is:

$$
\begin{aligned}
R_E &= R_f + \beta_E \times (R_M - R_f) \\
&= .06 + 1.2 \times .07 \\
&= .144, \text{ or } 14.4\%
\end{aligned}
$$

This suggests that 14.4 percent is Alpha's cost of equity. We next use the dividend growth model. The projected dividend is $D_0 \times (1 + g) = \$2 \times 1.08 = \$2.16$, so the expected return using this approach is:

$$
\begin{aligned}
R_E &= D_1/P_0 + g \\
&= \$2.16/\$30 + .08 \\
&= .152, \text{ or } 15.2\%
\end{aligned}
$$

Our two estimates are reasonably close, so we might just average them to find that Alpha's cost of equity is approximately 14.8 percent.

> ### Concept Questions
>
> **14.2a** What do we mean when we say that a corporation's cost of equity capital is 16 percent?
>
> **14.2b** What are two approaches to estimating the cost of equity capital?

14.3 The Costs of Debt and Preferred Stock

Excel Master It!

Excel Master coverage online

cost of debt
The return that lenders require on the firm's debt.

In addition to ordinary equity, firms use debt and, to a lesser extent, preferred stock to finance their investments. As we discuss next, determining the costs of capital associated with these sources of financing is much easier than determining the cost of equity.

THE COST OF DEBT

The **cost of debt** is the return the firm's creditors demand on new borrowing. In principle, we could determine the beta for the firm's debt and then use the SML to estimate the required return on debt just as we estimated the required return on equity. This isn't really necessary, however.

Unlike a firm's cost of equity, its cost of debt can normally be observed either directly or indirectly: The cost of debt is the interest rate the firm must pay on new borrowing, and we can observe interest rates in the financial markets. For example, if the firm already has bonds outstanding, then the yield to maturity on those bonds is the market-required rate on the firm's debt.

Alternatively, if we know that the firm's bonds are rated, say, AA, then we can find the interest rate on newly issued AA-rated bonds. Either way, there is no need to estimate a beta for the debt because we can directly observe the rate we want to know.

There is one thing to be careful about, though. The coupon rate on the firm's outstanding debt is irrelevant here. That rate tells us roughly what the firm's cost of debt was back when the bonds were issued, not what the cost of debt is today.[5] This is why we have to look at the yield on the debt in today's marketplace. For consistency with our other notation, we will use the symbol R_D for the cost of debt.

EXAMPLE 14.2 **The Cost of Debt**

Suppose the General Tool Company issued a 30-year, 7 percent bond 8 years ago. The bond is currently selling for 96 percent of its face value, or $960. What is General Tool's cost of debt?

Going back to Chapter 7, we need to calculate the yield to maturity on this bond. Because the bond is selling at a discount, the yield is apparently greater than 7 percent, but not much greater because the discount is fairly small. You can check to see that the yield to maturity is about 7.37 percent, assuming annual coupons. General Tool's cost of debt, R_D, is 7.37 percent.

THE COST OF PREFERRED STOCK

Determining the *cost of preferred stock* is quite straightforward. As we discussed in Chapters 6 and 8, preferred stock has a fixed dividend paid every period forever, so a share of preferred stock is essentially a perpetuity. The cost of preferred stock, R_P, is thus:

$$R_P = D/P_0$$

14.3

---

[5]The firm's cost of debt based on its historical borrowing is sometimes called the *embedded debt cost*.

where D is the fixed dividend and P_0 is the current price per share of the preferred stock. Notice that the cost of preferred stock is equal to the dividend yield on the preferred stock. Alternatively, because preferred stocks are rated in much the same way as bonds, the cost of preferred stock can be estimated by observing the required returns on other, similarly rated shares of preferred stock.

Alabama Power Co.'s Cost of Preferred Stock   EXAMPLE 14.3

On January 2, 2018, Alabama Power Co. had two issues of ordinary preferred stock with a $100 par value that traded on the NYSE. One issue paid $4.64 annually per share and sold for $99.70 per share. The other paid $4.92 per share annually and sold for $98.97 per share. What is Alabama Power's cost of preferred stock?

Using the first issue, we calculate that the cost of preferred stock is:

$R_P = D/P_0$
     $= \$4.64/\$99.70$
     $= .0465$, or 4.65%

Using the second issue, we calculate that the cost is:

$R_P = D/P_0$
     $= \$4.92/98.97$
     $=.0497$, or 4.97%

So, Alabama Power's cost of preferred stock appears to be about 4.81 percent.

Concept Questions

14.3a   Why is the coupon rate a bad estimate of a firm's cost of debt?
14.3b   How can the cost of debt be calculated?
14.3c   How can the cost of preferred stock be calculated?

The Weighted Average Cost of Capital   14.4

Now that we have the costs associated with the main sources of capital the firm employs, we need to worry about the specific mix. As we mentioned earlier, we will take this mix, which is the firm's capital structure, as given for now. Also, we will focus mostly on debt and ordinary equity in this discussion.

In Chapter 3, we mentioned that financial analysts frequently focus on a firm's total capitalization, which is the sum of its long-term debt and equity. This is particularly true in determining cost of capital; short-term liabilities are often ignored in the process. We will not explicitly distinguish between total value and total capitalization in the following discussion; the general approach is applicable with either.

Excel Master It!
xlsx Excel Master
coverage online

THE CAPITAL STRUCTURE WEIGHTS

We will use the symbol E (for equity) to stand for the *market* value of the firm's equity. We calculate this by taking the number of shares outstanding and multiplying it by the price per share. Similarly, we will use the symbol D (for debt) to stand for the *market* value of the firm's debt. For long-term debt, we calculate this by multiplying the market price of a single bond by the number of bonds outstanding.

If there are multiple bond issues (as there normally would be), we repeat this calculation of D for each and then add up the results. If there is debt that is not publicly traded (because it is held by a life insurance company, for example), we must observe the yield on similar publicly traded debt and then estimate the market value of the privately held debt using this yield as the discount rate. For short-term debt, the book (accounting) values and market values should be somewhat similar, so we might use the book values as estimates of the market values.

Finally, we will use the symbol V (for value) to stand for the combined market value of the debt and equity:

$$V = E + D$$ 14.4

If we divide both sides by V, we can calculate the percentages of the total capital represented by the debt and equity:

$$100\% = E/V + D/V$$ 14.5

These percentages can be interpreted just like portfolio weights, and they are often called the *capital structure weights*.

For example, if the total market value of a company's stock were calculated as $200 million and the total market value of the company's debt were calculated as $50 million, then the combined value would be $250 million. Of this total, E/V = $200 million/$250 million = .80, so 80 percent of the firm's financing would be equity and the remaining 20 percent would be debt.

We emphasize here that the correct way to proceed is to use the *market* values of the debt and equity. Under certain circumstances, such as when calculating figures for a privately owned company, it may not be possible to get reliable estimates of these quantities. In this case, we might go ahead and use the accounting values for debt and equity. Although this would probably be better than nothing, we would have to take the answer with a grain of salt.

TAXES AND THE WEIGHTED AVERAGE COST OF CAPITAL

There is one final issue we need to discuss. Recall that we are always concerned with aftertax cash flows. If we are determining the discount rate appropriate to those cash flows, then the discount rate also needs to be expressed on an aftertax basis.

As we discussed previously in various places in this book (and as we will discuss later), the interest paid by a corporation is deductible for tax purposes. Payments to stockholders, such as dividends, are not. What this means, effectively, is that the government pays some of the interest. In determining an aftertax discount rate, we need to distinguish between the pretax and the aftertax cost of debt.

To illustrate, suppose a firm borrows $1 million at 9 percent interest. The corporate tax rate is 21 percent. What is the aftertax interest rate on this loan? The total interest bill will be $90,000 per year. This amount is tax deductible, however, so the $90,000 interest reduces the firm's tax bill by .21 × $90,000 = $18,900. The aftertax interest bill is $90,000 − 18,900 = $71,100. The aftertax interest rate is $71,100/$1 million = .0711, or 7.11%.

Notice that, in general, the aftertax interest rate is equal to the pretax rate multiplied by 1 minus the tax rate. If we use the symbol T_C to stand for the corporate tax rate, then the aftertax rate can be written as $R_D \times (1 - T_C)$. Using the numbers from the preceding paragraph, we find that the aftertax interest rate is $9\% \times (1 - .21) = 7.11\%$.

To get a feel for actual, industry-level WACCs, visit Professor Aswath Damodaran at **pages .stern.nyu.edu/~adamodar/** and look for "cost of capital by sector."

The Tax Cuts and Jobs Act of 2017 placed limitations on the amount of interest that can be deducted in certain situations. Throughout this chapter, we will assume all interest can be deducted. We will discuss this issue in greater detail in a subsequent chapter.

Bringing together the various topics we have discussed in this chapter, we now have the capital structure weights along with the cost of equity and the aftertax cost of debt. To calculate the firm's overall cost of capital, we multiply the capital structure weights by the associated costs and add them up. The total is the **weighted average cost of capital (WACC)**:

$$\text{WACC} = (E/V) \times R_E + (D/V) \times R_D \times (1 - T_C)$$

 [14.6]

weighted average cost of capital (WACC)
The weighted average of the cost of equity and the aftertax cost of debt.

This WACC has a straightforward interpretation. It is the overall return the firm must earn on its existing assets to maintain the value of its stock. It is also the required return on any investments by the firm that have essentially the same risks as existing operations. So, if we were evaluating the cash flows from a proposed expansion of our existing operations, this is the discount rate we would use.

If a firm uses preferred stock in its capital structure, then our expression for the WACC needs a simple extension. If we define P/V as the percentage of the firm's financing that comes from preferred stock, then the WACC is:

$$\text{WACC} = (E/V) \times R_E + (P/V) \times R_P + (D/V) \times R_D \times (1 - T_C)$$

 [14.7]

where R_P is the cost of preferred stock.

Calculating the WACC   EXAMPLE 14.4

The B.B. Lean Co. has 1.4 million shares of stock outstanding. The stock currently sells for $20 per share. The firm's debt is publicly traded and was recently quoted at 93 percent of face value. It has a total face value of $5 million, and it is currently priced to yield 11 percent. The risk-free rate is 8 percent, and the market risk premium is 7 percent. You've estimated that Lean has a beta of .74. If the corporate tax rate is 21 percent, what is the WACC of Lean Co.?

We can first determine the cost of equity and the cost of debt. Using the SML, we find that the cost of equity is 8% + .74 × 7% = 13.18%. The total value of the equity is 1.4 million × $20 = $28 million. The pretax cost of debt is the current yield to maturity on the outstanding debt, 11 percent. The debt sells for 93 percent of its face value, so its current market value is .93 × $5 million = $4.65 million. The total market value of the equity and debt together is $28 million + 4.65 million = $32.65 million.

From here, we can calculate the WACC easily enough. The percentage of equity used by Lean to finance its operations is $28 million/$32.65 million = .8576, or 85.76%. Because the weights have to add up to 1, the percentage of debt is 1 − .8576 = .1424, or 14.24%. The WACC is:

$$\begin{aligned}
\text{WACC} &= (E/V) \times R_E + (D/V) \times R_D \times (1 - T_C) \\
&= .8576 \times .1318 + .1424 \times .11 \times (1 - .21) \\
&= .1254, \text{ or } 12.54\%
\end{aligned}$$

B.B. Lean has an overall weighted average cost of capital of 12.54 percent.

CALCULATING THE WACC FOR EASTMAN CHEMICAL

In this section, we illustrate how to calculate the WACC for Eastman Chemical Co., a leading international chemical company and maker of plastics such as those used in soft drink containers. It was created in 1993, when its former parent company, Eastman Kodak, split off the division as a separate company. Our goal is to take you through, on a step-by-step basis, the process of finding and using the information needed from online sources. As you will see, there is a fair amount of detail involved, but the necessary information is, for the most part, readily available.

Eastman's Cost of Equity   Our first stop is the main screen for Eastman available at finance.yahoo.com (ticker: EMN). As of early 2017, here's what it looked like:

Eastman Chemical Company (EMN)
NYSE - NYSE Real Time Price. Currency in USD

☆ Add to watchlist

77.72 -1.35 (-1.71%)
As of 2:01PM EST. Market open.

| Summary | Conversations | Statistics | Profile | Financials | Options | Holders | Historical Data | Analysts |

Previous Close	79.07	Market Cap	11.41B	
Open	78.71	Beta	1.35	
Bid	0.00 x	PE Ratio (TTM)	13.09	
Ask	0.00 x	EPS (TTM)	5.94	
Day's Range	76.99 - 79.23	Earnings Date	Jan 26, 2017	
52 Week Range	56.03 - 79.23	Dividend & Yield	2.04 (2.64%)	
Volume	730,190	Ex-Dividend Date	N/A	
Avg. Volume	1,463,619	1y Target Est	82.24	

1D 5D 1M 6M 1Y 2Y 5Y 10Y MAX   ⤢ Interactive chart

Next, we went to the "Statistics" screen. According to this screen, Eastman has 146.75 million shares of stock outstanding. The book value per share is $29.62, but the stock sells for $77.72. Total equity is therefore about $4.347 billion on a book value basis, but it is closer to $11.405 billion on a market value basis.

Balance Sheet

Total Cash (mrq)	207M
Total Cash Per Share (mrq)	1.41
Total Debt (mrq)	6.68B
Total Debt/Equity (mrq)	148.01
Current Ratio (mrq)	1.32
Book Value Per Share (mrq)	29.62

Stock Price History

Beta	1.35
52-Week Change [3]	25.49%
S&P500 52-Week Change [3]	17.36%
52 Week High [3]	79.23
52 Week Low [3]	56.03
50-Day Moving Average [3]	76.18
200-Day Moving Average [3]	69.95

Share Statistics

Avg Vol (3 month) [3]	1.46M
Avg Vol (10 day) [3]	1.33M
Shares Outstanding [5]	146.75M
Float	146M
% Held by Insiders [1]	0.68%
% Held by Institutions [1]	85.50%
Shares Short [3]	2.94M
Short Ratio [3]	1.98
Short % of Float [3]	2.00%
Shares Short (prior month) [3]	2.95M

To estimate Eastman's cost of equity, we will assume a market risk premium of 7 percent, similar to what we calculated in Chapter 12. Eastman's beta on Yahoo! is 1.35, which is higher than the beta of the average stock. To check this number, we went to the well-known Value Line *Investment Survey*, which uses an approach that moderates very large and very small betas. Here, the beta is reported as 1.30, so we will stick with the Yahoo! estimate. According to the Bonds section of finance.yahoo.com, T-bills were paying about .45 percent. Using the CAPM to estimate the cost of equity, we find:

$$R_E = .0045 + 1.35(.07) = .0990, \text{ or } 9.90\%$$

Eastman has paid dividends for only a few years, so calculating the growth rate for the dividend discount model is problematic. However, under the Analysts link at finance.yahoo.com, we found the following:

Growth Estimates	EMN
Current Qtr.	-6.30%
Next Qtr.	4.10%
Current Year	-7.40%
Next Year	8.20%
Next 5 Years (per annum)	5.06%
Past 5 Years (per annum)	11.06%

Analysts estimate the growth in earnings per share for the company will be 5.06 percent for the next five years. For now, we will use this growth rate in the dividend discount model to estimate the cost of equity; the link between earnings growth and dividends is discussed in a later chapter. The estimated cost of equity using the dividend discount model is:

$$R_E = \frac{\$2.04(1 + .0506)}{77.72} + .0506 = .0782, \text{ or } 7.82\%$$

Notice that our two estimates for the cost of equity are not identical. This is essentially always the case. Remember that each method of estimating the cost of equity relies on different assumptions, so different estimates of the cost of equity should not surprise us. If the estimates are different, there are two simple solutions. First, we could ignore one of the estimates. In this case, we would look at each estimate to see if one of them seemed too high or too low to be reasonable. Second, we could average the two estimates. For Eastman, our estimates of 9.90 percent and 7.82 percent are relatively close, so we would average them to get 8.86 percent as the cost of equity.

Eastman's Cost of Debt   Eastman has 13 relatively long-term bond issues that account for essentially all of its long-term debt. To calculate the cost of debt, we will have to combine these 13 issues. What we will do is compute a weighted average. We went to www .finra.org/marketdata to find quotes on the bonds. We should note here that finding the yield to maturity for all of a company's outstanding bond issues on a single day is unusual. If you remember our previous discussion of bonds, the bond market is not as liquid as the stock market; on many days, individual bond issues may not trade. To find the book value of the bonds, we went to www.sec.gov and found the 10-Q report dated September 30, 2016, and filed with the SEC on November 4, 2016. The basic information is as follows:

Coupon Rate	Maturity	Book Value (face value, in millions)	Price (% of par)	Yield to Maturity
2.40%	2017	$ 499	100.675	.920%
6.30	2018	166	109.498	1.077
5.50	2019	249	108.301	2.462
2.70	2020	795	101.276	2.245
4.50	2021	249	105.684	2.897
3.60	2022	890	102.866	3.014
1.50	2023	607	90.484	3.168
7.25	2024	244	124.376	3.322
7.625	2024	54	128.187	3.311
3.80	2025	792	101.611	3.565
7.60	2027	222	134.007	3.548
4.80	2042	492	102.564	4.626
4.65	2044	870	97.750	4.797
		$6,129		

To calculate the weighted average cost of debt, we take the percentage of the total debt represented by each issue and multiply by the yield on the issue. We then add to get the overall weighted average debt cost. We use both book values and market values here for comparison. The results of the calculations are as follows:

Coupon Rate	Book Value (face value, in millions)	Percentage of Total	Market Value (in millions)	Percentage of Total	Yield to Maturity	Book Values	Market Values
2.40%	$ 499	.08	$ 502.37	.08	.92%	.07%	.07%
6.30	166	.03	181.77	.03	1.08	.03	.03
5.50	249	.04	269.67	.04	2.46	.10	.11
2.70	795	.13	805.14	.13	2.25	.29	.29
4.50	249	.04	263.15	.04	2.90	.12	.12
3.60	890	.15	915.51	.14	3.01	.44	.44
1.50	607	.10	549.24	.09	3.17	.31	.28
7.25	244	.04	303.48	.05	3.32	.13	.16
7.625	54	.01	69.22	.01	3.31	.03	.04
3.80	792	.13	804.76	.13	3.57	.46	.45
7.60	222	.04	297.50	.05	3.55	.13	.17
4.80	492	.08	504.61	.08	4.63	.37	.37
4.65	875	.14	850.43	.13	4.80	.68	.65
	$6,129	1.00	$6,316.84	1.00		3.17%	3.16%

As these calculations show, Eastman's cost of debt is 3.17 percent on a book value basis and 3.16 percent on a market value basis. For Eastman, whether market values or book values are used makes no difference. The reason is that the market values and book values are similar. This will often be the case and explains why companies frequently use book values for debt in WACC calculations. Also, Eastman has no preferred stock, so we don't need to consider its cost.

Eastman's WACC   We now have the various pieces necessary to calculate Eastman's WACC. First, we need to calculate the capital structure weights. On a book value basis, Eastman's equity and debt are worth $4.347 billion and $6.129 billion, respectively. The total value is $10.476 billion, so the equity and debt weights are $4.347 billion/$10.476 billion = .41 and $6.129 billion/$10.476 billion = .59, respectively. Assuming a tax rate of 21 percent, Eastman's WACC is:

$$\text{WACC} = .41 \times .0886 + .59 \times .0317 \times (1 - .21) = .0514, \text{ or } 5.14\%$$

Using book value capital structure weights (and more decimal points than shown here), we get about 5.14 percent for Eastman's WACC.

If we use market value weights, the WACC will be higher. To see why, notice that on a market value basis, Eastman's equity and debt are worth $11.405 billion and $6.317 billion, respectively. The capital structure weights are therefore $11.405 billion/$17.722 billion = .64 and $6.317 billion/$17.722 billion = .36, so the equity percentage is much higher. With these weights (and more decimal points than shown here), Eastman's WACC is:

$$\text{WACC} = .64 \times .0886 + .36 \times .0316 \times (1 - .21) = .0659, \text{ or } 6.59\%$$

Using market value weights, we get about 6.59 percent for Eastman's WACC, which is noticeably larger than the 5.14 percent WACC we got using book value weights.

As this example illustrates, using book values can lead to trouble, particularly if equity book values are used. Going back to Chapter 3, recall that we discussed the market-to-book

WORK THE WEB

So how does our estimate of the WACC for Eastman Chemical compare to others? One place to find estimates for WACC is www.valuepro.net. We went there and found the following information for Eastman:

Online Valuation for EMN - 1 / 12 / 2017

Intrinsic Stock Value: 130.74 [Recalculate] [Value Another Stock]

Excess Return Period (yrs)	10	Depreciation Rate (% of Rev)	4.44
Revenues ($mil)	8588	Investment Rate (% of Rev)	5.8
Growth Rate (%)	11.5	Working Capital (% of Rev)	9.21
Net Oper. Profit Margin (%)	14.68	Short-Term Assets ($mil)	2737
Tax Rate (%)	32.583	Short-Term Liab. ($mil)	1335
Stock Price ($)	71.99	Equity Risk Premium (%)	3
Shares Outstanding (mil)	154.8	Company Beta	1.365
10-Yr Treasury Yield (%)	5	Value Debt Out. ($mil)	4779
Bond Spread Treasury (%)	1.5	Value Pref. Stock Out. ($mil)	0
Preferred Stock Yield (%)	7.5	Company WACC (%)	7.68

As you can see, ValuePro estimates the WACC (cost of capital) for Eastman as 7.68 percent, which is a little over one percent higher than our estimate of 6.59 percent. However, different inputs were used in the computations. For example, ValuePro uses an equity risk premium of only 3 percent. ValuePro also used the historic tax rate, which we chose not to change. Calculating WACC requires the estimation of various inputs, and you must use your best judgment in these estimates.

Questions

1. Go to www.valuepro.net and look up the current WACC for Eastman Chemical on this website. How has the WACC changed? What are the possible reasons for the change?

2. Celgene (CELG) is a biopharmaceutical company. Would you expect the WACC for this company to be higher or lower than the WACC for Eastman Chemical? Why? Go to www.valuepro.net and find the estimated WACC for CELG. Was your assumption correct?

ratio (the ratio of market value per share to book value per share). This ratio is usually substantially bigger than 1. For Eastman, for example, verify that it's about 2.62; so book values significantly overstate the percentage of Eastman's financing that comes from debt. In addition, if we were computing a WACC for a company that did not have publicly traded stock, we would try to come up with a suitable market-to-book ratio by looking at similar, publicly traded companies, and we would then use this ratio to adjust the book value of the company under consideration. As we have seen, failure to do so can lead to significant underestimation of the WACC.

Our nearby *Work the Web* box explains more about the WACC and related topics.

SOLVING THE WAREHOUSE PROBLEM AND SIMILAR CAPITAL BUDGETING PROBLEMS

Now we can use the WACC to solve the warehouse problem we posed at the beginning of the chapter. However, before we rush to discount the cash flows at the WACC to estimate NPV, we need to make sure we are doing the right thing.

Going back to first principles, we need to find an alternative in the financial markets that is comparable to the warehouse renovation. To be comparable, an alternative must be of the same level of risk as the warehouse project. Projects that have the same risk are said to be in the same risk class.

The WACC for a firm reflects the risk and the target capital structure of the firm's existing assets as a whole. As a result, strictly speaking, the firm's WACC is the appropriate discount rate only if the proposed investment is a replica of the firm's existing operating activities.

In broader terms, whether or not we can use the firm's WACC to value the warehouse project depends on whether the warehouse project is in the same risk class as the firm. We will assume that this project is an integral part of the overall business of the firm. In such cases, it is natural to think that the cost savings will be as risky as the general cash flows of the firm, and the project will be in the same risk class as the overall firm. More generally, projects like the warehouse renovation that are intimately related to the firm's existing operations are often viewed as being in the same risk class as the overall firm.

We can now see what the president should do. Suppose the firm has a target debt-equity ratio of 1/3. From Chapter 3, we know that a debt-equity ratio of $D/E = 1/3$ implies that E/V is .75 and D/V is .25. The cost of debt is 10 percent, and the cost of equity is 20 percent. Assuming a 21 percent tax rate, the WACC will be:

$$
\begin{aligned}
\text{WACC} &= (E/V) \times R_E + (D/V) \times R_D \times (1 - T_C) \\
&= .75 \times 20\% + .25 \times 10\% \times (1 - .21) \\
&= .1698, \text{ or } 16.98\%
\end{aligned}
$$

Recall that the warehouse project had a cost of $50 million and expected aftertax cash flows (the cost savings) of $12 million per year for six years. The NPV (in millions) is:

$$
\text{NPV} = -\$50 + \frac{12}{(1 + \text{WACC})^1} + \cdots + \frac{12}{(1 + \text{WACC})^6}
$$

Because the cash flows are in the form of an ordinary annuity, we can calculate this NPV using 16.65 percent (the WACC) as the discount rate as follows:

$$
\begin{aligned}
\text{NPV} &= -\$50 + 12 \times \frac{1 - [1/(1 + .1698)^6]}{.1698} \\
&= -\$50 + 12 \times 3.5915 \\
&= -\$6.90
\end{aligned}
$$

Should the firm take on the warehouse renovation? The project has a negative NPV using the firm's WACC. This means that the financial markets offer superior projects in the same risk class (namely, the firm itself). The answer is clear: The project should be rejected. For future reference, our discussion of the WACC is summarized in Table 14.1.

TABLE 14.1

Summary of Capital Cost Calculations

I.	**The Cost of Equity, R_E**

A. Dividend growth model approach (from Chapter 8):

$$R_E = D_1/P_0 + g$$

where D_1 is the expected dividend in one period, g is the dividend growth rate, and P_0 is the current stock price.

B. SML approach (from Chapter 13):

$$R_E = R_f + \beta_E \times (R_M - R_f)$$

where R_f is the risk-free rate, R_M is the expected return on the overall market, and β_E is the systematic risk of the equity.

II.	**The Cost of Debt, R_D**

A. For a firm with publicly held debt, the cost of debt can be measured as the yield to maturity on the outstanding debt. The coupon rate is irrelevant. Yield to maturity is covered in Chapter 7.

B. If the firm has no publicly traded debt, then the cost of debt can be measured as the yield to maturity on similarly rated bonds (bond ratings are discussed in Chapter 7).

III.	**The Weighted Average Cost of Capital, WACC**

A. The firm's WACC is the overall required return on the firm as a whole. It is the appropriate discount rate to use for cash flows similar in risk to those of the overall firm.

B. The WACC is calculated as:

$$\text{WACC} = (E/V) \times R_E + (D/V) \times R_D \times (1 - T_C)$$

where T_C is the corporate tax rate, E is the *market* value of the firm's equity, D is the *market* value of the firm's debt, and $V = E + D$. Note that E/V is the percentage of the firm's financing (in market value terms) that is equity, and D/V is the percentage that is debt.

EXAMPLE 14.5   **Using the WACC**

A firm is considering a project that will result in initial aftertax cash savings of $5 million at the end of the first year. These savings will grow at the rate of 5 percent per year. The firm has a debt-equity ratio of .5, a cost of equity of 29.2 percent, and a cost of debt of 10 percent. The cost-saving proposal is closely related to the firm's core business, so it is viewed as having the same risk as the overall firm. Should the firm take on the project?

Assuming a 21 percent tax rate, the firm should take on this project if it costs less than $30 million. To see this, first note that the PV is:

$$PV = \frac{\$5 \text{ million}}{\text{WACC} - .05}$$

This is an example of a growing perpetuity as discussed in Chapter 6. The WACC is:

$$
\begin{aligned}
\text{WACC} &= (E/V) \times R_E + (D/V) \times R_D \times \left(1 - T_C\right) \\
&= 2/3 \times 29.2\% + 1/3 \times 10\% \times (1 - .21) \\
&= 22.10\%
\end{aligned}
$$

The PV is thus:

$$PV = \frac{\$5 \text{ million}}{.2210 - .05} = \$29.2 \text{ million}$$

The NPV will be positive only if the cost is less than $29.2 million.

IN THEIR OWN WORDS ...

Bennett Stewart on EVA

A firm's weighted average cost of capital has important applications other than the discount rate in capital project evaluations. For instance, it is a key ingredient to measure a firm's true economic profit, or what I like to call EVA, standing for economic value added. Accounting rules dictate that the interest expense a company incurs on its debt financing be deducted from its reported profit, but those same rules ironically forbid deducting a charge for the shareholders' funds a firm uses. In economic terms, equity capital is in fact a very costly financing source, because shareholders bear the risk of being paid last, after all other stakeholders and investors are paid first. But according to accountants, shareholders' equity is free.

This egregious oversight has dire practical consequences. For one thing, it means that the profit figure accountants certify to be correct is inherently at odds with the net present value decision rule. For instance, it is a simple matter for management to inflate its reported earnings and earnings per share in ways that actually harm the shareholders by investing capital in projects that earn less than the overall cost of capital but more than the aftertax cost of borrowing money, which amounts to a trivial hurdle in most cases, a couple percentage points at most. In effect, EPS requires management to vault a mere three-foot hurdle when to satisfy shareholders managers must jump a ten-foot hurdle that includes the cost of equity. A prime example of the way accounting profit leads smart managers to do dumb things was Enron, where former top executives Ken Lay and Jeff Skilling boldly declared in the firm's 2000 annual report that they were "laser-focused on earnings per share," and so they were. Bonuses were funded out of book profit, and project developers were paid for signing up new deals and not generating a decent return on investment. Consequently, Enron's EPS was on the rise while its true economic profit—its EVA—measured after deducting the full cost of capital, was plummeting in the years leading up to the firm's demise—the result of massive misallocations of capital to ill-advised energy and new economy projects. The point is, EVA measures economic profit, the profit that actually discounts to net present value, and the maximization of which is every company's most important financial goal; yet, for all its popularity, EPS is just an accounting contrivance that is wholly unrelated to the maximization of shareholder wealth or sending the right decision signals to management.

Starting in the early 1990s, firms around the world—ranging from Coca-Cola, to Briggs & Stratton, Herman Miller, and Eli Lilly in America, Siemens in Germany, Tata Consulting and the Godrej Group out of India, Brahma Beer in Brazil, and many, many more—began to turn to EVA as a new and better way to measure performance and set goals, make decisions and determine bonuses, and to communicate with investors and to teach business and finance basics to managers and employees. Properly tailored and implemented, EVA is a natural way to bring the cost of capital to life and to turn everyone in a company into a capital conscientious, owner-entrepreneur.

Bennett Stewart is a cofounder of Stern Stewart & Co. and also the CEO of EVA Dimensions, a firm providing EVA data, valuation modeling, and hedge fund management. Stewart pioneered the practical development of EVA as chronicled in his original book, The Quest for Value, *and latest book,* Best-Practice EVA.

PERFORMANCE EVALUATION: ANOTHER USE OF THE WACC

Visit **www.sternstewart.com** for more about EVA.

Performance evaluation is another use of the WACC. Probably the best-known approach in this area is the economic value added (EVA) method developed by Stern Stewart & Co. Companies such as AT&T, Coca-Cola, Quaker Oats, and Briggs & Stratton are among the firms that have been using EVA as a means of evaluating corporate performance. Similar approaches include market value added (MVA) and shareholder value added (SVA).

Although the details differ, the basic idea behind EVA and similar strategies is straightforward. Suppose we have $100 million in capital (debt and equity) tied up in our firm, and our overall WACC is 12 percent. If we multiply these together, we get $12 million. Referring back to Chapter 2, if our cash flow from assets is less than this, we are, on an overall basis, destroying value; if cash flow from assets exceeds $12 million, we are creating value.

In practice, evaluation strategies such as these suffer to a certain extent from problems with implementation. For example, it appears that many companies make extensive use of book values for debt and equity in computing cost of capital. Even so, by focusing on value creation, WACC-based evaluation procedures force employees and management to pay attention to the real bottom line: Increasing share prices.

476   PART 6   Cost of Capital and Long-Term Financial Policy

---

Concept Questions

14.4a   How is the WACC calculated?

14.4b   Why do we multiply the cost of debt by $(1 - T_c)$ when we compute the WACC?

14.4c   Under what conditions is it correct to use the WACC to determine NPV?

14.5   Divisional and Project Costs of Capital

As we have seen, using the WACC as the discount rate for future cash flows is appropriate only when the proposed investment is similar to the firm's existing activities. This is not as restrictive as it sounds. If we are in the pizza business, for example, and we are thinking of opening a new location, then the WACC is the discount rate to use. The same is true of a retailer thinking of a new store, a manufacturer considering expanding production, or a consumer products company considering expanding its markets.

Despite the usefulness of the WACC as a benchmark, there will clearly be situations in which the cash flows under consideration have risks distinctly different from those of the overall firm. We consider how to cope with this problem next.

THE SML AND THE WACC

When we are evaluating investments with risks that are substantially different from those of the overall firm, use of the WACC will potentially lead to poor decisions. Figure 14.1 illustrates why.

In Figure 14.1, we have plotted an SML corresponding to a risk-free rate of 7 percent and a market risk premium of 8 percent. To keep things simple, we consider an all-equity company with a beta of 1. As we have indicated, the WACC and the cost of equity are exactly equal to 15 percent for this company because there is no debt.

FIGURE 14.1

The Security Market Line (SML) and the Weighted Average Cost of Capital (WACC)

If a firm uses its WACC to make accept–reject decisions for all types of projects, it will have a tendency toward incorrectly accepting risky projects and incorrectly rejecting less risky projects.

Suppose our firm uses its WACC to evaluate all investments. This means that any investment with a return of greater than 15 percent will be accepted and any investment with a return of less than 15 percent will be rejected. We know from our study of risk and return that a desirable investment is one that plots above the SML. As Figure 14.1 illustrates, using the WACC for all types of projects can result in the firm incorrectly accepting relatively risky projects and incorrectly rejecting relatively safe ones.

For example, consider Point A. This project has a beta of $\beta_A = .60$, as compared to the firm's beta of 1.0. It has an expected return of 14 percent. Is this a desirable investment? The answer is yes because its required return is only:

$$
\begin{aligned}
\text{Required return} &= R_f + \beta_A \times (R_M - R_f) \\
&= .07 + .60 \times .08 \\
&= .118, \text{ or } 11.8\%
\end{aligned}
$$

If we use the WACC as a cutoff, then this project will be rejected because its return is less than 15 percent. This example illustrates that a firm that uses its WACC as a cutoff will tend to reject profitable projects with risks less than those of the overall firm.

At the other extreme, consider Point B. This project has a beta of $\beta_B = 1.2$. It offers a 16 percent return, which exceeds the firm's cost of capital. This is not a good investment, because, given its level of systematic risk, its return is inadequate. Nonetheless, if we use the WACC to evaluate it, it will appear to be attractive. So the second error that will arise if we use the WACC as a cutoff is that we will tend to make unprofitable investments with risks greater than those of the overall firm. As a consequence, through time, a firm that uses its WACC to evaluate all projects will have a tendency to both accept unprofitable investments and become increasingly risky.

DIVISIONAL COST OF CAPITAL

The same type of problem with the WACC can arise in a corporation with more than one line of business. Imagine a corporation that has two divisions: A regulated electric company and an electronics manufacturing operation. The first of these (the electricity operation) has relatively low risk; the second has relatively high risk.

In this case, the firm's overall cost of capital is really a mixture of two different costs of capital, one for each division. If the two divisions were competing for resources, and the firm used a single WACC as a cutoff, which division would tend to be awarded greater funds for investment?

The answer is that the riskier division would tend to have greater returns (ignoring the greater risk), so it would tend to be the "winner." The less glamorous operation might have great profit potential that would end up being ignored. Large corporations in the United States are aware of this problem, and many work to develop separate divisional costs of capital.

THE PURE PLAY APPROACH

We've seen that using the firm's WACC inappropriately can lead to problems. How can we come up with the appropriate discount rates in such circumstances? Because we cannot observe the returns on these investments, there generally is no direct way of coming up with a beta. Instead, what we must do is examine other investments outside the firm that are in the same risk class as the one we are considering, and use the market-required return on these investments as the discount rate. In other words, we will try to determine what the cost of capital is for such investments by trying to locate some similar investments in the marketplace.

Going back to our electricity division, suppose we wanted to come up with a discount rate to use for that division. What we could do is identify several other electric companies that have publicly traded securities. We might find that a typical electric company has a beta of .80, AA-rated debt, and a capital structure that is about 50 percent debt and 50 percent equity. Using this information, we could develop a WACC for a typical electric company and use this as our discount rate.

Alternatively, if we were considering entering a new line of business, we would try to develop the appropriate cost of capital by looking at the market-required returns on companies already in that business. In the language of Wall Street, a company that focuses on a single line of business is called a *pure play*. If you wanted to bet on the price of crude oil by purchasing common stocks, you would try to identify companies that deal exclusively with this product because they would be the most affected by changes in the price of crude oil. Such companies would be called "pure plays on the price of crude oil."

What we try to do here is to find companies that focus as exclusively as possible on the type of project in which we are interested. Our approach, therefore, is called the **pure play approach** to estimating the required return on an investment. To illustrate, suppose McDonald's decides to enter the cell phone and tablet business with a line of electronics called McPhones. The risks involved are quite different from those in the fast-food business. As a result, McDonald's would need to look at companies already in the consumer electronics business to compute a cost of capital for the new division. An obvious pure play candidate would be Apple, which is predominantly in this line of business. Samsung, on the other hand, would not be as good a choice because it sells more product lines, such as televisions and appliances, which likely have a different level of risk.

In Chapter 3, we discussed the subject of identifying similar companies for comparison purposes. The same problems we described there come up here. The most obvious one is that we may not be able to find any suitable companies. In this case, how to objectively determine a discount rate becomes a difficult question. Even so, the important thing is to be aware of the issue so that we at least reduce the possibility of the kinds of mistakes that can arise when the WACC is used as a cutoff on all investments.

pure play approach
The use of a WACC that is unique to a particular project, based on companies in similar lines of business.

THE SUBJECTIVE APPROACH

Because of the difficulties that exist in objectively establishing discount rates for individual projects, firms often adopt an approach that involves making subjective adjustments to the overall WACC. To illustrate, suppose a firm has an overall WACC of 14 percent. It places all proposed projects into four categories as follows:

Category	Examples	Adjustment Factor	Discount Rate
High risk	New products	+6%	20%
Moderate risk	Cost savings, expansion of existing lines	+0	14
Low risk	Replacement of existing equipment	−4	10
Mandatory	Pollution control equipment	n/a	n/a

n/a = Not applicable.

The effect of this crude partitioning is to assume that all projects either fall into one of three risk classes or else are mandatory. In the last case, the cost of capital is irrelevant because the project must be taken. With the subjective approach, the firm's WACC may change through time as economic conditions change. As this happens, the discount rates for the different types of projects will also change.

Within each risk class, some projects will presumably have more risk than others, and the danger of making incorrect decisions still exists. Figure 14.2 illustrates this point.

FIGURE 14.2

The Security Market Line (SML) and the Subjective Approach

With the subjective approach, the firm places projects into one of several risk classes. The discount rate used to value the project is then determined by adding (for high risk) or subtracting (for low risk) an adjustment factor to or from the firm's WACC. This results in fewer incorrect decisions than if the firm simply used the WACC to make the decisions.

Comparing Figures 14.1 and 14.2, we see that similar problems exist; but the magnitude of the potential error is less with the subjective approach. The project labeled A would be accepted if the WACC were used, but it is rejected once it is classified as a high-risk investment. What this illustrates is that some risk adjustment, even if it is subjective, is probably better than no risk adjustment.

It would be better, in principle, to objectively determine the required return for each project separately. As a practical matter, it may not be possible to go much beyond subjective adjustments because either the necessary information is unavailable or the cost and effort required are not worthwhile.

Concept Questions

14.5a What are the likely consequences if a firm uses its WACC to evaluate all proposed investments?

14.5b What is the pure play approach to determining the appropriate discount rate? When might it be used?

Company Valuation with the WACC   14.6

When valuing a company, our approach is the same as the one we used for individual capital projects like the warehouse renovation, but there is one issue we have to deal with. When we look at an entire company, we will often see an interest deduction because the company has borrowed money. But as we have consistently emphasized, interest paid is a financing cost, not an operating cost. However, because interest paid is a tax deductible expense, a company's tax bill is lower than it would have been had the company not used debt financing. We will have much more to say about this in a later chapter.

For now, to calculate cash flow from assets, we need to first calculate what the firm's tax bill would have been if it had not used debt financing. To do that, we take earnings before interest and taxes (EBIT) and multiply it by the firm's tax rate (T_C) to get the firm's "would-have-been" tax bill, which we will call the "adjusted" taxes and label Taxes*:

$$\text{Taxes*} = \text{EBIT} \times T_c \qquad \text{(14.8)}$$

Next, we will calculate cash flow from assets the usual way, except we will use the adjusted taxes. We will call this the "adjusted" cash flow from assets, CFA*, which we calculate as:

$$
\begin{aligned}
\text{CFA*} &= \text{EBIT} + \text{Depreciation} - \text{Taxes*} \\
&\quad - \text{Change in NWC} - \text{Capital spending} \\
&= \text{EBIT} + \text{Depreciation} - \text{EBIT} \times T_c \\
&\quad - \text{Change in NWC} - \text{Capital spending}
\end{aligned}
\qquad \text{(14.9)}
$$

Our adjusted cash flow, CFA*, is often called "free cash flow," but as we mentioned much earlier in our book, that phrase means different things to different people, so we will stick with CFA* to avoid confusion.

Notice that we could simplify our CFA* calculation a bit by writing it as:

$$
\begin{aligned}
\text{CFA*} &= \text{EBIT} \times (1 - T_c) + \text{Depreciation} \\
&\quad - \text{Change in NWC} - \text{Capital spending}
\end{aligned}
\qquad \text{(14.10)}
$$

The term $\text{EBIT} \times (1 - T_C)$ is what net income would have been if the firm had used no debt, and the sum of the first two terms is our bottom-up definition of operating cash flow from Chapter 10.

At this point, if the firm is growing steadily, we can value it using our growing perpetuity formula (as we did earlier in this chapter). For example, suppose you project CFA* for the coming year as $\text{CFA}_1^* = \$120$ million. You think this amount will grow indefinitely at $g = 5$ percent per year. You've estimated the firm's WACC to be 9 percent, so the value of the firm today (V_0) is:

$$\text{Firm value today} = V_0 = \frac{\text{CFA}_1^*}{\text{WACC} - g} = \frac{\$120}{.09 - .05} = \$3 \text{ billion}$$

In sum, valuing a firm is no different from valuing a project, except for the fact that we have to adjust the taxes to remove the effect of any debt financing.

We can also consider the impact of nonconstant growth (as we did in an earlier chapter on stock valuation using the dividend growth model). In this case, we assume that constant growth begins at Time t in the future. In that case, we can write the value of the firm today as:

$$
V_0 = \frac{\text{CFA}_1^*}{1 + \text{WACC}} + \frac{\text{CFA}_2^*}{(1 + \text{WACC})^2} + \frac{\text{CFA}_3^*}{(1 + \text{WACC})^3} + \cdots \\
+ \frac{\text{CFA}_t^* + V_t}{(1 + \text{WACC})^t}
\qquad \text{(14.11)}
$$

Here, V_t is the value of the firm at Time t, which we again calculate using the growing perpetuity formula:

$$V_t = \frac{\text{CFA}_{t+1}^*}{\text{WACC} - g} \qquad \text{(14.12)}$$

As always, notice that the tricky part is that to get the value at Time t, we have to use the cash flow that occurs at the end of that period at Time $t + 1$. Also, the value of the firm in the future, V_t, is often referred to as the "terminal value."

Valuing a Company

EXAMPLE 14.6

A guest on the popular show *Great White Tank* is attempting to raise money for her new company, Feline Fancy, which makes cat toys. The potential investor wants to value the company, which is privately held. Because of this, she uses the pure play approach to determine that the appropriate WACC for the company is 8 percent. The relevant tax rate is 21 percent.

Feline Fancy currently has $40 million in debt and 3.5 million shares outstanding. Sales this year are expected to be $30 million, and that amount is expected to grow at 15 percent per year for the following four years. After that, sales are expected to grow at 2 percent indefinitely. EBIT this year will be $10 million. EBIT, depreciation, capital spending, and the change in net working capital will grow at the same rate as sales. What value would you assign to Feline Fancy as a whole? What price per share would you assign?

To value the company, we begin by estimating adjusted cash flow from assets (CFA*) for the next five years. The Year 1 values are the projections in millions for next year:

	Year 1	Year 2	Year 3	Year 4	Year 5
EBIT	$10.00	$11.50	$13.23	$15.21	$17.49
Depreciation	1.50	1.73	1.98	2.28	2.62
Taxes*	2.10	2.42	2.78	3.19	3.67
Change in NWC	.80	.92	1.06	1.22	1.40
Capital spending	2.40	2.76	3.17	3.65	4.20
CFA*	$ 6.20	$ 7.13	$ 8.20	$ 9.43	$10.84

Since the adjusted cash flow from assets will grow at 2 percent after Year 5, the terminal value of the company in Year 5 will be:

$$V_5 = \frac{\$10.84(1 + .02)}{.08 - .02} = \$184.35 \text{ million}$$

We can now find the value of the company today by discounting the first five CFA* values and the terminal value back to the present using the WACC. Doing so, we find:

$$V_0 = \frac{\$6.20}{1 + .08} + \frac{\$7.13}{(1 + .08)^2} + \frac{\$8.20}{(1 + .08)^3} + \frac{\$9.43}{(1 + .08)^4} + \frac{\$10.84 + 184.35}{(1 + .08)^5}$$
$$= \$158.14 \text{ million}$$

To find the value of equity, we subtract the $40 million in debt, resulting in a total equity value of $118.14 million. To find the share price, we divide this by the number of shares (3.5 million), which gives us a share price of:

Price per share = $118.14/3.5 = $33.75

Another common way to calculate the terminal value is to use a target ratio, similar to the way we used the PE and price-sales ratios in Chapter 8. For example, suppose the potential investor believes the appropriate price-sales ratio when the company's growth rate slows is three times. Sales in Year 5 are projected at $30 million × 1.15^4 = $52.47 million (notice that we compounded the $30 million forward four years because $30 million is sales by the end of Year 1, not sales from last year). So, the new estimated terminal value is:

$$V_5 = 3 \times \$52.47 \text{ million} = \$157.41 \text{ million}$$

With this new terminal value, the value of the company today will be:

$$V_0 = \frac{\$6.20}{1 + .08} + \frac{\$7.13}{(1 + .08)^2} + \frac{\$8.20}{(1 + .08)^3} + \frac{\$9.43}{(1 + .08)^4} + \frac{\$10.84 + 157.41}{(1 + .08)^5}$$
$$= \$139.80 \text{ million}$$

See for yourself if you don't agree that using this terminal value will result in an estimated per share value of $28.52.

> **Concept Questions**
>
> **14.6a** Why do we adjust a firm's taxes when we do a firm valuation?
> **14.6b** Why do you think we might prefer to use a ratio when calculating the terminal value when we do a firm valuation?

14.7 Flotation Costs and the Average Cost of Capital

So far, we have not included issue, or flotation, costs in our discussion of the weighted average cost of capital. If a company accepts a new project, it may be required to issue, or float, new bonds and stocks. This means that the firm will incur some costs, which we call *flotation costs*. The nature and magnitude of flotation costs are discussed in some detail in Chapter 15.

Sometimes it is suggested that the firm's WACC should be adjusted upward to reflect flotation costs. This is really not the best approach because, once again, the required return on an investment depends on the risk of the investment, not the source of the funds. This is not to say that flotation costs should be ignored. Because these costs arise as a consequence of the decision to undertake a project, they are relevant cash flows. We briefly discuss how to include them in project analysis.

THE BASIC APPROACH

We start with a simple case. The Spatt Company, an all-equity firm, has a cost of equity of 20 percent. Because this firm is 100 percent equity, its WACC and its cost of equity are the same. Spatt is contemplating a large-scale, $100 million expansion of its existing operations. The expansion would be funded by selling new stock.

Based on conversations with its investment banker, Spatt believes its flotation costs will run 10 percent of the amount issued. This means that Spatt's proceeds from the equity sale will be only 90 percent of the amount sold. When flotation costs are considered, what is the cost of the expansion?

As we discuss in more detail in Chapter 15, Spatt needs to sell enough equity to raise $100 million *after* covering the flotation costs. In other words:

$100 million = (1 − .10) × Amount raised
Amount raised = $100 million/.90 = $111.11 million

Spatt's flotation costs are $11.11 million, and the true cost of the expansion is $111.11 million once we include flotation costs.

Things are only slightly more complicated if the firm uses both debt and equity. Suppose Spatt's target capital structure is 60 percent equity, 40 percent debt. The flotation costs associated with equity are still 10 percent, but the flotation costs for debt are less—say 5 percent.

Earlier, when we had different capital costs for debt and equity, we calculated a weighted average cost of capital using the target capital structure weights. Here we will do much the same thing. We can calculate a weighted average flotation cost, f_A, by multiplying the equity flotation cost, f_E, by the percentage of equity (E/V) and the debt flotation cost, f_D, by the percentage of debt (D/V) and then adding the two together:

$$f_A = (E/V) \times f_E + (D/V) \times f_D$$
$$= .60 \times .10 + .40 \times .05$$
$$= .08, \text{ or } 8\%$$

[14.13]

The weighted average flotation cost is 8 percent. What this tells us is that for every dollar in outside financing needed for new projects, the firm must actually raise $1/(1 − .08) = $1.087. In our example, the project cost is $100 million when we ignore flotation costs. If we include them, then the true cost is $100 million/$(1 − f_A) = $100 million/.92 = $108.7 million.

In taking issue costs into account, the firm must be careful not to use the wrong weights. The firm should use the target weights, even if it can finance the entire cost of the project with either debt or equity. The fact that a firm can finance a specific project with debt or equity is not directly relevant. If a firm has a target debt-equity ratio of 1, for example, but chooses to finance a particular project with all debt, it will have to raise additional equity later on to maintain its target debt-equity ratio. To take this into account, the firm should always use the target weights in calculating the flotation cost.

| **Calculating the Weighted Average Flotation Cost** | **EXAMPLE 14.7** |

The Weinstein Corporation has a target capital structure that is 80 percent equity, 20 percent debt. The flotation costs for equity issues are 20 percent of the amount raised; the flotation costs for debt issues are 6 percent. If Weinstein needs $65 million for a new manufacturing facility, what is the true cost once flotation costs are considered?

We first calculate the weighted average flotation cost, f_A:

$$f_A = (E/V) \times f_E + (D/V) \times f_D$$
$$= .80 \times .20 + .20 \times .06$$
$$= .172, \text{ or } 17.2\%$$

The weighted average flotation cost is 17.2 percent. The project cost is $65 million when we ignore flotation costs. If we include them, then the true cost is $65 million/$(1 − f_A) = $65 million/.828 = $78.5 million, again illustrating that flotation costs can be a considerable expense.

FLOTATION COSTS AND NPV

To illustrate how flotation costs can be included in an NPV analysis, suppose the Tripleday Printing Company is currently at its target debt-equity ratio of 100 percent. It is considering building a new $500,000 printing plant in Kansas. This new plant is expected to generate aftertax cash flows of $73,150 per year forever. The tax rate is 21 percent. There are two financing options:

1. A $500,000 new issue of common stock: The issuance costs of the new common stock would be about 10 percent of the amount raised. The required return on the company's new equity is 20 percent.

2. A $500,000 issue of 30-year bonds: The issuance costs of the new debt would be 2 percent of the proceeds. The company can raise new debt at 10 percent.

What is the NPV of the new printing plant?

To begin, because printing is the company's main line of business, we will use the company's weighted average cost of capital to value the new printing plant:

$$\text{WACC} = (E/V) \times R_E + (D/V) \times R_D \times (1 - T_C)$$
$$= .50 \times .20 + .50 \times .10 \times (1 - .21)$$
$$= .1395, \text{ or } 13.95\%$$

Because the cash flows are $73,150 per year forever, the PV of the cash flows at 13.95 percent per year is:

$$\text{PV} = \frac{\$73,150}{.1395} = \$524,373$$

IN THEIR OWN WORDS ...

Samuel Weaver on Cost of Capital and Hurdle Rates at the Hershey Company

At Hershey, we reevaluate our cost of capital annually or as market conditions warrant. The calculation of the cost of capital essentially involves three different issues, each with a few alternatives:

· *Capital weights*
  book value or market value weights
  current or target capital structure
· *Cost of debt*
  Historical (coupon) interest rates
  Market-based interest rates
· *Cost of equity*
  Dividend growth model
  Capital asset pricing model, or CAPM

At Hershey, we calculate our cost of capital officially based on the projected "target" capital structure at the end of our three-year intermediate planning horizon. This allows management to see the immediate impact of strategic decisions related to the planned composition of Hershey's capital pool. The cost of debt is calculated as the anticipated weighted average aftertax cost of debt in that final plan year based on the coupon rates attached to that debt. The cost of equity is computed via the dividend growth model.

We conducted a survey of the 10 food processing companies that we consider our industry group competitors. The results of this survey indicated that the cost of capital for most of these companies was in the 7 to 10 percent range. Furthermore, without exception, all 10 of these companies employed the CAPM when calculating their cost of equity. Our experience has been that the dividend growth model works better for Hershey. We do pay dividends, and we do experience steady, stable growth in our dividends. This growth is also projected within our strategic plan. Consequently, the dividend growth model is technically applicable and appealing to management because it reflects their best estimate of the future long-term growth rate.

In addition to the calculation already described, the other possible combinations and permutations are calculated as barometers. Unofficially, the cost of capital is calculated using market weights, current marginal interest rates, and the CAPM cost of equity. For the most part, and due to rounding the cost of capital to the nearest whole percentage point, these alternative calculations yield approximately the same results.

From the cost of capital, individual project hurdle rates are developed using a subjectively determined risk premium based on the characteristics of the project. Projects are grouped into separate project categories, such as cost savings, capacity expansion, product line extension, and new products. For example, in general, a new product is more risky than a cost savings project. Consequently, each project category's hurdle rate reflects the level of risk and commensurate required return as perceived by senior management. As a result, capital project hurdle rates range from a slight premium over the cost of capital to the highest hurdle rate of approximately double the cost of capital.

Samuel Weaver, Ph.D., was formerly director, financial planning and analysis, for Hershey. He is a certified management accountant and certified financial manager. His position combined the theoretical with the pragmatic and involved the analysis of many different facets of finance in addition to capital expenditure analysis.

If we ignore flotation costs, the NPV is:

$$NPV = \$524{,}373 - 500{,}000 = \$24{,}373$$

With no flotation costs, the project generates an NPV that is greater than zero, so it should be accepted.

What about financing arrangements and issue costs? Because new financing must be raised, the flotation costs are relevant. From the information given, we know that the flotation costs are 2 percent for debt and 10 percent for equity. Because Tripleday uses equal amounts of debt and equity, the weighted average flotation cost, f_A, is:

$$f_A = (E/V) \times f_E + (D/V) \times f_D = .50 \times .10 + .50 \times .02$$
$$= .06, \text{ or } 6\%$$

Remember, the fact that Tripleday can finance the project with all debt or all equity is irrelevant. Because Tripleday needs $500,000 to fund the new plant, the true cost, once we include flotation costs, is $500,000/(1 − f_A) = $500,000/.94 = $531,915. Because the PV of the cash flows is $524,373, the plant has an NPV of $524,373 − 531,915 = −$7,542, so it is no longer a good investment.

INTERNAL EQUITY AND FLOTATION COSTS

Our discussion of flotation costs to this point implicitly assumes that firms always have to raise the capital needed for new investments. In reality, most firms rarely sell equity at all. Instead, their internally generated cash flow is sufficient to cover the equity portion of their capital spending. Only the debt portion must be raised externally.

The use of internal equity doesn't change our approach. We now assign a value of zero to the flotation cost of equity because there is no such cost. In our Tripleday example, the weighted average flotation cost would therefore be:

$$f_A = (E/V) \times f_E + (D/V) \times f_D$$
$$= .50 \times 0 + .50 \times .02$$
$$= .01, \text{ or } 1\%$$

Notice that whether equity is generated internally or externally makes a big difference because external equity has a relatively high flotation cost.

Concept Questions

14.7a   What are flotation costs?

14.7b   How are flotation costs included in an NPV analysis?

Summary and Conclusions   14.8

This chapter has discussed cost of capital. The most important concept is the weighted average cost of capital, or WACC, which we interpreted as the required rate of return on the overall firm. It is also the discount rate appropriate for cash flows that are similar in risk to those of the overall firm. We described how the WACC can be calculated, and we illustrated how it can be used in certain types of analyses.

We also pointed out situations in which it is inappropriate to use the WACC as the discount rate. To handle such cases, we described some alternative approaches to developing discount rates, such as the pure play approach. We also discussed how the flotation costs associated with raising new capital can be included in an NPV analysis.

CONNECT TO FINANCE

Do you use *Connect Finance* to practice what you learned? If you don't, you should—we can help you master the topics presented in this material. Log on to connect.mheducation.com to learn more!

486   **PART 6**   Cost of Capital and Long-Term Financial Policy

Can you answer the following *Connect* Quiz questions?

Section 14.2 A firm has paid dividends of $1.02, $1.10, $1.25, and $1.35 over the past four years, respectively. What is the average dividend growth rate?

Section 14.3 A semiannual, 7 percent bond matures in 14 years and has a face value of $1,000. The market quote on this bond is 101.4. What is the aftertax cost of debt if the tax rate is 21 percent?

Section 14.4 Why is the tax rate applied to the cost of debt but not to the cost of equity or preferred stock when computing a firm's weighted average cost of capital?

Section 14.5 What approach to a project's cost of capital entails the use of another firm's cost of capital rather than the use of your own firm's cost of capital?

Section 14.6 What is the flotation cost of equity for a firm that generates sufficient internal cash flows to cover the equity portion of any capital expenditure?

CHAPTER REVIEW AND SELF-TEST PROBLEMS

14.1 **Calculating the Cost of Equity** Suppose stock in Watta Corporation has a beta of .80. The market risk premium is 6 percent, and the risk-free rate is 6 percent. Watta's last dividend was $1.20 per share, and the dividend is expected to grow at 8 percent indefinitely. The stock currently sells for $45 per share. What is Watta's cost of equity capital?

14.2 **Calculating the WACC** In addition to the information given in the previous problem, suppose Watta has a target debt-equity ratio of 50 percent. Its cost of debt is 9 percent before taxes. If the tax rate is 21 percent, what is the WACC?

14.3 **Flotation Costs** Suppose in the previous problem Watta is seeking $30 million for a new project. The necessary funds will have to be raised externally. Watta's flotation costs for selling debt and equity are 2 percent and 16 percent, respectively. If flotation costs are considered, what is the true cost of the new project?

ANSWERS TO CHAPTER REVIEW AND SELF-TEST PROBLEMS

14.1 We start off with the SML approach. Based on the information given, the expected return on Watta's common stock is:

$$R_E = R_f + \beta_E \times (R_M - R_f)$$
$$= .06 + .80 \times .06$$
$$= .1080, \text{ or } 10.80\%$$

We now use the dividend growth model. The projected dividend is $D_0 \times (1 + g) = \$1.20 \times 1.08 = \$1.296$, so the expected return using this approach is:

$$R_E = D_1/P_0 + g$$
$$= \$1.296/\$45 + .08$$
$$= .1088, \text{ or } 10.88\%$$

Because these two estimates, 10.80 percent and 10.88 percent, are fairly close, we will average them. Watta's cost of equity is approximately 10.84 percent.

14.2 Because the target debt-equity ratio is .50, Watta uses $.50 in debt for every $1 in equity. In other words, Watta's target capital structure is 1/3 debt and 2/3 equity. The WACC is thus:

$$WACC = (E/V) \times R_E + (D/V) \times R_D \times (1 - T_C)$$
$$= 2/3 \times .1084 + 1/3 \times .09 \times (1 - .21)$$
$$= .0960, \text{ or } 9.60\%$$

14.3 Because Watta uses both debt and equity to finance its operations, we first need the weighted average flotation cost. As in the previous problem, the percentage of equity financing is 2/3, so the weighted average cost is:

$$f_A = (E/V) \times f_E + (D/V) \times f_D$$
$$= 2/3 \times .16 + 1/3 \times .02$$
$$= .1133, \text{ or } 11.33\%$$

If Watta needs $30 million after flotation costs, then the true cost of the project is $30 million/$(1 - f_A)$ = $30 million/.8867 = $33.83 million.

CONCEPTS REVIEW AND CRITICAL THINKING QUESTIONS

1. **WACC** [LO3] On the most basic level, if a firm's WACC is 12 percent, what does this mean?

2. **Book Values versus Market Values** [LO3] In calculating the WACC, if you had to use book values for either debt or equity, which would you choose? Why?

3. **Project Risk** [LO5] If you can borrow all the money you need for a project at 6 percent, doesn't it follow that 6 percent is your cost of capital for the project?

4. **WACC and Taxes** [LO3] Why do we use an aftertax figure for cost of debt but not for cost of equity?

5. **DCF Cost of Equity Estimation** [LO1] What are the advantages of using the DCF model for determining the cost of equity capital? What are the disadvantages? What specific piece of information do you need to find the cost of equity using this model? What are some of the ways in which you could get this estimate?

6. **SML Cost of Equity Estimation** [LO1] What are the advantages of using the SML approach to finding the cost of equity capital? What are the disadvantages? What specific pieces of information are needed to use this method? Are all of these variables observable, or do they need to be estimated? What are some of the ways in which you could get these estimates?

7. **Cost of Debt Estimation** [LO2] How do you determine the appropriate cost of debt for a company? Does it make a difference if the company's debt is privately placed as opposed to being publicly traded? How would you estimate the cost of debt for a firm whose only debt issues are privately held by institutional investors?

8. **Cost of Capital** [LO5] Suppose Tom O'Bedlam, president of Bedlam Products, Inc., has hired you to determine the firm's cost of debt and cost of equity capital.

   a. The stock currently sells for $50 per share, and the dividend per share will probably be about $5. Tom argues, "It will cost us $5 per share to use the stockholders' money this year, so the cost of equity is equal to 10 percent (= $5/50)." What's wrong with this conclusion?

   b. Based on the most recent financial statements, Bedlam Products's total liabilities are $8 million. Total interest expense for the coming year will be about

$1 million. Tom therefore reasons, "We owe $8 million, and we will pay $1 million interest. Therefore, our cost of debt is obviously $1 million/8 million = .125, or 12.5%." What's wrong with this conclusion?

c. Based on his own analysis, Tom is recommending that the company increase its use of equity financing because "Debt costs 12.5 percent, but equity costs only 10 percent; thus equity is cheaper." Ignoring all the other issues, what do you think about the conclusion that the cost of equity is less than the cost of debt?

9. **Company Risk versus Project Risk** [LO5] Both Dow Chemical Company, a large natural gas user, and Superior Oil, a major natural gas producer, are thinking of investing in natural gas wells near Houston. Both companies are all equity financed. Dow and Superior are looking at identical projects. They've analyzed their respective investments, which would involve a negative cash flow now and positive expected cash flows in the future. These cash flows would be the same for both firms. No debt would be used to finance the projects. Both companies estimate that their projects would have a net present value of $1 million at an 18 percent discount rate and a −$1.1 million NPV at a 22 percent discount rate. Dow has a beta of 1.25, whereas Superior has a beta of .75. The expected risk premium on the market is 8 percent, and risk-free bonds are yielding 12 percent. Should either company proceed? Should both? Explain.

10. **Divisional Cost of Capital** [LO5] Under what circumstances would it be appropriate for a firm to use different costs of capital for its different operating divisions? If the overall firm WACC were used as the hurdle rate for all divisions, would the riskier divisions or the more conservative divisions tend to get most of the investment projects? Why? If you were to try to estimate the appropriate cost of capital for different divisions, what problems might you encounter? What are two techniques you could use to develop a rough estimate for each division's cost of capital?

QUESTIONS AND PROBLEMS

BASIC
(Questions 1–19)

1. **Calculating Cost of Equity** [LO1] The Drogon Co. just issued a dividend of $2.80 per share on its common stock. The company is expected to maintain a constant 4.5 percent growth rate in its dividends indefinitely. If the stock sells for $58 a share, what is the company's cost of equity?

2. **Calculating Cost of Equity** [LO1] The Rhaegel Corporation's common stock has a beta of 1.07. If the risk-free rate is 3.5 percent and the expected return on the market is 10 percent, what is the company's cost of equity capital?

3. **Calculating Cost of Equity** [LO1] Stock in Daenerys Industries has a beta of 1.05. The market risk premium is 7 percent, and T-bills are currently yielding 3.4 percent. The company's most recent dividend was $2.35 per share, and dividends are expected to grow at an annual rate of 4.1 percent indefinitely. If the stock sells for $43 per share, what is your best estimate of the company's cost of equity?

4. **Estimating the DCF Growth Rate** [LO1] Suppose Stark, Ltd., just issued a dividend of $2.51 per share on its common stock. The company paid dividends of $2.01, $2.17, $2.25, and $2.36 per share in the last four years. If the stock currently sells for $43, what is your best estimate of the company's cost of equity capital using the arithmetic average growth rate in dividends? What if you use the geometric average growth rate?

5. **Calculating Cost of Preferred Stock** [LO1] Holdup Bank has an issue of preferred stock with a stated dividend of $4.25 that just sold for $93 per share. What is the bank's cost of preferred stock?

6. **Calculating Cost of Debt** [LO2] Viserion, Inc., is trying to determine its cost of debt. The firm has a debt issue outstanding with 23 years to maturity that is quoted at 103 percent of face value. The issue makes semiannual payments and has an embedded cost of 6 percent annually. What is the company's pretax cost of debt? If the tax rate is 21 percent, what is the aftertax cost of debt?

7. **Calculating Cost of Debt** [LO2] Jiminy's Cricket Farm issued a 30-year, 6 percent semiannual bond three years ago. The bond currently sells for 93 percent of its face value. The company's tax rate is 22 percent.

   a. What is the pretax cost of debt?

   b. What is the aftertax cost of debt?

   c. Which is more relevant, the pretax or the aftertax cost of debt? Why?

8. **Calculating Cost of Debt** [LO2] For the firm in Problem 7, suppose the book value of the debt issue is $95 million. In addition, the company has a second debt issue on the market, a zero coupon bond with eight years left to maturity; the book value of this issue is $40 million, and the bonds sell for 67 percent of par. What is the company's total book value of debt? The total market value? What is your best estimate of the aftertax cost of debt now?

9. **Calculating WACC** [LO3] Targaryen Corporation has a target capital structure of 70 percent common stock, 5 percent preferred stock, and 25 percent debt. Its cost of equity is 10 percent, the cost of preferred stock is 5 percent, and the pretax cost of debt is 6 percent. The relevant tax rate is 23 percent.

   a. What is the company's WACC?

   b. The company president has approached you about the company's capital structure. He wants to know why the company doesn't use more preferred stock financing because it costs less than debt. What would you tell the president?

10. **Taxes and WACC** [LO3] Lannister Manufacturing has a target debt-equity ratio of .55. Its cost of equity is 11 percent, and its cost of debt is 6 percent. If the tax rate is 21 percent, what is the company's WACC?

11. **Finding the Target Capital Structure** [LO3] Fama's Llamas has a weighted average cost of capital of 7.9 percent. The company's cost of equity is 11 percent, and its pretax cost of debt is 5.8 percent. The tax rate is 25 percent. What is the company's target debt-equity ratio?

12. **Book Value versus Market Value** [LO3] Dinklage Corp. has 7 million shares of common stock outstanding. The current share price is $68, and the book value per share is $8. The company also has two bond issues outstanding. The first bond issue has a face value of $70 million, a coupon rate of 6 percent, and sells for 97 percent of par. The second issue has a face value of $40 million, a coupon rate of 6.5 percent, and sells for 108 percent of par. The first issue matures in 21 years, the second in 6 years. Both bonds make semiannual coupon payments.

   a. What are the company's capital structure weights on a book value basis?

   b. What are the company's capital structure weights on a market value basis?

   c. Which are more relevant, the book or market value weights? Why?

13. **Calculating the WACC** [LO3] In Problem 12, suppose the most recent dividend was $3.25 and the dividend growth rate is 5 percent. Assume that the overall cost of debt is the weighted average of that implied by the two outstanding debt issues. Both bonds make semiannual payments. The tax rate is 21 percent. What is the company's WACC?

14. **WACC** [LO3] Starset, Inc., has a target debt-equity ratio of .85. Its WACC is 9.1 percent, and the tax rate is 23 percent.

   a. If the company's cost of equity is 14 percent, what is its pretax cost of debt?

   b. If instead you know that the aftertax cost of debt is 6.5 percent, what is the cost of equity?

15. **Finding the WACC** [LO3] Given the following information for Watson Power Co., find the WACC. Assume the company's tax rate is 21 percent.

Debt:	15,000 bonds with a 5.8 percent coupon outstanding, $1,000 par value, 25 years to maturity, selling for 108 percent of par; the bonds make semiannual payments.
Common stock:	575,000 shares outstanding, selling for $64 per share; the beta is 1.09.
Preferred stock:	35,000 shares of 2.8 percent preferred stock outstanding, currently selling for $65 per share.
Market:	7 percent market risk premium and 3.2 percent risk-free rate.

16. **Finding the WACC** [LO3] Titan Mining Corporation has 7.5 million shares of common stock outstanding, 250,000 shares of 4.2 percent preferred stock outstanding, and 140,000 bonds with a semiannual coupon of 5.1 percent outstanding, par value $1,000 each. The common stock currently sells for $51 per share and has a beta of 1.15, the preferred stock currently sells for $103 per share, and the bonds have 15 years to maturity and sell for 107 percent of par. The market risk premium is 7.5 percent, T-bills are yielding 2.4 percent, and the company's tax rate is 22 percent.

   a. What is the firm's market value capital structure?

   b. If the company is evaluating a new investment project that has the same risk as the firm's typical project, what rate should the firm use to discount the project's cash flows?

17. **SML and WACC** [LO1] An all-equity firm is considering the following projects:

Project	Beta	IRR
W	.85	8.9%
X	.92	10.8
Y	1.09	12.8
Z	1.35	13.3

   The T-bill rate is 4 percent, and the expected return on the market is 11 percent.

   a. Which projects have a higher expected return than the firm's 11 percent cost of capital?

   b. Which projects should be accepted?

   c. Which projects would be incorrectly accepted or rejected if the firm's overall cost of capital were used as a hurdle rate?

18. **Calculating Flotation Costs** [LO4] Suppose your company needs $24 million to build a new assembly line. Your target debt-equity ratio is .75. The flotation cost for new equity is 7 percent, but the flotation cost for debt is only 3 percent. Your boss has decided to fund the project by borrowing money because the flotation costs are lower and the needed funds are relatively small.

   a. What do you think about the rationale behind borrowing the entire amount?

   b. What is your company's weighted average flotation cost, assuming all equity is raised externally?

c. What is the true cost of building the new assembly line after taking flotation costs into account? Does it matter in this case that the entire amount is being raised from debt?

19. **Calculating Flotation Costs** [LO4] Cully Company needs to raise $80 million to start a new project and will raise the money by selling new bonds. The company will generate no internal equity for the foreseeable future. The company has a target capital structure of 70 percent common stock, 5 percent preferred stock, and 25 percent debt. Flotation costs for issuing new common stock are 7 percent, for new preferred stock, 4 percent, and for new debt, 2 percent. What is the true initial cost figure the company should use when evaluating its project?

20. **WACC and NPV** [LO3, 5] Sommer, Inc., is considering a project that will result in initial aftertax cash savings of $2.3 million at the end of the first year, and these savings will grow at a rate of 2 percent per year indefinitely. The firm has a target debt-equity ratio of .60, a cost of equity of 10 percent, and an aftertax cost of debt of 4.6 percent. The cost-saving proposal is somewhat riskier than the usual project the firm undertakes; management uses the subjective approach and applies an adjustment factor of +3 percent to the cost of capital for such risky projects. Under what circumstances should the company take on the project?

INTERMEDIATE
(Questions 20–25)

21. **Flotation Costs** [LO4] Being Human, Inc., recently issued new securities to finance a new TV show. The project cost $35 million, and the company paid $2.2 million in flotation costs. In addition, the equity issued had a flotation cost of 7 percent of the amount raised, whereas the debt issued had a flotation cost of 3 percent of the amount raised. If the company issued new securities in the same proportion as its target capital structure, what is the company's target debt-equity ratio?

22. **Calculating the Cost of Debt** [LO2] Ying Import has several bond issues outstanding, each making semiannual interest payments. The bonds are listed in the following table. If the corporate tax rate is 22 percent, what is the aftertax cost of the company's debt?

Bond	Coupon Rate	Price Quote	Maturity	Face Value
1	5.00%	103.18	5 years	$45,000,000
2	7.10	112.80	8 years	40,000,000
3	6.30	107.45	$15\frac{1}{2}$ years	50,000,000
4	5.90	102.75	25 years	65,000,000

23. **Calculating the Cost of Equity** [LO1] Minder Industries stock has a beta of 1.08. The company just paid a dividend of $.65, and the dividends are expected to grow at 4 percent. The expected return on the market is 10.5 percent, and Treasury bills are yielding 3.4 percent. The most recent stock price for the company is $72.

a. Calculate the cost of equity using the DCF method.

b. Calculate the cost of equity using the SML method.

c. Why do you think your estimates in (a) and (b) are so different?

24. **Adjusted Cash Flow from Assets** [LO3] Pearl Corp. is expected to have an EBIT of $1.8 million next year. Depreciation, the increase in net working capital, and capital spending are expected to be $155,000, $75,000, and $115,000, respectively. All are expected to grow at 18 percent per year for four years. The company currently has $9.5 million in debt and 750,000 shares outstanding. After Year 5, the adjusted cash flow from assets is expected to grow at 3 percent indefinitely. The company's

WACC is 8.5 percent and the tax rate is 21 percent. What is the price per share of the company's stock?

25. **Adjusted Cash Flow from Assets** [LO3] In the previous problem, instead of a perpetual growth rate in adjusted cash flow from assets, you decide to calculate the terminal value of the company with the price-sales ratio. You believe that Year 5 sales will be $16.9 million and the appropriate price-sales ratio is 2.9. What is your new estimate of the current share price?

CHALLENGE
(Questions 26–31)

26. **Adjusted Cash Flow from Assets** [LO3] You have looked at the current financial statements for Reigle Homes, Co. The company has an EBIT of $3.15 million this year. Depreciation, the increase in net working capital, and capital spending were $265,000, $105,000, and $495,000, respectively. You expect that over the next five years, EBIT will grow at 15 percent per year, depreciation and capital spending will grow at 20 percent per year, and NWC will grow at 10 percent per year. The company has $19.5 million in debt and 400,000 shares outstanding. After Year 5, the adjusted cash flow from assets is expected to grow at 3.5 percent indefinitely. The company's WACC is 9.25 percent, and the tax rate is 22 percent. What is the price per share of the company's stock?

27. **Adjusted Cash Flow from Assets** [LO3] In the previous problem, suppose you believe that sales in five years will be $29.2 million and the price-sales ratio will be 2.45. What is the share price now?

28. **Flotation Costs and NPV** [LO3, 4] Photochronograph Corporation (PC) manufactures time series photographic equipment. It is currently at its target debt-equity ratio of .60. It's considering building a new $65 million manufacturing facility. This new plant is expected to generate aftertax cash flows of $9.4 million in perpetuity. The company raises all equity from outside financing. There are three financing options:

    1. *A new issue of common stock*: The flotation costs of the new common stock would be 8 percent of the amount raised. The required return on the company's new equity is 14 percent.

    2. *A new issue of 20-year bonds*: The flotation costs of the new bonds would be 4 percent of the proceeds. If the company issues these new bonds at an annual coupon rate of 8 percent, they will sell at par.

    3. *Increased use of accounts payable financing*: Because this financing is part of the company's ongoing daily business, it has no flotation costs, and the company assigns it a cost that is the same as the overall firm WACC. Management has a target ratio of accounts payable to long-term debt of .15. (Assume there is no difference between the pretax and aftertax accounts payable cost.)

    What is the NPV of the new plant? Assume that PC has a 21 percent tax rate.

29. **Flotation Costs** [LO3] Lucas Corp. has a debt-equity ratio of .65. The company is considering a new plant that will cost $51 million to build. When the company issues new equity, it incurs a flotation cost of 7 percent. The flotation cost on new debt is 2.7 percent. What is the initial cost of the plant if the company raises all equity externally? What if it typically uses 60 percent retained earnings? What if all equity investment is financed through retained earnings?

30. **Project Evaluation** [LO3, 4] This is a comprehensive project evaluation problem bringing together much of what you have learned in this and previous chapters. Suppose you have been hired as a financial consultant to Defense Electronics, Inc. (DEI), a large, publicly traded firm that is the market share leader in radar detection systems (RDSs). The company is looking at setting up a manufacturing plant overseas to produce a new line of RDSs. This will be a five-year project.

The company bought some land three years ago for $2.7 million in anticipation of using it as a toxic dump site for waste chemicals, but it built a piping system to safely discard the chemicals instead. The land was appraised last week for $3.8 million on an aftertax basis. In five years, the aftertax value of the land will be $4.1 million, but the company expects to keep the land for a future project. The company wants to build its new manufacturing plant on this land; the plant and equipment will cost $34 million to build. The following market data on DEI's securities are current:

Debt:	195,000 bonds with a coupon rate of 6.2 percent outstanding, 25 years to maturity, selling for 106 percent of par; the bonds have a $1,000 par value each and make semiannual payments.
Common stock:	8,100,000 shares outstanding, selling for $63 per share; the beta is 1.1.
Preferred stock:	450,000 shares of 4.25 percent preferred stock outstanding, selling for $83 per share.
Market:	7 percent expected market risk premium; 3.1 percent risk-free rate.

DEI uses G.M. Wharton as its lead underwriter. Wharton charges DEI spreads of 7 percent on new common stock issues, 5 percent on new preferred stock issues, and 3 percent on new debt issues. Wharton has included all direct and indirect issuance costs (along with its profit) in setting these spreads. Wharton has recommended to DEI that it raise the funds needed to build the plant by issuing new shares of common stock. DEI's tax rate is 25 percent. The project requires $1,500,000 in initial net working capital investment to get operational. Assume DEI raises all equity for new projects externally.

a. Calculate the project's initial Time 0 cash flow, taking into account all side effects.

b. The new RDS project is somewhat riskier than a typical project for DEI, primarily because the plant is being located overseas. Management has told you to use an adjustment factor of +2 percent to account for this increased riskiness. Calculate the appropriate discount rate to use when evaluating DEI's project.

c. The manufacturing plant has an eight-year tax life, and DEI uses straight-line depreciation to a zero salvage value. At the end of the project (that is, the end of Year 5), the plant and equipment can be scrapped for $4.9 million. What is the aftertax salvage value of this plant and equipment?

d. The company will incur $6.9 million in annual fixed costs. The plan is to manufacture 12,100 RDSs per year and sell them at $11,450 per machine; the variable production costs are $9,500 per RDS. What is the annual operating cash flow (OCF) from this project?

e. DEI's comptroller is primarily interested in the impact of DEI's investments on the bottom line of reported accounting statements. What will you tell her is the accounting break-even quantity of RDSs sold for this project?

f. Finally, DEI's president wants you to throw all your calculations, assumptions, and everything else into the report for the chief financial officer; all he wants to know is what the RDS project's internal rate of return (IRR) and net present value (NPV) are. What will you report?

31. **Adjusted Cash Flow from Assets** [LO3] Suppose you are looking at a company with no change in capital spending, no change in net working capital, and no depreciation. Since the company is not increasing its assets, EBIT is constant. What is the value of the company?

EXCEL MASTER IT! PROBLEM

You want to calculate the WACC for auto parts retailer AutoZone (AZO). Complete the following steps to construct a spreadsheet that can be updated.

a. Using an input for the ticker symbol, create hyperlinks to the web pages that you will need to find all of the information necessary to calculate the cost of equity. Use a market risk premium of 7 percent when using CAPM.

b. Create hyperlinks to go to the FINRA bond quote website and the SEC EDGAR database and find the information for the company's bonds. Create a table that calculates the cost of debt for the company. Assume the tax rate is 21 percent.

c. Finally, calculate the market value weights for debt and equity. What is the WACC for AutoZone?

MINICASE

Cost of Capital for Swan Motors

You have recently been hired by Swan Motors, Inc. (SMI), in its relatively new treasury management department. SMI was founded eight years ago by Joe Swan. Joe found a method to manufacture a cheaper battery that will hold a larger charge, giving a car powered by the battery a range of 700 miles before requiring a charge. The cars manufactured by SMI are mid-sized and carry a price that allows the company to compete with other mainstream auto manufacturers. The company is privately owned by Joe and his family, and it had sales of $97 million last year.

SMI primarily sells to customers who buy the cars online, although it does have a limited number of company-owned dealerships. The customer selects any customization and makes a deposit of 20 percent of the purchase price. After the order is taken, the car is made to order, typically within 45 days. SMI's growth to date has come from its profits. When the company had sufficient capital, it would expand production. Relatively little formal analysis has been used in its capital budgeting process. Joe has just read about capital budgeting techniques and has come to you for help. For starters, the company has never attempted to determine its cost of capital, and Joe would like you to perform the analysis. Because the company is privately owned, it is difficult to determine the cost of equity for the company. Joe wants you to use the pure play approach to estimate the cost of capital for SMI, and he has chosen Tesla Motors as a representative company. The following questions will lead you through the steps to calculate this estimate.

QUESTIONS

1. Most publicly traded corporations are required to submit quarterly (10-Q) and annual (10-K) reports to the SEC detailing the financial operations of the company over the past quarter or year, respectively. These corporate filings are available on the SEC website at www.sec.gov. Go to the SEC website, follow the "Search for Company Filings" link, and search for SEC filings made by Tesla Motors (TSLA). Find the most recent 10-Q or 10-K, and download the form. Look on the balance sheet to find the book value of debt and the book value of equity.

2. To estimate the cost of equity for TSLA, go to finance .yahoo.com and enter the ticker symbol TSLA. Follow the links to answer the following questions: What is the most recent stock price listed for TSLA? What is the market value of equity, or market capitalization? How many shares of stock does TSLA have outstanding? What is the most recent annual dividend? Can you use the dividend discount model in this case? What is the beta for TSLA? Now go back to finance.yahoo.com and follow the "Bonds" link. What is the yield on three-month Treasury bills? Using the historical market risk premium, what is the cost of equity for TSLA using CAPM?

3. You now need to calculate the cost of debt for TSLA. Go to finra-markets.morningstar.com, enter TSLA as the company, and find the yield to maturity for each of TSLA's bonds. What is the weighted average cost of debt for TSLA using the book value weights and using the market value weights? Does it make a difference in this case if you use book value weights or market value weights?

4. You now have all the necessary information to calculate the weighted average cost of capital for TSLA. Calculate this using book value weights and market value weights, assuming TSLA has a 21 percent tax rate. Which number is more relevant?

5. You used TSLA as a pure play company to estimate the cost of capital for SMI. Are there any potential problems with this approach in this situation?

Raising Capital

15 Chapter

ON MARCH 2, 2017, in one of the most anticipated IPOs of the year, video messaging company Snap, operator of Snapchat, went public. Assisted by investment banks Morgan Stanley, Goldman Sachs, J.P. Morgan, and a host of others, the company offered 145 million shares of stock at a price of $17 per share. The first trade on the New York Stock Exchange was at $24 per share, a 41 percent jump from the initial stock price. The stock quickly rose to $26.05, before closing at $24.48. What made Snap's stock offering particularly unique was that the company sold Class A shares, which had no voting rights, in the IPO. The company also had Class B shares, with one vote per share, and Class C stock, with 10 votes per share. The Class C stock was held entirely by the company's founders. In this chapter, we will examine the process by which companies such as Snap sell stock to the public, the costs of doing so, and the role of investment banks in the process.

Learning Objectives

After studying this chapter, you should be able to:

LO1 Describe the venture capital market and its role in the financing of new, high-risk ventures.

LO2 Explain how securities are sold to the public and the role of investment banks in the process.

LO3 Define initial public offerings and some of the costs of going public.

LO4 Demonstrate how rights are issued to existing shareholders and how to value those rights.

©by_adri/iStockPhotoGetty/images

For updates on the latest happenings in finance, visit fundamentalsofcorporatefinance.blogspot.com.

All firms must, at varying times, obtain capital. To do so, a firm must either borrow the money (debt financing), sell a portion of the firm (equity financing), or both. How a firm raises capital depends a great deal on the size of the firm, its life-cycle stage, and its growth prospects.

In this chapter, we examine some of the ways in which firms actually raise capital. We begin by looking at companies in the early stages of their lives and the importance of venture capital for such firms. We then look at the process of going public and the role of investment banks. Along the way, we discuss many of the issues associated with selling securities to the public and their implications for all types of firms. We close the chapter with a discussion of sources of debt capital.[1]

---

[1]We are indebted to Jay R. Ritter of the University of Florida and M. Shane Hadden of *The Currency Report* (www.globalcurrencyreport.com) for helpful comments and suggestions for this chapter.

15.1 The Financing Life Cycle of a Firm: Early-Stage Financing and Venture Capital

One day, you and a friend have a great idea for a new computer software product that helps users communicate using the next-generation meganet. Filled with entrepreneurial zeal, you christen the product Megacomm and set about bringing it to market.

Working nights and weekends, you are able to create a prototype of your product. It doesn't actually work, but at least you can show it around to illustrate your idea. To actually develop the product, you need to hire programmers, buy computers, rent office space, and so on. Unfortunately, because you are both college students, your combined assets are not sufficient to fund a pizza party, much less a start-up company. You need what is often referred to as OPM—other people's money.

Your first thought might be to approach a bank for a loan. You would probably discover that banks are generally not interested in making loans to start-up companies with no assets (other than an idea) run by fledgling entrepreneurs with no track record. Instead your search for capital would likely lead you to the **venture capital (VC)** market.

venture capital (VC)
Financing for new, often high-risk, ventures.

VENTURE CAPITAL

The term *venture capital* does not have a precise meaning, but it generally refers to financing for new, often high-risk, ventures. For example, before it went public, Google was VC financed. Individual venture capitalists invest their own money; so-called "angels" are usually individual VC investors, but they tend to specialize in smaller deals. Venture capital firms specialize in pooling funds from various sources and investing them. The underlying sources of funds for such firms include individuals, pension funds, insurance companies, large corporations, and even university endowment funds. The broad term *private equity* is often used to label the rapidly growing area of equity financing for nonpublic companies.[2]

Venture capitalists and venture capital firms recognize that many or even most new ventures will not fly, but the occasional one will. The potential profits are enormous in such cases. To limit their risk, venture capitalists generally provide financing in stages. At each stage, enough money is invested to reach the next milestone or planning stage. For example, the *first-stage financing* might be enough to get a prototype built and a manufacturing plan completed. Based on the results, the *second-stage financing* might be a major investment needed to actually begin manufacturing, marketing, and distribution. There might be many such stages, each of which represents a key step in the process of growing the company.

Venture capital firms often specialize in different stages. Some specialize in very early "seed money," or ground floor, financing. In contrast, financing in the later stages might come from venture capitalists specializing in so-called mezzanine-level financing, where *mezzanine level* refers to the level just above the ground floor.

The fact that financing is available in stages and is contingent on specified goals being met is a powerful motivating force for the firm's founders. Often, the founders receive relatively little in the way of salary and have substantial portions of their personal assets tied up in the business. At each stage of financing, the value of the founders' stake grows and the probability of success rises.

In addition to providing financing, venture capitalists often actively participate in running the firm, providing the benefit of experience with previous start-ups as well as general business expertise. This is especially true when the firm's founders have little or no hands-on experience in running a company.

For more on the VC industry, check out **nvca.org**.

---

[2]So-called "vulture capitalists" specialize in high-risk investments in established, but financially distressed, firms. Vulgar capitalists invest in firms that have bad taste (**OK**, we made up this last bit).

SOME VENTURE CAPITAL REALITIES

Although there is a large venture capital market, the truth is that access to venture capital is really very limited. Venture capital companies receive huge numbers of unsolicited proposals, the vast majority of which end up in the circular file unread. Venture capitalists rely heavily on informal networks of lawyers, accountants, bankers, and other venture capitalists to help identify potential investments. As a result, personal contacts are important in gaining access to the venture capital market; it is very much an "introduction" market.

Another simple fact about venture capital is that it is incredibly expensive. In a typical deal, the venture capitalist will demand (and get) 40 percent or more of the equity in the company. Venture capitalists frequently hold voting preferred stock, giving them various priorities in the event that the company is sold or liquidated. The venture capitalist will typically demand (and get) several seats on the company's board of directors and may even appoint one or more members of senior management.

CHOOSING A VENTURE CAPITALIST

Some start-up companies, particularly those headed by experienced, previously successful entrepreneurs, will be in such demand that they will have the luxury of looking beyond the money in choosing a venture capitalist. There are some key considerations in such a case, some of which can be summarized as follows:

The Internet is a tremendous source of venture capital information, both for suppliers and demanders of capital. For example, the site at **www.dealflow.com** prompts you to search the firm's database as either an entrepreneur (capital seeker) or a venture capitalist (capital supplier).

1. *Financial strength is important:* The venture capitalist needs to have the resources and financial reserves for additional financing stages should they become necessary. This doesn't mean that bigger is necessarily better because of our next consideration.

2. *Style is important:* Some venture capitalists will wish to be very much involved in day-to-day operations and decision making, whereas others will be content with monthly reports. Which type is better depends on the firm and also on the venture capitalists' business skills. In addition, a large venture capital firm may be less flexible and more bureaucratic than a smaller "boutique" firm.

3. *References are important:* Has the venture capitalist been successful with similar firms? Of equal importance, how has the venture capitalist dealt with situations that didn't work out?

4. *Contacts are important:* A venture capitalist may be able to help the business in ways other than helping with financing and management by providing introductions to potentially important customers, suppliers, and other industry contacts. Venture capitalist firms frequently specialize in a few particular industries, and such specialization could prove quite valuable.

5. *Exit strategy is important:* Venture capitalists are generally not long-term investors. How and under what circumstances the venture capitalist will "cash out" of the business should be carefully evaluated.

CONCLUSION

If a start-up succeeds, the big payoff frequently comes when the company is sold to another company or goes public. Either way, investment bankers are often involved in the process. We discuss the process of selling securities to the public in the next several sections, paying particular attention to the process of going public.

Concept Questions

15.1a   What is venture capital?

15.1b   Why is venture capital often provided in stages?

15.2 Selling Securities to the Public: The Basic Procedure

Many rules and regulations surround the process of selling securities. The Securities Act of 1933 is the origin of federal regulations for all new interstate securities issues. The Securities Exchange Act of 1934 is the basis for regulating securities already outstanding. The Securities and Exchange Commission, or SEC, administers both acts.

A series of steps is involved in issuing securities to the public. In general terms, the basic procedure is as follows:

1. Management's first step in issuing any securities to the public is to obtain approval from the board of directors. In some cases, the number of authorized shares of common stock must be increased. This requires a vote of the shareholders.

registration statement
A statement filed with the SEC that discloses all material information concerning the corporation making a public offering.

2. The firm must prepare a **registration statement** and file it with the SEC. The registration statement is required for all public, interstate issues of securities, with two exceptions:

   a. Loans that mature within nine months.

   b. Issues that involve less than $5 million.

Regulation A
An SEC regulation that exempts public issues of less than $5 million from most registration requirements.

The second exception is known as the *small-issues exemption*. In such a case, simplified procedures are used. Under the basic small-issues exemption, issues of less than $5 million are governed by **Regulation A**, for which only a brief offering statement is needed. Normally, a registration statement contains many pages (50 or more) of financial information, including a financial history, details of the existing business, proposed financing, and plans for the future.

prospectus
A legal document describing details of the issuing corporation and the proposed offering to potential investors.

3. The SEC examines the registration statement during a waiting period. During this time, the firm may distribute copies of a preliminary **prospectus**. The prospectus contains much of the information in the registration statement, and it is given to potential investors by the firm. The preliminary prospectus is sometimes called a **red herring**, in part because bold red letters are printed on the cover.

red herring
A preliminary prospectus distributed to prospective investors in a new issue of securities.

A registration statement becomes effective on the 20th day after its filing unless the SEC sends a *letter of comment* suggesting changes. In that case, after the changes are made, the 20-day waiting period starts again. It is important to note that the SEC does not consider the economic merits of the proposed sale; it merely makes sure that various rules and regulations are followed. Also, the SEC generally does not check the accuracy or truthfulness of information in the prospectus.

The registration statement does not initially contain the price of the new issue. Usually, a price amendment is filed at or near the end of the waiting period, and the registration becomes effective.

4. The company cannot sell these securities during the waiting period. However, oral offers can be made.

5. On the effective date of the registration statement, a price is determined and a full-fledged selling effort gets under way. A final prospectus must accompany the delivery of securities or confirmation of sale, whichever comes first.

tombstone
An advertisement announcing a public offering.

Tombstone advertisements (or *tombstones*) are used by underwriters during and after the waiting period. An example is reproduced in Figure 15.1. The tombstone contains the name of the issuer (the World Wrestling Federation, now known as World Wrestling Entertainment). It provides some information about the issue, and it lists the investment banks (the underwriters) involved with selling the issue. The role of the investment banks in selling securities is discussed more fully in the following sections.

The investment banks on the tombstone are divided into groups called *brackets* based on their participation in the issue, and the names of the banks are listed alphabetically within each bracket. The brackets are often viewed as a kind of pecking order. In general,

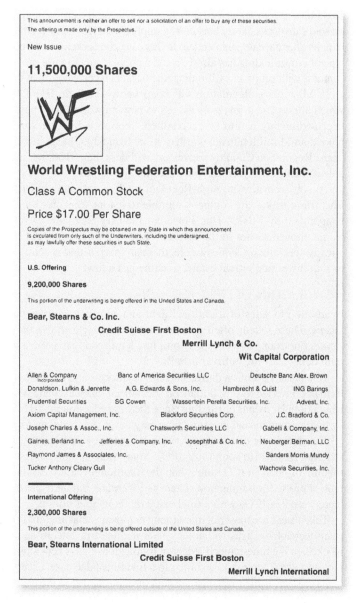

FIGURE 15.1

**An Example of
a Tombstone
Advertisement**

the higher the bracket, the greater is the underwriter's prestige. In recent years, the use of printed tombstones has declined, in part as a cost-saving measure.

CROWDFUNDING

On April 5, 2012, the Jumpstart Our Business Startups ("JOBS") Act was signed into law. A provision of this act allows companies to raise money through *crowdfunding*, which is the practice of raising small amounts of capital from a large number of people, typically via the Internet. Crowdfunding was first used to underwrite the U.S. tour of British rock band Marillion. The JOBS Act allows companies to sell equity by crowdfunding. Originally, the JOBS Act allowed a company to issue up to $1 million in securities in a 12-month period, although this limit was later raised to a maximum of $50 million.

We should make an important distinction about two types of crowdfunding—project crowdfunding and equity crowdfunding. As an example of project crowdfunding, consider the card game Exploding Kittens, which exploded on the crowdfunding website Kickstarter and raised

Learn more about crowdfunding at the Crowdfunding Professional Association website, **www.cfpa.org**.

Check out two of the more well-known project and charitable crowdfunding websites at **www.kickstarter.com** and **www.gofundme.com**.

Crowd Expert has a lot more info on equity crowdfunding at **www.crowdexpert.com**.

See upcoming ICOs at **tokenmarket.net/ico-calendar**.

The SEC has some warnings on ICOs at **www.sec.gov/news /public-statement/statement -clayton-2017-12-11**.

To see the market value of tokens at **coinmarketcap.com/**

$8.8 million from about 220,000 backers. During the crowdfunding campaign, the company presold card decks. Every backer was shipped a deck of cards for the game, beginning about six months after the campaign ended. In this case, the backers were purchasers, not investors. This type of crowdfunding has also become a popular way to raise money for charitable causes. In contrast, with equity crowdfunding, the backers receive equity in the company.

In May 2016, Regulation CF (also known as Title III of the JOBS Act) kicked in, which allows small investors access to new crowdfunding "portals." Previously, investors in crowdfunding had to be "accredited." For an individual, this requirement translates to more than $1 million in net worth or more than $200,000 in income for two of the past three years. Regulation CF allows investors with less than $100,000 in income or assets to invest at least $2,000 per year, up to a maximum of $5,000.

To sell securities through Regulation CF, a company must file a form with the SEC. This filing makes the company eligible to list its securities on a crowdfunding portal that is approved by FINRA (the Financial Industry Regulatory Authority), the same agency we mentioned earlier in the textbook for bond price reporting. Crowdfunding portals are already specializing. For example, there are portals that specialize in only accredited investors, all investors, or real estate, to name just a few.

INITIAL COIN OFFERINGS (ICOs)

In addition to sales of traditional debt and equity, a company can raise funds by selling *tokens*. These tokens often grant the holder the right to use the company's service in the future. For example, a company building a railroad may issue a token that can be used as a train ticket after the railroad is built.

Token sales occur on digital currency platforms and can be easily transferred on the platform or converted to U.S. dollars on specialized token exchanges. This liquidity has made tokens a popular means of funding since their introduction in 2015. Tokens are now purchased by both customers and investors who may never use the token for the service being offered.

The initial sale of a token on a digital currency platform is often called an Initial Coin Offering or ICO (to sound like IPO). Many start-up companies are now choosing to raise funding through an ICO rather than the traditional venture capital channels. The most common platform for issuing new tokens is Ethereum, but there are many competitors. In 2017, there were 234 ICOs with a total value of about $3.7 billion.

Token sales are most popular among companies that are building services based on blockchain technology. This technology is at the heart of bitcoin and other cryptocurrencies. A blockchain is a timestamped ledger of transactions that is kept among a network of users without centralized control. It is similar to a traditional database, except that cryptography is used to make it infeasible to change the data once it is added to the chain. Many industries, including finance, are now updating their recordkeeping infrastructure with blockchain technology.

Token sales can also serve as an effective marketing tool. This is especially true if the business benefits from network effects as the potential for price appreciation in the tokens attracts new customers. The increase in customers increases the value of the service, which in turn increases the value of the tokens. For example, Civic is building a blockchain-based identity platform, and its currency is used to purchase identity verification services from trusted parties. The company raised $33 million in June 2017 through an ICO of the CVC token. The total value of the tokens at the end of 2017 was $224 million.

Concept Questions

15.2a What are the basic procedures involved in selling a new issue?
15.2b What is a registration statement?

Alternative Issue Methods

15.3

When a company decides to issue a new security, it can sell it as a public issue or a private issue. In the case of a public issue, the firm is required to register the issue with the SEC. If the issue is to be sold to fewer than 35 investors, the sale can be carried out privately. In this case, a registration statement is not required.[3]

For equity sales, there are two kinds of public issues: a **general cash offer** and a **rights offer** (or *rights offering*). With a cash offer, securities are offered to the general public. With a rights offer, securities are initially offered only to existing owners. Rights offers are fairly common in other countries, but they are relatively rare in the United States, particularly in recent years. We therefore focus primarily on cash offers in this chapter.

The first public equity issue that is made by a company is referred to as an **initial public offering (IPO)**, or an *unseasoned new issue*. This issue occurs when a company decides to go public. Obviously, all initial public offerings are cash offers. If the firm's existing shareholders wanted to buy the shares, the firm wouldn't have to sell them publicly in the first place.

A **seasoned equity offering (SEO)** is a new issue for a company with securities that have been previously issued.[4] A seasoned equity offering of common stock can be made by using a cash offer or a rights offer.

These methods of issuing new securities are shown in Table 15.1. They are discussed in more detail in Sections 15.4 through 15.8.

general cash offer
An issue of securities offered for sale to the general public on a cash basis.

rights offer
A public issue of securities in which securities are first offered to existing shareholders. Also called a *rights offering*.

initial public offering (IPO)
A company's first equity issue made available to the public. Also called an *unseasoned new issue*.

seasoned equity offering (SEO)
A new equity issue of securities by a company that has previously issued securities to the public.

TABLE 15.1

The Methods of Issuing New Securities

Method	Type	Definition
Public Traditional negotiated cash offer	Firm commitment cash offer	The company negotiates an agreement with an investment banker to underwrite and distribute the new shares. A specified number of shares are bought by underwriters and sold at a higher price.
	Best efforts cash offer	The company has investment bankers sell as many of the new shares as possible at the agreed-upon price. There is no guarantee concerning how much cash will be raised.
	Dutch auction cash offer	The company has investment bankers auction shares to determine the highest offer price obtainable for a given number of shares to be sold.
Privileged subscription	Direct rights offer	The company offers the new stock directly to its existing shareholders.
	Standby rights offer	Like the direct rights offer, this contains a privileged subscription arrangement with existing shareholders. The net proceeds are guaranteed by the underwriters.
Nontraditional cash offer	Shelf cash offer	Qualifying companies can authorize all shares they expect to sell over a two-year period and sell them when needed.
	Competitive firm cash offer	The company can elect to award the underwriting contract through a public auction instead of negotiation.
Private	Direct placement	Securities are sold directly to the purchaser, who, at least until recently, generally could not resell securities for at least two years.

IPO information is widely available. Try IPO Scoop at **www.iposcoop.com**.

---

[3]A variety of different arrangements can be made for private equity issues. Selling unregistered securities avoids the costs of complying with the Securities Exchange Act of 1934. Regulation significantly restricts the resale of unregistered equity securities. For example, the purchaser may be required to hold the securities for at least one year (or more). Many of the restrictions were significantly eased in 1990 for very large institutional investors. The private placement of bonds is discussed in a later section.

[4]The terms *follow-on offering* and *secondary offering* are also commonly used.

> ### Concept Questions
>
> **15.3a**   What is the difference between a rights offer and a cash offer?
>
> **15.3b**   Why is an initial public offering necessarily a cash offer?

15.4   Underwriters

underwriters
Investment firms that act as intermediaries between a company selling securities and the investing public.

If the public issue of securities is a cash offer, **underwriters** are usually involved. Underwriting is an important line of business for large investment firms such as Morgan Stanley. Underwriters perform services such as the following for corporate issuers:

1. Formulating the method used to issue the securities.
2. Pricing the new securities.
3. Selling the new securities.

Typically, the underwriter buys the securities for less than the offering price and accepts the risk of not being able to sell them. Because underwriting involves risk, underwriters usually combine to form an underwriting group called a **syndicate** to share the risk and to help sell the issue.

syndicate
A group of underwriters formed to share the risk and to help sell an issue.

In a syndicate, one or more managers arrange, or co-manage, the offering. The lead manager typically has the responsibility of dealing with the issuer and pricing the securities. The other underwriters in the syndicate serve primarily to distribute the issue and produce research reports later on. In recent years, it has become fairly common for a syndicate to consist of only a small number of co-managers.

gross spread
Compensation to the underwriter, determined by the difference between the underwriter's buying price and the offering price.

The difference between the underwriter's buying price and the offering price is called the **gross spread**, or underwriting discount. It is the basic compensation received by the underwriter. Sometimes, on smaller deals, the underwriter will get noncash compensation in the form of warrants and stock in addition to the spread.[5]

CHOOSING AN UNDERWRITER

A firm can offer its securities to the highest bidding underwriter on a *competitive offer* basis, or it can negotiate directly with an underwriter. Except for a few large firms, companies usually offer new issues of debt and equity on a *negotiated offer* basis. The exception is public utility holding companies, which are essentially required to use competitive underwriting.

There is evidence that competitive underwriting is cheaper to use than negotiated underwriting. The underlying reasons for the dominance of negotiated underwriting in the United States are the subject of ongoing debate.

TYPES OF UNDERWRITING

Three basic types of underwriting are involved in a cash offer: firm commitment, best efforts, and Dutch auction.

firm commitment underwriting
The type of underwriting in which the underwriter buys the entire issue, assuming full financial responsibility for any unsold shares.

Firm Commitment Underwriting   In **firm commitment underwriting**, the issuer sells the entire issue to the underwriters, who then attempt to resell it. This is the most prevalent type of underwriting in the United States. This is really just a purchase-resale arrangement, and the underwriter's fee is the spread. For a new issue of seasoned equity, the underwriters can look at the market price to determine what the issue should sell for, and more than 95 percent of all such new issues are firm commitments.

If the underwriter cannot sell all of the issue at the agreed-upon offering price, it may have to lower the price on the unsold shares. Nonetheless, with firm commitment

---

[5] Warrants are options to buy newly issued stock at a fixed price for some fixed period.

underwriting, the issuer receives the agreed-upon amount, and all the risk associated with selling the issue is transferred to the underwriter.

Because the offering price usually isn't set until the underwriters have investigated how receptive the market is to the issue, this risk is usually minimal. Also, because the offering price usually is not set until just before selling commences, the issuer doesn't know precisely what its net proceeds will be until that time.

To determine the offering price, the underwriter will meet with potential buyers, typically large institutional buyers such as mutual funds. Often, the underwriter and company management will do presentations in multiple cities, pitching the stock in what is known as a *road show*. Potential buyers provide information on the price they would be willing to pay and the number of shares they would purchase at a particular price. This process of soliciting information about buyers and the prices and quantities they would demand is known as *bookbuilding*. As we will see, despite the bookbuilding process, underwriters frequently get the price wrong, or so it seems.

Learn more about investment banks at Merrill Lynch (**www.ml.com**).

Best Efforts Underwriting

In **best efforts underwriting**, the underwriter is legally bound to use "best efforts" to sell the securities at the agreed-upon offering price. Beyond this, the underwriter does not guarantee any particular amount of money to the issuer. This form of underwriting has become uncommon in recent years.

Dutch Auction Underwriting

With **Dutch auction underwriting**, the underwriter does not set a fixed price for the shares to be sold. Instead, the underwriter conducts an auction in which investors bid for shares. The offer price is determined based on the submitted bids. A Dutch auction is also known by the more descriptive name *uniform price auction*. This approach to selling securities to the public is relatively new in the IPO market and has not been widely used there, but it is very common in the bond markets. For example, it is the sole procedure used by the U.S. Treasury to sell enormous quantities of notes, bonds, and bills to the public.

The best way to understand a Dutch or uniform price auction is to consider a simple example. Suppose the Rial Company wants to sell 400 shares to the public. The company receives five bids as follows:

best efforts underwriting
The type of underwriting in which the underwriter sells as much of the issue as possible, but can return any unsold shares to the issuer without financial responsibility.

Dutch auction underwriting
The type of underwriting in which the offer price is set based on competitive bidding by investors. Also known as a *uniform price auction*.

Bidder	Quantity	Price
A	100 shares	$16
B	100 shares	14
C	200 shares	12
D	100 shares	12
E	200 shares	10

Bidder A is willing to buy 100 shares at $16 each, Bidder B is willing to buy 100 shares at $14, and so on. The Rial Company examines the bids to determine the highest price that will result in all 400 shares being sold. So, for example, at $14, A and B would buy only 200 shares, so that price is too high. Working our way down, all 400 shares won't be sold until we hit a price of $12, so $12 will be the offer price in the IPO. Bidders A through D will receive shares; Bidder E will not.

There are two additional important points to observe in our example. First, all the winning bidders will pay $12—even Bidders A and B, who actually bid a higher price. The fact that all successful bidders pay the same price is the reason for the name "uniform price auction." The idea in such an auction is to encourage bidders to bid aggressively by providing some protection against bidding a price that is too high.

Second, notice that at the $12 offer price, there are actually bids for 500 shares, which exceeds the 400 shares Rial wants to sell. There has to be some sort of allocation. How this is done varies a bit; but in the IPO market, the approach has been to compute the ratio of shares offered to shares bid at the offer price or better, which, in our example, is

Learn all about Dutch auction IPOs at **www.wrhambrecht.com**.

400/500 = .8, and allocate bidders that percentage of their bids. In other words, Bidders A through D would each receive 80 percent of the shares they bid at a price of $12 per share.

THE AFTERMARKET

The period after a new issue is initially sold to the public is referred to as the *aftermarket*. During this time, the members of the underwriting syndicate generally do not sell securities for less than the offering price.

The principal underwriter is permitted to buy shares if the market price falls below the offering price. The purpose of this would be to support the market and stabilize the price against temporary downward pressure. If the issue remains unsold after a time (for example, 30 days), members can leave the group and sell their shares at whatever price the market will allow.[6]

THE GREEN SHOE PROVISION

Green Shoe provision
A contract provision giving the underwriter the option to purchase additional shares from the issuer at the offering price. Also called the *overallotment option*.

Many underwriting contracts contain a **Green Shoe provision** (sometimes called the *overallotment option*), which gives the members of the underwriting group the option to purchase additional shares from the issuer at the offering price.[7] Essentially all IPOs and SEOs include this provision, but ordinary debt offerings generally do not. The stated reason for the Green Shoe option is to cover excess demand and oversubscriptions. Green Shoe options usually last for 30 days and involve 15 percent of the newly issued shares.

In practice, usually underwriters initially go ahead and sell 115 percent of the shares offered. If the demand for the issue is strong after the offering, the underwriters exercise the Green Shoe option to get the extra 15 percent from the company. If demand for the issue is weak, the underwriters buy the needed shares in the open market, thereby helping to support the price of the issue in the aftermarket.

LOCKUP AGREEMENTS

lockup agreement
The part of the underwriting contract that specifies how long insiders must wait after an IPO before they can sell stock.

Although they are not required by law, almost all underwriting contracts contain so-called **lockup agreements**. Such agreements specify how long insiders must wait after an IPO before they can sell some or all of their stock. Lockup periods have become fairly standardized in recent years at 180 days. Following an IPO, insiders can't cash out until six months have gone by, which ensures that they maintain a significant economic interest in the company going public.

Lockup periods are also important because it is not unusual for the number of locked-up shares to exceed the number of shares held by the public, sometimes by a substantial multiple. On the day the lockup period expires, there is the possibility that a large number of shares will hit the market on the same day and thereby depress values. The evidence suggests that, on average, venture capital-backed companies are particularly likely to experience a loss in value on the lockup expiration day.

THE QUIET PERIOD

Once a firm begins to seriously contemplate an IPO, the SEC requires that a firm and its managing underwriters observe a "quiet period." This means that all communications with the public must be limited to ordinary announcements and other purely factual matters. The quiet period ends 40 calendar days after an IPO (for most IPOs). The SEC's logic is that all relevant information should be contained in the prospectus. An important result of this requirement is that the underwriters' analysts are prohibited from making recommendations

---

[6] Occasionally, the price of a security falls dramatically when the underwriter ceases to stabilize the price. In such cases, Wall Street humorists (the ones who didn't buy any of the stock) have referred to the period following the aftermarket as the *aftermath*.

[7] The term *Green Shoe provision* sounds quite exotic, but the origin is relatively mundane. The term comes from the name of the Green Shoe Manufacturing Company, which, in 1963, was the first issuer that granted such an option.

to investors. As soon as the quiet period ends, the managing underwriters typically publish research reports, usually accompanied by a favorable "buy" recommendation.

In 2004, two firms experienced notable quiet period-related problems. Just before the Google (now Alphabet) IPO, an interview with Google cofounders Sergey Brin and Larry Page appeared in *Playboy*. The interview almost caused a postponement of the IPO, but Google was able to amend its prospectus in time. In May 2004, Salesforce.com's IPO was delayed because an interview with CEO Marc Benioff appeared in *The New York Times*. Salesforce.com finally went public two months later.

DIRECT LISTING

While firms usually use underwriters to help their stock become publicly traded, it is not required. If it wishes to do so, and it meets the requirements of the stock exchange, a company can do a **direct listing**. In this case, the firm arranges for its stock to be listed on the exchange without marketing and other help from an underwriter. Direct listings are not common for large firms, but music-streaming giant Spotify, with a valuation well into the billions of dollars, was proposing to do one on the NYSE in 2018. Among other things, a direct listing is much less expensive because there are no underwriting fees and other associated costs. Such fees are discussed in detail in a subsequent section, and they can be substantial.

direct listing
In a direct listing, a firm arranges for its stock to be listed on an exchange without marketing and other help from an underwriter.

Concept Questions
15.4a What do underwriters do?
15.4b What is the Green Shoe provision?

IPOs and Underpricing

15.5

Determining the correct offering price is the most difficult thing an underwriter must do for an initial public offering. The issuing firm faces a potential cost if the offering price is set too high or too low. If the issue is priced too high, it may be unsuccessful and have to be withdrawn. If the issue is priced below the true market value, the issuer's existing shareholders will experience an opportunity loss when the issuer sells shares for less than they are worth.

Underpricing is fairly common. It obviously helps new shareholders earn a higher return on the shares they buy. The existing shareholders of the issuing firm are not helped by underpricing. To them, it is an indirect cost of issuing new securities. For example, consider the 2017 Snap IPO. Snap sold 145 million shares in the IPO at a price of $17. The stock opened at $24 and rose to a first-day high of $26.05, before closing at $24.48. Based on these numbers, Snap was underpriced by about $7.48 per share, which means the company missed out on an additional $1.085 billion or so "left on the table." In 1999, eToys's 8.2-million-share IPO was underpriced by $57 per share, or almost a half a billion dollars in all. eToys could have used the money: It was bankrupt within two years.

Find out which firms are going public this week at **www.marketwatch.com**.

IPO UNDERPRICING: THE 1999–2000 EXPERIENCE

Table 15.2, along with Figures 15.2 and 15.3, shows that 1999 and 2000 were extraordinary years in the IPO market. Almost 900 companies went public, and the average first-day return across the two years was about 64 percent. During this time, 194 IPOs doubled, or more than doubled, in value on the first day. In contrast, only 39 did so in the preceding 24 years combined. One company, VA Linux, shot up 698 percent!

The dollar amount raised in 1999, $64.91 billion, was a record, followed closely by the $64.88 billion raised in 2000. The underpricing was so severe in 1999 that companies left

TABLE 15.2

Number of Offerings, Average First-Day Return, and Gross Proceeds of Initial Public Offerings: 1960–2016

Year	Number of Offerings*	Average First-Day Return, %†	Gross Proceeds, $ Millions‡
1960	269	17.8	553
1961	435	34.1	1,243
1962	298	−1.6	431
1963	83	3.9	246
1964	97	5.3	380
1965	146	12.7	409
1966	85	7.1	275
1967	100	37.7	641
1968	368	55.9	1,205
1969	780	12.5	2,605
1970	358	−.7	780
1971	391	21.2	1,655
1972	562	7.5	2,724
1973	105	−17.8	330
1974	9	−7.0	51
1975	12	−.2	261
1976	26	1.9	214
1977	15	3.6	128
1978	19	12.6	207
1979	39	8.5	313
1980	75	13.9	934
1981	196	6.2	2,367
1982	80	10.5	1,014
1983	524	8.9	11,370
1984	218	2.8	2,622
1985	218	6.5	4,964
1986	477	6.1	15,938
1987	336	5.7	12,481
1988	129	5.4	3,922
1989	122	7.8	5,308
1990	116	10.4	4,334
1991	293	11.8	16,431
1992	416	10.2	22,750
1993	527	12.7	31,756
1994	411	9.8	17,493
1995	464	21.1	29,511
1996	690	17.3	42,481
1997	486	13.9	32,559
1998	316	20.3	34,465
1999	486	69.7	64,913
2000	382	56.2	64,876
2001	79	14.2	34,241
2002	70	8.6	22,136
2003	68	11.9	10,075

Year	Number of Offerings*	Average First-Day Return, %[†]	Gross Proceeds, $ Millions[‡]
2004	183	12.3	31,927
2005	168	10.1	28,593
2006	162	11.9	30,648
2007	160	14.0	35,704
2008	21	5.7	22,762
2009	43	10.6	13,307
2010	100	9.2	30,708
2011	82	13.2	27,750
2012	105	17.1	32,074
2013	162	20.9	39,093
2014	224	14.9	46,940
2015	122	18.1	22,020
2016	77	14.4	12,736
1960–69	2,661	21.2	7,988
1970–79	1,536	7.1	6,663
1980–89	2,375	6.9	60,380
1990–99	4,205	21.0	296,693
2000–16	2,208	21.1	505,590
1960–2016	**12,985**	**16.8**	**877,314**

TABLE 15.2
(continued)

SOURCE: Data from 1960–1974 are taken from Ibbotson, Roger, Sindelar, Jody, and Ritter, Jay R., "The Market's Problems with the Pricing of Initial Public Offerings," *Journal of Applied Corporate Finance* 7, no. 1, Spring 1994, 66–74 (Table 1). Data from 1975–2016 are compiled by Jay R. Ritter using Thomson Financial, Dealogic, and other sources. The 1975–1993 numbers are different from those reported in the 1994 JACF article because the published article included IPOs that did not qualify for listing on Nasdaq, the Amex, or NYSE (mainly penny stocks).

*Beginning in 1975, the number of offerings excludes IPOs with an offer price of less than $5.00, ADRs, small best efforts offers, units, Regulation A offers (small issues, raising less than $1.5 million during the 1980s and $5 million until 2012), real estate investment trusts (REITs), natural resource limited partnerships, and closed-end funds. Banks and S&L IPOs are included. From 2012 and later, Regulation A offerings (issues raising up to $50 million are eligible) are included.

†First-day returns are computed as the percentage return from the offering price to the first closing market price.

‡Gross proceeds exclude overallotment options but include the international tranche, if any. No adjustments for inflation have been made.

FIGURE 15.2   **Average Initial Returns by Month for SEC-Registered Initial Public Offerings: 1960–2016**

SOURCE: Ibbotson, R. G., Sindelar, J. L., and Ritter, J. R., "The Market's Problems with the Pricing of Initial Public Offerings," *Journal of Applied Corporate Finance* 7, no. 1, Spring 1994, as updated by the authors.

WORK THE WEB

So, do the high returns IPOs sometimes earn have you excited? Do you wonder how recent IPOs have performed? You can find out at www.ipomonitor.com. We went to the website and looked in the Best-Worst Performers area. Here is part of what we found:

5 Best Performers			
Date	**Company**	**Symbol**	**% Chg.**
2017-01-27	JELD-WEN Holding, Inc.	JELD	+17.6%
2017-01-20	Keane Group, Inc.	FRAC	+16.7%
2017-01-27	REV Group, Inc.	REVG	+14.8%
2017-01-26	AnaptysBio, Inc.	ANAB	+10.8%
2017-01-27	Jounce Therapeutics, Inc.	JNCE	+6.8%

As you can see, in January 2017, JELD-WEN Holding and Keane Group had the largest first-day returns.

Questions

1. *Go to www.ipomonitor.com and find the companies that have had the biggest first-day gains in the most recent quarter. How do those gains compare with the biggest gains shown above? Which companies had the biggest first-day price drop?*
2. *Go to www.ipomonitor.com and find out which companies have filed for an IPO but have yet to start trading.*

FIGURE 15.3 **Number of Offerings by Month for SEC-Registered Initial Public Offerings: 1960–2016**

SOURCE: Ibbotson, R. G., Sindelar, J. L., and Ritter, J. R., "The Market's Problems with the Pricing of Initial Public Offerings," *Journal of Applied Corporate Finance* 7, no. 1, Spring 1994, as updated by the authors.

another $37 billion "on the table," which was substantially more than 1990–1998 combined; and in 2000, the amount was almost $30 billion. In other words, over the two-year period, companies missed out on $67 billion because of underpricing.

October 19, 1999, was one of the more memorable days during this time. The World Wrestling Federation (WWF) (now known as World Wrestling Entertainment, or WWE) and Martha Stewart Omnimedia both went public. When the closing bell rang, it was a

IN THEIR OWN WORDS ...

Jay Ritter on IPO Underpricing around the World

The United States is not the only country in which initial public offerings (IPOs) of common stock are underpriced. The phenomenon exists in every country with a stock market, although the extent of underpricing varies from country to country.

In general, countries with developed capital markets have more moderate underpricing than in emerging markets. During the Internet bubble of 1999–2000, however, underpricing in the developed capital markets increased dramatically. In the United States, for example, the average first-day return during 1999–2000 was 65 percent. Since the bursting of the Internet bubble in mid-2000, the level of underpricing in the United States, Germany, and other developed capital markets has returned to more traditional levels.

The underpricing of Chinese IPOs used to be extreme, but in recent years it has moderated. In the 1990s, Chinese government regulations required that the offer price could not be more than 15 times earnings, even when comparable stocks had a price-earnings ratio of 45. In 2011–2012, the average first-day return was 21 percent. But in 2013, there were no IPOs in China at all, due to a moratorium that the government imposed because it thought that an increase in the supply of shares would depress stock prices.

The following table gives a summary of the average first-day returns on IPOs in a number of countries around the world, with the figures collected from a number of studies by various authors.

Country	Sample Size	Time Period	Avg. Initial Return, %	Country	Sample Size	Time Period	Avg. Initial Return, %
Argentina	26	1991–2013	4.2	Malaysia	474	1980–2013	56.2
Australia	1,562	1976–2011	21.8	Mauritius	40	1989–2005	15.2
Austria	103	1971–2013	6.4	Mexico	123	1987–2002	11.6
Belgium	114	1984–2006	13.5	Morocco	33	2004–2011	33.3
Brazil	275	1979–2011	33.1	Netherlands	181	1982–2006	10.2
Bulgaria	9	2004–2007	36.5	New Zealand	242	1979–2013	18.6
Canada	720	1971–2013	6.5	Nigeria	122	1989–2013	13.1
Chile	81	1982–2013	7.4	Norway	209	1984–2013	8.1
China	2,637	1990–2014	113.5	Pakistan	80	2000–2013	22.1
Cyprus	73	1997–2012	20.3	Philippines	155	1987–2013	18.1
Denmark	164	1984–2011	7.4	Poland	309	1991–2014	12.7
Egypt	62	1990–2010	10.4	Portugal	32	1992–2006	11.9
Finland	168	1971–2013	16.9	Russia	64	1999–2013	3.3
France	697	1983–2010	10.5	Saudi Arabia	80	2003–2011	239.8
Germany	779	1978–2014	23.0	Singapore	609	1973–2013	25.8
Greece	373	1976–2013	50.8	South Africa	316	1980–2013	17.4
Hong Kong	1,486	1980–2013	15.8	Spain	143	1986–2013	10.3
India	2,983	1990–2014	88.0	Sri Lanka	105	1987–2008	33.5
Indonesia	464	1990–2014	24.9	Sweden	405	1980–2015	25.9
Iran	279	1991–2004	22.4	Switzerland	164	1983–2013	27.3
Ireland	38	1991–2013	21.6	Taiwan	1,620	1980–2013	38.1
Israel	348	1990–2006	13.8	Thailand	500	1987–2012	35.1
Italy	312	1985–2013	15.2	Tunisia	38	2001–2014	21.7
Japan	3,313	1970–2014	42.8	Turkey	404	1990–2014	9.6
Jordan	53	1999–2008	149.0	United Kingdom	4,932	1959–2012	16.0
Korea	1,758	1980–2014	58.8	United States	12,819	1960–2015	16.9

Jay R. Ritter is Cordell Professor of Finance at the University of Florida. An outstanding scholar, he is well known for his insightful analyses of new issues and going public.

SOURCE: Jay R. Ritter's website.

clear smack-down as Martha Stewart gained 98 percent on the first day compared to 48 percent for the WWF. If you're interested in finding out how IPOs have done recently, check out our nearby *Work the Web* box.

EVIDENCE ON UNDERPRICING

Figure 15.2 provides a more general illustration of the underpricing phenomenon. What is shown is the month-by-month history of underpricing for SEC-registered IPOs.[8] The period covered is 1960 through 2016. Figure 15.3 presents the number of offerings in each month for the same period.

Figure 15.2 shows that underpricing can be quite dramatic, exceeding 100 percent in some months. In such months, the average IPO more than doubled in value, sometimes in a matter of hours. Also, the degree of underpricing varies through time, and periods of severe underpricing ("hot issue" markets) are followed by periods of little underpricing ("cold issue" markets). For example, in the 1960s, the average IPO was underpriced by 21.2 percent. In the 1970s, the average underpricing was much smaller (7.1 percent), and the amount of underpricing was actually very small or even negative for much of that time. Underpricing in the 1980s ran about 6.9 percent. For 1990–1999, IPOs were underpriced by 21 percent on average, and they were underpriced by 21.1 percent in 2000–2016.

From Figure 15.3, it is apparent that the number of IPOs is also highly variable through time. Further, there are pronounced cycles in both the degree of underpricing and the number of IPOs. Comparing Figures 15.2 and 15.3, we see that increases in the number of new offerings tend to follow periods of significant underpricing by roughly six months. This probably occurs because companies decide to go public when they perceive that the market is highly receptive to new issues.

Table 15.2 contains a year-by-year summary of underpricing for the years 1960–2016. As indicated, a grand total of 12,985 companies were included in this analysis. The degree of underpricing averaged 16.8 percent overall for the 57 years examined. Securities were overpriced on average in only 5 of the 57 years. At the other extreme, in 1999, the 486 issues were underpriced, on average, by a remarkable 69.7 percent.

THE PARTIAL ADJUSTMENT PHENOMENON

When a company files its registration statement with the SEC, it will at some point in the process indicate a range of stock prices between which it expects to offer shares. This range is called the "file price range" or words to that effect. A file price range of $10 to $12 is common, but many others exist. For example, when Fitbit first filed its IPO on June 2, 2015, the company indicated a maximum anticipated price of $16.

Just before a company's shares are sold to investors, the final IPO offer price is determined. As shown in Section A of Table 15.3, that price can be above, within, or below the price range originally indicated by the company. Over the period 1980–2016, 48 percent of IPOs were within the file range, with 29 percent below and 23 percent above.

Section B of Table 15.3 illustrates an interesting and very clear pattern. IPO underpricing is much more severe when an offer is priced above the file range. Again over the 1980–2016 period, IPOs that priced above the file range were underpriced by 50 percent, on average, compared to only 3 percent for firms priced below it. The 1999–2000 period again stands out. Issues that "went off" above the file range were underpriced by an average of 121 percent!

This pattern is known as the "partial adjustment" phenomenon. The name refers to the fact that when firms raise their IPO offer prices, they only do so partially, meaning that they don't move the price high enough. In Fitbit's case, for example, the final offer price

---

[8]The discussion in this section draws on R. G. Ibbotson, J. L. Sindelar, and J. R. Ritter, "The Market's Problems with the Pricing of Initial Public Offerings," *Journal of Applied Corporate Finance* 7, no. 1 (Spring 1994).

A: Percentage of IPOs Relative to File Price Range			
	Below	Within	Above
1980–1989	30%	57%	13%
1990–1998	27	49	24
1999–2000	18	38	44
2001–2016	36	43	22
1980–2016	29	48	23
B: Average First-Day Returns Relative to File Price Range			
	Below	Within	Above
1980–1989	0%	6%	20%
1990–1998	4	11	31
1999–2000	8	26	121
2001–2016	3	11	37
1980–2016	3	11	50

TABLE 15.3

IPO Underpricing and File Price Range

was $20, an amount 25 percent higher than the original maximum price: The stock jumped 48 percent on the first day of trading. The Snap IPO we discussed to open the chapter is another good example. The company indicated a preliminary price range of $14–$16, but the final offer price was $17, and the stock soared on the first day of trading.

Why does the partial adjustment phenomenon exist? The answer is unknown. The question is related to the broader question of why IPO underpricing exists, which we consider next.

WHY DOES UNDERPRICING EXIST?

Based on the evidence we've examined, an obvious question is, Why does underpricing continue to exist? As we discuss, there are various explanations; but to date, there is a lack of complete agreement among researchers as to which of these is correct.

We present some pieces of the underpricing puzzle by stressing two important caveats to our preceding discussion. First, the average figures we have examined tend to obscure the fact that much of the apparent underpricing is attributable to the smaller, more highly speculative issues. This point is illustrated in Table 15.4, which shows the extent of underpricing for IPOs over the period from 1980 through 2016. Here, the firms are grouped based on their total sales in the 12 months prior to the IPO.

TABLE 15.4   Average First-Day Returns, Categorized by Sales, for IPOs: 1980–2016*

Annual Sales of Issuing Firms	1980–1989		1990–1998		1999–2000		2001–2016	
	Return	N	Return	N	Return	N	Return	N
0 ≤ sales < $10m	10.3%	420	17.2%	741	68.9%	331	9.7%	338
$10m ≤ sales < $20m	8.7	243	18.7	393	81.4	138	13.8	72
$20m ≤ sales < $50m	7.8	500	18.8	791	75.0	155	14.4	213
$50m ≤ sales < $100m	6.3	356	12.9	589	61.8	87	20.8	273
$100m ≤ sales < $200m	5.1	234	11.8	454	35.8	56	17.5	231
$200m ≤ sales	3.4	290	8.7	645	25.0	91	11.9	607
All	7.3	2,043	14.8	3,613	64.5	858	14.0	1,734

*Sales, measured in millions, are for the last 12 months prior to going public. All sales have been converted into dollars of 2003 purchasing power, using the Consumer Price Index. There are 8,248 IPOs, after excluding IPOs with an offer price of less than $5.00 per share, units, REITs, ADRs, closed-end funds, banks and S&Ls, firms not listed on CRSP within six months of the offering, and energy-related limited partnerships. Sales are from Thomson Financial's SDC, Dealogic, EDGAR, and the Graeme Howard-Todd Huxster collection of pre-EDGAR prospectuses. The average first-day return is 17.9 percent.
SOURCE: Professor Jay R. Ritter, University of Florida.

As illustrated in Table 15.4, the underpricing tends to be higher for firms with few to no sales in the previous year. These firms tend to be young firms, and such young firms can be very risky investments. Arguably, they must be significantly underpriced, on average, just to attract investors, and this is one explanation for the underpricing phenomenon.

The second caveat is that relatively few IPO buyers will actually get the initial high average returns observed in IPOs, and many will actually lose money. Although it is true that, on average, IPOs have positive initial returns, a significant fraction of them have price drops. Furthermore, when the price is too low, the issue is often "oversubscribed." This means investors will not be able to buy all of the shares they want, and the underwriters will allocate the shares among investors.

The average investor will find it difficult to get shares in a "successful" offering (one in which the price increases) because there will not be enough shares to go around. On the other hand, an investor blindly submitting orders for IPOs tends to get more shares in issues that go down in price.

To illustrate, consider this tale of two investors. Smith knows very accurately what the Bonanza Corporation is worth when its shares are offered. She is confident that the shares are underpriced. Jones knows only that prices usually rise one month after an IPO. Armed with this information, Jones decides to buy 1,000 shares of every IPO. Does he actually earn an abnormally high return on the initial offering?

The answer is no, and at least one reason is Smith. Knowing about the Bonanza Corporation, Smith invests all her money in its IPO. When the issue is oversubscribed, the underwriters have to somehow allocate the shares between Smith and Jones. The net result is that when an issue is underpriced, Jones doesn't get to buy as much of it as he wanted.

Smith also knows that the Blue Sky Corporation IPO is overpriced. In this case, she avoids its IPO altogether, and Jones ends up with a full 1,000 shares. To summarize this tale, Jones gets fewer shares when more knowledgeable investors swarm to buy an underpriced issue and he gets all he wants when the smart money avoids the issue.

This is an example of a "winner's curse," and it is thought to be another reason why IPOs have such a large average return. When the average investor "wins" and gets the entire allocation, it may be because those who knew better avoided the issue. The only way underwriters can counteract the winner's curse and attract the average investor is to underprice new issues (on average) so that the average investor still makes a profit.

Another reason for underpricing is that the underpricing is a kind of insurance for the investment banks. Conceivably, an investment bank could be sued successfully by angry customers if it consistently overpriced securities. Underpricing guarantees that, at least on average, customers will come out ahead.

A final reason for underpricing is that before the offer price is established, investment banks talk to big institutional investors to gauge the level of interest in the stock and to gather opinions about a suitable price. Underpricing is a way that the bank can reward these investors for truthfully revealing what they think the stock is worth and the number of shares they would like to buy.

Concept Questions

15.5a   Why is underpricing a cost to the issuing firm?

15.5b   Suppose a stockbroker calls you up out of the blue and offers to sell you "all the shares you want" of a new issue. Do you think the issue will be more or less underpriced than average?

New Equity Sales and the Value of the Firm   15.6

We now turn to a consideration of seasoned offerings, which, as we discussed earlier, are offerings by firms that already have outstanding securities. It seems reasonable to believe that new long-term financing is arranged by firms after positive net present value projects are put together. As a consequence, when the announcement of external financing is made, the firm's market value should go up. Interestingly, this is not what happens. Stock prices tend to decline following the announcement of a new equity issue, although they tend to not change much following a debt announcement. A number of researchers have studied this issue. Plausible reasons for this strange result include the following:

1. *Managerial information*: If management has superior information about the market value of the firm, it may know when the firm is overvalued. If it does, then it will attempt to issue new shares of stock when the market value exceeds the correct value. This will benefit existing shareholders. However, the potential new shareholders are not stupid, and they will anticipate this superior information and discount it in lower market prices at the new-issue date.

2. *Debt usage*: A company's decision to issue new equity may reveal that the company has too much debt or too little liquidity. One version of this argument says that the equity issue is a bad signal to the market. After all, if the new projects are favorable ones, why should the firm let new shareholders in on them? It could just issue debt and let the existing shareholders have all the gain.

3. *Issue costs*: As we discuss next, there are substantial costs associated with selling securities.

The drop in value of the existing stock following the announcement of a new issue is an example of an indirect cost of selling securities. This drop might typically be on the order of 3 percent for an industrial corporation (and somewhat smaller for a public utility); so, for a large company, it can represent a substantial amount of money. In our discussion of the costs of new issues (see Section 15.7), we label this drop the *abnormal return*.

To give a couple of recent examples, in December 2017, biopharmeceutical company Cascadian Therapeutics announced a secondary offering. Its stock fell about 3.4 percent on the day of the announcement. Also in December 2017, power systems company Digital Power announced a secondary offering. Its stock dropped 11.1 percent on the day of the announcement.

Concept Questions

15.6a What are some possible reasons why the price of a stock drops on the announcement of a new equity issue?

15.6b Explain why we might expect a firm with a positive NPV investment to finance it with debt instead of equity.

The Costs of Issuing Securities   15.7

Issuing securities to the public isn't free, and the costs of different methods are important determinants of which is used. These costs associated with *floating* a new issue are generically called *flotation costs*. In this section, we take a closer look at the flotation costs associated with equity sales to the public.

THE COSTS OF SELLING STOCK TO THE PUBLIC

The costs of selling stock are classified in the following list and fall into six categories: (1) the gross spread, (2) other direct expenses, (3) indirect expenses, (4) abnormal returns (discussed previously), (5) underpricing, and (6) the Green Shoe provision.

THE COSTS OF ISSUING SECURITIES

1. *Gross spread*	The gross spread consists of direct fees paid by the issuer to the underwriting syndicate—the difference between the price the issuer receives and the offer price.
2. *Other direct expenses*	These are direct costs, incurred by the issuer, that are not part of the compensation to underwriters. These costs include filing fees, legal fees, and taxes—all reported on the prospectus.
3. *Indirect expenses*	These costs are not reported on the prospectus and include the costs of management time spent working on the new issue.
4. *Abnormal returns*	In a seasoned issue of stock, the price of the existing stock drops on average by 3 percent on the announcement of the issue. This drop is called the *abnormal return*.
5. *Underpricing*	For initial public offerings, losses arise from selling the stock below the true value.
6. *Green Shoe option*	The Green Shoe option gives the underwriters the right to buy additional shares at the offer price to cover overallotments.

Table 15.5 reports direct costs as a percentage of the gross amount raised for IPOs, SEOs, straight (ordinary) bonds, and convertible bonds sold by U.S. companies over the 19-year period from 1990 through 2008. These are direct costs only. Not included are indirect expenses, the cost of the Green Shoe provision, underpricing (for IPOs), and abnormal returns (for SEOs).

As Table 15.5 shows, the direct costs alone can be very large, particularly for smaller issues (less than $10 million). On a smaller IPO, for example, the total direct costs amount to 25.22 percent of the amount raised. This means that if a company sells $10 million in stock, it will net only about $7.5 million; the other $2.5 million goes to cover the underwriter spread and other direct expenses. Typical underwriter spreads on an IPO range from about 5 percent up to 10 percent or so, but for well over half of the IPOs in Table 15.5, the spread is exactly 7 percent; so this is, by far, the most common spread.

Overall, four clear patterns emerge from Table 15.5. First, with the possible exception of straight debt offerings (about which we will have more to say later), there are substantial economies of scale. The underwriter spreads are smaller on larger issues, and the other direct costs fall sharply as a percentage of the amount raised—a reflection of the mostly fixed nature of such costs. Second, the costs associated with selling debt are substantially less than the costs of selling equity. Third, IPOs have higher expenses than SEOs, but the difference is not as great as might originally be guessed. Finally, straight bonds are cheaper to float than convertible bonds.

As we have discussed, the underpricing of IPOs is an additional cost to the issuer. To give a better idea of the total cost of going public, Table 15.6 combines the information in Table 15.5 for IPOs with data on the underpricing experienced by these firms. Overall, across all size groups, the total direct costs amount to about 10 percent of the amount raised, and the underpricing amounts to about 19 percent.

Finally, with regard to debt offerings, there is a general pattern in issue costs that is somewhat obscured in Table 15.5. Recall from Chapter 7 that bonds carry different credit

TABLE 15.5 Direct Costs as a Percentage of Gross Proceeds for Equity (IPOs and SEOs) and Straight and Convertible Bonds Offered by Domestic Operating Companies: 1990–2008

Proceeds ($ millions)	IPOs				SEOs			
	Number of Issues	Gross Spread	Other Direct Expense	Total Direct Cost	Number of Issues	Gross Spread	Other Direct Expense	Total Direct Cost
2.00–9.99	1,007	9.40%	15.82%	25.22%	515	8.11%	26.99%	35.11%
10.00–19.99	810	7.39	7.30	14.69	726	6.11	7.76	13.86
20.00–39.99	1,422	6.96	7.06	14.03	1,393	5.44	4.10	9.54
40.00–59.99	880	6.89	2.87	9.77	1,129	5.03	8.93	13.96
60.00–79.99	522	6.79	2.16	8.94	841	4.88	1.98	6.85
80.00–99.99	327	6.71	1.84	8.55	536	4.67	2.05	6.72
100.00–199.99	702	6.39	1.57	7.96	1,372	4.34	.89	5.23
200.00–499.99	440	5.81	1.03	6.84	811	3.72	1.22	4.94
500.00 and up	155	5.01	.49	5.50	264	3.10	.27	3.37
Total/Avg	**6,265**	**7.19**	**3.18**	**10.37**	**7,587**	**5.02**	**2.68**	**7.69**

Proceeds ($ millions)	Straight Bonds				Convertible Bonds			
	Number of Issues	Gross Spread	Other Direct Expense	Total Direct Cost	Number of Issues	Gross Spread	Other Direct Expense	Total Direct Cost
2.00–9.99	3,962	1.64%	2.40%	4.03%	14	6.39%	3.43%	9.82
10.00–19.99	3,400	1.50	1.71	3.20	23	5.52	3.09	8.61
20.00–39.99	2,690	1.25	.92	2.17	30	4.63	1.67	6.30
40.00–59.99	3,345	.81	.79	1.59	35	3.49	1.04	4.54
60.00–79.99	891	1.65	.80	2.44	60	2.79	.62	3.41
80.00–99.99	465	1.41	.57	1.98	16	2.30	.62	2.92
100.00–199.99	4,949	1.61	.52	2.14	82	2.66	.42	3.08
200.00–499.99	3,305	1.38	.33	1.71	46	2.65	.33	2.99
500.00 and up	1,261	.61	.15	.76	7	2.16	.13	2.29
Total/Avg	**24,268**	**1.38**	**.61**	**2.00**	**313**	**3.07**	**.85**	**3.92**

SOURCE: Lee, I. et al., "The Costs of Raising Capital," *Journal of Financial Research* 19, Spring 1996, updated by the authors.

TABLE 15.6

Direct and Indirect Costs, in Percentages, of Equity IPOs: 1990–2008

Proceeds ($ millions)	Number of Issues	Gross Spread	Other Direct Expense	Total Direct Cost	Underpricing
2.00–9.99	1,007	9.40%	15.82%	25.22%	20.42%
10.00–19.99	810	7.39	7.30	14.69	10.33
20.00–39.99	1,422	6.96	7.06	14.03	17.03
40.00–59.99	880	6.89	2.87	9.77	28.26
60.00–79.99	522	6.79	2.16	8.94	28.36
80.00–99.99	327	6.71	1.84	8.55	32.92
100.00–199.99	702	6.39	1.57	7.96	21.55
200.00–499.99	440	5.81	1.03	6.84	6.19
500.00 and up	155	5.01	.49	5.50	6.64
Total/Avg	**6,265**	**7.19**	**3.18**	**10.37**	**19.34**

SOURCE: Lee, I. et al., "The Costs of Raising Capital," *Journal of Financial Research* 19, Spring 1996, updated by the authors.

ratings. Higher-rated bonds are said to be investment grade, whereas lower-rated bonds are noninvestment grade. Table 15.7 contains a breakdown of direct costs for bond issues after the investment and noninvestment grades have been separated.

Table 15.7 clarifies two things regarding debt issues. First, there are substantial economies of scale here as well. Second, investment-grade issues have much lower direct costs, particularly for straight bonds.

THE COSTS OF GOING PUBLIC: A CASE STUDY

On July 21, 2016, Impinj, the Seattle-based radio-frequency identification company, went public via an IPO. Impinj issued 4.8 million shares of stock at a price of $14 each. The lead underwriter on the IPO was RBC Capital Markets, assisted by a syndicate of other investment banks. Even though the IPO raised a gross sum of $67.2 million, Impinj only got to keep $62.496 million after expenses. The biggest expense was the 7 percent underwriter spread, which is the usual spread for an offering of that size. Impinj sold each of the 4.8 million shares to the underwriters for $13.02, and the underwriters in turn sold the shares to the public for $14 each.

But wait—there's more. Impinj spent $7,458 in SEC registration fees and $11,609 in FINRA filing fees. The company also spent $125,000 in exchange listing fees, $1.6 million in legal fees, $417,000 on accounting to obtain the necessary audits, $5,000 for a transfer agent to physically transfer the shares and maintain a list of shareholders, $255,000 for printing and engraving expenses, and finally, $261,000 in miscellaneous expenses.

As Impinj's outlays show, an IPO can be a costly undertaking! In the end, Impinj's expenses totaled $7.39 million, of which $4.7 million went to the underwriters and $2.69 million went to other parties. All told, the total direct cost to Impinj was 11.8 percent of the issue proceeds raised by the company.

Concept Questions

15.7a   What are the different costs associated with security offerings?

15.7b   What lessons do we learn from studying issue costs?

TABLE 15.7   Average Gross Spreads and Total Direct Costs for Domestic Debt Issues: 1990–2008

Convertible Bonds

Proceeds ($ millions)	Investment Grade				Junk or Not Rated			
	Number of Issues	Gross Spread	Other Direct Expense	Total Direct Cost	Number of Issues	Gross Spread	Other Direct Expense	Total Direct Cost
2.00–9.99	—	—	—	—	14	6.39%	3.43%	9.82%
10.00–19.99	1	14.12%	1.87%	15.98%	23	5.52	3.09	8.61
20.00–39.99	—	—	—	—	30	4.63	1.67	6.30
40.00–59.99	3	1.92	.51	2.43	35	3.49	1.04	4.54
60.00–79.99	6	1.65	.44	2.09	60	2.79	.62	3.41
80.00–99.99	4	.89	.27	1.16	16	2.30	.62	2.92
100.00–199.99	27	2.22	.33	2.55	82	2.66	.42	3.08
200.00–499.99	27	2.03	.19	2.22	46	2.65	.33	2.99
500.00 and up	11	1.94	.13	2.06	7	2.16	.13	2.29
Total/Avg	**79**	**2.15**	**.29**	**2.44**	**313**	**3.31**	**.98**	**4.29**

Straight Bonds

Proceeds ($ millions)	Investment Grade				Junk or Not Rated			
	Number of Issues	Gross Spread	Other Direct Expense	Total Direct Cost	Number of Issues	Gross Spread	Other Direct Expense	Total Direct Cost
2.00–9.99	2,709	.62%	1.28%	1.90%	1,253	2.77%	2.50%	5.27%
10.00–19.99	2,564	.59	1.17	1.76	836	3.15	1.97	5.12
20.00–39.99	2,400	.63	.74	1.37	290	3.07	1.13	4.20
40.00–59.99	3,146	.40	.52	.92	199	2.93	1.20	4.14
60.00–79.99	792	.58	.38	.96	99	3.12	1.16	4.28
80.00–99.99	385	.66	.29	.96	80	2.73	.93	3.66
100.00–199.99	4,427	.54	.25	.79	522	2.73	.68	3.41
200.00–499.99	3,031	.52	.25	.76	274	2.59	.39	2.98
500.00 and up	1,207	.31	.08	.39	54	2.38	.25	2.63
Total/Avg	**20,661**	**.52**	**.35**	**.87**	**3,607**	**2.76**	**.81**	**3.57**

SOURCE: Lee, I. et al., "The Costs of Raising Capital," *Journal of Financial Research* 19, Spring 1996, updated by the authors.

15.8 Rights

When new shares of common stock are sold to the general public, the proportional owner-ship of existing shareholders is likely to be reduced. If a preemptive right is contained in the firm's articles of incorporation, the firm must first offer any new issue of common stock to existing shareholders. If the articles of incorporation do not include a preemptive right, the firm has a choice of offering the issue of common stock directly to existing shareholders or to the public.

An issue of common stock offered to existing stockholders is called a *rights offering* (or *offer*, for short) or a *privileged subscription*. In a rights offering, each shareholder is issued rights to buy a specified number of new shares from the firm at a specified price within a specified time, after which the rights are said to *expire*. The terms of the rights offering are evidenced by certificates known as *share warrants* or *rights*. Such rights are often traded on securities exchanges or over the counter.

Rights offerings have some interesting advantages relative to cash offers. For example, they appear to be cheaper for the issuing firm than cash offers. In fact, a firm can do a rights offering without using an underwriter; whereas, as a practical matter, an underwriter is almost a necessity in a cash offer. Despite this, rights offerings are fairly rare in the United States; in many other countries, they are more common than cash offers. Why this is true is a bit of a mystery and the source of much debate; but to our knowledge, no definitive answer exists.

THE MECHANICS OF A RIGHTS OFFERING

To illustrate the various considerations a financial manager faces in a rights offering, we will examine the situation faced by the National Power Company, whose abbreviated initial financial statements are given in Table 15.8.

As indicated in Table 15.8, National Power earns $2 million after taxes and has 1 million shares outstanding. Earnings per share are $2, and the stock sells for $20, or 10 times earnings (that is, the price-earnings ratio is 10). To fund a planned expansion, the company intends to raise $5 million worth of new equity funds through a rights offering.

TABLE 15.8

National Power Company Financial Statements Before Rights Offering

NATIONAL POWER COMPANY Balance Sheet			
Assets		**Shareholders' Equity**	
Assets	$15,000,000	Common stock	$ 5,000,000
		Retained earnings	10,000,000
Total	$15,000,000	Total	$15,000,000
Income Statement			
Earnings before taxes		$ 2,531,646	
Taxes (21%)		531,646	
Net income		$ 2,000,000	
Shares outstanding		1,000,000	
Earnings per share		$ 2	
Market price per share		$ 20	
Total market value		$20,000,000	

To execute a rights offering, the financial management of National Power will have to answer the following questions:

1. What should the price per share be for the new stock?
2. How many shares will have to be sold?
3. How many shares will each shareholder be allowed to buy?

Also, management will probably want to ask this:

4. What is likely to be the effect of the rights offering on the per-share value of the existing stock?

It turns out that the answers to these questions are highly interrelated. We will get to them in just a moment.

The early stages of a rights offering are the same as those for a general cash offer. The difference between a rights offering and a general cash offer lies in how the shares are sold. In a rights offer, National Power's existing shareholders are informed that they own one right for each share of stock they own. National Power will then specify how many rights a shareholder needs to buy one additional share at a specified price.

To take advantage of the rights offering, shareholders have to exercise the rights by filling out a subscription form and sending it, along with payment, to the firm's subscription agent (the subscription agent is usually a bank). Shareholders of National Power will actually have several choices: (1) Exercise their rights and subscribe for some or all of the entitled shares, (2) order some or all of the rights sold, or (3) do nothing and let the rights expire. As we will discuss, this third course of action is inadvisable.

NUMBER OF RIGHTS NEEDED TO PURCHASE A SHARE

National Power wants to raise $5 million in new equity. Suppose the subscription price is set at $10 per share. How National Power arrives at that price we will discuss later; but notice that the subscription price is substantially less than the current $20 per share market price.

At $10 per share, National Power will have to issue 500,000 new shares. This can be determined by dividing the total amount of funds to be raised by the subscription price:

$$\textbf{Number of new shares} = \frac{\textbf{Funds to be raised}}{\textbf{Subscription price}}$$

$$= \frac{\$5,000,000}{\$10} = 500,000 \text{ shares}$$

15.1

Because stockholders always get one right for each share of stock they own, 1 million rights will be issued by National Power. To determine how many rights will be needed to buy one new share of stock, we can divide the number of existing outstanding shares of stock by the number of new shares:

$$\frac{\textbf{Number of rights needed}}{\textbf{to buy a share of stock}} = \frac{\textbf{Old shares}}{\textbf{New shares}}$$

$$= \frac{1,000,000}{500,000} = 2 \text{ rights}$$

15.2

A shareholder will need to give up two rights plus $10 to receive a share of new stock. If all the stockholders do this, National Power will raise the required $5 million.

It should be clear that the subscription price, the number of new shares, and the number of rights needed to buy a new share of stock are interrelated. For example, National Power can lower the subscription price. If it does, then more new shares will have to be issued to raise $5 million in new equity. Several alternatives are worked out here:

Subscription Price	Number of New Shares	Number of Rights Needed to Buy a Share of Stock
$20	250,000	4
10	500,000	2
5	1,000,000	1

THE VALUE OF A RIGHT

Rights clearly have value. In the case of National Power, the right to buy a share of stock worth $20 for $10 is definitely worth something. In fact, if you think about it, a right is essentially a call option, which we will discuss in more detail in later chapters. The most important difference between a right and an ordinary call option is that rights are issued by the firm, so they more closely resemble warrants. In general, the valuation of options, rights, and warrants can be fairly complex, so we defer a full discussion of this subject to a later chapter. However, we can discuss the value of a right just prior to expiration to illustrate some important points.

Suppose a shareholder of National Power owns two shares of stock just before the rights offering is about to expire. This situation is depicted in Table 15.9. Initially, the price of National Power is $20 per share, so the shareholder's total holding is worth $2 \times $20 = 40. The National Power rights offer gives shareholders with two rights the opportunity to purchase one additional share for $10. The additional share does not carry a right.

The stockholder who has two shares will receive two rights. The holding of the shareholder who exercises these rights and buys the new share will increase to three shares. The total investment will be $40 + 10 = 50 (the $40 initial value plus the $10 paid to the company).

The stockholder now holds three shares, all of which are identical because the new share does not have a right and the rights attached to the old shares have been exercised. Because the total cost of buying these three shares is $40 + 10 = 50, the price per share must end up at $50/3 = 16.67 (rounded to two decimal places).

TABLE 15.9

The Value of Rights: The Individual Shareholder

Initial Position	
Number of shares	2
Share price	$20
Value of holding	$40
Terms of Offer	
Subscription price	$10
Number of rights issued	2
Number of rights for a new share	2
After Offer	
Number of shares	3
Value of holding	$50
Share price	$16.67
Value of one right: Old price − New price	$20 − 16.67 = $3.33

Initial Position	
Number of shares	1 million
Share price	$20
Value of firm	$20 million
Terms of Offer	
Subscription price	$10
Number of rights issued	1 million
Number of rights for a new share	2
After Offer	
Number of shares	1.5 million
Share price	$16.67
Value of firm	$25 million
Value of one right	$20 − 16.67 = $3.33

TABLE 15.10

National Power Company Rights Offering

Table 15.10 summarizes what happens to National Power's stock price. If all shareholders exercise their rights, the number of shares will increase to 1 million + .5 million = 1.5 million. The value of the firm will increase to $20 million + 5 million = $25 million. The value of each share will drop to $25 million/1.5 million = $16.67 after the rights offering.

The difference between the old share price of $20 and the new share price of $16.67 reflects the fact that the old shares carried rights to subscribe to the new issue. The difference must be equal to the value of one right—that is, $20 − 16.67 = $3.33.

An investor holding no shares of outstanding National Power stock who wants to subscribe to the new issue can do so by buying some rights. Suppose an outside investor buys two rights. This will cost $3.33 × 2 = $6.67 (to account for previous rounding). If the investor exercises the rights at a subscription price of $10, the total cost will be $10 + 6.67 = $16.67. In return for this expenditure, the investor will receive a share of the new stock, which, as we have seen, is worth $16.67.

Exercising Your Rights: Part 1	**EXAMPLE 15.1**

In the National Power example, suppose the subscription price is set at $8. How many shares will have to be sold? How many rights will you need to buy a new share? What is the value of a right? What will the price per share be after the rights offer?

To raise $5 million, $5 million/$8 = 625,000 shares will need to be sold. There are 1 million shares outstanding, so it will take 1 million/625,000 = 8/5 = 1.6 rights to buy a new share of stock (you can buy five new shares for every eight you own). After the rights offer, there will be 1.625 million shares, worth $25 million altogether, so the per-share value will be $25/1.625 = $15.38. The value of a right in this case is the $20 original price less the $15.38 ending price, or $4.62.

EX RIGHTS

National Power's rights have a substantial value. In addition, the rights offering will have a large impact on the market price of National Power's stock. That price will drop by $3.33 on the **ex-rights date**.

ex-rights date

The beginning of the period when stock is sold without a recently declared right, normally two trading days before the holder-of-record date.

FIGURE 15.4

Ex-Rights Stock Prices

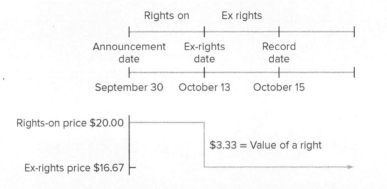

In a rights offering, there is a date of record, which is the last day on which a shareholder can establish legal ownership. However, stocks are sold ex rights two business days before the record date. Before the ex-rights date, the stock sells rights on, which means that the purchaser receives the rights.

holder-of-record date

The date on which existing shareholders on company records are designated as the recipients of stock rights. Also, the date of record.

The standard procedure for issuing rights involves the firm's setting a **holder-of-record date**. Following stock exchange rules, the stock typically goes ex rights two trading days before the holder-of-record date. If the stock is sold before the ex-rights date—"rights on," "with rights," or "cum rights"—the new owner will receive the rights. After the ex-rights date, an investor who purchases the shares will not receive the rights. This is depicted for National Power in Figure 15.4.

As illustrated, on September 30, National Power announces the terms of the rights offering, stating that the rights will be mailed on, say, November 1 to stockholders of record as of October 15. Because October 13 is the ex-rights date, only shareholders who own the stock on or before October 12 will receive the rights.

EXAMPLE 15.2 **Exercising Your Rights: Part II**

The Lagrange Point Co. has proposed a rights offering. The stock currently sells for $40 per share. Under the terms of the offer, stockholders will be allowed to buy one new share for every five that they own at a price of $25 per share. What is the value of a right? What is the ex-rights price?

You can buy five rights-on shares for 5 × $40 = $200 and then exercise the rights for another $25. Your total investment is $225, and you end up with six ex-rights shares. The ex-rights price per share is $225/6 = $37.50. The rights are worth $40 − 37.50 = $2.50 apiece.

EXAMPLE 15.3 **Right On**

In Example 15.2, suppose the rights sell for only $2 instead of the $2.50 we calculated. What can you do?

You can get rich quickly because you have found a money machine. Here's the recipe: Buy five rights for $10. Exercise them and pay $25 to get a new share. Your total investment to get one ex-rights share is 5 × $2 + 25 = $35. Sell the share for $37.50 and pocket the $2.50 difference. Repeat as desired.

THE UNDERWRITING ARRANGEMENTS

Rights offerings are typically arranged using **standby underwriting**. In standby underwriting, the issuer makes a rights offering, and the underwriter makes a firm commitment to "take up" (that is, purchase) the unsubscribed portion of the issue. The underwriter usually gets a **standby fee** and additional amounts based on the securities taken up.

Standby underwriting protects the firm against undersubscription, which can occur if investors throw away rights or if bad news causes the market price of the stock to fall below the subscription price.

In practice, only a small percentage (fewer than 10 percent) of shareholders fail to exercise valuable rights. This failure can probably be attributed to ignorance or vacations. Furthermore, shareholders are usually given an **oversubscription privilege**, which enables them to purchase unsubscribed shares at the subscription price. The oversubscription privilege makes it unlikely that the corporate issuer would have to turn to its underwriter for help.

standby underwriting
The type of underwriting in which the underwriter agrees to purchase the unsubscribed portion of the issue.

standby fee
An amount paid to an underwriter participating in a standby underwriting agreement.

oversubscription privilege
A privilege that allows shareholders to purchase unsubscribed shares in a rights offering at the subscription price.

EFFECTS ON SHAREHOLDERS

Shareholders can exercise their rights or sell them. In either case, the stockholder will neither win nor lose because of the rights offering. The hypothetical holder of two shares of National Power has a portfolio worth $40. If the shareholder exercises the rights, she or he ends up with three shares worth a total of $50. In other words, with an expenditure of $10, the investor's holding increases in value by $10, which means the shareholder is neither better nor worse off.

On the other hand, if the shareholder sells the two rights for $3.33 each, he or she would obtain $3.33 × 2 = $6.67 and end up with two shares worth $16.67 and the cash from selling the right:

$$\text{Shares held} = 2 \times \$16.67 = \$33.33$$
$$\text{Rights sold} = 2 \times \$3.33 \quad = \quad \underline{6.67}$$
$$\text{Total} = \qquad \qquad \underline{\$40.00}$$

The new $33.33 market value plus $6.67 in cash is exactly the same as the original holding of $40. Thus, stockholders cannot lose or gain by exercising or selling rights.

It is obvious that after the rights offering, the new market price of the firm's stock will be lower than the price before the rights offering. As we have seen, stockholders have suffered no loss because of the rights offering. The stock price decline is very much like that in a stock split, a device described in Chapter 17. The lower the subscription price, the greater is the price decline resulting from a rights offering. Because shareholders receive rights equal in value to the price drop, the rights offering does *not* hurt stockholders.

There is one last issue. How do we set the subscription price in a rights offering? If you think about it, you will see that the subscription price really does not matter. It has to be below the market price of the stock for the rights to have value; but beyond this, the price is arbitrary. In principle, it can be as low as we care to make it, as long as it is not zero. In other words, it is impossible to underprice a rights offer.

Concept Questions

15.8a How does a rights offering work?

15.8b What questions must financial managers answer in a rights offering?

15.8c How is the value of a right determined?

15.8d When does a rights offering affect the value of a company's shares?

15.8e Does a rights offering cause share prices to decrease? How are existing shareholders affected by a rights offering?

15.9 Dilution

dilution

Loss in existing shareholders' value in terms of ownership, market value, book value, or EPS.

A subject that comes up quite a bit in discussions involving the selling of securities is **dilution**. Dilution refers to a loss in existing shareholders' value. There are several kinds:

1. Dilution of percentage ownership.
2. Dilution of market value.
3. Dilution of book value and earnings per share.

The differences between these three types can be a little confusing, and there are some common misconceptions about dilution, so we discuss it in this section.

DILUTION OF PROPORTIONATE OWNERSHIP

The first type of dilution can arise whenever a firm sells shares to the general public. For example, Joe Smith owns 5,000 shares of Merit Shoe Company. Merit Shoe currently has 50,000 shares of stock outstanding; each share gets one vote. Joe controls 10 percent (= 5,000/50,000) of the votes and gets 10 percent of the dividends.

If Merit Shoe issues 50,000 new shares of common stock to the public via a general cash offer, Joe's ownership in Merit Shoe may be diluted. If Joe does not participate in the new issue, his ownership will drop to 5 percent (= 5,000/100,000). Notice that the value of Joe's shares is unaffected; he just owns a smaller percentage of the firm.

As this example illustrates, a rights offering ensures Joe Smith an opportunity to maintain his proportionate 10 percent share; therefore, dilution of the ownership of existing shareholders can be avoided by using a rights offering.

DILUTION OF VALUE: BOOK VERSUS MARKET VALUES

We now examine dilution of value by looking at some accounting numbers. We do this to illustrate a fallacy concerning dilution; we do not mean to suggest that accounting value dilution is more important than market value dilution. As we illustrate, quite the reverse is true.

Suppose Upper States Manufacturing (USM) wants to build a new electricity-generating plant to meet future anticipated demands. As shown in Table 15.11, USM currently has

TABLE 15.11

New Issues and Dilution: The Case of Upper States Manufacturing

	Initial	After Taking on New Project	
		With Dilution	With No Dilution
Number of shares	1,000,000	1,400,000	1,400,000
Book value	$10,000,000	$12,000,000	$12,000,000
Book value per share (B)	$10	$8.57	$8.57
Market value	$5,000,000	$6,000,000	$8,000,000
Market price (P)	$5	$4.29	$5.71
Net income	$1,000,000	$1,200,000	$1,600,000
Return on equity (ROE)	.10	.10	.13
Earnings per share (EPS)	$1	$.86	$1.14
EPS/P	.20	.20	.20
P/EPS	5	5	5
P/B	.5	.5	.67
Project cost $2,000,000		NPV = −$1,000,000	NPV = $1,000,000

1 million shares outstanding and no debt. Each share is selling for $5, and the company has a $5 million market value. USM's book value is $10 million total, or $10 per share.

USM has experienced a variety of difficulties in the past, including cost overruns, regulatory delays in building a nuclear-powered electricity-generating plant, and below-normal profits. These difficulties are reflected in the fact that USM's market-to-book ratio is $5/$10 = .50 (successful firms rarely have market prices below book values).

Net income for USM is currently $1 million. With 1 million shares, earnings per share are $1, and the return on equity is $1/$10 = .10, or 10%.[9] USM sells for five times earnings (the price-earnings ratio is 5). USM has 200 shareholders, each of whom holds 5,000 shares. The new plant will cost $2 million, so USM will have to issue 400,000 new shares ($5 × 400,000 = $2 million). There will be 1.4 million shares outstanding after the issue.

The ROE on the new plant is expected to be the same as for the company as a whole. In other words, net income is expected to go up by .10 × $2 million = $200,000. Total net income will be $1.2 million. The following will result if the plant is built:

1. With 1.4 million shares outstanding, EPS will be $1.2/1.4 = $.857, down from $1.
2. The proportionate ownership of each old shareholder will drop to 5,000/1.4 million = .0036, or .36 percent from .50 percent.
3. If the stock continues to sell for five times earnings, then the value will drop to 5 × $.857 = $4.29, representing a loss of $.71 per share.
4. The total book value will be the old $10 million plus the new $2 million, for a total of $12 million. Book value per share will fall to $12 million/1.4 million = $8.57.

If we take this example at face value, then dilution of proportionate ownership, accounting dilution, and market value dilution all occur. USM's stockholders appear to suffer significant losses.

A Misconception   Our example appears to show that selling stock when the market-to-book ratio is less than 1 is detrimental to stockholders. Some managers claim that the resulting dilution occurs because EPS will go down whenever shares are issued when the market value is less than the book value.

When the market-to-book ratio is less than 1, increasing the number of shares does cause EPS to go down. Such a decline in EPS is accounting dilution, and accounting dilution will always occur under these circumstances.

Is it also true that market value dilution will necessarily occur? The answer is no. There is nothing incorrect about our example, but why the market price has decreased is not obvious. We discuss this next.

The Correct Arguments   In this example, the market price falls from $5 per share to $4.29. This is true dilution, but why does it occur? The answer has to do with the new project. USM is going to spend $2 million on the new plant. As shown in Table 15.11, the total market value of the company is going to rise from $5 million to $6 million, an increase of only $1 million. This means that the NPV of the new project is −$1 million. With 1.4 million shares, the loss per share is $1/1.4 = $.71, as we calculated before.

So, true dilution takes place for the shareholders of USM because the NPV of the project is negative, not because the market-to-book ratio is less than 1. This negative NPV causes the market price to drop, and the accounting dilution has nothing to do with it.

---

[9] Return on equity, or ROE, is equal to earnings per share divided by book value per share, or, equivalently, net income divided by common equity. We discuss this and other financial ratios in some detail in Chapter 3.

Suppose the new project has a positive NPV of $1 million. The total market value rises by $2 million + 1 million = $3 million. As shown in Table 15.11 (third column), the price per share rises to $5.71. Notice that accounting dilution still takes place because the book value per share still falls, but there is no economic consequence of that fact. The market value of the stock rises.

The $.71 increase in share value comes about because of the $1 million NPV, which amounts to an increase in value of about $.71 per share. Also, as shown, if the ratio of price to EPS remains at 5, then EPS must rise to $5.71/5 = $1.14. Total earnings (net income) rises to $1.14 per share × 1.4 million shares = $1.6 million. Finally, ROE will rise to $1.6 million/$12 million = 13.33%.

Concept Questions

15.9a What are the different kinds of dilution?
15.9b Is dilution important?

15.10 Issuing Long-Term Debt

The general procedures followed in a public issue of bonds are the same as those for stocks. The issue must be registered with the SEC, there must be a prospectus, and so on. The registration statement for a public issue of bonds is different from the one for common stock. For bonds, the registration statement must indicate an indenture.

Another important difference is that more than 50 percent of all debt is issued privately. There are two basic forms of direct private long-term financing: Term loans and private placement.

term loans
Direct business loans of typically one to five years.

private placements
Loans (usually long-term) provided directly by a limited number of investors.

Term loans are direct business loans. These loans have maturities of between one and five years. Most term loans are repayable during the life of the loan. The lenders include commercial banks, insurance companies, and other lenders that specialize in corporate finance. **Private placements** are similar to term loans except that the maturity is longer.

The important differences between direct private long-term financing and public issues of debt are these:

1. A direct long-term loan avoids the cost of Securities and Exchange Commission registration.
2. Direct placement is likely to have more restrictive covenants.
3. It is easier to renegotiate a term loan or a private placement in the event of a default. It is harder to renegotiate a public issue because hundreds of holders are usually involved.
4. Life insurance companies and pension funds dominate the private placement segment of the bond market. Commercial banks are significant participants in the term loan market.
5. The costs of distributing bonds are lower in the private market.

The interest rates on term loans and private placements are usually higher than those on an equivalent public issue. This difference reflects the trade-off between a higher interest rate and more flexible arrangements in the event of financial distress, as well as the lower costs associated with private placements.

An additional, and very important, consideration is that the flotation costs associated with selling debt are much less than the comparable costs associated with selling equity.

Concept Questions

15.10a What is the difference between private and public bond issues?

15.10b A private placement is likely to have a higher interest rate than a public issue. Why?

Shelf Registration

15.11

To simplify the procedures for issuing securities, in March 1982, the SEC adopted Rule 415 on a temporary basis, and it was made permanent in November 1983. Rule 415 allows shelf registration. Both debt and equity securities can be shelf registered.

Shelf registration permits a corporation to register an offering that it reasonably expects to sell within the next two years and then sell the issue whenever it wants during that two-year period. For example, in March 2017, cargo ship operator DryShips announced a shelf registration of $2 billion in securities, including debt, preferred stock, common stock, and warrants. Not all companies can use Rule 415. The primary qualifications are these:

shelf registration
Registration permitted by SEC Rule 415, which allows a company to register all issues it expects to sell within two years at one time, with subsequent sales at any time within those two years.

1. The company must be rated investment grade.
2. The firm cannot have defaulted on its debt in the past three years.
3. The aggregate market value of the firm's outstanding stock must be more than $150 million.
4. The firm must not have violated the Securities Act of 1934 in the past three years.

Shelf registration allows firms to use a *dribble* method of new equity issuance. In dribbling, a company registers the issue and hires an underwriter as its selling agent. The company sells shares in "dribs and drabs" from time to time directly via a stock exchange (for example, the NYSE). Companies that have used dribble programs include Wells Fargo & Co., Pacific Gas and Electric Co., and Southern Company.

The rule has been controversial. The following arguments have been constructed against shelf registration:

1. The costs of new issues might go up because underwriters are unable to provide as much current information to potential investors as they would otherwise; therefore, investors may pay less. The expense of selling the issue piece by piece might therefore be higher than that of selling it all at once.
2. Some investment bankers have argued that shelf registration will cause a "market overhang" that will depress market prices. In other words, the possibility that the company may increase the supply of stock at any time will have a negative impact on the current stock price.

Concept Questions

15.11a What is shelf registration?

15.11b What are the arguments against shelf registration?

15.12 Summary and Conclusions

This chapter has looked at how corporate securities are issued. The following are the main points:

1. The costs of issuing securities can be quite large. They are much lower (as a percentage) for larger issues.

2. The direct and indirect costs of going public can be substantial. However, once a firm is public, it can raise additional capital with much greater ease.

3. Rights offerings are cheaper than general cash offers. Even so, most new equity issues in the United States are underwritten general cash offers.

CONNECT TO FINANCE

 For more practice, you should be using *Connect Finance*. Log on to connect .mheducation.com to get started!

Can you answer the following *Connect* Quiz questions?

Section 15.1 What stage of venture capital funding is most apt to provide the funding needed to actually commence the manufacturing operations of a firm?

Section 15.2 Smythe Enterprises is issuing securities under Regulation A. Given this, you know that the securities are valued at _____ or less, or are debt securities that mature in less than _____.

Section 15.4 The gross spread is defined as the difference between the _____ and the _____.

Section 15.7 What is referred to as the *abnormal return*?

CHAPTER REVIEW AND SELF-TEST PROBLEMS

15.1 Flotation Costs The L5 Corporation is considering an equity issue to finance a new space station. A total of $15 million in new equity is needed. If the direct costs are estimated at 7 percent of the amount raised, how large does the issue need to be? What is the dollar amount of the flotation cost?

15.2 Rights Offerings The Hadron Corporation currently has 3 million shares outstanding. The stock sells for $40 per share. To raise $20 million for a new particle accelerator, the firm is considering a rights offering at $25 per share. What is the value of a right in this case? The ex-rights price?

ANSWERS TO CHAPTER REVIEW AND SELF-TEST PROBLEMS

15.1 The firm needs to net $15 million after paying the 7 percent flotation costs. So the amount raised is given by:

$$\text{Amount raised} \times (1 - .07) = \$15 \text{ million}$$
$$\text{Amount raised} = \$15 \text{ million}/.93 = \$16.129 \text{ million}$$

The total flotation cost is thus $1.129 million.

15.2 To raise $20 million at $25 per share, $20 million/$25 = 800,000 shares will have to be sold. Before the offering, the firm is worth 3 million × $40 = $120 million. The issue will raise $20 million, and there will be 3.8 million shares outstanding. The price of an ex-rights share will therefore be $140 million/3.8 million = $36.84. The value of a right is thus $40 − 36.84 = $3.16.

CONCEPTS REVIEW AND CRITICAL THINKING QUESTIONS

1. **Debt versus Equity Offering Size** [LO2] In the aggregate, debt offerings are much more common than equity offerings and typically much larger as well. Why?

2. **Debt versus Equity Flotation Costs** [LO2] Why are the costs of selling equity so much larger than the costs of selling debt?

3. **Bond Ratings and Flotation Costs** [LO2] Why do noninvestment-grade bonds have much higher direct costs than investment-grade issues?

4. **Underpricing in Debt Offerings** [LO2] Why is underpricing not a great concern with bond offerings?

     Use the following information to answer the next three questions. Zipcar, the car-sharing company, went public in April 2011. Assisted by the investment bank Goldman, Sachs & Co., Zipcar sold 9.68 million shares at $18 each, thereby raising a total of $174.24 million. By the end of the first day of trading, the stock had zipped to $28 per share, down from a high of $31.50. Based on the end-of-day numbers, Zipcar shares were apparently underpriced by about $10 each, meaning that the company missed out on an additional $96.8 million.

5. **IPO Pricing** [LO3] The Zipcar IPO was underpriced by about 56 percent. Should Zipcar be upset at Goldman over the underpricing?

6. **IPO Pricing** [LO3] In the previous question, how would it affect your thinking to know that the company was incorporated about 10 years earlier, had only $186 million in revenues in 2010, and had never earned a profit? Additionally, the viability of the company's business model was still unproven.

7. **IPO Pricing** [LO3] In the previous two questions, how would it affect your thinking to know that in addition to the 9.68 million shares offered in the IPO, Zipcar had an additional 30 million shares outstanding? Of those 30 million shares, 14.1 million shares were owned by four venture capital firms, and 15.5 million shares were owned by the 12 directors and executive officers.

8. **Cash Offer versus Rights Offer** [LO4] Ren-Stimpy International is planning to raise fresh equity capital by selling a large new issue of common stock. Ren-Stimpy is currently a publicly traded corporation, and it is trying to choose between an underwritten cash offer and a rights offering (not underwritten) to current shareholders. Ren-Stimpy management is interested in minimizing the selling costs and has asked you for advice on the choice of issue methods. What is your recommendation and why?

9. **IPO Underpricing** [LO3] In 1980, a certain assistant professor of finance bought 12 initial public offerings of common stock. He held each of these for approximately one month and then sold them. The investment rule he followed was to submit a purchase order for every firm commitment initial public offering of oil and gas exploration companies. There were 22 of these offerings, and he submitted a purchase order for approximately $1,000 in stock for each of the companies. With 10 of these, no shares were allocated to this assistant professor. With 5 of the 12 offerings that were purchased, fewer than the requested number of shares were allocated.

The year 1980 was very good for oil and gas exploration company owners: On average, for the 22 companies that went public, the stocks were selling for 80 percent above the offering price a month after the initial offering date. The assistant professor looked at his performance record and found that the $8,400 invested in the 12 companies had grown to $10,000, representing a return of only about 20 percent (commissions were negligible). Did he have bad luck, or should he have expected to do worse than the average initial public offering investor? Explain.

10. **IPO Pricing** [LO3] The following material represents the cover page and summary of the prospectus for the initial public offering of the Pest Investigation Control Corporation (PICC), which is going public tomorrow with a firm commitment initial public offering managed by the investment banking firm of Erlanger and Ritter. Answer the following questions:

   a. Assume you know nothing about PICC other than the information contained in the prospectus. Based on your knowledge of finance, what is your prediction for

---

PROSPECTUS   PICC

200,000 SHARES
PEST INVESTIGATION CONTROL CORPORATION

Of the shares being offered hereby, all 200,000 are being sold by the Pest Investigation Control Corporation, Inc. ("the Company"). Before the offering there has been no public market for the shares of PICC, and no guarantee can be given that any such market will develop.

These securities have not been approved or disapproved by the SEC nor has the commission passed upon the accuracy or adequacy of this prospectus. Any representation to the contrary is a criminal offense.

	Price to Public	Underwriting Discount	Proceeds to Company*
Per share	$11.00	$1.10	$9.90
Total	$2,200,000	$220,000	$1,980,000

*Before deducting expenses estimated at $27,000 and payable by the Company.

This is an initial public offering. The common shares are being offered, subject to prior sale, when, as, and if delivered to and accepted by the Underwriters and subject to approval of certain legal matters by their Counsel and by Counsel for the Company. The Underwriters reserve the right to withdraw, cancel, or modify such offer and to reject offers in whole or in part.

Erlanger and Ritter, Investment Bankers

July 12, 2018

Prospectus Summary

The Company	The Pest Investigation Control Corporation (PICC) breeds and markets toads and tree frogs as ecologically safe insect-control mechanisms.
The Offering	200,000 shares of common stock, no par value.
Listing	The Company will seek listing on NASDAQ and will trade over the counter.
Shares Outstanding	As of June 30, 2018, 400,000 shares of common stock were outstanding. After the offering, 600,000 shares of common stock will be outstanding.
Use of Proceeds	To finance expansion of inventory and receivables and general working capital, and to pay for country club memberships for certain finance professors.

Selected Financial Information
(amounts in thousands except per-share data)

	Fiscal Year Ended June 30				As of June 30, 2018	
	2016	2017	2018		Actual	As Adjusted for This Offering
Revenues	$60.00	$120.00	$240.00	Working capital	$ 8	$1,961
Net earnings	3.80	15.90	36.10	Total assets	511	2,464
Earnings per share	.01	.04	.09	Stockholders' equity	423	2,376

the price of PICC tomorrow? Provide a short explanation of why you think this will occur.

   b. Assume you have several thousand dollars to invest. When you get home from class tonight, you find that your stockbroker, whom you have not talked to for weeks, has called. She has left a message that PICC is going public tomorrow and that she can get you several hundred shares at the offering price if you call her back first thing in the morning. Discuss the merits of this opportunity.

QUESTIONS AND PROBLEMS

1. **Rights Offerings** [LO4] Leah, Inc., is proposing a rights offering. Presently there are 375,000 shares outstanding at $67 each. There will be 50,000 new shares offered at $58 each.

   a. What is the new market value of the company?

   b. How many rights are associated with one of the new shares?

   c. What is the ex-rights price?

   d. What is the value of a right?

   e. Why might a company have a rights offering rather than a general cash offer?

2. **Rights Offerings** [LO4] The Clifford Corporation has announced a rights offer to raise $35 million for a new journal, the *Journal of Financial Excess*. This journal will review potential articles after the author pays a nonrefundable reviewing fee of $5,000 per page. The stock currently sells for $53 per share, and there are 3.9 million shares outstanding.

   a. What is the maximum possible subscription price? What is the minimum?

   b. If the subscription price is set at $47 per share, how many shares must be sold? How many rights will it take to buy one share?

   c. What is the ex-rights price? What is the value of a right?

   d. Show how a shareholder with 1,000 shares before the offering and no desire (or money) to buy additional shares is not harmed by the rights offer.

3. **Rights** [LO4] Red Shoe Co. has concluded that additional equity financing will be needed to expand operations and that the needed funds will be best obtained through a rights offering. It has correctly determined that as a result of the rights offering, the share price will fall from $49 to $47.60 ($49 is the rights-on price; $47.60 is the ex-rights price, also known as the *when-issued* price). The company is seeking $16.5 million in additional funds with a per-share subscription price equal to $34. How many shares are there currently, before the offering? (Assume that the increment to the market value of the equity equals the gross proceeds from the offering.)

4. **IPO Underpricing** [LO3] The Woods Co. and the Spieth Co. have both announced IPOs at $40 per share. One of these is undervalued by $9, and the other is overvalued by $4, but you have no way of knowing which is which. You plan to buy 1,000 shares of each issue. If an issue is underpriced, it will be rationed, and only half your order will be filled. If you *could* get 1,000 shares in Woods and 1,000 shares in Spieth, what would your profit be? What profit do you actually expect? What principle have you illustrated?

5. **Calculating Flotation Costs** [LO3] The Whistling Straits Corporation needs to raise $60 million to finance its expansion into new markets. The company will sell new shares of equity via a general cash offering to raise the needed funds. If the offer price is $21 per share and the company's underwriters charge a spread of 7 percent, how many shares need to be sold?

BASIC
(Questions 1–8)

6. **Calculating Flotation Costs** [LO3] In Problem 5, if the SEC filing fee and associated administrative expenses of the offering are $1.2 million, how many shares need to be sold?

7. **Calculating Flotation Costs** [LO3] The Raven Co. has just gone public. Under a firm commitment agreement, Raven received $21.39 for each of the 20 million shares sold. The initial offering price was $23 per share, and the stock rose to $28.41 per share in the first few minutes of trading. Raven paid $950,000 in direct legal and other costs and $320,000 in indirect costs. What was the flotation cost as a percentage of funds raised?

8. **Price Dilution** [LO3] Nemesis, Inc., has 165,000 shares of stock outstanding. Each share is worth $77, so the company's market value of equity is $12,705,000. Suppose the firm issues 30,000 new shares at the following prices: $77, $73, and $65. What effect will each of these alternative offering prices have on the existing price per share?

INTERMEDIATE
(Questions 9–15)

9. **Dilution** [LO3] Wayne, Inc., wishes to expand its facilities. The company currently has 6 million shares outstanding and no debt. The stock sells for $64 per share, but the book value per share is $19. Net income is currently $11.5 million. The new facility will cost $30 million, and it will increase net income by $675,000.

    a. Assuming a constant price-earnings ratio, what will the effect be of issuing new equity to finance the investment? To answer, calculate the new book value per share, the new total earnings, the new EPS, the new stock price, and the new market-to-book ratio. What is going on here?

    b. What would the new net income for the company have to be for the stock price to remain unchanged?

10. **Dilution** [LO3] The Metallica Heavy Metal Mining (MHMM) Corporation wants to diversify its operations. Some recent financial information for the company is shown here:

Stock price	$ 75
Number of shares	64,000
Total assets	$9,400,000
Total liabilities	$4,100,000
Net income	$ 980,000

    MHMM is considering an investment that has the same PE ratio as the firm. The cost of the investment is $1.5 million, and it will be financed with a new equity issue. The return on the investment will equal MHMM's current ROE. What will happen to the book value per share, the market value per share, and the EPS? What is the NPV of this investment? Does dilution take place?

11. **Dilution** [LO3] In Problem 10, what would the ROE on the investment have to be if we wanted the price after the offering to be $75 per share? (Assume the PE ratio remains constant.) What is the NPV of this investment? Does any dilution take place?

12. **Rights** [LO4] Bell Hill Mfg. is considering a rights offer. The company has determined that the ex-rights price would be $63. The current price is $68 per share, and there are 26 million shares outstanding. The rights offer would raise a total of $70 million. What is the subscription price?

13. **Value of a Right** [LO4] Show that the value of a right just prior to expiration can be written as:

$$\text{Value of a right} = P_{RO} - P_X = (P_{RO} - P_S)/(N + 1)$$

where P_{RO}, P_S, and P_X stand for the rights-on price, the subscription price, and the ex-rights price, respectively, and N is the number of rights needed to buy one new share at the subscription price.

14. **Selling Rights** [LO4] Prahm Corp. wants to raise $4.7 million via a rights offering. The company currently has 530,000 shares of common stock outstanding that sell for $55 per share. Its underwriter has set a subscription price of $30 per share and will charge the company a spread of 6 percent. If you currently own 5,000 shares of stock in the company and decide not to participate in the rights offering, how much money can you get by selling your rights?

15. **Valuing a Right** [LO4] Knight Inventory Systems, Inc., has announced a rights offer. The company has announced that it will take four rights to buy a new share in the offering at a subscription price of $35. At the close of business the day before the ex-rights day, the company's stock sells for $60 per share. The next morning, you notice that the stock sells for $53 per share and the rights sell for $3 each. Are the stock and the rights correctly priced on the ex-rights day? Describe a transaction in which you could use these prices to create an immediate profit.

MINICASE

S&S Air Goes Public

Mark Sexton and Todd Story have been discussing the future of S&S Air. The company has been experiencing fast growth, and the two see only clear skies in the company's future. However, the fast growth can no longer be funded by internal sources, so Mark and Todd have decided the time is right to take the company public. To this end, they have entered into discussions with the investment bank of Crowe & Mallard. The company has a working relationship with Renata Harper, the underwriter who assisted with the company's previous bond offering. Crowe & Mallard have assisted numerous small companies in the IPO process, so Mark and Todd feel confident with this choice.

Renata begins by telling Mark and Todd about the process. Although Crowe & Mallard charged an underwriter fee of 4 percent on the bond offering, the underwriter fee is 7 percent on all initial stock offerings of the size of S&S Air's offering. Renata tells Mark and Todd that the company can expect to pay about $2.1 million in legal fees and expenses, $12,000 in SEC registration fees, and $15,000 in other filing fees. Additionally, to be listed on the NASDAQ, the company must pay $100,000. There are also transfer agent fees of $6,500 and engraving expenses of $520,000. The company should also expect to pay $110,000 for other expenses associated with the IPO.

Finally, Renata tells Mark and Todd that to file with the SEC, the company must provide three years' audited financial statements. She is unsure about the costs of the audit. Mark tells Renata that the company provides audited financial statements as part of the bond covenant, and the company pays $300,000 per year for the outside auditor.

QUESTIONS

1. At the end of the discussion, Mark asks Renata about the Dutch auction IPO process. What are the differences in the expenses to S&S Air if it uses a Dutch auction IPO versus a traditional IPO? Should the company go public through a Dutch auction or use a traditional underwritten offering?

2. During the discussion of the potential IPO and S&S Air's future, Mark states that he feels the company should raise $85 million. However, Renata points out that if the company needs more cash in the near future, a secondary offering close to the IPO would be problematic. Instead she suggests that the company should raise $95 million in the IPO. How can we calculate the optimal size of the IPO? What are the advantages and disadvantages of increasing the size of the IPO to $95 million?

3. After deliberation, Mark and Todd have decided that the company should use a firm commitment offering with Crowe & Mallard as the lead underwriter. The IPO will be for $85 million. Ignoring underpricing, how much will the IPO cost the company as a percentage of the funds received?

4. Many employees of S&S Air have shares of stock in the company because of an existing employee stock purchase plan. To sell the stock, the employees can tender their shares to be sold in the IPO at the offering price, or the employees can retain their stock and sell it in the secondary market after S&S Air goes public. Todd asks you to advise the employees about which option is best. What would you suggest to the employees?

Chapter

16 | Financial Leverage and Capital Structure Policy

NO MATTER HOW YOU you look at it, 2017 was a tough year for brick-and-mortar retailers. In January, women's retailer The Limited announced it was filing for bankruptcy after more than 50 years in business. Then in March, electronics retailer RadioShack filed for bankruptcy. What made RadioShack's bankruptcy unique is that the company had emerged from a previous bankruptcy in 2015. After that bankruptcy, the company was left with 1,200 stores, which were co-branded as Sprint stores, but it quickly failed again. And in September, Toys "R" Us filed for Chapter 11 bankruptcy. The toy retailer had $4.9 billion in debt on its balance sheet at the time of the bankruptcy filing. Overall, more than 19 publicly traded retailers filed for bankruptcy during 2017.

A firm's choice of how much debt it should have relative to equity is known as a *capital structure decision*. Such a choice has many implications for a firm and is far from being a settled issue in either theory or practice. In this chapter, we discuss the basic ideas underlying capital structures and how firms choose them.

A firm's capital structure is really just a reflection of its borrowing policy. Should we borrow a lot of money, or just a little? At first glance, it probably seems that debt is something to be avoided. After all, the more debt a firm has, the greater is the risk of bankruptcy. What we learn is that debt is really a double-edged sword, and, properly used, debt can be enormously beneficial to a firm.

A good understanding of the effects of debt financing is important because the role of debt is so misunderstood, and many firms (and individuals) are far too conservative in their use of debt. Having said this, we can also say that firms sometimes err in the opposite direction, becoming much too heavily indebted, with bankruptcy as the unfortunate consequence. Striking the right balance is what the capital structure issue is all about.

Learning Objectives

After studying this chapter, you should be able to:

LO1 Explain the effect of financial leverage.

LO2 Show the impact of taxes and bankruptcy on capital structure choice.

LO3 Describe the essentials of the bankruptcy process.

Thus far, we have taken the firm's capital structure as given. Debt-equity ratios don't just drop on firms from the sky, of course, so now it's time to wonder where they come from. Going back to Chapter 1, recall that we refer to decisions about a firm's debt-equity ratio as *capital structure decisions*.[1]

For the most part, a firm can choose any capital structure it wants. If management so desired, a firm could issue some bonds and use the proceeds to buy back some stock, thereby increasing the debt-equity ratio. Alternatively, it could issue stock and use the money to pay off some debt, thereby reducing the debt-equity ratio. Activities such as these, which alter the firm's existing capital structure, are called capital *restructurings*. In general, such restructurings take place whenever the firm substitutes one capital structure for another while leaving the firm's assets unchanged.

Because the assets of a firm are not directly affected by a capital restructuring, we can examine the firm's capital structure decision separately from its other activities. This means that a firm can consider capital restructuring decisions in isolation from its investment decisions. In this chapter, then, we will ignore investment decisions and focus on the long-term financing, or capital structure, question.

What we will see in this chapter is that capital structure decisions can have important implications for the value of the firm and its cost of capital. We will also find that important elements of the capital structure decision are easy to identify, but precise measures of these elements are generally not obtainable. As a result, we are able to give only an incomplete answer to the question of what the best capital structure might be for a particular firm at a particular time.

The Capital Structure Question   16.1

How should a firm go about choosing its debt-equity ratio? Here, as always, we assume that the guiding principle is to choose the course of action that maximizes the value of a share of stock. As we discuss next, when it comes to capital structure decisions, this is essentially the same thing as maximizing the value of the whole firm, and, for convenience, we will tend to frame our discussion in terms of firm value.

FIRM VALUE AND STOCK VALUE: AN EXAMPLE

The following example illustrates that the capital structure that maximizes the value of the firm is the one financial managers should choose for the shareholders, so there is no conflict in our goals. To begin, suppose the market value of the J.J. Sprint Company is $1,000. The company currently has no debt, and J.J. Sprint's 100 shares sell for $10 each. Further suppose that J.J. Sprint restructures itself by borrowing $500 and then paying out the proceeds to shareholders as an extra dividend of $500/100 = $5 per share.

This restructuring will change the capital structure of the firm with no direct effect on the firm's assets. The immediate effect will be to increase debt and decrease equity. What will be the final impact of the restructuring? Table 16.1 illustrates three possible outcomes in addition to the original no-debt case. Notice that in Scenario II, the value of the firm is unchanged at $1,000. In Scenario I, firm value rises to $1,250; it falls by $250, to $750, in Scenario III. We haven't yet said what might lead to these changes. For now, we just take them as possible outcomes to illustrate a point.

Because our goal is to benefit the shareholders, we next examine, in Table 16.2, the net payoffs to the shareholders in these scenarios. We see that, if the value of the firm stays the

---

[1] It is conventional to refer to decisions regarding debt and equity as *capital structure decisions*. The term *financial structure decisions* would be more accurate, and we use the terms interchangeably.

TABLE 16.1

Possible Firm Values:
No Debt versus Debt
plus Dividend

| | | Debt plus Dividend | | |
	No Debt	I	II	III
Debt	$ 0	$ 500	$ 500	$500
Equity	1,000	750	500	250
Firm value	$1,000	$1,250	$1,000	$750

TABLE 16.2

Possible Payoffs to
Shareholders: Debt
plus Dividend

| | Debt plus Dividend | | |
	I	II	III
Equity value reduction	−$250	−$500	−$750
Dividends	500	500	500
Net effect	+$250	$ 0	−$250

same, shareholders will experience a capital loss exactly offsetting the extra dividend. This is Scenario II. In Scenario I, the value of the firm increases to $1,250 and the shareholders come out ahead by $250. In other words, the restructuring has an NPV of $250 in this scenario. The NPV in Scenario III is −$250.

The key observation to make here is that the change in the value of the firm is the same as the net effect on the stockholders. Financial managers can try to find the capital structure that maximizes the value of the firm. Put another way, the NPV rule applies to capital structure decisions, and the change in the value of the overall firm is the NPV of a restructuring. J.J. Sprint should borrow $500 if it expects Scenario I. The crucial question in determining a firm's capital structure is, of course, which scenario is likely to occur.

CAPITAL STRUCTURE AND THE COST OF CAPITAL

In Chapter 14, we discussed the concept of the firm's weighted average cost of capital, or WACC. You may recall that the WACC tells us that the firm's overall cost of capital is a weighted average of the costs of the various components of the firm's capital structure. When we described the WACC, we took the firm's capital structure as given. One important issue that we will want to explore in this chapter is what happens to the cost of capital when we vary the amount of debt financing, or the debt-equity ratio.

A primary reason for studying the WACC is that the value of the firm is maximized when the WACC is minimized. To see this, recall that the WACC is the appropriate discount rate for the firm's overall cash flows. Because values and discount rates move in opposite directions, minimizing the WACC will maximize the value of the firm's cash flows.

We will want to choose the firm's capital structure so that the WACC is minimized. For this reason, we will say that one capital structure is better than another if it results in a lower weighted average cost of capital. Further, we say that a particular debt-equity ratio represents the *optimal capital structure* if it results in the lowest possible WACC. This optimal capital structure is sometimes called the firm's *target* capital structure as well.

Concept Questions
16.1a Why should financial managers choose the capital structure that maximizes the value of the firm?
16.1b What is the relationship between the WACC and the value of the firm?
16.1c What is an optimal capital structure?

The Effect of Financial Leverage

16.2

The previous section described why the capital structure that produces the highest firm value (or the lowest cost of capital) is the one most beneficial to stockholders. In this section, we examine the impact of financial leverage on the payoffs to stockholders. As you may recall, *financial leverage* refers to the extent to which a firm relies on debt. The more debt financing a firm uses in its capital structure, the more financial leverage it employs.

As we describe, financial leverage can dramatically alter the payoffs to shareholders in the firm. Remarkably, financial leverage may not affect the overall cost of capital. If this is true, then a firm's capital structure is irrelevant because changes in capital structure won't affect the value of the firm. We will return to this issue a little later.

THE BASICS OF FINANCIAL LEVERAGE

We start by illustrating how financial leverage works. For now, we ignore the impact of taxes. Also, for ease of presentation, we describe the impact of leverage in terms of its effects on earnings per share, EPS, and return on equity, ROE. These are accounting numbers and, as such, are not our primary concern. Using cash flows instead of these accounting numbers would lead to precisely the same conclusions, but a little more work would be needed. We discuss the impact on market values in a subsequent section.

Financial Leverage, EPS, and ROE: An Example   The Trans Am Corporation currently has no debt in its capital structure. The CFO, Ms. Morris, is considering a restructuring that would involve issuing debt and using the proceeds to buy back some of the outstanding equity. Table 16.3 presents both the current and proposed capital structures. As shown, the firm's assets have a market value of $8 million, and there are 400,000 shares outstanding. Because Trans Am is an all-equity firm, the price per share is $20.

The proposed debt issue would raise $4 million; the interest rate would be 10 percent. Because the stock sells for $20 per share, the $4 million in new debt would be used to purchase $4 million/$20 = 200,000 shares, leaving 200,000. After the restructuring, Trans Am would have a capital structure that was 50 percent debt, so the debt-equity ratio would be 1. Notice that, for now, we assume that the stock price will remain at $20.

To investigate the impact of the proposed restructuring, Ms. Morris has prepared Table 16.4, which compares the firm's current capital structure to the proposed capital structure under three scenarios. The scenarios reflect different assumptions about the firm's EBIT. Under the expected scenario, the EBIT is $1 million. In the recession scenario, EBIT falls to $500,000. In the expansion scenario, it rises to $1.5 million.

To illustrate some of the calculations behind the figures in Table 16.4, consider the expansion case. EBIT is $1.5 million. With no debt (the current capital structure) and no taxes, net income is also $1.5 million. In this case, there are 400,000 shares worth $8 million total.

	Current	Proposed
Assets	$8,000,000	$8,000,000
Debt	$ 0	$4,000,000
Equity	$8,000,000	$4,000,000
Debt-equity ratio	0	1
Share price	$ 20	$ 20
Shares outstanding	400,000	200,000
Interest rate	10%	10%

TABLE 16.3

Current and Proposed Capital Structures for the Trans Am Corporation

TABLE 16.4

Capital Structure Scenarios for the Trans Am Corporation

Current Capital Structure: No Debt			
	Recession	**Expected**	**Expansion**
EBIT	$500,000	$1,000,000	$1,500,000
Interest	0	0	0
Net income	$500,000	$1,000,000	$1,500,000
ROE	6.25%	12.50%	18.75%
EPS	$ 1.25	$ 2.50	$ 3.75
Proposed Capital Structure: Debt = $4 million			
EBIT	$500,000	$1,000,000	$1,500,000
Interest	400,000	400,000	400,000
Net income	$100,000	$ 600,000	$1,100,000
ROE	2.50%	15.00%	27.50%
EPS	$ .50	$ 3.00	$ 5.50

EPS is $1.5 million/400,000 = $3.75. Also, because accounting return on equity, ROE, is net income divided by total equity, ROE is $1.5 million/$8 million = .1875, or 18.75%.[2]

With $4 million in debt (the proposed capital structure), things are somewhat different. Because the interest rate is 10 percent, the interest bill is $400,000. With EBIT of $1.5 million, interest of $400,000, and no taxes, net income is $1.1 million. Now there are only 200,000 shares worth $4 million total. EPS is therefore $1.1 million/200,000 = $5.50, versus the $3.75 that we calculated in the previous, no-debt, scenario. Furthermore, ROE is $1.1 million/$4 million = .275, or 27.5%. This is well above the 18.75 percent we calculated for the current capital structure.

EPS versus EBIT   The impact of leverage is evident when the effect of the restructuring on EPS and ROE is examined. In particular, the variability in both EPS and ROE is much larger under the proposed capital structure. This illustrates how financial leverage acts to magnify gains and losses to shareholders.

In Figure 16.1, we take a closer look at the effect of the proposed restructuring. This figure plots earnings per share, EPS, against earnings before interest and taxes, EBIT, for the current and proposed capital structures. The first line, labeled "No debt," represents the case of no leverage. This line begins at the origin, indicating that EPS would be $0 if EBIT were $0. From there, every $400,000 increase in EBIT increases EPS by $1 (because there are 400,000 shares outstanding).

The second line represents the proposed capital structure. Here, EPS is negative if EBIT is $0. This follows because $400,000 of interest must be paid regardless of the firm's profits. Because there are 200,000 shares in this case, the EPS is −$2 as shown. Similarly, if EBIT were $400,000, EPS would be exactly $0.

The important thing to notice in Figure 16.1 is that the slope of the line in this second case is steeper. In fact, for every $400,000 increase in EBIT, EPS rises by $2, so the line is twice as steep. This tells us that EPS is twice as sensitive to changes in EBIT because of the financial leverage employed.

Another observation to make in Figure 16.1 is that the lines intersect. At that point, EPS is exactly the same for both capital structures. To find this point, note that EPS is equal to EBIT/400,000 in the no-debt case. In the with-debt case, EPS is (EBIT − $400,000)/200,000. If we set these equal to each other, EBIT is:

$$EBIT/400{,}000 = (EBIT - \$400{,}000)/200{,}000$$
$$EBIT = 2 \times (EBIT - \$400{,}000)$$
$$= \$800{,}000$$

---

[2]ROE is discussed in some detail in Chapter 3.

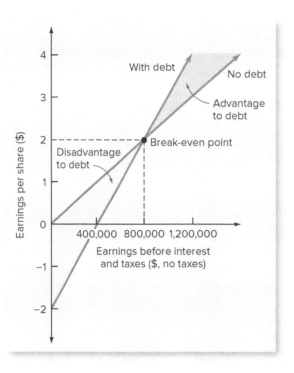

FIGURE 16.1

Financial Leverage: EPS and EBIT for the Trans Am Corporation

When EBIT is $800,000, EPS is $2 under either capital structure. This is labeled as the break-even point in Figure 16.1; we could also call it the indifference point. If EBIT is above this level, leverage is beneficial; if it is below this point, it is not.

There is another, more intuitive, way of seeing why the break-even point is $800,000. Notice that, if the firm has no debt and its EBIT is $800,000, its net income is also $800,000. In this case, the ROE is 10 percent. This is precisely the same as the interest rate on the debt, so the firm earns a return that is just sufficient to pay the interest.

Break-Even EBIT   **EXAMPLE 16.1**

The MPD Corporation has decided in favor of a capital restructuring. Currently, MPD uses no debt financing. Following the restructuring, debt will be $1 million. The interest rate on the debt will be 9 percent. MPD currently has 200,000 shares outstanding, and the price per share is $20. If the restructuring is expected to increase EPS, what is the minimum level for EBIT that MPD's management must be expecting? Ignore taxes in answering.

To answer, we calculate the break-even EBIT. At any EBIT above this, the increased financial leverage will increase EPS, so this will tell us the minimum level for EBIT. Under the old capital structure, EPS is EBIT/200,000. Under the new capital structure, the interest expense will be $1 million × .09 = $90,000. Furthermore, with the $1 million proceeds, MPD will repurchase $1 million/$20 = 50,000 shares of stock, leaving 150,000 shares outstanding. EPS will be (EBIT − $90,000)/150,000.

Now that we know how to calculate EPS under both scenarios, we set them equal to each other and solve for the break-even EBIT:

$$\text{EBIT}/200{,}000 = (\text{EBIT} - \$90{,}000)/150{,}000$$
$$\text{EBIT} = 4/3 \times (\text{EBIT} - \$90{,}000)$$
$$= \$360{,}000$$

Verify that, in either case, EPS is $1.80 when EBIT is $360,000. Management at MPD is apparently of the opinion that EPS will exceed $1.80.

CORPORATE BORROWING AND HOMEMADE LEVERAGE

Based on Tables 16.3 and 16.4 and Figure 16.1, Ms. Morris draws the following conclusions:

1. The effect of financial leverage depends on the company's EBIT. When EBIT is relatively high, leverage is beneficial.
2. Under the expected scenario, leverage increases the returns to shareholders, as measured by both ROE and EPS.
3. Shareholders are exposed to more risk under the proposed capital structure because the EPS and ROE are much more sensitive to changes in EBIT in this case.
4. Because of the impact that financial leverage has on both the expected return to stockholders and the riskiness of the stock, capital structure is an important consideration.

The first three of these conclusions are clearly correct. Does the last conclusion necessarily follow? Surprisingly, the answer is no. As we discuss next, the reason is that shareholders can adjust the amount of financial leverage by borrowing and lending on their own. This use of personal borrowing to alter the degree of financial leverage is called **homemade leverage**.

homemade leverage
The use of personal borrowing to change the overall amount of financial leverage to which the individual is exposed.

We will now illustrate that it actually makes no difference whether or not Trans Am adopts the proposed capital structure, because any stockholder who prefers the proposed capital structure can create it using homemade leverage. To begin, the first part of Table 16.5 shows what will happen to an investor who buys $2,000 worth of Trans Am stock if the proposed capital structure is adopted. This investor purchases 100 shares of stock. From Table 16.4, we know that EPS will be $.50, $3, or $5.50, so the total earnings for 100 shares will be either $50, $300, or $550 under the proposed capital structure.

Now, suppose that Trans Am does not adopt the proposed capital structure. In this case, EPS will be $1.25, $2.50, or $3.75. The second part of Table 16.5 demonstrates how a stockholder who prefers the payoffs under the proposed structure can create them using personal borrowing. To do this, the stockholder borrows $2,000 at 10 percent on his or her own. Our investor uses this amount, along with the original $2,000, to buy 200 shares of stock. As shown, the net payoffs are exactly the same as those for the proposed capital structure.

How did we know to borrow $2,000 to create the right payoffs? We are trying to replicate Trans Am's proposed capital structure at the personal level. The proposed capital structure results in a debt-equity ratio of 1. To replicate this structure at the personal level, the stockholder must borrow enough to create this same debt-equity ratio. Because the stockholder has $2,000 in equity invested, the borrowing of another $2,000 will create a personal debt-equity ratio of 1.

TABLE 16.5

Proposed Capital Structure versus Original Capital Structure with Homemade Leverage

Proposed Capital Structure			
	Recession	**Expected**	**Expansion**
EPS	$ .50	$ 3.00	$ 5.50
Earnings for 100 shares	50.00	300.00	550.00
Net cost = 100 shares × $20 = $2,000			
Original Capital Structure and Homemade Leverage			
EPS	$ 1.25	$ 2.50	$ 3.75
Earnings for 200 shares	250.00	500.00	750.00
Less: Interest on $2,000 at 10%	200.00	200.00	200.00
Net earnings	$ 50.00	$300.00	$550.00
Net cost = 200 shares × $20 − Amount borrowed = $4,000 − 2,000 = $2,000			

This example demonstrates that investors can always increase financial leverage themselves to create a different pattern of payoffs. It makes no difference whether Trans Am chooses the proposed capital structure.

Unlevering the Stock   EXAMPLE 16.2

In our Trans Am example, suppose management adopts the proposed capital structure. Further suppose that an investor who owns 100 shares prefers the original capital structure. Show how this investor could "unlever" the stock to re-create the original payoffs.

To create leverage, investors borrow on their own. To undo leverage, investors must lend money. In the case of Trans Am, the corporation borrowed an amount equal to half its value. The investor can unlever the stock by lending money in the same proportion. In this case, the investor sells 50 shares for $1,000 total and then lends the $1,000 at 10 percent. The payoffs are calculated in the following table:

	Recession	Expected	Expansion
EPS (proposed structure)	$ .50	$ 3.00	$ 5.50
Earnings for 50 shares	25.00	150.00	275.00
Plus: Interest on $1,000	100.00	100.00	100.00
Total payoff	$125.00	$250.00	$375.00

These are precisely the payoffs the investor would have experienced under the original capital structure.

Concept Questions

16.2a What is the impact of financial leverage on stockholders?

16.2b What is homemade leverage?

16.2c Why is Trans Am's capital structure irrelevant?

Capital Structure and the Cost of Equity Capital

16.3

Excel Master It!

xlsx Excel Master coverage online

We have seen that there is nothing special about corporate borrowing because investors can borrow or lend on their own. As a result, whichever capital structure Trans Am chooses, the stock price will be the same. Trans Am's capital structure is irrelevant, at least in the simple world we have examined.

Our Trans Am example is based on a famous argument advanced by two Nobel laureates, Franco Modigliani and Merton Miller, whom we will henceforth call M&M. What we illustrated for the Trans Am Corporation is a special case of **M&M Proposition I**. M&M Proposition I states that it is completely irrelevant how a firm chooses to arrange its finances.

M&M Proposition I
The proposition that the value of the firm is independent of the firm's capital structure.

M&M PROPOSITION I: THE PIE MODEL

One way to illustrate M&M Proposition I is to imagine two firms that are identical on the left side of the balance sheet. Their assets and operations are exactly the same. The right sides are different because the two firms finance their operations differently. In this case, we can view the capital structure question in terms of a "pie" model. Why we choose this

FIGURE 16.2

Two Pie Models of Capital Structure

name is apparent from Figure 16.2. Figure 16.2 gives two possible ways of cutting up the pie between the equity slice, *E*, and the debt slice, *D*: 40%–60% and 60%–40%. However, the size of the pie in Figure 16.2 is the same for both firms because the value of the assets is the same. This is precisely what M&M Proposition I states: The size of the pie doesn't depend on how it is sliced.

THE COST OF EQUITY AND FINANCIAL LEVERAGE: M&M PROPOSITION II

Although changing the capital structure of the firm does not change the firm's *total* value, it does cause important changes in the firm's debt and equity. We now examine what happens to a firm financed with debt and equity when the debt-equity ratio is changed. To simplify our analysis, we will continue to ignore taxes.

Based on our discussion in Chapter 14, if we ignore taxes, the weighted average cost of capital, WACC, is:

$$\text{WACC} = (E/V) \times R_E + (D/V) \times R_D$$

where *V* = *E* + *D*. We also saw that one way of interpreting the WACC is as the required return on the firm's overall assets. To remind us of this, we will use the symbol R_A to stand for the WACC and write:

$$R_A = (E/V) \times R_E + (D/V) \times R_D$$

If we rearrange this to solve for the cost of equity capital, we see that:

$$\boldsymbol{R_E = R_A + (R_A - R_D) \times (D/E)}$$

16.1

M&M Proposition II
The proposition that a firm's cost of equity capital is a positive linear function of the firm's capital structure.

This is the famous **M&M Proposition II**, which tells us that the cost of equity depends on three things: The required rate of return on the firm's assets, R_A; the firm's cost of debt, R_D; and the firm's debt-equity ratio, *D/E*.

Figure 16.3 summarizes our discussion thus far by plotting the cost of equity capital, R_E, against the debt-equity ratio. As shown, M&M Proposition II indicates that the cost of equity, R_E, is given by a straight line with a slope of $(R_A - R_D)$. The y-intercept corresponds to a firm with a debt-equity ratio of zero, so $R_A = R_E$ in that case. Figure 16.3 shows that as the firm raises its debt-equity ratio, the increase in leverage raises the risk of the equity and therefore the required return or cost of equity (R_E).

Notice in Figure 16.3 that the WACC doesn't depend on the debt-equity ratio; it's the same no matter what the debt-equity ratio is. This is another way of stating M&M Proposition I: The firm's overall cost of capital is unaffected by its capital structure. As illustrated, the fact that the cost of debt is lower than the cost of equity is exactly offset by the increase in the cost of equity from borrowing. In other words, the change in the capital structure weights (*E/V* and *D/V*) is exactly offset by the change in the cost of equity (R_E), so the WACC stays the same.

FIGURE 16.3

The Cost of Equity and the WACC: M&M Propositions I and II with No Taxes

$R_E = R_A + (R_A - R_D) \times (D/E)$ by M&M Proposition II

$R_A = \text{WACC} = \left(\dfrac{E}{V}\right) \times R_E + \left(\dfrac{D}{V}\right) \times R_D$

where $V = D + E$

The Cost of Equity Capital	EXAMPLE 16.3

The Ricardo Corporation has a weighted average cost of capital (ignoring taxes) of 12 percent. It can borrow at 8 percent. Assuming that Ricardo has a target capital structure of 80 percent equity and 20 percent debt, what is its cost of equity? What is the cost of equity if the target capital structure is 50 percent equity? Calculate the WACC using your answers to verify that it is the same.

According to M&M Proposition II, the cost of equity, R_E, is:

$$R_E = R_A + (R_A - R_D) \times (D/E)$$

In the first case, the debt-equity ratio is .2/.8 = .25, so the cost of the equity is:

$$R_E = .12 + (.12 - .08) \times .25$$
$$= .13, \text{ or } 13\%$$

In the second case, verify that the debt-equity ratio is 1.0, so the cost of equity is 16 percent.

We can now calculate the WACC assuming that the percentage of equity financing is 80 percent, the cost of equity is 13 percent, and the tax rate is zero:

$$\text{WACC} = (E/V) \times R_E + (D/V) \times R_D$$
$$= .80 \times .13 + .20 \times .08$$
$$= .12, \text{ or } 12\%$$

In the second case, the percentage of equity financing is 50 percent and the cost of equity is 16 percent. The WACC is:

$$\text{WACC} = (E/V) \times R_E + (D/V) \times R_D$$
$$= .50 \times .16 + .50 \times .08$$
$$= .12, \text{ or } 12\%$$

As we have calculated, the WACC is 12 percent in both cases.

IN THEIR OWN WORDS ...

Merton H. Miller on Capital Structure: M&M 30 Years Later

How difficult it is to summarize briefly the contribution of these papers was brought home to me very clearly after Franco Modigliani was awarded the Nobel Prize in Economics, in part—but, of course, only in part—for his work in finance. The television camera crews from our local stations in Chicago immediately descended upon me. "We understand," they said, "that you worked with Modigliani some years back in developing these M&M theorems, and we wonder if you could explain them briefly to our television viewers." "How briefly?" I asked. "Oh, take 10 seconds," was the reply.

Ten seconds to explain the work of a lifetime! Ten seconds to describe two carefully reasoned articles, each running to more than 30 printed pages and each with 60 or so long footnotes! When they saw the look of dismay on my face, they said, "You don't have to go into details. Just give us the main points in simple, common-sense terms."

The main point of the cost-of-capital article was, in principle at least, simple enough to make. It said that in an economist's ideal world, the total market value of all the securities issued by a firm would be governed by the earning power and risk of its underlying real assets and would be independent of how the mix of securities issued to finance it was divided between debt instruments and equity capital. Some corporate treasurers might well think that they could enhance total value by increasing the proportion of debt instruments because yields on debt instruments, given their lower risk, are, by and large, substantially below those on equity capital. But, under the ideal conditions assumed, the added risk to the shareholders from issuing more debt will raise required yields on the equity by just enough to offset the seeming gain from use of low-cost debt.

Such a summary would not only have been too long, but it relied on shorthand terms and concepts that are rich in connotations to economists, but hardly so to the general public. I thought, instead, of an analogy that we ourselves had invoked in the original paper. "Think of the firm," I said, "as a gigantic tub of whole milk. The farmer can sell the whole milk as is. Or he can separate out the cream and sell it at a considerably higher price than the whole milk would bring. (Selling cream is the analog of a firm selling low-yield and hence high-priced debt securities.) But, of course, what the farmer would have left would be skim milk, with low butterfat content, and that would sell for much less than whole milk. Skim milk corresponds to the levered equity. The M&M proposition says that if there were no costs of separation (and, of course, no government dairy support programs), the cream plus the skim milk would bring the same price as the whole milk."

The television people conferred among themselves for a while. They informed me that it was still too long, too complicated, and too academic. "Have you anything simpler?" they asked. I thought of another way in which the M&M proposition is presented that stresses the role of securities as devices for "partitioning" a firm's payoffs among the group of its capital suppliers. "Think of the firm," I said, "as a gigantic pizza, divided into quarters. If, now, you cut each quarter in half into eighths, the M&M proposition says that you will have more pieces, but not more pizza."

Once again whispered conversation. This time, they shut the lights off. They folded up their equipment. They thanked me for my cooperation. They said they would get back to me. But I knew that I had somehow lost my chance to start a new career as a packager of economic wisdom for TV viewers in convenient 10-second sound bites. Some have the talent for it; and some just don't.

The late Merton H. Miller was famous for his pathbreaking work with Franco Modigliani on corporate capital structure, cost of capital, and dividend policy. He received the Nobel Prize in Economics for his contributions shortly after this essay was prepared.

BUSINESS AND FINANCIAL RISK

business risk
The equity risk that comes from the nature of the firm's operating activities.

M&M Proposition II shows that the firm's cost of equity can be broken down into two components. The first component, R_A, is the required return on the firm's assets overall, and it depends on the nature of the firm's operating activities. The risk inherent in a firm's operations is called the **business risk** of the firm's equity. Referring back to Chapter 13, note that this business risk depends on the systematic risk of the firm's assets. The greater a firm's business risk, the greater R_A will be, and, all other things being the same, the greater will be the firm's cost of equity.

financial risk
The equity risk that comes from the financial policy (the capital structure) of the firm.

The second component in the cost of equity, $(R_A - R_D) \times (D/E)$, is determined by the firm's financial structure. For an all-equity firm, this component is zero. As the firm begins to rely on debt financing, the required return on equity rises. This occurs because the debt financing increases the risks borne by the stockholders. This extra risk that arises from the use of debt financing is called the **financial risk** of the firm's equity.

The total systematic risk of the firm's equity has two parts: Business risk and financial risk. The first part (the business risk) depends on the firm's assets and operations and is unaffected by capital structure. Given the firm's business risk (and its cost of debt), the second part (the financial risk) is completely determined by financial policy. As we have illustrated, the firm's cost of equity rises when the firm increases its use of financial leverage because the financial risk of the equity increases while the business risk remains the same.

Concept Questions

16.3a   What does M&M Proposition I state?

16.3b   What are the three determinants of a firm's cost of equity?

16.3c   The total systematic risk of a firm's equity has two parts. What are they?

M&M Propositions I and II with Corporate Taxes
16.4

Debt has two distinguishing features that we have not taken into proper account. First, as we have mentioned in a number of places, interest paid on debt is tax deductible. This is good for the firm, and it may be an added benefit of debt financing. Second, failure to meet debt obligations can result in bankruptcy. This is not good for the firm, and it may be an added cost of debt financing. Because we haven't explicitly considered either of these two features of debt, we realize that we may get a different answer about capital structure once we do. Accordingly, we consider taxes in this section and bankruptcy in the next one.

Our discussion here will assume that all interest paid is tax deductible. In reality, however, the Tax Cuts and Jobs Act of 2017 placed limits on the amount of interest that can be deducted. Specifically, for 2018 through 2021, the net interest deduction is limited to at most 30 percent of EBITDA. After 2021, it drops to 30 percent of EBIT. The term "net interest" means interest paid less interest earned (if any). Also, the limits aren't exactly based on EBITDA and EBIT because of some adjustments, but the differences will be minor in most cases. Importantly, any interest that can't be deducted in a particular year can be carried forward and deducted later. Thus, the tax deductibility isn't lost; it is deferred.

We can start by considering what happens to M&M Propositions I and II when we consider the effect of corporate taxes. To do this, we will examine two firms: Firm U (unlevered) and Firm L (levered). These two firms are identical on the left side of the balance sheet, so their assets and operations are the same.

We assume that EBIT is expected to be $1,000 every year forever for both firms. The difference between the firms is that Firm L has issued $1,000 worth of perpetual bonds on which it pays 8 percent interest each year. The interest bill is $.08 \times \$1,000 = \$80$ every year forever. Also, we assume that the corporate tax rate is 21 percent.

For our two firms, U and L, we can now calculate the following:

	Firm U	Firm L
EBIT	$1,000	$1,000.00
Interest	0	80.00
Taxable income	$1,000	$ 920.00
Taxes (21%)	210	193.20
Net income	$ 790	$ 726.80

THE INTEREST TAX SHIELD

To simplify things, we will assume that depreciation is zero. We will also assume that capital spending is zero and that there are no changes in NWC. In this case, cash flow from assets is equal to EBIT − Taxes. For Firms U and L, we have:

Cash Flow from Assets	Firm U	Firm L
EBIT	$1,000	$1,000.00
−Taxes	210	193.20
Total	$ 790	$ 806.80

We immediately see that capital structure is now having some effect because the cash flows from U and L are not the same even though the two firms have identical assets.

To see what's going on, we can compute the cash flow to stockholders and bondholders:

Cash Flow	Firm U	Firm L
To stockholders	$790	$726.80
To bondholders	0	80.00
Total	$790	$806.80

What we are seeing is that the total cash flow to L is $16.80 more. This occurs because L's tax bill (which is a cash outflow) is $16.80 less. The fact that interest is deductible for tax purposes has generated a tax savings equal to the interest payment ($80) multiplied by the corporate tax rate (21 percent): $80 × .21 = $16.80. We call this tax savings the **interest tax shield**.

interest tax shield
The tax savings attained by a firm from interest expense.

TAXES AND M&M PROPOSITION I

Because the debt is perpetual, the same $16.80 shield will be generated every year forever. The aftertax cash flow to L will be the same $790 that U earns plus the $16.80 tax shield. Because L's cash flow is always $16.80 greater, Firm L is worth more than Firm U, the difference being the value of this $16.80 perpetuity.

Because the tax shield is generated by paying interest, it has the same risk as the debt, and 8 percent (the cost of debt) is the appropriate discount rate. The value of the tax shield is:

$$PV = \frac{\$16.80}{.08} = \frac{.21 \times \$1,000 \times .08}{.08} = .21 \times \$1,000 = \$210$$

As our example illustrates, the present value of the interest tax shield can be written as:

Present value of the interest tax shield $= (T_c \times D \times R_D)/R_D$ **16.2**
$$= T_c \times D$$

We have now come up with another famous result, M&M Proposition I with corporate taxes. We have seen that the value of Firm L, V_L, exceeds the value of Firm U, V_U, by the present value of the interest tax shield, $T_c \times D$. M&M Proposition I with taxes states that:

$V_L = V_U + T_c \times D$ **16.3**

The effect of borrowing in this case is illustrated in Figure 16.4. We have plotted the value of the levered firm, V_L, against the amount of debt, D. M&M Proposition I with corporate taxes implies that the relationship is given by a straight line with a slope of T_c and a y-intercept of V_U.

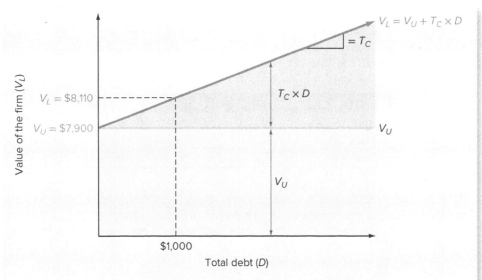

FIGURE 16.4

M&M Proposition I with Taxes

The value of the firm increases as total debt increases because of the interest tax shield. This is the basis of M&M Proposition I with taxes.

In Figure 16.4, we have also drawn a horizontal line representing V_U. As indicated, the distance between the two lines is $T_c \times D$, the present value of the tax shield.

Suppose that the cost of capital for Firm U is 10 percent. We will call this the **unlevered cost of capital**, and we will use the symbol R_U to represent it. We can think of R_U as the cost of capital a firm would have if it had no debt. Firm U's cash flow is $790 every year forever and, because U has no debt, the appropriate discount rate is $R_U = 10\%$. The value of the unlevered firm, V_U, is:

unlevered cost of capital
The cost of capital for a firm that has no debt.

$$V_U = \frac{\text{EBIT} \times (1 - T_c)}{R_U}$$
$$= \frac{\$790}{.10}$$
$$= \$7,900$$

The value of the levered firm, V_L, is:

$$V_L = V_U + T_c \times D$$
$$= \$7,900 + .21 \times 1,000$$
$$= \$8,110$$

As Figure 16.4 indicates, the value of the firm goes up by $.21 for every $1 in debt. In other words, the NPV *per dollar* of debt is $.21. It is difficult to imagine why any corporation would not borrow to the absolute maximum under these circumstances.

The result of our analysis in this section is the realization that, once we include taxes, capital structure definitely matters. However, we immediately reach the illogical conclusion that the optimal capital structure is 100 percent debt.

TAXES, THE WACC, AND PROPOSITION II

We can also conclude that the best capital structure is 100 percent debt by examining the weighted average cost of capital. From Chapter 14, we know that once we consider the effect of taxes, the WACC is:

$$\text{WACC} = (E/V) \times R_E + (D/V) \times R_D \times (1 - T_C)$$

To calculate this WACC, we need to know the cost of equity. M&M Proposition II with corporate taxes states that the cost of equity is:

$$\boldsymbol{R_E = R_U + (R_U - R_D) \times (D/E) \times (1 - T_C)}$$ **16.4**

To illustrate, recall that we saw a moment ago that Firm L is worth $8,110 total. Because the debt is worth $1,000, the equity must be worth $8,110 − 1,000 = $7,110. For Firm L, the cost of equity is:

$$R_E = .10 + (.10 - .08) \times (\$1,000/\$7,110) \times (1 - .21)$$
$$= .1022, \text{ or } 10.22\%$$

The weighted average cost of capital is:

$$\text{WACC} = (\$7,110/\$8,110) \times .1022 + (\$1,000/\$8,110) \times .08 \times (1 - .21)$$
$$= .0974, \text{ or } 9.74\%$$

Without debt, the WACC is over 10 percent; with debt, it is 9.74 percent. Therefore, the firm is better off with debt.

CONCLUSION

Figure 16.5 summarizes our discussion concerning the relationship between the cost of equity, the aftertax cost of debt, and the weighted average cost of capital. For reference,

FIGURE 16.5

The Cost of Equity and the WACC: M&M Proposition II with Taxes

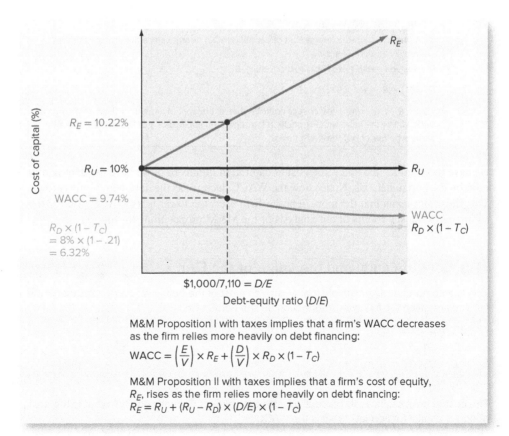

M&M Proposition I with taxes implies that a firm's WACC decreases as the firm relies more heavily on debt financing:

$$\text{WACC} = \left(\frac{E}{V}\right) \times R_E + \left(\frac{D}{V}\right) \times R_D \times (1 - T_C)$$

M&M Proposition II with taxes implies that a firm's cost of equity, R_E, rises as the firm relies more heavily on debt financing:

$$R_E = R_U + (R_U - R_D) \times (D/E) \times (1 - T_C)$$

TABLE 16.6

Modigliani and Miller Summary

I.	The No-Tax Case

A. Proposition I: The value of the firm levered (V_L) is equal to the value of the firm unlevered (V_U):

$$V_L = V_U$$

Implications of Proposition I:

1. A firm's capital structure is irrelevant.

2. A firm's weighted average cost of capital (WACC) is the same no matter what mixture of debt and equity is used to finance the firm.

B. Proposition II: The cost of equity, R_E, is:

$$R_E = R_A + (R_A - R_D) \times (D/E)$$

where R_A is the WACC, R_D is the cost of debt, and D/E is the debt-equity ratio.

Implications of Proposition II:

1. The cost of equity rises as the firm increases its use of debt financing.

2. The risk of the equity depends on two things: The riskiness of the firm's operations (*business risk*) and the degree of financial leverage (*financial risk*). Business risk determines R_A; financial risk is determined by D/E.

II.	The Tax Case

A. Proposition I with taxes: The value of the firm levered (V_L) is equal to the value of the firm unlevered (V_U) plus the present value of the interest tax shield:

$$V_L = V_U + T_C \times D$$

where T_C is the corporate tax rate and D is the amount of debt.

Implications of Proposition I:

1. Debt financing is highly advantageous, and, in the extreme, a firm's optimal capital structure is 100 percent debt.

2. A firm's weighted average cost of capital (WACC) decreases as the firm relies more heavily on debt financing.

B. Proposition II with taxes: The cost of equity, R_E, is:

$$R_E = R_U + (R_U - R_D) \times (D/E) \times (1 - T_C)$$

where R_U is the *unlevered cost of capital*—that is, the cost of capital for the firm if it has no debt. Unlike the case with Proposition I, the general implications of Proposition II are the same whether or not there are taxes.

we have included R_U, the unlevered cost of capital. In Figure 16.5, we have the debt-equity ratio on the horizontal axis. Notice how the WACC declines as the debt-equity ratio grows. This illustrates again that the more debt the firm uses, the lower is its WACC. Table 16.6 summarizes the key results of our analysis of the M&M propositions for future reference.

The Cost of Equity and the Value of the Firm	EXAMPLE 16.4

This is a comprehensive example that illustrates most of the points we have discussed thus far. You are given the following information for the Format Co.:

EBIT = $126.58

T_C = .21

D = $500

R_U = .20

The cost of debt capital is 10 percent. What is the value of Format's equity? What is the cost of equity capital for Format? What is the WACC?

This one's easier than it looks. Remember that all the cash flows are perpetuities. The value of the firm if it has no debt, V_U, is:

$$V_U = \frac{\text{EBIT} - \text{Taxes}}{R_U} = \frac{\text{EBIT} \times (1 - T_c)}{R_U}$$
$$= \frac{\$100}{.20}$$
$$= \$500$$

From M&M Proposition I with taxes, we know that the value of the firm with debt is:

$$V_L = V_U + T_c \times D$$
$$= \$500 + .21 \times \$500$$
$$= \$605$$

Because the firm is worth $605 total and the debt is worth $500, the equity is worth $105:

$$E = V_L - D$$
$$= \$605 - 500$$
$$= \$105$$

Based on M&M Proposition II with taxes, the cost of equity is:

$$R_E = R_U + (R_U - R_D) \times (D/E) \times (1 - T_c)$$
$$= .20 + (.20 - .10) \times (\$500/\$105) \times (1 - .21)$$
$$= .5762, \text{ or } 57.62\%$$

Finally, the WACC is:

$$\text{WACC} = (\$105/\$605) \times .5762 + (\$500/\$605) \times .10 \times (1 - .21)$$
$$= .1653, \text{ or } 16.53\%$$

Notice that this is lower than the cost of capital for the firm with no debt ($R_U = 20\%$), so debt financing is advantageous.

Concept Questions

16.4a   What is the relationship between the value of an unlevered firm and the value of a levered firm once we consider the effect of corporate taxes?

16.4b   If we consider only the effect of taxes, what is the optimal capital structure?

16.5 Bankruptcy Costs

One limiting factor affecting the amount of debt a firm might use comes in the form of *bankruptcy costs*. As the debt-equity ratio rises, so too does the probability that the firm will be unable to pay its bondholders what was promised to them. When this happens, ownership of the firm's assets is ultimately transferred from the stockholders to the bondholders.

In principle, a firm becomes bankrupt when the value of its assets equals the value of its debt. When this occurs, the value of equity is zero, and the stockholders turn over control of the firm to the bondholders. When this takes place, the bondholders hold assets whose value is exactly equal to what is owed on the debt. In a perfect world, there are no costs associated with this transfer of ownership, and the bondholders don't lose anything.

This idealized view of bankruptcy is not, of course, what happens in the real world. Ironically, it is expensive to go bankrupt. As we discuss, the costs associated with bankruptcy may eventually offset the tax-related gains from leverage.

DIRECT BANKRUPTCY COSTS

When the value of a firm's assets equals the value of its debt, then the firm is economically bankrupt in the sense that the equity has no value. However, the formal turning over of the assets to the bondholders is a *legal* process, not an economic one. There are legal and administrative costs to bankruptcy, and it has been remarked that bankruptcies are to lawyers what blood is to sharks.

For example, in September 2008, famed investment bank Lehman Brothers filed for bankruptcy in the largest U.S. bankruptcy to date. The company emerged from bankruptcy in March 2012 as a liquidating trust, with the goal of selling off assets and paying creditors. The direct bankruptcy costs were eye-watering: Lehman spent more than $2.2 billion (that's "billion" with a "b") on lawyers, accountants, consultants, and examiners for its U.S. and European operations. The individual costs submitted by one law firm were equally amazing: The firm requested $200,000 for business meals, $439,000 for computerized and other research, $115,000 for local transportation, and $287,000 for copying charges at 10 cents per page. The other costs of bankruptcy may have been even larger. Some experts estimated that because Lehman rushed into bankruptcy it lost out on $75 billion that it could have earned if the sale of many of its assets had been better planned.

Because of the expenses associated with bankruptcy, bondholders won't get all that they are owed. Some fraction of the firm's assets will "disappear" in the legal process of going bankrupt. These are the legal and administrative expenses associated with the bankruptcy proceeding. We call these costs **direct bankruptcy costs**.

These direct bankruptcy costs are a disincentive to debt financing. If a firm goes bankrupt, then, suddenly, a piece of the firm disappears. This amounts to a bankruptcy "tax." So a firm faces a trade-off: Borrowing saves a firm money on its corporate taxes, but the more a firm borrows, the more likely it is that the firm will become bankrupt and have to pay the bankruptcy tax.

direct bankruptcy costs
The costs that are directly associated with bankruptcy, such as legal and administrative expenses.

INDIRECT BANKRUPTCY COSTS

Because it is expensive to go bankrupt, a firm will spend resources to avoid doing so. When a firm is having significant problems in meeting its debt obligations, we say that it is experiencing financial distress. Some financially distressed firms ultimately file for bankruptcy, but most do not because they are able to recover or otherwise survive.

The costs of avoiding a bankruptcy filing incurred by a financially distressed firm are called **indirect bankruptcy costs**. We use the term **financial distress costs** to refer generically to the direct and indirect costs associated with going bankrupt or avoiding a bankruptcy filing.

The problems that come up in financial distress are particularly severe, and the financial distress costs are larger, when the stockholders and the bondholders are different groups. Until the firm is legally bankrupt, the stockholders control it. They, of course, will take actions in their own economic interests. Because the stockholders can be wiped out in a legal bankruptcy, they have a very strong incentive to avoid a bankruptcy filing.

The bondholders, on the other hand, are primarily concerned with protecting the value of the firm's assets and will try to take control away from stockholders. They have a strong incentive to seek bankruptcy to protect their interests and keep stockholders from further dissipating the assets of the firm. The net effect of all this fighting is that a long, drawn-out, and potentially quite expensive legal battle gets started.

indirect bankruptcy costs
The costs of avoiding a bankruptcy filing incurred by a financially distressed firm.

financial distress costs
The direct and indirect costs associated with going bankrupt or experiencing financial distress.

Meanwhile, as the wheels of justice turn in their ponderous ways, the assets of the firm lose value because management is busy trying to avoid bankruptcy instead of running the business. Normal operations are disrupted, and sales are lost. Valuable employees leave, potentially fruitful programs are dropped to preserve cash, and otherwise profitable investments are not taken.

For example, in 2008, both General Motors and Chrysler were experiencing significant financial difficulty, and many people felt that one or both companies would eventually file for bankruptcy (both later did). As a result of the bad news surrounding them, there was a loss of confidence in the companies' automobiles. A study showed that 75 percent of Americans would not purchase an automobile from a bankrupt company because the company might not honor the warranty, and it might be difficult to obtain replacement parts. This concern resulted in lost potential sales for both companies, which only added to their financial distress.

These are all indirect bankruptcy costs, or costs of financial distress. Whether or not the firm ultimately goes bankrupt, the net effect is a loss of value because the firm chose to use debt in its capital structure. It is this possibility of loss that limits the amount of debt that a firm will choose to use.

Concept Questions

16.5a   What are direct bankruptcy costs?
16.5b   What are indirect bankruptcy costs?

16.6 Optimal Capital Structure

Our previous two sections have established the basis for determining an optimal capital structure. A firm will borrow because the interest tax shield is valuable. At relatively low debt levels, the probability of bankruptcy and financial distress is low, and the benefit from debt outweighs the cost. At very high debt levels, the possibility of financial distress is a chronic, ongoing problem for the firm, so the benefits from debt financing may be more than offset by the financial distress costs. Based on our discussion, it would appear that an optimal capital structure exists somewhere in between these extremes.

THE STATIC THEORY OF CAPITAL STRUCTURE

static theory of capital structure
The theory that a firm borrows up to the point where the tax benefit from an extra dollar in debt is exactly equal to the cost that comes from the increased probability of financial distress.

The theory of capital structure that we have outlined is called the **static theory of capital structure**. It says that firms borrow up to the point where the tax benefit from an extra dollar in debt is exactly equal to the cost that comes from the increased probability of financial distress. We call this the static theory because it assumes that the firm is fixed in terms of its assets and operations and it considers only possible changes in the debt-equity ratio.

The static theory is illustrated in Figure 16.6, which plots the value of the firm, V_L, against the amount of debt, D. In Figure 16.6, we have drawn lines corresponding to three different stories. The first represents M&M Proposition I with no taxes. This is the horizontal line extending from V_U, and it indicates that the value of the firm is unaffected by its capital structure. The second case, M&M Proposition I with corporate taxes, is represented by the upward-sloping straight line. These two cases are exactly the same as the ones we previously illustrated in Figure 16.4.

FIGURE 16.6   **The Static Theory of Capital Structure: The Optimal Capital Structure and the Value of the Firm**

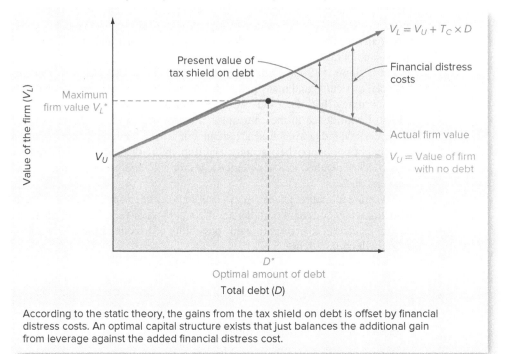

According to the static theory, the gains from the tax shield on debt is offset by financial distress costs. An optimal capital structure exists that just balances the additional gain from leverage against the added financial distress cost.

The third case in Figure 16.6 illustrates our current discussion: The value of the firm rises to a maximum and then declines beyond that point. This is the picture that we get from our static theory. The maximum value of the firm, V_L^*, is reached at D^*, so this point represents the optimal amount of borrowing. Put another way, the firm's optimal capital structure is composed of D^*/V_L^* in debt and $(1 - D^*/V_L^*)$ in equity.

The final thing to notice in Figure 16.6 is that the difference between the value of the firm in our static theory and the M&M value of the firm with taxes is the loss in value from the possibility of financial distress. Also, the difference between the static theory value of the firm and the M&M value with no taxes is the gain from leverage, net of distress costs.

OPTIMAL CAPITAL STRUCTURE AND THE COST OF CAPITAL

As we discussed earlier, the capital structure that maximizes the value of the firm is also the one that minimizes the cost of capital. Figure 16.7 illustrates the static theory of capital structure in terms of the weighted average cost of capital and the costs of debt and equity. Notice in Figure 16.7 that we have plotted the various capital costs against the debt-equity ratio, D/E.

Figure 16.7 is much the same as Figure 16.5 except that we have added a new line for the WACC. This line, which corresponds to the static theory, declines at first. This occurs because the aftertax cost of debt is cheaper than equity, so, at least initially, the overall cost of capital declines.

At some point, the cost of debt begins to rise, and the fact that debt is cheaper than equity is more than offset by the financial distress costs. From this point, further increases in debt actually increase the WACC. As illustrated, the minimum WACC* occurs at the point D^*/E^*, just as we described before.

FIGURE 16.7

The Static Theory of Capital Structure: The Optimal Capital Structure and the Cost of Capital

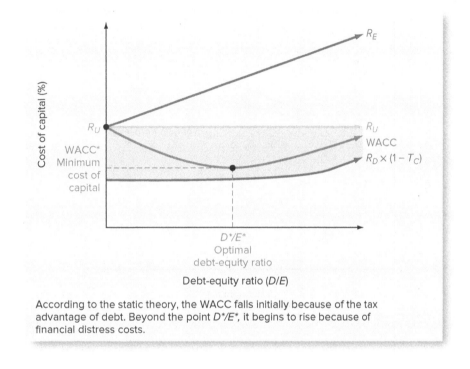

According to the static theory, the WACC falls initially because of the tax advantage of debt. Beyond the point D^*/E^*, it begins to rise because of financial distress costs.

OPTIMAL CAPITAL STRUCTURE: A RECAP

With the help of Figure 16.8, we can recap (no pun intended) our discussion of capital structure and cost of capital. As we have noted, there are essentially three cases. We will use the simplest of the three cases as a starting point and then build up to the static theory of capital structure. Along the way, we will pay particular attention to the connection between capital structure, firm value, and cost of capital.

Figure 16.8 presents the original Modigliani and Miller no-tax, no-bankruptcy argument as Case I. This is the most basic case. In the top part of the figure, we have plotted the value of the firm, V_L, against total debt, D. When there are no taxes, bankruptcy costs, or other real-world imperfections, we know that the total value of the firm is not affected by its debt policy, so V_L is constant. The bottom part of Figure 16.8 tells the same story in terms of the cost of capital. Here, the weighted average cost of capital, WACC, is plotted against the debt-equity ratio, D/E. As with total firm value, the overall cost of capital is not affected by debt policy in this basic case, so the WACC is constant.

Next, we consider what happens to the original M&M argument once taxes are introduced. As Case II illustrates, we now see that the firm's value critically depends on its debt policy. The more the firm borrows, the more it is worth. From our earlier discussion, we know this happens because interest payments are tax deductible, and the gain in firm value is equal to the present value of the interest tax shield.

In the bottom part of Figure 16.8, notice how the WACC declines as the firm uses more and more debt financing. As the firm increases its financial leverage, the cost of equity does increase; but this increase is more than offset by the tax break associated with debt financing. As a result, the firm's overall cost of capital declines.

To finish our story, we include the impact of bankruptcy, or financial distress costs, to get Case III. As shown in the top part of Figure 16.8, the value of the firm will not be as large as we previously indicated. The reason is that the firm's value is reduced by the present value of the potential future bankruptcy costs. These costs grow as the

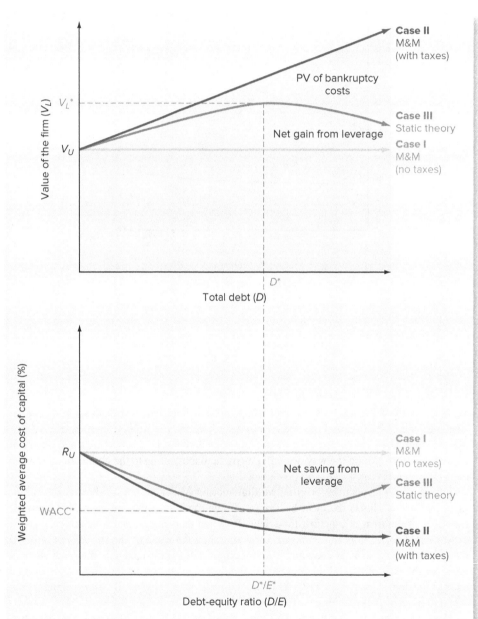

FIGURE 16.8

The Capital Structure Question

Case I
With no taxes or bankruptcy costs, the value of the firm and its weighted average cost of capital are not affected by capital structures.

Case II
With corporate taxes and no bankruptcy costs, the value of the firm increases and the weighted average cost of capital decreases as the amount of debt goes up.

Case III
With corporate taxes and bankruptcy costs, the value of the firm, V_L, reaches a maximum at D^*, the point representing the optimal amount of borrowing. At the same time, the weighted average cost of capital, WACC, is minimized at D^*/E^*.

firm borrows more and more, and they eventually overwhelm the tax advantage of debt financing. The optimal capital structure occurs at D^*, the point at which the tax savings from an additional dollar in debt financing is exactly balanced by the increased bankruptcy costs associated with the additional borrowing. This is the essence of the static theory of capital structure.

The bottom part of Figure 16.8 presents the optimal capital structure in terms of the cost of capital. Corresponding to D^*, the optimal debt level, is the optimal debt-equity ratio, D^*/E^*. At this level of debt financing, the lowest possible weighted average cost of capital, $WACC^*$, occurs.

CAPITAL STRUCTURE: SOME MANAGERIAL RECOMMENDATIONS

The static model that we have described is not capable of identifying a precise optimal capital structure, but it does point out two of the more relevant factors: Taxes and financial distress. We can draw some limited conclusions concerning these.

Taxes   First of all, the tax benefit from leverage is obviously important only to firms that are in a tax-paying position. Firms with substantial accumulated losses will get little value from the interest tax shield. Furthermore, firms that have substantial tax shields from other sources, such as depreciation, will get less benefit from leverage.

Also, firms all face the same 21 percent federal tax rate beginning in 2018, but other taxes (such as state taxes) create different effective tax rates. The higher the effective tax rate, the greater the incentive to borrow.

Financial Distress   Firms with a greater risk of experiencing financial distress will borrow less than firms with a lower risk of financial distress. For example, all other things being equal, the greater the volatility in EBIT, the less a firm should borrow.

In addition, financial distress is more costly for some firms than for others. The costs of financial distress depend primarily on the firm's assets. In particular, financial distress costs will be determined by how easily ownership of those assets can be transferred.

For example, a firm with mostly tangible assets that can be sold without great loss in value will have an incentive to borrow more. For firms that rely heavily on intangibles, such as employee talent or growth opportunities, debt will be less attractive because these assets effectively cannot be sold.

Concept Questions

16.6a   Can you describe the trade-off that defines the static theory of capital structure?

16.6b   What are the important factors in making capital structure decisions?

16.7 The Pie Again

Although it is comforting to know that the firm might have an optimal capital structure when we take into account real-world matters such as taxes and financial distress costs, it is disquieting to see the elegant original M&M intuition (that is, the no-tax version) fall apart in the face of these matters.

Critics of the M&M theory often say that it fails to hold as soon as we add in real-world issues and that the M&M theory is really just that: A theory that doesn't have much to say about the real world that we live in. In fact, they would argue that it is the M&M theory that is irrelevant, not capital structure. As we discuss next, taking that view blinds critics to the real value of the M&M theory.

THE EXTENDED PIE MODEL

To illustrate the value of the original M&M intuition, we briefly consider an expanded version of the pie model that we introduced earlier. In the extended pie model, taxes represent just another claim on the cash flows of the firm. Because taxes are reduced as leverage is increased, the value of the government's claim (G) on the firm's cash flows decreases with leverage.

Bankruptcy costs are also a claim on the cash flows of the firm. They come into play as the firm comes close to bankruptcy and has to alter its behavior to attempt to stave off the event itself, and they become large when bankruptcy actually takes place. The value of this claim (B) on the cash flows rises with increases in the debt-equity ratio.

The extended pie model holds that all of these claims can be paid from only one source: The cash flows (CF) of the firm. Algebraically, we must have:

CF = Payments to stockholders
     + Payments to creditors
     + Payments to the government
     + Payments to bankruptcy courts and lawyers
     + Payments to any and all other claimants to the cash flows of the firm

The extended pie model is illustrated in Figure 16.9. Notice that we have added a few slices for the additional groups. Notice also the change in the relative sizes of the slices as the firm's use of debt financing is increased.

With the list we have developed, we have not even begun to exhaust the potential claims to the firm's cash flows. To give an unusual example, we might say that everyone reading this book has an economic claim on the cash flows of General Motors. After all, if you are injured in an accident, you might sue GM, and, win or lose, GM will expend some of its cash flow in dealing with the matter. For GM, or any other company, there should be a slice of the pie representing potential lawsuits. This is the essence of the M&M intuition

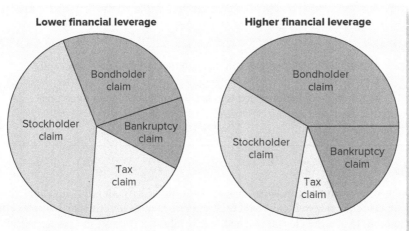

FIGURE 16.9

The Extended Pie Model

In the extended pie model, the value of all the claims against the firm's cash flows is unaffected by capital structure, but the *relative* values of claims change as the amount of debt financing is increased.

and theory: The value of the firm depends on the total cash flow of the firm. The firm's capital structure just cuts that cash flow up into slices without altering the total. What we recognize now is that the stockholders and the bondholders may not be the only ones who can claim a slice.

MARKETED CLAIMS VERSUS NONMARKETED CLAIMS

With our extended pie model, there is an important distinction between claims such as those of stockholders and bondholders, on the one hand, and those of the government and potential litigants in lawsuits on the other. The first set of claims are *marketed claims*, and the second set are *nonmarketed claims*. A key difference is that the marketed claims can be bought and sold in financial markets and the nonmarketed claims cannot be sold in financial markets.

When we speak of the value of the firm, we are generally referring to just the value of the marketed claims, V_M, and not the value of the nonmarketed claims, V_N. If we write V_T for the total value of *all* the claims against a corporation's cash flows, then:

$$V_T = E + D + G + B + \cdots$$
$$= V_M + V_N$$

The essence of our extended pie model is that this total value, V_T, of all the claims to the firm's cash flows is unaltered by capital structure. However, the value of the marketed claims, V_M, may be affected by changes in the capital structure.

Based on the extended pie model, any increase in V_M must imply an identical decrease in V_N. The optimal capital structure is the one that maximizes the value of the marketed claims or, equivalently, minimizes the value of nonmarketed claims such as taxes and bankruptcy costs.

Concept Questions

16.7a   What are some of the claims to a firm's cash flows?

16.7b   What is the difference between a marketed claim and a nonmarketed claim?

16.7c   What does the extended pie model say about the value of all the claims to a firm's cash flows?

16.8 The Pecking-Order Theory

The static theory we have developed in this chapter has dominated thinking about capital structure for a long time, but it has some shortcomings. Perhaps the most obvious is that many large, financially sophisticated, and highly profitable firms use little debt. This is the opposite of what we would expect. Under the static theory, these are the firms that should use the *most* debt because there is little risk of bankruptcy and the value of the tax shield is substantial. Why do they use so little debt? The pecking-order theory, which we consider next, may be part of the answer.

INTERNAL FINANCING AND THE PECKING ORDER

The pecking-order theory is an alternative to the static theory. A key element in the pecking-order theory is that firms prefer to use internal financing whenever possible.

A simple reason is that selling securities to raise cash can be expensive, so it makes sense to avoid doing so if possible. If a firm is very profitable, it might never need external financing; so it would end up with little or no debt. For example, in late 2017, Alphabet's balance sheet showed assets of $189.5 billion, of which almost $100.3 billion were classified as either cash or marketable securities. In fact, Alphabet held so much of its assets in the form of securities that, at one point, it was in danger of being regulated as a mutual fund!

There is a more subtle reason that companies may prefer internal financing. Suppose you are the manager of a firm, and you need to raise external capital to fund a new venture. As an insider, you are privy to a lot of information that isn't known to the public. Based on your knowledge, the firm's future prospects are considerably brighter than outside investors realize. As a result, you think your stock is currently undervalued. Should you issue debt or equity to finance the new venture?

If you think about it, you definitely don't want to issue equity in this case. The reason is that your stock is undervalued, and you don't want to sell it too cheaply. So, you issue debt instead.

Would you ever want to issue equity? Suppose you thought your firm's stock was overvalued. It makes sense to raise money at inflated prices, but a problem crops up. If you try to sell equity, investors will realize that the shares are probably overvalued, and your stock price will take a hit. In other words, if you try to raise money by selling equity, you run the risk of signaling to investors that the price is too high. In fact, in the real world, companies rarely sell new equity, and the market reacts negatively to such sales when they occur.

So, we have a pecking order. Companies will use internal financing first. Then, they will issue debt if necessary. Equity will be sold pretty much as a last resort.

IMPLICATIONS OF THE PECKING ORDER

The pecking-order theory has several significant implications, a couple of which are at odds with our static theory:

1. *No target capital structure*: Under the pecking-order theory, there is no target or optimal debt-equity ratio. Instead, a firm's capital structure is determined by its need for external financing, which dictates the amount of debt the firm will have.

2. *Profitable firms use less debt*: Because profitable firms have greater internal cash flow, they will need less external financing and will therefore have less debt. As we mentioned earlier, this is a pattern that we seem to observe, at least for some companies.

3. *Companies will want financial slack*: To avoid selling new equity, companies will want to stockpile internally generated cash. Such a cash reserve is known as *financial slack*. It gives management the ability to finance projects as they appear and to move quickly if necessary.

Which theory, static or pecking-order, is correct? Financial researchers have not reached a definitive conclusion on this issue, but we can make a few observations. The static theory speaks more to long-run financial goals or strategies. The issues of tax shields and financial distress costs are plainly important in that context. The pecking-order theory is more concerned with the shorter-run, tactical issue of raising external funds to finance investments. So both theories are useful ways of understanding corporate use of debt. For example, it is probably the case that firms have long-run, target capital structures, but it is also probably true that they will deviate from those long-run targets as needed to avoid issuing new equity.

> **Concept Questions**
>
> **16.8a** Under the pecking-order theory, what is the order in which firms will obtain financing?
> **16.8b** Why might firms prefer not to issue new equity?
> **16.8c** What are some differences in implications of the static and pecking-order theories?

16.9 Observed Capital Structures

No two firms have identical capital structures. Nonetheless, we see some regular elements when we start looking at actual capital structures. We discuss a few of these next.

The most striking thing we observe about capital structures, particularly in the United States, is that most corporations seem to have relatively low debt-equity ratios. In fact, most corporations use much less debt financing than equity financing. To illustrate, Table 16.7 presents median debt ratios and debt-equity ratios for various U.S. industries classified by SIC code (we discussed such codes in Chapter 3).

In Table 16.7, what is most striking is the wide variation across industries, ranging from essentially no debt for drug and computer companies to relatively heavy debt usage in the airline and cable television industries. Notice that these last two industries are the only ones for which more debt is used than equity, and most of the other industries rely far more heavily on equity than debt. This is true even though many of the companies in these industries pay substantial taxes. Table 16.7 makes it clear that corporations have not, in general, issued debt up to the point that tax shelters have been completely used up, and we conclude that there must be limits to the amount of debt corporations can use. Take a look at our nearby *Work the Web* box for more about actual capital structures.

TABLE 16.7

Capital Structures for U.S. Industries

SOURCE: *Ibbotson Cost of Capital Yearbook.* Chicago: Morningstar, 2010.

Industry	Ratio of Debt to Total Capital*	Ratio of Debt to Equity	Number of Companies	SIC Code	Representative Companies
Electric utilities	48.54%	94.31%	33	491	American Electric Power, Southern Co.
Computer equipment	9.09	10.02	48	357	Apple, Cisco
Paper	27.75	38.40	24	26	Avery Dennison, Weyerhaeuser
Petroleum refining	32.27	47.65	18	29	Chevron, Sunoco
Airlines	63.92	177.19	10	4512	Delta, Southwest
Pay television	63.56	193.88	5	484	Dish Network, TiVo
Motor vehicles	17.77	21.60	25	371	Ford, Winnebago
Fabric apparel	15.86	18.84	14	23	Guess, Nine West
Department stores	27.40	37.73	8	531	J.C. Penney, Macy's
Eating places	23.40	30.54	42	5812	McDonald's, Papa John's
Drugs	7.80	8.46	194	283	Merck, Pfizer
Steel works	19.96	24.95	9	331	Nucor, U.S. Steel

*Debt is the book value of preferred stock and long-term debt, including amounts due in one year. Equity is the market value of outstanding shares. Total capital is the sum of debt and equity. Median values are shown.

WORK THE WEB

When it comes to capital structure, all companies (and industries) are not created equal. To illustrate, we looked up some capital structure information on American Airlines (AAL) and Pfizer (PFE) using the Financials area of www.reuters.com. American Airlines's capital structure looks like this (note that leverage ratios are expressed as percentages on this site):

FINANCIAL STRENGTH			
	Company	industry	sector
Quick Ratio (MRQ)	0.68	0.90	2.07
Current Ratio (MRQ)	0.76	0.97	2.49
LT Debt to Equity (MRQ)	490.66	92.30	65.25
Total Debt to Equity (MRQ)	531.61	143.06	90.49
Interest Coverage (TTM)	8.55	13.73	14.40

For every dollar of equity, American Airlines has long-term debt of $4.9066 and total debt of $5.3161. Compare this result to Pfizer:

FINANCIAL STRENGTH			
	Company	industry	sector
Quick Ratio (MRQ)	0.89	2.29	2.41
Current Ratio (MRQ)	1.11	3.21	3.31
LT Debt to Equity (MRQ)	48.08	21.38	21.99
Total Debt to Equity (MRQ)	69.61	30.44	30.99
Interest Coverage (TTM)	23.64	38.25	38.48

For every dollar of equity, Pfizer has only $.4808 of long-term debt and total debt of $.6961. When we examine the industry and sector averages, the differences are again apparent. Although the choice of capital structure is a management decision, it is clearly influenced by industry characteristics.

Questions

1. *The ratios shown for these companies were based on January 2017 figures. Go to www.reuters.com and find the current long-term debt-to-equity and total debt-to-equity ratios for both American Airlines and Pfizer. How have these ratios changed over this time?*

2. *Go to www.reuters.com and find the long-term debt-to-equity and total debt-to-equity ratios for Bank of America (BAC), Cisco (CSCO), and Chevron (CVX). Why do you think these three companies use such differing amounts of debt?*

Because different industries have different operating characteristics in terms of, for example, EBIT volatility and asset types, there does appear to be some connection between these characteristics and capital structure. Our story involving tax savings, financial distress costs, and potential pecking orders undoubtedly supplies part of the reason; but, to date, there is no fully satisfactory theory that explains these regularities in capital structures.

Concept Questions

16.9a   Do U.S. corporations rely heavily on debt financing?
16.9b   What regularities do we observe in capital structures?

16.10 A Quick Look at the Bankruptcy Process

As we have discussed, one consequence of using debt is the possibility of financial distress, which can be defined in several ways:

1. *Business failure*: This term is usually used to refer to a situation in which a business has terminated with a loss to creditors; but even an all-equity firm can fail.

2. *Legal bankruptcy*: Firms or creditors bring petitions to a federal court for bankruptcy. **Bankruptcy** is a legal proceeding for liquidating or reorganizing a business.

3. *Technical insolvency*: Technical insolvency occurs when a firm is unable to meet its financial obligations.

4. *Accounting insolvency*: Firms with negative net worth are insolvent on the books. This happens when the total book liabilities exceed the book value of the total assets.

We now very briefly discuss some of the terms and more relevant issues associated with bankruptcy and financial distress.

bankruptcy
A legal proceeding for liquidating or reorganizing a business.

LIQUIDATION AND REORGANIZATION

Firms that cannot or choose not to make contractually required payments to creditors have two basic options: Liquidation or reorganization. **Liquidation** means termination of the firm as a going concern, and it involves selling off the assets of the firm. The proceeds, net of selling costs, are distributed to creditors in order of established priority. **Reorganization** is the option of keeping the firm a going concern; it often involves issuing new securities to replace old securities. Liquidation or reorganization is the result of a bankruptcy proceeding. Which occurs depends on whether the firm is worth more "dead or alive."

liquidation
Termination of the firm as a going concern.

reorganization
Financial restructuring of a failing firm to attempt to continue operations as a going concern.

Bankruptcy Liquidation   Chapter 7 of the Federal Bankruptcy Reform Act of 1978 deals with "straight" liquidation. The following sequence of events is typical:

1. A petition is filed in a federal court. Corporations may file a voluntary petition, or involuntary petitions may be filed against the corporation by several of its creditors.

2. A trustee-in-bankruptcy is elected by the creditors to take over the assets of the debtor corporation. The trustee will attempt to liquidate the assets.

3. When the assets are liquidated, after payment of the bankruptcy administration costs, the proceeds are distributed among the creditors.

4. If any proceeds remain, after expenses and payments to creditors, they are distributed to the shareholders.

The SEC has a good overview of the bankruptcy process in its "Online Publications" section at **www.sec.gov**.

The distribution of the proceeds of the liquidation occurs according to the following priority list:

1. Administrative expenses associated with the bankruptcy.
2. Other expenses arising after the filing of an involuntary bankruptcy petition but before the appointment of a trustee.
3. Wages, salaries, and commissions.
4. Contributions to employee benefit plans.
5. Consumer claims.
6. Government tax claims.
7. Payment to unsecured creditors.
8. Payment to preferred stockholders.
9. Payment to common stockholders.

This priority list for liquidation is a reflection of the **absolute priority rule (APR)**. The higher a claim is on this list, the more likely it is to be paid. In many of these categories, there are various limitations and qualifications that we omit for the sake of brevity.

 Two qualifications to this list are in order. The first concerns secured creditors. Such creditors are entitled to the proceeds from the sale of the security and are outside this ordering. If the secured property is liquidated and provides cash insufficient to cover the amount owed, the secured creditors join with unsecured creditors in dividing the remaining liquidated value. In contrast, if the secured property is liquidated for proceeds greater than the secured claim, the net proceeds are used to pay unsecured creditors and others. The second qualification to the APR is that, in reality, what happens, and who gets what, in the event of bankruptcy are subject to much negotiation; as a result, the APR is frequently not followed.

absolute priority rule (APR)
The rule establishing priority of claims in liquidation.

Bankruptcy Reorganization Corporate reorganization takes place under Chapter 11 of the Federal Bankruptcy Reform Act of 1978. The general objective of a proceeding under Chapter 11 is to plan to restructure the corporation with some provision for repayment of creditors. A typical sequence of events follows:

Get the latest on bankruptcy at **www.bankruptcydata.com**.

1. A voluntary petition can be filed by the corporation, or an involuntary petition can be filed by creditors.
2. A federal judge either approves or denies the petition. If the petition is approved, a time for filing proofs of claims is set.
3. In most cases, the corporation (the "debtor in possession") continues to run the business.
4. The corporation (and, in certain cases, the creditors) submits a reorganization plan.
5. Creditors and shareholders are divided into classes. A class of creditors accepts the plan if a majority of the class agrees to the plan.
6. After its acceptance by creditors, the plan is confirmed by the court.
7. Payments in cash, property, and securities are made to creditors and shareholders. The plan may provide for the issuance of new securities.
8. For some fixed length of time, the firm operates according to the provisions of the reorganization plan.

The corporation may wish to allow the old stockholders to retain some participation in the firm. Needless to say, this may involve some protest by the holders of unsecured debt.

So-called prepackaged bankruptcies are a relatively common phenomenon. What happens is that the corporation secures the necessary approval of a bankruptcy plan from a majority of its creditors first, and then it files for bankruptcy. As a result, the company enters bankruptcy and reemerges almost immediately.

For example, one of the largest Chapter 11 prepackaged bankruptcies to date began when business lender CIT Group filed for bankruptcy on November 1, 2009. Under the terms of the agreement, stockholders were wiped out entirely and bondholders' claims were reduced by $10.5 billion. At the same time, the maturity on the company's debt was extended by three years. An additional debt reduction occurred when $2.3 billion in "bailout" funds received by the company under the U.S. government's Troubled Asset Relief Program (TARP) were wiped out. Thanks to the prepack, the company moved quickly through the bankruptcy process, emerging from bankruptcy proceedings on December 10, 2009.

In another recent example, on October 24, 2016, Houston-based Key Energy Services filed for a prepack bankruptcy. Under the terms of the plan, the company's debt would be reduced from $1.2 billion to $250 million, existing creditors would be granted shares of the company's new stock, and rights would be issued on the company's new stock to repay principal and interest on an outstanding loan. Surprisingly, existing shareholders received a reduced number of shares of new stock, with rights and warrants to buy more. Key Energy Services exited its prepack bankruptcy on December 15, 2016, only 52 days after entering bankruptcy.

In some cases, the bankruptcy procedure is needed to invoke the "cram-down" power of the bankruptcy court. Under certain circumstances, a class of creditors can be forced to accept a bankruptcy plan even if they vote not to approve it—hence the remarkably apt description "cram down."

In 2005, Congress passed the most significant overhaul of U.S. bankruptcy laws in the last 25 years, the Bankruptcy Abuse Prevention and Consumer Protection Act of 2005 (BAPCPA). Most of the changes were aimed at individual debtors, but corporations were also affected. Before BAPCPA, a bankrupt company had the exclusive right to submit reorganization plans to the bankruptcy court. It has been argued that this exclusivity is one reason some companies have remained in bankruptcy for so long. Under the new law, after 18 months, creditors can submit their own plan for the court's consideration. This change is likely to speed up bankruptcies and also lead to more prepacks.

One controversial change made by BAPCPA has to do with so-called key employee retention plans, or KERPs. Strange as it may sound, bankrupt companies routinely give bonus payments to executives, even though the executives may be the same ones who led the company into bankruptcy in the first place. Such bonuses are intended to keep valuable employees from moving to more successful firms, but critics have argued they are often abused. The new law permits KERPs only if the employee in question actually has a job offer from another company.

Recently, Section 363 of the bankruptcy code has been in the news. In a traditional Chapter 11 filing, the bankruptcy plan is described to creditors and shareholders in a prospectus-like disclosure. The plan must then be approved by a vote involving the interested parties. A Section 363 bankruptcy is more like an auction. An initial bidder, known as a *stalking horse*, bids on all or part of the bankrupt company's assets. Other bidders are then invited into the process to determine the highest bid for the company's assets. The main advantage of a Section 363 bankruptcy is speed. Since a traditional bankruptcy requires the approval of interested parties, it is not uncommon for the process to take several years, while a Section 363 bankruptcy is generally much quicker. For example, in the middle of 2009, both General Motors and Chrysler sped through the bankruptcy process in less than 45 days with the help of Section 363 sales.

FINANCIAL MANAGEMENT AND THE BANKRUPTCY PROCESS

It may seem a little odd, but the right to go bankrupt is very valuable. There are several reasons why this is true. First, from an operational standpoint, when a firm files for bankruptcy, there is an immediate "stay" on creditors, usually meaning that payments to creditors will cease, and creditors will have to await the outcome of the bankruptcy process to find out if and how much they will be paid. This stay gives the firm time to evaluate its options, and it prevents what is usually termed a "race to the courthouse steps" by creditors and others.

Beyond this, some bankruptcy filings are actually strategic actions intended to improve a firm's competitive position, and firms have filed for bankruptcy even though they were not insolvent at the time. Probably the most famous example is Continental Airlines. In 1983, following deregulation of the airline industry, Continental found itself competing with newly established airlines that had much lower labor costs. Continental filed for reorganization under Chapter 11 even though it was not insolvent.

Continental argued that, based on pro forma data, it would become insolvent in the future, and a reorganization was therefore necessary. By filing for bankruptcy, Continental was able to terminate its existing labor agreements, lay off large numbers of workers, and slash wages for the remaining employees. In other words, at least in the eyes of critics, Continental essentially used the bankruptcy process as a vehicle for reducing labor costs. Congress subsequently modified bankruptcy laws to make it more difficult, though not impossible, for companies to abrogate a labor contract through the bankruptcy process. For example, Delta Air Lines filed for bankruptcy in 2005, in part to renegotiate the contracts with its union employees.

Other famous examples of strategic bankruptcies exist. For example, Manville (then known as Johns-Manville) and Dow Corning filed for bankruptcies because of expected future losses resulting from litigation associated with asbestos and silicone breast implants, respectively. Similarly, in the then-largest-ever bankruptcy, Texaco filed in 1987 after Pennzoil was awarded a $10.3 billion judgment against the company. Texaco later settled for $3.5 billion and emerged from bankruptcy. As of early 2018, the largest bankruptcies in the United States in terms of assets were the 2008 bankruptcy of Lehman Brothers (with $691 billion in assets) and the collapse of Washington Mutual (with $328 billion in assets), also in 2008. However, the 2003 bankruptcy filing of Italian dairy company Parmalat may have topped them both in terms of relative importance. This company, by itself, represented 1.5 percent of the Italian gross national product!

AGREEMENTS TO AVOID BANKRUPTCY

When a firm defaults on an obligation, it can avoid a bankruptcy filing. Because the legal process of bankruptcy can be lengthy and expensive, it is often in everyone's best interest to devise a "workout" that avoids a bankruptcy filing. Much of the time, creditors can work with the management of a company that has defaulted on a loan contract. Voluntary arrangements to restructure or "reschedule" the company's debt can be, and often are, made. This may involve *extension*, which postpones the date of payment, or *composition*, which involves a reduced payment.

Concept Questions

16.10a   What is the APR?
16.10b   What is the difference between liquidation and reorganization?

16.11 Summary and Conclusions

The ideal mixture of debt and equity for a firm—its optimal capital structure—is the one that maximizes the value of the firm and minimizes the overall cost of capital. If we ignore taxes, financial distress costs, and any other imperfections, we find that there is no ideal mixture. Under these circumstances, the firm's capital structure is irrelevant.

If we consider the effect of corporate taxes, we find that capital structure matters a great deal. This conclusion is based on the fact that interest is tax deductible and generates a valuable tax shield. Unfortunately, we also find that the optimal capital structure is 100 percent debt, which is not something we observe in healthy firms.

When we introduce costs associated with bankruptcy, or, more generally, financial distress, we see that these costs reduce the attractiveness of debt financing. We conclude that an optimal capital structure exists when the net tax savings from an additional dollar in interest just equals the increase in expected financial distress costs. This is the essence of the static theory of capital structure.

In this chapter we also considered the pecking-order theory of capital structure as an alternative to the static theory. This theory suggests that firms will use internal financing as much as possible, followed by debt financing if needed. Equity will not be issued if possible. As a result, a firm's capital structure just reflects its historical needs for external financing, so there is no optimal capital structure.

When we examine actual capital structures, we find two regularities. First, firms in the United States typically do not use great amounts of debt, but they pay substantial taxes. This suggests that there is a limit to the use of debt financing to generate tax shields. Second, firms in similar industries tend to have similar capital structures, suggesting that the nature of their assets and operations is an important determinant of capital structure.

CONNECT TO FINANCE

 Connect Finance offers you plenty of opportunities to practice mastering these concepts. Log on to connect.mheducation.com to learn more. If you like what you see, ask your professor about using *Connect Finance*!

Can you answer the following *Connect* Quiz questions?

Section 16.1 Maximizing what will maximize shareholder value?
Section 16.3 What is most closely related to a firm's use of debt in its capital structure?
Section 16.5 Give an example of a direct cost of bankruptcy.
Section 16.7 What claims increase when the debt-equity ratio is increased?

CHAPTER REVIEW AND SELF-TEST PROBLEMS

16.1 EBIT and EPS Suppose the BDJ Corporation has decided in favor of a capital restructuring that involves increasing its existing $80 million in debt to $125 million. The interest rate on the debt is 9 percent and is not expected to change. The firm currently has 10 million shares outstanding, and the price per share is $45. If the restructuring is expected to increase the ROE, what is the minimum level for EBIT that BDJ's management must be expecting? Ignore taxes in your answer.

16.2 **M&M Proposition II (no taxes)** The Habitat Corporation has a WACC of 16 percent. Its cost of debt is 13 percent. If Habitat's debt-equity ratio is 2, what is its cost of equity capital? Ignore taxes in your answer.

16.3 **M&M Proposition I (with corporate taxes)** Gypco expects an EBIT of $10,000 every year forever. Gypco can borrow at 7 percent. Suppose Gypco currently has no debt, and its cost of equity is 17 percent. If the corporate tax rate is 21 percent, what is the value of the firm? What will the value be if Gypco borrows $15,000 and uses the proceeds to repurchase stock?

ANSWERS TO CHAPTER REVIEW AND SELF-TEST PROBLEMS

16.1 To answer, we can calculate the break-even EBIT. At any EBIT above this, the increased financial leverage will increase EPS. Under the old capital structure, the interest bill is $80 million × .09 = $7,200,000. There are 10 million shares of stock; so, ignoring taxes, EPS is (EBIT − $7.2 million)/10 million.

Under the new capital structure, the interest expense will be $125 million × .09 = $11.25 million. Furthermore, the debt rises by $45 million. This amount is sufficient to repurchase $45 million/$45 = 1 million shares of stock, leaving 9 million outstanding. EPS is thus (EBIT − $11.25 million)/9 million.

Now that we know how to calculate EPS under both scenarios, we set the two calculations equal to each other and solve for the break-even EBIT:

$$(\text{EBIT} - \$7.2 \text{ million})/10 \text{ million} = (\text{EBIT} - \$11.25 \text{ million})/9 \text{ million}$$
$$\text{EBIT} - \$7.2 \text{ million} = 1.11 \times (\text{EBIT} - \$11.25 \text{ million})$$
$$\text{EBIT} = \$47,700,000$$

Verify that, in either case, EPS is $4.05 when EBIT is $47.7 million.

16.2 According to M&M Proposition II (no taxes), the cost of equity is:

$$R_E = R_A + (R_A - R_D) \times (D/E)$$
$$= .16 + (.16 - .13) \times 2$$
$$= .22, \text{ or } 22\%$$

16.3 With no debt, Gypco's WACC is 17 percent. This is also the unlevered cost of capital. The aftertax cash flow is $10,000 × (1 − .21) = $7,900, so the value is just $V_U = \$7,900/.17 = \$46,471$.

After the debt issue, Gypco will be worth the original $46,471 plus the present value of the tax shield. According to M&M Proposition I with taxes, the present value of the tax shield is $T_C \times D$, or .21 × $15,000 = $3,150; so the firm is worth $46,471 + 3,150 = $49,621.

CONCEPTS REVIEW AND CRITICAL THINKING QUESTIONS

1. **Business Risk versus Financial Risk [LO1]** Explain what is meant by *business risk* and *financial risk*. Suppose Firm A has greater business risk than Firm B. Is it true that Firm A also has a higher cost of equity capital? Explain.

2. **M&M Propositions [LO1]** How would you answer in the following debate?

   Q: Isn't it true that the riskiness of a firm's equity will rise if the firm increases its use of debt financing?

   A: Yes, that's the essence of M&M Proposition II.

Q: And isn't it true that, as a firm increases its use of borrowing, the likelihood of default increases, thereby increasing the risk of the firm's debt?

A: Yes.

Q: In other words, increased borrowing increases the risk of the equity *and* the debt?

A: That's right.

Q: Well, given that the firm uses only debt and equity financing, and given that the risks of both are increased by increased borrowing, does it not follow that increasing debt increases the overall risk of the firm and therefore decreases the value of the firm?

A: ?

3. **Optimal Capital Structure** [LO1] Is there an easily identifiable debt-equity ratio that will maximize the value of a firm? Why or why not?

4. **Observed Capital Structures** [LO1] Refer to the observed capital structures given in Table 16.7 of the text. What do you notice about the types of industries with respect to their average debt-equity ratios? Are certain types of industries more likely to be highly leveraged than others? What are some possible reasons for this observed segmentation? Do the operating results and tax history of the firms play a role? How about their future earnings prospects? Explain.

5. **Financial Leverage** [LO1] Why is the use of debt financing referred to as financial "leverage"?

6. **Interest Deductibility and Financial Ratios** [LO1] Take a look back at the times interest earned (TIE) ratio we discussed in Chapter 3. For interest paid to be fully deductible by a company after the Tax Cuts and Jobs Act of 2017, what must be true about this ratio? Assume the company has no interest income.

7. **Bankruptcy and Corporate Ethics** [LO3] As mentioned in the text, some firms have filed for bankruptcy because of actual or likely litigation-related losses. Is this a proper use of the bankruptcy process?

8. **Bankruptcy and Corporate Ethics** [LO3] Firms sometimes use the threat of a bankruptcy filing to force creditors to renegotiate terms. Critics argue that in such cases, the firm is using bankruptcy laws "as a sword rather than a shield." Is this an ethical tactic?

9. **Bankruptcy and Corporate Ethics** [LO3] As mentioned in the text, Continental Airlines filed for bankruptcy, at least in part, as a means of reducing labor costs. Whether this move was ethical, or proper, was hotly debated. Give both sides of the argument.

10. **Capital Structure Goal** [LO1] What is the basic goal of financial management with regard to capital structure?

QUESTIONS AND PROBLEMS

BASIC

(Questions 1–15)

1. **EBIT and Leverage** [LO1] Ghost, Inc., has no debt outstanding and a total market value of $185,000. Earnings before interest and taxes, EBIT, are projected to be $29,000 if economic conditions are normal. If there is strong expansion in the economy, then EBIT will be 30 percent higher. If there is a recession, then EBIT will be 40 percent lower. The company is considering a $65,000 debt issue with an interest rate of 7 percent. The proceeds will be used to repurchase shares of stock. There are currently 7,400 shares outstanding. Ignore taxes for this problem.

   a. Calculate earnings per share (EPS) under each of the three economic scenarios before any debt is issued. Also calculate the percentage changes in EPS when the economy expands or enters a recession.

    b. Repeat part (a) assuming that the company goes through with recapitalization. What do you observe?

2. **EBIT, Taxes, and Leverage** [LO2] Repeat parts (a) and (b) in Problem 1 assuming the company has a tax rate of 21 percent, a market-to-book ratio of 1.0, and the stock price remains constant.

3. **ROE and Leverage** [LO1, 2] Suppose the company in Problem 1 has a market-to-book ratio of 1.0 and the stock price remains constant.

    a. Calculate return on equity (ROE) under each of the three economic scenarios before any debt is issued. Also calculate the percentage changes in ROE for economic expansion and recession, assuming no taxes.

    b. Repeat part (a) assuming the firm goes through with the proposed recapitalization.

    c. Repeat parts (a) and (b) of this problem assuming the firm has a tax rate of 21 percent.

4. **Break-Even EBIT** [LO1] Round Hammer is comparing two different capital structures: An all-equity plan (Plan I) and a levered plan (Plan II). Under Plan I, the company would have 180,000 shares of stock outstanding. Under Plan II, there would be 130,000 shares of stock outstanding and $1.925 million in debt outstanding. The interest rate on the debt is 8 percent, and there are no taxes.

    a. If EBIT is $400,000, which plan will result in the higher EPS?

    b. If EBIT is $600,000, which plan will result in the higher EPS?

    c. What is the break-even EBIT?

5. **M&M and Stock Value** [LO1] In Problem 4, use M&M Proposition I to find the price per share of equity under each of the two proposed plans. What is the value of the firm?

6. **Break-Even EBIT and Leverage** [LO1, 2] Bellwood Corp. is comparing two different capital structures. Plan I would result in 12,700 shares of stock and $109,250 in debt. Plan II would result in 9,800 shares of stock and $247,000 in debt. The interest rate on the debt is 10 percent.

    a. Ignoring taxes, compare both of these plans to an all-equity plan assuming that EBIT will be $79,000. The all-equity plan would result in 15,000 shares of stock outstanding. Which of the three plans has the highest EPS? The lowest?

    b. In part (a), what are the break-even levels of EBIT for each plan as compared to that for an all-equity plan? Is one higher than the other? Why?

    c. Ignoring taxes, when will EPS be identical for Plans I and II?

    d. Repeat parts (a), (b), and (c) assuming that the corporate tax rate is 21 percent. Are the break-even levels of EBIT different from before? Why or why not?

7. **Leverage and Stock Value** [LO1] Ignoring taxes in Problem 6, what is the price per share of equity under Plan I? Plan II? What principle is illustrated by your answers?

8. **Homemade Leverage** [LO1] FCOJ, Inc., a prominent consumer products firm, is debating whether to convert its all-equity capital structure to one that is 30 percent debt. Currently, there are 5,800 shares outstanding, and the price per share is $57. EBIT is expected to remain at $32,000 per year forever. The interest rate on new debt is 8 percent, and there are no taxes.

    a. Allison, a shareholder of the firm, owns 100 shares of stock. What is her cash flow under the current capital structure, assuming the firm has a dividend payout rate of 100 percent?

    b. What will Allison's cash flow be under the proposed capital structure of the firm? Assume she keeps all 100 of her shares.

    c. Suppose the company does convert, but Allison prefers the current all-equity capital structure. Show how she could unlever her shares of stock to re-create the original capital structure.

    d. Using your answer to part (c), explain why the company's choice of capital structure is irrelevant.

9. **Homemade Leverage and WACC** [LO1] ABC Co. and XYZ Co. are identical firms in all respects except for their capital structure. ABC is all-equity financed with $720,000 in stock. XYZ uses both stock and perpetual debt; its stock is worth $360,000 and the interest rate on its debt is 7 percent. Both firms expect EBIT to be $73,000. Ignore taxes.

    a. Rico owns $43,500 worth of XYZ's stock. What rate of return is he expecting?

    b. Show how Rico could generate exactly the same cash flows and rate of return by investing in ABC and using homemade leverage.

    c. What is the cost of equity for ABC? What is it for XYZ?

    d. What is the WACC for ABC? For XYZ? What principle have you illustrated?

10. **M&M** [LO1] Thrice Corp. uses no debt. The weighted average cost of capital is 8.4 percent. If the current market value of the equity is $16.3 million and there are no taxes, what is EBIT?

11. **M&M and Taxes** [LO2] In Problem 10, suppose the corporate tax rate is 22 percent. What is EBIT in this case? What is the WACC? Explain.

12. **Calculating WACC** [LO1] Blitz Industries has a debt-equity ratio of 1.25. Its WACC is 8.3 percent, and its cost of debt is 5.1 percent. The corporate tax rate is 21 percent.

    a. What is the company's cost of equity capital?

    b. What is the company's unlevered cost of equity capital?

    c. What would the cost of equity be if the debt-equity ratio were 2? What if it were 1? What if it were zero?

13. **Calculating WACC** [LO1] Citee Corp. has no debt but can borrow at 6.1 percent. The firm's WACC is currently 9.4 percent, and the tax rate is 21 percent.

    a. What is the company's cost of equity?

    b. If the firm converts to 25 percent debt, what will its cost of equity be?

    c. If the firm converts to 50 percent debt, what will its cost of equity be?

    d. What is the company's WACC in part (b)? In part (c)?

14. **M&M and Taxes** [LO2] Meyer & Co. expects its EBIT to be $97,000 every year forever. The firm can borrow at 8 percent. The company currently has no debt, and its cost of equity is 13 percent. If the tax rate is 24 percent, what is the value of the firm? What will the value be if the company borrows $195,000 and uses the proceeds to repurchase shares?

15. **M&M and Taxes** [LO2] In Problem 14, what is the cost of equity after recapitalization? What is the WACC? What are the implications for the firm's capital structure decision?

INTERMEDIATE
(Questions 16–18)

16. **M&M** [LO2] Tool Manufacturing has an expected EBIT of $51,000 in perpetuity and a tax rate of 21 percent. The firm has $126,000 in outstanding debt at an interest rate of 5.35 percent, and its unlevered cost of capital is 9.6 percent. What is the value of the firm according to M&M Proposition I with taxes? Should the company change its debt-equity ratio if the goal is to maximize the value of the firm? Explain.

17. **Firm Value** [LO2] Change Corporation expects an EBIT of $31,200 every year forever. The company currently has no debt, and its cost of equity is 11 percent.

    a. What is the current value of the company?

    b. Suppose the company can borrow at 6 percent. If the corporate tax rate is 22 percent, what will the value of the firm be if the company takes on debt equal to 50 percent of its unlevered value? What if it takes on debt equal to 100 percent of its unlevered value?

    c. What will the value of the firm be if the company takes on debt equal to 50 percent of its levered value? What if the company takes on debt equal to 100 percent of its levered value?

18. **Homemade Leverage** [LO1] The Day Company and the Knight Company are identical in every respect except that Day is not levered. Financial information for the two firms appears in the following table. All earnings streams are perpetuities, and neither firm pays taxes. Both firms distribute all earnings available to common stockholders immediately.

	Day	Knight
Projected operating income	$ 375,000	$ 375,000
Year-end interest on debt	—	$ 54,000
Market value of stock	$2,300,000	$1,650,000
Market value of debt	—	$ 900,000

    a. An investor who can borrow at 6 percent per year wishes to purchase 5 percent of Knight's equity. Can he increase his dollar return by purchasing 5 percent of Day's equity if he borrows so that the initial net costs of the strategies are the same?

    b. Given the two investment strategies in (a), which will investors choose? When will this process cease?

19. **Weighted Average Cost of Capital** [LO1] In a world of corporate taxes only, show that the WACC can be written as $WACC = R_U \times [1 - T_C(D/V)]$.

20. **Cost of Equity and Leverage** [LO1] Assuming a world of corporate taxes only, show that the cost of equity, R_E, is as given in the chapter by M&M Proposition II with corporate taxes.

21. **Business and Financial Risk** [LO1] Assume a firm's debt is risk-free, so that the cost of debt equals the risk-free rate, R_f. Define β_A as the firm's *asset* beta—that is, the systematic risk of the firm's assets. Define β_E to be the beta of the firm's equity. Use the capital asset pricing model (CAPM) along with M&M Proposition II to show that $\beta_E = \beta_A \times (1 + D/E)$, where D/E is the debt-equity ratio. Assume the tax rate is zero.

22. **Stockholder Risk** [LO1] Suppose a firm's business operations are such that they mirror movements in the economy as a whole very closely; that is, the firm's asset beta is 1.0. Use the result of Problem 21 to find the equity beta for this firm for debt-equity ratios of 0, 1, 5, and 20. What does this tell you about the relationship between capital structure and shareholder risk? How is the shareholders' required return on equity affected? Explain.

CHALLENGE
(Questions 19–22)

EXCEL MASTER IT! PROBLEM

The TL Corporation currently has no debt outstanding. Josh Culberson, the CFO, is considering restructuring the company by issuing debt and using the proceeds to repurchase outstanding equity. The company's assets are worth $40 million, the stock price is $25 per share, and there are 1,600,000 shares outstanding. In the expected state of the economy, EBIT is predicted to be $3 million. If there is a recession, EBIT would fall to $1.8 million, and in an expansion, EBIT would increase to $4.3 million. If the company issues debt, it will issue a combination of short-term debt and long-term debt. The ratio of short-term debt to long-term debt will be .20. The short-term debt will have an interest rate of 3 percent and the long-term debt will have an interest rate of 8 percent.

a. On the next worksheet, fill in the values in each table. For the debt-equity ratio, create a spinner that changes the debt-equity ratio. The resulting debt-equity ratio should range from 0 to 10 at increments of .1.

b. Graph the EBIT and EPS for the TL Corporation on the same graph using a scatter plot.

c. What is the break-even EBIT between the current capital structure and the new capital structure?

d. To illustrate the new capital structure, you would like to create a pie chart. Another pie chart that is available is the pie in pie chart. Using the pie in pie chart, graph the equity and total debt in the main pie chart and the short-term debt and long-term debt in the secondary pie chart. Note, if you right-click on a data series in the chart and select Format Data Series, the Series Options will permit you to display the series by a customized choice. In the customization, you can select which data series you want displayed in the primary pie chart and the secondary pie chart.

MINICASE

Stephenson Real Estate Recapitalization

Stephenson Real Estate Company was founded 25 years ago by the current CEO, Robert Stephenson. The company purchases real estate, including land and buildings, and rents the property to tenants. The company has shown a profit every year for the past 18 years, and the shareholders are satisfied with the company's management. Prior to founding Stephenson Real Estate, Robert was the founder and CEO of a failed alpaca farming operation. The resulting bankruptcy made him extremely averse to debt financing. As a result, the company is entirely equity financed, with 8 million shares of common stock outstanding. The stock currently trades at $37.80 per share.

Stephenson is evaluating a plan to purchase a huge tract of land in the southeastern United States for $85 million. The land will subsequently be leased to tenant farmers. This purchase is expected to increase Stephenson's annual pretax earnings by $14.125 million in perpetuity. Jennifer Weyand, the company's new CFO, has been put in charge of the project. Jennifer has determined that the company's current cost of capital is 10.2 percent. She feels that the company would be more valuable

if it included debt in its capital structure, so she is evaluating whether the company should issue debt to entirely finance the project. Based on some conversations with investment banks, she thinks that the company can issue bonds at par value with a 6 percent coupon rate. From her analysis, she also believes that a capital structure in the range of 70 percent equity/30 percent debt would be optimal. If the company goes beyond 30 percent debt, its bonds would carry a lower rating and a much higher coupon because the possibility of financial distress and the associated costs would rise sharply. Stephenson has a 23 percent corporate tax rate (state and federal).

QUESTIONS

1. If Stephenson wishes to maximize its total market value, would you recommend that it issue debt or equity to finance the land purchase? Explain.

2. Construct Stephenson's market value balance sheet before it announces the purchase.

3. Suppose Stephenson decides to issue equity to finance the purchase.

 a. What is the net present value of the project?

 b. Construct Stephenson's market value balance sheet after it announces that the firm will finance the purchase using equity. What would be the new price per share of the firm's stock? How many shares will Stephenson need to issue to finance the purchase?

 c. Construct Stephenson's market value balance sheet after the equity issue but before the purchase has been made. How many shares of common stock does Stephenson have outstanding? What is the price per share of the firm's stock?

 d. Construct Stephenson's market value balance sheet after the purchase has been made.

4. Suppose Stephenson decides to issue debt to finance the purchase.

 a. What will the market value of the Stephenson Real Estate Company be if the purchase is financed with debt?

 b. Construct Stephenson's market value balance sheet after both the debt issue and the land purchase. What is the price per share of the firm's stock?

5. Which method of financing maximizes the per-share stock price of Stephenson's equity?

Chapter 17 | Dividends and Payout Policy

ON JANUARY 26, 2017, cable TV giant Comcast announced a broad plan to reward stockholders for the recent success of the firm's business. Under the plan, Comcast would (1) boost its annual dividend by 15 percent, from $1.10 per share to $1.26 per share; (2) undertake a two-for-one stock split, meaning each share of common stock would be replaced with two new shares; and (3) repurchase about $5 billion of Comcast's common stock during the next year. Investors cheered, bidding up the stock price by about 3 percent on the day of the announcement, on a day when the stock market as a whole fell. Why were investors so pleased? To find out, this chapter explores these actions and their implications for shareholders.

Learning Objectives

After studying this chapter, you should be able to:

LO1 Define dividend types and how dividends are paid.

LO2 Explain the issues surrounding dividend policy decisions.

LO3 Describe the difference between cash and stock dividends.

LO4 Explain why share repurchases are an alternative to dividends.

For updates on the latest happenings in finance, visit fundamentalsofcorporatefinance.blogspot.com.

Dividend policy is an important subject in corporate finance, and dividends are a major cash outlay for many corporations. For example, S&P 500 companies paid about $397 billion in dividends in 2016, an increase from the $383 billion paid in 2015, and a record for dividends paid. In fact, dividends globally were $1.024 trillion. ExxonMobil and Apple were the biggest payers. How big? ExxonMobil paid out about $12.5 billion in dividends during 2016 and Apple paid out about $12 billion. In contrast, about 16 percent of the companies in the S&P 500 paid no dividend at all.

At first glance, it may seem obvious that a firm would always want to give as much as possible back to its shareholders by paying dividends. It might seem equally obvious that a firm could always invest the money for its shareholders instead of paying it out. The heart of the dividend policy question is this: Should the firm pay out money to its shareholders, or should the firm take that money and invest it for its shareholders?

In this chapter, we will cover a variety of topics related to dividends and corporate payout policies. We first discuss the various types of cash dividends and how they are paid. We ask whether dividend policy matters, and we consider arguments in favor of both high and low dividend payouts. Next, we examine stock repurchases, which have become an important alternative to cash dividends. We then bring together several decades of research on dividends and corporate payouts to describe the key trade-offs involved in establishing a payout policy. We conclude the chapter by discussing stock splits and stock dividends.

Cash Dividends and Dividend Payment

17.1

The term **dividend** usually refers to cash paid out of earnings. If a payment is made from sources other than current or accumulated retained earnings, the term **distribution**, rather than *dividend*, is used. It is acceptable to refer to a distribution from earnings as a dividend and a distribution from capital as a liquidating dividend. More generally, any direct payment by the corporation to the shareholders may be considered a dividend or a part of dividend policy.

Dividends come in several different forms. The basic types of cash dividends are these:

1. Regular cash dividends.
2. Extra dividends.
3. Special dividends.
4. Liquidating dividends.

Later in the chapter, we discuss dividends paid in stock instead of cash. We also consider another alternative to cash dividends: Stock repurchase.

dividend
A payment made out of a firm's earnings to its owners, in the form of either cash or stock.

distribution
A payment made by a firm to its owners from sources other than current or accumulated retained earnings.

CASH DIVIDENDS

The most common type of dividend is a cash dividend. Commonly, public companies pay **regular cash dividends** four times per year. As the name suggests, these are cash payments made directly to shareholders, and they are made in the regular course of business. In other words, management sees nothing unusual about the dividend and no reason why it won't be continued.

Sometimes firms will pay a regular cash dividend and an *extra cash dividend*. By calling part of the payment "extra," management is indicating that the "extra" part may or may not be repeated in the future. A *special dividend* is similar, but the name usually indicates that this dividend is viewed as a truly unusual or one-time event and won't be repeated. For example, in December 2004, Microsoft paid a special dividend of $3 per share. The total payout of $32 billion was the largest one-time corporate dividend in history. Founder Bill Gates received about $3 *billion*, which he pledged to donate to charity. To give you another idea of the size of the special dividend, consider that in December, when the dividend was sent to investors, personal income in the United States rose 3.7 percent. Without the dividend, personal income rose only .3 percent, so the dividend payment accounted for about 3 percent of all personal income in the United States for the month! Finally, the payment of a *liquidating dividend* usually means that some or all of the business has been liquidated—that is, sold off.

However it is labeled, a cash dividend payment reduces corporate cash and retained earnings, except in the case of a liquidating dividend (which may reduce paid-in capital).

regular cash dividend
A cash payment made by a firm to its owners in the normal course of business, usually paid four times per year.

For a list of companies that are paying dividends today, go to **www.thestreet.com /dividends/**.

STANDARD METHOD OF CASH DIVIDEND PAYMENT

The decision to pay a dividend rests in the hands of the board of directors of the corporation. When a dividend has been declared, it becomes a debt of the firm and cannot easily be rescinded. Sometime after it has been declared, a dividend is distributed to all shareholders as of some specific date.

576   **PART 6**   Cost of Capital and Long-Term Financial Policy

1. *Declaration date*: The board of directors declares a payment of dividends.
2. *Ex-dividend date*: A share of stock goes ex-dividend on the date the seller is entitled to keep the dividend; under NYSE rules, shares are traded ex dividend on and after the second business day before the record date.
3. *Record date*: The declared dividends are distributable to people who are shareholders of record as of this specific date.
4. *Payment date*: The dividend checks are mailed to shareholders of record.

Commonly, the amount of the cash dividend is expressed in terms of dollars per share (*dividends per share*). As we have seen in other chapters, it is also expressed as a percentage of the market price (the *dividend yield*) or as a percentage of net income or earnings per share (the *dividend payout*).

DIVIDEND PAYMENT: A CHRONOLOGY

The mechanics of a cash dividend payment can be illustrated by the example in Figure 17.1 and the following description:

declaration date
The date on which the board of directors passes a resolution to pay a dividend.

ex-dividend date
The date two business days before the date of record, establishing those individuals entitled to a dividend.

1. **Declaration date**: On January 15, the board of directors passes a resolution to pay a dividend of $1 per share on February 16 to all holders of record as of January 30.

2. **Ex-dividend date**: To make sure that dividend checks go to the right people, brokerage firms and stock exchanges establish an ex-dividend date. This date is two business days before the date of record (discussed next). If you buy the stock before this date, you are entitled to the dividend. If you buy on this date or after, the previous owner will get the dividend.

   In Figure 17.1, Wednesday, January 28, is the ex-dividend date. Before this date, the stock is said to trade "with dividend" or "cum dividend." Afterward, the stock trades "ex dividend."

   The ex-dividend date convention removes any ambiguity about who is entitled to the dividend. Because the dividend is valuable, the stock price will be affected when the stock goes "ex." We examine this effect in a moment.

date of record
The date by which a holder must be on record to be designated to receive a dividend.

3. **Date of record**: Based on its records, the corporation prepares a list on January 30 of all individuals believed to be stockholders. These are the *holders of record*, and January 30 is the date of record (or record date). The word *believed* is important here. If you buy the stock just before this date, the corporation's records may not reflect that fact because of mailing or other delays. Without some modification, some of the dividend checks will get mailed to the wrong people. This is the reason for the ex-dividend date convention.

date of payment
The date on which the dividend checks are mailed.

4. **Date of payment**: The dividend checks are mailed on February 16.

MORE ABOUT THE EX-DIVIDEND DATE

The ex-dividend date is important and is a common source of confusion. We examine what happens to the stock when it goes ex, meaning that the ex-dividend date arrives.

Ex date

Price = $10

-t   •••   -2   -1   0   +1   +2   •••   t

$1 is the ex-dividend price drop

Price = $9

The stock price will fall by the amount of the dividend on the ex date
(Time 0). If the dividend is $1 per share, the price will be $10 − 1 = $9
on the ex date:

        Before ex date (Time −1), dividend = $0   Price = $10
        On ex date (Time 0), dividend = $1   Price = $9

FIGURE 17.2

**Price Behavior around
the Ex-Dividend Date
for a $1 Cash Dividend**

To illustrate, suppose we have a stock that sells for $10 per share. The board of directors declares a dividend of $1 per share, and the record date is set to be Tuesday, June 12. Based on our previous discussion, we know that the ex date will be two business (not calendar) days earlier, on Friday, June 8.

If you buy the stock on Thursday, June 7, just as the market closes, you'll get the $1 dividend because the stock is trading cum dividend. If you wait and buy it just as the market opens on Friday, you won't get the $1 dividend. What happens to the value of the stock overnight?

If you think about it, you will see that the stock is worth about $1 less on Friday morning, so its price will drop by this amount between close of business on Thursday and the Friday opening. In general, we expect that the value of a share of stock will go down by about the dividend amount when the stock goes ex dividend. The key word here is *about*. Because dividends are taxed, the actual price drop might be closer to some measure of the aftertax value of the dividend. Determining this value is complicated because of the different tax rates and tax rules that apply for different buyers.

The series of events described here is illustrated in Figure 17.2.

"Ex" Marks the Day   EXAMPLE 17.1

The board of directors of Divided Airlines has declared a dividend of $2.50 per share payable on Tuesday, May 30, to shareholders of record as of Tuesday, May 9. Cal Icon buys 100 shares of Divided on Tuesday, May 2, for $150 per share. What is the ex date? Describe the events that will occur with regard to the cash dividend and the stock price.

The ex date is two business days before the date of record, Tuesday, May 9; so the stock will go ex on Friday, May 5. Cal buys the stock on Tuesday, May 2, so Cal purchases the stock cum dividend. In other words, Cal will get $2.50 × 100 = $250 in dividends. The check will be mailed on Tuesday, May 30. Just before the stock does go ex on Friday, its value will drop overnight by about $2.50 per share.

As an example of the price drop on the ex-dividend date, we examine the large dividend paid by Warrior Met Coal, operator of coal mines in Alabama, in November 2017. The dividend was $11.21 per share at a time when the stock price was around $30, so the dividend was about 40 percent of the total stock price, a truly special dividend. The stock went ex dividend on November 24, 2017. The stock price chart here shows the change in Warrior stock four days prior to the ex-dividend date and on the ex-dividend date.

The stock closed at $29.90 on November 22 (November 23 was a holiday) and opened at $18.65 on November 24—a drop of $11.25. With a 20 percent tax rate on dividends, we would have expected a drop of about $9, so the actual price dropped more than we would have expected. We discuss dividends and taxes in more detail in a subsequent section.

Concept Questions	
17.1a	What are the different types of cash dividends?
17.1b	What are the mechanics of the cash dividend payment?
17.1c	How should the price of a stock change when it goes ex dividend?

17.2 Does Dividend Policy Matter?

To decide whether or not dividend policy matters, we first have to define what we mean by dividend *policy*. All other things being the same, of course dividends matter. Dividends are paid in cash, and cash is something that everybody likes. The question we will be discussing here is whether the firm should pay out cash now or invest the cash and pay it out later. Dividend policy is the time pattern of dividend payout. In particular, should the firm pay out a large percentage of its earnings now or a small (or even zero) percentage? This is the dividend policy question.

AN ILLUSTRATION OF THE IRRELEVANCE OF DIVIDEND POLICY

A powerful argument can be made that dividend policy does not matter. We illustrate this by considering the simple case of Wharton Corporation. Wharton is an all-equity firm that has existed for 10 years. The current financial managers plan to dissolve the firm in two years. The total cash flows the firm will generate, including the proceeds from liquidation, will be $10,000 in each of the next two years.

Current Policy: Dividends Set Equal to Cash Flow   At the present time, dividends at each date are set equal to the cash flow of $10,000. There are 100 shares outstanding, so the dividend per share is $100. In Chapter 6, we showed that the value of the

stock is equal to the present value of the future dividends. Assuming a 10 percent required return, the value of a share of stock today, P_0, is:

$$P_0 = \frac{D_1}{(1 + R)^1} + \frac{D_2}{(1 + R)^2}$$
$$= \frac{\$100}{1.10} + \frac{\$100}{1.10^2} = \$173.55$$

The firm as a whole is worth $100 \times \$173.55 = \$17,355$.

Several members of the board of Wharton have expressed dissatisfaction with the current dividend policy and have asked you to analyze an alternative policy.

Alternative Policy: Initial Dividend Greater than Cash Flow   Another possible policy is for the firm to pay a dividend of $110 per share on the first date (Date 1), which is, of course, a total dividend of $11,000. Because the cash flow is only $10,000, an extra $1,000 must somehow be raised. One way to do this is to issue $1,000 worth of bonds or stock at Date 1. Assume that stock is issued. The new stockholders will desire enough cash flow at Date 2 so that they earn the required 10 percent return on their Date 1 investment.[1]

What is the value of the firm with this new dividend policy? The new stockholders invest $1,000. They require a 10 percent return, so they will demand $1,000 \times 1.10 = \$1,100$ of the Date 2 cash flow, leaving only $8,900 to the old stockholders. The dividends to the old stockholders will be as follows:

	Date 1	Date 2
Aggregate dividends to old stockholders	$11,000	$8,900
Dividends per share	110	89

The present value of the dividends per share is:

$$P_0 = \frac{\$110}{1.10} + \frac{89}{1.10^2} = \$173.55$$

This is the same value we had before.

The value of the stock is unaffected by this switch in dividend policy even though we have to sell some new stock to finance the new dividend. In fact, no matter what pattern of dividend payout the firm chooses, the value of the stock will always be the same in this example. In other words, for the Wharton Corporation, dividend policy makes no difference. The reason is simple: Any increase in a dividend at some point in time is exactly offset by a decrease at some other time; so the net effect, once we account for time value, is zero.

HOMEMADE DIVIDENDS

There is an alternative and perhaps more intuitively appealing explanation of why dividend policy doesn't matter in our example. Suppose individual Investor X prefers dividends per share of $100 at both Dates 1 and 2. Would she be disappointed if informed that the firm's management was adopting the alternative dividend policy (dividends of $110 and $89 on the two dates, respectively)? Not necessarily: She could easily reinvest the $10 of unneeded

---

[1] The same results would occur after an issue of bonds, though the arguments would be less easily presented.

funds received on Date 1 by buying more Wharton stock. At 10 percent, this investment would grow to $11 by Date 2. Investor X would receive her desired net cash flow of $110 − 10 = $100 at Date 1 and $89 + 11 = $100 at Date 2.

Conversely, imagine that Investor Z, preferring $110 of cash flow at Date 1 and $89 of cash flow at Date 2, finds that management will pay dividends of $100 at both Dates 1 and 2. This investor can sell $10 worth of stock to boost his total cash at Date 1 to $110. Because this investment returns 10 percent, Investor Z gives up $11 at Date 2 (= $10 × 1.1), leaving him with $100 − 11 = $89.

Our two investors are able to transform the corporation's dividend policy into a different policy by buying or selling on their own. The result is that investors are able to create a **homemade dividend policy**. This means that dissatisfied stockholders can alter the firm's dividend policy to suit themselves. As a result, there is no particular advantage to any one dividend policy the firm might choose.

Many corporations actually assist their stockholders in creating homemade dividend policies by offering *automatic dividend reinvestment plans* (ADRs or DRIPs). McDonald's, Walmart, and Procter & Gamble, for example, have set up such plans. As the name suggests, with such a plan, stockholders have the option of automatically reinvesting some or all of their cash dividend in shares of stock. In some cases, they actually receive a discount on the stock, which makes such plans very attractive.

homemade dividend policy
The tailored dividend policy created by individual investors who undo corporate dividend policy by reinvesting dividends or selling shares of stock.

For more information on DRIPs, check out the Motley Fool at **www.fool.com**.

A TEST

Our discussion to this point can be summarized by considering the following true-false test questions:

1. True or false: Dividends are irrelevant.
2. True or false: Dividend policy is irrelevant.

The first statement is surely false, and the reason follows from common sense. Clearly, investors prefer higher dividends to lower dividends at any single date if the dividend level is held constant at every other date. To be more precise regarding the first question, if the dividend per share at a given date is raised while the dividend per share at every other date is held constant, the stock price will rise. The reason is that the present value of the future dividends must go up if this occurs. This action can be accomplished by management decisions that improve productivity, increase tax savings, strengthen product marketing, or otherwise improve cash flow.

The second statement is true, at least in the simple case we have been examining. Dividend policy by itself cannot raise the dividend at one date while keeping it the same at all other dates. Rather, dividend policy merely establishes the trade-off between dividends at one date and dividends at another date. Once we allow for time value, the present value of the dividend stream is unchanged. In this simple world, dividend policy does not matter because managers choosing either to raise or to lower the current dividend do not affect the current value of their firm. However, we have ignored several real-world factors that might lead us to change our minds; we pursue some of these in subsequent sections.

Concept Questions

17.2a   How can an investor create a homemade dividend?
17.2b   Are dividends irrelevant?

Real-World Factors Favoring
a Low Dividend Payout

17.3

The example we used to illustrate the irrelevance of dividend policy ignored taxes and flotation costs. In this section, we will see that these factors might lead us to prefer a low dividend payout.

TAXES

U.S. tax laws are complex, and they affect dividend policy in a number of ways. The key tax feature has to do with the taxation of dividend income and capital gains. For individual shareholders, *effective* tax rates on dividend income are higher than the tax rates on capital gains. Historically, dividends received have been taxed as ordinary income. Capital gains have been taxed at somewhat lower rates, and the tax on a capital gain is deferred until the stock is sold. This second aspect of capital gains taxation makes the effective tax rate much lower because the present value of the tax is less.[2]

Recent tax law changes have led to a renewed interest in the effect of taxes on corporate dividend policies. As we previously noted, historically, dividends have been taxed as ordinary income (at ordinary income tax rates). In 2003, under President G. W. Bush, this changed dramatically. Tax rates on dividends and capital gains were lowered from a maximum in the 35–39 percent range to 15 percent, giving corporations a much larger tax incentive to pay dividends. In 2018, the tax rate on dividends was 0 percent, 15 percent, or 20 percent, depending on the individual's marginal tax rate.

FLOTATION COSTS

In our example illustrating that dividend policy doesn't matter, we saw that the firm could sell some new stock if necessary to pay a dividend. As we mentioned in Chapter 15, selling new stock can be very expensive. If we include flotation costs in our argument, then we will find that the value of the stock decreases if we sell new stock.

More generally, imagine two firms identical in every way except that one pays out a greater percentage of its cash flow in the form of dividends. Because the other firm plows back more cash, its equity grows faster. If these two firms are to remain identical, then the one with the higher payout will have to periodically sell some stock to catch up. Because this is expensive, a firm might be inclined to have a low payout.

DIVIDEND RESTRICTIONS

In some cases, a corporation may face restrictions on its ability to pay dividends. For example, as we discussed in Chapter 7, a common feature of a bond indenture is a covenant prohibiting dividend payments above some level. Also, a corporation may be prohibited by state law from paying dividends if the dividend amount exceeds the firm's retained earnings.

---

[2]In fact, capital gains taxes can sometimes be avoided altogether. Although we do not recommend this particular tax avoidance strategy, the capital gains tax may be avoided by dying. Your heirs are not considered to have a capital gain, so the tax liability dies when you do. In this instance, you *can* take it with you.

Concept Questions

17.3a What are the tax benefits of low dividends?
17.3b Why do flotation costs favor a low payout?

17.4 Real-World Factors Favoring a High Dividend Payout

In this section, we consider reasons why a firm might pay its shareholders higher dividends even if it means the firm must issue more shares of stock to finance the dividend payments.

In a classic textbook, Benjamin Graham, David Dodd, and Sidney Cottle argue that firms should generally have high dividend payouts because:

1. "The discounted value of near dividends is higher than the present worth of distant dividends."
2. Between "two companies with the same general earning power and same general position in an industry, the one paying the larger dividend will almost always sell at a higher price."[3]

Two additional factors favoring a high dividend payout have also been mentioned frequently by proponents of this view: The desire for current income and the resolution of uncertainty.

DESIRE FOR CURRENT INCOME

It has been argued that many individuals desire current income. The classic example is the group of retired people and others living on a fixed income (the proverbial widows and orphans). It is argued that this group is willing to pay a premium to get a higher dividend yield. If this is true, then it lends support to the second claim made by Graham, Dodd, and Cottle.

It is easy to see that this argument is irrelevant in our simple case. An individual preferring high current cash flow but holding low-dividend securities can easily sell off shares to provide the necessary funds. Similarly, an individual desiring a low current cash flow but holding high-dividend securities can just reinvest the dividend. This is just our homemade dividend argument again. In a world of no transaction costs, a policy of high current dividends would be of no value to the stockholder.

The current income argument may have relevance in the real world. Here the sale of low-dividend stocks would involve brokerage fees and other transaction costs. These direct cash expenses could be avoided by an investment in high-dividend securities. In addition, the expenditure of the stockholder's own time in selling securities and the natural (though not necessarily rational) fear of consuming out of principal might further lead many investors to buy high-dividend securities.

Even so, to put this argument in perspective, remember that financial intermediaries such as mutual funds can (and do) perform these "repackaging" transactions for individuals at very low cost. Such intermediaries could buy low-dividend stocks and, through a controlled policy of realizing gains, they could pay their investors at a higher rate.

[3]Graham, B., Dodd, D., and Cottle, S., *Security Analysis*. New York: McGraw-Hill, 1962.

TAX AND OTHER BENEFITS FROM HIGH DIVIDENDS

Earlier, we saw that dividends were taxed unfavorably for individual investors (at least until very recently). This fact is a powerful argument for a low payout. However, there are a number of other investors who do not receive unfavorable tax treatment from holding high-dividend yield, rather than low-dividend yield, securities.

Corporate Investors   A significant tax break on dividends occurs when a corporation owns stock in another corporation. A corporate stockholder receiving either common or preferred dividends is granted a 50 percent (or more) dividend exclusion (reduced from 70 percent or more in the 2017 Tax Cuts and Jobs Act). Because the 50 percent exclusion does not apply to capital gains, this group is taxed unfavorably on capital gains.

As a result of the dividend exclusion, high-dividend, low-capital gains stocks may be more appropriate for corporations to hold. As we discuss elsewhere, this is why corporations hold a substantial percentage of the outstanding preferred stock in the economy. This tax advantage of dividends also leads some corporations to hold high-yielding stocks instead of long-term bonds because there is no similar tax exclusion of interest payments to corporate bondholders.

Tax-Exempt Investors   We have pointed out both the tax advantages and the tax disadvantages of a low dividend payout. Of course, this discussion is irrelevant to those in zero tax brackets. This group includes some of the largest investors in the economy, such as pension funds, endowment funds, and trust funds.

CONCLUSION

Overall, individual investors (for whatever reason) may have a desire for current income and may be willing to pay the dividend tax. In addition, some very large investors such as corporations and tax-free institutions may have a very strong preference for high dividend payouts.

Concept Questions

17.4a   Why might some individual investors favor a high dividend payout?

17.4b   Why might some nonindividual investors prefer a high dividend payout?

A Resolution of Real-World Factors?   17.5

In the previous sections, we presented some factors that favor a low-dividend policy and others that favor a high-dividend policy. In this section, we discuss two important concepts related to dividends and dividend policy: The information content of dividends and the clientele effect. The first topic illustrates both the importance of dividends in general and the importance of distinguishing between dividends and dividend policy. The second topic suggests that, despite the many real-world considerations we have discussed, the dividend payout ratio may not be as important as we originally imagined.

INFORMATION CONTENT OF DIVIDENDS

To begin, we quickly review some of our earlier discussion. Previously, we examined three different positions on dividends:

1. Based on the homemade dividend argument, dividend policy is irrelevant.
2. Because of tax effects for individual investors and new issue costs, a low-dividend policy is best.
3. Because of the desire for current income and related factors, a high-dividend policy is best.

If you wanted to decide which of these positions is the right one, an obvious way to get started would be to look at what happens to stock prices when companies announce dividend changes. You would find with some consistency that stock prices rise when the current dividend is unexpectedly increased, and they generally fall when the dividend is unexpectedly decreased. What does this imply about any of the three positions just stated?

At first glance, the behavior we describe seems consistent with the third position and inconsistent with the other two. In fact, many writers have argued this position. If stock prices rise in response to dividend increases and fall in response to dividend decreases, then isn't the market saying that it approves of higher dividends?

Other authors have pointed out that this observation doesn't really tell us much about dividend policy. Everyone agrees that dividends are important, all other things being equal. Companies cut dividends only with great reluctance. Thus, a dividend cut is often a signal that the firm is in trouble.

More to the point, a dividend cut is usually not a voluntary, planned change in dividend policy. Instead, it usually signals that management does not think that the current dividend policy can be maintained. As a result, expectations of future dividends should generally be revised downward. The present value of expected future dividends falls, and so does the stock price.

In this case, the stock price declines following a dividend cut because future dividends are generally expected to be lower, not because the firm has changed the percentage of its earnings it will pay out in the form of dividends.

For example, on February 4, 2016, oil company ConocoPhillips announced that it was cutting its dividend by two-thirds, from $.74 per year to $.25 per year. The company stated that the drastic fall in oil prices was to blame. Shareholders were in for a big shock. On a typical day, about 7.1 million shares of the company stock traded hands. Following the announcement, about 50 million shares were traded and the stock lost about 9 percent of its value.

Of course, the phenomenon of a stock price decrease in the face of a dividend cut is not restricted to the United States. In February 2016, Australian natural resource company BHP Billiton announced that its annual dividend would be 14 cents, well below the previous year's dividend of 62 cents. In response, the stock dropped by about 5 percent.

In a similar vein, an unexpected increase in the dividend signals good news. Management will raise the dividend only when future earnings, cash flow, and general prospects are expected to rise to such an extent that the dividend will not have to be cut later. A dividend increase is management's signal to the market that the firm is expected to do well. The stock price reacts favorably because expectations of future dividends are revised upward, not because the firm has increased its payout.

In both of these cases, the stock price reacts to the dividend change. The reaction can be attributed to changes in the expected amount of future dividends, not necessarily a change in dividend payout policy. This reaction is called the **information content effect** of the dividend. The fact that dividend changes convey information about the firm to the market makes it difficult to interpret the effect of the dividend policy of the firm.

information content effect
The market's reaction to a change in corporate dividend payout.

THE CLIENTELE EFFECT

In our earlier discussion, we saw that some groups (wealthy individuals, for example) have an incentive to pursue low-payout (or zero-payout) stocks. Other groups (corporations, for example) have an incentive to pursue high-payout stocks. Companies with high payouts will attract one group, and low-payout companies will attract another.

These different groups are called *clienteles*, and what we have described is a **clientele effect**. The clientele effect argument states that different groups of investors desire different levels of dividends. When a firm chooses a particular dividend policy, the only effect is to attract a particular clientele. If a firm changes its dividend policy, then it attracts a different clientele.

What we are left with is a simple supply and demand argument. Suppose 40 percent of all investors prefer high dividends, but only 20 percent of the firms pay high dividends. Here the high-dividend firms will be in short supply; their stock prices will rise. Consequently, low-dividend firms will find it advantageous to switch policies until 40 percent of all firms have high payouts. At this point, the *dividend market* is in equilibrium. Further changes in dividend policy are pointless because all of the clienteles are satisfied. The dividend policy for any individual firm is now irrelevant.

To see if you understand the clientele effect, consider the following statement: In spite of the theoretical argument that dividend policy is irrelevant or that firms should not pay dividends, many investors like high dividends; because of this fact, a firm can boost its share price by having a higher dividend payout ratio. True or false?

The answer is false if clienteles exist. As long as enough high-dividend firms satisfy the dividend-loving investors, a firm won't be able to boost its share price by paying high dividends. An unsatisfied clientele must exist for this to happen, and there is no evidence that this is the case.

clientele effect
The observable fact that stocks attract particular groups based on dividend yield and the resulting tax effects.

Concept Questions

17.5a How does the market react to unexpected dividend changes? What does this tell us about dividends? About dividend policy?

17.5b What is a dividend clientele? All things considered, would you expect a risky firm with significant but highly uncertain growth prospects to have a low or a high dividend payout?

Stock Repurchases: An Alternative to Cash Dividends   17.6

Thus far in our chapter, we have considered cash dividends. Cash dividends are not the only way corporations distribute cash. Instead, a company can **repurchase** its own stock. Repurchases (or *buybacks*) have become an increasingly popular tool, and the amount spent on repurchases has become huge. For example, in 2016, about $536 billion in share repurchases were announced, a 6 percent decrease over the $572 billion of repurchases in 2015. The record amount of stock buybacks in a single year was the $589 billion announced in 2007.

Another way to see how important repurchases have become is to compare them to cash dividends. Consider Figure 17.3, which shows the aggregate real (inflation-adjusted) dividends and stock repurchases by publicly held U.S. industrial firms for the period 1971–2015, along with the combined total. Aggregate real dividends have grown relatively

stock repurchase
The purchase, by a corporation, of its own shares of stock; also known as a *buyback*.

586   **PART 6**   Cost of Capital and Long-Term Financial Policy

FIGURE 17.3

Aggregate Real (2012) Dividends and Stock Repurchases by Publicly Held U.S. Industrial Firms: 1971–2015

SOURCE: Redrawn by authors using Compustat data, following Farre-Mensa, J., Michaely, R., and Schmaltz, M., "Payout Policy," *Annual Review of Financial Economics* 6, 2014, pp. 75–134.

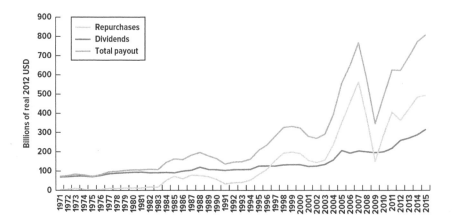

steadily through time, but repurchases have exploded in the last two decades. They reached a peak in 2007 of about 2.5 times the size of aggregate dividends. Repurchases plunged in the 2008–2009 recession as firms conserved cash, but they rebounded in 2010.

Share repurchases are typically accomplished in one of three ways. First, companies may purchase their own stock, just as anyone would buy shares of a particular stock. In these *open market purchases*, the firm does not reveal itself as the buyer. The seller does not know whether the shares were sold back to the firm or sold to another investor.

Second, the firm could institute a *tender offer*. Here, the firm announces to all of its stockholders that it is willing to buy a fixed number of shares at a specific price. For example, suppose Arts and Crafts (A&C), Inc., has 1 million shares of stock outstanding, with a stock price of $50 per share. The firm makes a tender offer to buy back 300,000 shares at $60 per share. A&C chooses a price above $50 to induce shareholders to sell, that is, tender, their shares. In fact, if the tender price is set high enough, shareholders may very well want to sell more than the 300,000 shares. In the extreme case where all outstanding shares are tendered, A&C will buy back 3 out of every 10 shares that a shareholder holds.

Finally, firms may repurchase shares from specific individual stockholders. This procedure has been called a *targeted repurchase*. For example, suppose the International Biotechnology Corporation purchased approximately 10 percent of the outstanding stock of the Prime Robotics Company (P-R Co.) in April at around $38 per share. At that time, International Biotechnology announced to the Securities and Exchange Commission that it might eventually try to take control of P-R Co. In May, P-R Co. repurchased the International Biotechnology holdings at $48 per share, well above the market price at that time. This offer was not extended to other shareholders.

CASH DIVIDENDS VERSUS REPURCHASE

Imagine an all-equity company with excess cash of $300,000. The firm pays no dividends, and its net income for the year just ended is $49,000. The market value balance sheet at the end of the year is represented here:

Market Value Balance Sheet (before paying out excess cash)			
Excess cash	$ 300,000	Debt	$ 0
Other assets	700,000	Equity	1,000,000
Total	$1,000,000	Total	$1,000,000

There are 100,000 shares outstanding. The total market value of the equity is $1 million, so the stock sells for $10 per share. Earnings per share (EPS) are $49,000/100,000 = $.49, and the price-earnings ratio (PE) is $10/$.49 = 20.4.

One option the company is considering is a $300,000/100,000 = $3 per share extra cash dividend. Alternatively, the company is thinking of using the money to repurchase $300,000/$10 = 30,000 shares of stock.

If commissions, taxes, and other imperfections are ignored in our example, the stockholders shouldn't care which option is chosen. Does this seem surprising? It shouldn't, really. What is happening here is that the firm is paying out $300,000 in cash. The new balance sheet is represented here:

Market Value Balance Sheet (after paying out excess cash)			
Excess cash	$ 0	Debt	$ 0
Other assets	700,000	Equity	700,000
Total	$700,000	Total	$700,000

If the cash is paid out as a dividend, there are still 100,000 shares outstanding, so each is worth $7.

The fact that the per-share value fell from $10 to $7 is not a cause for concern. Consider a stockholder who owns 100 shares. At $10 per share before the dividend, the total value is $1,000.

After the $3 dividend, this same stockholder has 100 shares worth $7 each, for a total of $700, plus 100 × $3 = $300 in cash, for a combined total of $1,000. This illustrates what we saw early on: A cash dividend doesn't affect a stockholder's wealth if there are no imperfections. In this case, the stock price fell by $3 when the stock went ex dividend.

Also, because total earnings and the number of shares outstanding haven't changed, EPS is still 49 cents. The price-earnings ratio falls to $7/$.49 = 14.3. The reason why we are looking at accounting earnings and PE ratios will be apparent in just a moment.

Alternatively, if the company repurchases 30,000 shares, there are 70,000 shares left outstanding. The balance sheet looks the same:

Market Value Balance Sheet (after share repurchase)			
Excess cash	$ 0	Debt	$ 0
Other assets	700,000	Equity	700,000
Total	$700,000	Total	$700,000

The company is worth $700,000 again, so each remaining share is worth $700,000/70,000 = $10. Our stockholder with 100 shares is obviously unaffected. For example, if she was so inclined, she could sell 30 shares and end up with $300 in cash and $700 in stock, just as she has if the firm pays the cash dividend. This is another example of a homemade dividend.

In this second case, EPS goes up because total earnings remain the same while the number of shares goes down. The new EPS is $49,000/70,000 = $.70. The important thing to notice is that the PE ratio is $10/$.70 = 14.3, as it was following the dividend.

This example illustrates the important point that, if there are no imperfections, a cash dividend and a share repurchase are essentially the same thing. This is another illustration of dividend policy irrelevance when there are no taxes or other imperfections.

REAL-WORLD CONSIDERATIONS IN A REPURCHASE

The example we have just described shows that a repurchase and a cash dividend are the same thing in a world without taxes and transaction costs. In the real world, there are some accounting differences between a share repurchase and a cash dividend, but the most important difference is in the tax treatment.

Under current tax law, a repurchase has a significant tax advantage over a cash dividend. A dividend is taxed, and a shareholder has no choice about whether or not to receive the dividend. In a repurchase, a shareholder pays taxes only if (1) the shareholder actually chooses to sell and (2) the shareholder has a capital gain on the sale.

For example, suppose a dividend of $1 per share is taxed at ordinary rates. Investors in the 28 percent tax bracket who own 100 shares of the security pay $100 × .28 = $28 in taxes. Selling shareholders would pay far lower taxes if $100 worth of stock were repurchased. This is because taxes are paid only on the profit from a sale. The gain on a sale would be only $40 if shares sold at $100 were originally purchased at $60. The capital gains tax would be .28 × $40 = $11.20. Note that the 2003 reductions in dividend and capital gains tax rates do not change the fact that a repurchase has a potentially large tax edge.

To give a few recent examples, in January 2017, Apple announced that it had repurchased $11 billion of its stock in the previous quarter. And General Motors announced that it was increasing its $9 billion repurchase, which it had begun in 2015, by another $5 billion. Also in January 2017, both Pfizer and Swiss drugmaker Novartis announced repurchases of $5 billion.

IBM is well known for its aggressive repurchasing policies. In the first nine months of 2016, it repurchased $2.6 billion of its own stock. Since 2003, the company had spent about $138.8 billion on buybacks through the end of 2016. In fact, from the beginning of 2003 through the end of 2016, the number of shares in the company fell from 1.72 billion shares to 951 million shares.

One thing to note is that not all announced stock repurchase plans are completed. Based on research covering the 2004–2007 period, average completion rates were only 81 percent.[4]

SHARE REPURCHASE AND EPS

You may read in the popular financial press that a share repurchase is beneficial because it causes earnings per share to increase. As we have seen, this will happen. The reason is that a share repurchase reduces the number of outstanding shares, but it has no effect on total earnings. As a result, EPS rises.

---

[4]See A. A. Bonaimé, "Mandatory Disclosure and Firm Behavior: Evidence from Share Repurchases," *The Accounting Review* 90 (2015).

The financial press may place undue emphasis on EPS figures in a repurchase agreement. In our preceding example, we saw that the value of the stock wasn't affected by the EPS change. In fact, the PE ratio was exactly the same when we compared a cash dividend to a repurchase.

Concept Questions

17.6a   Why might a stock repurchase make more sense than an extra cash dividend?

17.6b   What is the effect of a stock repurchase on a firm's EPS? Its PE?

What We Know and Do Not Know about Dividend and Payout Policies

17.7

DIVIDENDS AND DIVIDEND PAYERS

As we have discussed, there are numerous good reasons favoring a dividend policy of low (or no) payout. Nonetheless, in the United States, aggregate dividends paid are quite large. For example, in 1978, U.S. industrial firms listed on the major exchanges paid $31.3 billion in total dividends. By 2000, that number had risen to $101.6 billion (unadjusted for inflation), an increase of over 200 percent (after adjusting for inflation, the increase is smaller, 22.7 percent, but still substantial).

While we know dividends are large in the aggregate, we also know that the number of companies that pay dividends has declined. Over the same 1978–2000 period, the number of industrial companies paying dividends declined from over 2,000 to just under 1,000, and the percentage of these firms paying dividends declined 65 percent, to 19 percent.[5]

The fact that aggregate dividends grew while the number of payers fell so sharply seems a bit paradoxical, but the explanation is straightforward: Dividend payments are heavily concentrated in a relatively small set of large firms. In 2000, for example, about 80 percent of aggregate dividends were paid by just 100 firms. The top 25 payers, which include such well-known giants as ExxonMobil and General Electric, collectively paid about 55 percent of all dividends. The reason that dividends grew while dividend payers shrank is that the decline in dividend payers is almost entirely due to smaller firms, which tend to pay smaller dividends in the first place.

One important reason that the percentage of dividend-paying firms has declined is that the population of firms has changed. There has been a huge increase in the number of newly listed firms over the last 25 or so years. Newly listed firms tend to be younger and less profitable. Such firms need their internally generated cash to fund growth and typically do not pay dividends.

Another factor at work is that firms appear to be more likely to begin making payouts using share repurchases, which are flexible, rather than committing to making cash distributions. Such a policy seems quite sensible given our previous discussions. However, after

---

[5]These figures and those in the following paragraph are from H. DeAngelo, L. DeAngelo, and D. J. Skinner, "Are Dividends Disappearing? Dividend Concentration and the Consolidation of Earnings," *Journal of Financial Economics* 72 (2004).

FIGURE 17.4

Proportion of Dividend Payers, Repurchasers, and Firms with Positive Total Payout among All Publicly Held U.S. Industrial Firms: 1971–2015

SOURCE: Redrawn by authors using Compustat data, following Farre-Mensa, J., Michaely, R., and Schmaltz, M., "Payout Policy," *Annual Review of Financial Economics* 6, 2014, pp. 75–134.

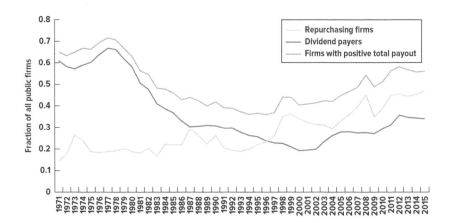

controlling for the changing mix of firms and the increase in share repurchasing activity, there still appears to be a decreased propensity to pay dividends among certain types of older, better established firms, though further research is needed on this question.

The fact that the number of dividend-paying firms has declined so sharply is an interesting phenomenon. Making matters even more interesting is evidence showing that the trend may have begun to reverse itself. Take a look at Figure 17.4, which shows the percentage of industrial firms paying dividends over the period 1971–2015, along with the percentage of (1) firms doing repurchases and (2) firms with a positive payout of one type or the other (or both). As shown, there is a pronounced downward trend, but that trend appears to bottom out in 2000 and then sharply reverse in 2002. So what's going on?

Part of the apparent rebound in Figure 17.4 is probably an illusion. The percentage of firms paying dividends rose because nonpayers dropped out in large numbers.[6] The number of firms listed on the major stock markets dropped sharply, from over 5,000 to under 4,000, during the period 2000–2005. About 2,000 firms delisted over this period, 98 percent of which were not dividend payers. By 2013, the number of listed firms had declined to below 3,000, and the percentage of dividend payers reached 36 percent.

Once we control for the drop-out problem, there is still an increase in the number of dividend payers, but it happens in 2003. As shown in Figure 17.5, the uptick is concentrated in the months following May 2003. What is so special about this month? The answer is that in May 2003, top personal tax rates on dividends were slashed from about 38 to 15 percent. Consistent with our earlier tax arguments, a reduction in personal tax rates led to increases in dividends.

It is important not to read too much into Figure 17.5. It seems clear that the reduction in tax rates did have an effect, but, on balance, what we see is a few hundred firms initiating dividends. There are still thousands of firms that did not initiate dividends, even though the tax rate reduction was very large. The evidence suggests that tax rates matter, but they are not a primary determinant of dividend policy. This interpretation is consistent with the results of a 2005 survey of financial executives, more than two-thirds of whom said that the tax rate cut probably or definitely would not affect their dividend policies.[7]

---

[6]These numbers and this explanation are from R. Chetty and E. Saez, "The Effects of the 2003 Dividend Tax Cut on Corporate Behavior: Interpreting the Evidence," *American Economic Review* Papers and Proceedings 96 (2006).

[7]See A. P. Brav, J. R. Graham, C. R. Harvey, and R. Michaely, "Managerial Response to the May 2003 Dividend Tax Cut," *Financial Management* 37 (2008), pp. 611–624.

FIGURE 17.5   **Regular Dividend Initiations, 2001–2006**

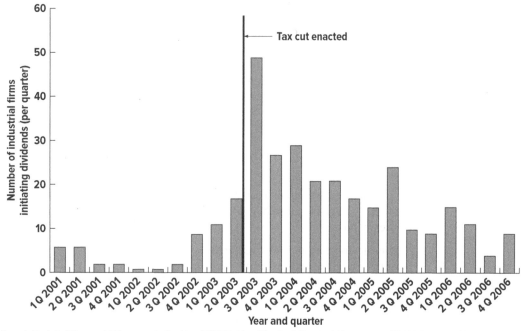

SOURCE: Brav, A. P. et al., "Managerial Response to the May 2003 Dividend Tax Cut," *Financial Management* 37, 2008, pp. 611–624.

A second force that may be at work over time is the maturing of many of the (surviving) newly listed firms we mentioned earlier. As these firms have become better established, their profitability has increased (and, potentially, their investment opportunities have decreased), and they have begun to pay dividends.

A third factor that may be contributing to the increase in the number of dividend payers is a little more subtle. The technology-heavy NASDAQ index plummeted in the spring of 2000 (due to the "dot-com" crash), and it became clear that many newly listed companies were likely to fail. Shortly thereafter, major accounting scandals at companies such as Enron and WorldCom left investors unsure of the trustworthiness of reported earnings. In such an environment, companies may have chosen to initiate dividends in an attempt to signal to investors that they had the cash to make dividend payments now and in the future.

The apparent reversal in the decline of dividend payers is a recent phenomenon, so its significance remains to be seen. It may prove to be just a transient event in the middle of a long decline. We will have to wait and see.

CORPORATIONS SMOOTH DIVIDENDS

As we previously observed, dividend cuts are frequently viewed as very bad news by market participants. As a result, companies only cut dividends when there is no other acceptable alternative. For the same reason, companies are also reluctant to increase dividends unless they are sure the new dividend level can be sustained.

In practice, what we observe is that dividend-paying companies tend to raise dividends only after earnings have risen, and they don't increase or cut dividends in response to temporary earnings fluctuations. In other words, (1) dividend growth lags earnings growth and (2) dividend growth will tend to be much smoother than earnings growth.

To see how important dividend stability and steady growth are to financial managers, consider that, in 2016, 2,634 companies in the United States increased their dividend payments, while only 659 companies decreased their dividend payments. Two companies with long histories of dividend increases are Procter & Gamble and Colgate-Palmolive. At the end of 2016, Procter & Gamble had increased its dividend for 61 consecutive years, and Colgate-Palmolive had increased its dividend for 53 consecutive years. Overall, as of early 2017, 51 companies in the S&P 500 had increased dividends for at least 25 consecutive years.

PUTTING IT ALL TOGETHER

Much of what we have discussed in this chapter (and much of what we know about dividends from decades of research) can be pulled together and summarized in the following five observations:[8]

1. Aggregate dividend and stock repurchases are massive, and they have increased steadily in nominal and real terms over the years.
2. Dividends are heavily concentrated among a relatively small number of large, mature firms.
3. Managers are very reluctant to cut dividends, normally doing so only due to firm-specific problems.
4. Managers smooth dividends, raising them slowly and incrementally as earnings grow.
5. Stock prices react to unanticipated changes in dividends.

The challenge now is to fit these five pieces into a reasonably coherent picture. With regard to payouts in general, meaning the combination of stock repurchases and cash dividends, a simple life cycle theory fits Points 1 and 2. The key ideas are straightforward. First, relatively young and less profitable firms generally should not make cash distributions. They need the cash to fund investments (and flotation costs discourage the raising of outside cash).

As a firm matures, it begins to generate free cash flow (which, you will recall, is internally generated cash flow beyond that needed to fund profitable investment activities). Significant free cash flow can lead to agency problems if it is not distributed. Managers may become tempted to pursue empire building or otherwise spend the excess cash in ways not in the shareholders' best interests. Firms come under pressure to make distributions rather than hoard cash. And, consistent with what we observe, we expect large firms with a history of profitability to make large distributions.

The life cycle theory says that firms trade off the agency costs of excess cash retention against the potential future costs of external equity financing. A firm should begin making distributions when it generates sufficient internal cash flow to fund its investment needs now and into the foreseeable future.

The more complex issue concerns the type of distribution, cash dividends versus repurchases. The tax argument in favor of repurchases is a clear and strong one. Further,

[8]This list is distilled in part from a longer list in DeAngelo, H., and DeAngelo, L., "Payout Policy Pedagogy: What Matters and Why," *European Financial Management* 13, 2007.

repurchases are a much more flexible option (and managers greatly value financial flexibility), so the question is: Why would firms ever choose a cash dividend?

If we are to answer this question, we have to ask a different question. What can a cash dividend accomplish that a share repurchase cannot accomplish? One answer is that when a firm makes a commitment to pay a cash dividend now and into the future, it sends a two-part signal to the markets. As we have already discussed, one signal is that the firm anticipates being profitable, with the ability to make the payments on an ongoing basis. Note that a firm cannot benefit by trying to fool the market in this regard because the firm would ultimately be punished when it couldn't make the dividend payment (or couldn't make it without relying on external financing). A cash dividend may let a firm distinguish itself from less profitable rivals.

A second, and more subtle, signal takes us back to the agency problem of free cash flow. By committing to pay cash dividends now and in the future, the firm signals that it won't be hoarding cash (or at least not as much cash), thereby reducing agency costs and enhancing shareholder wealth.

This two-part signaling story is consistent with Points 3–5 above, but an obvious objection remains. Why don't firms just commit to a policy of setting aside whatever money would be used to pay dividends and use it instead to buy back shares? After all, either way, a firm is committing to pay out cash to shareholders.

A fixed repurchase strategy suffers from two drawbacks. The first is verifiability. A firm could announce an open market repurchase and then not do it. By suitably fudging its books, it would be some time before the deception was discovered. It would be necessary for shareholders to develop a monitoring mechanism, meaning some sort of way for stockholders to know for sure that the repurchase was in fact done. Such a mechanism wouldn't be difficult to build (it could be a simple trustee relationship such as we observe in the bond markets), but it currently does not exist. Of course, a tender offer repurchase needs little or no verification, but such offers have expenses associated with them. The beauty of a cash dividend is that it needs no monitoring. A firm is forced to cut and mail checks four times per year, year in and year out.

A second objection to a fixed repurchase strategy is more controversial. Suppose managers, as insiders, are better able than stockholders to judge whether their stock price is too high or too low. (Note that this idea does not conflict with semistrong market efficiency if inside information is the reason.) In this case, a fixed repurchase commitment forces management to buy back stock even in circumstances when the stock is overvalued. In other words, it forces management into making negative NPV investments.

More research on the cash dividend versus share repurchase question is needed, but the historical trend seems to be favoring continued growth in repurchases relative to dividends.

Total corporate payouts seem to be relatively stable over time at roughly 20 percent of aggregate earnings (see Figure 17.3), but repurchases are becoming a larger portion of that total. The split reached about 50-50 in the latter part of the 1990s, but it looks like aggregate repurchases have recently passed aggregate dividends.

One aspect of aggregate cash dividends that has not received much attention is that there may be a strong legacy effect. Before 1982, the regulatory status of stock repurchases was somewhat murky, creating a significant disincentive. In 1982, the SEC, after years of debate, created a clear set of guidelines for firms to follow, thereby making repurchases much more attractive.

The legacy effect arises because many of the giant firms that pay such a large portion of aggregate dividends were paying dividends before (and perhaps long before) 1982. To the extent that these firms are unwilling to cut their dividends, aggregate cash dividends will be large, but only because of a "lock-in" effect for older firms. If locked-in, legacy payers account for much of the aggregate dividend, what we should observe is (1) a sharply reduced tendency for maturing firms to initiate dividends and (2) a growth in repurchases relative to cash dividends over time. We actually do see evidence of both of these trends; legacy effects alone can't account for all cash dividend payers.

The Pros and Cons of Paying Dividends	
Pros	**Cons**
1. Cash dividends can underscore good results and provide support to the stock price.	1. Dividends are taxed to recipients.
2. Dividends may attract institutional investors who prefer some return in the form of dividends. A mix of institutional and individual investors may allow a firm to raise capital at lower cost because of the ability of the firm to reach a wider market.	2. Dividends can reduce internal sources of financing. Dividends may force the firm to forgo positive NPV projects or to rely on costly external equity financing.
3. Stock price usually increases with the announcement of a new or increased dividend.	3. Once established, dividend cuts are hard to make without adversely affecting a firm's stock price.
4. Dividends absorb excess cash flow and may reduce agency costs that arise from conflicts between management and shareholders.	

SOME SURVEY EVIDENCE ON DIVIDENDS

A recent study surveyed a large number of financial executives regarding dividend policy. One of the questions asked was, "Do these statements describe factors that affect your company's dividend decisions?" Table 17.1 shows some of the results.

As shown in Table 17.1, financial managers are very disinclined to cut dividends. Moreover, they are very conscious of their previous dividends and desire to maintain a relatively steady dividend. In contrast, the cost of external capital and the desire to attract "prudent man" investors (those with fiduciary duties) are less important.

TABLE 17.1

Survey Responses on Dividend Decisions*

SOURCE: Adapted from Table 4 of Brav, A. el at., "Payout Policy in the 21st Century," *Journal of Financial Economics*, 2005.

Do These Statements Affect Your Dividend Policy?	Percent Who Agree or Strongly Agree
1. Avoiding dividend cuts	93.8%
2. Maintaining a "smooth" dividend over time	89.6
3. Size of recently paid dividends	88.2
4. Making sure that any changes we make won't have to be reversed later	77.9
5. The rate at which dividends are changing or growing	66.7
6. The cost of cutting dividends exceeds the cost of raising external capital	42.8
7. Using dividends to attract investors subject to "prudent man" investment restrictions	41.7

*Survey respondents were asked the question, "Do these statements describe factors that affect your company's dividend decisions?"

IN THEIR OWN WORDS ...

Fischer Black on Why Firms Pay Dividends

I think investors like dividends. They believe that dividends enhance stock value (given the firm's prospects), and they feel uncomfortable spending out of their capital.

We see evidence for this everywhere: Investment advisers and institutions treat a high-yield stock as both attractive and safe, financial analysts value a stock by predicting and discounting its dividends, financial economists study the relation between stock prices and actual dividends, and investors complain about dividend cuts.

What if investors were neutral toward dividends? Investment advisers would tell clients to spend indifferently from income and capital and, if taxable, to avoid income; financial analysts would ignore dividends in valuing stocks; financial economists would treat stock price and the discounted value of dividends as equal, even when stocks are mispriced; and a firm would apologize to its taxable investors when forced by an accumulated earnings tax to pay dividends. This is not what we observe.

Furthermore, changing dividends seems a poor way to tell the financial markets about a firm's prospects. Public statements can better detail the firm's prospects and have more impact on both the speaker's and the firm's reputations.

I predict that under current tax rules, dividends will gradually disappear.

The late Fischer Black was a partner at Goldman, Sachs & Co., an investment banking firm. Before that, he was a professor of finance at MIT. He is one of the fathers of option pricing theory, and he is widely regarded as one of the preeminent financial scholars. He is well known for his creative ideas, many of which were dismissed at first only to become part of accepted lore when others finally came to understand them. He is sadly missed by his colleagues.

Table 17.2 is drawn from the same survey, but here the responses are to the question, "How important are the following factors to your company's dividend decision?" Not surprisingly given the responses in Table 17.1 and our earlier discussion, the highest priority is maintaining a consistent dividend policy. The next several items are also consistent with our previous analysis. Financial managers are very concerned about earnings stability and future earnings levels in making dividend decisions, and they consider the availability of good investment opportunities. Survey respondents also believed that attracting both institutional and individual (retail) investors was relatively important.

In contrast to our discussion of taxes and flotation costs in the earlier part of this chapter, the financial managers in this survey did not think that personal taxes paid on dividends by shareholders were very important. Even fewer financial managers thought that equity flotation costs were relevant.

How Important Are the Following?	Percent Who Think This Is Important or Very Important
1. Being consistent with our historic dividend policy	84.1%
2. Future earnings stability	71.9
3. Sustainable earnings changes	67.1
4. Attracting institutional investors	52.5
5. Good quality investments	47.6
6. Attracting retail investors	44.5
7. Personal taxes paid by our shareholders on dividends we pay	21.1
8. Costs associated with issuing new equity	9.3

TABLE 17.2

Survey Responses on Dividend Decisions*

SOURCE: Adapted from Table 5 of Brav, A. el at., "Payout Policy in the 21st Century," *Journal of Financial Economics*, 2005.

*Survey respondents were asked the question, "How important are the following factors to your company's dividend decision?"

17.8 Stock Dividends and Stock Splits

stock dividend
A payment made by a firm to its owners in the form of stock, diluting the value of each share outstanding.

Another type of dividend is paid out in shares of stock. This type of dividend is called a **stock dividend**. A stock dividend is not a true dividend because it is not paid in cash. The effect of a stock dividend is to increase the number of shares that each owner holds. Because there are more shares outstanding, each is worth less.

A stock dividend is commonly expressed as a percentage; for example, a 20 percent stock dividend means that a shareholder receives one new share for every five currently owned (a 20 percent increase). Because every shareholder receives 20 percent more stock, the total number of shares outstanding rises by 20 percent. As we will see in a moment, the result is that each share of stock is worth about 20 percent less.

stock split
An increase in a firm's shares outstanding without any change in owners' equity.

A **stock split** is essentially the same thing as a stock dividend, except that a split is expressed as a ratio instead of a percentage. When a split is declared, each share is split up to create additional shares. For example, in a three-for-one stock split, each old share is split into three new shares.

SOME DETAILS ABOUT STOCK SPLITS AND STOCK DIVIDENDS

Stock splits and stock dividends have essentially the same impacts on the corporation and the shareholder: They increase the number of shares outstanding and reduce the value per share. The accounting treatment is not the same and it depends on two things: (1) Whether the distribution is a stock split or a stock dividend and (2) the size of the stock dividend if it is called a dividend. In recent years, stock splits have slowed considerably. During the 1990s, an average of 64 S&P 500 companies split each year. From 2008 through 2012, the number fell to about 12 per year.

By convention, stock dividends of less than 20 to 25 percent are called *small stock dividends*. The accounting procedure for such a dividend is discussed next. A stock dividend greater than this range of 20 to 25 percent is called a *large stock dividend*. Large stock dividends are not uncommon. For example, the Comcast two-for-one stock split we discussed at the beginning of the chapter was to be in the form of a 100 percent stock dividend. In June 2016, Facebook announced its 200 percent stock dividend in the form of a three-for-one stock dividend that created the company's nonvoting Class C shares. Except for some relatively minor accounting differences, a stock dividend has the same effect as a stock split.

Information on upcoming stock splits is available on the splits calendar at **www.investmenthouse.com** and **finance.yahoo.com**.

Example of a Small Stock Dividend   The Peterson Co., a consulting firm specializing in difficult accounting problems, has 10,000 shares of stock outstanding, each selling at $66. The total market value of the equity is $66 × 10,000 = $660,000. With a 10 percent stock dividend, each stockholder receives one additional share for each 10 owned, and the total number of shares outstanding after the dividend is 11,000.

Before the stock dividend, the equity portion of Peterson's balance sheet might look like this:

Common stock ($1 par, 10,000 shares outstanding)	$ 10,000
Capital in excess of par value	200,000
Retained earnings	290,000
Total owners' equity	$500,000

A seemingly arbitrary accounting procedure is used to adjust the balance sheet after a small stock dividend. Because 1,000 new shares are issued, the common stock account is increased by $1,000 (1,000 shares at $1 par value each), for a total of $11,000. The market price of $66 is $65 greater than the par value, so the "excess" of $65 × 1,000 shares = $65,000 is added to the capital surplus account (capital in excess of par value), producing a total of $265,000.

Total owners' equity is unaffected by the stock dividend because no cash has come in or out, so retained earnings are reduced by the entire $66,000, leaving $224,000. The net effect of these machinations is that Peterson's equity accounts now look like this:

Common stock ($1 par, 11,000 shares outstanding)	$ 11,000
Capital in excess of par value	265,000
Retained earnings	224,000
Total owners' equity	$500,000

Example of a Stock Split A stock split is conceptually similar to a stock dividend, but it is commonly expressed as a ratio. For example, in a three-for-two split, each shareholder receives one additional share of stock for each two held originally, so a three-for-two split amounts to a 50 percent stock dividend. Again, no cash is paid out, and the percentage of the entire firm that each shareholder owns is unaffected.

The accounting treatment of a stock split is a little different from (and simpler than) that of a stock dividend. Suppose Peterson decides to declare a two-for-one stock split. The number of shares outstanding will double to 20,000, and the par value will be halved to $.50 per share. The owners' equity after the split is represented as follows:

Common stock ($.50 par, 20,000 shares outstanding)	$ 10,000
Capital in excess of par value	200,000
Retained earnings	290,000
Total owners' equity	$500,000

For a list of recent stock splits, try **www.stocksplits.net**.

Note that, for all three of the categories, the figures on the right are completely unaffected by the split. The only changes are in the par value per share and the number of shares outstanding. Because the number of shares has doubled, the par value of each is cut in half.

Example of a Large Stock Dividend In our example, if a 100 percent stock dividend were declared, 10,000 new shares would be distributed, so 20,000 shares would be outstanding. At a $1 par value per share, the common stock account would rise by $10,000, for a total of $20,000. The retained earnings account would be reduced by $10,000, leaving $280,000. The result would be the following:

Common stock ($1 par, 20,000 shares outstanding)	$ 20,000
Capital in excess of par value	200,000
Retained earnings	280,000
Total owners' equity	$500,000

VALUE OF STOCK SPLITS AND STOCK DIVIDENDS

The laws of logic tell us that stock splits and stock dividends can (1) leave the value of the firm unaffected, (2) increase its value, or (3) decrease its value. Unfortunately, the issues are complex enough that we cannot easily determine which of the three relationships holds.

The Benchmark Case A strong case can be made that stock dividends and splits do not change either the wealth of any shareholder or the wealth of the firm as a whole. In our preceding example, the equity had a total market value of $660,000. With the small stock dividend, the number of shares increased to 11,000, so it seems that each would be worth $660,000/11,000 = $60.

For example, a shareholder who had 100 shares worth $66 each before the dividend would have 110 shares worth $60 each afterward. The total value of the stock is $6,600 either way; so the stock dividend doesn't really have any economic effect.

After the stock split, there are 20,000 shares outstanding, so each should be worth $660,000/20,000 = $33. In other words, the number of shares doubles and the price halves. From these calculations, it appears that stock dividends and splits are just paper transactions.

Although these results are relatively obvious, reasons are often given to suggest that there may be some benefits to these actions. The typical financial manager is aware of many real-world complexities; for that reason, the stock split or stock dividend decision is not treated lightly in practice.

trading range
The price range between the highest and lowest prices at which a stock is traded.

Popular Trading Range   Proponents of stock dividends and stock splits frequently argue that a security has a proper **trading range**. When the security is priced above this level, many investors do not have the funds to buy the common trading unit of 100 shares, called a *round lot*. Although securities can be purchased in *odd-lot* form (fewer than 100 shares), the commissions are greater. Firms will split the stock to keep the price in this trading range.

For example, Microsoft has split nine times since the company went public in 1986. The stock has split three-for-two on two occasions and two-for-one a total of seven times. So for every share of Microsoft you owned in 1986 when the company first went public, you would own 288 shares as of the most recent stock split. Similarly, since Walmart went public in 1970, it has split its stock two-for-one 11 times, and Apple has split seven-for-one once and two-for-one three times since going public in 1980. For a really long split history, consider Procter & Gamble, which has split five-for-one twice, 1.5-to-1 once, and two-for-one eight times since 1920. Each share of P&G purchased prior to the company's first stock split would now be worth 9,600 shares.

Although this argument is a popular one, its validity is questionable for a number of reasons. Mutual funds, pension funds, and other institutions have steadily increased their trading activity since World War II and now handle a sizable percentage of total trading volume (on the order of 90 percent of NYSE trading volume, for example). Because these institutions buy and sell in huge amounts, the individual share price is of little concern.

Furthermore, we sometimes observe share prices that are quite large that do not appear to cause problems. To take a well-known case, Berkshire Hathaway, a widely respected company headed by legendary investor Warren Buffett, sold for about $300,000 per share in early 2018.

Finally, there is evidence that stock splits may actually decrease the liquidity of the company's shares. Following a two-for-one split, the number of shares traded should more than double if liquidity is increased by the split. This doesn't appear to happen, and the reverse is sometimes observed.

REVERSE SPLITS

reverse split
A stock split in which a firm's number of shares outstanding is reduced.

A less frequently encountered financial maneuver is the **reverse split**. For example, in May 2017, Cobalt Energy announced a 1-for-15 reverse stock split. Also in May 2017, Xerox underwent a 1-for-4 reverse split. In a 1-for-4 reverse split, each investor exchanges 4 old shares for one new share. The par value is increased by a factor of 4 in the process. In what will probably be one of the biggest reverse splits ever (in terms of market cap), banking giant Citigroup announced in March 2011 that it would do a 1-for-10 reverse split, thereby reducing the number of shares outstanding from 29 billion to 2.9 billion. As with stock splits and stock dividends, a case can be made that a reverse split has no real effect.

Given real-world imperfections, three related reasons are cited for reverse splits. First, transaction costs to shareholders may be less after the reverse split. Second, the liquidity and marketability of a company's stock might be improved when its price is raised to the popular trading range. Third, stocks selling at prices below a certain level are not considered respectable, meaning that investors underestimate these firms' earnings, cash flow, growth, and stability. Some financial analysts argue that a reverse split can achieve instant respectability. As was the case with stock splits, none of these reasons is particularly compelling, especially not the third one.

There are two other reasons for reverse splits. First, stock exchanges have minimum price per share requirements. A reverse split may bring the stock price up to such a minimum. For example, NASDAQ begins the delisting process for companies whose stock price drops below $1 per share for 30 days. Following the collapse of the Internet boom in 2001–2002, a large number of Internet-related companies found themselves in danger of being delisted and used reverse splits to boost their stock prices. Second, companies sometimes perform reverse splits and, at the same time, buy out any stockholders who end up with less than a certain number of shares.

For example, in January 2017, Lime Energy completed a reverse/forward split. In this case, the company first did a 1-for-300 reverse stock split and then repurchased all shares held by stockholders with less than one share of stock, eliminating smaller shareholders thus reducing the total number of shareholders. This process allowed the company to delist its stock, or "go dark." What made the proposal especially imaginative was that immediately after the reverse split, the company did a 300-for-1 ordinary split to restore the stock to its original cost!

Concept Questions

17.8a What is the effect of a stock split on stockholder wealth?

17.8b How does the accounting treatment of a stock split differ from that used with a small stock dividend?

Summary and Conclusions 17.9

In this chapter, we first discussed the types of dividends and how they are paid. We then defined dividend policy and examined whether or not dividend policy matters. Next, we illustrated how a firm might establish a dividend policy and described an important alternative to cash dividends, a share repurchase.

In covering these subjects, we discussed the following points:

1. Dividend policy is irrelevant when there are no taxes or other imperfections because shareholders can effectively undo the firm's dividend strategy. Shareholders who receive dividends greater than desired can reinvest the excess. Conversely, shareholders who receive dividends smaller than desired can sell off extra shares of stock.

2. Individual shareholder income taxes and new issue flotation costs are real-world considerations that favor a low dividend payout. With taxes and new issue costs, the firm should pay out dividends only after all positive NPV projects have been fully financed.

3. There are groups in the economy that may favor a high payout. These include many large institutions such as pension plans. Recognizing that some groups prefer a high payout and some prefer a low payout, the clientele effect argument supports the idea that dividend policy responds to the needs of stockholders. For example, if 40 percent of the stockholders prefer low dividends and 60 percent of the stockholders prefer high dividends, approximately 40 percent of companies will have a low dividend payout, and 60 percent will have a high payout. This sharply reduces the impact of any individual firm's dividend policy on its market price.

4. A stock repurchase acts much like a cash dividend, but it has a significant tax advantage. Stock repurchases are therefore a very useful part of overall dividend policy.

5. We discussed recent research and thinking on dividend policy. We saw that dividends are heavily concentrated in a relatively small number of larger, older firms and that the use of share repurchases continues to grow. We described a simple life cycle theory of distributions in which firms trade off the agency costs of excess cash retention against the future costs of external equity financing. The implication is that younger firms with significant growth opportunities will not distribute cash, but older, profitable firms with significant free cash flow will distribute cash.

To close our discussion of dividends, we emphasize one last time the difference between dividends and dividend policy. Dividends are important because the value of a share of stock is ultimately determined by the dividends that will be paid. What is less clear is whether the time pattern of dividends (more now versus more later) matters. This is the dividend policy question, and it is not easy to give a definitive answer to it.

CONNECT TO FINANCE

 Connect Finance offers you plenty of opportunities to practice mastering these concepts. Log on to connect.mheducation.com to learn more. If you like what you see, ask your professor about using *Connect Finance*!

Can you answer the following *Connect* Quiz questions?

Section 17.1   Dividends are paid to the parties listed as shareholders on what date?

Section 17.3   What factors favor a high dividend payout?

Section 17.4   Which parties are most apt to prefer a low dividend payout?

Section 17.8   Tomas currently owns 300 shares of Doo Little Corp. How many shares will he own if the firm does a four-for-five reverse stock split?

CONCEPTS REVIEW AND CRITICAL THINKING QUESTIONS

1. **Dividend Policy Irrelevance** [LO2] How is it possible that dividends are so important, but at the same time, dividend policy is irrelevant?

2. **Stock Repurchases** [LO4] What is the impact of a stock repurchase on a company's debt ratio? Does this suggest another use for excess cash?

3. **Dividend Chronology** [LO1] On Tuesday, December 5, Hometown Power Co.'s board of directors declares a dividend of 75 cents per share payable on Wednesday,

January 17, to shareholders of record as of Wednesday, January 3. When is the ex-dividend date? If a shareholder buys stock before that date, who gets the dividends on those shares, the buyer or the seller?

4. **Alternative Dividends** [LO1] Some corporations, like one British company that offers its large shareholders free crematorium use, pay dividends in kind (that is, offer their services to shareholders at below-market cost). Should mutual funds invest in stocks that pay these dividends in kind? (The fundholders do not receive these services.)

5. **Dividends and Stock Price** [LO1] If increases in dividends tend to be followed by (immediate) increases in share prices, how can it be said that dividend policy is irrelevant?

6. **Dividends and Stock Price** [LO1] Last month, Central Virginia Power Company, which had been having trouble with cost overruns on a nuclear power plant that it had been building, announced that it was "temporarily suspending payments due to the cash flow crunch associated with its investment program." The company's stock price dropped from $28.50 to $25 when this announcement was made. How would you interpret this change in the stock price (that is, what would you say caused it)?

7. **Dividend Reinvestment Plans** [LO1] The DRK Corporation has recently developed a dividend reinvestment plan, or DRIP. The plan allows investors to reinvest cash dividends automatically in DRK in exchange for new shares of stock. Over time, investors in DRK will be able to build their holdings by reinvesting dividends to purchase additional shares of the company.

A large number of companies offer dividend reinvestment plans. Most companies with DRIPs charge no brokerage or service fees. In fact, the shares of DRK will be purchased at a 10 percent discount from the market price.

A consultant for DRK estimates that about 75 percent of DRK's shareholders will take part in this plan. This is somewhat higher than the average.

Evaluate DRK's dividend reinvestment plan. Will it increase shareholder wealth? Discuss the advantages and disadvantages involved here.

8. **Dividend Policy** [LO2] For initial public offerings of common stock, 2017 was a slow year, with about $24.53 billion raised by the process. Relatively few of the 108 firms involved paid cash dividends. Why do you think that most chose not to pay cash dividends?

Use the following information to answer the next two questions:

Historically, the U.S. tax code treated dividend payments made to shareholders as ordinary income. Thus, dividends were taxed at the investor's marginal tax rate, which was as high as 38.6 percent in 2002. Capital gains were taxed at a capital gains tax rate, which was the same for most investors and fluctuated through the years. In 2002, the capital gains tax rate stood at 20 percent. In an effort to stimulate the economy, President George W. Bush presided over a tax plan overhaul that included changes in dividend and capital gains tax rates. The new tax plan, which was implemented in 2003, called for a 15 percent tax rate on both dividends and capital gains for investors in higher tax brackets. For lower-tax bracket investors, the tax rate on dividends and capital gains was set at 5 percent through 2007, dropping to zero in 2008.

9. **Ex-Dividend Stock Prices** [LO1] How do you think this tax law change affected ex-dividend stock prices?

10. **Stock Repurchases** [LO4] How do you think this tax law change affected the relative attractiveness of stock repurchases compared to dividend payments?

QUESTIONS AND PROBLEMS

BASIC

(Questions 1–9)

1. **Dividends and Taxes** [LO2] Ginger, Inc., has declared a $5.35 per share dividend. Suppose capital gains are not taxed, but dividends are taxed at 15 percent. New IRS regulations require that taxes be withheld at the time the dividend is paid. The company's stock sells for $74.20 per share, and the stock is about to go ex dividend. What do you think the ex-dividend price will be?

2. **Stock Dividends** [LO3] The owners' equity accounts for Vidi International are shown here:

Common stock ($.50 par value)	$ 25,000
Capital surplus	215,000
Retained earnings	642,700
Total owners' equity	$882,700

   a. If the company's stock currently sells for $32 per share and a 10 percent stock dividend is declared, how many new shares will be distributed? Show how the equity accounts would change.

   b. If the company declared a 25 percent stock dividend, how would the accounts change?

3. **Stock Splits** [LO3] For the company in Problem 2, show how the equity accounts will change if:

   a. The company declares a four-for-one stock split. How many shares are outstanding now? What is the new par value per share?

   b. The company declares a one-for-five reverse stock split. How many shares are outstanding now? What is the new par value per share?

4. **Stock Splits and Stock Dividends** [LO3] Simmons Mineral Operations, Inc. (SMO), currently has 530,000 shares of stock outstanding that sell for $68 per share. Assuming no market imperfections or tax effects exist, what will the share price be after:

   a. SMO has a five-for-three stock split?

   b. SMO has a 15 percent stock dividend?

   c. SMO has a 42.5 percent stock dividend?

   d. SMO has a four-for-seven reverse stock split?

   Determine the new number of shares outstanding in parts (a) through (d).

5. **Regular Dividends** [LO1] The balance sheet for Sinking Ship Corp. is shown here in market value terms. There are 14,000 shares of stock outstanding.

Market Value Balance Sheet			
Cash	$ 53,700	Equity	$438,700
Fixed assets	385,000		
Total	$438,700	Total	$438,700

   The company has declared a dividend of $1.30 per share. The stock goes ex dividend tomorrow. Ignoring any tax effects, what is the stock selling for today? What will it sell for tomorrow? What will the balance sheet look like after the dividends are paid?

6. **Share Repurchase** [LO4] In Problem 5, suppose the company has announced it is going to repurchase $18,200 worth of stock. What effect will this transaction have on the equity of the firm? How many shares will be outstanding? What will the price per

share be after the repurchase? Ignoring tax effects, show how the share repurchase is effectively the same as a cash dividend.

7. **Stock Dividends** [LO3] The market value balance sheet for Bobaflex Manufacturing is shown here. The company has declared a 25 percent stock dividend. The stock goes ex dividend tomorrow (the chronology for a stock dividend is similar to that for a cash dividend). There are 12,000 shares of stock outstanding. What will the ex-dividend price be?

Market Value Balance Sheet			
Cash	$ 79,000	Debt	$116,000
Fixed assets	545,000	Equity	508,000
Total	$624,000	Total	$624,000

8. **Stock Dividends** [LO3] The company with the common equity accounts shown here has declared a 15 percent stock dividend when the market value of its stock is $53 per share. What effects will the distribution of the stock dividend have on the equity accounts?

Common stock ($1 par value)	$ 245,000
Capital surplus	618,000
Retained earnings	2,758,300
Total owners' equity	$3,621,300

9. **Stock Splits** [LO3] In Problem 8, suppose the company instead decides on a four-for-one stock split. The firm's 65-cent per-share cash dividend on the new (postsplit) shares represents an increase of 10 percent over last year's dividend on the presplit stock. What effect does this have on the equity accounts? What was last year's dividend per share?

10. **Homemade Dividends** [LO2] You own 1,000 shares of stock in Avondale Corporation. You will receive a $3.15 per share dividend in one year. In two years, the company will pay a liquidating dividend of $57 per share. The required return on the company's stock is 15 percent. What is the current share price of your stock (ignoring taxes)? If you would rather have equal dividends in each of the next two years, show how you can accomplish this by creating homemade dividends. *Hint:* Dividends will be in the form of an annuity.

INTERMEDIATE
(Questions 10–12)

11. **Homemade Dividends** [LO2] In Problem 10, suppose you want only $1,500 total in dividends the first year. What will your homemade dividend be in two years?

12. **Stock Repurchase** [LO4] Awake Corporation is evaluating an extra dividend versus a share repurchase. In either case, $17,500 would be spent. Current earnings are $1.89 per share, and the stock currently sells for $64 per share. There are 2,000 shares outstanding. Ignore taxes and other imperfections in answering the first two questions.

   a. Evaluate the two alternatives in terms of the effect on the price per share of the stock and shareholder wealth.

   b. What will be the effect on the company's EPS and PE ratio under the two different scenarios?

   c. In the real world, which of these actions would you recommend? Why?

13. **Expected Return, Dividends, and Taxes** [LO2] The Gecko Company and the Gordon Company are two firms that have the same business risk but different dividend policies. Gecko pays no dividend, whereas Gordon has an expected dividend yield of 2.9 percent. Suppose the capital gains tax rate is zero, whereas the income tax rate is 35 percent. Gecko has an expected earnings growth rate of 12 percent annually, and its stock price is expected to grow at this same rate. If the aftertax expected returns on the two stocks are equal (because they are in the same risk class), what is the pretax required return on Gordon's stock?

14. **Dividends and Taxes** [LO2] As discussed in the text, in the absence of market imperfections and tax effects, we would expect the share price to decline by the amount of the dividend payment when the stock goes ex dividend. Once we consider the role of taxes, however, this is not necessarily true. One model has been proposed that incorporates tax effects into determining the ex-dividend price:[9]

$$(P_0 - P_X)/D = (1 - T_P)/(1 - T_G)$$

where P_0 is the price just before the stock goes ex, P_X is the ex-dividend share price, D is the amount of the dividend per share, T_P is the relevant marginal personal tax rate on dividends, and T_G is the effective marginal tax rate on capital gains.

   a. If $T_P = T_G = 0$, how much will the share price fall when the stock goes ex?
   b. If $T_P = 15$ percent and $T_G = 0$, how much will the share price fall?
   c. If $T_P = 15$ percent and $T_G = 30$ percent, how much will the share price fall?
   d. Suppose the only owners of stock are corporations. Recall that corporations get at least a 50 percent exemption from taxation on the dividend income they receive, but they do not get such an exemption on capital gains. If the corporation's income and capital gains tax rates are both 35 percent, what does this model predict the ex-dividend share price will be?
   e. What does this problem tell you about real-world tax considerations and the dividend policy of the firm?

15. **Dividends versus Reinvestment** [LO2] National Business Machine Co. (NBM) has $4 million of extra cash after taxes have been paid. NBM has two choices to make use of this cash. One alternative is to invest the cash in financial assets. The resulting investment income will be paid out as a special dividend at the end of three years. In this case, the firm can invest in Treasury bills yielding 2.5 percent or in 4.3 percent preferred stock. Assume IRS regulations allow the company to exclude from taxable income 70 percent of the dividends received from investing in another company's stock. Another alternative is to pay out the cash now as dividends. This would allow the shareholders to invest on their own in Treasury bills with the same yield, or in preferred stock. The corporate tax rate is 21 percent. Assume the investor has a 31 percent personal income tax rate, which is applied to interest income and preferred stock dividends. Also assume the personal dividend tax rate is 15 percent on common stock dividends. Should the cash be paid today or in three years? Which of the two options generates the highest aftertax income for the shareholders?

16. **Dividends versus Reinvestment** [LO2] After completing its capital spending for the year, Carlson Manufacturing has $1,000 extra cash. Carlson's managers must choose between investing the cash in Treasury bonds that yield 3 percent or paying the cash out to investors who would invest in the bonds themselves.

---

[9]N. Elton and M. Gruber, "Marginal Stockholder Tax Rates and the Clientele Effect," *Review of Economics and Statistics* 52 (February 1970).

a. If the corporate tax rate is 35 percent, what personal tax rate would make the investors equally willing to receive the dividend or to let Carlson invest the money?

b. Is the answer to (a) reasonable? Why or why not?

c. Suppose the only investment choice is preferred stock that yields 6 percent. The corporate dividend exclusion of 70 percent applies. What personal tax rate will make the stockholders indifferent to the outcome of Carlson's dividend decision?

d. Is this a compelling argument for a low dividend payout ratio? Why or why not?

MINICASE

Electronic Timing, Inc.

Electronic Timing, Inc. (ETI), is a small company founded 15 years ago by electronics engineers Tom Miller and Jessica Kerr. ETI manufactures integrated circuits to capitalize on the complex mixed-signal design technology and has recently entered the market for frequency timing generators, or silicon timing devices, which provide the timing signals or "clocks" necessary to synchronize electronic systems. Its clock products originally were used in PC video graphics applications, but the market has subsequently expanded to include motherboards, PC peripheral devices, and other digital consumer electronics, such as digital television boxes and game consoles. ETI also designs and markets custom application-specific integrated circuits (ASICs) for industrial customers. The ASIC's design combines analog and digital, or mixed-signal, technology. In addition to Tom and Jessica, Nolan Pittman, who provided capital for the company, is the third primary owner. Each owns 25 percent of the 1 million shares outstanding. The company has several other individuals, including current employees, who own the remaining shares.

Recently, the company designed a new computer motherboard. The company's design is both more efficient and less expensive to manufacture, and the ETI design is expected to become standard in many personal computers. After investigating the possibility of manufacturing the new motherboard, ETI determined that the costs involved in building a new plant would be prohibitive. The owners also decided that they were unwilling to bring in another large outside owner. Instead, ETI sold the design to an outside firm. The sale of the motherboard design was completed for an aftertax payment of $30 million.

QUESTIONS

1. Tom believes the company should use the extra cash to pay a special one-time dividend. How will this proposal affect the stock price? How will it affect the value of the company?

2. Jessica believes the company should use the extra cash to pay off debt and upgrade and expand its existing manufacturing capability. How would Jessica's proposals affect the company?

3. Nolan favors a share repurchase. He argues that a repurchase will increase the company's PE ratio, return on assets, and return on equity. Are his arguments correct? How will a share repurchase affect the value of the company?

4. Another option discussed by Tom, Jessica, and Nolan would be to begin a regular dividend payment to shareholders. How would you evaluate this proposal?

5. One way to value a share of stock is the dividend growth, or growing perpetuity, model. Consider the following: The dividend payout ratio is 1 minus b, where b is the "retention" or "plowback" ratio. So, the dividend next year will be the earnings next year, E_1, times 1 minus the retention ratio. The most commonly used equation to calculate the sustainable growth rate is the return on equity times the retention ratio. Substituting these relationships into the dividend growth model, we get the following equation to calculate the price of a share of stock today:

$$P_0 = \frac{E_1(1-b)}{R_s - \text{ROE} \times b}$$

What are the implications of this result in terms of whether the company should pay a dividend or upgrade and expand its manufacturing capability? Explain.

6. Does the question of whether the company should pay a dividend depend on whether the company is organized as a corporation or an LLC?

Credits

Online Supplements

Connect Online Access for Fundamentals of Corporate Finance, 12th Edition

McGraw-Hill Connect is a digital teaching and learning environment that improves performance over a variety of critical outcomes. With Connect, instructors can deliver assignments, quizzes and tests easily online. Students can practice important skills at their own pace and on their own schedule.

HOW TO REGISTER

Using a <u>Print Book</u>?
To register and activate your Connect account, simply follow these easy steps:
1. **Go to the Connect course web address provided by your instructor or visit the Connect link set up on your instructor's course within your campus learning management system.**
2. **Click on the link to register.**
3. **When prompted, enter the Connect code found on the inside back cover of your book and click Submit. Complete the brief registration form that follows to begin using Connect.**

Using an <u>eBook</u>?
To register and activate your Connect account, simply follow these easy steps:
1. **Upon purchase of your eBook, you will be granted automatic access to Connect.**
2. **Go to the Connect course web address provided by your instructor or visit the Connect link set up on your instructor's course within your campus learning management system.**
3. **Sign in using the same email address and password you used to register on the eBookstore. Complete your registration and begin using Connect.**

Note: Access Code is for one use only. If you did not purchase this book new, the access code included in this book is no longer valid.

Need help? Visit mhhe.com/support